Helga's Diary

Helga Weiss was born in Prague in 1929. Her father, Otto, was employed in the state bank in Prague and her mother, Irena, was a dressmaker. Of the 15,000 children brought to Terezín and later deported to Auschwitz, only 100 survived the Holocaust. Helga was one of them. On her return to Prague she studied art and has become well known for her paintings. The drawings and paintings that Helga made during her time in Terezín, which accompany this diary, were published in 1998 in the book *Draw What You See* (*Zeichne, was Du siehst*). Her father's novel *And God saw that it was bad*, written during his time in Terezín and which she illustrated, was published in 2010. In 1954 Helga married the musician Jirí Hošek. She has two children, three grandchildren and lives to this day in the flat where she was born.

Helga's Diary

A Young Girl's Account of Life in a Concentration Camp

HELGA WEISS

Translated by Neil Bermel

VIKING
an imprint of
PENGUIN BOOKS

VIKING

Published by the Penguin Group
Penguin Books Ltd, 80 Strand, London WC2R 0RL, England
Penguin Group (USA) Inc., 375 Hudson Street, New York, New York 10014, USA
Penguin Group (Canada), 90 Eglinton Avenue East, Suite 700, Toronto, Ontario, Canada M4P 2Y3
(a division of Pearson Penguin Canada Inc.)
Penguin Ireland, 25 St Stephen's Green, Dublin 2, Ireland (a division of Penguin Books Ltd)
Penguin Group (Australia), 707 Collins Street, Melbourne, Victoria 3008, Australia
(a division of Pearson Australia Group Pty Ltd)
Penguin Books India Pvt Ltd, 11 Community Centre, Panchsheel Park, New Delhi – 110 017, India
Penguin Group (NZ), 67 Apollo Drive, Rosedale, Auckland 0632, New Zealand
(a division of Pearson New Zealand Ltd)
Penguin Books (South Africa) (Pty) Block D, Rosebank Office Park, 181 Jan Smuts Avenue,
Parktown North, Gauteng, 2193, South Africa

Penguin Books Ltd, Registered Offices: 80 Strand, London WC2R 0RL, England

www.penguin.com

First published 2013
001

A shortened version of the diary of Helga Weiss was included in the book *Deníky dětí (Children's Diaries)*,
published by Naše vojsko (Our Armed Forces) in 1961, and in the book *Terezín*, which was published by the
Council of Jewish Communities in the Czech Lands in Prague in 1965. Quotations from the diary were
also used in several documentaries, such as Zuzana Justmanová's 1997 film *Voices of the Children*.

Text copyright © Helga Weiss, 2013
Translation copyright © Neil Bermel, 2013
Paintings copyright © Wallstein Verlag, Göttingen, 1998
The Illustration Credits on pages 225–6 constitute an extension of this copyright page

Maps drawn by Michael Hill at Maps Illustrated

Set in Ehrhardt MT 11.75/15 pt
Typeset by Palimpsest Book Production Limited, Falkirk, Stirlingshire
Printed in Great Britain by Clays Ltd, St Ives plc

A CIP catalogue record for this book is available from the British Library

Hardback ISBN: 978–0–670–92141–6
Trade Paperback ISBN: 978–0–670–92142–3

www.greenpenguin.co.uk

ALWAYS LEARNING   PEARSON

To my granddaughters, D., N. and S., and to all
young people, in the hope that they will keep the past alive
in their memories, and that they will never experience for
themselves what my generation has had to live through.

Contents

Translator's Note

Helga's surviving manuscripts consist of two stapled school notebooks and a stack of paper that she used once the notebooks ran out. Over the years, she worked on them several times, writing over and into her original scripts in pencil and making several revised versions of them, one an early typescript that survives as well.

Although the current edition presents Helga's journals as a daily diary, according to her wishes, the original composition of the work is more varied.

∼

The notebooks
The surviving notebooks recount Helga's time in Prague and later at Terezín internment camp. Textual evidence shows that she did not keep daily entries; instead, she picked up the journal at greater intervals and wrote long entries covering months at a stretch. This explains in part what would have been an uncanny awareness of the significance of events, as well as accounting for the occasional chronological hiccup, when two events close in time are transposed in order.

The first notebook begins with a reminiscence about Helga's 'childhood' (remember that at the time she started writing she was a child herself, certainly no older than fourteen) and continues by recounting scenes and events from the early wartime years, documented in a mixture of past and present narration. The narrative style is, with the exception of the first few pages, remarkably consistent, with Helga telling her stories as if she is reliving them just moments later.

In the current edition, which follows a version of the text that Helga put together after the war, she has rewritten the passages about 1938 and the first half of 1939, stripping out some of her childish purple prose and putting them in a format more like that of the remaining sections, and she has added dates throughout the work. Although these now read like daily diary entries, therefore, they were not originally so. This explains the maturity of the style, which would have been highly improbable for a child of eight or nine.

Helga edited the text of the notebooks after the war as she made her typescript version. In her edits, Helga has removed some comments and episodes that perhaps seemed to her overly critical of people (who were possibly still alive at that point) and cut down some of the discursive and repetitive episodes that she felt were of little interest. This editing has been retained at Helga's express wishes, so what readers have in front of them is the post-war version, rather than the text of the original notebooks. Roughly a quarter of the notebooks' text was excised, and a further quarter underwent some stylistic editing. In a few places, Helga added further observations after the war, and these have been signalled in the endnotes.

Helga's second notebook ends with an entry concerning the family's arrival at Terezín in 1941 and their separation. This was apparently written in 1943, as in the notebook Helga says she remembers this scene 'even now, two years later'.

The loose-leaf papers

What survives in manuscript form from after that date are individual sheets of paper, some possibly written down while she was at the camp and many others written after the war. At this point, we can only take educated guesses as to which pages date from when, based on the paper itself and the handwriting. Here, more than in the notebooks, substantial editing is visible right on the manuscript pages. Because the pages were not numbered or dated, as they got misfiled and reshuffled over the years, the original order was lost. Furthermore, when Helga was writing and editing her work after the war, reference works about the Holocaust were few and far between, so rather than working to a strict chronology, she often wrote and grouped entries thematically. For example, where she had mentioned a cultural event, she included the names of one or two others that she attended later as well.

Some research and interpretation was thus needed to put this section into an order that made sense, without traducing what was on the original pages. In translating this section, I have used Helga's authorized, edited text, and have as far as possible followed the ordering in that text. However, in some places I have placed entries in a different order from Helga's original guesses, as long as in doing so I was able to respect the composition of the original manuscripts. Some discrepancies remain, due to the thematic way in which the entries were composed, but notes will direct readers to many of the remaining issues with the timeline of events.

✗

The remaining text

The final section of the diary is similarly written in diary format, but was composed necessarily, as Helga explains in her Preface, on her return to Prague after the war during 1945 and 1946. There is no surviving manuscript of this section, so it relies entirely on the post-war typescript. The composition of it is still in diary form, continuing in the same vein as Helga had done in her wartime account. In our interview (see page 188), Helga explains why she wrote this third section in the format of a diary.

✗

The translation and the format

In my translation, I have tried to respect Helga's vision of a text that is readable for modern sensibilities while keeping to her authorized version. This is not a definitive scholarly edition, and my own changes to the text have thus been minimal. The gaps, awkward bits, jumps and repetitions are there to begin with, and it's our job as modern readers to try to bridge the gulf between our world and Helga's childhood world.

For this reason, readers will find notes at the back to explain some of the references that Helga would have taken for granted. In very occasional places, I have inserted an extra explanatory word or two into the main text to make a reference point clear, but for the most part these references are explained in the notes. Helga's original paragraphs are often very long, so in places I have taken the liberty of breaking them in two to offer readers a pause between thoughts.

Helga wrote her journal as an adolescent and, as is understandable for a child living in dramatic times, she mentioned dates only occasionally. Dates as entry headings appear first sporadically, as later insertions on some of the loose-leaf pages, and are not found consistently until the post-war typescript; these were thus inserted retrospectively as best as Helga could recall or figure out after the war.

We have left Helga's reconstructed dates as an aid to readers, but rather than try to add further dates throughout the text, which would be well nigh impossible, we have attempted to forestall confusion in readers' minds, as Helga switches tenses and subjects, with two further sorts of break within the text. A larger gap with a scroll (⌒) indicates the beginning of a fresh episode in the diary, the introduction of a new subject or concern, often but not necessarily preceded by a larger, or at least a definite, passage of time. A small gap with a star (*) simply indicates that some time may have passed between paragraphs, perhaps only a few hours, perhaps a couple of days, but the subject remains the same and the narrative is essentially continuous. These gaps do not correspond to gaps in the original manuscript, and should not be taken to indicate that Helga has put her diary down and returned to it afresh.

Similarly, the diary is presented here in three parts – the first covers her experiences in Prague, the second her time in Terezín and the third her experiences thereafter – but readers should know that these divisions are not original to the text.

I have followed Helga in citing place names in Czech, unless there is a common English version, such as Prague, or unless the German name is more familiar. Sometimes, as in the case of Brüx–Most, she uses both terms, in which case I have stuck with the modern Czech place name so as not to confuse readers.

Helga's Diary contains a number of German words that describe places and activities in the camps. As she wrote in Czech and it was her native tongue, I've preserved many of these interlopers to give a flavour of the original. Czech readers of today would struggle with these alien words if anything more than English speakers do. Some readers may find it strange that frequently a German word is mixed with an English ending (*Krankenträgers*, meaning 'stretcher-bearers'). This again reflects the original text, in which Helga increasingly incorporates the official language of the camp – German – into her own language, adapting it to the flective demands of her native Czech. In many places, however, I have provided a translation or explanation in English so as not to disrupt readers too greatly. A short German glossary can be found at the end of the text that contains many of the more frequent German words Helga uses. (Helga and I discussed some of these words in greater detail in her interview.)

Many of the places mentioned in the book are, of course, still there to this day and can be visited. Terezín, designated by the Germans as a transit camp for Jews to be deported to labour and extermination camps elsewhere in the Reich, and later tarted up to claim to the international community that the Jews were being treated humanely, is a Czech national monument. The Trade Fair Palace, a 1920s building in the northern Prague suburb of Holešovice, is now an art gallery belonging to the National Gallery (although the Radio Palace next door, where the actual internments took place, has been knocked down; a plaque, designed by Helga, marks its location). And other camps where Helga was interned, such as Auschwitz-Birkenau and Mauthausen, are open to the public as well.

Helga, incidentally, still lives in the flat where she was born and where the opening events of her journal take place.

❧

Acknowledgments

In preparing this translation, I had recourse to many sources, including the official websites of the Terezín National Monument, the educational portal Holocaust.cz, the Vedem project, the United States Holocaust Memorial Museum, the YIVO encyclopedia, the Prague Jewish Museum, the town of Terezín, the Czech National Gallery, the Prague Information Service, Mauthausen Memorial, Czech Radio and the Terezín Initiative Institute. The websites www.ghetto-theresienstadt.info, www.fronta.cz, www.jewishgen.org and vysocina-news.cz were further important sources. Other interviews on the web with Holocaust survivors provided valuable context and corroborating information, such as those on www.hermanova.de, www.holocaustresearchproject.org, historycz.edublogs.org and www.holocaustcenterbuff.com.

Among the books I consulted were Hans Günther Adler's *Theresienstadt: das Antlitz einer Zwangsgemeinschaft*, Norbert Troller's *Theresienstadt: Hitler's Gift to the Jews*, *The Terezin Diary of Gonda Redlich* (ed. Saul Friedman and trans. Laurence Kutler), Joža Karas's *Music in Terezín, 1941–45*, Alena Heitlinger's *In the*

Shadows of the Holocaust and Communism: Czech and Slovak Jews since 1945 and *Pokoj 127*, a memoir by six Terezín survivors, Tom Luke, Mordechaj Livni, Chava Livni, Petr Herrmann, Eva Ročková and Jan Roček.

I'm also grateful to Edgar de Bruin for his invaluable collaboration in reconstructing the chronology of the diary; to Luděk Knittl for his linguistic assistance; to Andrew Swartz for his moral support; and to the UK editor, Will Hammond, for his patient and assured shepherding of this project from beginning to end.

Neil Bermel
Sheffield University, 2012

Maps

HELGA'S JOURNEY

WARSAW

THE
GENERAL
GOVERNMENT
OF
POLAND
(OCCUPIED BY GERMAN REICH)

BRESLAU

KATOWICE

CRACOW

BIRKENAU

AUSCHWITZ

ORATE OF
MORAVIA

OSTRAVA

BRNO

SLOVAKIA

VIENNA

HUNGARY

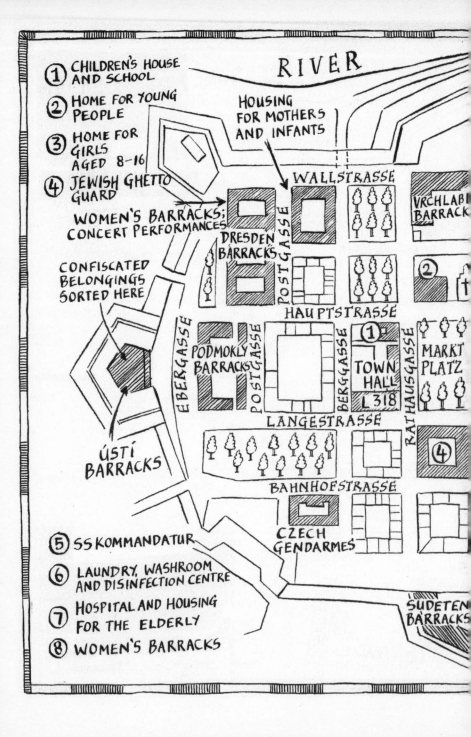

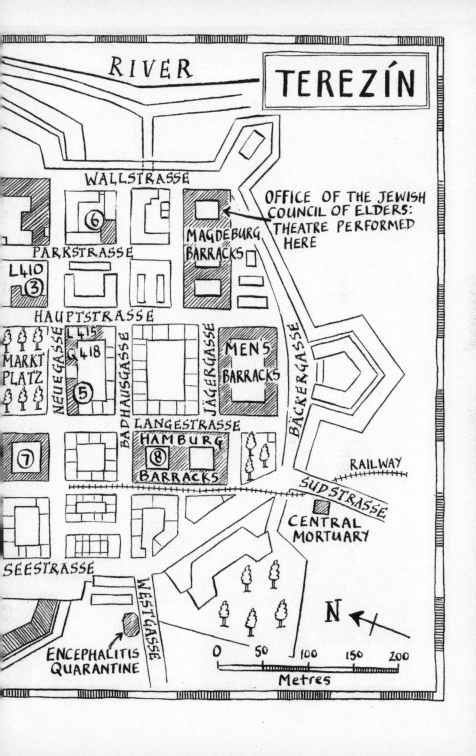

HELGA'S DIARY

Preface

With age, one returns increasingly to the past. To my surprise, I now find that I essentially never left it. After some years I read my diary again – carefully, from beginning to end – with a bit of nostalgia, I admit, and in many places with great emotion.

I don't really know how to start writing a preface to my diary, or why I should do so. Everything essential I recorded more than sixty years ago. I wrote down my experiences and thoughts, at first in school notebooks, then on individual sheets of paper. The writing is childish, the style prolix, naïve. Still, it is a faithful picture of the time in which my generation lived, grew up and died. Much has already been written, many things have been forgotten, occasionally matters have been deliberately suppressed and distorted. I like things tidy and don't want to leave a mess behind. It's high time I put my effects in order.

Over the years a large number of documents have accumulated. I don't enjoy sorting through papers and so mine are a bit chaotic. Thus I came upon my journal, put away years ago and almost forgotten at the bottom of a drawer. It's a stack of yellowed papers, written in pencil, in places hardly readable. I move with the times; I learned to use a computer and so page by page I typed it up and printed it out.

I found myself deleting things, shortening long sentences, omitting clauses, choosing more appropriate words and expressions.

[3]

Some might object that it needs professional editing. However, my experiences with this have not been good ones. Many articles, radio programmes and reports have already been written about my adventures. Editorial interventions have frequently changed the point of them completely, distorting or falsifying true events. I fear that, with changes, the authenticity and force of the narration would be lost. May readers treat this diary charitably and accept it for what it is.

My diary begins in Prague in 1938; it describes the occupation of Czechoslovakia and the conditions there – primarily the anti-Jewish directives in the Protectorate and life in the ghetto at Terezín. Before our deportation from Terezín to Auschwitz (September–October 1944), I gave the diary to my uncle Josef Polák, who took it and my drawings and bricked them into the wall of a building, thus preserving them. Shortly after the war (1945–6) I finished off my Terezín diary and wrote down everything I had experienced in the other concentration camps (Auschwitz, Freiberg, Mauthausen), where there had been absolutely no opportunity to write.

I recorded these events as they occurred to me in my memories, writing spontaneously, quickly, under the pressure of the experiences that filled me. I wrote on unbound sheets of paper, without even numbering the pages. It did not occur to me to check the dates – in many cases I hadn't even noted them down – and anyway at the time historians were only just starting work on their studies. Scholarly publications did not come out until much later, after I had finished my diary.

When I was preparing my diary for publication in book form, it was not easy to put the events in chronological order. If I have not been successful, may my readers be tolerant of this. I am not a historian and my diary is not a work of scholarship. My priority, the most fundamental thing for me, was the events and experiences, and these I remember quite precisely to this day.

Reliable facts can be found in the scholarly literature. From history textbooks, students can learn that during the Second World War six million Jews perished. The precise figures have been tallied and preserved in databases. All you need to do is click on your computer; the dates and numbers will appear.

Each number, however, contains one human fate, one story. My diary is only one of these.

I finished my notes with our May 1945 return to Prague and the words 'finally home'. However, there was no home to return to. My mother and I had nowhere to go; my father never returned and our former flat had been occupied. I was fifteen and a half and most of all needed to make up my missed school years. We began a new life.

Helga Weiss
Prague, 2012

1. Prague

What do they mean by 'mobilization'? All young men have to join up. Why? Not long ago it was all about Austria, and now it's mobilization again. People can't talk about anything else. But what is it? Why aren't Mum and Dad home today? Instead of telling me what this mobilization's about, they've gone to listen to the radio. Anyway, it's just an excuse, because they could listen to the radio at home. They must have gone to their friends' house so they could talk about the mobilization. What must they think of me? That I'm still just a little girl, with whom they can't talk about anything? I'm a big girl already, I'll be nine soon. My God, what time are the bells tolling? I have to go to school tomorrow and I'm still not asleep. This silly mobilization has made me forget about school completely.

What air raid? Into the cellar – now, at night? Why are you getting me up, Mummy? What's wrong, what's happening? What are you doing; you can't put my clothes on over my pyjamas . . .

The gong just sounded in the hallway, summoning us to the shelter. Dad was pacing impatiently in the vestibule and Mum just barely managed to pull my gym clothes on before we fled down to the cellar. The porter opened the old storeroom, which was supposed to serve as a shelter. There wasn't a lot of room; we were packed together, but at least we all fit in. At first no one spoke, but their fearful eyes asked: 'What will happen; what does it mean?'

However, in a little while the mood improved. The men tried to calm the women down, although they were just as upset themselves. They had more self-control and could crack jokes. About a half-hour later the blare of the sirens announced the end of the air raid. Everyone went back to their flats. The parents of my friend invited us to spend the rest of the night at their house. They sent Eva and me to sleep; our parents stayed in the other room, where they listened to the radio. Sleeping was out of the question. Why should we kids have to go to sleep when everyone else was up? And when we finally closed our eyes, the siren wailed again. It happened three more times that night and each time we went to the shelter.

We didn't sleep at all that night. We children couldn't wait till morning. We'd have so much to tell people tomorrow at school. Maybe there wouldn't even be school; that would be brilliant. The grown-ups had other things to worry about and so they weren't so happy when the siren went off. But fortunately everything turned out OK. They were just false alarms and there was no air raid.

*

In the morning, I went to school. The classes weren't much use. All of us were excited and tired from the previous night. We told each other our night-time adventures. There was stuff to talk about all day. After lunch (which wasn't much good; no one was in the right frame of mind to cook) the whole building met in the shelter again. This time it wasn't because of an air raid, but so that we could clean up the shelter, in case we had to spend another night in it. We threw out all the things that belonged in the rubbish; the women set to sweeping and scrubbing while the men put together first-aid kits and made a secret exit. The mothers made bunks for us using the goods lockers. Finally, everyone brought a suitcase with supplies down. We spent a bit of time chatting and then everyone went home and waited anxiously to see what the night would bring. Against all expectations it passed peacefully. Despite that, Eva's father and mine decided that it was too dangerous to stay in Prague. That very afternoon they went to find a suitable flat outside Prague where we could stay until the danger was past. They rented us two rooms in a small detached house in the village of Úvaly. In the meantime our mums packed up and the next day we left.

❦

When we saw that there was no danger threatening Prague, we returned home. In the meantime our president, Eduard Beneš, had resigned and Emil Hácha had taken his place. That was called the Second Republic. Then there was peace for a while, but not for long. One day our new president was called to Berlin, where there were going to be discussions about the future of Czechoslovakia. There was great excitement everywhere in the country. People felt nothing good would come of this. And they were not mistaken.

❦

15 March 1939

In the morning, when I woke up, Mum and Dad were sitting by the radio, their heads hung low. At first I didn't know what had happened, but soon I figured it out. A trembling voice came from the radio: 'This morning at 6.30 the German army crossed the Czechoslovak border.' I didn't really understand the meaning of those words, but I felt there was something terrible in them. The announcer said several more times: 'Stay calm and collected!' I remained in bed for a bit longer. Dad came and sat next to me on the bed. He was serious and I could see he was very upset. He didn't say a word. I took his hand; I could feel it trembling. It was quiet, broken only by the weak ticking of the clock. There was something heavy in the air. No one wanted to break the awkward silence. We stayed that way for several minutes. Then I got dressed and went to school. Mum went with me. Along the way we met familiar and unfamiliar faces. You could read the same things in everyone's eyes: fear, sadness and the question 'What will happen next?'

At school, the mood was sad. The happy chatter and carefree laughter of children had changed into frightened whispers. Clutches of girls deep in conversation could be seen in the hallways and the classrooms. After the bell rang, we went off to our classes. Not much teaching went on. We were all distracted and felt relieved once the bell rang again. After classes lots of our parents were waiting for us. My mum came for me. On the way home we saw loads of German cars and tanks. The weather was chilly; it was raining, snow fell, the wind howled. It was as if nature was protesting.

In this way we came under the 'protection' of the German Reich, without knowing how or what from. We also got a new name.

Instead of Czechoslovakia we are now called the Protectorate of Bohemia and Moravia.

Since 15 March there has not been a single calm day. There have been orders one after another that repress and wound us more and more. Not a day goes by without bringing some new turmoil. The worst of it has landed on us Jews. They heap everything on our backs. We're the cause of one thing after another, everything is our fault, even though we didn't do anything. We can't help being Jews, and nor can we help any of these other things. No one asks; they just feel they have to pour out their anger on someone and who's better for that than – of course – the Jews. Anti-Semitism is rising; the newspapers are full of anti-Jewish articles.

*

Anti-Jewish orders are on the rise. The news that Jews couldn't be employed in government jobs any more caused an uproar in Jewish families. Then, no Aryan (previously an unfamiliar word) could employ a non-Aryan Jew. Now they keep coming, time and time again, order after order. You barely know what you can and can't do. It is forbidden to visit cafés, cinemas, theatres, playgrounds, parks . . . there are so many things that I can't remember them all. Among others there was also an order that really upset me: the expulsion of Jewish children from state schools. When I found out, I was unhappy. After the holidays I was supposed to go into Year 5. I like school and the thought that I will never be able to sit at a school desk with the other students brings tears to my eyes. But I have to bear up; there are other things waiting for me and many of them will undoubtedly be much worse.

Signs in German and Czech at a children's park in Prague, 1939.
The uppermost sign reads 'Jews Not Allowed'.

❧

1 September 1939

War has broken out. No one was surprised. The way events
turned out, we had to count on it. However horrid the prospect
that this could lead to a world war, it's the only hope – not only
for us, but for all enslaved peoples – to have a happier tomorrow.

*

Before I got back from the holidays, Dad signed me up for a group so I could keep up my studies. It's not like being in school, but I'm getting used to it and am starting to like this new way of learning. Our group is made up of five Jewish girls. Our teachers are two young students who had to give up their studies for the same reason we did. We take turns meeting in each other's flats. Instead of a school building like we were used to, it's an ordinary tenement; instead of a classroom, a child's bedroom. School desks are replaced by simple chairs and a table, the big school blackboard by a child's small slate.

꩜

28 October 1939

Another disruptive order. This time, for a change, it doesn't concern Jews, but university students. All the colleges will be closed down – because a few students tried to hold a protest. One of them was killed. At his funeral there was a repeat of the protest. But nothing was achieved except that a lot of students were dragged off to the concentration camps.

The arrests never stop. The German 'Gestapo' police rampage through Prague and arrest everyone it suits them to, as they say. Prague is full of these uniformed and plain-clothes Gestapo men. They spread terror wherever they go and everyone takes great care not to fall into their clutches. Despite people trying their hardest to stay clear, there are many unlucky ones who fall victim to their cleverly laid traps. Danger lurks at every step. When you leave your house, you never know if you will return. By now there are very few families who don't have one of their nearest and dearest in a concentration camp. Thank God we have been spared that so far.

⌐

Autumn 1940

Slowly we got used to the new regime. We grew numb. Even the sharpest decrees don't nettle us much. And there are a fair number of them.

All businesses have to be German-Czech. (Some enthusiasts take it too much to heart and only have German on their shop-fronts.) A notice was added to the menu in every restaurant, printed in bold letters so no one could miss it: 'Jews not allowed – *Juden nicht zugänglich*'. This sign appeared at the entrance to all entertainment establishments, sweet shops and barbers. Contact with Jews is being curtailed.

Despite this my Aryan friends have not stopped visiting me. They always bring their school notebooks, which Dad uses as a guide, because since Christmas he's been teaching me himself.

So I muddled through a whole year that way. I passed my exam at the Jewish school and got my report. All A's. Why don't I feel satisfied the way I used to? The marks still make me happy, but the knowledge that I'll be spending the forthcoming holidays in Prague fills me with sadness.

Last year, even though it wasn't as nice as the previous year, at least we were in the countryside. In a small town – more like a village – called Cerhenice. Dad was employed there on a farm, by the farmer. He went voluntarily, like many others, so he wouldn't be called up for other manual work. Staying there certainly wasn't ideal, but since there weren't many summer flats Jews were allowed to rent, I was happy enough with it. It was a long way to the woods and I only went swimming a couple of times at the beginning before the ban came in: 'Jews are forbidden to swim in the river' – just in case, God forbid, they pollute the water before the Aryans can bathe in it. But the relatives we were staying with had a big garden and a pool in it – a small one, but a pool nonetheless. Four of my distant cousins lived in the village and our other relatives had two daughters themselves. So there were seven of us and that was enough for us to play to our hearts' content.

We had a good time that summer and still I wasn't satisfied. It hadn't been like other holidays. What I wouldn't give now to be able even to go there! But that's not possible. Jews are not permitted to go more than 30 kilometres from their place of residence. Prague in summertime, dusty streets, ugh! It will be the first holidays I've ever spent in Prague.

These thoughts whirl around my head; it's why my school report hasn't brought me any joy. But so what: there are kids who have never ever been to the countryside. Why shouldn't I try it for once? After all, it is only once. Next year the holidays will be better. Of course they will; after all, this won't last forever.

⚬﹘

Summer 1941

And the holidays are here. All the Aryan children have left. The only one of my friends who has stayed is Eva – but not the Eva from our building, she's not my friend any more, not for a long time now. Since Hitler came she looks down on me; she probably thinks she's better than me. If it makes her happy, I'm not going to spoil it for her.

So only Eva stayed. We spend all day together. Eva's building has a small garden where we play. The shady area takes the place of a forest; the tub filled with water stands in for a river. We play for days on end and we're very good friends. Our parents have also grown close. On Sunday, when the weather is good, we take short trips together. When it's nasty out we visit each other. We come over soon after lunch and stay together till late in the evening. That is, until a quarter to eight, because after eight we are not allowed outside. We never want to go home and always look forward to the next day when we'll meet again. So day after day passes, the evenings grow shorter, the air grows cooler. The holidays are nearing an end.

It went by so fast. It wasn't all that bad in Prague; I had imagined it being much worse. The kids are returning from their holidays; school will be starting soon. I can't wait. I'll be going to the group again. I'm curious about our new teacher, our studies and my classmates. Why does time drag so? I'm counting the days till the new school year.

31 August 1941

Finally: school starts tomorrow. For a long time I can't fall asleep; I'm thinking. How will I like the group; will the classes be difficult? What will my fellow students be like? Will there be any boys among them? Lots of questions and no answers. I toss in my bed and can't sleep. I hear the clock strike eleven. I still can't sleep. Now I'm afraid I won't be well rested tomorrow. I try to force myself to drift off. I count to a hundred but it doesn't help. One more time, and again, I'm falling asleep . . .

My sleep is restless; I toss and turn and have strange dreams. In the morning, I'm the first one up; I'm afraid of being late and can't stay in bed. There's still plenty of time till we have to go and I'm already ready. I hurry Dad, who is supposed to be accompanying me. Why is he moving so slowly? He's taking his time with everything and I'm going to be late!

Finally he's ready and we set off. We're taking the tram. It's not far, only three stops. My God, everything's dragging today. The tram moves slowly; I wish we were there already. Time to get off! I jump down from the tram, from the back carriage – where else, of course, surely not the front one? That's only for Aryans.

We enter the building whose number we were given and stop at a door on the second floor. My heart is beating rapidly when Dad's hand touches the bell. I feel like a little girl going to school for the first time. The door opens slowly and there is a young woman standing there, my teacher-to-be. I look her over with a searching gaze. After a short conversation with her, Dad goes away, leaving me here alone. The teacher takes me into her room, our classroom. There is a long table and ten chairs. So we'll be ten, I suppose. I thought I'd be first but there's one boy here already, my future classmate.

I sit down on one of the chairs and look around at the room. Time is dragging again. I exchange several glances with the boy, but we've not yet spoken to each other. And now the doors open again and three boys come in. And then one more and another two. My goodness, is it going to be all boys? They all know each other; all of them came here last year. They have lots to talk about and they barely notice me.

I look them over curiously. I don't know any of them. Or do I? This, if I'm not wrong, is Honza. We knew each other years ago, when we were in Year 1 together, and over there, that must be Jirka. We took the exam together. A little while later a girl comes in. I relax – my fears were groundless. I quickly start a conversation with her. One more boy comes in. It's nine o'clock and the lesson starts.

During the break we introduce ourselves. I already feel at home. I know what each of their names is; I have to go over and over them so as not to forget. The one sitting next to me is Petr, then Jirka and then that one – what's he called? Aha, that's Pavel, and then another Jirka and Honza. Then after that is a second Pavel, next to him Luki and his neighbour, the little kid, has a strange name: Aristides. We call him Ari. Then there's Rutka and I. That's our whole group. I'll have to repeat it a few more times – maybe that'll help me remember.

After the break we had one more lesson and then we broke up with a cheerful 'See you tomorrow'. I hurried home, where Mum was waiting; she was curious how I liked the group. After lunch I'll go over to Eva's – she was at her group for the first time today, so we'll have a lot to talk about. At three – the time Jews are allowed to shop – we'll buy some school supplies. I'm looking forward to tomorrow.

5 October 1941

A month has passed. I'm completely at home in my group. Otherwise nothing has changed. In the morning I go off to school and return at noon, even though we finish at eleven. That's because the whole group goes to the playground – the Jewish one, of course. Meanwhile, Dad is at home, cooking. It might sound a bit strange, but almost all the Jews do that. What else should they do all day? After all, it's three years since they lost their jobs. It's wonderful what progress you can make in three years. Before, Dad couldn't even make tea, and now he bakes desserts and cooks entire lunches all by himself. He and Eva's dad compete to see who can clean up quicker and they visit each other to see whose floors gleam more brightly and who has the most sparkling stove or dishes.

After lunch, when I have finished all my homework, I go for a walk with Eva. Usually to the Jewish playground. We're both learning English from my father. I'm getting on well with it and I enjoy each new word that I learn. It feels like we could survive another few years of this life. But unfortunately the Germans think we are too well off and are now thinking of more things to spice up our peaceful life. This time they came up with a great idea that even the Middle Ages would have been proud of. Conspicuously labelling the Jews. Stars! Bright yellow, with the word *JUDE*.

It's almost a quarter to nine. Quickly, coat on, swift glance in the mirror to see how the new, bright yellow star sticks out, and now it's high time to get off to school. Dad's waiting; who knows how the Aryans will behave once they've seen us marked in this way. That's why, unusually, he's going with me today. The first person we meet is our building's caretaker. Why is he staring at us that way? But of course: he has to see how our new badges suit us.

On the street we meet with various sorts of glances. One person will pass by not noticing, at least apparently (no one can resist peeking just a bit); another will smile sympathetically or encouragingly; with a third, a mocking and sneering jeer will cross his mouth. Sometimes we have to put up with comments, but we're used to that already. We get into the tram, into the last carriage. Here things look a bit different: one star after another. And once we get closer to the city centre it's positively swarming with stars. We've reached our stop. I reassure Dad that he doesn't have to come and pick me up. I'm not afraid to come home alone; I can see nothing will happen. The reaction hasn't been as strong as the Germans imagined.

At school we all boast about whose star is sewn on best. Even though it's not pleasant to have to wear it, we make light of it. We've got used to other things; we'll get used to this.

In fact, nothing did happen and I got home safely.

In the afternoon, I go for a walk with Eva. Not to the playground today – we deliberately stay on the busy streets. It amuses us when we meet other Jews. They always smile, as if to say: 'Looks good on us, doesn't it?' We count how many stars we meet and compete to see who can count more. We talk gaily and laugh loudly. Let the Germans see that we're not bothered. We deliberately put on cheerful faces and make ourselves laugh. Deliberately, to make them angry.

*

Jewish schoolchildren in Prague wearing the yellow star.

A further month passed. The stars became something we took for granted, as if we'd been wearing them forever. But another new thing is coming to disrupt Jewish families. It's horrible; there's never been anything like it here before. No one knows anything definite, people just sense it. Supposedly there will be *transports*. Let's hope it's not true. No, it certainly won't be true, it mustn't! All it takes is someone to think it up and the news spreads like wildfire. Still, everyone would rather be prepared. We can't know what will happen and it's better to be ready and not go anywhere than to get the transport unexpectedly. And so Jewish flats are turning slowly, or actually quite quickly, into warehouses of things needed for the journey.

All the Jewish flats have been turned upside down, and ours is no exception. Everywhere – on the tables, the chairs and the ground – are stacked suitcases, rucksacks, haversacks, sleeping bags, warm underwear, sturdy shoes, flasks, mess tins, torches, pocket first-aid kits, canteens, solid alcohol, candles. If I wanted to write it all out, even the whole notebook wouldn't be enough.

*

Everyone is getting ready for travel.

The news about the transports wasn't made up and the preparations weren't in vain.

~

12 October 1941

So it's a fact now. 'They're sending out the announcements tonight' – everywhere you can hear the Jews talking about it.

Last night several hundred Jewish families got summonses for transport. Poor things, they couldn't even prepare properly; it was Saturday night. The day after, the shops would be closed and on Monday they'll have to go. If only we knew where it was going.

There is talk of Poland, but who really knows.

In all the excitement over one thing you lose track of another. We pack feverishly, bake, and at the last moment there are good-byes. Thank God, this time there was no one from our family in it, only a few acquaintances. But what will come next?

No sooner had the first ones set foot in the 'Trade Fair' than there is talk of a second transport. Only now does the real packing begin. In all of Prague there is not a single proper suitcase, backpack or mess tin to be had. Every time you go past a Jewish flat there is the smell of fresh-baked goods. People are baking crackers, biscuits, Christmas cake. Everyone is getting ready for travel.

15 October 1941

I sit in the tram on my way to lessons. Last night there were more summonses. Again, my whole family and Eva's were lucky enough to escape. Now we'll see what happens at school. The woman sitting next to me, poor thing: she's crying. Someone close to her must be in it.

I've arrived; I'm afraid to enter the building. Which of us will be in it? And suddenly I can't stand it any longer; I want to know as soon as possible. I run upstairs and fly right into the flat. I stop, hesitate, open the classroom door with a trembling hand. I look around with an enquiring glance. I don't even have to form the question. 'Luki's in it,' I hear a choked voice say. I take my seat quietly. So Luki's in it.

Today our good mood falters, somehow. The doors open and Luki appears. We want to drive away his sad thoughts and make his last hours among us pleasant. We try to be as cheerful as usual, but the jokes just don't come. Luki's smile, too, is fixed. During the break we make plans; each of us is ready to bring something from what we've purchased to make up for what Luki still lacks. And they'll need a lot; after all, they've had so little time to prepare. Luki modestly refuses our help, but soon we convince him. Fine friends we'd be not to help him in such a situation.

That afternoon the whole group goes to the playground. All

together, for the last time. Tomorrow we'll be one poorer. We try not to let it show, so Luki can forget about it a little, although not entirely. The thought keeps coming back to us and we can't shake the mood. The smiles always die on our lips.

It slowly gets dark; the time for goodbyes has come. I'd like to go home already, but I can't bring myself to say it; I can't get the words out. And when finally that fateful 'farewell' passes my lips, I have to add quickly: 'I mean, goodbye, I'll be right back.' And so three times, I come back. Every time I'm about to leave, I have to turn round. After all, it's the last evening we'll be together. The last. We'll never see each other again. Until maybe 'some day'. It's childish to believe in it, but we have no other comfort.

At last it's completely dark. Now there's nothing for it, I have to just say: 'So farewell, then, Luki.' How meagre it is compared to what I'd like to say, but I can't force myself to say anything more. I feel my throat seize up and that one, meagre sentence comes out in such a strange voice that it frightens even me. 'Farewell', comes his quiet answer.

*

There were more summonses. Once again nothing. Now as long as Eva isn't in it . . . I stop at her house before going to school. I don't even have a proper breakfast; I just run to the Vohryzeks'. For a long time I stand at the door and am afraid to ring the bell. Until I do, I can always hope, but once I ring – no, I can't imagine it. I don't have the courage to ring. Through the door I can hear worried voices. Eva's at the door now. I hear three words: 'We're in it.' Only three words. I can't come up with even one. I have to go and get Mum so she can help pack.

At home I pour out, flustered, what I heard and then hurry

off to school, it's high time. Now all we need is for someone from the group to be in it. I arrive all out of breath. This time no one's in it; they were only afraid it was me since I took so long getting there. In the lessons I'm distracted; the teacher hears about Eva and doesn't call on me. At the break I don't talk to anyone. I keep thinking about Eva. If only lessons were over so I could go to see her. One more hour. I get nothing from the lessons. Half an hour more, a quarter, finally it's half past eleven, lessons are over.

From school I took the tram, grabbed some food at home and hurried over to the Vohryzeks'. The place has been turned upside down. Luggage thrown everywhere, clothing, food, agitated people. There's plenty of work for everyone. Numbers get written on suitcases, sewn on backpacks, haversacks, bedrolls. Underwear and clothes are sorted: what to put on, what to put in the rucksack – because what you have on, you can count on; only the less necessary items will go in a suitcase. Who knows whether they'll be delivered. They send Eva and me out, we're just getting in the way.

We go over to our place. We try to play as usual, but it doesn't work. The realization keeps coming back to us that these are the last hours we will spend together. We don't even talk much. Around eight I walk Eva home and come back with my parents. After dinner I go straight to bed. My head aches and I'm on the verge of tears. While I was with Eva I managed to suppress it, but now, alone, I feel fully conscious of it for the first time. I don't fall asleep till late that night.

*

Today again I get nothing from the lessons. I'm poorly prepared and my homework is full of mistakes. When I am called on, I don't know what I'm supposed to be answering.

That afternoon Eva is at our place again. We finish sewing outfits for our dolls. When we're done, we go to the Vs' to pack the toys. It's so difficult to choose the ones we love most. Eva has a whole cabinet full of them; she'd like to take them all with her. However, there are more important things to have with you on the road. For toys, the only room left is a small handbag. Finally Eva manages to speak and admits that since she's losing everything she owns, she will have to give up her toys as well. We chose a couple of her most beloved things. There are so few of them compared to the heaps of toys that are staying. And still they barely fit in the handbag.

Working together and eliminating a few more small items, we finally fit them all into the bag. On top goes the bag with the outfits we finally finished. Eva will carry the dolls themselves in the pocket of her coat, in their own sleeping bags and clothing with transport numbers. What if the handbag were to get lost? Then at least the dolls would be saved. Tomorrow is Sunday; Eva will spend the whole day and night with us.

There's been lots of progress with the packing, but there's still plenty to do. We keep coming up with new ideas for taking as many things as possible, for hiding contraband so they won't find it during the searches.

*

The three-day period has passed; tomorrow they have to leave. This evening the whole family is over at the Vohryzeks'. Together one last time. Will we ever meet again? Maybe, but it's more likely that we will follow them than that they will return. No, that can't be, some day we'll meet again in a well-heated flat and we'll remember things and talk about our sad, long-gone exile.

It might be a long way off, but some day it will happen and we will survive. We won't give in!

~

28 October 1941

5 o'clock in the morning. It's time to get up. The Vohryzeks report at six.

I don't even know how I got to the Vohryzeks' house. For the last time, I enter that friendly flat where Eva and I spent so many happy hours together.

The Vohryzeks are ready and just waiting for us. Their packed luggage lies ready on the floor of the entrance hall. On every piece, and on the coats of each member of the family, are pinned their transport numbers: 248, 249, 250. So they're no longer people, just numbers. A last scan through the flat to see if anything's been forgotten and then we are leaving the flat for the last time.

Eva and I go first. We don't speak. It's not necessary. We both have the same thought, and even if we wanted to, our choked-up throats won't let out a single sound. I try with all my might to stop from crying, so as not to make this difficult farewell even harder for Eva. Eva is also fighting her tears, but at the building gate she can't hold them back any longer. I want to comfort her, but my attempt at a consoling word ends up as a quiet sob. Now we can't stop crying. We walk silently side by side, holding hands, and the early-morning greyness is broken only by the occasional sobbing.

In this way we arrive at the stop, our parents following behind. They feel uncomfortable as well.

The tram carriage we board is completely empty. It is barely a quarter to 6. There are a few labourers on their way to work. The closer we get to Prague, the more the car fills up with members of the transport. The tram we transfer to several stops from the Trade Fair is completely packed. We have to wait on the platform. 'Trade Fair Palace!' the conductor announces. The carriage empties out. This is where our journey has led us.

Alongside the Trade Fair is a sprawling queue, which we too now join. The queue moves slowly, and yet we wish it wouldn't move at all. With every movement we're closer to the moment when we have to say farewell. The waiting is endless and still the moment of leave-taking grows irrevocably closer.

We're quite close to the entrance now. We can't go any further together. We have to say goodbye. But instead of words a torrent of tears pours forth. Now even our parents don't have the strength to hold back. The last kiss, the last handshake, and the marshals are coming to tear us apart. 'No goodbyes: anyone not on the transport has no business here!' One final glance, a wave of the hands and the Vs are lost among the mass of bodies.

And so I lost my last friend. Now I only see Rutka, Doda and sometimes the boys from the group. But none of them is as close to me as Eva. I think of her always. I will never forget her.

⌒⟋

1 November 1941

Two further transports have left, but thank God we made it through, luckily. I have only one wish now. To celebrate my birthday, which is ten days from now, at home. Eva and I were so looking forward to it and now I'll be alone. I'll be sad. Last year a few of my Aryan friends came, but this year I wouldn't even dare invite them. They wouldn't come anyway; I couldn't ask it of them, it's too risky.

⌒

The days go quickly by and 14 quiet days have passed since my 12th birthday. But today we got a fright. Mum and I were coming back from shopping and we saw an unfamiliar man with a star and a briefcase in his hand going into our building. By the signs of it, from the Council. There are no other Jews in the building besides us. What if he's bringing us transport orders? The thought flashed through our heads and we hurried quickly up the steps. The man was in fact about to ring our bell. We breathed easier – it was 'only' registration. Tomorrow at 1 o'clock we have to appear in Střešovice.

*

Registration is behind us now and we're just waiting to see when they bring the summons to transport. Though the news is circulating around Prague that the transports have been halted, no one believes it; it's too beautiful to be true.

But something has come true. Not completely, but at least in part. The transports supposedly won't go to Poland, but somewhere in the Protectorate. To a place called Terezín. It's an old military fortress, there would be plenty of room there for accommodation. We'll see whether there's anything to it.

*

We didn't have to wait long to see what came out of it. A few days after our registration there was a new summons. Once again we're not in it, but Uncle Pepa is. It's mostly men going; it's a work transport for the AK (*Aufbaukommando*).

⌒

4 December 1941

The clock has struck nine. Dad is reading the newspaper, I'm reading a book for fun, Mum has also sat down with a book – for the first time, now that she's finished sewing things for the transport. 'The transport could come any time now,' Dad says in a calm voice. Calm, because this isn't the first time we've waited this way. We've waited out several such evenings; will we get through this one as well?

Night-time quiet, interrupted by the sharp sound of the bell. Dad goes with an uncertain tread to the door. 'It's for you today, don't be afraid – after all, it's only *Terezín*!' says the man with the summons, trying to calm us down. 'Only': easy for him to say; he'd feel differently if the order was directed at him. Dad signs the summons with trembling fingers. After the man leaves we sit, motionless, for a while. I don't even realize that two huge tears are running down my cheeks. The moment I notice, I wipe them away. I won't cry! Dad and Mum aren't crying either. Mum has pulled herself together; she is hustling me off to bed and has already put the washing water on to heat up. Everything dirty will need to be washed overnight.

*

In the morning I wake up early. Still, both my parents are already dressed. Did they sleep at all last night? I hurry to get dressed; there's lots of work waiting for me. I have to let Grandma know, while Dad goes to tell our aunts. If only they were in it too! We could all go together.

We stand at the stop, waiting for the tram. As if on purpose, none of them has a rear carriage. We've already decided we'll have to walk. Finally one comes with a rear carriage. Dad gets out first and I continue a couple of further stops on my own. At Grandma's I'm slightly at a loss how to give her the news, but she sees it in my face before I can open my mouth. I come home with my aunt; she's helping us pack.

It looks awful here. Suitcases strewn everywhere, just like at the Vohryzeks' recently. Aryan visitors come by every day; there are lots of things to Aryanize. Each of them brings us something for the journey.

*

The time has flown quickly; tomorrow is Thursday and we have to go to sign up. Although a rumour is flying across Prague: 'The transport's been halted; there won't be any more of them.' We don't believe it.

Let's just have it; the delay won't last long in any case and waiting like this without knowing is horrid. The only good thing is that we can get packed in peace.

*

List of Possessions (7 January 1943)

Before being deported, the Jews had to hand in an inventory of all their property. This painting shows my mother counting the items of linen in the chest of drawers, while my father notes down the figures.

Today we found out that we have to board on Sunday. We'll have plenty to do to make sure we're ready with everything on time.

*

It's Saturday. Tomorrow we say goodbye to our home, our relatives and everything that was dear and close to us.

Our friends were here till late in the night. They came to say farewell. A sad evening – our last at home!

Tonight I'll sleep in my bed again, but tomorrow . . .? The visitors left long ago. I lie here and can't fall asleep. How long has it been since I couldn't sleep because of worrying about school. Barely three months. How silly it seems to me today. Back then I was afraid they'd not accept me in the group, and yet we all got used to each other. How hard today's goodbyes were. It's just a few hours since I said farewell to Jirka. He stayed till evening; he couldn't say goodbye.

After all, it was only yesterday that the whole group saw each other for the last time. Already it seems so long ago. And still I can hear their voices, feel the press of their hands. It's all gone now; I'll never see them again, never talk to them again. All I have left is a token from each one to remember them by.

I can't fall asleep and don't even want to. If I stay up, I'll prolong the night and put off the moment of departure . . .

⌒

7 December 1941

Five o'clock in the morning. The light is on in the living room; my parents are also up. My underclothes and dress are laid out on the chair. There are some notebooks on the desk; probably mine from school. On the doorframe opposite are hooks for the exercise rings. The piano stands in the corner. My eyes wander around the room from one object to another. Lying on my back, hands beneath my head, I etch all these familiar things into my memory so they will never disappear.

We sit down to breakfast – our last. Today everything, no matter what we do, is the last. Always the same thought: never again! My aunt and uncle arrive. We can go. I put on my coat; on it is my transport number, 520. And now it's irrevocable – we have to leave. Dad has locked the door of the flat and we go downstairs.

The building is quiet; all the inhabitants are still asleep. We go out on to the deserted street. Here and there the figure of a workman passes by, hurrying to work. Some give us a sympathetic glance; others pay no attention, or look at us with undisguised glee. Glee at our suffering, but by now we're used to such behaviour and no stupid smile or remark can bother us today. I notice nothing, automatically hurrying along so as not to be left behind. I can't manage a single word, sob, a single tear. Although I feel their pressure, I swallow their bitterness. As if in a dream, I walk, turning once to the windows of our flat vanishing in the distance, but my parents are already a way ahead and I have to run to catch up with them.

In the tram we meet several people we know who are going to the same place as us: the Trade Fair Palace. After half an hour, we get off. Not far away is that ragged queue; we join it – this time with the difference that we will not return from it. Instead, we'll go into the open gates of the Trade Fair, which will close behind us, and we will never again see our home.

But there's no time for such thoughts now. The queue in front of us grows ever shorter; the number of those waiting dwindles and the time grows closer when we too will have to enter those gates that await us so eagerly, open wide like a mouth lying in wait for its victims, so it can swallow us. The '*Ordners*' – marshals – are here again, with their yellow armbands, to tear us away from our relatives. It has to be fast; there's still a long queue behind us. 'Hurry up, Auntie, one more kiss, don't cry – after all, you'll be coming soon too . . .' But the *Ordners* are impatient;

the goodbyes are lasting too long for them. We turn around a few more times, wave and then we're ripped away by the crowd, which carries us off.

All of this – farewells, leaving home and all these morning impressions – happened so quickly that we didn't even have time to absorb it. We stand at a massive table in front of a man checking us in. '518, 519, 520,' says Dad, announcing our arrival. We are sent to search out our allocated places.

The Trade Fair Palace is swarming with people. There are squares two metres in size painted in white on the floor. In each of them is a number and here and there are mounds of filthy, dusty mattresses. We finally get to the place marked with our transport numbers. We take two mattresses each from the mound lying nearest and sit down on them. We're tired, worn out and hungry. From our haversack we take out our snack prepared at home and start to eat. The Trade Fair is filling up. Everyone is on the lookout for his place, mattresses, luggage. I manage to find some kids I know who are in the same transport as us and, together with a few girls, we help distribute the luggage.

*

The Trade Fair is now full up. I return to my place. Some of our suitcases are already here and Mum is trying in vain to put together something that could pass for comfortable seating. We introduce ourselves to our neighbours, look around the Trade Fair and the courtyard and it's already 10.30; they are starting to give out lunch. We're called up by number; each person gets a coupon and we get in line with our mess tins. The hours pass quickly and it isn't even 12.30 when I approach the window in the kitchen – of course it's no luxurious kitchen, just a few

[35]

cauldrons, an awning and a tub in which there is a cooked lunch. The cook puts a couple of potatoes into my mess tin, pours the so-called gravy over them and takes the ticket off me, so that, God forbid, I can't come back for seconds. We eat our lunch in the courtyard, where we then wash up our dishes at the spigot and go to have a rest for a bit.

I can't stay lying down for long and set off with a newly found friend to look round the whole building. Inside we soon grow weary: everywhere is nothing but dirt, dust, an unbearably heavy atmosphere, suitcases and between them people stretched out. We go out into the courtyard, past the kitchen, and get to two enclosures with the signs '*Damen und Herrenlatrinen*'. The sharp stench of chlorine is enough for us and we don't even want to know how it looks inside. We meet a few other children and when we have had enough fresh air we go back to our parents.

Milk is being given out for children: more time waiting in the queue. After this snack I write a letter to Grandma. I add a little drawing of the Trade Fair to the envelope. With any luck the letter will get there – I hope so; there is a barber we know here who might deliver it for a cigarette or two.

*

The afternoon flowed past like water in a constant rearranging of suitcases, waiting in queues, the arrival of a few more '*Nachtrage*' – latecomers – confusion and noise, interrupted only by a few '*Achtungs*'.

After dinner we all stay in our places to prepare them for sleeping. But there's no thought of sleep. Our neighbours are talking loudly among themselves; a bit of humour is coming back.

We are interrupted from our lively conversation for the

hundredth time by a sharp growl, this time in a hoarse voice: '*Achtung, Achtung!*' An announcement follows that a German delegation is arriving. After this a deathly silence descends on the Trade Fair and shortly afterwards people in our area get up and stand at attention. I barely manage to jump up when several soldiers in heavy boots pass by us, looking severely around. After they leave I go with Mum to the '*Latrine*'. I've never seen one before and so I am curious how it looks inside. My curiosity, however, soon leaves me, for the moment I enter the gap in the fence under the sign '*Damenlatrine*' my stomach heaves in revulsion. Beyond the entrance is a narrow passageway: on one side is a wooden wall, on the other is the enclosure. Underneath an awning a board has been nailed and behind it a row of buckets has been placed. On them and around them chlorine has been spread. The ground is covered in puddles, or more accurately ice patches, because it is December and below freezing.

*

We get ready for bed. My day outfit is easily transformed into a night one: all I do is take off my shoes. Not exactly in the most comfortable position, but nonetheless I fall instantly asleep.

We are right next to the clinic and so we are woken every few minutes by the arrival of patients on stretchers. At first the sight of them makes me ill, but I soon get used to it. I will not let anything disturb me and I sleep without waking until morning.

*

It is barely six and everyone is already up. The noise here is like in the busiest of Prague streets. Everyone makes his 'bed' and then quickly rushes to the courtyard to wash. Mum and I go to the 'washroom'. Of course, this is no tiled bathroom with running water, but a rather ordinary shed with two benches and several nails in the wall. In the corner is a cauldron with hot water. It's not exactly ideal, but we're completely content, even ecstatic. What about the poor men? They have to wash in the courtyard. Brr, stripping half naked under the open sky and washing in icy water from the troughs, where your hands freeze to the taps.

After washing we go for breakfast. There is even white coffee – that's fantastic; it doesn't matter that it's not really white, more like grey, but at least there's some milk in it. It has no smell either, but so what? If nothing else, at least it's warm and the Christmas cake we can still treat ourselves to today will make up for its deficiencies.

'*Achtung!*' The whole Trade Fair shakes again with its sound. No one can leave his assigned place. We wait for the *Ordners* to come and they lead us away to a queue in the courtyard, and from there to an office where we deposit all our valuables. Money, jewellery, silver and the keys to our flats. Of course, only the things we took with us – there's no mention of the property already Aryanized. Understandably we declare a lot less than we have already hidden.

Our turn came around half nine and by lunchtime we were done. From queue to queue and the morning's already over. True, there's never a dull moment here. In the afternoon all the men had to go and have their heads shaved. Dad made use of the occasion to give the aforementioned barber his letter. He promised he'd deliver it; let's hope he does – after all, we gave him the cigarettes and the money we'd kept back that morning. It's certainly enough for such a small favour. We fill in a few more official papers and they're giving out children's milk again.

It's four o'clock. How time flies! It's almost two days since we left home.

I spend the rest of the afternoon playing with other kids; then dinner is given out. Soon after we go to bed. The noise at bedtime doesn't even bother me any more; I might not even be able to fall asleep without it. I'm woken up a few times by an *Ordner* who comes to shake Dad by the leg so he won't stop people from sleeping with his snoring.

*

Today wasn't at all interesting; everything was just like the preceding two days. Several queues, '*Achtung!*', a German visit, a walk in the courtyard, fill in a few more forms, and it's evening again. We don't cover ourselves with duvets today; they're already rolled up into '*Bettrolle*', so coats take their place. Our suitcases have been handed over; all we have on us is our '*Handgepäck*', because we're leaving tomorrow.

2. Terezín

5 a.m.

The alarm: time to get up! At six we start to board. We hurry to get washed – today just a little bit, only face and hands. We have to go and get coffee and fill our flasks with it, so we have something warm for the train. Shove everything packed into our rucksacks, put on shoes, get dressed and wait until they come for us.

'*Achtung, Achtung!* All numbers up to 50 board now; everyone else remain in your place.' The hours pass, we wait. '*Achtung!* Numbers up to 150, 200, 300, 500.' I am number 520. We're ready, waiting for the command. '*Achtung!* Numbers up to 550.' We go. They lead us to the courtyard; several hundred members of the transport are assembled here. We take up our assigned place.

Within an hour all thousand members of the transport are assembled in the courtyard. Several German soldiers stand with each group, their bayonets at the ready. Careful: everything goes quiet. A German officer (or something like that?) strides to the centre of the courtyard and prepares to give another speech. Deathly silence. A single booming voice sounds through the courtyard.

We receive some instructions regarding our journey, and afterwards we learn something that surprises all of us. That is, it would surprise us if it were true. Except we, unfortunately, are so used to these speeches and promises and have had several opportunities to see how true they are.

We are supposedly off to a new land to avoid persecution, so that we can start a new life. We will be taken care of, things will go well for us. We may be thankful that we are among the first and can help to build the ghetto and prepare it for the others who will soon follow us. This and other flattery come to our ears. It's just strange that none of this corresponds with the letters sent secretly from Terezín. We stare at the speaker and silently calculate how long we think he can keep speaking.

*

8 a.m.

The speech is over; the first 'crew' leaves for the station. We stare impatiently at the departing group. We're freezing; if only we could take our seats on the train. We shift from foot to foot, count the minutes. The hour hand is on its second time round and we're still standing in the same place.

We go out on to the street. In front of us and behind us are soldiers on bicycles. Pedestrians stop on the pavements and stare curiously at us. Tears even appear in some of their eyes; once in a while someone stands rooted to the spot with his mouth open as if he has seen a ghost. There must be something odd about us; the inhabitants of Prague don't get to see such a spectacle every day: people being led along the main streets in broad daylight under military guard, carrying all their possessions on their backs. Children, pensioners, doesn't matter, all with stars and transport numbers on their coats. It must be a spectacle, but it wouldn't stop the inhabitants of buildings near the Trade Fair in their tracks, because these days they must be presented with this view fairly often.

We take no notice of the curious looks; our thoughts are far ahead of us. After all, we don't even know where we'll sleep tonight, whether they'll tear families apart, what we'll have to eat tomorrow and other similar worries. We gaze at the streets of Prague for one last time. Who knows how long it will be before we see them again, if ever. A last walk through Prague. Many – no, certainly all of us – are crying silently, but we don't let our emotions show. What, and give the Germans the pleasure? Never! We all have the strength to control ourselves. Or should we be ashamed of how we look? Of the stars? Of the numbers? No, they're not our fault; that's for someone else to be ashamed of. The world is just a strange place.

The train station. They seat us in – or rather, load us into – one of the empty carriages. For now they're done with us. We take our seats, each in the place marked with his number. The luggage we put either above or beneath the seat. We can even remove our coats; the cold air warms up quickly with the breath of so many people. Outside it's a scramble; more groups are coming.

*

11 o'clock

All thousand travellers are in their places. So why aren't we leaving? The wagons are closed, each has its *Ordner*, armed soldiers stand on the steps.

Why aren't we moving? Perhaps so we can feast our eyes on Prague one last time? Thanks very much, what a lovely thought. What's the point in looking through closed windows? We're not allowed to open them. If only, for God's sake, we'd leave already; don't torture us with this waiting.

The train slowly starts to move. Are we really on our way? No, the train stops again, goes back to the station. More waiting. Everyone is sitting in their seats, many unwrap their sandwiches and start to eat.

Once more the wheels clatter beneath us, we think we're under way, but again the brakes screech. This is even worse than standing in one place. Could it be – finally – and again, no. And still nothing. Here, there, here, always in the same place.

*

Twelve

Two hours in the train. Again we leave the platform, pass the station, but we do not go back; instead, the train picks up speed. Everyone has gone quiet. Despite the fact that we had all wished to be gone, now that we're actually travelling an oppressive mood seizes us.

We will never see Prague again. Never! Why doesn't the train return once more? Once, just one more time. Let us say farewell to Prague for the last time. To our dear, beloved Prague, let us take our leave of her forever.

However, the train does not return, nor halt; it rushes mercilessly onwards without ever stopping . . .

Prague is far behind us. The factories and tenements have changed into small country houses, blackened streets have changed into meandering tracts of snow-covered fields. Prague is far away. The depressive mood lifts a bit.

We don't think so much about what has happened, but about what will come. More worries and pointless agonizing. None of us has ever been to Terezín before; no one knows anything –

just fuzzy, indefinite ideas. How does it look there; will our uncle meet us at the train station? A sharp opening of the doors interrupts my thoughts. Several SS men enter. '*Achtung!*' The word flies through the silenced compartment. Everyone stands to attention. '*Achtundzwanzig Frauen, sechs Kinder und sechsundzwanzig Männer*' – twenty-eight women, six children and twenty-six men – the pale *Ordner* reports with his heels together and arms at his sides. The SS man surveys him from top to bottom, casts a glance across the compartment and without a word leaves. We take our seats again. The conversation resumes its flow. A blow is heard from the next compartment. A woman by the door looks about to faint. It's the mother of our *Ordner*. Through a crack in the door she saw the SS man's heavy fist fall on her son's face. In his excitement he got his count wrong.

The woman has calmed down. The hobnailed boots in the next compartment have gone quiet. The *Ordner* comes back. He's fine, only his face is red and puffy, but he's laughing already. 'I won't die from a slap.'

*

Where are we now? That over there is Říp. I'd forgotten for a long time to look out of the window and meanwhile we'd travelled some distance. In a little while we'll be in Terezín.

The travellers are searching for their luggage, putting their coats on. Utter confusion everywhere. There's a scrum at the window. Outside are loads of men, each searching for people he knows. The train slows, there are several jolts and then it stops completely. The door of our compartment opens, letting us out. 'Anything you can't carry, leave in the train; you'll get everything.' We leave one bag and get off. Men in overalls, heavy boots, jumpers, riding breeches and caps. Lorries. The elderly and children can ride; the rest go on foot.

A bumpy road and a thaw. Our heavy feet sink into the mud and dirty yellow water squirts out from beneath the carriages laden with luggage. Behind each 'crew' there are carts in case anyone can't carry his luggage, and the men who push them readily answer our questions. We learn lots of unpleasant things. The worst – and we'd figured this would happen – is that men and women live separately.

*

Three o'clock

The first houses in the village. Curious faces look out of the windows at us; children run out in front of the houses to get a better glimpse. Why are there so few people on the street? After all, several transports have already arrived. I don't understand. What is over there, that big building? People are crowding at the windows, waving, but I can't make out any faces at this distance. Why are they all squeezed at the windows instead of going outside? 'That's Sudetenland, the men's barracks. They're not allowed out,' a man in overalls explains.

'Hello, Mr Hirsch,' a woman behind me calls. 'So, you too?' 'Yes, and how long have you been here?' 'I'm AK,' the man boasts. 'You've tried already, haven't you?' 'Don't even ask.' 'And how about your wife; is she at home?' 'Thank God, I was so worried she might come today.' 'Just be grateful for every day she's still at home. Even just the Trade Fair . . .' 'You're telling me . . .' I have no more time to take an interest in Mr Hirsch or even in the woman behind me.

In front of us is a large building – barracks, apparently. They lead us inside. 'Men to the left, women straight on.' But what's this – can't I hold my father's hand? 'Quickly, quickly, didn't you hear?' 'Farewell, Dad!' and then the current of people sweeps me along towards the courtyard. Arched windows one after the other, like a colonnade. Some people are already here, so we're not the first. All women, must be the women's barracks. Will we have to stand? I won't be able to hold out. Up since five, then the trip, I really can't, I'm terribly sleepy and tired. If only my feet didn't hurt.

'No, Mum, I'm fine, I'm just a little tired.' After all, I'm not going to tell Mum I can't hold out. How could she help? After all, she's no less tired than I am, poor thing. But it shouldn't have to go on this long. If only they'd take us somewhere, no matter where; if only I could sit down, even on the ground, just so I wouldn't have to stand any more.

*

Complete darkness, six o'clock. Is it possible we're finally on our way? Turn right, up the steps, keep going, one more flight. Along the hall to the left, turn the corner, into that room.

Number 215. Thank God, at least we're in a room. But where are we supposed to sit? There's just four bare walls. I really can't stay on my feet any longer. I sit down on the bedroll; next to me are Anita and another girl. Her name is Helena; we don't ask any more questions, we're too tired even to talk, our eyes are closing. If only I could sleep, lie down somewhere and sleep, that's the only thing I want right now. Just to sleep, sleep and forget about everything.

'Here you go, divide it up between yourselves.' Mattresses! I manage to get hold of one and now I couldn't care less, I can go to sleep. Goodnight.

Arrival in Terezín (1942)

*Each person was allowed fifty kilos of luggage. One suitcase could be
sent. People had to carry the rest themselves.*

Is it morning already? But I only just went to sleep. I'm still so
tired; my legs and back hurt. Nothing for it; everyone is getting
up, where I'm lying is in the way. Our bedrolls are all here – I
hadn't even noticed. Dad brought them by last night. Poor Dad,
didn't even lie down himself, just so I could get some sleep. God
knows where he found them.

We have to go and get some coffee, but where? How should I know where the kitchen is? Who could be expected to find their way around here? Hallways and more hallways, door after door.

After a quarter-hour of wandering I join the queue near the kitchen. I obtain coffee and after a bit more wandering return to our room. After breakfast – we still had some Christmas cake, but we have to be sparing with it, our supplies are clearly dwindling – I go to the *Waschraum*. There are a few of us together and so it's easier to find it. It's just around the corner from the kitchen.

For now the men are living in the same barracks as us, just one floor down. Soon, however, they'll be moving, maybe today or tomorrow. I'm going to look in on Dad and then go to search for our suitcases. There's a whole courtyard full of them and they're still bringing in more.

*

After a half-hour of almost hopeless wandering I found Dad in his out-of-the-way billet. He's still missing one suitcase but otherwise he's got all of our luggage. It's a horrible mess out in the courtyard; I didn't even try to look in that bedlam. I'm happy to be sitting down again finally. It took ages for me to find my way back to our quarters. It's terrible; I'll never learn my way around here. But so what; we won't be here for long.

*

'Today the men are moving!' The announcement resounds through the barracks, buzzes through the corridors, echoes back from the opposite wall of the courtyard. The women are busy packing. How many times already have we done this? We get

Dad's luggage ready. From today he'll be living on his own, having to take care of himself. That will be something! Mum anxiously repacks Dad's suitcase, thinking of thousands of new problems, advising Dad what to do – there's no way he can remember all of it.

*

Half one

'Men embark!' We accompany Dad to the courtyard. For now we can be together. For now, but in a few minutes, maybe an hour or half an hour and then – farewell – and – maybe – no, I won't think about it. But thoughts go where they will. What comes next? Perhaps we'll never see each other again. 'Dad,' no, I won't, I can't speak. A whistle. We have to go. 'Helga, be good and if it turns out that . . . we can't know what will happen . . .' I bite my lip and hold back my sobs. I squeeze Dad's hand; it is hot and in his eyes – for the first time in my life – I see tears.

We feel – I can't find the word, and maybe none exists that could express the sorrow of this moment. And yet Mum and I will stay together, while Dad will be alone. It must be a hundred times worse for him.

Again the whistle, this time for real.

*

Half five

Hardly light enough to see and I'm still standing at the window. Around me everywhere are women with eyes red from crying, fixed on a single point down there in the courtyard, where the heads of our loved ones are disappearing into the darkness.

It's so dark now that we can't make out the individuals. Everything has blended into a single surface blurred by our screen of tears. No one leaves the windows. With hungry, longing eyes, we stare at the last spot where we saw our husbands, fathers, brothers and sons. Even fourteen-year-old boys are counted as grown-ups and can't stay with their mothers.

13 December 1941

Three days in Terezín. We finally have all our luggage, we've tidied up our space – it doesn't exactly look pretty, but we've done what we can. There are 21 of us in quite a small room. Mum and I have 1.20 square metres. At night people lie in the middle as well and if anyone goes out they have to jump over them. We stick our feet in other people's faces – truly horrible. If you've not seen it with your own eyes, you would never believe it, and one day even we will find it difficult to believe that people could live in such conditions.

We've not seen Dad since Friday, but he sent us a letter through a man who has a pass. So one great worry of ours has been lifted: we know he's still in the same town as us. We can't have any contact with him, not even by writing – only when someone with a pass comes by and takes the letter with him. Of course a letter doesn't mean writing paper and a sealed envelope; it's just a scrap of skilfully rolled paper that can be hidden in shoes, stockings or elsewhere. They often have

The Dormitory in the Barracks (1942)

'There are 21 of us in quite a small room. Mum and I have 1.20 square metres. At night people lie in the middle as well and if anyone goes out they have to jump over them.'

pocket searches and God forbid if they should find a letter on someone.

*

A transport is supposed to arrive again today. I can't wait – maybe some of our relatives will be on it.

*

3 o'clock

I'm completely frozen. I've been waiting since 11 o'clock, and it must be coming any moment now. I can't let them slip by. Aunt Marta will be coming (my uncle spoke with her at the train station). I have to be here to welcome her.

～

16 December 1941

Tomorrow we'll have been here a week. A week already, or just a week? A week is only a few days and yet everything – leaving home, the Trade Fair – seems like an eternity.

There was a men's brigade here the day before yesterday. Dad wasn't among them. Maybe he'll come next time. Actually I'm sort of glad he didn't come this time. It would have been worse than not seeing him at all. They brought the group of men into the courtyard of Dresden (that's the name of our barracks). They left them standing there for a while, wouldn't let anyone through to see them and then led them away. That was it. The women thronged at the windows just so they could catch a glimpse of their loved ones and send greetings with a gesture.

Yesterday another group came, still no Dad. For days Mum and I keep a lookout, so we won't miss him. Dad writes to us daily; he signed up to carry suitcases and they've promised him, supposedly, that they'll come here as well. Perhaps one day it will actually happen.

*

Today it finally worked out. They were bringing suitcases to Dresden. As usual, Mum and I waited in the gateway – more out of habit than any belief that he'd come. Suddenly a group of men with suitcases on their shoulders appeared, and Dad was among them. I was overjoyed – but made sure no one could see it. A kiss or something similar was out of the question, perish the thought – how could a man be allowed to meet with a woman, let alone speak to her? Even if it is his own wife. Here you're a prisoner and that's the end of it; such things don't happen here. But we understand each other even so, and we got lucky as well. The gendarme turned away. The men were not allowed to stay a moment longer once they'd dropped off the suitcases upstairs. We ran up to Dad, one on each side, and he didn't know who to listen to first. He didn't even get a word in edgeways, poor fellow. We had so much to say, but we had to say goodbye. We couldn't even show him where we're living. Let's hope he manages to come again soon. Perhaps he'll be able to stay longer. At the end of the stairs we said farewell. The gendarme 'coincidentally' turned around again.

Three days later Dad came again. This time it was with an official visit brigade. The men weren't allowed to go to our quarters, but we didn't bother asking. Dad just had a spot of tea and then we rushed back to the courtyard, so no one would find him in the room. We had a quarter-hour till departure time. We walked around the hallways for a while, but when we got back to the courtyard at half five, there was no one there.

Is the clock fast? Surely not. It's definitely half five; it's already dark. Could the others have left already? Gradually nervousness took hold of us. Maybe they're waiting in the other courtyard. It was already too dark to see properly. On top of everything it started to rain.

We were utterly desperate. We ran from place to place, turned our torches on, all for nothing – the courtyard was empty. What now? We stood helpless in the middle of the courtyard, so wet that the water was literally dripping off us, and not a living soul in sight who could advise or help us.

Should Dad stay overnight and worm his way into a brigade tomorrow? No point. At eight o'clock they check on us at *Standt*; by that time he absolutely has to be at home. There was nothing for it but to go to the gendarme and voluntarily announce the fact. But who knows if he's even on duty today. What if it's someone beastly who is on duty and he makes a stink over it? We were in a desperate situation.

At that moment the cooks rode by with a cart. A small spark of hope: maybe they can help or at least advise us. We were lucky. They hadn't been counted and so they could take Dad with them. How happily Dad grabbed the cart and helped push with all his might! The gendarme couldn't even suspect that Dad didn't belong among them. Let's hope that things go just as easily for Dad back at Magdeburg and no one will have the least inkling of our adventure. It's not even half seven; by the time they take attendance Dad will be long since home.

A View of the Barracks Courtyard (11 July 1943)

If only Dad had come today. So many people we know are here, just not Dad – he's never pushy enough. Nothing left for it but to send the bread and sardines to him with someone. We had one tin left; Mum hid it away for today so at least we'd have fish for dinner. It's Christmas Eve. What a shame; it would have tasted better if we were all together.

We waited in vain until it got dark. We could have guessed that Dad wouldn't make it. He doesn't know how to work the system. Also, you have to grease a few palms, but Dad and greasy palms don't go together.

It's a crummy Christmas. I won't even see Dad and it's been

a fortnight since he was here. And on top of it they made caraway soup. Somehow the kitchen mixed up the menus. But what of it; we have it every day, so why not today as well? Because it's Christmas Eve? Stomachs don't know that and won't complain, and that's the main thing, after all.

In the room next door the girls prepared a show. Everyone from the rooms nearby came to see.

It was beautiful. We sang, the girls even acted out a short play. For a while we forgot completely. It was as if we were home, somewhere at the theatre, as if the candles set on suitcases and mugs were shining on a Christmas tree and we were at liberty and free.

No one is listening any more; no one notices the girls' songs and dances. They're not even dancing any more, actually. Their thoughts are somewhere else. They're no longer prisoners in these cold, dirty barracks. No longer do they face each new day with empty stomachs and constant fear. We're free, far beyond the ramparts and gates of the ghetto that hide so much suffering and woe, where death lurks for its thousands of victims – far from there, around a packed table, among so many dear faces and things – that's where everyone's thoughts are, and in the glow of the candles burning they see that beautiful, unforgettable image come alive before them . . . Home.

We were up long into the night, remembering our homes with tears in our eyes.

*

A week later we celebrated the New Year, 1942, in similar fashion, in the hope that it would be better than the last few. However, its beginning promised nothing pleasant.

I can't even write, my hand is trembling so much just from thinking about it. If I hadn't seen it with my own eyes, I would not have believed that today, in the 20th century, something like this could happen. This morning they ordered us to shut all the windows. We already suspected something. We knew that behind Ústí barracks they had put up a gallows. Around nine we saw (you can see through closed windows) a small group enter Ústí barracks. In the front and rear were the SS, in the middle nine young men with shovels on their shoulders – so they could dig their own graves! Nine condemned to death. What did these boys do that was so terrible to be dealt with so cruelly? Twenty-year-olds, maybe even younger, sent news about themselves to their mothers. So they sent the messages illegally? How else could they send them, when contact with home is forbidden? That's why they were executed. Why shouldn't it be possible? These days nothing is impossible.

I know they can be harsh and cruel, but today was the limit. They promised us we could go and visit our fathers on Sunday. All week we looked forward to it, couldn't wait, our fathers too; they'd put together a sort of concert, a festive welcome. My God, after all, it was to be the first time we'd been officially permitted to go on a visit. Our brigade was supposed to go at 2 o'clock.

Starting at 12, the courtyard was full of well-scrubbed and combed children in holiday clothes. After all, isn't it a holiday when we get to go and visit our fathers?

Then the order came to go back to our rooms. We wouldn't be going over to Magdeburg. A case of scarlet fever had been found among us; they didn't want us to spread the infection. We tried to protest, but of course to no effect. So we returned home with heads hung low, and this longed-for day ended in disappointment and tears. I got a letter from Dad in which he describes all the things they had planned for us and how they'd been looking forward to it. Perhaps they'll let us visit next Sunday.

Now I go every day with Pavel (an eleven-year-old boy from our room) to collect milk from the canisters in front of the commissary. A few times we had a row over it with some other children, but now we get there at half two. Then we're first and we have dibs on the milk. In the commissary they know us by now and sometimes they deliberately don't pour out the whole bucket, so there's up to $\frac{1}{8}$ of a litre of milk left. Today we collected three-quarters of a litre all told. This morning we got hold of some turnips: one for Pavel and two for me. Yesterday they were putting them in the former mortuary for storage, but so what? Who would think about such things; hunger is unpleasant and turnip fills the stomach. Almost nothing is left of our stores from home and bread has to be hoarded. Our ration is a half-loaf for three days, and what's more it's mouldy.

Most of all we mustn't get caught. We crawled in through the window; it was easy, there was a cart standing beneath it from yesterday. Mum doesn't yet know; she's in Magdeburg with the 'Putzkolonne', the cleaning brigade. She goes every day so she can talk to Dad. (I wanted to go too, but they wouldn't take me.) She'll be pleased when she gets back. I want to surprise her and get hold of some potatoes as well. You can collect them from the peelings in the room below in the passageway where they throw the kitchen rubbish. I've got the milk already; if I can acquire a couple of potatoes as well, Mum can make mashed potatoes. My mouth is watering already.

'Putzkolonne' *(Cleaning Brigade) (5 January 1943)*

Working in the cleaning brigade allowed one to visit other barracks. At a time when it was still not permitted to move freely in the town, before the original inhabitants had been evacuated, this was the only opportunity for men and women to meet or at least see one another from afar.

I'm uneasy about this transport. Dad said (this morning he managed to get over here again after three weeks) that it's stupid; where would it be going? But when people start talking about something, there's always some truth in it.

This afternoon, as I was coming back with the milk I'd collected, I found not a single person in the room. Where is everyone? I ran out into the corridor – not a peep. Where had everyone vanished to?

I made my way downstairs to the courtyard. What was happening? The courtyard was full of people and each of them was just pointing: 'Psst, quiet, there's going to be a roll-call . . .'

'Unfortunately, you were right,' Dad wrote to us. Yes, unfortunately, it was true. A transport of a thousand people will be going further east, they told us at roll-call. Everyone up to number 300 from our room will have to get ready. We're 500s, but who believes 'them'. 'I hope it all turns out all right,' Dad continued in his letter, 'but get packing just in case.' Well, that's nice. We thought at least now that we're in Terezín, we'd be spared any more of this. Now it seems to me that we'll never be finished with all this 'transporting', ever.

Last night the summons went out (thank God, we weren't included). This morning the transport boarded. Of course we didn't sleep all night. No one could know whether he'd be in it and so everyone packed just in case or helped those who already had the summons in hand. Many people we knew left.

Now in the barracks it's like after someone's died. The transport has left and the mood among those left has soured.

Prague has come. Three aunts and an uncle have arrived: Ola, Micka, and Frieda and Jindra. They're in the *Schleuse* in Hamburg barracks. We have to get to see them at any cost. It won't be easy, especially for me. They won't take me on any of the brigades, because I'm too small. I've not been away from the barracks since the time I went to Podmokly to gather potatoes. I've no hope of getting to the *Schleuse*, but at least Mum might. Frieda is in bed; she's got a high temperature – she fell ill at the Trade Fair. As long as it's not pneumonia. The doctor prescribed compresses. Who should put them on her? Jindra has already had to move out – people she doesn't even know? Here everyone's got enough worries of their own without taking care of anyone else. Mum has to get over there.

*

Frieda is in a bad way; Mum went to see her. They wouldn't take her to the infirmary; today they're supposed to be moving over here, to Dresden. There are some free places in our room since the others left. I hope we manage to get them all here.

*

We're all living together now. They brought Frieda on a stretcher; I've got to get a mattress allocated for her. Finally she'll be seen to.

*

No sooner was Frieda a bit better than Micka took to her bed. Both had pneumonia. Mum had her hands full. She's not going to work at all; for now they're not taking it too seriously. Now Dad can get to see us more often; he doesn't have to lug suitcases or shift potatoes. He got a place in the office and a pass, and so it's always possible somehow to work it out so he can get an official trip over to Dresden.

*

Micka was still in her bed and Frieda had barely got out of hers when the news flew round again that another transport was to leave. That morning Jindra wrote that he was very worried and in the afternoon they brought Frieda the news. The office job protects Dad a little, so we don't need to quake as much as the others, but you can never know what will occur to 'them'. Tomorrow a different order might come. No one here can be sure.

*

There were a lot of people from our dormitory in this one: another wakeful night.

*

The next day, the transport was supposed to board after lunch. Frieda was all prepared to leave when they brought her the recall notice. It took Dad and Pepa some doing to get her pulled out.

What's all this about Křivoklát again? It probably isn't even true, but anyway I don't have to go on the 'programme'. That's what we call studies, because school or anything like it is forbidden.

Our schooling moves around among the dormitories. Somewhere in a corner they free up a bit of space, everyone brings a chair (which our dads steal from somewhere – pardon, I should say they 'sluice' it, because there's a big difference – or they trade bread for wood, from which they bang together benches and shelves), a notebook and a pencil, and so we study. Sometimes we make too much noise and they throw us out of the room with our teacher. Other times a German visit comes through – someone always warns us in time, then we pack our things as quickly as we can and disperse.

So there's no programme again today. We have the whole day free. Except – is there any truth in the Křivoklát rumour? Supposedly a working transport of women is going to Křivoklát to do agricultural work. The summonses should be distributed this afternoon.

*

The transport has left. My aunts Ola, Micka and Marta have gone. I hope it's true that they will come back. They weren't even allowed to take all their luggage with them, only the barest necessities. That's not definitive, but it's generally said that it's just a working group and that they'll come back again. Let's hope.

We've moved over to the window, into the unoccupied places.

After all, it was time we moved away from the door. It's not as cold now as when we chipped ice off it, but given how freezing it was over there, I think we deserve a slightly better location. Dad still wants me to move out; they have set up special housing for children, the '*Kinderheims*'. Supposedly it'll be better for me there. I went to have a look; it is actually nice there, but I'd just rather live with Mum.

Our schooling is more regular now. Classes take place either in the loft or in the *Kinderheims*. Maybe I will move there after all. It's better to live with kids than among adults in the dormitory.

~

It's nice here in the *Kinderheim*, but I am really homesick. I know it's silly – after all, Mum is just one floor up – but I can't help it. It's fun here during the day, we're all the same age here, we study together and in our free time we play. We take turns doing '*Zimmertour*', cleaning up in the room; we call it '*Toranuth*'. We have dinner together round the table and then we make up the couches, always two and two; I'm together with Dita. Now we hear they're even going to put up bunks for us. In short, everything's better here than in the dormitory. If only I weren't homesick all the time. If it were up to me, I'd move back, but Dad won't let me. I suppose I'll get used to it.

~

What kind of Mother's Day is it when I don't even have a flower for my mum. But where to get it, when I can't get out of the barracks? I know; I'll make it out of paper – I've got crêpe paper in several colours. I'm sure I can manage it. But what else? A flower on its own, and not even a real one, isn't a proper present, after all.

I have an idea. The girls and I will make paper hearts together and Dad will write a message inside. This afternoon, kids get dessert rations; I'll hide mine and this evening, before Mum comes from work, I'll get it ready for her.

*

By some quirk I got lucky; I don't even know how it happened. In the kitchen they gave me an extra dessert. They're quite large slices of cake; I'll make the two into four and I'll have a present for Mum. I went to look in the *Schleuse* – some people we know have arrived and I got a few biscuits. I added them to the plate with the dessert and it looks really pretty.

It's not much, but after all, Mum knows there's not a lot of choice. Anyway, next year I'll make it up to her. By that time we'll surely be home! If only Dad could come see us as well – then it would really be a holiday.

*

Křivoklát has returned. So this time they were right. Everyone's gorgeously suntanned – especially compared to us, since we're still locked up in the barracks. They were in contact with some Aryans and brought back lots of stuff (eggs, cheeses – things we've not seen for the longest time) and, even better, good news. It'll all be over in two months, they say.

Now only the Vrbas are missing and we'll all be here. Grandma and Aunt Vally arrived yesterday. Hopefully they won't get shoved straight on to a transport. People are talking about transports again.

It's nice here now, as nice as it can be in this place. We got Grandma and Vally here in 217. Mum has a couch she shares with Frieda and Marta; Ola and Micka live in another room. I'm the only one who has to live apart. I'm desperate to move back in with Mum, but Dad won't hear of it. He says I should be glad I'm living in the *Kinderheim* and one day I might be glad when I think back on it.

Maybe he's right. Grown-ups have other worries. The transports are starting again. A commission is meeting at night; they've started to draw up the roster. We hear that they're mostly for the women from Křivoklát.

*

Two days have passed and I won't forget them soon. How could it be that they only put Ola in, and left Micka out? That's gratitude for you – after all that donkey work at Křivoklát. First they promised them the earth and then stuffed them all in a transport. But did we really expect anything better from them? It turned out well, we got Ola out. Other than that no one was in it.

1 July 1942

I must be sure to remember this date. The opening of the ghetto. We're allowed to walk freely in the streets. Only with a pass during the day, but at night everyone can. What a wonderful feeling it is to walk alone, without surveillance – where I want, like a free person. It must be a small step on the way to freedom; the end of the war must be near.

They got permission to build a playground on a huge field on the citadel ramparts. I go there every day. We're doing better for food; Mum has started sewing for people. You can't earn a lot, it's true – for a dress sewn completely by hand you get a loaf of bread – but even that means a lot to us. In general it's all much better than when we came. After all, back then there was absolutely nothing here, not even nails in the wall. We began to build like real pioneers, from the ground up, with bare hands. Today, half a year later, we've got a decent bit of work done. They started with building bunks; theatres are being set up in the lofts. I have been to a couple of shows already. Soon will be the premiere of *The Bartered Bride*. The houses the Aryans moved out of have been cleaned, the streets divided into blocks and signed, vertical ones with L and cross-streets with Q. The new transports get moved right into the blocks.

In the next few days we should start moving: all the working women into Hamburg, the office workers will go from Magdeburg to 'Sun' (the former hotel), mothers with infants to *Säuglingsheim*, the infants' home; children to *Kriechlingsheim* and *Kinderheim*, the toddlers' and children's homes; older girls to *Mädchenheim*, the girls' home; the boys to *Jugendheim* and *Lehrlingsheim*, the boys' home and apprentices' home. The officers, the so-called 'upper crust', got their own rooms in Magdeburg.

The L410 Dormitory (1943)

'They divided us into rooms by year of birth. So I was put in twenty-four. There are 33 of us here; we have triple-decker bunks.'

Our Dresden *Heim* has moved to the former German commander's house on the square by the church, to *Mädchenheim* L410. They divided us into rooms by year of birth. So I was put in twenty-four. There are 33 of us here; we have tripledecker bunks. During the day we study together and can only go out as a brigade. Mum is ill; she has a middle-ear infection and I can only go and see her for an hour each evening. I'm horribly homesick.

I live with one girl who's four days younger than me; her name is Francka. Our mums figured out that we were both born in the same maternity ward. From that day on we were friends. It's just interesting that we met this way. We should be sharing a bunk since we're friends, but Francka didn't want to leave her single bunk. In an unfortunate accident, however, she fell off it and her mum wouldn't let her go on sleeping on the third level. She was lucky that basically nothing happened to her. She cracked her head a bit, but only a little. It's not nice of me, but I'm just a bit glad it happened, because by coincidence there was a free spot next to me and so Francka moved over. Now I'm not as homesick – neither of us is, because Francka's just the same as me that way. In bed, we talk long into the night and have no time for crying. Anyway, why should we be weeping? We're all young girls, after all, we're supposed to be cheerful, no snivelling allowed. That's everyone's view and if we want to be on good terms with them (and we do), we can't go against that motto.

In any event there's no reason for crying. Maybe because we're imprisoned, because we can't go to the cinema, the theatre or even on walks like other children? Quite the opposite. That's exactly why we have to be cheerful. No one ever died for lack of a cinema or theatre. You can live in overcrowded hostels (there are relatively few of us here, only 33), on bunks with fleas and bedbugs. It's rather worse without food, but even a bit of hunger can be tolerated. 'Where there's a will, there's a way . . .', only you mustn't take everything so seriously and start sobbing. They want to destroy us, that's obvious, but we won't give in. We'll hold out these last few months.

I wouldn't move out of here now, even if I could. We have a fabulous group. We study Czech, geography, history and maths under the leadership of a *Betreuer*. We're thirteen, after all, and we've only finished primary school. What will happen to us after the war? We usually read in the evenings. Sometimes on our own, sometimes we read aloud to each other. There's a good choice of books here. That's understandable. When we packed our fifty kilos of luggage, there wasn't much room left for books; nonetheless, each of us took his most valued ones. Together we read Čapek's *First Team*, *R.U.R.*, *The Mother* and Hugo's *Les Misérables*. We read the poems of Jan Neruda, Jiří Wolker; I know by heart 'The Ballad of the Stoker's Eyes', 'The Sailor', 'The Unborn Child'.

Yesterday I went to see *The Kiss*. It's playing in Magdeburg, up in the loft. Even though it's sung only to the accompaniment of a piano, with no curtains or costumes, the impression it makes couldn't be greater even in the National Theatre.

The Vrbas have arrived. Now, of all times, when a transport will be leaving and there aren't many people. My cousin has been here for a month already; the whole time he's been working on the *Bahnbau* and they promised him that this would protect his whole family from the transport, but as there are five of them, that will probably be difficult. It really doesn't look good with this transport in general. They don't even want to let them off the *Schleuse*.

Opera in the Loft *(December 1943)*

There were many artists and scientists in Terezín, and in spite of the inhumane conditions the cultural life was rich. Literary recitals, concerts, plays and lectures were held in the dormitories, lofts and courtyards. They were a source of hope and strength, and people, including children, took a great interest in them.

*

Dad, Pepa and Frieda did what they could, but there were too many of them. Pepa would have been able to stay – the *Bahnbau* protects him – but not his family. He didn't want to let them go alone; he went voluntarily. They left this morning. Straight from the *Schleuse*.

*

The Vrbas had hardly left when a new transport was announced. Grandma and Vally were in it. We couldn't get them out. Mum wanted to join voluntarily, and then Frieda did. In the end, though, they stayed.

⌒

Altertransports. 10,000 sick, lame, dying, everyone over 65.

It's horrendously hot. Sunbeams fall directly on my bunk; they reach further and further as I shrink from them in vain, withdrawing into the shade.

Today I'm not going to volunteer to help out with the *Hilfs-dienst*. I've not missed a day so far, but I'm too exhausted to see all that misery and suffering. *Altertransports.* Young people aren't allowed to join them voluntarily. Children have to let their elderly parents leave and can't help them.

Why send defenceless people away? If they wanted to get rid of us young ones, that I would understand. They're probably afraid of us; they don't want more Jewish children born. But what danger are these people to them? They've already had to come here to Terezín; isn't that enough – can't they let them die here in peace? After all, that's what awaits them. Half of them already die in the *Schleuse* and the train.

The ghetto guards are shouting and running about beneath our windows; they're closing off the street. Another group's on its way. There's a stretcher, a two-wheeled cart with corpses, baggage and a *Leichenwagen*, a hearse. The street glazed with

August glare is shrouded in thick, filthy dust. Suitcases, stretchers, corpses. That's how it goes, all week long. Corpses on the two-wheeled carts and the living on the hearses. Everything here gets transported on these vehicles: dirty laundry, bread – we have one of them in our *Heim* standing in the courtyard. It has a sign on it: '*Jugendfürsorge*' – 'Child Welfare'.

What of it; a car's a car, no one's stopped to give it any thought – but for it to be carrying people, that's a bit much.

Again the rumble of carts beneath our windows. Two *Transportleiters* – the transport organizers – are walking; their cargo; and behind, several *Krankenträgers* – stretcher-bearers – and the *Hilfsdienst*.

Are those corpses among the suitcases? No, one of them is moving; through the screen of dust whipping around the vehicle a yellow armband shines. Who could forget them? We met them daily near the kitchen. On crutches, blind, with a little bowl in their hands, asking for a bit of coffee, soup, scraping out the unwashed tubs and basins used for cooking, or raking through the mounds of rotten potatoes, peelings and rubbish. Yes, it's them: emaciated, hungry, pitiful. They, the living on the funeral wagons. How many of them will make it there, how many will come back?

All the hearses are in use. For the first time, they carry a living load. And yet for these people nothing could be more appropriate. Where will these wrecks of human beings go; where will their bodies be thrown? No one will weep for them, no one will lament their passing. Until some day there will be a mention of them in our textbooks. Then the only fitting title will read: 'Buried Alive'.

Scraping out the Leftovers (10 March 1943)

Old people were the worst off as they received the smallest rations.

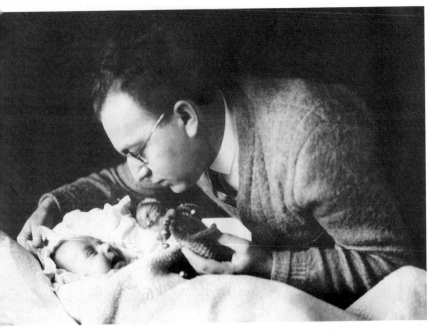

Helga as a baby with her father, Otto, February 1930.

Helga aged one, February 1931.

Helga's first day at school, 1936.

Helga with her paternal grandmother, Sofie, outside the house where Otto was born.

Helga with her parents and grandmother.

Wenceslas Square in the centre of Prague, before 1939.

The Germany army entering Prague, March 1939.

A transport passing through the town of Bohušovice, just south of Terezín.

A rooftop view of an unidentified concentration camp.

A large group of Dutch Jews who have just arrived at Terezín are herded into the camp, 20 January 1944 (photographed under supervision of the SS for propaganda).

Members of the transport of Dutch Jews eating their first meal in the courtyard of Terezín (photographed under supervision of the SS for propaganda).

A photograph of the main courtyard within the Terezín fortress, taken by one of the leaders of the Red Cross delegation during their visit, 23 June 1944.

A street scene in Terezín, 20 January 1944 (photographed under supervision of the SS for propaganda).

Prisoners in a workshop in the Kovno ghetto in Lithuania, 1942–4.

Slave labour at
the Plaszow camp
in Poland, 1943.

The Flossenbürg
concentration camp
in Germany shortly
after its liberation
by US troops on
23 April 1945.

A note smuggled in Terezín from Helga's mother to her father, describing her attempts to arrange for her sister and relatives to stay in the same barracks as her.

Notes smuggled in Terezín to Helga's uncle, Josef Polák, who saved her diary, and to her father, Otto.

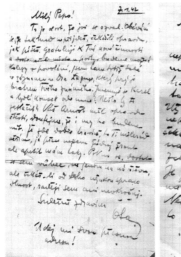

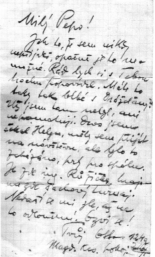

Two notes written in Terezín from Otto to Josef, describing the pain of being separated from his family, his frustration at being unable to leave his barracks and how sorry he is that Helga and the other children were not allowed to make the visit they were promised (see page 57).

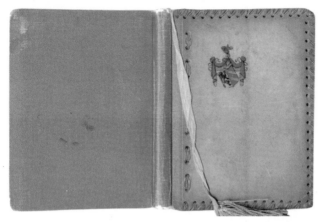

The cover of Helga's copybook, in which she transcribed poems and kept notes and drawings.

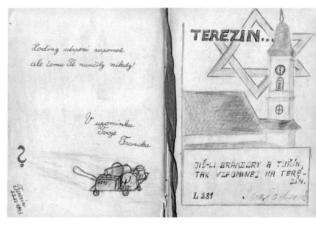

A page from Helga's copybook. The note on the left reads: 'Forget the hours of suffering, / But never the lessons they've taught you. / In memory, Francka.' The note on the right reads: 'When on potatoes and turnips you've dined, / Let Terezín be on your mind!'

A page from Helga's copybook with the signatures of her fellow Jewish classmates after their expulsion from the state schools.

Three young lads escaped. For that, we've had *Kasernensperre* – curfew – and *Lichtsperre* – blackout – for a week already. We can only go to work in brigades; no one is allowed out on the street after six. We come back from work in the dark; in the morning we leave when it's still dark as well. We get dressed and undressed by memory. The windows have to be darkened and it is forbidden to shine any sort of light. Tomorrow I'll go to Hamburg barracks for bread; maybe I'll manage to pop in to see Mum.

*

Kasernensperre has been called off, but apparently *Lichtsperre* will remain all winter. We have to save electricity. It hits each block in turn every third day. We're allowed to light candles, but they don't last us long. Our reserves from home are running low and we won't be allocated any more. It's horribly silly; we can't even read in the evenings.

Without light, everything's sad and gloomy. I miss Prague horribly. Night after night Francka and I relive it endlessly; often we dream of it in our sleep.

Today I had a beautiful dream. I dreamed I was home; I saw our flat and our street absolutely clearly. Now I'm disappointed and in a bad mood, because I woke up in this bunk instead of in my own bed. Maybe, however, it's some sort of sign the end is near. But then there should be an eternal *Lichtsperre* across all of Germany.

It's incredible how time flies. In a couple of days we'll have been here a year. Last year I never thought I'd be spending my birthday here. And it was pretty nice. I got several cakes – of course, only Terezín ones – a charm – my transport number – and lots more things. We just got a package too. Packages have been permitted for about a month now.

With so few opportunities for amusement here, we seek out every possibility, such as one of our birthdays, to have a bit of refreshment, put on a play, etc. And because there are mixed-race girls with us in the *Heim*, we decided to celebrate both Chanukah and Christmas. We can't wait, and because Chanukah is before Christmas, the main preparations have gone into the first holiday. Each of us has to prepare 32 presents, one for each, or even more. Chanukah is in a fortnight. Starting today, none of us can eat sugar or margarine; our whole ration gets saved for cake. Anyone who has someone in the kitchen or gets a package puts their jam in. The day before the celebration we're not going to have dinner; we'll save all our potatoes for the meal together.

A potato gateau for the holidays? Here in Terezín we have fabulous recipes, of a sort not known elsewhere. For instance, bread cake with poor-man's cream; it's a delicacy.

*

We didn't have a Christmas celebration together, because the majority of the girls wanted to be with their parents. On New Year's Eve there was a masked ball; we were up until half one. All the *Heims* went visiting to wish people a happy new year. So many of them have disappointed us; will this one be better?

14 days after the New Year (1943)

'Girls, Vilík is on his way; he was just on the first floor. From number thirteen Dáša, Věra and Hanka are in it. He's in number twenty-five now. Dita, Eva, Danka and Líza.'

Vilík stands on the threshold of our door; all eyes hang on his lips. Who – am I in it as well? A couple of white paper slips tremble in Vilík's fingers. He looked slowly around the room and his eyes stopped at me. 'Helga, come sign this for me.' I'd never been out of bed so quickly and so quickly dressed.

It was late in the evening and we were all in bed already. Meanwhile, my aunt came and took me with her to Magdeburg. We waited in Dad's office until around midnight. They'd promised him; we wouldn't even have to pack.

I spent the rest of the night at Mum's and didn't return to the *Heim* until morning. The girls waited impatiently to see what my news would be and were tremendously glad that we'd had a promise. However, promises don't count for much, so just in case we set to packing.

The transport would board that evening and by eight we still had not had a recall notice. Dad got a confirmation, finally, so we didn't have to board and overnight they brought the recall notice.

This isn't a *Heim* any more; it's a regular hospital. Everyone avoids us; half of L410 is in bed. The thermometers won't drop below forty. The number of sick rises every day; the infirmary can't cope. The rooms are full of sick people and the doctor doesn't know what to do.

I don't feel very well; I'll probably take to my bed as well. I've had every illness that's passed through here . . . 'Girls, whichever of you is going over to Hamburg, tell my mum I won't be coming today. My temperature's at 38.'

They took Zorka to the infirmary yesterday; she's in a bad way. The doctor doesn't have much hope. It'll probably be typhus. They want to quarantine us; they suspect all of us.

It looks awful here. No more than three of us in each room are well. Even Dáša, our *Betreuerin*, didn't come in today. She's been walking around with a 38-degree fever all week.

*

Yesterday they took Lilka's sister to Vrchlabí barracks; she's unconscious. They're setting up a new infirmary. Brr, I'm so cold again; I definitely have a fever . . .

*

Yesterday I had 40.3. My nose was bleeding. I was in horribly bad shape. They couldn't stop the bleeding; finally the doctor came. I thought I'd die, that's how ill I was. Today I feel a bit better; I just hope my temperature doesn't rise.

I was lucky; my temperature broke on the very day when everyone with a fever higher than 38 degrees had to move to the infirmary. It's typhus. I don't know – maybe I had it, maybe not. At any rate, my temperature wasn't up and they didn't send me to the infirmary.

There's an enormous sign on the doors of L410: '*Achtung* –

Infektionsgefahr'. Everyone's fleeing. Lilka's sister died and Lilka herself has typhus. Věra, Olina and Marta have gone to the infirmary. Yesterday they took Milča to Vrchlabí barracks; I hear she's in agony. Dáša and Zorka have died.

*

Typhus raged terribly across the whole of Terezín. The hospital and infirmaries were packed. They emptied out a whole house and made it into a typhus ward. Everywhere you can see signs: '*Achtung – Typhus*'; all the water pipes and pumps have '*Nie vergessen Hände waschen*' – Do Not Forget to Wash Your Hands. However, there's almost never any running water.

*

Shops are opening and we hear everyone will receive money for their work. What are we supposed to think about this? It's laughable, after all. Shops, money! What for, and for whom?

*

We thought it was strange that they were really going to start selling things here, but no one ever imagined they'd do it in this way. A whole transport simply had its luggage confiscated, and immediately there are goods for sale. There is a shop here with dishes, suitcases, clothing and sheets, a perfume shop and a grocery. Our pay is divided into four groups; special money is printed – *Ghettogeld*. We received points for everything. Every six weeks it's our turn for groceries. Mustard, caraway, celery salt and spread are available.

It does look like a real town here now, but I simply don't understand what they mean by doing this. If the rooms serving as shops were freed up for people to live in, it would definitely be more useful. On the one hand they're sending transports away from here, while on the other they're playing games like this.

*

And now another transport. We hear it won't go to Poland; the front's already there. It's for a new camp on the Polish border, somewhere near Bohumín. It's probably the same everywhere.

*

Things look a bit livelier here again. Girls are slowly returning from the hospital. Even Miluška will be getting out. We had very little hope for her. Even the doctors had their doubts; her life was hanging by a thread. Tomorrow Olina, Růža, Alena and Marta will come back. Thank God. It's the old twenty-four again.

⌒

We all signed up for work in the garden.

It's great there. We are working outside the ghetto and have a group pass. We all got into the same group. It's fun even just being out in the air. That's the difference between there and here. You can even see it in the way we look. We've been going there for barely a fortnight and we've all got red cheeks – and it hasn't even been that nice out; wait till the sun starts to shine! If only we didn't have to get up so early. And that endless hoeing – I can't wait till we're done and can start sowing.

I'm really looking forward to bringing Mum some vegetables. Maybe even today, if we go to Kréta to pick spinach. I have to get ready in any case, so I can 'sluice' some through. It'll work if I put on plus-fours, or should I put my gardening trousers on over them? Oh, Katka has a great idea. She unstitched the lining of her sleeve; it makes a wonderful pocket. It's a quarter past; in a little while we'll be forming up.

~

A lecture on Rembrandt was held in the boys' house, with lantern slides. It was very interesting. I hope they keep having these lectures; I'll definitely go again.

We all went to a cultural evening; they recited Villon's poems. It had a powerful effect on me. They're frightening and beautiful at the same time. 'I'm dying of thirst beside the fountain, / Hot as fire, and with chattering teeth: / In my own land, I'm in a far domain: / Near the flame, I shiver beyond belief'. I have to borrow these poems from somewhere.

Mum is moving again. Out of the blue some women from the *Landwirtschaft* – the agriculture department – came and of all places it was her room that took their fancy. Because it's the *Landwirtschaft* and in addition they probably have some pull in the *Raumwirtschaft*, our space management unit, they got the room allocated to them and the rest of the women had to move out within 24 hours. We've been here a year and a half, but what does that count for if we don't have any pull? Mum wasn't allocated to another room and so she has had to move to the loft.

~

Finally, after three months, Mum got a place in room 84, again with Frieda, on the third floor by the window. Pretty nice – most importantly it's not visible, so in the evenings when we all meet, we can climb up there and have supper in peace, without getting in anyone's way or anyone getting in ours.

~

September 1943

The girls are crowding at the *Waschraum* door; some have taken washbasins and laundry out to the courtyard. The benches, bunk ladders, everything that touches your hand stings. The stove can't heat all the water; the washing gets done cold. Between the puddles of water and the dirty laundry, on the bunks, the corridors, anywhere there's a bit of space, are piled suitcases, rucksacks and all our luggage. Nimble fingers mend everything that's torn. 'Girls, which of you will be finished first; I need to reserve a washtub. Where have you been, Eva, in Magdeburg? What's the news – how many, 1,500?!'

That afternoon the announcement came. Máša, our *Betreuerin*,

Renka, Gita and Ema. For now we're not in it, but they've still to announce the reserve list.

*

'Helga, get up, we're in the transport,' said Mum when she came to wake me early this morning. A little while later, Vily brought me the summons. We're way up in the reserves.

The reserve list is running the *Schleuse* in the brewery. It's 5 in the afternoon. I have to board. Vily is calling already. 'So, Máša, goodbye, I won't say farewell – after all, we'll see each other again soon and we'll found a new number 24 in Birkenau or wherever it's going. Franci, I'll hold a bunk for you next to me. Girls, come have a look in the *Schleuse*. Gita, Renka, are you ready? So once more, girls, farewell. Farewell, number twenty-four.'

*

Rather than be on the reserve list again I'd rather just leave straight away. How much luggage have we hauled? We kept not wanting to send our suitcases off, in case they sent them onward while we stayed here – and the fear of it happening the other way around. We could ignore all that – the fact that we didn't sleep all night and that we dragged our baggage at least twice from the loft down to the courtyard and back up again – if it weren't for the dreadful uncertainty. If only they'd just run it correctly, by the numbers, but *Transportleitung* – the transport administration – did whatever they felt like. In the end the highest reserve numbers went and the rest stayed here. I can't remember how many times we were assembled in the

Summons to Join the Transport *(24 February 1942)*

The summons to join a transport was delivered mostly at night. The location and the time to assemble were written on a slip of paper.

courtyard; I only know that at some point I just wanted to be on that train.

One time we were already on the way to the train. If not for Mum, we'd already be gone. On the way she turned around and saw there was no one behind us. We came back to the *Schleuse*, hid out for a while in the courtyard and then they let us in. Luckily we were among the first to get out of the *Schleuse*, because then suddenly they didn't have enough people and they were taking anyone they could find, even right off the street. Our girls – Gita also stayed – were waiting in front of the brewery and walked us back to the *Heim* in a festive parade. Francka made my bed up for me straight away and soon after that I fell asleep. I've never slept so well in my bunk. Now I want nothing more than to wait out the end of the war in it.

◦⟞

The buildings near the Sokol hall have to be cleared out. A special dinner is being cooked; we're preparing an *Entwesung*, a disinfestation. Some Polish children are supposedly coming. It's all so incomprehensible. Why and for what purpose are they bringing them here from Poland?

They arrived yesterday at 5 p.m. No one is allowed in to see them. Overnight a few nurses, *Betreuers* and doctors were permitted in; aside from them no one is allowed to go near the buildings.

*

We've managed to get some news from the buildings. None of the kids know Czech at all; we don't even know if they're Jewish, Polish or something else. We can see them a bit from the tower; this morning they went to the *Entwesung*. They look awful. It's not even possible to guess their age. They all have old, worn-down faces and tiny little bodies. Most of them have no stockings and only a few of them have shoes. They return from the *Entwesung* shaven bare; we hear they have fleas. They all have terrified eyes and resisted fearfully when shown to the baths. Were they afraid it was gas?

Yesterday afternoon they were taken away. The doctors, nurses and *Betreuers* went with them. The whole time they were quarantined they were specially cooked for and clothing was scrounged for them. The only person who managed to get in touch with them was Fredy Hirsch. Now, as a result, he's locked in a bunker at the command centre.

They've left. We never learned where they were from or where they were taken. All that's left of them is a couple of lines scrawled on the wall of the building, which we can barely decipher. And that horrible, inexplicable rumour – gas!

I spent November 10th in bed. I had a fever again. Despite that, it was a lovely birthday. I got a little present from each of the girls: a pudding from Francka, a new charm from Jindra and that's not even including Mum and Dad. Where they got it all, I don't know. So many beautiful things that I couldn't have had a nicer birthday even at home. The next day, though, was less lovely, and in time will be remembered in all of Terezín.

11 November 1943

Unfortunately, or perhaps fortunately, I didn't take part myself due to illness, and so I regret not being able to make more detailed notes.

The morning count didn't add up, and supposedly someone had run away; it was probably true, although maybe the Germans just made it up. It was necessary to undertake a full census of the inhabitants – and not in the barracks, the way it had been done before when someone was missing, but outside the ghetto. That night all the sick from the hostels and the building infirmaries were transferred to infirmaries in the barracks. Other than that, all the ghetto inhabitants, from the very youngest infants in the *Säuglingsheim* to the very oldest, were taken out to a huge meadow (the Bohušovice basin), lined up by the hundreds and left standing from daybreak until deepest darkness, constantly being rearranged and recounted, with the horrible thoughts that they would never be let back in the ghetto, that they'd be taken away and shot etc. – something they deduced from the SS men's many spiteful taunts and remarks. Although I wasn't there, I can easily imagine myself in that situation.

Others thought I was better off in my bed in Vrchlabí, although I'm not convinced. That morning was OK. Lízinka and I were sharing a bed for lack of space and we were in a pretty good mood. They came to count us too, and so we believed it was nothing more than a census. However, when by three and then by four and finally by six o'clock there was no sign that anyone else had come back, we started to worry. Our worries were the same as the people outside: the most horrible visions and finally self-reproach for not going with the rest so we could all perish together. If only we were allowed to go out in the corridor to look out of the window into the street – but that too was forbidden.

Eyes fastened on the door, ears pricked, we listened tensely for even the slightest sign of life. We waited, hunched under the bedcovers. In vain. Silence, grim and unusual, was the only response to all our questions. Will I ever see my mum and dad again? What has happened to them? Our tense, unsettled nerves, irritated by our day-long fast, gave in, and hot tears welled up in our eyes.

Around eight in the evening finally steps resounded outside. The barrack corridors came alive. The door opened and the relatives of the ill came in and told us everything. Dad came to see me too and brought me something to eat. We stayed in the hospital till morning.

No one ever returned to the gates of Terezín so happily or fell asleep so contentedly as on that night of 11th November.

An international committee is coming, we hear. A huge clean-up and reorganization of the town is in progress: *Verschönerung der Stadt*. A plan is all ready as to where the committee will go and the work is being carried out accordingly. In Hamburg barracks, the third layer of bunks must be gone within 24 hours from all the rooms whose windows face on to the street. One transport has left already, true, but that is not nearly enough to free up enough spaces.

Cutting Down Bunks (1944)

'*So it happened that early one morning they came, sawed off the top bunks and their tenants had no choice but to grab their bags and move on.*'

So it happened that early one morning they came, sawed off the top bunks and their tenants had no choice but to grab their bags and move on. There were no other places to go, but within two days it had all been worked out. Some people moved into other buildings, the rest found *Notbelags*. Mum was among those affected; fortunately after three days of desperate searching she got a place in a bunk bed in room 211.

Christmas. We had been looking forward to it, and for a while it seemed they'd leave us alone. Even though we've had enough opportunities to get to know the Germans, we are still so naïve. There hasn't yet been a holiday where they've left us in peace. Nor would this Christmas be an exception. Aunt Ola and many of our girls left. It'll be a sad holiday.

A freshly scrubbed floor and perfectly made-up bunks. In the middle of a white tablecloth, a new, beautifully carved wooden menorah, a gigantic cake and 33 mess tin lids with slices of bread. In the corner of the room, a basket with the presents we prepared. Girls in ironed white blouses and blue skirts. Everything is ready. The Chanukah celebration begins.

The cramped loft space of building L410 filled up with the figures of girls. The first candle on the menorah flared into life and objects stretched into long, scary shadows. 360 pairs of eyes lit up. Our *Heimleiter* approached the menorah and prayed. '*Ma'oz tzur yeshu'ati* . . .' echoed quietly through the loft . . . when suddenly: 'A German's in the building!' shouted the watch, who had run up from downstairs.

The candle went out; the shadows vanished. 'Everyone into your rooms!' came the order. 'Careful, don't let them hear you.' How will it turn out? If he figures out that we were celebrating . . .! Or if he goes into our rooms and see the tables laid! This could turn into a right mess.

We'd barely got back to our room when the German – it

Chanukah in the Loft (16 January 1944)
'The cramped loft space of building L410 filled up with the figures of girls. The first candle on the menorah flared into life and objects stretched into long, scary shadows. 360 pairs of eyes lit up.'

was Lagerkommandant Burgr himself – got up to the third floor and burst into 24, our room. He went right to the table, sat down on the bench and started to question us. How was it that we had such a prettily laid table, where had we got so much bread, etc. At least we'd had the foresight to hide the menorah in time. We didn't give anything away and so he left empty-handed.

We breathed a sigh of relief, waited until they came up from downstairs to tell us he'd left the building, had our supper and gave out the presents. It was very nice and could have been even nicer if that awful man hadn't spoiled our plans.

[121]

Jaundice and typhus are out of fashion. A new illness has appeared – encephalitis. They cleared out the entire Sokol hall, formerly our typhus ward. L410 has, as always, the most cases. We've been quarantined for several days. I think they should just set up an infirmary here, otherwise the whole *Heim* will move over to the Sokol hall anyway. They've enlarged our infirmary by one room already, number 17.

The illness is running its course without too many serious cases. We're having fun with it. We know all the signs of this odd illness and we spend days examining each other. Today the girls diagnosed me with poor stomach and eye reflexes and they say my tongue is crooked. Also, I can't touch my nose with my finger when my eyes are closed.

In fact, the girls were right. On his visit today, the doctor explained what the tongue looks like when you have encephalitis. He had me stick out my tongue and that was that.

He examined me and announced it was a typical case of encephalitis. I have to go to Vrchlabí barracks for an examination.

*

At Vrchlabí they confirmed the finding. I'm in number 17. It's unbelievably disorganized and cold here. I've got my duvet and mattresses ready for disinfection. Tomorrow I go to the Sokol hall. I'm looking forward to a bath. The girls wrote that everyone has to bathe first. That will be wonderful: a bath, for the first time in three years.

*

I've been lying here over a week. There's nothing wrong with me, but no one can be released before a fortnight is up. My bed is next to Katka's. We've got nothing to do all day. I'm painting and reading a lot. Katka and I read *Quo Vadis* by Henryk Sienkiewicz together. It's a tremendously interesting book. The persecution of Christians was horrid. And it's horrid that so many centuries later similar things are happening. We also read Hora's poems; I liked them so much that I copied some of them out.

◦—

15 January 1944

I missed a big event: the move from Hamburg barracks. According to the letters and stories, it must have been a terrible madhouse: to move 4,000 people and all their luggage within 24 hours. Mum didn't even come this afternoon; she just wrote to say that I should be glad I wasn't there. By the time I get back, supposedly everything will be in order. Fortunately she got a pretty good place in Q610.

The doctor was here today; Pucka and I will be released. Tomorrow morning they'll bring us our *Übersiedlungschein* and we can go. Poor Francka; she was so looking forward to my coming home and now she's in the infirmary herself.

◦—

Pucka and I got up at half five so we could be home before the girls get up. We were surprised. The bunks have been rebuilt, covered in brown paint, the curtains dyed green and on the main wall, covered by a sheet dyed the same shade of green, there's a huge painted picture of Prague. I was silly to want to go back to Mum. Today I wouldn't trade our room 24 for anything on this earth. Except for the end of the war, but even then I'll probably miss it.

Francka has been in the infirmary almost three weeks. We were worried it would turn out to be pneumonia. Now, thank God, it's safely behind her and tomorrow she's coming home. I've got everything ready and tidied for her, so that she'll like it here. We've pasted dark red and black paper on her bunk, on the outside it's covered in pictures and on the inside are three post-cards from Prague. It feels to me like being in a little room and the postcards serve as windows. We have a view out on to Hradčany and the River Vltava. If only it were morning already and I could go fetch Francka.

The committee, for whose sake a transport had left and the triple-decker bunks were destroyed, left and was apparently satisfied. They didn't see much – they were here only a half-day. But it was probably only a general review. From the *Kommandatur* new orders were sent out about the *Verschönerung*, the 'beautification', which must be completed within two months.

It's funny, but it looks as if they're trying to change Terezín into a spa town. It's like in the fairy tale about the wishing-table.

In the evening the order comes, and by morning we all roll our eyes in surprise at how this or that has happened.

For three whole years it never occurred to anyone that the streets should be named anything other than L and Q. Every little child knew where Magdeburg, Jägrovka or any of the other barracks, just as any Praguer knows where Wenceslas Square is. The Germans suddenly got an idea and overnight there had to be signs hung on every corner house with the street name and at the junctions arrows pointing '*Zum Park*', '*Zum Bad*', etc. The barracks are no longer called Magdeburg, but B-five; I no longer live at L410, but at Hauptstrasse 10. All the patients were moved overnight out of the school by the *Bauhof*, which had till today been serving as our hospital; the whole building was painted, scrubbed, school desks were brought in and by morning a huge sign shone into the distance: '*Knaben und Mädchenschule*' – 'The Boys' and Girls' School'. It really does look beautiful, like a real school, except it's got no pupils or teachers. However, this drawback was fixed quite simply: a small sign announcing '*Ferien*' – 'Holidays'.

Freshly sown grass is already coming up on the town square; the middle is decorated with a huge bed of roses. The paths have been strewn with clean yellow sand and newly lacquered benches line them in two rows. The boards, whose purpose we mused over for several days, have turned into a music pavilion. We even have a café with a lovely sign, '*Kaffeehaus*'. All the shops have got new names as well. The houses too will be repainted; over on Langestrasse they have already started.

The building behind Magdeburg, which used to be for manufacture and *Glimmer*, is now the *Speisehalle*, or dining hall. Several girls are employed there heating up food. They have to wear white caps and aprons. The Sokol hall, as of this writing, has become a restaurant with carved furniture; there are plush chairs in the main hall and huge vases with flowers. On the first floor there is a library and reading room, and there are tables with coloured sunshades on the terrace.

There has been significant progress with the house painting. Several Danish hostels have received furniture. Bunks and shelves painted yellow were put up in two buildings along with blue curtains. In the park in front of the *Säuglingsheim*, they've built a luxurious pavilion with cribs and pale blue embroidered coverlets. One room has toys, a rocking horse etc. Then there's a pool, a merry-go-round and see-saws. None of us can explain why they are doing all this. Do they really care so much about this committee? Perhaps we don't even know how good the situation is.

⟳

Mum isn't working in the factory any more; she got a job in one of the *Kinderheims* as a seamstress. I'm going out to the garden again, but I applied late, so they allocated me to a different group from the other girls.

⟳

Now, instead of celebrating Mother's Day we have to pack. How many weeks were we looking forward to this; how much self-denial and self-control it took for us to save those few dozen grams of sugar and margarine for a cake. Which of us this time will be in it?

Francka is in the *Schleuse*. And several other girls beside her. The whole orphanage is in it. What did those innocent children ever do to them? I helped the kids from L318 through the *Schleuse*. Some of them can't even really speak yet. Two- and three-year-old children with transport numbers around their necks and the word *Waisenkind* – orphan – added in pencil.

I don't know who to think of first. Pucka, Doris, Hanka, Růža, Francka. It's so dead here, so quiet that it hurts. No one's bouncing above me, no one laughing, and an empty bunk next to me. My God, please let Francka out of the transport.

*

I don't know what time I fell asleep. It must have been really late; the girls were boarding on the *Hilfsdienst*'s second night shift. When we got up, it was still dark. They sent us back from the *Schleuse*; by yesterday they wouldn't take any more comers on the *Hilfsdienst* and without an armband they weren't letting anyone in. I saw them letting in people with red armbands; we cut up some shorts and made the bands ourselves.

We spent about an hour in the *Schleuse*; then they sent us away so we wouldn't get underfoot. The Germans were on a rampage and more than once they shoved someone on the train just as he was. The rest of the afternoon I stood under Francka's window and never took my eyes off the scrap of paper tied to a string. It was a sign that they were still up there and had not yet boarded. At half six the locomotive's whistle sounded and the train moved off past Jägrovka barracks. The paper still hung from the string. Francka had been recalled.

~

From the garden, we go to Travčice to help with the hay. The journey leads past the Small Fortress and we meet groups of prisoners. Is Hanka's or Lála's father among them? Do they know anything about them? And whose fathers, husbands, sons are these? We're not allowed to speak to them.

How we'd like just to greet them, raise their hung heads and give them strength for the coming – possibly their last – days! We mustn't stop, we can't give any sign; they probably aren't allowed to look at us either. SS men with guns surround them, shouting, slapping, throwing stones. We exchange quick glances with them. We belong to you, friends, take courage, hold on a while longer. We're prisoners too, we also long to go home.

There's so much we'd like to tell them, but we mustn't . . . yet, the thought has already crossed our minds and we start to sing. Songs by Voskovec and Werich; how could the Germans understand? '*As long as I've still got my head, I'll use it to sing songs instead . . .*' Their marching improves and smiles of recognition appear on their faces. Well, comrades, heads up. '*Freedom can't be snared in chains. Chains rust, old iron can't hold us again.*'

*

Rutka's parents have been in prison for two years. She last saw her mum last year picking chestnuts, when she went into the fields with the prisoners from the Small Fortress. She had no news of her father until she saw him three weeks ago in a group of prisoners from the Small Fortress. Every day she gets up at half five and waits by the fence near the road the prisoners take to get to work. At six a.m. going, and after five p.m. on the way back. For a fortnight now Rutka has been watching in vain and letting herself get shouted at by the SS. Her dad is not with the prisoners any more. Perhaps he's been transported somewhere else, or sent for further interrogation to Prague; maybe he's ill – or has died. No one dares to mention it aloud. We console Rutka and now she's getting up at five again so as not to miss a single group.

Number 24 is a convent? They won't be saying that about us. Old maids? No one will make fun of us again. Number 24 is organizing a dance.

The invitations are ready; the cellar has been reserved; the accordion player has promised to come. We'll do a buffet in the back room of the cellar with open-faced sandwiches and lemonade. We've got everything arranged and the margarine set aside for the accordionist (he'll play all evening for half a kilo). We kind of know how to dance; Šára and Tonička are patient teachers. All that's left is to distribute the invitations.

*

It worked out marvellously. Much better than we'd expected. We'd been afraid that the boys wouldn't come, that we wouldn't know how to dance and that it would all be a huge embarrassment. But in the end everyone who was invited came and the atmosphere was superb. Some of the boys probably got their feet stepped on a bit, but by and large we got through it. Almost all evening I danced with one boy. He didn't ask practically any of the others to dance, only me. The girls are predicting a relationship, but I don't fancy him in the least. Anyway, he didn't even ask me for a date.

*

'Number 24's been corrupted,' that's what the girls from other rooms are whispering about us. For God's sake, what's the problem if some of the girls are seeing boys? Are the rest of them just sitting around at home? Did they think we'd stay a convent forever?

We had another dancing lesson. He came again and only danced with me. His name is Ota; he has curly, light brown hair and he's 25. The girls won't leave me alone about it. I make fun of them, but I don't know how long I'll be able to keep up the pretence. I'm actually starting to like him.

Mum went for an X-ray today. She has had an elevated temperature for several months and they still won't certify her as ill. She has a lingering pneumonia and should be resting. I hope they don't find anything on her lungs as a result. Dad wants her to go into hospital.

This afternoon there's a celebration on the tower; I'm really looking forward to it. Ota will probably come as well. It's been a fortnight since the second dance lesson and he still hasn't asked me on a date. Each time he meets me he stops for a while, but that's all. I just hope he comes this afternoon. If even today nothing happens, then it's probably a lost cause.

*

He was there. He walked me home and asked me on a date this evening. He's a great guy; we had a nice conversation. He's not one of those crazy boys, like the ones some of our girls date. After all, he's 25. It's a bit much for me at my age, but it doesn't really matter, since we understand each other so well. The girls are rooting for me; my act didn't work, they knew I liked him. Francka is a bit jealous, but I forgive her her silly words. Did I really insist just a month ago that I would buy myself a canary and a cat and stay an old maid? I'm looking forward to tomorrow. At half six again, at the corner of L410.

*

Beneath our windows, a band is bawling; the cleanly scrubbed pavements contrast sharply with the newly painted houses; freshly ironed curtains shine in the windows. The café is overflowing, the park benches fully occupied and the playground in front of the *Säuglingsheim* is in use for the first time. Behind Magdeburg a vehicle is waiting, but this is no *Leichenwagen*, no hearse – it's a nice, clean vehicle with bread and men in white aprons, caps and gloves. A group of the prettiest, most healthy-looking girls have been chosen from the *Landwirtschaft*, who will bring a basket of fresh fruits, singing all the while. The children are rehearsing one final time their joyous greeting for 'Uncle Rahm', turning up their noses at the snack they are offered. '*Schon wieder Sardinen?*' – 'Sardines again?' Today we'll have two bread rolls and pâté for supper, tomorrow there will be meat for dinner. The menu has been written for the whole week ahead, and of course for last week too. Everything is ready; the ghetto guards are running madly here and there to make sure they let everyone know in time. We're just waiting until the first cars from the International Committee appear on the road from Bohušovice and the comedy can begin.

The Arrival of the International Red Cross Committee (1944)

To give the impression that the Jews in Terezín were well looked after, everything was thoroughly cleaned, brightened up and arranged like a stage set. The committee was duped and believed that everything was in the best of order.

I've been transferred to Kréta. I've wanted it for a long time, but now I'm not so happy about it. I don't know how I'm going to fit everything in. Mum has been in the hospital since yesterday. In Kréta we work from six to half six, with an hour break. So two hours more than I'd done up till now. At noon we have a lesson and then in the evening from eight to nine we have maths. At least the people living in Mum's room in Q610 are nice and will help me cook something. Then I can take it to Gran and Dad when he's got the evening shift. On the other hand, in Kréta I'll be able to 'sluice' things more often and besides, every other day I'll have a *Zusatz* – a supplement – and every week ¾ of a loaf of bread and two pâtés. I've got to get hold of these things myself now that Mum can't sew. Today we got a package, too, so I hope it might work out.

If only Heinl didn't carry on so. It's his fault that no one wants to join the *Landwirtschaft*. He guards us like a madman; every day he catches someone. Everyone knew his motorcycle and the moment they heard it they were on their guard. So he came up with a new method of silent skulking. Now he rides a bicycle and watches us from the opposite ramparts with a telescope. Now that I've finally got into Kréta, it might turn out to be impossible to take things at all. But regardless of how things are, I have to get Mum some vegetables.

*

It has been possible to 'sluice' things, but we're watched awfully closely. Today Heinl beat one boy for a single cucumber peel

[103]

found tossed in the greenhouse. Almost all of us had something on us, but evidently he was satisfied with a blow and a mild punishment: by evening we had to level the fields along the fence. We have to be very careful bringing things in, but outside we can stuff ourselves to bursting. At the moment we've mostly got cucumbers; I eat them with bread, salt, even sugar – I'm utterly sick of them. The carrot situation is pretty bad; the field is right by the road, where Heinl can appear at any moment. However, I'm getting more experienced. I have a new skirt for gardening, very frilly, and the gendarmes are by and large good-natured. Except for Heinl, but he's got eyes everywhere.

Today it's exactly five weeks from that celebration at the tower – five weeks since our first date. People might say it's a ridiculously short time, but can one really compare time here with what it is outside? Does our life have anything in common with the rest of the world? We're only separated from it by a couple of ramparts, but isn't it something else that broke the bonds connecting us with them? When Terezín's gates open one day, once the barbed wire is torn down and the ramparts levelled, will we be able to walk on in life alongside those who stayed outside and went their own uninterrupted way through life?

Five Sundays, no more. How close we grew in those few weeks. The thing that binds us here to each other also deepens the gulf between us and those from whose midst we were violently ripped.

It was not just five weeks, but five times seven long days, when there was not an hour without some emotional tension. Hunger, filth, illnesses, epidemics and that horrible fear from the constant threat of deportation. When will there be an end to all this? What is the political situation? If it were at least possible to believe the news here, but it's all half-invented, twisted and embellished, always those stupid, optimistic *bonkes*, rumours.

It's impossible to talk with Mum about these matters; she's always snowed under with work and trying to scrape together enough food. Dad is worn out after a full day at the office and if he doesn't have the evening shift he's happy to be able to relax a bit after work. There's no talking with the girls about these things. Except a little bit with Francka. But now I have Ota, with whom I can have long, intelligent debates.

Ota was in Lípa for two years before Terezín. He tells awful tales from there. It was only a work camp, but the treatment was similar to a concentration camp. He's all alone here. He hasn't had a mother since he was twelve; his father he lost at twenty. Out of four siblings, two are in Poland and only one sister is for now still at home; she married an Aryan. Before he was expelled from school he studied chemistry; he has two semesters to go. Even here he's constantly lugging his textbooks around. He works in the laundry room as a stoker. His shifts alternate; he prefers the night shift, because next to the laundry room is a fruit garden and he can 'sluice' apples there. Every evening I get one and he's always bringing me food and forcing it on me. I really don't like taking it from him; he's got so little himself other than a bit of bread, margarine and sugar, which he gets for odd jobs. He looks miserable, and yet the little he has, he shares with me. A wonderful fellow!

I stayed home today; yesterday I'd had a temperature. There's nothing wrong with me, but the doctor wrote me a sick note.

And what of it – for a month I clocked in every day, I can play hookey just this once. If only the *Toranut* girls were here with supper already. By 7 o'clock I have to nip over to Mum's, then a bit of time with Ota and at 8 o'clock it's maths.

Night, ¼ to 2

Ugh, these revolting bedbugs! It's impossible to sleep. There are only six of us left here; the rest have moved out to the courtyard and the corridor. We have the light on, but it doesn't help. That's why they say 'as nosy as a bedbug'. They crawl around the walls, across the duvets, all over your body, fall from the bunks right into your face. Up till now they've more or less left me alone, but today they seem to have got a taste for my blood. I don't even bother killing them any more; I sacrificed a whole stack of paper to them and still can't bring myself to squash them with my hands. We compete to see who can catch more of them. I'm losing – so far I've only got 30, Hanka is in the lead: 66 personal and 33 community ones, caught on the floor, walls, tables and benches. Three more days till disinfection. If I'm not quick enough to grab a place outside tomorrow (even next to the toilets, as long as it's not in here), that will be three nights without sleeping a wink.

*

During the disinfection the girls are staying over in Hamburg; I'm in Mum's free bunk. I've got a temperature again, but this afternoon I have to go to work. I hear we're loading carrots and I can't let an opportunity like this slip by.

*

Mum is out of hospital; there's only a small shadow left on her lungs. Still, she has to conserve her strength. Yesterday we got a package, so at least there's something to help her convalesce.

*

Back in L410, but not in 24 any more. Despite our loud protests and requests they moved us to 27. Our initial prejudice against this *Heim* is subsiding and it seems like it might even be nicer here than our old home – but still, we were and will always remain number twenty-four.

There are only 21 of us here, not a single empty bunk. I've got a place by the window again in a single; Francka is next to me, underneath me is Rutka, and Hanka's on the third level. The boys are making us some shelves to share, for our shoes, dishes and food. The suitcases are up in the loft, clothes are in the wardrobe in the corridor. Nothing must be under the bunk – no rubbish, everything in its place. We entrusted Ota with dyeing our curtains and tablecloths.

It'll be fine here; if only we were done with cleaning already. But enough writing for now – and hey ho, on to painting the bunks . . .

17 September 1944

Ironed curtains, bunks all made up the same, and it's clean, ever so clean here and all around the building. The girls are hurrying to get dressed (everyone's in white blouses and blue skirts today) and fix supper. We whisper among ourselves – really, you don't even dare speak aloud, that's how beautiful and festive it is today. It's the evening of the holiday Rosh Hashanah.

*

A competition for the cleanest, best-decorated and prettiest *Heim*. We won. I think we rightfully deserve the first prize. Number twenty-seven was truly exemplary. Not only in looks, but also in behaviour.

A party is in the works; every room will contribute a number. We've already got a programme and are rehearsing diligently every day.

*

This afternoon we hoed the celery; I brought back three bunches. The spinach is ever so slowly coming out; the lettuce hearts are coming along . . .

That was a week ago, yesterday, and this afternoon. An hour ago Ota and I went outside; we had no idea . . .

And no? Oh, girls, I sit here among you – no, I won't tell you anything. Rehearse your lines, laugh, play, be merry – at least for today. Once I tell you – maybe you'll never laugh again. Sing, frolic – how much I'd like to join you, but now I know, so I won't be able to.

An hour ago we were on our way back from a walk over by Magdeburg. Cheerful, carefree. Clumps of people were standing in front of the building. 'Five thousand men.'

Farm Work *(13 March 1943)*

There were advantages to cultivating vegetables for the Germans. One laboured outside the ghetto in the fresh air, and in spite of prohibitions one could manage to smuggle in some food or at least eat something surreptitiously.

I didn't catch Dad in the office. Still, I didn't need him to confirm it. The corridors of Magdeburg speak for themselves. The booming footfalls, rustling clothes, roaring ghetto guards, slamming doors, and hysterical crying always sound the same and mean the same thing.

Five thousand, all men. Supposedly for work, to build a new ghetto. Somewhere near Königstein. Two and a half thousand tomorrow, two and a half the day after. Uncle Jindra is in the first, Dad and Ota in the second.

*

The *Schleuse* is in Hamburg. Jindra boards early morning. I have to help Ota finish packing his bags. Dad is ready. He probably wouldn't even have to go; he could get himself recalled. He might get out, but that wouldn't be him. 'Ask on my own behalf? Five thousand are going, why shouldn't I go as well? Someone else would have to go in my place.'

28 September 1944

Yom Kippur. I'm fasting and no one had better tell me it's pointless. Not this year, not right now.

The first group are still in the *Schleuse*. The second have not had to board yet. The train carriages haven't arrived. I'm fasting and – it's probably foolish – I believe there will be a miracle.

The carriages have come, the first two and a half thousand are gone, but the second deportation is not boarding. Rumour is they're having to combine – no trains, supposedly, the tracks are broken; maybe they won't go. The optimists are unpacking their luggage.

*

9 p.m.

A chill breeze blows through the open windows into the room. Outside it's quiet, here and there a cart rattles, a recalled person returns from the *Schleuse*.

Number twenty-seven today. Unmade beds, shelves over-turned, ripped and darned socks, men's shirts and handkerchiefs hung over the stove, underneath it washbasins with water to be poured out. Suitcases under the bunks, rucksacks on the floor, there a pot of margarine, a piece of bread.

Each of us has someone in it – a father, brother, some of us both. This is the former number twenty-four, which only three days ago was rehearsing a play; these are the girls who could laugh so heartily.

We sit around the table; Milan, Miluška's boyfriend, and Ota are here as well. We're singing. Folk songs, Terezín parodies. The boys sing too, and loudly, drowning us out, cracking jokes. The girls are laughing, and I laugh with them. Then suddenly silence, and again the boys rescue the situation with their humour. For God's sake, be quiet now, don't pretend, you're deceiving us and yourselves as well. Don't laugh, it only makes things worse. This is what you call a good mood? Gallows humour, that's what it is; don't play the hero. Maybe I'm a coward, but my tears are more sincere than your laughter. Let me cry . . .

[111]

*

The boys have left; we're in bed, no one is asleep. The light is on; it helps the night pass faster.

*

The darkness is broken by the first rays of daylight. It's still peaceful outside. We wait. Any moment the carriage wheels might rumble – and then all hope is gone; it means the end is here.

～

29 September 1944

The train carriages are here, the second transport is starting the *Schleuse*. Mum is quickly getting supper ready, so Dad can have one last real meal. Ota is here too, this whole week of transports he's been having supper with us. I stuff myself with food; I don't know what I'm eating. Does it even matter? I swallow mouthfuls; I'm not hungry, but with each spoonful I swallow a single tear. There is not enough food; there are far more tears.

Dad and Ota are rolling cigarettes in the Russian style, filling them with tea and laughing. Gallows humour again!

A quarter to six; we have to go.

Roll-ups laid aside on the bench, and laughter abandoned along with them. All three of us used to sit here, every evening – not for long, only this last three-quarters of a year. This was our best time at Terezín, our happiest days here.

If only the war had ended already . . . it would have been too beautiful.

So here we sit today for the last time. From tomorrow, Mum and I are alone. And you, Dad? His hand tosses the still-smouldering cigarette away, clutches me to him and Mum on the other side. We can't hold back the tears; we've stored up too many of them this past week and we can't resist them any longer. With my head pressed to Dad's chest I can distinctly hear the beating of his heart. Halting, sad, like the mood this evening. Oh, Dad, if only your hands were so strong that no one could rip me from their embrace. I hear your heart; I feel it trembling and yet its beats are firm and resolved. Resolved to face the battle that awaits it, ready for the wounds it will receive, bleeding from a wound that struck it in the most vulnerable of places: a farewell. And still it beats, it will beat and must beat on! Our hearts will be with him; they will fight and suffer with him, hope and believe. And just as ours do, his will beat for us . . .

*

Hamburg, third courtyard. Half one at night. We're boarding. We have white dresses and *Hilfsdienst* armbands; we can accompany them as far as the gates. Ota must already be on the train. What a shame; I couldn't even help him with his luggage, or I wouldn't have got back from the second courtyard.

'We didn't know each other for long, but . . . they were wonderful times. I'll remember them happily, and don't you forget them either. You know the address to come to after the war. Maybe we'll meet again.' He gave me his photo to remember him by. On the back side he wrote a verse from Nezval's *Manon Lescaut*: 'When the key rattles the dark seminary gates, don't leave me there, come stroke my face.' A kiss, a squeeze of my hand, then he helped me climb over the fencing. Now he's in the train and in a few hours he'll be leaving . . .

We approach the gate quickly; forty people more, now thirty. Dad takes his luggage from us, here it goes again . . . Twenty people in front of us. What's this? They're closing the gates . . . 'Everyone back to the barracks!' No more boarding; they don't have enough train carriages. Is it possible; will they really get to stay? Perhaps a miracle has occurred . . .

Five hundred women have to volunteer to join the thousand men left. Mum wants to come forward; Dad won't let her. He says he knows what he's doing. But we want to go, Mum and I. After all, if he's going, it's our responsibility to go with him. No, it's his responsibility to see that we stay here.

All the men talk that way. Why isn't it obvious that we want to go with them? Would they let us go alone if it was the other way round? They won't let us; they were promised that we'd be spared from any future transports.

⌒

1 October 1944

I can still see him standing on the steps, waving, smiling . . . Oh, God, what sort of smile was that? I've never seen him like that before. He probably meant it to be a laugh, but all that came out was a failed grimace. The corners of his mouth twitched oddly. 'Daddy!'

He's gone, lost in the crowd among the rest of them. Mum and I looked in vain for him from the window. But he was nowhere to be seen. He probably couldn't get out past the luggage. But his stretched lips, that forced attempt at a smile. Daddy, why wouldn't you let us volunteer? You didn't believe you were going to build a new ghetto! Your eyes glittered strangely and your hand shook as you pressed me to yourself for the last time. What did it mean? Goodbye, or farewell? Daddy, did you believe we'd ever meet again?

The Departure of a Transport (4 April 1943)
Ghettowache *(ghetto guards) form a chain to separate those leaving and prevent others from reaching them.*

3 October 1944

This afternoon they're bringing the summonses for another transport. 1,500 family members of those who left. Of course they promised them that their families would be spared. So that was just another big lie. We could have left straight away yesterday and at least we would have been together. Who knows if they'll send us to the same place. If we'd had our way, we'd already be gone, but Dad didn't want it. And now we'll be in different places. We're almost certain to be in it. And if not today, then tomorrow or the day after. There'll be no respite. I'll go and see Mum; maybe she knows something already. I hope we were right not to volunteer – that's fate and there's nothing that can be done about it. Maybe we'd have had second thoughts one day if things had turned out badly.

*

I'm ending my Terezín diary here. One stage of my life has ended. Only the memories remain.

I'm opening a new notebook; I'll start to fill its empty pages tomorrow. Will I see this next one through to the end as well?

3. Auschwitz, Freiberg, Mauthausen, Home

4 October 1944

We might have been able to get out of it, but we didn't want to. Since we're in it, we're going. In this case it's best to leave things as you find them. We've been allowed to take all our luggage – a good sign. Maybe they were right and we're following the men. I'm looking forward to it; perhaps I'll see Dad by the end of the day.

It's 12 o'clock; the train has left the station. We were lucky to get on the train. We're in the last carriage. It's a good thing we went out to the courtyard early; there was a mêlée at the gate. I feel as if my back's broken. It wasn't easy pushing my way through starting at four a.m. with a rucksack on my back. It's never happened in a transport before that people fought so hard to get on the train. Today's transport is different from the others. We're following our men. I'm following Dad and Ota.

I wonder if a *Transportleitung* will come and help us with our luggage, like when we arrived at Terezín? Maybe Dad or Ota will be at the station. They'll be surprised to see us. We should be there soon – Königstein, they said, it must be close already. We've been travelling about six hours.

*

For God's sake, aren't we there yet? We've been travelling all night. That's not possible. Königstein isn't even that far away. What's happened – the train's stopped for a while. No, now it's flying onwards – that was a siren, there must be an air raid somewhere. What if it hits here? We're in Germany now, there are air raids here. Why is the train going so horribly fast?

*

It's getting light out. Where are we now? We've just passed through a station. Katowice. My God, that's the Polish border. Where are they taking us? The front's in Poland now. Could it be to Birkenau? But we heard it had been wound up, that transports weren't going there any more. So where are we headed? Are our men there? If so, then it doesn't matter where we go, so long as we stay together.

*

We've been travelling for twenty-four hours. Where, only God knows. We're all starting to get nervous. People were saying all sorts; listen to them and the front must be far behind us, and yet we've been travelling across Poland for half a day now and there's no sign of it. Now the train has started to slow. Could we finally be there? I don't want to believe it – I'd started to think this trip would never end. We're getting close, definitely – you can see buildings over there. And so many of them – it's a huge camp. I can see people, but what are they wearing? It looks like pyjamas, and they've all got the same ones.

My God, those are prisoners' clothes! Where have they taken us?! This is a concentration camp! There are some men working over there, stacking boards. Why is that man beating them so hard? It must hurt horribly, he took a cudgel to them. How can he be so cruel? He isn't even a German – he's also in a striped jumper, but he's got a band on his arm.

I must have been wrong; we can't be stopping here. Why would they take us to a concentration camp? It's not as if we've done anything. It's horrible how they treat people here. I can't watch; it makes me ill. He's walloped another one, an old man. What a stinker; he's barely twenty. Shame on him; that man could be his father and to treat him that way. He kicked him again till the poor old man staggered.

So that's what a concentration camp looks like; I could never imagine it. People have been living this way for several years. And we complained about Terezín. That was an absolute paradise compared to this.

What's this? The train has stopped. A whole group of striped people is running towards us. Is there anyone among them from Terezín? Maybe they've come to help with our baggage. Perhaps Dad's among them. But no, they've probably just come to see what sort of train this is. We're not getting off here, surely? Or – why didn't it occur to me earlier? – this is Auschwitz, of course. Birkenau is nearby, maybe the trains don't go there, so we'll have to walk that bit. Definitely, that's the way it is. This is Auschwitz, the concentration camp, and we're going to Birkenau, the work camp.

*

The carriage next to us is already alighting. Why so much noise over there? They're banging on our door. I suppose it's our turn now. Why are there so many SS men outside? Are they all here to guard us? Where would we run to? It would be pointless anyway. We're in it; there's no helping us.

'Everyone out! Leave your luggage where it is! *Alle heraus, schneller!!!*' Leave everything here, hand luggage too? Why are they shouting so much, what's with the spiteful smiles? They're grabbing everyone by the wrist; what are they looking for, watches? If only they wouldn't yell at us so much, and what do those grimaces and comments mean? They're treating us as if we belong in that concentration camp. One woman just got a slap for trying to take a loaf of bread with her. Is this Birkenau?

Why is my throat so scratchy? I don't want them to know how I feel.

Stupid eyes – why are they smarting? I mustn't cry! For all the world, not now!! '*Alles da lassen!*' – 'Leave everything as is!' – '*Schneller, heraus!!!*'

*

They sort us into two groups. One – older women and mothers with young children – goes to the left; the other goes to the right. 'Sick people shouldn't say anything,' hushed voices repeat; 'you're all healthy,' one of the ones in prisoner's clothes whispers in Czech just behind me. A Czech, then. The queues in front of us move; soon it will be our turn. As long as they leave me and Mum together. Surely they can't separate us if I say we belong together. Or will it be better not to say we're together? Probably; maybe they deliberately wouldn't let us stay together if they knew how much it mattered to us.

They're even taking mothers away from their children. I know that girl there; she's going to the right and her mum's going left. But the mum's quite old; she's got grey hair. My mum still looks young. But . . . maybe I look too much like a child? Maybe they'll ask me how old I am. Should I tell the truth? Fifteen; no, that's too little – they'd send me left and separate me from Mum. I'd better say I'm older, maybe eighteen. Do I look it? Sure, maybe they'll believe me.

The queue is getting shorter; the group of five in front of us has gone. Oh Lord, I pray to you, leave me and Mum together. Don't let them send us each a different way.

Two more people and it's our turn. For God's sake, what if he asks me what year I was born? Quickly: 1929 and I'm fifteen, so if I'm eighteen . . . 29, 28, 27, that makes 1926. Mum is standing in front of the SS man, he's sent her to the right. Lord, let us stay together! '*Rechts!*' the SS man snarled at me and pointed the way with his finger. Praise be, we're both on the same side. Thank you, God, a thousand thanks for making it work out.

⌒

First they led us to the baths, where they took from us everything we still had. Quite literally there wasn't even a hair left. I've sort of got used to the shaven heads, but the first impression was horrid. I didn't even recognize my own mother till I heard her voice. But so what, hair will grow back, it's not such a tragedy, as long as we survive. I don't hold out much hope. As soon as we got here, they held us up with a long speech, of which I remember nothing beyond the first sentence, which was plenty: '*Ihr seid in Vernichtungslager!*' *You are in an extermination camp.* Upon which they drove us here, into this building, on to bunks from which we are not allowed to move.

Hungarian Jews on the selection ramp at Auschwitz, May / June 1944. Those deemed fit to work were sent to the right; those sent to the left were immediately gassed.

I'm seriously hungry; we've not eaten since morning, it must be seven o'clock already, but it doesn't look as if we'll be getting any supper. Who knows, maybe they won't feed us at all and will leave us to die of hunger. If only we'd eaten that pâté on the train; we were saving it for Dad, so we'd have something to give him right away.

My God, we're such idiots, what were we thinking? 'You're following your men to a new ghetto.' And we believed them. Some people even volunteered to come. That's why they let us take all our luggage. A nice pile of things they can put in their warehouse today.

[122]

We're better off going to bed and sleeping off our hunger. Maybe they'll leave us alone for today. Figuring out how to fit ten into a space for four will be a problem, of course, but we'll manage somehow. If we all lie on our sides in one direction, it might work. We have three covers (that's not really the right word, but I can't find another term for the filthy rags that perhaps at one time used to be covers) that we have to share; we'll put our clothes under our heads – so yes, it'll work. We won't be comfortable, but after all the events and afflictions of the last twenty-four hours I'm so tired that I think I could sleep well even on these bare boards.

What must the girls in the *Heim* be doing? Francka, Šáry and the others? Will they remember me? And what about my lovely bunk? I won't see out the end of the war on it now.

*

So they're not letting us die of hunger. By this I don't mean that there was plenty of tasty food, not by any reckoning, but it doesn't matter, the main thing is that there was something at all.

Early in the morning came the wake-up call, after which each bunk received a pot with scrapings in it. They said that we're new here so there was no more left for us. I was utterly miserable. If that's how they're going to feed us, then it's the end for us. Although it wasn't at all edible – cold, thick and bitter – we forced it down. Partially to fill our stomachs with something, anything, and also because we were afraid that they would punish us for leaving food.

After breakfast was roll-call, where they counted us, left us standing there for an hour, maybe two, I don't know exactly, because I don't have a watch – in any case it was endless. Why I don't know; apparently it's part of the daily programme. They only let us back in the building once it seemed to them that we were sufficiently tired and frozen through and through. It's only October, but it was freezing cold standing there at four in the morning (it must have been around then, it was still completely dark), almost naked, for the rags they dressed us in can't be called clothes, our bare feet stuck in Dutch clogs (sometimes only one clog, if you're not clever and energetic enough to clamber down from the bunk in time and there aren't enough to go round) – and the worst thing of all, with a shaven head; that's the part that gets coldest.

Besides that, this Polish climate is awfully odd. During the day the sun beats down till people faint from the heat, while in the early morning it freezes worse than at home in December. I have to laugh when I remember how Mum always got mad when I wouldn't want to put on a cap or long stockings in winter. If I ever get home again, I will never wear anything on my head till the day I die.

No sooner had we crawled (in the true sense of the word; there are no ladders here like there were at Terezín) back on our bunks and wrapped our numb legs and hands in rags than it was time to get up again, from whence we went to the latrine and the *Waschraum*. Everything went by at such a pace that it was absolutely impossible to use either of these two rooms. We'd barely taken two steps inside and the guards were chasing us out again, using cudgels and suchlike.

Marching at a pace quick enough to lose your clogs in the mud so abundant here, we returned to the building. Shortly thereafter they brought soup – called *zupa* here – not too tasty, with everything possible (and impossible) floating in it. Rotten

[124]

turnip, corn cobs, bits of frozen marrow, stalks and beetroot, which gave the mixture a pinkish colour. As earlier that morning, five to ten people ate from a single pot. That didn't help the taste, because we don't even have spoons. Many people turned up their noses or didn't even eat, but not me. You have to eat – doesn't matter how or what. Like the proverb 'A good pig eats everything', I stuffed myself as full as I could. I used my teeth and my hands – just like the others who understand what's what and don't give themselves airs.

In the evening there was roll-call again, when bread rations were given out – a quarter-loaf of dark rye for each person and a spoonful of jam. We have no knives, so we just broke off bits and spread the jam with the crust. Mum and I hid one portion for the next morning and ate the other for supper. One of the guards gave me a handkerchief – I was surprised, since they're all such pigs. She saw Mum covering my head with her bare hands and it must have awakened a bit of human kindness in her; the rest aren't susceptible.

*

I'm so angry with myself; I let myself be waited on like a small child and I just sob all day. I can't help it; everything here is so horrible. Bedtime is drawing near and I'm already good for nothing. Lying unmoving in one position until morning. Last night I didn't even wake up once, but this morning I was all bruised, my bones felt as if they'd been broken, dreadful. You can't sleep well on a hard surface and now here it is again. Oh, God, why are you punishing us like this? *'Ruhe, alle schlafen, schneller!'* – 'Silence, everyone to sleep, hurry up!' The block warden patrols the middle of the building and the guards tear about shouting like madwomen. '*Schlafen, schneller!*' The lights have gone out.

*

The morning was the same as yesterday except that they would not let us back from the latrines into block 9, where we'd come from, and sent us into another block two further down. After lunch they moved us somewhere else again, where we spent several trying moments. It was already *Lagerruhe*, camp curfew; outside it was dark and suddenly . . . gunfire, a shout, the noise of footsteps fleeing and another shot . . . A wail, frightened voices, the door to our barracks opened slightly and several child-ish figures, their eyes wide with fear, slipped through the small crack. They spread out and clambered into the bunks among the others. Mum and I were sitting on the third level and three of them climbed into the bottom bunk.

We stared, frozen, into space and only a while later, from a few fearfully whispered words, did we understand what was going on. They were moving children from our camp over to the other side. The other side! People talk about it so much; the guards use it to threaten us over every silly thing, but as far as what it looks like there and what happens, I can't find out. A mysterious phrase – the other side – that makes everyone shiver. I understand it to mean gas . . .

Now clattering again, angry male voices, cries, more gunfire and loud wailing. The thud of heavy, hobnailed boots right in front of the building. They're coming here! They saw the chil-dren running to us! We are sitting on the first bunk next to the entrance and the hidden children are beneath us. They'll find them. They'll shoot. They'll shoot all of us. It's the end! These thoughts flashed through my mind; I hugged Mum even closer and started to pray: 'God, if I must die, then at least let Mum and me die together. Don't leave me alone here. Don't let me die after Mum does. Although I don't want to die – let me live, let Mum and me survive till the war ends.'

The steps slowly faded into the distance; the crying ceased. We were safe, and the children who'd run to us were too.

⌒

Before we came here to number eighteen, they left us sitting for a while in a building where Mum found a bucket of cooked potatoes. Probably a guard forgot them there. We divided them among everyone in the bunk; there were only eight potatoes left over. But they'll be good too: we're covered in case there's another day when we don't get any bread. Yesterday with all the moving they either forgot or it happens here more frequently; I don't know. In the morning I even managed to wash my face.

Today it was horribly hot; lots of people fainted during roll-call. I learned something interesting: they have an odd way of reviving people who have fainted. No artificial breathing or dousing with cold water. At first it seemed strange to me, but I came to see that no scientific or medical procedures work better or more quickly than this simple method: slapping. Everyone comes to, immediately.

*

They allowed us to write to Terezín. There isn't much point in it; I doubt they will even send our letters and we can't write the truth in them anyway. For our address, we were told to write: 'Arbeitslager Birkenau'. From the name, no one will imagine this and won't know that it's the same as Auschwitz. Just as we had no idea from the letters that reached Terezín from here.

However, we have some agreed signs: they'll know that everything we write is the precise opposite. The main thing is for them to have some word from us; the question, of course, is whether the letters will get there. They also told us to write that we'll be travelling onwards for work. There's been talk of it from the moment we arrived and I kept hoping for it to happen, but now, since they've let us write about it, I don't believe it any more at all.

We lived in number eighteen for two days. One guard took a liking to me; I helped her clean up and at noon I got as a reward three pans of *zupa*. She's Polish; her name is Broche. A really nice girl; she's not like the other guards, which is why I've become friends with her. I wouldn't have anything to do with the other ones; they're monsters – not even if they gave me a whole cauldron of *zupa*.

If only they'd left us in number eighteen. Perish the thought – here apparently you sleep in a different place every night. They must save a lot of bread this way, because in the confusion one building always gets forgotten about, as happened to us today for the second time.

*

At noon a transport from Terezín arrived. We were waiting by the latrine when they went by. I saw Laška and Růža Vogelová;

they said their mum, Líza and Zuzka had gone to the other side. What about Rutka? She arrived with me and I've not seen her again. Rutka is shorter than I; she probably went to the left. And Mrs Spitzová and Anita too. I can't believe it's possible that none of them are still alive, or that they'll be gassed any day now. Cheerful, smiling Rutka, our little Rutka; little Líza and her tiny sister Zuzka, who was born in Terezín.

Maybe the guards are just trying to frighten us and give us the creeps. Have any of them been on the other side? Are there really gas chambers there? I look in vain towards where that awful place is supposed to be. All our questions are pointless. The only things I see, which serve as an answer, are two chimneystacks that pour smoke day and night. The crematorium, they say.

The boards wouldn't even hurt me so much, but last night was woefully bad. It started with the so-called *Entwesung,* disinfestation. I kept thinking they were going to gas us. It wasn't that bad, but I'm fed up.

We had to take off our clothes and then they left us there. The first people's turn came after two hours; some weren't done until morning. The main purpose was probably to ensure we caught a proper cold and changed our clothing. I expected I'd get some different, disinfected ones, but perish the thought! They gave them out from the same pile where we'd taken them off – of course we got someone else's and each of us got either a dress or underclothes but not both, as we'd had before.

The bathing was over in a trice. Each of us walked through some showers and finally they sprayed us with Lysol. To make sure it all went off smartly and with no fuss, there were SS watching us, fairly young snotty-nosed boys, who must have been having great fun. We didn't have towels, of course, and so there was no choice but to wriggle into our clothes wet. There would have been no point drying off anyway, because it was pouring outside and we got even wetter.

There was shooting, much more noticeable than the night before. We hear they're shelling Cracow, the front's approaching. Maybe they'll come liberate us soon. God willing.

*

This building has a block warden; she must be a real pig. She struts around like a peahen in a satin bathrobe and a nightshirt. She left one woman kneeling on the bricks for asking for permission to use the toilet. Pig – well, there's no other word for her. Even that's too nice, the comparison is an insult to pigs everywhere.

They didn't even give us blankets, only a single paper-like coverlet made of straw to cover five people. But now I'm not even chilled; I've not caught the flu and I don't think anyone will even catch cold. You can withstand a lot, much more than you think. It's almost unbelievable: Mum just got over pneumonia and since we've been here she's completely stopped coughing.

*

A little while after roll-call (we were allowed to stay on our bunks; they just counted our legs – perhaps they felt a little bit sorry since we froze all night) an SS guy flew into the building; he must have been about sixteen. '*Alle nackt ausziehen und heraus!*' – 'Everyone strip naked and outside!' Again they divided us into two groups. Another moment of nervousness; would we stay together? It worked out OK. No sooner had we pulled our

Counting Legs (1945/6)

'. . . *we were allowed to stay on our bunks; they just counted our legs –*
perhaps they felt a little bit sorry since we froze all night . . .'

clothes back on than they were herding us onwards. People in
the building gazed at us sorrowfully and it occurred to me that
they were taking us to be gassed. I tried every which way to
banish this thought. Everyone said we were going to be put
to work and we should be happy. All pointless – gas, the gas
chambers, went round and round in my head and wouldn't
stop.

We went through the gate of C-camp, then a bit of the path
ran right alongside the *Mänerlager*, the men's camp; I kept an
eye out for Dad – perhaps he was in one of the buildings, he
must have been sent here, to Auschwitz. But I quickly gave up

any hope I'd had of actually finding him. It would have been an incredible coincidence: we were walking so fast that there was no time to look round. It was all we could do to keep up with the pace and not lose our clogs in the mud. Then came another order: '*Stehen bleiben!*' – 'Halt!'

At that moment a huge downpour began. We were soaked to the skin in no time. We clung tightly to each other to protect our bodies from the weather. Our clothes stuck to us and the dye from them ran down our legs in little streams.

Despite all our curses, appeals and prayers, the rain didn't stop until late in the afternoon. The setting sun briefly landed on us and the water began to evaporate; we disappeared completely in the steam. Only after that did our teeth start to chatter and goosebumps appeared.

It was already getting dark when the line began to move again a bit. They wrote everyone down; for safety's sake I said 1926 again and Mum took four years off, so the age difference wouldn't be so great. We've not told anyone that we're mother and daughter; supposedly it's better that way.

The baths were very similar to yesterday's *Entwesung*, just a lot bigger; they called it a sauna. There was awfully little time for bathing; we didn't get a chance to wash at all. After bathing we waited in an empty room with the windowpanes bashed out. Towels would have been unnecessary; the draught dried us off completely. Everything took place beneath the strict gaze of the youngest SS men.

I got incredibly lucky when clothes were distributed. I have a dress with long sleeves, high shoes (they don't match, but that's OK, everyone's are like that) and a coat with padding. It comes down to my ankles and can be buttoned at the neck. I have never been, nor will I ever again be, so pleased with anything as I am with this coat. I'm so beautifully warm in it; I'm so happy.

*

Late that night we got into a train (covered cattle cars). At the camp gates we each got a loaf of bread, a bit of margarine and a slice of salami. I tore into the bread as we walked and while boarding. We hadn't eaten since yesterday evening. Now I've got the salami into me as well and I'm feeling good again. Mum and I wrapped the margarine into a bit of the lining of my coat and hung it on a nail. We also tore off a bit of the padding for our heads.

We're sitting on the floor; there are fifty of us in the middle of this car. Somehow we have to lie down to sleep. There's something hard behind me, a board or something; it's pressing into me horribly, but I can't stand up now. In the morning I'll have to fix it. I'm curious where we're going. Supposedly it's a good transport. We'll see; it could be like with Königstein again. But nowhere could it be worse than here. At least I hope not.

After a twenty-four hour ride they decanted 500 of us at the station in Freiberg. The rest travelled on. After a bit of a walk, we came to a huge building. It's probably a factory. An SS man was waiting – all signs indicate he's the camp director; they call him *Unterscharführer* – with lots of *Aufsehers*, overseers. He read out the roll to see if we were all here, told us how to behave and then divided us into rooms. It was already late at night.

We couldn't believe our eyes. We're going to live here. In a proper building with walls, not in those awful shacks like at Auschwitz. To sleep on proper bunks and not in those horrid cages. Always two and two on one. I've got an advantage in that I'm with Mum and don't have to sleep with a stranger. We crawled up on to the third row. It's lovely lying here – it's so soft, and so warm. There's even central heating. We were really lucky to get out – this certainly won't be a bad camp.

*

I've never slept as well as last night. It was only on straw, with my coat folded under my head, but to me it felt like lying on a feather bed. I'm so happy that we've ended up here. I feel like a human being again. We were each allocated a coverlet (there are three now on each bunk), a towel for every two of us, and everyone got a bowl, mug and spoon. The last makes me happiest; we don't have to eat with our hands like animals any more; we're like people again.

We all live on the same corridor. Supposedly there are some Polish women on the second floor, but we're not allowed to go up there – or off this hallway at all. Still, that doesn't matter. We have everything we need here. Even flush toilets and a tiled washroom. If only there were running water. I'd like to have a wash; I think the grime will never come off. We don't have any soap and the whole time we were in Auschwitz, even at bathing hours, there was no time for washing. Also, we've not had any liquids for 24 hours and the exhaustion after the trip . . . I am terribly thirsty.

*

I fainted at roll-call. Thirst is dreadful, worse than hunger. Mum wiped the drains in the washroom; there were a few drops of water there, and so she revived me. The water began to run that night; I heard it and went for a drink. Immediately I felt better.

At noon there was marrow soup; there were even pieces of meat in it. Everyone could have as much as she wanted. As long as they keep feeding us this way, then we'll be able to survive. If only Dad is doing as well.

We've been here for a fortnight, but it seems like forever. Every day we have marrow soup – a litre per person, not as much as we want, like that first day. It's nothing but water and an hour later the hunger is back. We're allocated 400 grams of bread, but the guards are horrendous cheats.

We should already be working, but there have been a few cases of scarlet fever, so we're quarantined. We can't even go out in the corridor; we've not moved from this room for a fortnight. If we could at least be in our bunks, I'd sleep all day; at night it's impossible due to the bedbugs. In my whole life I've never seen as many as there are here; Terezín was nothing. They crawl around the walls even in broad daylight. During the day we have to have our bunks made perfectly and sit elsewhere. We sit on the ground; there isn't room for everyone on the chairs. Our daily programme consists of waiting for food and endless boredom. If no more scarlet fever breaks out, we'll go to work tomorrow.

We're working in a building here that is a factory for aeroplanes. We work in shifts, from 12 to 12. Last week we started at noon; that was OK. This week we start at midnight; we never get enough sleep. We come home at noon, then we stand at roll-call for an hour while our soup gets completely cold. After lunch we go to wash; it's three o'clock before we get to bed. We sleep for an hour and a half and then bread is distributed. By the time they give out the *Zulags* (the 'bonuses' consist of 10 grams of margarine and a spoonful of jam) it's six o'clock and at eight they bring round coffee. Between the two distributions the guards make such a racket that it's impossible to sleep. After coffee we sleep two hours and at 10 o'clock it's wake-up. We have to be ready within half an hour and lined up for roll-call.

*

If we have to stay on this shift any longer, I don't know how we'll survive. The hunger's a lot worse on this shift too. We get dinner just before bed and the bread has to last us for the whole twelve hours at work – and the work is so stupid at that. The whole time we are not allowed to sit down and yet there's nothing at all to do. That's the worst thing, because we can't let it be known and we have to keep pretending we're working. We're polishing aeroplane parts, horribly annoying. You stand in one place, doing the same motions with your hands. It's also terribly unhealthy to be swallowing iron filings the whole time and we never get out in the fresh air.

I thought something would happen on 28 October, but there wasn't even an air raid. In a fortnight it'll be my birthday. If only the end would come by then. That would be a present.

⌖

Now the day shift works from six to six. However, I'm not so lucky; our particular hall works till eight. It's still the same monotonous polishing. Mum was transferred to the second floor, assembling small wings.

*

Every morning at roll-call, Šára (that's what we call the *Unter-scharführer*, or sometimes Uša as well) finds an excuse to slap someone. I'm unlucky enough that it always happens right nearby. At first it made me ill, but now I'm past caring about such things. It was worse when one time he remembered that someone had left her papers in the *Waschraum* and he didn't give us any bread. Otherwise I'm becoming completely indifferent to everything.

⌖

'They're in Görlitz already and Bautzen, 80 km from here. By New Year it will all be over. A peace conference is meeting. The newspapers admit Cologne is gone.' All that was making the rounds here, but for now, the only fact is that it's a week after Christmas, the soup is getting weaker and weaker and we're down to 300 grams of bread.

We hear we'll be moving into real buildings.

The work halls are completely unheated. The floor here is cement; our shoes are shredded and we have no stockings. Šára has forbidden us to wear coats. We couldn't bear the cold and so we took the stuffing (for those of us who happened to have greatcoats) and the linings from our coats and made foot-rags, kerchiefs for our heads and vests for underneath our dresses. Today Šára took them all away. So now we've got thin coats and we're still freezing. The cold is horrible, maybe even worse than thirst and hunger.

*

I was at home for three days with a 40-degree fever and tonsillitis. I fainted twice in the ward. Today they certified me fit for work again.

⟿

We've been afraid of it for so long, and now it's here. We're moving into the buildings. Outside in the fresh air for the first time in four months. It was terribly cold: a snowstorm. The factory is about half an hour from here. I thought I wouldn't make it. Yesterday I still had a temperature, but now I'm OK and I think it will pass. Then I'm sure I'll never catch cold again in my life.

Snowman (December 1941)
The first picture that I made in Terezín. I smuggled it to my father in
the men's barracks and he wrote back: 'Draw what you see!'

In the Queue in Front of the Kitchen (1942)
For every meal – three times a day – one stood in an endless queue.

The Washroom (1942)
There was only cold running water and we had to use it sparingly.

Children Go to Lessons (1942)
Before the establishment of the '*Kinderheims*' (children's homes), children
brought their own benches and gathered together in a corner to learn.

Concert in the Dormitory (1942)
Despite the gloomy circumstances, we made time for culture
and entertainment.

The Corridor in Dresden Barracks (1942)
The little girl in the makeshift bed is suffering from TB. They made a bed for
her in the open corridor in an attempt to provide her with fresh air, but there was
hardly any fresh air anywhere. The overcrowded town was rife with disease.

A Parcel Arrived (11 July 1943)

It was a great event when somebody in the children's home received a parcel. The contents would be modest – bread, biscuits, sugar, a chunk of salami – but these wer treasures for hungry children. Some kept the parcel for themselves and others share with their best friend, while some gave everyone a piece of bread or biscuit.

For Her Fourteenth Birthday (November 1943)

A picture for my friend Francka. We were born in the same maternity home and shared a bunk and became best friends in Terezín. We imagined what it would be like in fourteen years, when we would both be mothers and go for walks in Prague. Francka died in Auschwitz before her fifteenth birthday.

Birthday Wish I (1943)
Everything in Terezín was transported in old hearses, even this
enormous imaginary birthday cake from Prague!

Birthday Wish II (1943)
What I desired most: going
home to Prague.

The Waiting Room of the Emergency Clinic (26 July 1943)
Because of the poor living conditions, this waiting room was always full.

A Visit to the Hospital (7 January 1944)
At the time of the encephalitis epidemic a hospital was established in the former Sokol hall. Visitors were allowed only as far as the door.

Bread on the Hearses (27 December 1942)
The word on the side of this hearse is '*Jugendfürsorge*' (Welfare for the Young).

People on Stretchers Included in the Transport (1942)
Those who were sick and too feeble to walk were carried on stretchers.

The 'Sluice' in the Courtyard (9 September 1943)

On arrival from and departure for the transports, everyone was assembled in the so-called '*Schleuse*' (sluice), where they were registered and checked. They would have to wait for hours or even days in the heat or the cold until they were called.

The Transport of Polish Children (29 August 1943)

These children arrived in deplorable condition and were quarantined during their entire stay in Terezín. For some reason they were supposed to be sent to Switzerland but they ended up in Auschwitz. When they were due to go into the showers they tried to resist and shouted: 'Gas!' They knew more than other Terezín inmates at that time.

Apparently they have stockings and clogs in the storeroom, but they're not giving them out. I don't know what they're waiting for.

*

The buildings were only recently finished and they've not dried out yet. Water drips from the ceiling, so every evening, our coverings and straw mattresses are completely wet. It might be better to sleep on the lower bunks – they're only two levels here – but there the moisture seeps in from below. There's hoar frost on the walls and they never light the stove. We're allocated two buckets of coal a day, but the guards steal half of it while we're at work. As of yet we have not been able to wash, only a bit in secret in the factory, at the water pipe in the lavatory. But Šára will slap you for that. The *Waschraum* is four buildings along from where we live; at the moment the water there is frozen.

We don't even undress at night; we sleep three to a bunk, as there are not enough straw mattresses. It's dreadful here. Unless a miracle occurs, we won't survive this. Maybe the end will be here soon. Supposedly they're in Bautzen already, for real this time; one of the foremen said so.

*

Shocking as it seems, Šára has taken pity on us. He admitted it's not possible to live in this damp. It's not that he actually cares about us, but he realized that we would all fall ill and what would the factory do without us? We're a trained workforce and many of the specialists have already gone off to the front. It was for the factory's sake that they moved us into a better building. It's also freezing cold in here, but at least the ceilings aren't dripping wet (at least not as much).

*

There's running water in the washroom now, but it's not possible to wash there; all the windows are broken. We stole buckets from the factory and wash ourselves in the buildings. Of course, Šára found out and at roll-call he explicitly forbade us from doing it. He or the overseers come round each morning to check. We wash at night; it's the safest way.

⌒

It's 29 January.

They distributed the stockings and clogs. We were lucky; Mum and I got both. There weren't enough for everyone; some people will have to go barefoot all winter. There are more in the storeroom, but apparently they're not giving them out.

I finally got out of polishing. They put me on the ground floor, in assembly. It's men's work, horribly hard. We're assembling enormous wings, standing on scaffolding to do it. My fingers are shot through from riveting; I can't seem to learn how to do it. I'm afraid the *Salmeister* in charge of us will complain to Šára. He's a real swine; even the specialists are afraid of him. Some of the rivet guns are so heavy that I can't even lift them.

We work from one in the afternoon till one in the morning. Wake-up call is at nine – supposed to be ten, but the guards are always in a hurry. At half eleven we leave the building; at half past midnight we have to be in the factory lined up for roll-call. Šára is always in a desperate hurry and waits on the steps with a strap in hand.

We used to save our bread and eat it before roll-call, but Šára won't permit it. He says we have to finish eating before we leave. We eat secretly at work, because it's impossible to hold out till evening on an empty stomach. Dinner is at seven p.m. The breaks are horribly short. By the time they distribute 1,000 portions the last people don't even have enough time to drink the water down (that's all it is by now).

The portions are awfully unequal, but that's the guards' fault for not stirring the cauldron at all. As if it were so much work. This way some people get a plate of water skimmed off the top and others get all the solid bits. Of course that's only for the guards' favourites. For ordinary mortals like me there's only ever water. It's the same with the bread, which we get at the same time as the soup. Šára walks around as they give it out and keeps order with his strap. If only he'd use it as they divided up the portions; that's where it's needed. But he and the guards are thick as thieves, otherwise they wouldn't be so mean to us. Of course – he's got no need to be fair.

*

My favourite part of the whole day is the time after we come back to the work hall. The specialists aren't yet back from dinner and the lights are out. Šára sends us back to work pointlessly early. I always climb up to the top of the scaffolding, to have a few minutes alone. It's the one moment of the whole day when I don't see other people. I remember . . . Dad and I promised we'd always think of each other at seven o'clock in the evening.

It's not possible in the confusion, crush and noise at mealtime. So this is half an hour later. Maybe Dad doesn't have time at seven o'clock either. Maybe he's asleep after the day shift; perhaps he's just starting work, or has a break at exactly the same time and is thinking of us.

◦⟋

I can rivet as well as any specialist now, but I don't really care whether we finish this plane or not. Although I would like to get the bonus. It's silly to get a reward for working for the Germans, but it wouldn't kill us. Once Mum and I got a package of soap powder. It lasted us almost two months. Yesterday I bought three spoonfuls of powder for two slices of bread. It's a hard price to pay, but there's no helping it. We're still wearing the same undergarments we got at Auschwitz. Mum got a bonus of 300 grams of bread. We ate it all at one sitting; for once we felt we had something in our stomachs. The *Salmeister* promises me every day that he'll put me forward, but it hasn't happened yet. By the time it's finally my turn, they won't be giving out bonuses. That's just my luck: I've never got anything in life, whether it's *Nachschub* – an extra portion – bonuses or anything else. Almost everyone has jumpers already, but I always get there too late.

Getting overalls without having to give up my stockings was a real piece of luck; I don't know where I got the courage and gall to do it. I simply took off my stockings, hid them under my coat and said I didn't have any. It was a big risk – what if Šára had come to check up? – but that's the only way to do things here. I have to learn a bit from the Poles; they know how such things work.

They gave out special *Zulags*, half a ration of bread and farmer's cheese for children. I got nothing, because I'm down as born in 1926. Also, when we worked until eight, children could go home at six, but not me. Once in my life I lied and all I've had from it are disadvantages. Of course it could also have turned out that, if I'd told the truth, they'd have split up me and Mum. They can keep their cheese, then.

*

There are air raids every day now, more and more often. The siren is endlessly going off and the *Voralarm* before the raids never stops. Yesterday there was a big air raid on Dresden. Shooting could be heard and at night, as we were coming back from work, the sky was completely crimson. Even today the glow is still visible.

For days, vehicles with refugees have been streaming constantly past along the road. It makes me feel so good; I'm always more cheerful on my way to work now. Three years ago it was us fleeing the air raids. They used to let us into the shelter here, but then thought better of it; they're afraid of not getting to safety in time themselves. So we always deliberately walked slowly. It's down to fate whether we perish or stay alive. Life matters so little to us; we have nothing to lose.

The one thing I'm afraid of is that only one of us will be killed. The moment the siren sounds, I'm up on the second floor by Mum's side. Then I couldn't care less whether we're hit or not.

So they won't let us into the shelter any more; we stay in the hall, all the women down on the ground floor. For now there have not been any air raids directly on Freiberg, but a number of times planes have circled over the factory. Today one plane was shot down; the specialists went mad with joy. They talked about it all day until by evening they'd turned one downed plane into three. Personally I am quite fond of air raids (and I think I'm not the only one). We don't have to work, I can spend a bit of time with Mum, and it's also terribly good fun to watch the specialists – sorry for the expression – wet themselves.

Kapteiner, my *Salmeister*, the one who shouts so much and drives us so hard, the one everyone quails before, is always the first out of the hall. A while back one of the specialists even broke his leg running to the shelter. Just wait till the real air raids start, every day, let them show the Germans what they can do – those idiots still believe they will win the war. With the very planes we're making here?!

～

I'm on day shift again. It's beautiful outside today. The sun is shining, the birds are singing; it's spring. And we're locked in this cold, grey factory. I've not done anything yet, I can't – I have to keep looking outside. I'm far from the window; all I can see is a bit of sky and the treetops. They're starting to bud. On the way from work we saw children playing marbles, spinning tops – in short, spring is here.

The specialists don't notice us much; there are so few of them here now, most have gone off to the front. We work completely independently – if only that Kapteiner didn't pay such close attention. Geňa – a Polish girl I work with – and I deliberately broke several light bulbs so we'd be able to go and get new ones. I don't feel like working today; it never interests me, but recently we're not even doing anything. Except we always have to be vigilant, so that Kapteiner or Šára don't catch us. I keep my hammer to hand; as soon as someone comes, I start riveting. Geňa, on the other hand, understands me. Always the same work. How long is there to go? Will this war never end?

*

Mum's legs got scalded when they were distributing coffee. Those awful Dutch girls – they always fight over the food like madwomen. Mum is in the infirmary. It's sad being alone here. Now I see how lucky we are to have stayed together.

*

Supposedly we won't be working in the factory any more. It will be liquidated; the front is getting close. We'll leave here – there are no trains; the specialists say we'll go on foot. That can't be possible, how far would we get? We'll see – not everything that's said has to be true. For now, work goes on as before.

This morning we started work as usual; the specialists didn't say anything at all and probably didn't even know. Suddenly the order came: 'Tools down.' Apparently we're not going back to the factory.

The last day we were at work, one woman disappeared. They threatened to cut off our hair if we didn't tell them what we knew. But would they really find her? They only found out twelve hours after it happened. Let them try to find her. Supposedly she fled with one of the specialists. By now she'll be who knows where.

They did frighten me a bit with the hair cutting. In Auschwitz I didn't really care, but now I wouldn't like it. The end is surely coming soon and it wouldn't be pleasant to go back to Prague with a shaved head. We won't escape it anyway; Šára has been in a bad mood recently and shaves people for every little thing. For example, he had one woman's hair cut off because he could see her hair underneath her kerchief (in the winter we were allowed to wear kerchiefs on the way to work). Another woman had made a ring out of a piece of wire, and a third had washed herself all over. All things that had been explicitly forbidden to us.

*

Šára left a few days ago. They say he went to arrange our departure for Flossenbürg. That's the concentration camp we belong to and that issued our prisoner numbers (*Häftlingsnummern*). My number is 54391. The number is imprinted on a metal disc and it is affixed to our clothing.

*

Šára has returned. He mocked us at roll-call, saying he'd heard some silly rumours about leaving. He knew nothing of it and forbade us to spread stories of this sort. So it is definitely true, otherwise he wouldn't be making so many excuses.

Mum decided to return from the infirmary. If we did go

anywhere, maybe the sick would have to remain behind or would all be shot. We can never know what might happen and the most important thing now is to stay together.

⌔

There's no work here at all, but they keep at us to do it. Hoeing the beds, fixing the paths, digging up bushes and all sorts of pointless work. There are tools for maybe a hundred people and there are a thousand of us. Anyone who doesn't get a tool has to carry and break up rocks. It's still horribly cold outside – our buildings are located high up in the mountains – but Šára has resolved that we will work without coats. He and his *Aufsehers* are warm enough; they've got full stomachs.

It's a fortnight since we've worked in the factory. There isn't a single stone left lying anywhere in the whole camp, but we still have to move them. We carry them from one pile to another, just so it'll look as if we're doing something.

The situation with food is terrible. We don't even get a full litre of soup any more. It's unsalted; they've run out of salt. Only 170 grams of bread.

Mum looks awfully bad; she's skin and bones. Recently she's started having heart trouble. She's so weak she can barely stay on her feet. We're almost all that way; although I'm young, even my knees give way as I walk.

We were always hungry; hope sustained us. We were no longer living off that litre of water and slice of bread; you can't live off that. Now we live off the strength of our will. And we will survive! Some day, after all, the end must come.

Explosions can be heard. From one side they're attacking Dresden, from the other Chemnitz.

During the day there was a *Hochalarm* four times; apparently they're already at Dresden and in Chemnitz parachutists have gone in. A few women went to clean at the factory and brought back a newspaper. There are huge battles near Berlin, that's what it says in the newspaper – they must definitely already be in Berlin.

Often I sit by the window and look out at the white road in front of us. Soon, maybe tomorrow, the day after. That's how they'll come. God, when the first tanks arrive! They'll come to liberate us, we'll be free. And the end will soon come. After all, in the papers they almost admit that Berlin has fallen.

*

This morning they called Šára to the phone from roll-call. '*Vorbereiten zum Abmarsch! Schüssel und Decken mitnahmen!*' – 'Prepare to march! Bowls and blankets with you!' That was at three a.m.; at four we had roll-call and at five we set off.

I wanted to hide instead of forming up. Maybe in a pallet or one of the pits behind the building that we dug yesterday. They wouldn't waste time looking for us; Šára was terribly upset and in a hurry. The front must be very close. It might even reach Freiberg today. If only I knew for sure that it wouldn't last long – but what if it takes them a week to get here, or a fortnight? With a loaf of bread in hand I wouldn't have hesitated, but it would be hard to hold out a fortnight without any food at all.

I might just have stayed anyway, but Mum started having second thoughts. And kept having them until it was too late.

They split us into groups of five, counted us and off we went. At a clip. We'd always walked quickly on our way to work, but nowhere near like today.

Along the way and at the train station were refugees, one after the other, carrying bundles. The *Aufsehers* were taking their luggage with them. Šára had his wife along. They're all fleeing, the whole town has taken to its feet. They've only just realized? It's taken them a while to see the light. It's not the Americans they're fleeing; they're dreadfully afraid of the Russians. But they won't get away from them all the same.

They loaded us into open coal wagons, sixty to eighty persons in each. At eight o'clock the train left the station.

I'll never see Freiberg again. I won't miss it, although it saddens me that I won't see the troops come. Maybe they're there already, coming down the road I looked at so longingly. Why didn't I hide, in the end?

⌒

We are crossing the Sudetenland. From the *Aufsehers*' conversation (there are two in each wagon) we caught something about Bavaria. Flossenbürg.

It's starting to get dark. They've not let us out of the wagons all day and have given us nothing to eat.

So, we're going to Flossenbürg. I didn't think I'd see the inside of another concentration camp. This morning I was in a good mood as I watched the Germans flee, but Flossenbürg!? We kept thinking that once danger threatened, they'd flee and stop worrying about us. And now this. In the end they'll just bump off all of us and it'll be over.

I can't even believe this will ever end. The war has lasted so long already. It was always 'in the autumn, in the autumn' and now it's almost summer and still nothing. The day before yesterday, even yesterday we were making plans, imagining them coming to liberate us, and now we're off to another concentration camp. They'll always have enough time for us.

We crossed through Most and are travelling on towards Chomutov. Everything here is all smashed up and the alarm just sounded. One railway worker, a Czech, shouted at us that they'd be here in two days. Within a week, he said, it'll all be over. If only he were right.

Now we're going the other direction again. Maybe the train's being shunted aside. No, it's returning back along the same route. Why? I can't worry about it now; we've got to lie down and get some sleep. In the morning we'll see where we are.

*

We didn't sleep, just dozed a bit sitting up. The fog is lifting and the sun is starting to come out. Please let it be nice out. The whole night beneath the open sky, covered only by a thin blanket. Will I ever get warm again? I feel like I won't.

Daybreak. We recognize places from yesterday. We're standing on the tracks outside Most. In front of us are rows of buildings, barbed wire. A concentration camp. Maybe they'll leave us here. We probably won't get to Flossenbürg now. They sent us back from Chomutov; apparently we can't go any further because of the front. There are people, men walking in front of the buildings. Maybe Dad's there. If only they'd unload us here, on the ground, let us sleep, even without blankets, just so we'd have a roof over our heads.

*

They have sent us on to a dead-end siding. It's been five days. We probably won't get out of the wagons till the war's over. All day, trains carrying wounded soldiers pass by. Twenty-four hours later they go back in the direction they came from. The front is on all sides; they don't even sound sirens for the air raids. There are constantly planes overhead. They shoot at them without interruption; the anti-aircraft fire bursts right over our heads. The first day we were a bit afraid, but now it doesn't bother us at all. A bomb could fall here, but I don't think about it. I believe nothing will happen to us. And if it does, at least we won't know about it. We won't be freezing and hungry any more.

The camp is named Triebschitz. We get food from there. A slice of bread and a half-litre of coffee. We drink half of it and use the rest to wash. In doing so we're cheating our bodies of a bit of liquid that they're yearning for, but we don't want to get lice. Each morning, even if it's cold, we strip and at least air out our undergarments and clothes. We've swept out the coal dust and we each have our own place. We had to get things organized; who knows how long we'll be on this train.

During the day it's bearable, but the nights can drive you mad. We've figured out there's only one way for everyone to lie down. We line up like sardines, starting the process before dusk, so we can get ready while it's still light. We all lie on our right side and if anyone turns over – which we've forbidden ourselves to do – the whole car has to do the same at precisely that moment.

Three of my toes have got frostbite – one so badly that I can't get it into my clog. We're lucky; the weather is relatively good, even though there are frosts at night, since it's only April.

*

I'm afraid of the nights; they are the worst ordeal. If only these women could be more understanding of each other. Each thinks only of herself and is indifferent to everyone else. Egoists, selfish people. As long as she can sleep, everyone else can be up. Each thinks she's got the worst place and blames the others for having more space and for tormenting her. She gets up and in doing so wakes up the whole wagon. All the evening's counting and measuring was in vain; we won't be able to lie back down before morning again.

The *Posten*, our sentry, came twice, there was so much noise here. I thought it was only us, but when it gets dark you can hear arguments from all the wagons. It's probably also the hunger that makes us all so nervous.

Now it's even worse for me – someone is constantly stepping on my foot and the frostbite hurts horribly. They stepped on a blister on my big toe, broke it and it bled. I wrapped it in the old bandage from Mum's scalding, which is healing already – even here, in this filth!

This will be our sixth night in the train, a week in Triebschitz. I can't take it any longer. Every evening I think about it; tonight I might just do it. I'll jump under a passing train and commit suicide. I can't stand even one more night like this. But what if it is the end, what if this is the last time? I'll try it once more.

*

They've added two transports to ours. Greek women and Polish men. They're in terrible shape, much worse than us. They said they've not eaten for a week and have epidemic typhus. At night you can hear the wailing from there; they're calling out for water. They have a much worse Šára and *Aufsehers* than we do. They treat them horribly. We can't meet them; we only saw them when they went to the camp for food. They can't even walk, they just stagger. The men have striped clothes and look even worse than the women. My God, maybe Dad looks like that!

In the morning a men's transport from Buchenwald went by. They shouted at us. There were Poles, Hungarians, Slovaks and Czechs, but no one from Terezín. The way they looked! In comparison we're fat and beautifully dressed. They probably look so awful because they haven't been shaved. But all the same, they've gone through a lot. They were packed in even tighter than we are; they couldn't even all sit down and had to stand up so they'd fit.

We looked for Dad among them, but we probably wouldn't even recognize him. What can be left of a person – how can they treat someone that way?! I don't really even believe that Dad's still alive. He wouldn't survive it. And still there's no end.

*

Overnight there was a big air raid on Chomutov and Most. It looked like the end for us, but miraculously no bombs fell here. The *Aufsehers* and *Postens* fled, but we weren't allowed to leave the wagon. We were just as happy not to have to get up and we slept on peacefully. I only crawled out to look at the Stalin candles, which lit up the whole sky. Then I had to remain sitting till morning; I couldn't fit back in.

It was a huge air raid, but there was no siren at all; the front is certainly only a couple of kilometres from here. Maybe we'll live to be liberated after all.

During the air raid at night, a Slovak woman gave birth. In the dark, by the weak light of a torch that the *Posten* shone beneath the covers. For now the mother and child are both healthy. The fuss people would have made over a newborn at home – and here they simply wrapped him in a dirty, coal-smeared blanket. It's the second baby; the first was born the night before we left Freiberg.

The *Postens*, *Aufsehers* and Šára are awfully worked up. The Americans are already in Chomutov. We're travelling at great speed towards Most. They're shipping us with them as they themselves flee the advancing front. It's the second time it's come so close to us and once again we're going to miss out.

It's been raining more and more heavily all afternoon. The covers we're wrapped in are soaked through and sagging towards the ground. Soon it will be evening. We're travelling at great speed. If only it would stop pouring; we can't make it through the night like this in wet blankets. Perhaps they'll offload us somewhere for the night, maybe into a barn of some sort, if only to have a roof over our heads.

We're passing through a small village. Children are playing in front of the houses. They look at us, eyes agog, wave, those over there are shouting something. '*Nazdar!*' – 'Hello!' It's in Czech – they're Czech children. We're home, in Bohemia. The adults join in, the '*Nazdar!*' swells. My God, how beautiful it is to hear Czech again. What a difference between these Czech kids, the way they greet us, and those German brats who threw stones at us as we walked to work.

We pass a forest: a hare flees, a squirrel jumps through the trees. Nature is so beautiful. And the forest smells different from in Germany. A Czech forest. To be that hare, or that squirrel. Living free, breathing free. How happy those animals are. And where are we off to? Has Šára found a way to get us to Flossenbürg? Then this is the last forest I will see. The last bit of freedom. Tomorrow I might not even be alive. Is there a gas chamber in Flossenbürg? Oh, to jump from the train, hide in the forest, escape.

We stopped for a moment at a Czech train station. People run up to the train, throwing bread and rolls at us. My God, they are nice. They're all speaking Czech to us, saying it will soon be over.

Then we move onwards. It's pouring non-stop, but I don't even feel it. I don't care. My blanket has slipped off, people are treading on it underfoot, but I'm not bothered. One woman shares with us the bread that she got. We've not eaten since morning, I'm tremendously hungry, but I can't eat the bread. I clutch it to my chest; I don't feel the cold, rain or even the tears running down my face. I can't eat. It's bread from Czech people, our bread – we're home, in the Czech lands!

Two women have jumped out of our car. The *Posten* pretended not to see; the sentries don't care any more. I would like to escape, but it's harder with two. What if something happens to one of you as you're jumping; what if they catch one? If Mum were strong enough . . . but in the state she's in now, she couldn't escape. What if she ended up lying somewhere along the way? I won't jump; I'll leave it up to fate. There's no sign of life here. I have no idea where we are.

*

We're at the station in Horní Bříza. It's about midnight. It hasn't stopped pouring. The railway workers are shouting that in the morning we'll get covered cars. Morning – at least six hours to go. My frostbite is starting to burn and my neck hurts from the weight of my waterlogged blanket. Six more hours. The rain does not stop.

They transferred us into covered cattle cars. Now let it pour outside, at least we've got a roof. If only there were dry blankets – we'll never warm up this way.

*

The blankets have almost dried out; it doesn't feel cold any more. They've uncoupled us from that other transport. It's better that way; there were lots of sick people there and all we need is to catch an infection.

*

We left Horní Bříza early in the morning; we're probably headed for Plzeň. Šára knows that two women escaped, but he doesn't seem at all upset by it. We're probably not his concern any more.

By noon the train reached Plzeň. It stopped behind the train station, by a forest. Immediately loads of people converged on us with food. I don't understand where they got it all so quickly. It's Sunday; they must have already been baking. They're carrying full baskets and hampers full of bread, pastries, fruit. Except they're giving them all to Šára, who tells them he'll distribute it all to us. That I want to see.

For a bit they left our car open – there are a couple of women from Plzeň among us and they let people know, so we tossed out a few notes. We call out to the people to give the food to us themselves or make sure they're there when it's distributed. Šára will certainly keep it all for himself and his *Aufsehers*.

All the people here are so nice. All day they brought us food and made us soup. From morning till evening they brought it out here from the town. We each got a full bowl of real Czech potato soup. After two days, something hot to eat. They gave it out themselves – Šára was beside himself but couldn't do anything. He can't get away with as much as he used to.

We heard his conversation with the stationmaster, who was trying to convince him to leave us here. They would take care of us, he said, food, everything. He advised Šára not to travel onwards with us – apparently we won't get anywhere. But Šára wouldn't hear of it. He wants to leave here at any cost. He feels the end coming and is afraid to be among Czechs. He asked which direction it was to Bavaria. The stationmaster claims he can't get there, but Šára is beyond persuasion.

～

We're in a dead-end siding again. No sign of life here at all. We have no idea where we are. We think it might be near Domažlice. Šára is trying to get something to eat, but can't find anything anywhere. He's got no supplies, not even for his *Aufsehers*. Today they're eating all the pastries they didn't give us yesterday. Why didn't Šára stay in Plzeň? We'd have had food supplied; here we'll die of hunger.

We can't go any further. They turned us back at one station. It's awfully strange here, so dead. We are evidently in the war zone.

Yesterday they gave us no food at all, today they made tea on a campfire and sweetened it. Šára still has a bit of sugar. We don't even leave the carriages when they allow us to. It takes too much energy to clamber down. We can't even stand on our feet any more.

*

They gave each of us two spoonfuls of sugar. You wouldn't believe what it did for us. Instantly it set us aright. Mum and I went for a walk in front of the cars. We got a cup of water for washing. We're horribly dirty. Did we once wash ourselves in Triebschitz in a quarter-litre of coffee?

*

Šára scrounged some potatoes from somewhere with his own hands. They cooked them in buckets over a fire. Each of us got two. If we don't leave here soon, we'll perish. How long can we survive without food?

⌒

We're in Klatovy. Once again people come from all sides with food, but Šára won't let them close. There's a stream nearby; we're allowed to go and wash ourselves.

I tossed my jumper out of the window; there were lice in it. I'll be cold, but that's easier to endure than lice. Something's always biting me and I end up thinking about it constantly. We were so afraid of them that in Freiberg we tried hard to keep clean. Once they're here, we'll never get rid of them.

Mum is cross with me; she says I'm too highly strung, lice won't kill me and it's far worse that we've got no food. That's true, but the lice bother me more than the food does. It makes me miserable.

People would be happy to help us; why won't Šára let them? One girl, a mixed-race, has parents here in Klatovy. At night they called her name. She could have escaped, but is seriously ill. She'd been in the camp infirmary since Christmas. It's horrible, for her and her parents. So close to home, without food, without help.

*

They've moved us one station further on. The mother of the girl has been standing outside the train since morning. She was asking Šára and the *Aufsehers* to take her off the train and leave her here; even the block warden would have permitted it, since she's so sick. But Šára wouldn't allow it and wouldn't even let the woman come over.

The *Aufsehers* go into the town to beg for food. They return with full rucksacks and baskets, even bringing several jugs of milk, fruit, but it all disappears into the carriages with the *Aufsehers* and Šára. If only we could give people a sign. They certainly don't have food to waste – they're giving the best they have and Šára is scoffing all of it.

Tonight I'll escape. I'll definitely scarper – I've been planning it for a couple of days. The people here will certainly help us.

Šára changed his mind and let them come to the train. Even the mother of that girl. They made us white coffee and bread to go with it. A huge slice for each of us and pastries for the infirmary. What bread that was! The best pastry in the world couldn't taste better. And the coffee! Milky and sweet. The way a Czech kitchen smelled. It was high time they gave us something to eat. Aside from those two potatoes, half a mug of tea and two spoons of sugar we hadn't eaten in four days. That morning Mum fainted twice from weakness. In a little while they'll let us out of the cars; I'll look around outside and tonight, without fail, I'll leg it.

*

I still have to think it through. There's a watch posted all along the train. I looked to see if it would be possible to lie down under the train. But there are locomotives at both ends of the train and I don't know which direction we're going. There's still one option left. If they leave the windows open at night (the doors are locked from outside the whole time), we can jump. The people I've had the opportunity to speak with have warned us off this. There are apparently still constant searches. They can get us food, but where will we hide? We can't ask people to hide us and bring misfortune on themselves.

If I could be sure the end was near, then we'd hold out somehow. We'd sleep in the forests, in haystacks . . . after all, we're used to worse. However, how long could we live like that? At some point they'd certainly catch us. Mum still doesn't want to flee; she's afraid she's too weak. I don't want to try to talk her round. I'm just waiting on her word. If she says it, then I'll run for it with no further hesitations.

I'm waiting, maybe she'll say yes.

*

I stood by the window long into the night and looked out. Our place is right below the window, so I wasn't disturbing anyone. Around eleven we left Klatovy. We were going quite slowly, so it would have been perfect for jumping. But Mum was silent.

I suppose we can't go any further. The stationmaster in Plzeň was telling the truth that we wouldn't get any further than Horažďovice.

*

Hello, how did these people know we'd be coming this way? All of them are carrying loaves of bread under their arms. A railway worker threw Mum his own snack. Another asks if we're all Czechs. He passed us a loaf of bread and another one through the next window. 'Berlin has fallen. It'll be over within two days . . .' but then Šára ran up and hammered on the windows angrily with his gun.

It's dark in here, but at least he didn't see them passing us the bread. We divided it up; everyone got a slice. We hadn't eaten since yesterday; Šára said it wasn't necessary since we'd got food off people.

*

We rode onwards. Where to? After all, the track to České Budějovice is blocked.

We asked and called out for them to open the windows; it was suffocating in here. The *Posten* took pity on us and opened one, at least. A military train was standing opposite; they gave us a can of bean soup. We divided it up and each got a spoonful. At any rate, something warm for our stomachs. They would have given us more – they'd had some slices of bread ready – but Šára frightened them off by running over and banging on the window again. Only a small crack stayed open. The soldiers made a few remarks about inhuman behaviour. Maybe they're not all that evil; they're just afraid of one another, and mostly of the SS.

*

All the trains are going back towards Horažd'ovice but Šára apparently doesn't intend to. He always has to have his way and is intent on it this time too. He'll go where he wants to.

We asked one railway worker whether he knows where we're going. 'Mauthausen, probably.' Probably? No, people don't say things like that lightly. Ten women jumped out of our car overnight. The Germans shot at them, but I don't think anything happened to any of them. Probably even the *Postens* didn't want to hit them. They don't care what happens to us; one of them has even disappeared.

Still, I wouldn't try anything here. If I wouldn't escape in Bohemia, should I risk it here in České Budějovice, which is full of Germans?

Now it's too late. I'll stay and hold out till the end. If I'm fated to die, so be it. Let God's will be done.

*

They've figured out that there are ten fewer of us. They threatened to punish us, but what else can happen to us? Is there anything worse than Mauthausen?

'Water, drink, only a drop, wet our lips. *Wasser, bitte, trinken!*' They don't hear, they don't want to hear. We don't feel hunger any more – we're used to going without food, but thirst, unbridled thirst, tortures us.

*

Through the cracks rays of sunlight filter in. You can see a bit of the sky, here and there a tree trunk or treetop. That must be a forest. Oh, looking at a forest makes me saddest of all. I love them so. Dad loved them too. The grass over there is rippling. God, the world is so beautiful.

Šára won after all. So, what of all those pronouncements that we'd never get anywhere? How many times did they say the end was coming? Our sixteen-day journey is at an end. The cars are open, and on the wall opposite is written in large, black letters: 'MAUTHAUSEN'.

*

I saw myself in the window glass. And frightened myself. How can a person change so much in sixteen days? We're all altered beyond recognition. Sunken cheeks, bulging eyes. Who cares? It's trivial to notice such details – here, at Mauthausen.

They lead, or rather force, us along the road through the town. People look out of the windows, curious children run out into our path. How many transports have gone down this road? How many breaths, tears, beads of sweat and blood have soaked into its dust?

Yesterday at this time we were still in Bohemia. I saw the Czech land, I heard the Czech language. I will no longer see or hear either. And no one will ever find out that we perished here in Mauthausen.

*

I can't go on. I can't move any further. I'll lie down here – let them shoot me. The blanket is so heavy; I can't even hold my bowl. If they'd only let us rest a moment, an instant, just to catch our breath. Or allow us a drink. If we'd been allowed to drink from the pump at the train station, we'd be able to go on. The road climbs a hill, ever steeper. They drive us on at a mad pace. A drop of water, a single swallow . . . I can't go on.

The road narrows to a trail. We must be there already. Just a bit further. I gather my last strength. I must make it. There – what is it? A spring, water flowing down a slope. Maybe it's a stream, rainwater, maybe overflow from the canal. No point thinking about it – quickly, Šára is in front and the *Aufseher* has her back turned. One more gulp, how it cools and refreshes . . .

A stone wall comes into view, towers, the camp gates. Does anyone return from here alive?

*

We stopped so they could count us. Our last minutes in the free air. In a couple of minutes, five, maybe ten, those tremendous gates will close behind us and then . . .?

The setting sun leans into our backs and the fresh green grass ripples in a light breeze. A beetle crosses the path and a bit further along a butterfly settles on a flower. I never knew how much I loved this world. How much of it have I experienced? Fifteen years; of those, three and a half in the camp. And now, when I've made so many plans, now, when life can really begin . . .

*

We're off. The gate is wide open and waiting. Now they'll split me and Mum up. Maybe we're going right into the gas. 'Mum, thank you for everything and if you ever see Dad again and I don't, thank him for me. For everything.' One more kiss and the gates swallowed us up. 'God, do not abandon us . . .'

On one side, a stone wall with barbed wire; opposite, an even larger stone building. We sit on the ground, while among us run the '*Schupo*', the state police, in yellow uniforms. Šára has turned us over to the local authorities.

We get coffee, a full bowl, and can go for seconds, as much as we want. I pour a third portion into myself; where's it all going? I can only feel my slightly moist tongue, but inside nothing, dusty, dry. Maybe I don't have anything inside any more. The *Schupo* give out cigarettes, chocolate, talk with us, calm us down, comfort us. Aren't we going to be gassed? Won't we be put to work? Aren't they going to cut our hair off again? Will we stay together? No, nothing will happen to us, there's no one to work for. The front will be here within a week.

Why the ironic answer to that girl who was looking for her sister: '"Sister" does not exist; here you are things.' Why did they beat back the prisoners so cruelly when we went by the buildings? I don't want their chocolate; anyway it's stolen from the packages for prisoners. They can keep their cigarettes. There's nothing true in what they're saying. They're lying, playing with our fears, having fun at our expense. I don't believe them.

*

They line us up in pairs. We get coffee again and – bread! Really, bread, a whole 300-gram ration and 20 grams of margarine. Bread, my God, to bite into it again after sixteen days, a whole 300 grams will belong to me alone; I can eat it all at one sitting. I can already feel how my jaws will break up and grind the pieces, the crumbs melting on my tongue, the bitter taste of ration loaf. We're moving up, in a few minutes, a few seconds I'll be holding it in my hands. Bread, a whole chunk of bread!

I got a beautiful ration, the heel. Then they took us along the other side behind the building. The *Schupo* started to shout, beat us with cat-o'-nine-tails: the ones in front pushed us back and those in the rear wouldn't let us out. Straps, insults, blows. Confusion. They threw me on the ground, poured out my coffee and snatched my bread. Mum stayed at the back. Afraid of losing her, I call out, she sees me, pushes forward; they knock her down and the bread vanishes in the scrum.

The *Schupo* calmed down; we pick ourselves off the ground. The Polish women are fighting; the Hungarians are arguing;

puddles of coffee, shards. Mum made her way to me, giving up our bundle of things (a piece of soap, shirts, a washcloth, a bit of jacket lining, a handkerchief, some washing powder – a bonus from Freiberg – a spoon, a cup, my pencil, a piece of paper). What of it? We won't need anything any more, we're in Mauthausen and that's the end. The end of the war might not be far off, but even if it's only a week away, our end will come first.

We go back to our former place to wait for our baths – not for the gas . . .? I split my margarine – the one thing left in my hand – with Mum.

*

In fact, it was not gas and they let us keep our hair. Just a bath, lovely hot water and plenty of time to wash.

How long would I need to wash off all this filth? It doesn't matter; the worst is down the drain, and mainly it's just having that feeling of cleanliness again. We took off our old clothes; the only things we're allowed to keep are the clogs.

They distribute underwear. Men's boxers and undershirts. That's all we get, but despite that they are completely new shirts, never worn. Finally we're rid of the lice. And then – they didn't gas us, didn't cut our hair off, clean underclothes and decent behaviour. Have we finally made it?

*

Through the main gate, the mud and up the stairs, and we're here. Our teeth chatter, but that's nothing, they're sorting us out into buildings. They shove us on to overfilled bunks, three, four on each. Some people are up. The Poles, Hungarians, Greeks, a few Czechs. The rest sleep on uninterrupted. Or are they corpses? You can't tell the living from the dead: it's dark, the lights aren't on. We'll see in the morning. I suspect we're in the infirmary.

At the doorway they shoved a bowl of soup at each of us. 'Do you want more?' they ask. We do not understand. We grope at the contents: a bowl full to the brim, its bottom hot. A pleasing smell and warm steam wafts to our noses. I sip as I walk. And the taste so well known from Auschwitz. At the time I didn't like it, but today it's superb.

Someone tugs at my sleeve, shoves her portion at me. Thank you, and a second serving vanishes instantly into my innards. My cheeks flush, a pleasant warmth runs through my body, my intestines start to work, my legs are steadier and I can stand more firmly on them. I no longer regret my lost bread; I have a full stomach and thus good cheer. No one is hounding us, shouting at us; what can it mean?

A group of men arrives: Czechs bringing us food, searching for blankets for us, places for us to sleep. They help us on to the bunks, promise to help, tomorrow they'll come again.

*

No roll-call, nothing. We can do what we want. Empty tins of food roll about on the bunks, chocolate wrappers, boxes and papers with the Red Cross's label. I truly do not understand. The end? But, God, now I can finally look round at where we are. An infirmary, without a doubt, but the state of it! Last night we were tired and couldn't have cared less. We were overjoyed at the clean shirts and covers. But at night everything looks different from during the day. The shirts are clean, true, but horribly lice-infested. The covers kept us nicely warm and thus

I don't throw mine off, although all night I knew what that repulsive smell was. An infirmary where the only illnesses are typhus and diarrhoea. What else could blankets look like that have done duty here for years on end . . .

Stench, filth, lice, the sick and the dead. Men or women? The elderly? Children? It's day already, but I was wrong to think I'd be able to tell in the morning. They don't move. Their breath, the only sign of life, is so feeble that I can hardly even make it out on the person in the neighbouring bed. Some people are still standing, or rather wobbling on their feet. Apathetic, speaking with no one, their eyes are cloudy, expressionless. Sunken cheeks, limbs and body parts, bared with cracks in dirty lines, bones visible beneath ashy grey, yellowed skin bitten by lice and covered in boils from the dirt, malnutrition and vitamin deficiencies.

You want to start talking to them, catch their attention, make them happy, say, perhaps, that it's over already (after all, maybe now it really is), but something stops you, you're almost afraid of them – you feel that before your eyes, Death herself is walking past. (That's how she must look.) You try it with a smile, but no luck, their sight is fixed on an indefinite point; without noticing you they grasp and support themselves on the headboard, walking – no, floating past the bunks. From their spot to the latrine and back.

You want to entice a smile on to these people's faces? Fool! Weeks, maybe months without food and drink. Yes, that's the last system. Physical and spiritual torture became commonplace and then – the mortality rate wasn't high enough – here in the *Krankenlager*, the sickbed, at the whim of lice and the typhus bacilli, what have these – people? – gone through?

Yes, they were once people. Healthy, strong, with their own will and thoughts, with feelings, interests and love. Love for life, for good things, for beauty, with faith in a better tomorrow. What's left are phantoms, bodies, skeletons without souls.

*

The Czechs are here again, bringing several spoons as promised, pieces of bread. They have a bit of time with us, looking for and asking after people they know. We talk about Prague, Brno, our homes, life in the camps, news from the front. They ask and answer . . . 'Are there any Jews here?' 'There were, ten days ago.' 'Not any more? What happened to them?'

They don't want to give an answer to these questions. They skip over them silently, or with some excuse, or simply, 'Don't ask.' Fine, that's enough, we know everything. 'And one more thing.' It seeps out of them slowly, but it's out. What was done here recently, especially with the Jews, simply can't be told. Even our transport was destined for the gas chambers! They gassed the last thousand on Wednesday, then the Red Cross stepped in. Today is Monday. So we came four days too late. If not for that attempt to get to Flossenbürg . . . it was the one thing that saved us. Luck? Coincidence? Fate?

'Dishes for dinner!' We have none; we gave ours back yesterday. There are tins and bowls rolling about under the bunks. The sick must have used them as washbowls or perhaps for other purposes. No matter; after all, in the train we too ate and washed from the same vessel, they'll do.

*

A figure sits motionless on an overturned box by the stove. I've been watching her since morning and I think she had been sitting here last night when we arrived. A little while ago someone threw a blanket over her. So that's it – but why doesn't anyone take her away?! Children scurry past, a bit further away an infant cries. It's the one that was born in the car on the way from the train up to the camp.

*

They brought a pile of clothes to the front of the building; they're ours, supposedly disinfected. We can't find our own, so once again we take someone else's. We are not allowed back in the building. We got our dinner: dried vegetables cooked in water. They write us down in the card ledger, for the third time or so today.

*

We walk for about a half-hour. The camp is a good way behind us. Steps, an awful lot of steps. There's one quarry after another, here and there we meet prisoners. We're being moved, to a women's camp, they say. And what if it's to be gassed? The ones up there said that's over with, but who believes the Germans? So, the Czechs confirmed it? They just didn't want to frighten us. 'Mum, we're going to be gassed, you'll see.' 'So let's go, then, what am I supposed to do?'

That's an answer for you! I know we're powerless, but can I really just not care? To perish now, when the end might come any day, any hour? Gas! Gas? No, we're being moved to a women's camp.

*

It wasn't the gas chambers, or a women's camp. A huge wooden shack in the forest with a sign: 'Wienergraben'. A barbed-wire fence round it, a row of taps with running water, underneath them a trough and a latrine next to it. Inside, pallets and mud. Russian women live here; the guards are Gypsies.

We lie four to a pallet crammed into the aisle. There was a two-hour roll-call this morning; since then we've not been allowed to move or the Gypsy women are here immediately with cudgels and whips. The Russians are at work; they go to dig roads somewhere. We got nothing for supper, a scant quarter-litre of coffee for two persons for breakfast, a half-litre of soup for dinner.

---

1 May 1945

Second day in the Gypsy camp. Second day without bread, with a quarter-litre of coffee and the same amount of soup. Long morning roll-calls in the cold and mud. My clogs are so full of holes that I'm basically barefoot, with water running into them. Curses, blows.

*

It's three in the afternoon. We've still had nothing to eat. I can barely get Mum to roll-call in the morning and then off to the latrine. She lies down; it's all the same to her. I begged some potato peelings off the Russian women and cooked a soup from them. It made Mum sick; I put some grass I picked into it, and it must have been poisonous. The *Schupo* are giving out cigarettes. I wheedled three of them. Yesterday the Russian women were trading potatoes for them. They bring them from outside; they must be working near a field. Two potatoes for one cigarette.

Maybe they'll be trading them again today. Three cigarettes is six potatoes, they could save Mum. If only they'd come already; Mum's so ill. Maybe . . . I don't even want to finish the thought. They aren't accepting people in the clinic. I'm so helpless. Desperate.

*

So it's the first of May. The day we waited and hoped for. Rumbling can be heard in the distance, but that's probably the quarries. And to top it all those repulsive lice. Every time I check I find at least twenty of them. I've not washed since I got here. I don't have enough strength. I'm just glad I can still stand on my own two feet.

Outside the kettle is clanging; they've brought the soup. A quarter-litre per person. That's our First of May celebration. I don't believe anything any more. World, I bid thee farewell.

⌒

5 May 1945

Early morning. I sit behind the building by the campfire and wait to see if one of the Russian women throws away any potato peelings. They don't want to give them to us any more; they keep them and cook them for themselves. They've not been to work since Thursday and don't have any fresh supplies of potatoes. At the time they came back with much rejoicing, saying they didn't have to work any more because it would all be over. We celebrated with them – but as it turned out, prematurely.

Every night we hear the shooting; supposedly they're in Linz already, 27 km from here. If only it were true. The whole week we've only had a sixteenth of a loaf, twice, that's 70 grams. The Gypsies are worse than Germans. They beat us, cursing, threaten us with all-day roll-calls, and of the little bit of food we get, they steal half, if not all of it.

*

Mum is getting weaker day by day. A little while ago I led her outside into the fresh air and it made her so dizzy that she couldn't walk back. She was already weakened in Freiberg; the sixteen-day trip made things worse and now she's been here a week without food. I'm really frightened for her. I look dreadful myself, it's true, but at least I still feel strong; I can make it another month. I have to make it! I want to live, to return home. God, have mercy, give Mum enough strength so she too can see us liberated.

*

Late morning. Loads of Germans are here: the *Schupo*, *Postens*, *Aufsehers*. They are after civilian clothing to change into. The Gypsies are packing up; vehicles full of luggage pass through the forest. The explosions last night were very strong, several times they shook the building and now the Germans are starting to flee. Actually, individuals have been disappearing since Thursday. I'm starting to believe again.

*

Noon

The guard booth in front of the entrance is empty. The *Schupo* aren't promenading as usual in front of the building; the Gypsies are gone. Where have they gone? Half an hour ago they were still here. They even pushed me away roughly when I tried to take new clogs from out of the pile to replace my broken ones. (I still managed to steal a pair.)

What's happening?

They start to distribute soup. Today we'll get a bit to eat again: I have some boiled potato peelings, in salted water, even – one of the Russians gave me some salt.

What's happening? They've stopped giving out soup. Near the entrance everyone stands up, runs out, people hug one another. Why don't they stop playing around and give out the food? That's more important than anything else. Mum is ill, she's waiting for a bit of that water – after eating a little of her strength always returns.

People are gathering outside, the rejoicing reaches all the way to us. Some more *bonkes*, rumours like the ones the Russians came back with that time? I quickly finish my peelings and listen.

I can pick out individual voices now in the clamour. Am I hearing right? I put down my unfinished bowl and run outside. The voices grow, all of them blending into a single tone. 'Peace, peace, peace!!!' flies from mouth to mouth across the whole building. I stop in front of the gate. Everyone's gaze is fixed upwards; I turn my head in that direction. What is it I see? Am I dreaming? Can I really believe it, can it be true?

I'm not sleeping, I'm awake. I am standing behind the barbed wire of a Gypsy camp and up high, on the tower of Mauthausen – a white flag flutters! A flag of peace.

Mauthausen has capitulated, peace has come to us. 'PEACE,' I repeat to myself and every nerve in my body trembles beneath this word like a string. My legs break into a run all by themselves. Muddied, in my bare stockings just the way I'd run out, I arrive back at our space. Mum stands up – where has she found the strength all of a sudden? – I hang myself around her neck and, between kisses, I spill out, jubilantly, the word we've dreamed of for years. The word we indulged ourselves with in the most secret corner of our being and feared to pronounce aloud. That sacred word, which contains so many beautiful, unbelievable things: liberty, freedom. The end of tyranny, misery, slavery, hunger. Today I can pronounce it in public, without cringing, today it has come true.

The voices thrum and people repeat as if in a fevered ecstasy: PEACE, PEACE, PEACE . . . It seems as if everyone's singing with me. The woods, nature, the building is friendlier; I feel like dancing, whooping. We made it. We survived the war. PEACE IS HERE.

⌒

Night-time, 21 May 1945

16 days after liberation, 12 days after the end of the war.

In clean clothes, sewn by hand from SS bedcovers, with a full stomach, in a second-class local train. The final screech of the brakes and the loudspeaker announces up and down the platform: 'The train from Mauthausen is departing on track three!'

The platform of Wilson Station. The clock shows a quarter to two. I stand at the window and large, hot tears run down my cheeks. Tears of joy and happiness. Finally: Prague, the city we yearned for.

Finally home.

Children watch an outdoor performance at one of the homes set up for young Displaced Persons in Czechoslovakia after the war, 1945–7.

Interview with Helga Weiss

Neil Bermel spoke with Helga in her flat in Prague on 1 December 2011. The following is an edited version of their conversation, translated from the Czech. Additions and clarifications made by the translator and editor are in square brackets.

Could you tell us something about your parents: what their names were, what they did, what they were like before the war? From the diary we learn only that they were Mum and Dad . . .

My father's name was Otto Weiss; he was very educated, loved music, wrote poetry as well. He worked as a bank clerk. In the First World War, when he was eighteen, he was badly wounded in his right arm. My mother, Irena, born Fuchsová, trained as a dressmaker; she stayed home and ran the household. We weren't rich, but my parents created a home that was full of love. I had a happy childhood.

What was the fate of your friends, acquaintances, relatives?

In general things ended badly. Sadly . . . My father probably went to the gas chambers. But we never found out for sure. There's even a book, *The Terezín Memory Book*, where people's details are recorded in brief. There's always the date they were sent to Terezín, the date they were sent onwards and, if it's known, the concentration camp they were sent to. But for Dad the last mention is the date he left Terezín. That's the last trace of him.

Even with all those reports, daily attendances, and so forth . . . ?

Later we searched everywhere, combed through all those papers, asked people who came back from various camps whether they'd seen him. There's no further trace. Probably he went straight off the train to the gas chambers. Dad was forty-six, but one reason might have been the fact that he wore glasses – that was a mark of the intelligentsia, and they got liquidated first – or he also had a scar on his arm, because he'd been badly wounded in the First World War. So there could have been two reasons: glasses and that scar.

They didn't need reasons, though, did they?

And so in all probability he went straight to the gas chambers.

And Ota?

I don't know anything further about Ota. After the war I visited his sister; he'd given me her address. She was in a mixed marriage and even had a child during the war. I went to see her after the war, but couldn't find him anywhere. Finally I found his name; it's written here in Prague. It's in the old Pinkas Synagogue, which is now a memorial. The walls are covered from top to bottom with the names of the eighty thousand people who perished. So I found him inscribed there.

And I think you've written about Francka that . . .

Francka didn't come back.

You've written that of the fifteen thousand children who passed through Terezín, about a hundred survived . . .

That's true. Of the ones who were sent on from Terezín, only a few were saved and they were mixed-race kids, the children of mixed marriages. It's interesting: I don't know why, but the mixed-race boys were sent onwards [to other camps], while the girls somehow managed to stay in Terezín, so some of them survived.

So of that whole group of yours that was there . . .?

Well, now there are only a few of us.

I'd like to ask you about how you lived in Terezín . . .

Terezín had been an ordinary town, a regimental town with lots of barracks. And around the barracks lived the normal civilian population. When the transports started in November 1941, the civilians were still living there. So at the beginning we just lived in the barracks. These were enormous dormitory barracks; sixty or a hundred people could live there. But the number of people kept increasing. Terezín was originally for about seven thousand inhabitants including the soldiers and all of a sudden there were about sixty thousand of us there. After a few months the civilian population had to move out, and then they divided us up and we lived everywhere, even in the civilians' homes. Of course, it wasn't as if we were allocated flats; they were just rooms and we lived the same way there. So each person had 1.80 square metres of space. And people filled up the barracks. Some then stayed in the barracks and others were sent into housing blocks, and later people lived in lofts and former shops and various warehouses – basically everywhere.

Is it true that some of the inhabitants felt themselves to be somewhat better than others?

Yes, of course, such castes did exist there to some extent. First there was the *Ältestenrat* [the Council of Elders]. That was our self-governing body. So they were the highest society, and yes – maybe I mentioned it somewhere – some of them came across as a bit arrogant. The first transport was 24 November [1941] and the second a few days later. And those were all male; they were called the AK, which was from the German word *Aufbaukommando*, construction squad. And they were the ones who went to get the ghetto ready. They were given certain benefits, and for a time they were even protected from further deportations. Because they said: 'We built all this' and 'We slept on the concrete.' By implication: 'You have something better to sleep on.' So that was the *Ältestenrat*, and the gradations went on down from there.

As far as accommodation goes, one of the best things that the *Ältestenrat* did was to try first of all to protect the children from the difficult conditions, to the extent that they could. So they identified suitable buildings from those in the vicinity and set up children's homes. There was a children's home; there was even a home for mothers with small children, newborns, because a few children were born there. That was the *Säuglingsheim*, from *Säugling*, baby. Then there was the *Kinderheim*, for younger children;

[182]

then two homes, one for boys and one for girls: *Knabenheim* and *Mädchenheim*. The *Mädchenheim* is the one where I lived. It was for girls from about ten to seventeen. And then there was the *Lehrlingsheim*, which was for adolescents. And that's where we were cared for by the *Betreuers*.

So is that why your father was so insistent on you moving to the girls' home?

Yes, of course, because things were better for us there. Conditions there were basically the same as for the adults. We had only 1.80 metres of living space, a bunk, but of course it was better and easier to be among children than to live with the elderly, where people were ill, they were nervous, there were various misunderstandings, people were dying and . . . Well, it was just better for the children to live separately.

Whenever you were summoned for deportation from Terezín, you immediately had to find a way to get the notice rescinded. How did that work?

Of course, the fear of being allocated to a transport was always with us, and everyone tried to avoid it. So it happened that when people found themselves in a transport, they tried to get themselves recalled from it. One excuse, for instance, was infectious diseases. The Germans were horribly afraid of people spreading infections. So if someone got, I don't know, scarlet fever or something, then at least for the moment that would protect him from deportation and his family along with him.

Later people also started to appeal to their bosses in various departments, arguing that their work was indispensable. And if the work truly was indispensable, then they would leave them there. For example, there was one German in Terezín named Kursavy, who oversaw a group of women agricultural labourers. And he did in fact protect them. Sometimes it would happen that, I don't know, the mother of one of the women would be in a transport and the daughter would volunteer to go with her mother, and he wouldn't give her permission. Because we didn't know what was coming, only that it would be something worse. But they really did know, and he didn't let them go. I think he even permitted her to save her mother. So that was one of those recalls.

But you felt that there was something going on in those other camps and that, at the least, it would be worse.

We knew it would be worse. But we had no idea even where the transports were going. We did know, to some extent, that concentration camps existed – they'd existed before the war, in Germany. But that we were being sent to other camps, that gas chambers existed, and death trains, where we'd . . . We had no idea of that at all.

At least that was the case while you were still at Terezín. Because later, at Auschwitz . . .

But even there we had no idea until the moment we got there.

But when you were at Birkenau, there you must have known, because the wardens were threatening you directly.

There we did know, because when we arrived, they just showed us the chimneys back there where we thought it was some sort of factory – and they told us straight off it was a crematorium. And there was dark humour: for example, 'The soot will fly up the chimney tomorrow and that's you done for.' So there we knew about the gas chambers, but we hadn't known until the moment we got there.

That constant threat of deportation from Terezín must have affected you in some way.

Of course it did. Some more highly placed people almost certainly knew what was coming. Because there were one, maybe two prisoners, Vrba and Lederer, who got out of Auschwitz, and they brought a message, a warning, with them. The message got to England, I think to Churchill, and to America. No one believed it. No one, nothing. Either they didn't believe it or wouldn't lift a finger. And I think the leaders in the ghetto who did know didn't tell us, because panic would have broken out.

Probably the only one who said he'd tell us and that it wouldn't happen here was Jakob Edelstein. The leaders had to pick up their orders at the German *Kommandatur*, a building in Terezín – today it's a bank – and beneath it was a bunker, which was the prison. Edelstein went to pick up some order or another, told them he was going to tell people and they never let him out. He stayed in that bunker and then left in a prisoners' transport. Actually it was a normal deportation train to which they added one special carriage with a notice saying that it was for prisoners. Immediately upon arrival those people were liquidated. It's known that they shot Edelstein's wife and son in front of him, and only then did they shoot him.

You described all this as a child. It must have looked to you like senseless confusion at the time, but there had to have been rigorous planning involved.

It did look like confusion on the surface, but it was an extremely well-thought-out operation. It had been thought through from beginning to end, starting with small decrees and escalating into that final liquidation.

What led you to start writing your diary?

Well, events were such that I started to write them down; I thought it would be important for them to be recorded.

And can you remember one specific impulse, an event of some sort?

Not at the beginning . . . Of course, I always followed the political situation. My father was quite active in politics, so people we knew used to meet at our house and debates went on – and I listened to all of it. I even remember when once they forgot to mention something to me and I was so insulted; why hadn't they told me? So I think I understood the situation well enough – in my own way, maybe, but I did understand it. And so I started to write things down.

Who were you writing for? Was it just for yourself?

I was writing only for myself, and I don't think that I had any special plans beyond that. Well, maybe I did, maybe I didn't; I don't know. But I drew as well. I drew for myself, although maybe I was also thinking – just a little bit, if I try today to follow my train of thought at the time and if I can put those thoughts in order – about the fact that this needed to be recorded. Mainly I was writing for myself, but perhaps there was just a little bit of that [idea] in there somewhere.

Were there many children who kept diaries?

Yes, I think there were a lot. In Terezín loads of children kept diaries; and not only children, adults as well, because people needed to come to terms with the situation and so they started to write. They wrote poems as well – people who had never done so before and wanted to take part in the cultural life [of the camp]. So there are a number of these diaries around.

Some of the events at the beginning of your account were originally described retrospectively, but eventually you move to a style of narration that is very immediate, describing things almost as if they were just happening. Where approximately in the notebooks does that retrospective stance end and this more immediate stance begin?

I used the past tense in the first few pages, where I'm describing the mobilization of 23 September 1938 and the occupation of 15 March 1939. Then there are eight more pages in the past and gradually I move over into the present. I changed these first pages into the present right after the war, when I was writing up my experiences from the other concentration camps. At the time I wanted the diary to form a cohesive whole – a testimony about those times. I did the same thing with my drawings: in Terezín I also painted an event that had occurred before our deportation ['List of Possessions', see page 32].

In the part you wrote upon returning to Prague, you continued to narrate events as if they were going on right now, as you were writing them down.

At the time I was already thinking about the fact that I had to write everything down chronologically, and I was writing just after the war, probably still in 1945, or at the latest 1946. And at the time I was still so vividly inside it all that I can say that it was as if I was writing it there and then. It was deliberate: I wrote it in the present tense, even though it was written afterwards.

And was that connected with the way you'd written earlier: that you'd always written that way, as things were happening?

Well, I followed on from where I'd left off [at fourteen]. And in the same manner. When I came back [from the camps], I was fifteen and a half. So it wasn't all that great an age difference, but I think that psychologically I was much further along at that point.

So would it make any sense to put it back into a past form of narration, or not?

No, I think it's more effective in the present. And when I wrote it, I lived through it all again. Even today, they invite those few of us who came back to visit various schools and gatherings to talk about ourselves. And I think it wrecks us; physically, of course, it wrecks us, but it wrecks us psychologically as well. Because I catch myself as I'm talking about it, and when I talk, I relive it; I'm still in it. So it's still the present, even though it's the past. And it's still just as vivid.

As you re-read your diary in preparing the manuscript for publication, did any absences surprise you? I mean things that were so self-evident to you back then that it didn't even occur to you to describe them?

I think I wrote down most of the main things. There were a couple of things, maybe a few things I mentioned where I said to myself later that this could have been a bit longer, so I sometimes added a word or term here or there. But basically I think I'd written down all the main things. When I read it recently after all these years, I even noticed some things in it that I'd since forgotten about. Of course, I used Terezín slang in my diary, which these days no one understands, and it needs some explanation.

One very specific word from Terezín slang is šlojska.

The word *šlojska* comes from the German word *Schleuse*, which means a sluice. When a transport of people came into Terezín or as they were leaving, they had to be channelled through a place – in other words, a sluice – where they would take various things out of people's luggage that weren't supposed to be there. That activity became a verb, *šlojzovat*, 'to sluice'. So it has two meanings: either it's a noun, the sluice as a place, or a verb, meaning 'to pilfer'. And in Terezín there was a huge difference between stealing and 'sluicing'. You 'sluiced' from common property, like when we were working in the fields, where we'd 'sluice' some vegetables, which was forbidden. But of course, if I'd taken something that belonged to a particular person, from his suitcase or his shelf, then that was stealing. There practically wasn't any theft there; at least in our children's home, I can't remember anything like that ever existing. And I think that it really didn't, but there was an awful lot of sluicing.

You also wrote about how you went to help out in the Schleuse.

I even have two pictures from it. One is in pencil, I think it was an arrival. And I have another picture called 'The "Sluice" in the Courtyard' [see colour inset]. People were channelled into various places for the sluice and that courtyard was one of them. Some of the people boarding were old and sick, and so services were provided. We even used to volunteer for this; we'd help the old people, we'd lead them, help with their luggage and so forth. So that was helping out in the *Schleuse*.

A few more specific points about Terezín: for example, daily attendance.

A roster was written out daily showing how many people were there. Every day the so-called *Zimmerälteste* [the room's elder] would make a report. He'd hand it in and it would get passed onwards. And these reports were brought daily to the German *Kommandatur*. So they would always have an overview and know whether anyone was missing. They constantly had to announce how many people were there today, how many had died. And the roster had to agree. Every day. And each day the so-called *Tages-befehl* would come back from the *Kommandatur*; those were the daily orders.

And roll-call, which happened more often in those other camps . . .

Terezín didn't have roll-calls, but Auschwitz and the other camps did, and there they would count us. Physically. It wasn't just writing something down, and I think it wasn't always just for the purpose of counting us, because that could have been done more quickly. At roll-calls we would stand there for hours. Hours in the cold, the rain, the snow – we always had to go outside somewhere and stand in groups of five as they counted us over and over. Constantly.

So it had a psychological purpose . . .

That too, or physically breaking us. You would stand there with no food, in the cold or the heat, no going to the loo. And they'd count us. So that was roll-call.

You also came into contact with people of various nationalities in the camps – Czechs, Poles, Germans . . .

In Terezín the Jews were primarily Czech, and later people from Germany, Holland, Denmark and Hungary were deported there as well. So we could encounter them, but by and large each national group stuck together. For instance, in our girls' home we were all Czechs. Then there was another home where the kids from Germany lived.

Could you explain some of the terms you used for people? For example, in Terezín I noticed Betreuer, Heimleiter, betreuerka . . .?

That's right. Because these were official matters, the language was German. And so all the announcements and orders that were brought each day from the *Kommandatur* were also in German. But of course we put these forms into Czech, because in correct

German it's *Betreuer/Betreuerin*, a male or female caregiver, but we didn't use those words; instead it was kind of half-Czech, *betreuerka*. The ending of the word is Czech.

How did things run in the camp at Terezín?

In Terezín all the orders came from the Germans; the head was a *Lagerkommandant*, and then there were some others under him. They could come round for checks at any time. We never knew when it was going to be. But internal order-keeping was divided. There were Czech gendarmes who kept watch over us; they were by and large decent and in many cases they tried to help us. For example, they would help smuggle various letters or packages out, and for that goodwill, of course, many of them paid with their lives. So those were the Czech gendarmes, who were on watch at all the entry gates. When we went to work, they would do pocket searches, count us again – how many left, how many arrived – that was their job. And there were other elements, because in Terezín they set up so-called self-governance. By the Jews.

So the Betreuers, Heimleiters, *they were all . . .?*

They were all part of the Jewish self-governing body. And at the most local level, order was kept by the *Ghettowache*.

Yes, who you called the get'áci. *And they were also Jews.*

Yes, of course. *Ghettowache*, shortened in Czech to *get'áci*. That's more Terezín slang, which you need to understand. The *Ghettowache* didn't specifically have uniforms – but they did have caps

– sort of round, black ones with a yellow stripe; they had a belt and strap. I drew it in several pictures [see 'Children Go to Lessons' in the colour inset].

Could you tell me a bit about what happened to you after the war?

For a long time there was no interest in what happened afterwards. People thought: the war has ended and everything's OK. Of course it wasn't at all, and that's another era that needs to be recorded; it's only recently that people have started to ask what happened after the war was over. My mother and I returned from Mauthausen on 29 May [1945]. We arrived in the middle of the night, they let us sleep somewhere and in the morning they told us: 'You're free, go home.' And there was nowhere to go. And that's how it began.

So how did you find a place to live?

We had nowhere to go. So the first place we went was to our old neighbours, who lived next door to us in our building, and who had behaved very decently to us, even during the war. And that was the address – I think all Jewish families did this – where we'd said to each other: after the war we'll meet here. So the first thing we did was go to them. Their name was Pěchoč. And of course they invited us in, welcomed us, let us sleep on their feather beds and gave us white coffee and rolls the next morning for breakfast. We were so weakened that we couldn't eat anything rich. Sometimes people gave the returnees a huge meal and it cost them their lives. They announced that everywhere on the radio, so people would know not to do it.

But the interesting thing is, we'd survived everything, and

your body will hold out just as long as it has to. And now that everything was over it just gave out: we stayed there one day and got a fever. Everywhere there were announcements that the people who were returning from the camps had typhus, so they took us to the typhus ward. So I ended up being treated for typhus. That family had a grocery shop, so we caused them a lot of unpleasantness, because after we left they had to have everything disinfected, the shop and so forth.

They released me from the hospital before my mum. I didn't want to burden the Pěchoč family any more, but I had no place to go. We literally walked the streets looking for somewhere to sleep. There were some shelters where they would let us stay the night, but only ever one night, I don't know why. So each morning we'd walk round trying to find somewhere to sleep that night. And various charities would cook meals for people in certain places, so each morning we'd go to Wilson Station, where they made coffee and gave us a bit of bread or something. And we'd carry it in our hands – we didn't have a bag, or money, or anything. At noon there'd be soup somewhere else, so we'd go and have some soup, and then sleep in one of the shelters.

So the beginning was very difficult. Then they released my mum, and then there was another shelter where we lived for a week or so. Then we started to look for a flat and that was quite complicated.

This was the flat I left to go to Terezín; I was born in this flat. This was what we left when we were deported. But when Jews abandoned their flats, the first thing that happened was that the flats were emptied; they carted away everything that was there, put it into various warehouses and allocated the flat to a German. And that German would then go to the warehouses and requisition some furnishings. So a German lived here during the war; his name was Otto Werner. The only thing that remained of his in the flat [when he left] was a brass plaque he had on the door with his name on it: he did take it off the door, but it stayed in the flat. In those revolutionary days [in May 1945] he fled – I heard he left on a bicycle – but he gave the apartment keys to the building manager; he was at least decent enough to do that. And people were terribly curious: they must have thought everything here belonged to the Germans, so people from the building piled into the flat and took what they could, and . . . well, it was complicated.

But in the end you got your flat back.

We got the flat back some time that summer; we were somewhere in a convalescent facility. In September I started school. I was fifteen and a half, and my last education in a school had been in Year 5 of primary school.

So you went to the academic high school, the gymnázium . . .

I started in Year 4 of secondary school, the *kvarta*. I should have been in *kvinta*, Year 5, but I went one year back and belatedly took the entrance exam.

And from there you went . . .?

Well, I wanted to paint. So I transferred to a different high school, but it was a school of graphic design, a technical school. The subjects were mostly technical in nature and I regretted not having a more rounded education. So I went to that school during the day and did the academic course at the *gymnázium* as an external student. And after four years of that, I did two sets of school-leaving exams: at the graphics school and at the academic high school.

And was it then that you decided to make painting your career?

I decided then that it would be my profession, so I took the entrance exams for the Academy of Arts, Architecture and Design [in Prague]. But even that wasn't so simple.

Tell me about when you got your diary back.

Yes, I'd been lucky, because my uncle actually was in that one profession in Terezín that was basically indispensable: he worked in the records department. So he had access to all the documents, which he hid, and then after the war he and Dr Lagus even published a book using them. I think it's one of the best books about Terezín to come out, because it has all the facts from those documents. Even today, when I need to check something, I can find it in that book. It's called *Město za mřížemi* [*City behind Bars*].

He hid those documents, and because I knew worse things were coming, fortunately I didn't take my diary or my drawings with me. Before I left for Auschwitz I gave them to him. And he hid them together with his documents; he bricked them into a wall in Magdeburg barracks.

It was his occupation that protected him. He managed to shield his wife as well. After the war he went back [to Terezín]; he knew where he'd hidden them. So he removed them and brought them to me.

At that point you had your papers and drawings back; what happened with them?

What happened? Not much of anything. Now and then an article would come out somewhere. I think I told them at the [State Jewish] museum that I had the diary. A bit of it came out in English. And also in 1960 or thereabouts there was one publisher, Naše vojsko [Our Armed Forces], who put out a book called *Deníky dětí* [*Children's Diaries*]. A bit of it was published there, in Czech. But that was heavily edited, shortened – I might even have done that myself, because I knew only a bit of it would be published, so I cut it down.

In general, what was the attitude in post-war Czechoslovakia towards Jews and their wartime experiences?

Well, it varied, of course. First of all, no one had figured on us returning. And when we did, it was rather a surprise for people. We threw them. They'd say: 'Wow, so you've come back? Who would ever have thought?' And 'What a shame that your dad didn't come back as well.' That's the sort of reactions they had. And then they'd start to say: 'Don't think we had it easy or anything; we were hungry too.' And they'd start to tell us their stories, which seemed completely ludicrous to us. Because their hunger was nothing compared to our hunger and their difficulties were laughable.

So people weren't very interested in it. We'd even hidden some of our things with these people. We could only take 50 kilograms of luggage with us; we had to leave the rest of it in our flat and even hand in a list of what we were leaving. People tried to hide a few things with Aryans they knew – the removal of the Jews was called

Aryanization, because there were 'Aryans' and 'non-Aryans'; we were the 'non-Aryans' and they were the 'Aryans' – and the results were varied. Some of the Aryans behaved quite awfully. We were rather lucky to get our things back. Not all of them, of course: I remember that one woman said a ring of ours had rolled away from them in the loft. Or my mum had exchanged her gold watch for a chrome one before we left, so she'd be allowed to take it with her, although in the end she had to give it up anyway. And those people told us: 'You have to understand – it was wartime and there was nothing to eat, so we traded it for some lard.' Or something like that. So we had a little of that too, but it happened to a lot of Jews that people denied them their things and didn't return them.

And then came 1948, the Communist coup.

Yes, that was a bad year. The situation for Jews here was pretty ugly.

And I assume the end of the 1940s and the beginning of the 1950s were too?

Yes, they were. You're probably thinking of the Slánský trials. That was a truly bad time. At the time I was going to the Academy of Arts. My original professor, Mr Fila, who taught monumental painting, which is what I was studying, unfortunately died while I was in my second year. So they divided us up between the other studios. That's how I got into the studio of Antonín Pelc, who taught political caricature. No one there tried to force me to do caricatures, because they'd taken me in from another department, but what the students there were doing . . . those were awful things. And it was very anti-Semitic;

that whole trial was anti-Semitic. Ninety per cent of the accused were Jewish. They hadn't even been religious, they had been Communists, but each of them had to start his confession with the words: 'I, of Jewish origin . . .' And they said it. What things they must have done to make them . . . It was a terrible time.

So when was there renewed interest in your story? Maybe the 1960s? I'm assuming that while there were various trials against 'cosmopolitans' going on, no one would want to talk much about the war, or at least about the Jews' experiences.

True, but that was the whole Communist regime – it just was that way.

Sort of contradictory, almost . . .

And then came '68. But a bit before then the situation loosened up a little. There were good relations originally between Czechoslovakia and Israel. In Israel they remember it even today, because Czechoslovakia helped them at the time; they even trained Israeli soldiers here as pilots. Relations were so good at the time that a scholarship was offered for one Czech artist to spend ten weeks in Israel and I got it. It was the most beautiful time of my life. I even changed my whole style of painting – we haven't spoken much about that, but you can read about it elsewhere. When I returned, I put together an exhibition from the sketches I'd brought back; it was very successful. I had invitations from abroad to mount exhibitions – and then came August '68 and the gate slammed shut. The end of everything for twenty more years.

But still, you stayed here that whole time, when many Jews emigrated to various countries.

Yes, a large number of those who came back and particularly the young ones, those few who survived, emigrated right after the war. They went to various places: to the US or wherever they had relatives who'd left in time. Whereas here they'd lost their whole family – young people, my age, for example, by themselves – so their families abroad invited them and took them in. So some emigrated to their relatives and those who had nowhere to go went to Israel. They volunteered for the [Israeli] army, the Haganah – that was right after the war. I wanted to do that too. I was in contact with them, but I don't know – maybe it was just an excuse on my part. I wanted to go, but I was just a bit afraid. I'm not the brave type for emigration, but on the other hand – and this was one of my main reasons – my mum was here and she didn't dare go. And to leave my mother behind was just out of the question. So I stayed.

Various political and cultural periods have come and gone here, and I'm interested to know whether your own opinions about your experiences and your diary have changed over that time as well.

My whole artistic oeuvre depicts my life. And in it you can read everything about me.

First I finished my course, then I did various studies, sketches and normal drawings, and then in the 1960s I started to come to terms with my past. I painted the Holocaust; I think I wanted to do something like Goya did, *The Disasters of War*. But then in '64 I wanted to finish with that and I told myself: 'I've painted that now, that's the end.'

[200]

Then I got that scholarship to Israel and there everything changed. Suddenly it was optimism and sun, and the colours all changed, and so forth. Then came '68 and I stopped painting completely for a few years, because I didn't want to paint war any more and I couldn't paint what I wanted to. Because suddenly everything was anti-Israeli. Even at that exhibition I had, I was cautious enough not to mention Israel. It was called *Travels in the Holy Land*. Because by then even the word 'Israel' had become dangerous, and later it was completely taboo. I didn't want more war, I couldn't paint Israel, so for a few years I just stopped painting altogether.

Then I finally went to do something I had never wanted to do, even though I had the qualifications for it: I started to teach. I taught at a people's art school. Originally I just went to stand in for a colleague who said it would be for two months. Then she went to Switzerland and wrote that she wasn't coming back; she emigrated. I stayed at that school for fourteen years. For a few years I didn't paint; then I started going back to it, but it wasn't about Israel any more. Or there were a few reminiscences about Israel, but it was more about the Holocaust again, although not exactly. It was more like war in general and everything I'd lived through. Another cycle of paintings came out of it called *Devastations*. And in it are paintings like 'Overturned Roots', 'Wounded Earth', 'Devastation', and so forth. You can read everything from those paintings, the way life was then.

What did people say in those days about Terezín and the Holocaust?

People didn't talk about Terezín at all. There are two fortresses in the town: the main fortress and the small fortress. The small fortress was always a political prison. Then it was a Gestapo prison. And they turned the large fortress, where the town was, into the ghetto. There's a national cemetery in the small fortress and they would celebrate various days of remembrance there. But no one spoke about Terezín. Even the building where the museum is today: there was a plan to make it into a museum of the ghetto even back then, but they wouldn't approve it. They turned it into a Museum of the National Security Forces. And when, for instance, people from as far away as America would come here, wanting to see where their parents had died, they'd ride through Terezín and say: 'Yes, we've been there, there was nothing there anyway.' So Terezín was hushed up.

After the war, they wrote the names of all the people who'd perished on [the walls of] the Pinkas Synagogue. Then, under the Socialists, they said that the building needed repair, put up scaffolding all around it and the 'reconstruction work' lasted forty years. It was inaccessible. And only after the revolution, in 1990, did they take the scaffolding down and rewrite all the names there. So that's what the situation looked like. Terezín wasn't there, the names weren't there. I think it's important you know about this; it says quite a lot about the times.

So the synagogue was like that the whole time from 1948 until 1989?

Yes, it was surrounded by scaffolding and 'under reconstruction'.

I think I remember that from when I was here shortly before the revolution in 1989.

So you'll remember what it looked like; there was construction all around it. But that just wasn't the case. They just took down the names and put up scaffolding.

Could you tell me something about your family now?

I got married while I was studying at the art academy. And in my second to last year, I gave birth prematurely to twins, but one of them died the day after. So I had to break off my studies for a year and finish up later. And four years after that my daughter was born.

So I have a son and a daughter. My son is a well-known musician, a cellist; he's on the senior staff at the Music Academy in Prague. His daughter, my granddaughter Dominika, is a top-flight solo cellist. She studied for two years in Israel and one of her main focuses is Jewish music. She's even managed to really bring me back to Judaism, so that subject has reappeared in my more recent work now. I do keep going back to the war as well, of course, but that also involves Jewish themes.

My husband was a musician too, a bass player and member of the Czechoslovak Radio Symphony Orchestra. And one other granddaughter, Dominika's sister, has gone in the other direction and is studying fine art. It stays in the family.

So you have three generations of artists . . .

It was slightly more complicated than that, because we had a mixed marriage. My husband was even from a very devout Catholic family, but nonetheless we had a great deal of mutual respect. Because religion was repressed here during Communism, his family was persecuted for their Catholicism. His brother was in prison for thirteen years; my sister-in-law did about twelve, another brother-in-law three and a half. So my whole life I was involved with prisons. I think that's also important to know.

Over the past sixty years a large number of memoirs have been published about the Holocaust; films have been made about people's experiences.

A lot of things have come out. Not all of them are good; some are even very bad. And some distort matters; there's misinformation, things that didn't happen or even couldn't have happened . . .

Human memory is a strange thing.

But it's not even about memory. In places it can be intentional. An intention to hush up certain things or pass over them, not to speak of some things and to exaggerate others . . .

It's difficult to film things of this sort. Every book or every film has within it the personal experience of the author. But it has to be truthful. And there are actually very few truthful ones. One of the best [people], who tells the truth, is, for example, Elie Wiesel, whose words I often quote when I'm interviewed – although I always make it clear that they're his words; I don't take them as my own. As far as Terezín goes, Ruth Bondy's book is a true account. She's originally from Prague but has lived in Israel for years; she wrote a book called *'Elder of the Jews': Jakob Edelstein of Theresienstadt*, so that's a good book. Then I read an excellent book by Imre Kertész called *Fateless*. So there are a few books like that, and then there are some that are utterly poor, fictitious, distorted.

What would you say is the contribution of your diary? Why should we read another account of the Holocaust?

Mostly because it is truthful. I've put my own sentiments into it as well, but those sentiments themselves are emotional, moving and most of all truthful. And maybe because it's narrated in that half-childish way, it's accessible and expressive, and I think it will help people to understand those times.

Notes

Helga's Diary

p. 7 'mobilization': On 23 September 1938, the Czechoslovak government declared a general mobilization for an impending state of war.

p. 7 all about Austria: A reference to the *Anschluss*, the annexation of Austria in 1938.

p. 7 I'll be nine soon: As mentioned in the Translator's Note, these first few entries were rewritten extensively by Helga after the war. They were probably composed at Terezín or shortly before, but, as might be expected, there is no mention of age in the original manuscript.

p. 9 Úvaly: Today a suburb of Prague on the eastern outskirts of the city.

p. 9 the Second Republic: The First Czechoslovak Republic existed from the declaration of independence in 1918 until Beneš's resignation in the wake of the Munich agreement of 1938 and the occupation of the Sudetenland by Germany. The Second Republic lasted only a few months thereafter, until the dismemberment of Czechoslovakia after the Nazi invasion in 1939.

p. 11 Aryan: The Nazis' term for members of superior 'races', typically depicted as light-skinned, light-haired Northern Europeans, who were favoured by German legislation and orders throughout the Nazi era. Jews were by definition non-Aryans.

p. 13 'Gestapo': Short for *Geheime Staatspolizei* or 'Secret State Police'. By the time Czechoslovakia was annexed, the Gestapo also included the security services and the criminal police; they were in charge of the incarceration, deportation and internment of the Jews.

p. 14 Autumn 1940: This date has been inserted to help the reader make sense of the timing.

p. 14 I passed my exam: According to Helga, the Jewish community in Prague organized exams for pupils who were being home-educated since they had been excluded from regular schooling.

p. 15 Summer 1941: This date has been inserted to help the reader make sense of the timing.

p. 19 A month has passed: The German Interior Minister's decree mandating that all Jews over the age of six wear yellow stars of David sewn to their clothing dates from 1 September 1941. This entry, despite its date, seems to cover events from early September to early October. Thus when Helga writes later 'A further month passed' (see below), she is actually only bringing us forward to early October (the date for the next entry is just a week later, on 12 October).

p. 21 A further month passed: The month referred to here is apparently between the decree (early September) and these events (early October).

p. 21 *transports*: This German term has been co-opted into both Czech and English to describe the forced deportation of the Jews and other 'undesirables' to the camps and other fates. Helga often uses it as well to refer to the trains that were usually used for this purpose.

p. 22 solid alcohol: A kind of fuel used for lighting or cooking; it comes in blocks or cakes.

p. 22 the shops would be closed: There is a slight discrepancy in the dates here as 12 October was a Sunday, but some of the references ('Last night', 'Tomorrow') seem to be written from the point of view of Saturday.

p. 22 'Trade Fair': Alternately referred to here as *Veletrh* or 'Trade Fair' and *Veletržní palác* or 'Trade Fair Palace', this grand exhibition hall for hosting trade fairs was built in 1929 in Prague's Holešovice district. Jews reported to the nearby *Rádiotrh*, 'Radio Market', to be processed and housed during deportation proceedings. (These run-down wooden barracks have since been demolished.) According to Helga, people referred to the whole area as *Veletrh*, which is reflected in her usage.

p. 23 in it: Helga writes of people being 'in it' or 'not in it', by which she means ordered to report for deportation or not.

p. 29 Střešovice: District of Prague where the headquarters of the Centre for Jewish Deportations (later renamed the Central Office for the Resolution of the Jewish Question in Bohemia and Moravia) was located. All Jews had to undergo processing here in advance of the transports.

p. 30 AK (*Aufbaukommando*): The first construction squad (the 'construction commandos'), which was sent to make Terezín ready for the influx of new inhabitants, the AK formed part of the highest 'caste' of Terezín society (see page 182 for more details).

p. 30 4 December 1941: This entry starts with events several days before this; the date specified is the Thursday on which they had to go to sign up.

p. 31 rear carriage: Remember that – as Helga said earlier – Jews had to ride in a specially designated rear carriage of the tram. If there was only one carriage, they had to wait for the next tram.

p. 35 The Trade Fair Palace is swarming with people: Here Helga evidently means the Radio Market; in the original manuscript it does not say what building they were in, and the specific mention was evidently added later, erroneously.

p. 44 his count: The *Ordners* were Jews, hence they were both wardens and prisoners. His count (Helga calls it the *Standt*) was the number of Jews under his watch.

p. 44 Říp: An odd-shaped hill that sticks straight out of the flat, central Bohemian plain. Legend has it that the forefather of the Czech nation climbed the hill, liked what he saw and decided to settle his tribe here. Říp's distinctive shape is recognizable to every Czech schoolchild.

p. 45 Sudetenland: Many of the barracks at Terezín were named after cities or places in the Third Reich (Sudetenland, Dresden, Magdeburg, Hamburg, etc.)

p. 45 AK: Short for *Aufbaukommando* (see note on page 209).

p. 52 men's brigade: Movement around Terezín was strictly

controlled and normally the Jews were only allowed out in organized groups, typically for work purposes. I have called these groups 'brigades'; Helga uses the Czech word *kolona*, borrowed from the German *Kolonne*.

p. 52 they'll come here as well: Helga means that her father will be sent over in a group of Jews to carry suitcases.

p. 53 'coincidentally': See page 192, where Helga talks about the small kindnesses shown to them by some of the Czech gendarmes.

p. 61 in the *Schleuse*: Literally 'in the sluice', this was the process upon entry to and exit from the camp during which the Germans divested the Jews of their possessions and valuables. In this meaning it is specific to Terezín and even gets borrowed into Czech in the form *šlojska* (as Helga explains on page 189).

p. 62 in the office: Helga's father worked in the finance office (*Wirtschaftsabteilung*) at Terezín.

p. 63 'sluice' it: The Terezín Jews also used the term *Schleuse* as a verb, meaning 'to scrounge' (Czech *šlojzovat*). In their view this was distinct from *stealing*; it was more like *lifting* something, as no disapproval accrued to taking from one's captors (as Helga explains on page 189).

p. 64 '*Toranuth*': Sometimes written *Toranut*, this is a Hebrew term.

p. 66 only the Vrbas are missing: The Vrbas were close relatives – Helga's mother's sister and her family.

p. 67 *The Bartered Bride*: An opera by Czech composer Bedřich

Smetana. The premiere took place on 28 November 1942. Helga at a later point inserted this extra line into the manuscript; it works thematically, but comes several months too early.

p. 70 I wouldn't move out of here now: These two paragraphs appear to have been written later, as they are not in Helga's original manuscript. The mention of *The Kiss* is even later, as it is handwritten into a post-war typescript. Although Helga did see this production, she could not have done so until after the premiere in July 1943, so the mention here is thematic rather than chronological.

p. 70 Čapek's *First Team, R.U.R., The Mother*: Three works by Czech author Karel Čapek.

p. 70 *The Kiss*: Another opera by Bedřich Smetana.

p. 72 *Altertransports*: Chronologically this passage belongs at this point in the manuscript, although Helga clearly did not write it this way originally; it is on a separate page, in a different and later hand. The maturity of the style here suggests this might have been written after the war as she was recalling the rest of her experiences.

p. 75 Three young lads escaped: This passage was written on a separate sheet of paper in a much later hand, so its place in the manuscript is unclear. There was a similar event in Terezín that occurred in April 1943, but the mention of 'winter' seems to contradict that, so this passage has been left where Helga put it originally.

p. 76 With so few opportunities for amusement: We have removed a sentence just before this that was added during a later edit and is clearly an error. The sentence it replaced is unreadable in the original pages and could not be reconstructed.

p. 76 mixed-race girls: In Nazi Germany, Jews and Aryans were considered different races. Here, then, Helga means that one parent was Christian and the other Jewish.

p. 76 Chanukah is before Christmas: The Jewish Festival of Lights has a fixed date in the Jewish calendar. In the Christian calendar it comes at varying points in December, often quite close to Christmas. Chanukah involves a festive meal and the lighting of the *chanukiah*, a nine-branched *menorah* or candelabra.

p. 76 poor-man's cream: From the Czech Yiddish *daleskrém*; Helga says this was made by whipping water with sugar in it.

p. 77 14 days after the New Year: This date appears in the loose-leaf pages, but without the year. Helga has reconstructed it as being 1943, which matches both with the information about the transport (which took place on 20 January 1943) and the typhus epidemic, which peaked in February 1943.

p. 79 Shops are opening: These three paragraphs are written together in a later hand on a separate sheet of paper; we have inserted them here because the mention of *Ghettogeld* is tied clearly to May 1943, when this scrip was introduced in Terezín.

p. 79 *Ghettogeld*: Scrip printed for the residents of Terezín to use in the camp's shops.

p. 81 to pick spinach: Kréta was an area on the edge of the ghetto used at the time as a garden for the camp.

p. 81 A lecture on Rembrandt: These two paragraphs are not in the original manuscript and Helga must have added them later, after the war.

p. 81 'I'm dying of thirst . . .': The Villon translation is taken from http://www.poetryintranslation.com/PITBR/French/Villon.htm. Translated by A. S. Kline © 2004 All Rights Reserved. Reproduced here by permission of A. S. Kline.

p. 85 the Sokol hall: An early Czech version of the Boy Scouts, focusing on patriotism and exercise.

p. 85 *Entwesung*: Helga frequently uses this word, which in German refers to pest control. The Czech equivalent that also crops up in her diaries, *desinfekce*, 'disinfection', is somewhat broader in meaning.

p. 86 And that horrible, inexplicable rumour – gas!: The Polish children arrived in Terezín during the summer of 1943 and were deported to Auschwitz in October. This entry is therefore thematic, overlapping with the previous one, and appears to have been written later, perhaps after Helga realized the significance of their arrival and subsequent deportation.

p. 89 the rest found *Notbelags*: In other words, they found places to sleep up in the lofts or between other bunks.

p. 90 The Chanukah celebration begins: This description is closely associated in Helga's mind with the drawing 'Chanukah in the Loft', which is dated 16 January 1944. In 1943 Chanukah fell shortly before Christmas, and just after the 18 December transport that took away many of Helga's friends and relatives; this is referred to in the preceding paragraph.

p. 90 *Heimleiter*: The warden was part of the *samospráva* or self-governing apparatus of the Jewish community within Terezín.

p. 90 *'Ma'oz tzur yeshu'ati . . .'*: The opening words of a traditional Chanukah song, sung in Hebrew after the lighting of the candles.

p. 91 Burgr: Helga evidently spelled this name the way she heard it. He himself spelled it Burger.

p. 92 encephalitis: The epidemic peaked in December 1943, and the moving of Hamburg barracks took place in January 1944.

p. 93 Hora's poems: Josef Hora was a Czech poet of the early twentieth century. Pictures of Helga's copybook can be found in the photographic inset. Helga apparently added this passage later, as it is not in the original manuscript.

p. 94 Hradčany and the River Vltava: Hradčany is the famous castle in Prague and the River Vltava runs just at its foot.

p. 94 a general review: Helga thinks this was not about the Red Cross committee that visited later in 1944; it probably concerned a preparatory visit by the Germans. The Red Cross visit is described further along in the text.

p. 94 the wishing-table: The Brothers Grimm fairy tale 'The Wishing-table, the Golden Ass and the Cudgel in the Sack' is a favourite in the Czech lands, although less well known in Anglo-Saxon countries. The wishing-table can make a magnificent feast appear magically.

p. 95 *'Zum Park'*, *'Zum Bad'*: 'To the Park', 'To the Baths'.

p. 95 *Glimmer*: Processing of the mineral mica (used in German aeroplane manufacture).

p. 96 Danish hostels: Approximately 500 Danish Jews were deported to Terezín. Their presence there was one of the prime motivators for the Red Cross visit that caused all this sudden renovation.

p. 96 instead of celebrating Mother's Day: Mother's Day was traditionally celebrated on the second Sunday in May – in this case, 14 May 1944.

p. 96 those few dozen grams: Throughout her manuscript, Helga uses decagrams (units of ten grams), a common Czech measure for foodstuffs; we have converted these to grams to aid the non-Czech reader.

p. 98 Voskovec and Werich: A popular Czech variety act with Prague's Liberated Theatre (*Osvobozené divadlo*), starting in 1927. They quickly came into conflict with the Nazi regime and emigrated to the USA in 1939, returning after the war was over.

p. 102 'Uncle Rahm': Karl Rahm was the *Gruppenführer* (commandant) of Terezín for the SS. Other eyewitness testimonies also recall how he made children address him as 'Onkel Rahm' in front of the Red Cross committee.

p. 105 Lípa: A small village near Havlíčkův Brod, in the eastern part of Bohemia.

p. 106 the *Toranut* girls: The Hebrew word *Toranut* is used here of chores done for others or for the common good.

p. 106 'as nosy as a bedbug': A Czech phrase (*dotěrná jako štěnice*).

p. 108 Rosh Hashanah: The Jewish New Year has a fixed date in the Jewish calendar, which usually falls in September in the Christian calendar. In Judaism, the 'day' starts at sundown, so the holiday starts on the evening of the previous day.

p. 110 Yom Kippur: The Jewish Day of Atonement falls ten days after the New Year and is marked with a day-long fast.

p. 113 *Manon Lescaut*: Czech poet Vítězslav Nezval wrote a verse play in 1940 based on the novel by Abbé Prévost.

p. 116 a new notebook: This does not correspond to any surviving notebook or loose-leaf pages. In any event, anything Helga had taken with her from Terezín would have been confiscated upon arrival at Auschwitz-Birkenau and lost. This and all subsequent entries were written after her return to Prague in 1945.

p. 119 Birkenau, the work camp: Birkenau was in fact not a work camp, but Helga said they discovered this only later (see the interview with her on page 184).

p. 126 *Lagerruhe*: According to Helga, during camp curfew inmates were required to lie on their bunks and keep quiet. Any activity or movement was forbidden.

p. 137 28 October: Helga was referring here to the national holiday commemorating Czechoslovak independence in 1918.

p. 137 Šára . . . Uša: The first bit of each of these nicknames sounds in Czech like part of the German *Unterscharführer*. Not only were they conveniently shorter, but they offered the added bonus that any Germans overhearing them would not know who was being spoken about.

p. 146 Flossenbürg: The main concentration camp to which Freiberg, a satellite work camp, was affiliated.

p. 150 Most . . . Chomutov: These northern Czech towns and the rest of the border area, called the Sudetenland, were annexed to the Reich at the start of the war. Their populations were mixed German and Czech.

p. 151 Triebschitz: A work camp just outside Most.

pp. 153–4 Stalin candles: The Soviets dropped magnesium flare bombs to illuminate the terrain below them at night, improving their bombing accuracy. These commonly went by the name 'Stalin candles'.

p. 171 'Wienergraben': A quarry belonging to Mauthausen concentration camp.

Interview with Helga Weiss

p. 185 Jakob Edelstein: served as *Judenälteste* (Elder of the Jews) from 1941 to 1943 and as the Deputy to the *Judenälteste* from January to December 1943, when he was deported to Auschwitz. Edelstein and his family were executed in June 1944.

p. 194 We literally walked: 'We' here refers to Helga and her aunt, who had also been released from quarantine at the same time.

p. 195 entrance exam: At the time Helga went to school, Czech children attended a primary school for five years, after which they could take entrance exams for further schooling. Two of the possibilities were a technical high school, which prepared them for a trade or entrance into a technical college, or a *gymnázium*, an academic high school preparing them for entrance to a university. *Gymnázium* lasted eight years; the years had Latin-derived names, so *kvarta* was the fourth year of study and *kvinta* was the fifth year.

p. 196 *Město za mřížemi*: Karel Lagus served as curator of the State Jewish Museum in Prague and was on the board of directors of the Terezín Memorial. He had spent the war years in Terezín alongside Helga's uncle, Josef Polák; their book was published in 1962. It has not been translated into English.

p. 197 came out in English: Excerpts from Helga's diary were published in *Terezín*, edited by František Ehrmann, Otta Heitlinger and Rudolf Iltis (Council of Jewish Communities in the Czech Lands, Prague, 1965), pp. 106–9.

p. 198 Slánský trials: A series of purge trials within the Czechoslovak Communist Party in the early 1950s, starting with the eminent Party member Rudolf Slánský. As Helga says, most of the accused were Jewish and they were said to have been 'cosmopolitans', a code word for bourgeois Jews or Zionists. They were forced to recant their supposed infractions and eleven of the fourteen tried were put to death.

p. 199 '68: After a few years of growing liberalization in Czechoslovakia, in early 1968 Communist Party Secretary Alexander Dubček announced that there would be further loosening of controls on freedom of speech and economic activity and increasing democratization. This brief experiment in 'socialism with a human face', known as the Prague Spring, ended in August of that same year, when Warsaw Pact troops, acting on orders from Moscow, invaded Czechoslovakia and re-established tighter controls.

Glossary

Although Helga came from a Czech-speaking Jewish family and began her life in the independent Czechoslovak state, where Czech was the first official language, the imposition of Nazi rule and, later, life at the camps meant that the presence of German loomed ever larger in her world. She refers to many places and events by their German names, frequently adapted into Czech and conjugated or declined as a Czech word would be. These words have been 'translated' into English in a similar way, to ensure that the English reader has the flavour of her text in the same way that a Czech reader would. Helga also occasionally uses words from Yiddish or Hebrew, but these are explained in the text or notes and do not appear in this glossary.

Achtung	*warning, attention*
alle heraus	*everybody out*
alles da lassen	*leave everything where it is*
Altertransport	*deportation of the elderly*
Arbeitslager	*work camp*
Aufbaukommando	*construction squad*
Aufseher	*overseer*
Bahnbau	*railway construction*
Bauhof	*yard*
Betreuer, Betreuerin	*caregiver*

Bettrolle	bedrolls
Damen und Herrenlatrinen	women's and men's WCs
Entwesung	disinfestation
Ferien	holidays
Häftlingsnummer	prisoner number
Handgepäck	hand luggage
Heim	home, house
Heimleiter	warden (in Terezín)
heraus	(get) out
Hilfsdienst	volunteer unit
Hochalarm	red alert
Infektionsgefahr	risk of infection
Jude	Jew
Jugendfürsorge	child welfare
Jugendheim	boys' home
Kaffeehaus	coffee house
Kasernensperre	curfew, confinement to quarters
Kinderheim	children's home
Knaben und Mädchenschule	boys' and girls' school
Kommandatur	camp headquarters
Krankenlager	sickbed
Krankenträger	stretcher-bearer
Kriechlingsheim	toddlers' home
Lagerkommandant	camp commander
Lagerruhe	silence in the camp, camp curfew
Landwirtschaft	agriculture department
Lehrlingsheim	apprentices' home
Leichenwagen	hearse
Lichtsperre	blackout

Mädchenheim	girls' home
Mänerlager	men's camp
Nachschub	extra portion
Nachtrage	latecomers
Notbelag	emergency billet – i.e. sleeping in lofts or between bunks
Ordner	marshal
Posten	sentry
Putzkolonne	cleaning brigade
Raumwirtschaft	space management department
rechts	to the right
ruhe	silence, quiet
Salmeister	workroom manager
Säuglingsheim	infants' home
Schleuse	'the sluice', a name for the camp entry and departure process, in which Jews were systematically shaken down for any valuable possessions
schneller	hurry up
Schupo	state police
Speisehalle	dining hall
Standt	attendance
stehen bleiben	stay put, halt
Tagesbefehl	daily orders
Transport	deportation and also the trains used in the process
Transportleiter	deportation manager
Transportleitung	deportation administration
Übersiedlungschein	relocation ticket
Unterscharführer	sergeant

Verschönerung der Stadt	*beautification of the town*
Voralarm	*advance alarm*
Waisenkind	*orphan*
Waschraum	*washroom*
Zimmerälteste	*room's elder*
Zimmertour	*room duty*
Zulag	*bonus*
Zum Bad	*to the baths*
Zum Park	*to the park*
Zusatz	*supplement*

Illustration Credits

All paintings and drawings are by Helga Weiss. © Wallstein Verlag, Germany, 1998. All rights reserved.

Endpapers: Facsimile of pages from Helga Weiss's diaries, reproduced by permission of the author.

Photographs within the diary: page 12, © bpk; page 21, Jewish Museum Prague / Yad Vashem Archive; page 122, Courtesy of Yad Vashem Archive; page 177, United States Holocaust Memorial Museum / Yad Vashem Archive. Courtesy of Olga Fierzova. © United States Holocaust Memorial Museum.

Photographs in the plate section are used by permission of the author unless stated otherwise: page 2, bottom, akg-images / ullstein bild; page 3, top, Courtesy of Yad Vashem Archive; middle, Jewish Museum Prague / Yad Vashem Archive; bottom, Courtesy of Yad Vashem Archive; page 4, top, United States Holocaust Memorial Museum / Czechoslovak News Agency / Pamatnik Terezin nardoni kulturni pamatka. Courtesy of Ivan Vojtech Fric. © United States Holocaust Memorial Museum; bottom, United States Holocaust Memorial Museum / Czechoslovak News Agency / Pamatnik Terezin nardoni kulturni pamatka. Courtesy of Ivan Vojtech Fric. © United States

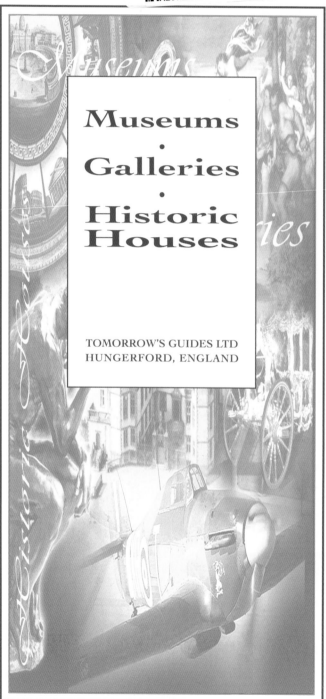

Museums
·
Galleries
·
Historic Houses

TOMORROW'S GUIDES LTD
HUNGERFORD, ENGLAND

Acknowledgements

We are indebted to curators, owners and their staff who have provided us with profiles and photographs of their wonderful and diverse collections from over 1600 museums, art galleries, historic houses and sites.

All National Trust property photographs are reproduced by courtesy of the National Trust Photographic Library.

Publisher: Davina Ludlow
Editor: Victoria Rowlands
Assistant Editor: Nicola Hunt
Assistant Editor: Nicola Furr
Production: Oli Blackwell
Mapping & Imaging: Phil Cory
Design: Zai Khan

This edition edited and designed by:

Tomorrow's Guides
PO Box 7677, Hungerford RG17 0FX
Subscription sales Tel: 0800 387342
sales@tomorrows.co.uk
www.tomorrows.co.uk

Distribution in the UK by Portfolio

Printed in Spain

Third edition 2004

© Tomorrow's Guides Ltd 2003

ISBN 1 85890 041 7

Introduction

Welcome to the 2004 edition of 'Collections in Museums, Galleries and Historic Houses'. We would like to thank those of you who have taken the time to contact us with comments and recommendations and, as you will see, many of those suggestions have been included within the book.

Once again we have included many of the greatest treasures in the world which are exhibited in both British and Irish museums and art galleries. The stately homes and historic country houses featured have superb collections of fine pictures, furniture and decorative art. In this edition there are many more historic houses listed than in previous editions.

The curators, owners and their staff have provided us with a wealth of information, profiles and photographs of their wonderful and diverse collections from over 1600 museums, art galleries, historic houses and sites - and now many, including our national museums and art galleries, have free entry for everyone.

Our book caters for all ages and will assist you in finding whatever you are looking for. Refer to the three indexes at the back of the book to search by Classification, Town or Name of Entry. There are 32 different and specialist classifications ranging from Anthropology to Victoriana (listed on page 9).

If there are any museums, art galleries or historic houses that you feel have been omitted and should have been listed, please email us on info@tomorrows.co.uk or return the report form located at the back of the book.

To search online visit our website www.mghh.co.uk which includes all of the museums, galleries and historic houses listed in this publication.

And finally, we would like to thank all of you who have bought this book, whether for the first time or as a previous purchaser. We do hope you enjoy visiting some of the places listed and we look forward to receiving your comments and recommendations through the year.

Davina Ludlow
Publisher

Contents

Contents

Ireland Counties Map

UK Counties Map

SHETLAND ISLANDS

ORKNEY ISLANDS

OUTER HEBRIDES

HIGHLANDS & ISLANDS

CENTRAL, EAST & NORTHEAST SCOTLAND

EDINBURGH, GLASGOW & SOUTHERN SCOTLAND

NORTHUMBRIA

ISLE OF MAN

CUMBRIA

LANCASHIRE, CHESHIRE, MANCHESTER & MERSEYSIDE

YORKSHIRE

LEICESTERSHIRE, LINCOLNSHIRE & NOTTINGHAMSHIRE

DERBYSHIRE & STAFFORDSHIRE

NORTH WALES

CAMBRIDGESHIRE & NORTHAMPTONSHIRE

SHROPSHIRE

WARWICKSHIRE & WEST MIDLANDS

HEREFORD & WORCESTER

MID-WALES

NORFOLK

ESSEX & SUFFOLK

SOUTH & SOUTHWEST WALES

GLOUCESTERSHIRE

LONDON

OXFORDSHIRE

BATH, BRISTOL & NORTH EAST SOMERSET

SOMERSET

KENT

CORNWALL

DEVON

DORSET

SUSSEX

HAMPSHIRE & ISLE OF WIGHT

BEDFORDSHIRE, BERKSHIRE, BUCKINGHAMSHIRE, HERTFORDSHIRE, & SURREY

WILTSHIRE

GUERNSEY

JERSEY

ISLES OF SCILLY

How to use

Finding the right Museum, Gallery, Historic House
We have divided the publication into England, Scotland, Wales, Ireland, Isle of Man and Channel Islands. Each section has its own colour coding. The maps on pages 6-7 detail the Areas/Counties for each Country, and the contents (pages 4-5) provide a page reference to each Area/County, where you will find a more detailed map showing Map References for Museums, Art Galleries and Historic Houses listed within that Area/County. You should use these Map References to locate Museums etc within the Town or Area that you wish to visit. Also refer to the quick reference indexes at the back which provide page references by Classification, Town and, if you are looking for a particular Museum, by Name.

Sequence of Entries
The listings within each Area (i.e North Wales) or within each County (i.e Cumbria) are sequenced by Town Name. Multiple listings within the same town are shown in alphabetical order.

Profiles
Each entry has a profile of its Collection/s written by the Museum's Curator (or in some cases its owner).

Opening Times
The periods of the year, the days of the week and opening times (24 hour clock) are provided.

Admission Charges
Admission charges for England, Scotland, Wales, Northern Ireland, Isle of Man and the Channel Islands are shown in British £, and for Ireland in Euros (€).

Key to Symbols

🖙	Guided or Private Tours	☕	Café or Refreshments
♿	Disabled Access (Please check for exact details)	🍴	Restaurant
🎁	Gift Shop or Sales Point	🚚	Car Parking

How to use

Locations
Each listing has a brief description of its location as well as a Map Reference which is shown on the Map at the start of each Area/County.

Exhibitions & Events 2004
The dates and subject matter are listed for Exhibitions and Events scheduled to take place during 2004 in many of the major Museums, Galleries and Historic Houses listed.

Indexes
At the back of the book there are quick reference indexes by Classification (see key below), Town Name and Entry Name.

Feedback
There is a Report Form on page 464 and this should be used to let us know about Museums etc that you visit (we value your comments, good or bad), also to advise us of any Collections that are not listed in our book that you feel should be listed. Feedback is essential for the integrity of our book.

www.mghh.co.uk
Visit our website to order copies of this book and search online for museums, galleries and historic houses.

Key to Classifications
see Classifications Index on page 423

Anthropology	Horticultural	Police, Prisons
Archaeological	Jewellery	& Dungeons
Art Galleries	Literature & Libraries	Railways
Arts, Crafts & Textiles	Maritime	Religion
China, Glass & Ceramics	Military & Defence	Roman
Communications	Multicultural	Science - Earth & Planetary
Egyptian	Music & Theatre	Sculpture
Fashion	Natural History	Sporting History
Geology	Oriental	Toy & Childhood
Health & Medicine	Palaces	Transport
Historic Houses	Photography	Victoriana

9

re:source

The Council for Museums, Archives and Libraries

Resource: The Council for Museums, Archives and Libraries is an international leader in harnessing the knowledge contained across museums, archives and libraries, establishing the UK as a global leader of cultural innovation.

There are more than 1860 museums Registered as part of the Resource Registration Scheme for Museums and Galleries. They range from world class National Museums and Galleries to small independent, largely volunteer run organisations such as the Weald and Downland Open Air Museum. Registration means that we can be confident of the ability of these museums to care for and manage their collections for the benefit of the public.

Collections in 62 of England's Registered museums, have also been identified as being of outstanding quality and significance by the Designation Scheme. Resource administers this scheme on behalf of the Department of Culture Media and Sport.

Through these schemes and initiatives such as the development of toolkits to promote learning, cultural diversity, social inclusion and disabled access, Resource seeks to support museums in their mission to care for, display and interpret their collections.

Museums as places of learning can offer the visitor life changing experiences through access to their objects and the stories they tell. Museums have been shown to have a key role in local economies and social regeneration, promoting strong community pride and a shared commitment to our cultural heritage.

Museums, archives and libraries connect people to knowledge and information, creativity and inspiration. Resource is leading the drive to unlock this wealth for all.

You can find further information about our work on the Resource website at www.resource.gov.uk.

THE NATIONAL TRUST

The National Trust is now Europe's largest conservation charity with a membership of more than 3.3 million.

It was founded in 1895 by three Victorian philanthropists, Miss Octavia Hill, Sir Robert Hunter and Canon Hardwicke Rawnsley, all of whom were concerned about the impact of uncontrolled development and industrialisation. They set up the Trust to act as a guardian for the nation in the acquisition and protection of threatened coastline, countryside and buildings.

In those ensuing 109 years, more than 630 buildings have been opened to the public by the Trust. Some 300 of these are country houses with gardens for which the Trust is best known.

The other 330 vary from a workhouse in Nottinghamshire to John Lennon's childhood home in Liverpool to a very early textile mill at Quarry Bank in Cheshire to a seminal Modernist home in London.

With many of the buildings came some of the country's finest and most unusual collections, ranging from furniture owned by royalty to historic costumes through to lawnmowers.

Knole at Sevenoaks in Kent is one of England's great treasure houses whose collection of 17th-century Stuart furniture and textiles were acquired by the 6th Earl of Dorset around 1700. The practical purpose of the collection was to refurnish Knole after it had been stripped of its original contents in the English Civil War. The furniture owned by James I is of the highest possible quality and includes state beds, chairs and the famous silver looking glass, table and candlestands.

Dunham Massey in Cheshire was home since the 17th century to the staunchly Protestant Booth family. When the second Earl of Warrington

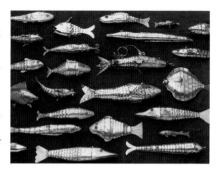

THE NATIONAL TRUST

commissioned his massive silver collection in the early 18th century, it was the renowned Huguenot silversmiths he patronised. The magnificent collection which went on display two years ago is only one sixth of the original but is still one of the largest groups of plate to remain in the house for which it was made.

One particularly unusual collection of silver the Trust holds is at Ickworth House in Suffolk. A case is devoted to a shoal of silver ornate fishes - some designed as ornamental pendants, others as scent containers - which belonged to Geraldine, Marchioness of Bristol.

Charlecote Manor in Warwickshire houses one of the Trust's finest libraries, built to house the Lucy family's fine collection of books, in Elizabethan-style bookcases carved by Willcox. Sir Thomas Lucy III formed the nucleus of the book collection in the early 17th century. It was then considerably increased by George Hammond Lucy's purchases from the famous early Victorian bookseller and publisher William Pickering, who stayed at Charlecote several times. The collection includes a first edition of Hollinshed's 'Chronicles', a source used by Shakespeare for his historical plays.

Musical instruments were also an important feature of the great houses. Fenton House in Hampstead, London, was built at the time of William and Mary. Early keyboard instruments stand in nearly every room. The collection includes harpsichords by the prominent 18th-century makers Jacob Kirckman and Burckhardt Shudi. A virginals dated 1664 could have been the instrument Pepys saw being rescued by boat from the Great Fire of 2 September 1666.

THE NATIONAL TRUST

Petworth House in West Sussex contains the Trust's finest art collection comprising more than 300 paintings on display in the staterooms are by Van Dyck, Reynolds, Titian, Blake, Bosch and Turner.

One of the best collections of modern art can be found at 2 Willow Road, Hampstead, home of Modernist architect Ernö Goldfinger. The important collection reflects the Goldfingers' close links with the avant-garde with works by Henry Moore and Max Ernst displayed alongside some of Ernö's prototype furniture.

At Sudbury House in Derbyshire, the old servants' wing houses the National Trust Museum of Childhood and has some jolting reminders of how children lived in the past, including a chimney climb for 'sweep-sized' children. The Betty Cadbury collection of playthings from the past is also on display.

The Paulise de Bush collection of 18th- to 20th-century costume gives a sense of the 220 year history of Killerton in Devon as the outfits are displayed on life-size dummies in carefully composed historical settings. The clothing on display comes right up to the 1930s, including feminine floral chiffon evening gowns of the sort that would have been worn at weekend parties that took place at the house between the two World Wars.

Arlington Court near Barnstaple in Devon houses the Trust's large collection of horse-drawn carriages while the splendid Tudor house at Trerice in Cornwall is the rather unexpected setting for a madcap collection of lawnmowers, displayed in the hayloft of the former stable. An informative exhibition traces the history of this humble but important invention from its very first incarnation, patented by a Mr. Budding, in 1831.

ENGLISH HERITAGE

Kenwood House

Carisbrooke Castle

Battle Abbey

Osborne House

It's our job at English Heritage to look after the historic environment of England for future generations. With some of the country's best conservationists, archaeologists and historians, we help make England's unique landscapes, buildings and castles available, relevant and fun for all.

Many English Heritage properties are home to a range of exhibitions and collections. You'll find more details on the collections in this book.

www.english-heritage.org.uk

ENGLISH HERITAGE

Secure a place in history

Half a million people are already members of English Heritage. You can join them and enjoy 15 months' membership for the price of 12*

The benefits of membership include:

- Free entry to over 400 historic properties
- Full-colour handbook, map and events diary
- Award-winning quarterly magazine, Heritage Today

AND

- Free or reduced-price admission to hundreds of special events

Kenwood House

- Half-price entry to historic sites in Scotland, Wales and the Isle of Man – free after the first year
- Free or discounted admission to over 30 other historic attractions in England
- Exclusive behind-the-scenes tours

Call 0870 333 1182, quoting MUSE

To find out more about English Heritage, take a look at our website: www.english-heritage.org.uk.

English Heritage, Membership department, FREEPOST, PO Box 570, Swindon, Wiltshire SN2 2UR.

*When you join by direct debit before 31st December 2004

The Long Gallery at Parham House

Of Britain's many outstanding attributes, it is perhaps the range and diversity of our built heritage, together with the history that has shaped it, of which we can be most proud.

Britain is unique in regard to the number, and quality, of houses that have survived over the centuries, despite the uncompromising social and economic conditions that have existed from time to time. But it is not just the houses themselves that add to the wealth of our heritage, important though they are, it is the gardens and parkland that are sustained by them and the artistic collections for which they stand as custodians, that gives Britain its pre-eminence. Historic Museums provide untold care and protection for a significant number of collections which have, for whatever reason, been forced out of private ownership - indeed this splendid book shines a light on

Powderham Castle

some of the very best. But for many people, seeing art and furniture as part of a wider collection, within the private house or setting for which they were originally commissioned or collected, is a particularly memorable experience.

The Historic Houses Association established in 1973 represents the interests of those houses, still in private ownership, which together form the greater part of

Longleat House

HISTORIC HOUSES ASSOCIATION

Britain's built heritage. Over 1,500 owners are members and we have more houses open to the public than both the National Trust and English Heritage (and their Scottish and Welsh equivalents) combined. Unlike our counterparts in most other European countries, however, we receive no fiscal help from government towards the main-

Berkeley Castle from Queen Elizabeth 1st's Bowling Green

tenance of these buildings - despite the high cost of sustaining and enhancing the fabric of the buildings themselves and the important collections and artefacts they house. The upshot has been a marked

Racing Room at Woburn Abbey

increase in the number of sales of works of art to fund all important maintenance, a clearly unsustainable position.

Nonetheless, with the support of visitors and our Friends scheme, as well as the determination of owners, these houses remain largely in good health and ready to welcome the 12 million people who come to share in their exhibits every year.

Over 26,000 people have joined our Friends Scheme, allowing them free access to the 300 or so houses which open to the public. If you would like to join the scheme, or would like more information about the Historic Houses Assoc-iation, take a look at our website, www.hha.org.uk or call 020 7259 5688.

The State Drawing Room at Scone Palace

Bath, Bristol & Northeast Somerset

Bristol, the largest university city in the southwest of England with its beautiful cathedral, is an industrial and commercial centre with a long history of maritime adventure and commerce and housing a wealth of historic treasures.

The jewel of this lovely region is undoubtedly Bath, built on hills rising steeply from the River Avon. This delightful city, a spa centre since Roman times, became a centre of fashion and manners during the eighteenth century. The tradition and history of this region is innovatively and fascinatingly revealed to the visitor through a wealth of fine galleries, museums and displays.

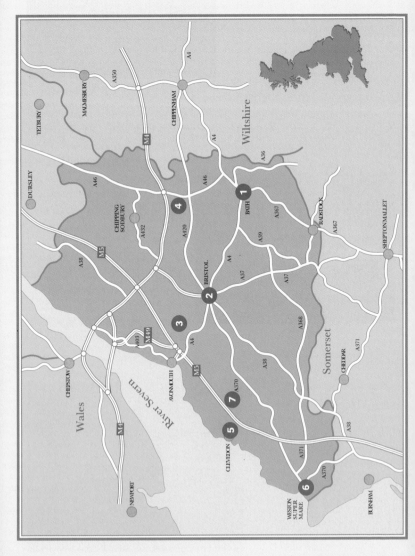

The Red Map References should be used to locate Museums etc on the pages that follow

Bath, Bristol & Northeast Somerset

American Museum in Britain

Claverton Manor, Bath BA2 7BD   Tel: 01225 460503   Fax: 01225 469160
Email: info@americanmuseum.org   Web: www.americanmuseum.org

The American Museum shows in a series of 18 period rooms how Americans lived between the late 17th and mid 19th centuries. There are galleries devoted to Folk Art and to an extensive textile collection. The grounds contain an arboretum of American trees and shrubs as well as a replica of part of the garden at Mount Vernon, George Washington's Virginia home.

Opening Times: 20 Mar to 31 Oct Tue to Sun 12:00-17:30. 20 Nov to 15 Dec Tue to Sun 13:00-16:00. Closed Mon except in Aug & BH. Admission: Adult £6.50, Child £4.00, OAP £6.00. Location: Two miles south east of Bath Exhibitions & Events 2004 : 20 Mar to 31 Oct: 'Stars, Strips & Spirals' Welsh & American Quilts.   Map Ref: 1

Bath Abbey Heritage Vaults

13 Kingston Buildings, Bath BA1 1LT   Tel: 01225 422462
Email: laj@heritagevaults.fsnet.co.uk

A pageant of the Abbey's past from the 8th century to the present day in words and pictures, sights and sounds.

Opening Times: Daily 10:00-16:00, closed Xmas & New Year and Good Friday.
Admission: Adult £2.50, Child Free, OAP/Student £1.50. Location: In the centre of Bath, alongside Bath Abbey.   Map Ref: 1

Beckford's Tower & Museum

Lansdown Road, Bath BA1 9BH   Tel: 01225 422212/460705   Fax: 01225 481805
Email: beckford@bptrust.demon.co.uk   Web: www.bath-preservation-trust.org.uk

The recently restored Tower, built in 1827 for William Beckford, boasts a spiral staircase and elegant Belvedere offering panoramic views. It contains a museum collection, with paintings, prints, models and art objects, illustrating Beckford's life and interests.

Opening Times: Easter to end Oct Sat Sun & BH 10:30-17:00. Admission: Adult £2.50, Child/OAP £2.00, Family £6.00. Location: One and a half miles north from Bath centre on Lansdown Road towards the racecourse.   Map Ref: 1

Building of Bath Museum

Countess of Huntingdon's Chapel, The Vineyards, Bath BA1 5NA   Tel: 01225 333895
Fax: 01225 445473   Email: cathryn@bathmuseum.co.uk   Web: www.bath-preservation-trust.org.uk

Situated in the beautiful Gothic chapel built in 1765 is the complete guide to how Georgian Bath was conceived and built. The exhibition is illustrated with a number of models, artefacts, paintings and touch screen computer.

Opening Times: 15 Feb to 30 Nov, Tue to Sun & BH 10:30-17:00. Closed 1 Dec to 14 Feb.
Admission: Adult £4.00, Child £1.50, Concession £3.00. Location: Short walk from Bath Town Centre on The Paragon which runs parellel with Lansdown and Walcot Street.   Map Ref: 1

Holburne Museum of Art

Great Pulteney Street, Bath BA2 4DB   Tel: 01225 466669   Fax: 01225 333121   Email: holburne@bath.ac.uk   Web: www.bath.ac.uk/holburne

This jewel in Bath's crown was once the Georgian Sydney Hotel, whose glittering society Jane Austen watched from her house opposite. It displays the treasures collected by Sir William Holburne: superb English and continental silver, porcelain, maiolica, glass and Renaissance bronzes. The Picture Gallery contains works by Turner, Guardi, Stubbs and other artists plus portraits of Bath society by Thomas Gainsborough.

Opening Times: Mid Feb to Mid Dec Tue to Sat 10:00-17:00, Sun 14:30-17:30. Admission: Adult £4.00, Child £1.50, OAP £3.50, Family £9.00. Location: Five minutes walk from town centre.   Map Ref: 1

Bath, Bristol & Northeast Somerset

Museum of Bath at Work

Camden Works, Julian Road, Bath BA1 2RH   Tel / Fax: 01225 318348
Email: mobaw@hotmail.com   Web: www.bath-at-work.org.uk

Stories of working life in Bath, of Bath stone and building industry, Victorian ironmongers, mineral water factory and engineering works, furniture making and car factory. Temporary exhibitions.

Opening Times: Apr to Nov daily, Nov to Apr Sat & Sun 10:00-17:00.   Admission: Adult £3.50, Concession £2.50, Family £10.00.   Location: North of city centre, five minutes walk.   Map Ref: 1

Museum of Costume

Assembly Rooms, Bennett Street, Bath BA1 2QH
Tel: 01225 477785   Fax: 01225 477743
Email: costume_bookings@bathnes.gov.uk   Web: www.museumofcostume.co.uk

One of the most prestigious and extensive collections of its kind. Displays include over 150 dressed figures illustrating the changing styles in fashionable dress for men, women and children from the late 16th century to the present day. The modern collection contains work by many of the world's top designers. Personal audio guides included. Special exhibition for 2004, 'Jane Austen: Film & Fashion'.

18th Century Gallery
Court dress of brocaded silk, c.1760-65

Opening Times: Open daily Jan & Feb 11:00-16:00, Mar to Oct 11:00-17:00, Nov to Dec 11:00-16:00. Last exit one hour after closing. Closed 25-26 Dec.   Admission: 2004 Adult £6.00, Child £4.00, Concession £5.00, Family £16.50. Group rates and Saver tickets with Roman Baths are available.   Location: Ten minute walk from city centre, 15 minute walk from bus and railway stations.   Map Ref: 1

Museum of East Asian Art

12 Bennett Street, Bath BA1 2QJ   Tel: 01225 464640
Fax: 01225 461718   Email: info@meaa.org.uk
Web: www.meaa.org.uk

A unique museum housing a fine collection of objects from all over East Asia, ranging in date from circa 5000 BC to the present day. The exquisite collection includes Chinese ceramics and metalware, Japanese lacquer and a range of south east Asian ceramics, as well as some outstanding examples of Chinese jade.

Opening Times: Tue to Sat 10:00-17:00, Sun 12:00-17:00, some BH. Closed Mon, Xmas & New Year.   Admission: Adult £3.50, Child (under 12) £1.00, OAP £3.00.   Location: Upper town area of city; just off The Circus. 20 minutes walk from railway/bus station.

Gilt bronze statue of a standing
monk with begging bowl

Map Ref: 1

No 1 Royal Crescent

Bath BA1 2LR   Tel: 01225 338727   Fax: 01225 481850   Email: admin@bptrust.demon.co.uk
Web: www.bath-preservation-trust.org.uk

A grand town house of the late 18th century accurately restored and furnished with authentic furniture, paintings and carpets. On the ground floor are the study and dining room and on the first floor a lady's bedroom and drawing room. In the basement is a period kitchen and a museum shop.

Opening Times: Mid-Feb to end Oct Tue to Sun 10:30-17:00, Nov Tue to Sun 10:30-16:00. Closed Good Friday, open BH.   Admission: Adult £4.00, Child/Concession/Student £3.50, Family £10.00, Schools £2.50, Groups £3.00 .   Location: Central.   Map Ref: 1

The Lady's Bedroom

Bath, Bristol & Northeast Somerset

Postboy 18th/19th century

Postal Museum in Bath

8 Broad Street, Bath BA1 5LJ   Tel / Fax: 01225 460333   Email: info@bathpostalmuseum.org
Web: www.bathpostalmuseum.org

We cover 4,000 years of communication from clay-mail to e-mail. This time-line also includes exhibitions in the Education Room on the Victorians, an essential ingredient in school curricula. Four computer games demonstrate how the post was 'carried'. Constantly playing videos plus an international airmail room showing early aviation films, a reconstructed 1930s post office and special displays will intrigue the visitor.

Opening Times: Mon to Sat 11:00-17:00. Last entry 16:30.
Admission: Adult £2.90, Student £1.90, Child £1.50, OAP £2.40, Family ticket £6.90.   Location: In town centre, one minute walk from General Post Office.   Map Ref: 1

Roman Baths

Pump Room, Stall Street, Bath BA1 1LZ
Tel: 01225 477785   Fax: 01225 477743
Email: romanbaths_bookings@bathnes.gov.uk   Web: www.romanbaths.co.uk

The Roman Baths contain the remains of one of the greatest religious spas in the ancient world and a fine Roman museum. Bath's unique thermal springs rise at the heart of the site. It is the most popular visitor attraction in the West Country and is among the UK's major heritage sites. Free audio tours are available in seven languages.

Opening Times: Jan to Feb & Nov to Dec 09:30-16:30, Mar to Jun & Sep to Oct 09:00-17:00, Jul to Aug 09:00-21:00. Last exit 1/2 hour after closing. Closed 25-26 Dec.
Admission: 2004 Adult £9.00, Child £5.00, OAP £8.00, Family £24.00. Group rates and saver tickets with

Great Bath, Roman Baths

Museum of Costume are available.   Location: City centre.   Map Ref: 1

Victoria Art Gallery

Bridge Street, Bath BA2 4AT   Tel: 01225 477233
Fax: 01225 477231   Email: victoria_enquiries@bathnes.gov.uk
Web: www.victoriagal.org.uk

Bath and North East Somerset's art gallery, housing a substantial permanent collection in addition to major touring exhibitions. Paintings by Gainsborough, Turner and Sickert hang in the recently refurbished Upper Gallery and are described on free audio guides. Decorative arts newly on display include collections of pottery, porcelain, glass and watches.

Opening Times: Tue to Fri 10:00-17:30, Sat 10:00-17:00, Sun 14:00-17:00. Closed BH.   Admission: Free.

The permanent collection at the Victoria Art Gallery

Location: City centre.   Map Ref: 1

William Herschel Museum

19 New King Street, Bath BA1 2BL   Tel: 01225 311342/446865   Fax: 01225 446865
Web: www.bath-preservation-trust.org.uk

Home of 18th century astronomers William and Caroline Herschel. A charming Georgian townhouse furnished in the style of the period, includes workshop where Herschel made telescopes and discovered the planet Uranus in 1781. Collection of astronomical and musical instruments. 'Star Vault' attraction showing astronomy programmes. Delightful Georgian garden. Out of hours tours.

Opening Times: 9 Feb to 30 Nov Mon to Fri 14:00-17:00, Sat & Sun 11:00-17:00. Closed Wed.
Admission: Adult £3.50, Child £2.00, Family £7.50. Local residents & Bath Preservation Trust Museums Concession.   Location: Six minutes walk from central bus and railway stations, near city centre.   Map Ref: 1

Bath, Bristol & Northeast Somerset

Arnolfini

ARNOLFINI

16 Narrow Quay, Bristol BS1 4QA   Tel: 0117 917 2300   Fax: 0117 917 2303
Email: info@arnolfini.org.uk   Web: www.arnolfini.org.uk

Arnolfini is one of Europe's leading centres for the contemporary arts, presenting new and innovative work in the visual arts, performance, dance and film. From 29 Sep 2003 Arnolfini is closing temporarily to undertake a major £12million refurbishment project. Arnolfini will re-open in Spring 2005 with upgraded and expanded facilities. A temporary Arnolfini bookshop and information point is planned for the harbourside and Arnolfini is organising an Interlude programme of events in and around the city while building work is being carried out.

Photo: Woodley and Quick

Location: Located on the harbourside, near to the town centre, 15 minute walk from Bristol Temple Meads Railway Station.   Map Ref: 2

Blaise Castle House Museum

Bristol
Museums &
Art Gallery

Henbury Road, Henbury, Bristol BS10 7QS   Tel: 0117 903 9818
Fax: 0117 903 9820   Email: general_museum@bristol-city.gov.uk
Web: www.bristol-city.gov.uk/museums

Steeped in history and set in beautiful parkland, discover everyday objects from times past including kitchen and laundry equipment; sumptuous costume and accessories; a Victorian school room; Victorian baths; model trains, dolls and toy soldiers and more.

Opening Times: Apr to Oct Sat to Wed 10:00-17:00.   Admission: Free.   Map Ref: 3

Bristol City Museum & Art Gallery

Bristol
Museums &
Art Gallery

Queens Road, Bristol BS8 1RL   Tel: 0117 922 3571   Fax: 0117 922 2047
Email: general_museum@bristol-city.gov.uk
Web: www.bristol-city.gov.uk/museums

Be amazed by countless, wonderful objects. Some of the treasures include: minerals and fossils; Egyptian galleries; Far Eastern art; wildlife galleries; archaeology; ceramics and glass; seven galleries of art. Temporary exhibitions and special events are held throughout the year.

Opening Times: Daily 10:00-17:00.   Admission: Free.
'La Belle Dame/Sans Merci' Frank Dicksee 1902   Map Ref: 2

Bristol Industrial Museum

Bristol
Museums &
Art Gallery

Princes Wharf, Wapping Road, Bristol BS1 4RN   Tel: 0117 925 1470
Fax: 0117 929 7318   Email: general_museums@bristol-city.gov.uk
Web: www.bristol-city.gov.uk/museums

Bringing the past to life. Discover loads of things to see and do. The Museum's exhibits based on Bristol's rich industrial past include: The story of the Port of Bristol's trading past and present; Bristol's involvement in transatlantic slave trade; Bristol-made cars, buses, bicycles and motorbikes; how printing and packaging was made; how the aircraft industry developed in the city, with real aircraft and engines.

Tobacco and Aircraft
two of Bristol's major industries

Opening Times: Sat to Wed 10:00-17:00.
Admission: Free.   Map Ref: 2

Guided or Private Tours	Disabled Access	Gift Shop or Sales Point	Café or Refreshments	Restaurant	Car Parking

Bath, Bristol & Northeast Somerset

The British Empire & Commonwealth Museum   ♿ ❂ ▭

Station Approach, Temple Meads, Bristol BS1 6QH   Tel: 0117 9254 980   Fax: 0117 9254 983
Email: admin@empiremuseum.co.uk   Web: www.empiremuseum.co.uk

An award-winning national museum which presents the 500 year history of the rise and fall of the British empire and examines its legacy on modern Britain and the Commonwealth. It has sixteen permanent galleries and regulary presents additional special exhibitions.

Opening Times: 10:00-17:00. Closed 25 & 26 Dec.   Location: Near Temple Meads, one minute walk from the station.   Map Ref: 2

Georgian House

7 Great George Street, Bristol BS1 5RR   Tel: 0117 921 1362
Email: general_museum@bristol-city.gov.uk   Web: www.bristol-city.gov.uk/museums

Bristol
Museums &
Art Gallery

The Georgian House is an exquisite example of a town house of about 1790. The house is furnished to illustrate life both above and below stairs.

Opening Times: Apr to Oct Sat to Wed 10:00-17:00.   Admission: Free.   Map Ref: 2

Red Lodge

Park Row, Bristol BS1 5LJ   Tel: 0117 921 1360
Email: general_museum@bristol-city.gov.uk
Web: www.bristol-city.gov.uk/museums

Bristol
Museums &
Art Gallery

Red Lodge is an Elizabethan house built around 1590, with the city's last surviving suite of 16th century rooms. There is also an impressive Tudor-style knot garden.

Opening Times: Apr to Oct Sat to Wed 10:00-17:00.   Admission: Free.   Map Ref: 2

Dyrham Park   ▦ ♿ ❂ ▭ ⊞

near Chippenham SN14 8ER   Tel: 01179 372501   Fax: 01179 371353
Email: dyrhampark@nationaltrust.org.uk   Web: www.nationaltrust.org.uk

One of the Blackmoor torcheres in Balcony Room

This 17th century mansion was built in the baroque style between 1692 and 1704 for William Blathwayt, secretary of state to William III. The rooms have changed little since they were furnished by Blathwayt and their contents are recorded in his housekeeper's inventory. There are family portraits, paintings and a state bed made for the house. The items of Delftware reflect the contemporary taste for Dutch fashions. Victorian domestic rooms open include kitchen, bakehouse, larders and dairy.

Opening Times: House: 26 Mar to 31 Oct Fri to Tue 12:00-17:00. Garden: 26 Mar to 31 Oct Fri to Tue 11:00-17:30. Timed tickets on BHs. Closed Xmas.   Admission: Adult £8.30, Child £4.10, Family £20.50. Garden & park only: Adult £3.20, Child £1.60, Family £7.30. NT Members Free. Location: Eight miles north of Bath, 12 miles east of Bristol, two miles south of Tormarton interchange with M4, exit18.   Map Ref: 4

Clevedon Court   ▦ ♿ ⊞

Tickenham Road, Clevedon BS21 6QU   Tel: 01275 872257   Fax: 0871 433 9294
Web: www.nationaltrust.org.uk

Brightly coloured glass rolling pins mounted on a wall in the Justice Room

An outstanding 14th century manor house with much of the original building still evident. It has been home to the Elton Family since 1709. The house contains many striking Eltonware pots and vases and a fascinating collection of Nailsea glass. There is a beautiful 18th century terraced garden.

Opening Times: 4 Apr to 30 Sep Wed, Thu & Sun 14:00-17:00. Admission by timed ticket in High season. Open BH Mons.   Admission: Adult £5.00, Child £2.50. NT Members Free.   Location: One and a half miles east of Clevedon, on Bristol road (B3130), signposted from M5 exit 20.   Map Ref: 5

Bath, Bristol & Northeast Somerset

The Helicopter Museum

The Heliport, Locking Moor Road, Weston-super-Mare BS24 8PP   Tel: 01934 635227
Fax: 01934 645230   Email: office@helimuseum.fsnet.co.uk
Web: www.helicoptermuseum.co.uk

Britain's only helicopter museum is a fascinating place to visit with many rare and unique helicopters on display under cover. Group/school visits welcome by prior arrangement. Restoration hangar, adventure play area, open cockpit days and sight-seeing flights.

Opening Times: Apr to Oct Wed to Sun 10:00-18:00, Nov to Mar 10:00-16:00. Open daily for BH, Easter and summer school holidays.   Admission: Adult £3.95, Child £2.75, OAP £3.25, Family (2 adults and 2 children) £11.00, Concessions for groups.   Location: Museum is on A368/A371, three miles from Weston-super-Mare seafront. Approx one and a half miles from junction 21 on M5.   Map Ref: 6

North Somerset Museum

Burlington Street, Weston-super-Mare BS23 1PR   Tel: 01934 621028   Fax: 01934 612526
Email: museum.service@n-somerset.gov.uk   Web: www.n-somerset.gov.uk/museum

Victorian museum featuring galleries of archaelogy, social and natural history, The Seaside Gallery and the unique Clara's Cottage make up the static displays. Exhibitions, Peoples Collection, events and seminars make this a very popular attraction. Disabled access downstairs only. Cafe and shop.

Opening Times: Mon to Sat 10:00-16:30.   Admission: Adult £3.50, OAP £2.50, Child Free.
Location: Town centre, five minutes walk from all car parks.   Map Ref: 6

Tyntesfield

Wraxall BS48 1NT   Tel: 0870 458 4500   Web: www.nationaltrust.org.uk

This is a spectacular Victorian country house, remodelled in 1864. It is an extraordinary Gothic Revival, with towers, turrets and its original interior intact. There is an unrivalled collection of decorative arts and a sumptuously decorated private Chapel. It is surrounded by 500 acres of landscaped gardens.

Opening Times: By guided tour, booking in advance only.   Admission: Telephone for details.   Location: Off B3130.   Map Ref: 7

Bedfordshire, Berkshire, Buckinghamshire & Hertfordshire

These four counties encapsulate much of the English way of life. At the very heart of the country and surrounding the capital, the region was the culmination of ancient tracks and trade routes, the Ridgeway and the Icknield Way, dating back to the Bronze Age. The Romans too in their turn left their road building mark. In a country of magnificent medieval castles, this area being so close to the country's heart felt safe from invaders and as a consequence, what it lacks in military architecture it more than makes up for with its glorious domestic architecture.

The marks indelibly stamped on these four counties by their early occupants are thankfully well recorded in their splendid museums and heritage centres.

The Red Map References should be used to locate Museums etc on the pages that follow

Beds, Berks, Bucks & Herts

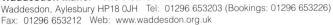

Buckinghamshire County Museum
& The Roald Dahl Children's Gallery

Church Street, Aylesbury HP20 2QP Tel: 01296 331441 Fax: 01296 334884
Email: museum@buckscc.gov.uk Web: www.buckscc.gov.uk/museum

You really can awaken your senses at this award-winning museum with its innovative touchable displays, exciting programme of family exhibitions, and regular events and activities. Let your imagination run wild.

Opening Times: Mon to Sat 10:00-17:00, Sun 14:00-17:00. On school days the Dahl Gallery is reserved for school use only until 15:00. Admission: Bucks County Museum - Free. Roald Dahl Children's Gallery: Adult £3.50, Child £2.75. Location: In the old part of Aylesbury near the town centre, three minutes walk from bus station. Map Ref: 1

Waddesdon Manor - The Rothschild Collection

Waddesdon, Aylesbury HP18 0JH Tel: 01296 653203 (Bookings: 01296 653226)
Fax: 01296 653212 Web: www.waddesdon.org.uk

*Dining Room 19th Century setting,
Photo Tim Imrie ©Waddesdon,
The Rothschild Collection (The National Trust)*

Waddesdon Manor was built between 1874 and 1889, in the style of a 16th century French chateau, for Baron Ferdinand de Rothschild. There is a large display of French 18th century decorative arts. The furniture, carpets and porcelain are internationally important. Outstanding portraits by Gainsborough and Reynolds and works by Dutch and Flemish Masters of the 17th century. Waddesdon has one of the finest Victorian gardens in Britain, renowned for its seasonal displays, colourful shrubs, mature trees and parterre. Thousands of bottles of vintage Rothschild wines line the cellars.

*Green Boudoir, Photo John Freeman
©Waddesdon, The Rothschild
Collection (The National Trust)*

Opening Times: House: 31 Mar to 31 Oct Wed to Sun 11:00-16:00. Grounds: 3 Mar to 31 Oct Wed to Sun 10:00-17:00, 3 Nov to 23 Dec Wed to Sun 11:00-17:00. Open BH Mons. Admission: House & Grounds: Adult £11.00, Child (5-16 inc) £8.00, Bachelor's Wing £1.00. Groups: Adult £8.80, Child £6.40, Bachelor's Wing £1.00. Grounds only: Adult £4.00, Child £2.00. Groups: Adult £3.20, Child £1.60. NT Members: Free. Location: Access via Waddesdon village, six miles north west of Aylesbury on A41. Map Ref: 2

Bedford Museum

Castle Lane, Bedford MK40 3XD Tel: 01234 353323 Fax: 01234 273401
Email: bmuseum@bedford.gov.uk Web: www.bedfordmuseum.org

Embark on a fascinating journey through the human and natural history of North Bedfordshire. Go back in time to visit the delightful rural room sets and the Old School Museum.

Opening Times: Tue to Sat 11:00-17:00, Sun & BH Mon 14:00-17:00. Closed Good Friday, Xmas & New Year. Admission: Adult £2.20, Child/OAP/Concession Free. Annual ticket £8.80.
Location: Close to two town centre car parks and a short walk from Allhallows Bus Station and the Midland Road Railway Station. Map Ref: 3

Cecil Higgins Art Gallery
see Page opposite
Map Ref: 3

John Bunyan Museum

Bunyan Meeting Free Church, Mill Street, Bedford MK40 3EU Tel / Fax: 01234 213722
Email: bmeeting@dialstart.net

Walk through the life and times of the famous 17th century preacher, pastor and author. The collection includes copies of John Bunyan's most celebrated work in over 170 languages.

Opening Times: 2 Mar to 30 Oct Tue to Sat 11:00-16:00. Closed Good Friday.
Admission: Free Location: Near town centre, just off the High Street. Map Ref: 3

The Burges Room,
Victorian Mansion

'The Vitriol Thrower' 1894
by Eugène-Samuel Grasset

Cecil Higgins Art Gallery

Castle Lane, Bedford MK40 3RP
Tel: 01234 211222   Fax: 01234 327149
Email: chag@bedford.gov.uk   Web: www.cecilhigginsartgallery.org

Housed in an elegantly converted and extended Victorian mansion, the Gallery is home to one of the most outstanding fine and decorative art collections outside London. A remarkable collection of British and European watercolours from the 18th to the 20th centuries and international prints from Impressionism to the present. Ceramics and glass from the Renaissance to the 20th century, with particular focus on 18th century porcelain, Whitefriars glass and ceramics of the Art & Crafts movement. Authentically reconstructed Victorian room settings, including the William Burges Room, a complete Gothic experience. Thomas Lester lace collection and changing exhibitions, programme events, lectures and workshops for all ages.

'St George' c. 1899
by Sir Alfred Gilbert

'Falling Star' Enamel Plaque c.1905
by P.O. Reeves

Glass Flask, 1686
by Willem Van Heemskerk

Opening Times: Tue to Sat 11:00-17:00, Sun & BH Mon 14:00-17:00.
Admission: Adult £2.20, Child/Concession Free.
Location: Centre of Bedford, just off the Embankment.
Exhibitions & Events 2004 : Please ring for current exhibition programme.

Beds, Berks, Bucks & Herts

BIGGLESWADE *Beds*

Shuttleworth Collection
Old Warden Aerodrome, Biggleswade SG18 9EA   Tel: 01767 627288

A collection of historic aeroplanes kept in flying condition housed in eight hangars in a quiet countryside setting on an established all-grass runway. Flying displays during summer months.

Opening Times: Daily Apr to Oct 10:00-17:00, Nov to Mar 10:00-16:00. Closed Xmas & New Year.   Admission: Adult £7.50, Seniors £6.00 (not event days). Flying Display Days & Evenings £15.00 per person.   Location: Three miles west of A1 at the Biggleswade roundabout, nearest railway station - Biggleswade.   Map Ref: 4

BUCKINGHAM *Bucks*

Claydon House

Middle Claydon, Buckingham MK18 2EY
Tel: 01296 730349   Fax: 01296 738511
Email: claydon@nationaltrust.org.uk Web: www.nationaltrust.org.uk

National Trust property with family museum containing mementoes of Florence Nightingale, military uniforms, weapons, costume and musical instruments. Exuberant Rococo and Chinoiserie style throughout. Second hand bookshop.

Opening Times: 27 Mar to 24 Oct Sat to Wed 13:00-17:00, 25 Oct to 31 Oct Sat to Wed 13:00-16:00.   Admission: Adult £4.70, Child £2.30, Family £11.70. Group (15+) £3.60. NT Members Free.
Location: In Middle Claydon 13 miles north west of Aylesbury, three and a half miles south west of Winslow.   Map Ref: 5

Sir Francis Verney as 'The Barbary Pirate' (1583-1615)

The Old Gaol Museum
Market Hill, Buckingham MK18 1JX   Tel: 01280 823020

One of the first purpose bulit county gaols in England, now a museum proudly displaying aspects of historical Buckingham.

Opening Times: Mon to Sat 10:00-16:00.   Admission: Adult £1.50, Child/Concession £1.00.
Location: One minute walk from town centre car park.   Map Ref: 6

BUSHEY *Herts*

Bushey Museum & Art Gallery

Rudolph Road, Bushey WD23 3HW   Tel: 020 8420 4057
Fax: 020 8420 4923   Email: busmt@bushey.org.uk
Web: www.busheymuseum.org

An award-winning community museum telling the unique story of Bushey from the earliest times to the present day. Art galleries and special displays show two hundred years of art teaching and practice in Bushey from the early watercolours of the Monro Circle to the social realism and portraiture of the Herkomer Art School, to the animal painting of Lucy Kemp-Welch and Marguerite Frobisher Schools.

Opening Times: Thu to Sun 11:00-16:00.   Admission: Free.
Location: Just off Bushey High Street.   Map Ref: 7

CHALFONT ST GILES *Bucks*

Milton's Cottage
Deanway, Chalfont St Giles HP8 4JH   Tel: 01494 872313   Email: info@miltonscottage.org
Web: www.miltonscottage.org

Probably the finest collection of Milton 17th century 1st editions in the world. Milton memorabilia and civil war artefacts. All housed in the 16th century grade I listed cottage to which he escaped from the plague in 1665.

Opening Times: 1 Mar to 31 Oct Tue to Sun 10:00-13:00 & 14:00-18:00. Closed Mon except BH.
Admission: Adult £3.00, Child £1.00, Group (20+) £2.00. Location: Centre of village. Map Ref: 8

Beds, Berks, Bucks & Herts

Hatfield House, Park & Gardens

Hatfield AL9 5NQ   Tel: 01707 287010   Fax: 01707 287033   Email: curator@hatfield-house.co.uk   Web: www.hatfield-house.co.uk

Celebrated Jacobean house, steeped in Elizabethan and Victorian political history with exquisite furniture, tapestries and paintings, standing within its own Great Park. Constantly developing gardens reflect historic origins.

Opening Times: Easter Sat to 30 Sep daily 12:00-16:00.   Admission: £7.50.   Location: Two miles from J4 A1 (M). Opposite Hatfield rail station.   Map Ref: 9

Mill Green Museum & Mill

Mill Green, Hatfield AL9 5PD   Tel: 01707 271362   Email: museum@welhat.gov.uk   Web: www.welhat.gov.uk

An 18th century watermill, restored to working order, with a museum in the adjoining miller's house complete with Victorian kitchen. The museum also features regular special exhibitions and events.

Opening Times: Tue to Fri 10:00-17:00 Sat, Sun & BH 14:00-17:00. Closed Mon. Admission: Free.   Location: In hamlet of Mill Green. One mile from Hatfield railway station.   Map Ref: 9

Stondon Museum

Station Road, Lower Stondon, Henlow SG16 6JN   Tel: 01462 850339   Fax: 01462 850824   Email: enquiries@transportmuseum.co.uk   Web: www.transportmuseum.co.uk

Largest private collection in the country, covering one hundred years of motoring, plus military vehicles, fire engines etc, even a full size replica of Captain Cook's ship, 'Endeavour'.

Opening Times: Daily 10:00-17:00. Closed Xmas. Re-opens New Years Day.   Admission: Adult £6.00, Child £3.00, Concession £5.00, Family £16.00. Group rates available, please pre-book.   Location: Off A600 Hitchin - Bedford road, four miles from Hitchin.   Map Ref: 10

Hertford Museum

18 Bull Plain, Hertford SG14 1DT   Tel: 01992 582686   Fax: 01992 552100   Email: info@hertfordmuseum.org   Web: www.hertfordmuseum.org

HERTFORD MUSEUM

Located in 17th century town house with attractive Jacobean style garden. Century old collections of local and social history, geology, archaeology, photographs and fine art, changing exhibitions, events and activity room for schools.

Opening Times: Tue to Sat 10:00-17:00.   Admission: Free.   Location: Town centre.   Map Ref: 11

Hughenden Manor

Valley Road, High Wycombe HP14 4LA   Tel: 01494 755573   Fax: 01494 474284   Email: hughenden@nationaltrust.org.uk   Web: www.nationaltrust.org.uk

The home of Victorian prime minister Benjamin Disraeli from 1848 until his death in 1881. Most of his furniture, pictures and books remain here, which was his private retreat from parliamentary life in London. A collection of personal memorabilia is also shown. The garden was largely created by his wife Mary Anne Disraeli.

Opening Times: 6 Mar to 28 Mar Sat & Sun 13:00-17:00, 31 Mar to 31 Oct Wed to Sun 13:00-17:00.Open BH Mons.   Admission: Adult £4.70, Child £2.30, Family £12.00. Group Adult £4.20, Child £2.10. Garden: Adult £1.70, Child 80p. NT Members Free.   Location: One and a half miles north of High Wycombe on west side of the Great

'Mary Anne Disraeli', 1829 by F. Rochard in the Disraeli Room

Missenden road (A4128).   Exhibitions & Events 2004 : Disraeli bicentenary.   Map Ref: 12

Beds, Berks, Bucks & Herts

West Wycombe Park

West Wycombe HP14 3AJ   Tel: 01494 513569   Web: www.nationaltrust.org.uk

The house is among the most theatrical and Italianate in England, its facades formed as classical temples. The interior has Palmyrene ceilings and decoration, with pictures, furniture, sculpture and tapestries dating from the time of Sir Francis Dashwood. The landscaped gardens were created in the mid-18th century.

The Tapestry Room

Opening Times: House: 1 Jun to 31 Aug Sun to Thu 14:00-18:00. Grounds: 1 Apr to 31 Aug Sun to Thu 14:00-18:00. Admission: Adult £5.20, Child £2.60, Family £13.00. Grounds only: Adult £2.70, Child £1.30. NT Members Free. Location: At west end of West Wycombe, south of the Oxford road (A40).   Map Ref: 13

Wycombe Museum

Priory Avenue, High Wycombe HP13 6PX   Tel: 01494 421895   Fax: 01494 421897
Email: museum@wycombe.gov.uk   Web: www.wycombe.gov.uk/museum

Friendly local museum set in 18th century house with attractive grounds. Modern displays include interactive exhibits and children's activities. Collections include historic Windsor chairs from the Chiltern's traditional furniture industry.

Opening Times: Mon to Sat 10:00-17:00 & Sun 14:00-17:00. Closed BH. Admission: Free.
Location: Five minute walk from High Street. ten minute walk from bus station, two minute walk from railway station.   Map Ref: 12

Hitchin Museum & Art Gallery

Paynes Park, Hitchin SG5 1EW   Tel: 01462 434476   Fax: 01462 431316
Email: caroline.frith@nhdc.gov.uk   Web: www.north-herts.gov.uk

Hitchin Museum is housed in a beautiful Georgian town house build by George Kershaw in 1825, who ran a coaching service between the town and London. In this historical setting we tell the story of Hitchin's past through imaginative displays. Explore Hitchin's industrial and domestic life, contemplate the clothes people have worn for the last 170 years and fabulous art collection. Keepers of the Herts Yeomanry on permanent display.

Opening Times: Mon, Tue, Thur to Sat 10:00-17:00. Closed Wed, Sun & BH. Admission: Free.
Location: 20 minute walk from Hitchin Railway Station situated next door to Hitchin Library, two minute walk from Market Place.   Map Ref: 14

Knebworth House, Gardens & Park

Knebworth SG3 6PY   Tel: 01438 812661   Fax: 01438 811908
Email: info@knebworthhouse.com   Web: www.knebworthhouse.com

Home to the Lytton family since 1490, the romantic Victorian gothic exterior of Knebworth House does little to prepare the visitor for what to expect inside. The house, it's décor and contents encapsulate 500 years of English history from early Tudor times to the present day through the 19 generations of one family. Knebworth is famous world wide for its rock concerts and as the home of Victorian novelist Edward Bulwer Lytton, auther of the words, 'The pen is mightier than the sword'. Formal gardens and country park.

Opening Times: Daily 3-18 Apr, 29 May to 6 Jun, 3 Jul to 31 Aug. Weekends & BH 27-28 Mar, 24 Apr to 23 May, 12-27 Jun, 4-26 Sep. Admission: Adult £8.50, OAP/Child £8.00, Family (4) £29.00. Location: Off A1(M) junction 7.   Map Ref: 15

Beds, Berks, Bucks & Herts

Ascott House

Ascott Estate Office, Wing, Leighton Buzzard LU7 0PS   Tel: 01296 688242
Fax: 01296 681904   Email: info@ascottestate.co.uk
Web: www.nationaltrust.org.uk

Originally a half timbered Jacobean farmhouse, Ascott was bought in 1876 by the de Rothschild family and considerably transformed and enlarged. It now houses a quite exceptional collection of fine paintings, Oriental porcelain, English and French furniture. The extensive gardens are a mixture of formal and natural.

Opening Times: House & Gardens: 16 Mar to 30 Apr Tue to Sun 14:00-18-00, 4 May to 29 Jul Tue to Thu 14:00-18:00, I Aug to 31 Aug Tue to Sun 14:00-18:00.
Admission: House & Gardens: Adult £6.00, Child £3.00.
Gardens: Adult £4.00, Child £2.00 NT Members Free.
Location: Half a mile east of Wing, two miles south west of Leighton Buzzard on A418.   Map Ref: 16

Landscape with Animals,
by Nicholaes Berchem (1620-1683)

Leighton Buzzard Railway

Pages Park Station, Billington Road, Leighton Buzzard LU7 4TN   Tel: 01525 373888
Fax: 01525 377814   Email: info@buzzrail.co.uk   Web: www.buzzrail.co.uk

A working passenger railway, using the line of the narrow-gauge Leighton Buzzard Light Railway, built in 1919 to carry sand trains. Displays of photographs and actual locomotives and rolling stock. Regular working displays.

Opening Times: Mar to Oct Sun & BH weekends, extra days Jul & Aug.   Admission: Adult £5.50, Child £2.50, Under 2s Free, OAP £4.50.   Location: On A4146 Hemel Hempstead road, near roundabout with A505 from Dunstable and A5.   Map Ref: 17

Letchworth Museum & Art Gallery

The Broadway, Letchworth SG6 3PF   Tel: 01462 685647   Fax: 01462 481879
Email: letchworth.museum@north-herts.gov.uk   Web: www.north-herts.gov.uk

Letchworth Museum opened in 1914 to house the collections of the Letchworth Naturalists Society, but since then has expanded greatly. The attractive downstairs Natural History Gallery shows local wildlife in realistic settings, including the famous Letchworth black squirrel. The Archaeology Gallery upstairs displays fascinating Celtic and Roman collections, while the Art Gallery is home to a wide range of temporary exhibitions.

Opening Times: Mon to Sat 10:00-17:00. Closed Wed, Sun & BH.   Admission: Free.
Location: Near Broadway Cinema, next door to Letchworth Library, five minutes walk from railway station.   Map Ref: 18

Luton Museum & Gallery

Wardown Park, Luton LU2 7HA   Tel: 01582 746722
Email: museum.gallery@luton.gov.uk
Web: www.luton.gov.uk/enjoying/museums

The collections present the story of the people of Luton from earliest times to the present century. Highlights include a spectacular hoard of Roman gold coins, wonderful Saxon jewellery, the nationally important lace collection and the straw plait and hat collections, and the Bedfordshire and Hertfordshire Regimental Gallery. Events & exhibitions throughout the year.

Opening Times: Tue to Sat 10:00-17:00, Sun 13:00-17:00.   Admission: Free.
Location: Situated in beautiful Wardown Park, one mile north of town centre, Bus 24 & 25.
Follow brown signs.   Map Ref: 19

Stockwood Craft Museum & Gardens
& Mossman Collection

Stockwood Park, Farley Hill, Luton LU1 4BH   Tel: 01582 738714
Email: museum.gallery@luton.gov.uk   Web: www.luton.gov.uk/enjoying/museums

The Craft Museum collections focus on the rural life, crafts and trades of Bedfordshire. In the

Beds, Berks, Bucks & Herts

Mossman Building, visitors can enjoy the largest collections of horse-drawn vehicles on public display in Britain. In addition, the Transport Gallery brings the story into the 20th century with vintage cars, bicycles and a model of Luton's trams. Beautiful period gardens show influences of nine centuries of gardening history.

Opening Times: Apr to Oct Tue to Sun 10:00-17:00. Nov to Mar Sat to Sun 10:00-16:00.
Admission: Free. Location: In Stockwood Country Park, five minutes drive from junction 10 of the M1, Buses 1 & 4 from Park Square, town centre five minutes.   Map Ref: 19

MAIDENHEAD *Bucks*

Cliveden
Taplow, Maidenhead SL6 0JA   Tel: 01628 605069   Web: www.nationaltrust.org.uk

The present house, the third on the site, was built by Charles Barry in 1851. It has an opulent panelled hall and study and early 18th century tapestries. There are a series of gardens, featuring topiary, water gardens and a formal parterre.

Opening Times: House: 1 Apr to 31 Oct Thu & Sun 15:00-17:30. Estate & garden: 15 Mar to 31 Oct daily 11:00-18:00, 1 Nov to 12 Dec daily 11:00-16:00. Admission: Grounds: Adult £6.50, Child £3.20, Family £16.20. Group £5.50. House £1.00 extra, Child 50p. NT Members Free.
Location: Two miles north of Taplow; leave M4 at exit 7 onto A4, or M40 at exit 4 onto A404 to Marlow and follow brown signs.   Map Ref: 20

MILTON KEYNES *Bucks*

Bletchley Park
The Mansion, Wilton Avenue, Bletchley,
Milton Keynes MK3 6EB   Tel: 01908 640404   Fax: 01908 274381
Email: info@bletchleypark.org.uk   Web: www.bletchleypark.org.uk

Bletchley Park, also known as 'Station X', was home to the famous codebreakers of the Second World War and the birthplace of modern computing and communications. Museum, historic war-time buildings, Churchill Collection, exhibitions and guided tours.

Opening Times: Please telephone for details or check website.
Admission: Please telephone for details or check website. Under 13 Free.   Location: Two minute walk from Bletchley Railway Station.   Map Ref: 21

Milton Keynes Gallery
900 Midsummer Boulevard, Central Milton Keynes MK9 3QA   Tel: 01908 676900
Fax: 01908 558308   Email: mkgallery@mktgc.co.uk   Web: www.mkweb.co.uk/mkg

This successful new contemporary art gallery offers 8-10 solo and group exhibitions a year, presenting all media, including painting, sculpture, photography, printmaking and installation. There are regular talks, tours and weekend and holiday activities for children. Recorded information (01908) 558307.

Opening Times: Tue to Sat 10:00-17:00, Sun 11:00-17:00. Closed Mon & BH.
Admission: Free. Location: City Centre.   Map Ref: 22

Milton Keynes Museum
McConnell Drive, Wolverton, Milton Keynes MK12 5EL   Tel: 01908 316222   Fax: 01908 319148   Email: mkmuseum@mkmuseum.org.uk   Web: www.mkmuseum.org.uk

Victorian/Edwardian room settings, schoolroom and nursery provide a link with times past. The Shopping Street is now open. In the Hall of Transport the restored Wolverton to Stony Stratford Tramcar provides an eye-catching centre piece. Jessie the shire horse can be seen working in the extensive grounds.

Opening Times: Nov to Apr weekends only 11:00-16:30. Also BH Mon & Spring half term.
Admission: Adult £3.50, Concession £2.50, Family £8.00. Location: Five minutes by car from Milton Keynes Station or Wolverton Station.   Map Ref: 23

Beds, Berks, Bucks & Herts

Forge Museum & Victorian Cottage Garden

The Forge, High Street, Much Hadham SG10 6BS   Tel / Fax: 01279 843301
Email: christinaharrison@hotmail.com   Web: www.hertsmuseums.org.uk

The museum displays tell fascinating stories of how the crafts of blacksmithing and farriery have developed over the years, as well as smaller exhibits of local village life. There is a resident working blacksmith at the museum.

Opening Times: Mar to Dec Fri to Sun & BH 11:00-17:00. Jan & Feb by appointment.
Admission: Adult £1.00, Child/OAP 50p. Group rates available.   Location: Situated on B1004 between Bishop's Stortford and Ware on Much Hadham High Street, opposite the village hall.

Map Ref: 24

West Berkshire Museum

The Wharf, Newbury RG14 5AS   Tel: 01635 30511   Fax: 01635 38535
Email: heritage@westberks.gov.uk   Web: www.westberks.gov.uk

West Berkshire Museum is situated in two historic buildings in the heart of Newbury. The 17th century Cloth Hall and 18th century granary overlooking the Kennet & Avon Canal house fascinating displays of local history and archaeology, decorative arts, costume and rural crafts. There are galleries devoted to the Civil War battles of 1643 and 1644 and the history of Greenham Common.

Opening Times: Apr to Sep Mon to Fri 10:00-17:00, Sat 10:00-16:30. Oct to Mar Mon to Sat 10:00-16:00. Closed Wed except school holidays. Closed Sun and BH.   Admission: Free.
Location: Town centre, five minute walk from bus and railway station.   Map Ref: 25

The Cowper and Newton Museum

Orchard Side, Market Place, Olney MK46 4AJ   Tel: 01234 711516   Fax: 0870 164 0662
Email: cnm@mkheritage.co.uk   Web: www.cowperandnewtonmuseum.org

Home of 18th century poet and letter-writer, William Cowper. Artefacts of Cowper and former slave trader, John Newton, author of 'Amazing Grace'. Period gardens. Collections of bobbin lace, dinosaur bones and local history.

Opening Times: 1 Mar to 23 Dec Tue to Sat 10:00-13:00 & 14:00-17:00. Also Sun in June, Jul & Aug 14:00-17:00, BH 10:00-17:00. Closed Good Friday.   Admission: Adult £3.00, Child £1.50, Concession £2.00, Family £7.50. Group/Tour rates available. Garden only £1.00.   Location: In south east corner of Market Place in centre of Olney on A509. Five miles from junction 14 off M1.

Map Ref: 26

Basildon Park

Lower Basildon, Reading RG8 9NR
Tel: 0118 9843040   Fax: 0118 9767370
Email: basildonpark@nationaltrust.org.uk
Web: www.nationaltrust.org.uk

An 18th century Palladian mansion set in 400 acres of parkland, contains fine plasterwork, an important collection of furniture and paintings, a decorative shell room and Graham Sutherland's studies for the tapestry 'Christ in Glory'.

Opening Times: 31 Mar to 31 Oct Wed to Sun 13:00-17:30. Open BH Mons.   Admission: Adult £4.70, Child £2.30, Family £11.70. Group (15+) £3.50. Park and garden only: Adult £2.30, Child £1.10, Family £5.70. NT Members Free.   Location: On A329 between Pangbourne and Streatley, one mile walk from Pangbourne Station.

St John The Evangelist,
by Pompeo Batoni (1708-1787)

Map Ref: 27

Englefield House

Englefield, Reading RG7 5EN   Tel: 0118 930 2221   Fax: 0118 930 3226
Email: benyon@englefield.co.uk

Built in the Tudor period, extensive alterations and additions were made in the mid-18th and 19th centuries. The 12th century Church, redesigned and enlarged by Sir Gilbert Scott in 1874, stands close by.

Opening Times: House: By appointment (minimum 20). Garden: Every Mon all year, 1 Apr to 1 Nov Mon to Thur. (No dogs). Admission: House £6.00, Garden £3.00 Location: Six miles west of Reading on A340. Map Ref: 28

Museum of Reading
The Town Hall, Blagrave Street, Reading RG1 1QH Tel: 0118 939 9800 Fax: 0118 939 9881
Web: www.readingmuseum.org.uk

Excellent collections of archaeology including Roman Silchester, Reading Abbey, art and natural history. Now featuring 12 hands-on galleries.

Opening Times: Tue to Sat 10:00-16:00, Sun & BH Mon 11:00-16:00. Closed Mon.
Admission: Free. Location: In town centre, two minutes from railway station. Map Ref: 29

REME Museum of Technology
Isaac Newton Road, Arborfield Garrison, Reading RG2 9NJ Tel / Fax: 0118 9763375
Email: reme-museum@gtnet.gov.uk Web: www.rememuseum.org.uk

Reflective of the skills and training REME has employed since 1942. Displays include avionics, aeronautical instruments, control equipment, optics, radar and radios. The museum exhibition hall displays 19 specialist vehicles, a helicopter and an education area.

Opening Times: Mon to Thu 09:00-16:30, Fri 09:00-16:00, Sun 11:00-16:00. Closed Xmas & New Year. Admission: Adult £3.00, Child £2.00, OAP/Concession £2.50, Family £8.00, Group rates available, School visits please enquire and book in advance. Location: Off Biggs Lane, three miles from Wokingham in Berkshire countryside. Map Ref: 30

Royston & District Museum
Lower King Street, Royston SG8 5AL Tel: 01763 242587
Email: curator@roystonmuseum.org.uk Web: www.roystonmuseum.org.uk

Local history and archaeology. Changing Exhibitions. Excellent ceramic collection covering late 19th and 20th century.

Opening Times: Wed, Thu & Sat 10:00-16:45 open all year round. Sun & BH Mon 14:00-16:45 from Easter Sun to last Sun in Sep. Closed Xmas & New Year. Admission: Free. Groups by appointment. Location: Five minutes from railway station, ten minutes from bus station. Car parking within two minutes. Map Ref: 31

Clock Tower
Market Place, St Albans AL3 5DR Tel: 01727 751810 Fax: 01727 859919
Email: museum@stalbans.gov.uk Web: www.stalbansmuseums.org.uk

S'ALBANS MUSEUMS

Built between 1403 and 1412 this four-staged tower is the only Medieval town belfry in England. Its fine bell has also survived almost 600 years of use.

Opening Times: Easter to Oct Sat, Sun & BH 10:30-17:00. Admission: 30p. Location: In town centre. Map Ref: 32

De Havilland Aircraft Heritage Centre
(inc the Mosquito Aircraft Museum)
PO Box 107, Salisbury Hall, London Colney, St Albans AL2 1EX Tel: 01727 822051 Fax: 01727 826400 Web: www.dehavillandmuseum.co.uk

A secret wartime site waiting to be discovered by you. Home of the prototype Mosquito. On display there is a variety of de Havilland aircraft, ranging from Tiger Moth to modern military and civil jets including various sections. A working museum. Comprehensive collection of de Havilland engines and memorabilia.

Opening Times: First Sun in Mar to last Sun in Oct, Tue to Thu & Sat 14:00-17:00, Sun & BH 10:30-17:00.
Admission: Adult £5.00, Child/OAP £3.00, Family £13.00. Groups by arrangement. Location: Junction 22 of M25, follow signs (near St Albans). Map Ref: 32

de Havilland Aircraft Heritage Centre

Beds, Berks, Bucks & Herts

Kingsbury Watermill Museum
St Michaels Village, St Albans AL3 4SJ   Tel: 01727 853502

Elizabethan Watermill on three floors with working waterwheel. Fine display of milling machinery and comprehensive selection of 19th century dairy and farming implements. Pottery, gift shop and Waffle House Restaurant.

Opening Times: Mon to Sat 10:00-18:00 Sun & BH 11:00-18:00. Winter closing time 17:00. Admission: Adult £1.10, Child 60p, Concession 75p.   Location: Ten minute walk from town centre.   Map Ref: 33

Museum of St Albans

Hatfield Road, St Albans AL1 3RR   Tel: 01727 819340   Fax: 01727 837472
Email: a.coles@stalbans.gov.uk   Web: www.stalbansmuseums.org.uk

The story of historic St Albans from the departure of the Romans to the present day. Also home to the Saloman Collection of craft tools. Regular exhibitions and wildlife garden.

Opening Times: Mon to Sat 10:00-17:00, Sun 14:00-17:00.   Admission: Free.   Location: Five minutes walk from town centre, ten minutes walk from railway station.   Map Ref: 32
Photo Caption:

The Roman Theatre of Verulamium
Bluehouse Hill, St Albans AL3 6AH   Tel: 01727 835035   Email: stalbans@struttandparker.co.uk
Web: www.romantheatre.co.uk

The Roman Theatre of Verulamium was built in 140 AD as a theatre with a stage, rather than an amphitheatre. The current ruins were found in 1847 but were not fully excavated until 1930-1935.

Opening Times: Daily all year - summer 10:00-17:00, winter 10:00-16:00.   Admission: Adult £1.50, Child 50p, Concession £1.00, Under 5s Free.   Location: On the western outskirts of St Albans, just off the A4147 and on the road known as Bluehouse Hill.   Map Ref: 32

Verulamium Museum & Hypocaust

St Michaels, St Albans AL3 4SW   Tel: 01727 751810   Fax: 01727 859919
Email: a.coles@stalbans.gov.uk   Web: www.stalbansmuseums.org.uk

Discover the life and times of a major Roman city, set in attractive parkland. Nearby Roman theatre, walls, hypocaust. Demonstrations by Roman soldiers every second weekend of the month.

Opening Times: Mon to Sat 10:00-17:30, Sun 14:00-17:30.   Admission: Adult £3.30 Child/Concession £2.00 Family £8.00.   Location: Ten minutes from St Albans City Centre
                                                                                                                      Map Ref: 32

Calleva Museum
Bramley Road, Silchester RG7 2LU   Tel: 0118 9700825

Calleva Museum is unmanned and gives a pictorial record of life in Roman times. The museum acts as an information point.

Opening Times: Daily 09:30 to dusk.   Admission: Free.   Location: In the village of Silchester, Bramley Road.   Map Ref: 34

Slough Museum
278/286 High Street, Slough SL1 1NB   Tel / Fax: 01753 526422
Email: info@sloughmuseum.co.uk   Web: www.sloughmuseum.co.uk

Slough has a unique and fascinating history stretching back thousands of years. The museum traces this history in its exhibition 'A Journey Through Time', telling the story of Slough from mammoths to the modern day. Work by local groups is on display in the temporary exhibition room and there are lots of special activities for schools, children and families.

Opening Times: Wed to Sat 11:30-16:00.   Admission: Free.   Location: East end of Slough High Street, ten minutes walk from train/bus station.   Map Ref: 33

Beds, Berks, Bucks & Herts

Stevenage Museum

St Georges Way, Stevenage SG1 1XX   Tel: 01438 218881   Fax: 01438 218882
Email: museum@stevenage.gov.uk   Web: www.stevenage.gov.uk/museum

The main galleries focus on the history of the town, from the Stone Age right up to the present day. Frequently changing exhibitions on a wide range of topics.

Opening Times: Mon to Sat 10:00-17:00, Sun 14:00-17:00. Closed BH.   Admission: Free.
Location: Three minutes walk from town centre.   Map Ref: 35

The Walter Rothschild Zoological Museum

Akeman Street, Tring HP23 6AP   Tel: 020 7942 6171   Fax: 020 7942 6150
Web: www.nhm.ac.uk/museum/tring

Once the private collection of Lionel Walter, 2nd Baron Rothschild, now part of The Natural History Museum. More than 4000 mounted specimens of animals in a unique Victorian setting. The Discovery Room on the first floor is a hands-on interactive centre that encourages a sense of wonder about the natural world.

Opening Times: Mon to Sat 10:00-17:00, Sun 14:00-17:00. Admission: Free. Exhibitions & Events 2004 : A changing programme of exhibitions - please phone for details.   Map Ref: 36

Watford Museum

194 High Street, Watford WD17 2DT   Tel: 01923 232297   Fax: 01923 224772
Email: museum@artsteam-watford.co.uk   Web: www.hertsmuseums.org.uk

Watford Museum tells the story of Watford and its people from the earliest times to the present. Special exhibitions of printing and brewing and regularly changing temporary exhibitions offer something for everyone.

Opening Times: Mon to Fri 10:00-17:00, Sat 10:00-13:00 & 14:00-17:00. Closed Sun & BH.
Admission: Free.   Location: Near town centre, five minute walk from Harlequin Shopping Centre.   Map Ref: 37

Shaw's Corner

Ayot St Lawrence, Welwyn AL6 9BX   Tel / Fax: 01438 820307
Email: shawscorner@nationaltrust.org.uk   Web: www.nationaltrust.org.uk

An arts and crafts inspired house, home to playwright and socialist G Bernard Shaw for over 40 years. The rooms are much as he left them, a faithful reflection of pre-war furniture and decoration.

Opening Times: House: 20 Mar to 31 Oct Wed to Sun 13:00-17:00 (Last admission 16:30). Garden: 20 Mar to 31 Oct Wed to Sun 12:00-17:30. Open BH Mons.   Admission: Adult £3.80, Child £1.90. Family £9.50 (2 Adults and up to 3 Children). Group (15+) Adult £3.20, Child £1.60. NT Members Free.   Location: A1(M) junction 4, five miles Welwyn Garden City, five miles Harpenden. Two miles north west of Wheathampstead.   Exhibitions & Events 2004 : Please telephone for details.   Map Ref: 38

Dorney Court

Windsor SL4 6QP   Tel: 01628 604638   Fax: 01628 665772
Email: palmer@dorneycourt.co.uk   Web: www.dorneycourt.co.uk

Home of the Palmer family through thirteen generations. It shows the evolution of the squirearchy in English Country Life and of particular interest are the early family portraits, furniture and needlework.

Opening Times: May BH Mon & Sun 13:30-16:30, last entry 16:00. Aug Sun to Fri 13:30-16:30, last entry 16:00. Admission: Adult £5.50, Child over 10 £3.50. Location: Close to Junction 7 M4, Windsor Castle & Eton College.   Map Ref: 39

Beds, Berks, Bucks & Herts

Museum of Eton Life

Eton College, Windsor SL4 6DW   Tel: 01753 671177   Fax: 01753 671265
Email: rhunkin@etoncollege.org.uk   Web: www.etoncollege.com

The Museum of Eton illustrates the history and function of Eton College. There is a short video which depicts life and work of the school today. A visit to the Museum usually follows a guided tour of the College although it is open to visitors who do not take a tour.

Opening Times: 27 Mar to 20 Apr & 3 Jul to 7 Sep 10:30-16:30. 21 Apr to 2 Jul & 8 Sep to 3 Oct 14:00-16:30. Admission: Please telephone for details. Location: 15 minutes walk from Windsor. Map Ref: 39

School Yard, Eton College

Town & Crown Exhibition

Royal Windsor Information Centre, 24 High Street, Windsor SL4 1LH   Tel: 01628 796829
Fax: 01628 796859   Email: museum.collections@rbwm.gov.uk   Web: www.rbwm.gov.uk
Small display of Windsor history from its origins as a hilltop fort through to Victorian times.
Opening Times: Daily as per Tourist Centre opening hours.   Admission: Free.   Map Ref: 39

Windsor Castle

Windsor SL4 1NJ   Tel: 020 7766 7304   Fax: 020 7930 9625
Email: information@royalcollection.org.uk   Web: www.royal.gov.uk

Windsor Castle - view from Winchester Tower.
Photo by John Freeman.
The Royal Collection © 2003

The largest and oldest occupied castle in the world, encapsulates 900 years of British history and is furnished with some of the finest works of art from the Royal Collection. The current exhibition in the Drawings Gallery: The Stuarts at Windsor Castle, 27 Sep 2003 to 3 Oct 2004, marks the 400th anniversary of the Union of the Crowns. On display are some of the most exceptional artefacts from the Stuart dynasty.

Opening Times: Mar to Oct 09:45-17:15 (last admission 16:00), Nov to Feb 09:45-16:15 (last admission 15:00). Admission: Adult £12.00, Under 17s £6.00, OAP/Student £10.00, Family (2 adults and 3 children) £31.50. Location: Windsor, Berkshire. Map Ref: 39

Woburn Abbey

Woburn MK17 9WA   Tel: 01525 290666   Fax: 01525 290271
Email: enquiries@woburnabbey.co.uk   Web: www.woburnabbey.co.uk

Woburn Abbey has been home to the Dukes of Bedford for almost 450 years. Over the centuries the Russell family have, with their love of art, created one of the finest private collections in England. There are paintings by Van Dyck, Gainsborough, Reynolds and Velazquez. 21 views of Venice by Canaletto can be seen in the Venetian Room in the Private Apartments. The Vaults contain beautiful porcelain from France, Japan, Germany, England and China, including the famous Sevres dinner service given to the 4th Duchess by Louis XV. The 3,000 acre deer park contains nine species of deer and there are two gift shops, a pottery and an Antique Centre with 40 shops.

Racing Room at Woburn Abbey

Opening Times: 13 Mar to 31 Oct Mon to Fri 11:00-16:00, Sat & Sun 11:00-17:00. Open 1 Jan to 13 Mar weekends only. Admission: Adult £9.00, OAP £8.00, Child £4.50. Group Adult £7.50, Group OAP £6.50, Group Child £3.50. Location: Woburn Village one mile distance, Flitwick Railway Station five miles. No local transport available. Map Ref: 40

Cambridgeshire & Northamptonshire

Cambridgeshire, which includes the Soke of Peterborough and the Isle of Ely, boasts a wealth of historic sites and spectacular buildings. Northamptonshire, 'the county of spires and squires', is primarily a farming county.

Both Cambridgeshire and Northamptonshire can be considered to be counties of personalities, their stories carefully preserved in collections of memorabilia.

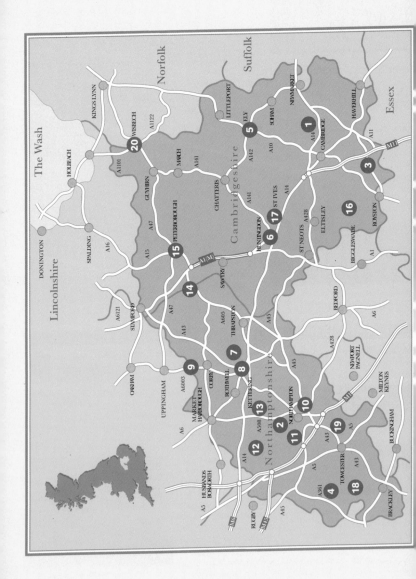

The Red Map References should be used to locate Museums etc on the pages that follow

Cambridgeshire & Northamptonshire

Early C16th cedarwood figure of St.Florian

Anglesey Abbey, Gardens and Lode Mill

Quy Road, Lode, Cambridge CB5 9EJ   Tel: 01223 810080 Fax: 01223 811200
Email: angleseyabbey@nationaltrust.org.uk
Web: www.nationaltrust.org.uk

The house dating from 1600 was built on the site of a twelfth century Augustinian Priory. It houses a unique collection of over 750 paintings, watercolours and prints. There are fine examples of furniture, silver and tapestries and one of the largest collections of clocks. The 100-acre landscaped garden and arboretum has over 100 pieces of sculpture.

Opening Times: 24 Mar to 7 Nov Wed to Sun 13:00-17:00 (Closed Good Friday). Open BH Mons. Admission: House & Garden Summer: Adult £6.60, Child £3.30. Garden Summer: Adult £4.10, Child £2.05. NT Members Free. Location: Six miles north east of Cambridge on B1102. Signposted from A14. Exhibitions & Events 2004 : Please telephone for details.   Map Ref: 1

Cambridge & County Folk Museum

2/3 Castle Street, Cambridge CB3 0AQ   Tel: 01223 355159 Email: info@folkmuseum.org.uk
Web: www.folkmuseum.org.uk

The museum is housed in a superb late 15th century timber-framed building. The displays reflect the everyday life of the people of Cambridge and the surrounding county from 1700 to the present day.

Opening Times: Apr to Sep Mon to Sat 10:30-17:00, Sun 14:00-17:00. Oct to Mar Tue to Sat 10:30-17:00, Sun 14:00-17:00. Admission: Adult £2.50, Child 75p, Concession £1.50. Location: Near the town centre, a five minute walk from central shopping area and two minutes drive from M11.
Map Ref: 2

Imperial War Museum Duxford

Cambridge CB2 4QR Tel: 01223 835000 Fax: 01223 837267
Email: duxford@iwm.org.uk Web: www.iwm.org.uk

Photo credit John M Dibbs

Europe's premier aviation museum stands on a wartime airfield and is home to a unique and fascinating collection of aircraft and military exibits. This historic airfield was built during the First World War and played an important role in the Battle of Britain during the Second World War. Much of the airfield is preserved as it was during the early 1940s, including the hangars and the Battle of Britain Operations Room. Duxford also has one of the finest collections of tanks, military vehicles and artillery in the country and features the Normandy Experience and Monty exhibitions. There are 200 aircraft on display including the legendary Spitfire, Lancaster,

Concorde and the amazing SR-71 Blackbird spy plane which flew on the edge of space. Over 50 working historic aircraft are based at Duxford and regularly take to the sky over the Museum. The award winning American Air Museum located at Duxford houses the largest collection of US aircraft outside of America including the beautifully restored B-24 Liberator. The American Air Museums stands as a memorial to the 30,000 US airmen who gave their lives while flying from British bases, including Duxford, during the Second World War.

Opening Times: Mid-Mar to Mid-Oct 10:00-18:00 (summer) 10:00-16:00 (winter). Closed Xmas. Admission: Please telephone 01223 835000 for details. Prices vary on Air Show days, Children under 12 must be accompanied by an adult. Location: Off junction 10 on M11, near Cambridge. Exhibitions & Events 2004 : Imperial War Museum Duxford plays host to four Air Shows in 2004 plus many other events.
Map Ref: 3

Kettle's Yard

🔍 ♿ **KETTLE'S YARD**

Castle Street, Cambridge CB3 0AQ   Tel: 01223 352124   Fax: 01223 324377
Email: mail@kettlesyard.cam.ac.uk   Web: www.kettlesyard.co.uk

Interior of Kettle's Yard

Kettle's Yard is a house with a permanent collection and a Gallery showing a changing programme of exhibitions. Founded by Jim Ede, once a curator at the Tate Gallery, it was intended as a 'refuge of peace and order, of the visual arts and music'. Works of art by Ben and Winifred Nicholson, Christopher Wood, Alfred Wallis, Barbara Hepworth, Constantin Brancusi and Henri Gaudier-Brzeska.

Opening Times: House: 10 Apr to 29 Aug Tue to Sun 13:30-16:30, 30 Aug to 25 Mar Tue to Sun 14:00-16:00.
Gallery: Tue to Sun 11:30-17:00.   Admission: Free.
Location: Near town centre.   Map Ref: 2

Scott Polar Research Institute Museum

♿ ♿

Lensfield, Cambridge CB2 1ER   Tel: 01223 336540   Fax: 01223 336549
Web: www.spri.cam.ac.uk

Displays include materials from the Antarctic expeditions of Robert Falcon Scott and Sir Ernest Shackleton, and the Arctic expeditions of Sir John Franklin and others searching for the 19th century.

Opening Times: Tue to Sat 14:00-16:00.   Admission: Free.   Location: Ten minutes walk from railway station and central bus station.   Map Ref: 2

Sedgwick Museum of Geology

♿

Dept of Earth Sciences, Downing Street, Cambridge CB2 3EQ   Tel: 01223 333456
Web: www.sedgwickmuseum.org

Fossils and minerals, mounted skeletons, important local displays, historical material. Major new displays opening early summer 2002.

Opening Times: Mon to Fri 09:00-13:00 and 14:00-17:00, Sat 10:00-13:00. Closed Xmas and Easter.   Admission: Free.   Location: Near town centre, two minutes walk from bus station.
                    Map Ref: 2

University Museum of Archaeology & Anthropology

♿

Downing Street, Cambridge CB2 3DZ   Tel: 01223 333516   Fax: 01223 333517
Email: cumaa@hermes.cam.ac.uk   Web: htpp://museum-server.archanth.cam.ac.uk/

The collections and their associated photographic and archival material are of outstanding research and historical value; they cover the ethnography and pre-history of the world together with local archaeology. The museum is an important national resource in archaeology and anthropology.

Opening Times: Tue to Sat 14:00-16:30, closed Sun, Mon & BH.   Admission: Free.
Location: City centre.   Map Ref: 2

University Museum of Zoology at Cambridge

♿

Downing Street, Cambridge CB2 3EJ   Tel: 01223 336650   Fax: 01223 336679
Email: umzc@zoo.cam.ac.uk   Web: www.zoo.cam.ac.uk/museum

Spectacular displays of internationally important zoological specimens, including fossils, dinosaurs, mammal skeletons, birds, beautiful shells and a huge whale. Temporary exhibitions throughout the year.

Opening Times: Mon to Fri 10:00-13:00 & 14:00-16:45. Closed Xmas & Easter.
Admission: Free.   Location: City centre.   Map Ref: 2

Cambridgeshire & Northamptonshire

Whipple Museum of the History of Science

Free School Lane, Cambridge CB2 3RH   Tel: 01223 330906
Fax: 01223 334554   Email: hps-whipple-museum@lists.cam.ac.uk
Web: www.hps.cam.ac.uk/whipple/

The Whipple Museum is a pre-eminent collection of scientific instruments and models, dating from the Middle Ages to the present. Microscopes and telescopes, sundials, early slide rules, pocket electronic calculators, teaching and demonstration apparatus, as well as laboratory equipment are included in this outstanding collection. Part of the Department of History and Philosophy of Science, it plays an important role in the Department's teaching and research.

The main gallery of the Whipple Museum

Opening Times: Mon to Fri 13:30-16:30. Closed Sat, Sun & BH. Please check beforehand as the Museum is not always open during the University vacations.   Admission: Free.   Location: In town centre.
Map Ref: 2

Canons Ashby House

Canons Ashby, Daventry NN11 3SD   Tel: 01327 861900   Fax: 01327 861909
Email: canonsashby@nationaltrust.org.uk
Web: www.nationaltrust.org.uk

Built in the mid 16th century it has survived more or less unaltered since 1710. The interior contains murals and plasterwork of the highest quality. There is a good collection of furniture, pewter, tapestries and family portraits. The formal garden has an orchard featuring a variety of fruit trees from the 16th century.

The Armorial Stained glass panels by the Staircase at Canons Ashby

Opening Times: 22 Mar to 29 Sep Sat to Wed 13:00-17:30, 2 Oct to 3 Nov Sat to Wed 12:00-16:30. Open Good Friday.
Admission: Adult £5.60, Child £2.80, Family £14.00. Group (15+) Adult £4.70, Child £2.35. NT Members Free.   Location: Access from either M40, exit 11 or M1, exit 16.
Map Ref: 4

Oliver Cromwell's House

29 St Marys Street, Ely CB7 4HF   Tel: 01353 662062   Fax: 01353 668518
Email: tic@eastcambs.gov.uk   Web: www.eastcambs.gov.uk

Cromwell's family home from 1636. Period rooms, exhibitions and displays tell the story of Ely's most famous resident.

Opening Times: Summer daily 10:00-17:30, winter Mon to Fri & Sun 11:00-16:00, Sat 11:00-17:00.   Admission: Adult £4.50. Wide range of concessions available.   Location: In heart of conservation area, 300 yards from cathedral.
Map Ref: 5

Stained Glass Museum

South Triforium, The Cathedral, Ely CB7 4DL   Tel: 01353 660347
Fax: 01353 665025   Email: curator@stainedglassmuseum.com
Web: www.stainedglassmuseum.com

A unique museum with an exhibition of stained glass from 1210 to the present. The exhibition contains examples of stained glass from all over Britain and explains the history of the craft.

Opening Times: Mon to Fri 10:30-17:00, Sat 10:30-17:30 (winter 10:30-17:00), Sun 12:00-18:00 (winter 12:00-4:30). Closed Xmas & New Year and Good Friday.   Admission: Adult £3.50, Child (over 12)/Concession £2.50. Group rates available.   Location: In the centre of city, ten minute walk from the railway station.
Map Ref: 5

Guided or Private Tours	Disabled Access	Gift Shop or Sales Point	Café or Refreshments	Restaurant	Car Parking

Cambridgeshire & Northamptonshire

Elton Hall

Elton, Peterborough PE8 6SH   Tel: 01832 280468   Fax: 01832 280584
Email: office@eltonhall.com

An historic house and gardens open to the public with a fine collection of paintings, furniture, books and Henry VIII's prayer book. There is also a restored rose garden and sunken garden.

Opening Times: BH. Wed in Jun. Wed, Thu & Sun in Jul & Aug. 14:00-17:00.   Admission: Hall & Gardens £6.00. Garden only £3.00.   Map Ref: 14

Peterborough Museum & Art Gallery

Priestgate, Peterborough PE1 1LF   Tel: 01733 343329   Fax: 01733 341928
Email: museum@peterborough.gov.uk   Web: www.peterboroughheritage.org.uk

Exhibitions of the permanent collection covering the history and community of Peterborough. Collections include local archaeology, social history and geology. Unique collections of Jurassic marine reptiles and French Napoleonic prisoner of war craft work. Changing historical and art exhibition programme, plus events and activities at weekends.

Opening Times: Sat 10:00-17:00, Sun & BH 12:00-16:00, Tue to Fri 12:00-17:00 (termtime) 10:00-17:00 (school holidays). Closed Mon, Xmas & New Year.   Admission: Free. Small charge for some events or exhibitions.   Location: City centre, just off Main Street, within five minutes walk of both railway and bus stations.   Map Ref: 15

Peterborough Sculpture Trust

c/o 50 St Pega's Road, Peakirk, Peterborough PE6 7NF   Tel: 01733 253 212

Sculpture by major artists of the last 25 years, including Gormley and Caro.

Opening Times: Year round.   Admission: Free.   Location: 20 minutes walk from city centre. The Sculpture Park is on either side of the one kilometre long Rowing Lake.   Map Ref: 15

Railworld

Oundle Road, Peterborough PE2 9NR   Tel / Fax: 01733 344240   Web: www.railworld.net

Railworld's exhibition centre and museum highlights modern trains worldwide and environmental concerns. Railworld's model railway is impressive. Railworld also has 'Age of Steam' exhibits, flower beds and 'Stephenson' the cat!

Opening Times: Mar to Oct daily 11:00-16:00, Nov to Feb Mon to Fri 11:00-16:00. Xmas & New Year by appointment.   Admission: Adult £4.00, Child £2.00, Concession £3.00, Family £10.00. Location: Near city centre, 15 minute walk from bus and railway station.   Map Ref: 15

Wimpole Hall & Home Farm

Wimpole Hall, Arrington, Royston SG8 0BW   Tel: 01223 207257   Fax: 01223 207838   Email: wimpolehall@nationaltrust.org.uk   Web: www.wimpole.org

This magnificent 18th century house is the largest in Cambridgeshire. The interior is a rich mixture of 1800s decoration, including furniture, paintings and porcelain. The Great Barn has a collection of farm implements dating back 200 years. The garden has extensive walks through the grounds.

Opening Times: Hall:20 Mar to 31 Jul Tue to Thu, Sat & Sun 13:00-17:00, 1 Aug to 31 Aug Tue to Sun 13:00-17:00, 1 Sep to 31 Oct Tue to Thu, Sat & Sun 13:00-17:00, 7 Nov to 28 Nov Sun only 13:00-16:00. Open BH Mons & Good Friday.   Admission: Hall: Adult £6.60, Child £3.20. Group (12+) Adult £5.60 Child £2.70. NT

The Ante Room with panelling was installed by Flitcroft in the 1740's

Members Free.   Location: Eight miles south west of Cambridge off A603. Six miles north of Royston (A1198).   Exhibitions & Events 2004 : Please telephone for details.   Map Ref: 16

![Guided]	![Disabled]	![Gift Shop]	![Café]	![Restaurant]	![Car]
Guided or Private Tours	Disabled Access	Gift Shop or Sales Point	Café or Refreshments	Restaurant	Car Parking

Cambridgeshire & Northamptonshire

ST IVES *Cambs*

Norris Museum

The Broadway, St Ives PE27 5BX Tel: 01480 497314

History of Huntingdonshire: fossils and dinosaurs, archaeology, history, the Civil War, Fen skating, art gallery with regular special exhibitions.

Opening Times: May to Sep Mon to Fri 10:00-13:00 & 14:00-17:00, Sat 10:00-12:00 & 14:00-17:00, Sun 14:00-17:00. Oct to Mar Mon to Fri 10:00-13:00 & 14:00-16:00, Sat 10:00-12:00.
Admission: Free. Location: West end of town centre, beside the river and near the parish church.

Map Ref: 17

SULGRAVE *Northants*

Sulgrave Manor

Manor Road, Sulgrave, Banbury OX17 2SD Tel: 01295 760205 Fax: 01295 768056
Email: sulgrave-manor@talk21.com Web: www.sulgravemanor.org.uk

A Tudor manor house and gardens, the ancestral home of George Washington. Well known for the excellence of the guided tours and the quality of the special events.

Opening Times: 1 Apr to 30 Oct 14:00-17:30. Closed Mon and Fri, except BH.
Admission: Adult £5.00, Child £2.50. Garden only £2.50. Location: In the village of Sulgrave, seven miles from M40 junction 11.

Map Ref: 18

TOWCESTER *Northants*

Canal Museum

Stoke Bruerne, Towcester NN12 7SE Tel: 01604 862229 Fax: 01604 864199

An old cornmill housing a colourful collection depicting 200 years of inland waterways, situated in a rich historical site by the busy Grand Union Canal.

Opening Times: Easter to Oct daily 10:00-17:00, Oct to Easter Tue to Sun 10:00-16:00. Closed Xmas. Location: Village four miles from junction 15 of M1.

Map Ref: 19

WISBECH *Cambs*

Peckover House and Garden

North Brink, Wisbech PE13 1JR Tel: 01945 583463
Web: www.nationaltrust.org.uk

This town house, built in 1722 is renowned for its fine plaster and wood rococo decoration. It houses a mixed collection of paintings and portraits. The outstanding 2-acre Victorian garden includes an orangery, summer houses, herbaceous borders and croquet lawn.

Opening Times: 21 Mar to 28 Apr Wed, Sat & Sun only 13:30-16:30, 1 May to 29 Aug Wed, Thu, Sat & Sun only 13:30-16:30, 1 Sep to 31 Oct Wed, Sat & Sun only 13:30-16:30. Open BH Mons & Good Friday. Admission: Adult £4.25, Child £2.00. Groups (15+) £3.75. NT Members Free.
Location: On north bank of River Nene in Wisbech.

Map Ref: 20

Wisbech & Fenland Museum

Museum Square, Wisbech PE13 1ES Tel: 01945 583817 Fax: 01945 589050
Email: wisbechmuseum@beeb.net

A purpose built Victorian Museum, dating from 1847, with much of its original fittings and charm. Decorative art, ceramics, archaeology, natural history, geology, fossils, social history, egyptology, ethnography and numismatics. Exhibition on The Fenland, and Thomas Clarkson and his campaign to abolish slavery.

Opening Times: Summer Tue to Sat 10:00-17:00, winter Tue to Sat 10:00-16:00. Location: At centre of town's Georgian Crescent, opposite Wisbech Castle and next to St Peter's Church.

Map Ref: 20

Chester, a port until silting-up forced it to relinquish its sea trade to its neighbour Liverpool, is a city of great age, remarkable charm and some of the finest half-timbered buildings in the world. Manchester, despite dating back to the Roman era, is predominantly Victorian, and in Liverpool, though the days of the great ocean going liners have gone, much of the associated architecture remains.

Nearly 80 museums, galleries and historic houses combine to display the military, shipping and industrial history of this region.

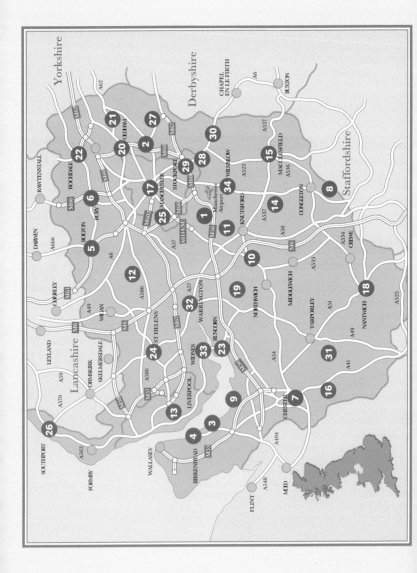

The Red Map References should be used to locate Museums etc on the pages that follow

Cheshire, Manchester & Merseyside

Dunham Massey Hall, Park & Garden

The National Trust, Dunham Massey Hall, Altrincham WA14 4SJ   Tel: 0161 941 1025
Fax: 0161 929 7508 Email: dunhammassey@nationaltrust.org.uk
Web: www.nationaltrust.org.uk

An early Georgian house, which was extensively re-worked in the early years of of the 20th century. The result is one of the most sumptuous Edwardian interiors housing exceptional collections that include Huguenot silver, paintings and walnut furniture. There is an extensive below stairs complex. The gardens have richly planted borders and majestic trees, as well as an orangery, Victorian bark house and well house.

The Saloon at Dunham Massey

Opening Times: 27 Mar to 23 Oct Sat to Wed 12:00-17:00, 24 Oct to 3 Nov Sat to Wed 12:00-16:00. House open Good Friday and BH Sun & Mon 11:00-17:00. Admission: House & Garden: Adult £6.00, Child £3.00, Family £15.00. Group (15) £5.00. NT Members Free. Location: Three miles south west of Altrincham off A56; exit 19 off M6; exit 7 off M56.   Map Ref: 1   Pair of Elizabethan gauntlet mittens

Central Art Gallery

Old Street, Ashton-under-Lyne OL6 7SF   Tel: 0161 342 2650

The Central Art Gallery is on Old Street in Ashton-under-Lyne. The first floor of this fine Victorian Gothic building provides three excellent galleries. A varied programme of temporary exhibitions has been established featuring a wide range of work including paintings, sculptures and textiles from regional artists and touring exhibitions.

Opening Times: Tue, Wed & Fri 10:00-17:00 Thur 13:00-19:30 Sat 09:00-12:30 & 13:00-16:00. Admission: Free. Location: Five minutes walk from Ashton railway and bus station. Map Ref: 2

Museum of the Manchesters: Social & Regimental History

Town Hall, Ashton-under-Lyne OL6 6DL   Tel: 0161 342 3078

Two galleries display the history of the Manchester Regiment and the experience of war back home away from the front line. Features include a First World War trench, an Anderson Shelter and fine collections of medals and uniforms.

Opening Times: Mon to Sat 10:00-16:00. Admission: Free. Location: Two minute walk from Ashton-under-Lyne railway and bus stations.   Map Ref: 2

Lady Lever Art Gallery

NATIONAL MUSEUM LIVERPOOL

Port Sunlight Village, Lower Road, Bebington, Wirral CH62 5EQ   Tel: 0151 478 4136
Fax: 0151 478 4140 Web: www.ladyleverartgallery.org.uk

The jewel in the crown of the garden village of Port Sunlight, housing the magnificent personal collection of the first Lord Leverhulme. Built by the soap magnate and philanthropist in 1922, the gallery includes Pre-Raphaelites, paintings by Turner and Constable alongside 18th century furniture, ceramics, Wedgwood, sculpture, tapestries and Napoleonic memorabilia.

Opening Times: Mon to Sat 10:00-17:00, Sun 12:00-17:00. Closed 24-26 Dec & 1 Jan. Admission: Free. Location: Signposted from A41 New Chester Road. Bebington railway station.   Exhibitions & Events 2004 : 31 Jan to 16 May: Animal Magic - small display of ceramics.   Map Ref: 3

47

Cheshire, Manchester & Merseyside

Port Sunlight Heritage Centre
95 Greendale Road, Port Sunlight, Bebington, Wirral CH62 4XE   Tel: 0151 644 6466
Fax: 0151 645 8973 Web: www.portsunlightvillage.com

Port Sunlight Heritage Centre explores the fascinating story about the village and its community. Old photographs and early film footage depict a quality of life for residents unimaginable in most 19th century industrial communities.

Opening Times: Mon to Fri 10:00-16:00, Sat & Sun (Apr to Oct) 10:00-16:00, (Nov to Mar) 11:00-16:00. Closed Xmas. Admission: Small admission charge. Group discount.
Location: 20 minutes by road or rail from Chester and Liverpool.   Map Ref: 3

Williamson Art Gallery & Museum
Slatey Road, Birkenhead CH43 4UE   Tel: 0151 652 4177   Fax: 0151 670 0253

Large but unintimidating gallery and museum with excellent picture and maritime displays, and active exhibition programme.

Opening Times: Tue to Sun 10:00-17:00. Closed Mon except BH. Admission: Free.
Location: 20 minute walk from Birkenhead Park or Birkenhead Central Stations; five minute drive from town centre.   Map Ref: 4

Wirral Museum - Birkenhead Town Hall
Hamilton Street, Birkenhead CH41 5BR   Tel: 0151 666 4010

Refurbished Victorian Town Hall developed as a local history museum and access point for archives service.

Opening Times: Tue to Sun 10:00-17:00. Closed Mon except BH. Admission: Free.
Location: One minute walk from Hamilton Square Station.   Map Ref: 4

Wirral Transport Museum
1 Taylor Street, Birkenhead CH41 1BG   Tel: 0151 647 2128

The home of Birkenhead Tramways, with restored trams in use and as static displays. Also buses under restoration, cars, motorbikes and models.

Opening Times: Apr to Oct Sat & Sun 13:00-17:00, Nov to Mar Sat & Sun 12:00-16:00. Easter, Whitsun, Summer School Hols & BH Wed to Sun 13:00-17:00. Admission: Free.   Map Ref: 4

Bolton Museum, Art Gallery & Aquarium
Le Mans Crescent, Bolton BL1 1SE Tel: 01204 332211
Fax: 01204 332241 Email: museums@bolton.gov.uk
Web: www.boltonmuseums.org.uk

Bolton Museum, Art Gallery and Aquarium is one of the largest regional art galleries in the North West, housing an impressive collection of fine and decorative art dating from the 18th to the 20th century. This includes watercolours and drawings, a prominent collection of modern British art prints, along with 20th century sculpture and contemporary ceramics. The Museum has recently purchased the Thomas Moran painting 'Nearing Camp on the Upper Colorado River' after a national campaign. The Museum has extensive collections of Egyptology, ethnography, natural, local and industrial history, with examples of machinery and working models. The Natural History department includes the Wildlife on your

'The Perspective of Idleness', E. Wadsworth (1930)

www.mghh.co.uk

For current information on the outstanding Collections in over 1600 Museums, Galleries & Historic Houses in England, Scotland, Wales and Ireland

Cheshire, Manchester & Merseyside

Doorstep Gallery and an award winning, interactive Wildlife Study Centre and dinosaurs. The art gallery has a constantly changing programme of events and exhibitions. The aquarium is heavily involved in conservation and has a highly specialised breeding programme. It features a wide variety of species of fish from around the world, some now extinct in their natural habitat. The education department plays a prominent and important role in the Museum's success and works closely with schools and other groups, particularly in subject areas included in the national curriculum.

Opening Times: Mon to Sat 10:00-17:00. Closed Sun & BH. Admission: Free.
Location: Town centre, behind town hall, five minutes from train and bus stations. Exhibitions & Events 2004 : For Exhibitions and Events please telephone for details. Map Ref: 5

Fusiliers Museum (Lancashire)
Wellington Barracks, Bolton Road, Bury BL8 2PL Tel / Fax: 0161 764 2208

The museum contains uniforms, arms, medals, records, military art and regimental silver dating from 1688 to present day. Artefacts are also held of General Wolfe, Napoleon and General Robert Ross of Bladenburg.

Opening Times: Daily except Wed & Sun 09:30-16:30. Admission: Adult £2.00, Child Free, OAP £1.00. Location: One mile from town centre on the Bolton Bury Road (A58). Bus service from Bury Interchange/Metroline. Map Ref: 6

Cheshire Military Museum
The Castle, Chester CH1 2DN Tel / Fax: 01244 327617
Web: www.chester.ac.uk/militarymuseum

An attractive and interesting exhibition depicting the history of four famous regiments and their military connection with the county of Cheshire.

Opening Times: Daily 10:00-17:00. Location: From town centre, follow castle signs. We are the left wing building of Greek Revival Castle buildings, next to the Crown Court. Map Ref: 7

Grosvenor Museum

27 Grosvenor Street, Chester CH1 2DD
Tel: 01244 402008 Fax: 01244 347587
Email: s.rogers@chestercc.gov.uk
Web: www.chestercc.gov.uk/heritage/museum/home.html

The museum to visit for the 21st century family. Step-free access to ground floor. Fascinating audio-visual introduction to the city's history. Unique Roman cemetery with world-renowned tombstone collection. Paintings by local artists. Work from Chester's silversmiths. Period rooms in a townhouse. Cheshire's wildlife. Temporary exhibitions. Interactives. Keeper-guided video tours of first floor galleries. Computerised collections.

Opening Times: Mon to Sat 10:30-17:00, Sun 13:00-16:00.
Admission: Free. There is a charge for guided tours.
Face to face with yesterday
Location: Near town centre and drop-off point for open bus tours.
Exhibitions & Events 2004 : 21 Feb to 18 Apr: John Witt, 1 May to 27 Jun: Group 75, 10 Jul to 5 Sep: Chris Achilleos, 18 Sep to 14 Nov: Baudelaire, Limouse and their Heroic Art, 27 Nov to 23 Jan: Beasts of the Nile For further information on these exhibitions please ring 01244 402008.
Map Ref: 7

Little Moreton Hall
Congleton CW12 4SD Tel: 01260 272018 Web: www.nationaltrust.org.uk

Britain's most famous and arguably finest timber-framed moated manor house. It houses interesting painted murals, heraldic glass and plasterwork figures. There is a knot garden and yew tunnel in 16th century style.

Opening Times: 20 Mar to 31 Oct Wed to Sun 11:30-17:00. 6 Nov to 19 Dec Sat & Sun only 11:30-16:00. Open BH Mons. Admission: Adult £5.00, Child £2.50, Family £12.00. Group £4.25. NT Members Free. Special openings (inc NT Members) £7.50. 4 Dec to 19 Dec Free.
Location: Four miles south west of Congleton, on east side of A34. Map Ref: 8

Cheshire, Manchester & Merseyside

Boat Museum

South Pier Road, Ellesmere Port CH65 4FW   Tel: 0151 355 5017   Fax: 0151 355 4079
Email: bookings@thewaterwaystrust.org   Web: www.boatmuseum.org.uk

Set within a historic dock complex, see the world's largest floating collection of canal craft. A video sets the scene while eight indoor exhibitions tell the history of canals. Together with four period cottages, power hall, blacksmiths forge, shop, cafe, disabled access, boat trips (seasonal).

Opening Times: Apr to Oct daily 10:00-17:00. Nov to Mar Sat to Wed 11:00-16:00. Closed Thu & Fri.
Admission: Adult £5.50, Child £3.70, Concession £4.30, Family £16.50. Group rates available.   Location: Just off J9 M53. Ten minute walk from railway station, 15 minute walk from central bus station, free parking.   Map Ref: 9

The Boat Museum is situated on the Shropshire Union Canal

Tabley House Stately Home

Tabley House, Knutsford WA16 0HB   Tel: 01565 750151   Fax: 01565 653230
Email: inquiries@tableyhouse.co.uk   Web: www.tableyhouse.co.uk

The finest Palladian House in the north west, containing fascinating Leicester family memorabilia, furniture by Chippendale, Gillow and Bullock, and the first collection of English paintings ever made, shown in the State Rooms.

Opening Times: Apr to end Oct Thu, Fri, Sat, Sun and BH 14:00-17:00. Admission: Adult £4.00, Child/Student £1.50.   Location: Rural, two and a half miles west of Knutsford on A5033 off A556 South (M6 J19).   Map Ref: 10

Tatton Park

Knutsford WA16 6QN   Tel: 01625 534400   Fax: 01625 534403
Email: tatton@cheshire.gov.uk   Web: www.tattonpark.org.uk

This is one of the most complete historic estates open to visitors. The house sits amid a landscaped deer park and is opulently decorated, providing a fine setting for the family's collections. These include family portraits, paintings, books, china, glass, silver and specially commisioned Gillow furniture. The garden extends to a fernery, orangery, rose garden, pinetum, also Italian and Japanese gardens. There are many walks including a trail around the lake.

The Music Room

Opening Times: House: 27 Mar to 3 Oct Tue to Sun 13:00-17:00 (guided tours 12:00 & 12:15). Tudor Old Hall: 27 Mar to 3 Oct Sat & Sun 12:00-16:00. Guided tours only,hourly. Admission: Mansion: Adult £3.00, Child £2.00, Family £8.00. Group (12+) Adult £2.40 Child £1.60. NT Members Free, but must pay for guided tours and gardens and a reduced rate for entry to Tudor Old Hall.
Location: Two miles north of Knutsford, five miles from M6, exit 19, three miles from M56, exit 7.   Map Ref: 11

The Stoning of St Stephen, by Sir Anthony van Dyck (1599-1641)

Turnpike Gallery

Civic Square, Leigh WN7 1EB   Tel: 01942 404469   Fax: 01942 404447
Email: turnpikegallery@wlct.org   Web: www.wlct.org

The gallery presents contemporary art through exhibitions, projects, residencies, arts outreach and education. The exhibition programme reflects the broad variety of current visual arts practice by regional, national and international artists.

Opening Times: Mon, Thu & Fri 09:30-17:30, Tue 10:00-17:30, Wed 09:30-17:00, Sat 10:00-15:00. Closed Sun & BH. Admission: Free. Location: In town centre, three minute walk from bus station.   Map Ref: 12

Cheshire, Manchester & Merseyside

Conservation Centre

Whitechapel, Liverpool L1 6HZ   Tel: 0151 478 4999
Fax: 0151 478 4990   Web: www.conservationcentre.org.uk

The award-winning Conservation Centre is dedicated to the preservation of precious items, from ceramics and paintings to textiles and sculpture. It is the only centre of its kind to open its doors to the public revealing the fascinating techniques with its weekly studio tours.

Opening Times: Mon to Sat 10:00-17:00, Sun 12:00-17:00. Closed 24-26 Dec & 1 Jan. Admission: Free. Location: Lime Street Station and Queen Square bus station - five minute walk.
Exhibitions & Events 2004 : 20 Dec to 1 Feb: 'Come Dancing' photographic exhibition, 14 Feb to 18 Apr: 'Strands' contemporary textiles exhibition.   Map Ref: 13

Croxteth Hall & Country Park

Croxteth Hall Lane, West Derby, Liverpool L12 0HB   Tel: 0151 228 5311   Fax: 0151 228 2817
Web: www.croxteth.uk

The Hall depicts the lifestyle of the Earl and family, where visitors can appreciate an Edwardian country house with character figures of the family and of the servants working below stairs. Over 100 paintings, family portraits and sporting pictures. No visit to the Earl's estate would be complete without also visiting the Victorian walled garden and home farm which contains rare breeds.

Opening Times: Apr to Oct 10:30-17:00. Admission: Hall & Farm: Adult £2.00, Child/OAP £1.18. Walled Garden: Adult £1.18, Child/OAP 67p. Location: Six miles from the city centre.
                                                                         Map Ref: 13

HM Customs & Excise National Museum

Merseyside Maritime Museum, Albert Dock, Liverpool L3 4AQ   Tel: 0151 478 4499
Fax: 0151 478 4590   Web: www.customsandexcisemuseum.org.uk

Enter into the intriguing world of customs and excise. This surprising museum demonstrates how the battle against smuggling is undertaken by sniffer dogs and customs officers, from uncovering endangered species to drugs and replica goods. Meet some of the museum's colourful characters, including Mother Redcap, spot suspect travellers and learn about the latest technology used by customs officers.

HM Customs & Excise National Museum
endangered species

Opening Times: Mon to Sun 10:00-17:00. Closed 24-26 Dec & 1 Jan. Admission: Free. Location: James Street Station ten minute walk.   Map Ref: 13

Liverpool Museum

William Brown Street, Liverpool L3 8EN
Tel: 0151 478 4393 Fax: 0151 478 4350
Web: www.liverpoolmuseum.org.uk

A popular family destination, exploring the secrets of the natural world and the mysteries of outer space. A truly world class museum with important and diverse collections covering archaeology, ethnology and the natural and physical sciences. Liverpool Museum is currently undergoing extensive building improvements and refurbishments. The project will see the museum double in size with new attractions like The Bug House and The Exploration Zone. Expected completion date - early 2005.

Opening Times: Mon to Sat 10:00-17:00, Sun 12:00-17:00. Closed 24-26 Dec & 1 Jan. Admission: Free. Location: Lime Street train station five minute walk. Exhibitions & Events 2004 : 19 Jul to 29 Feb: Grossology exhibition.
                                                                         Map Ref: 13

Cheshire, Manchester & Merseyside

Merseyside Maritime Museum

Albert Dock, Liverpool L3 4AQ Tel: 0151 478 4499 Fax: 0151 478 4590 Web: www.merseysidemaritimemuseum.org.uk

Liverpool's seafaring heritage brought to life in the historic Albert Dock. The museum's collections reflect the international importance of Liverpool as a gateway to the world, including the city's role in the transatlantic slave trade and emigration, the merchant navy and the Titanic. During the summer visitors can also explore the adjacent ships and quaysides.

Opening Times: Mon to Sun 10:00-17:00. Closed 24-26 Dec & 1 Jan. Admission: Free. Location: James Street train and Paradise Street bus station - ten minute walk. Exhibitions & Events 2004 : 10 Jul to 6 Jun: Spirit of the Blitz exhibition. Map Ref: 13

Museum of Liverpool Life

Pier Head, Liverpool L3 1PZ Tel: 0151 478 4080 Fax: 0151 478 4090 Web: www.museumofliverpoollife.org.uk

The Museum of Liverpool Life celebrates the unique character of this vibrant city and its contribution to national life from Brookside to the Grand National. Recently expanded to include three new galleries, City Lives explores the richness of Liverpool's cultural diversity, The River Room features life around the River Mersey and City Soldiers tells the story of the Kings Regiment.

Opening Times: Mon to Sun 10:00-17:00. Closed 24-26 Dec & 1 Jan Admission: Free. Location: James Street train station and Paradise Street bus station - ten minute walk. Exhibitions & Events 2004 : 24 Oct to 3 May 04:

Museum of Liverpool Life, River Room

David Jacques 'As if in a dream dreamt by another'. Map Ref: 13

Speke Hall, Garden and Estate

The Walk, Liverpool L24 1XD Tel: 0151 427 7231 Fax: 0151 427 9860 Web: www.nationaltrust.org.uk

A half-timbered house dating from 16th century. It has an interesting collection of furniture, tapestries and plasterwork. Some of the rooms are hung with William Morris wallpapers. The restored garden has a rose garden, summer border and a stream garden.

Opening Times: 20 Mar to 31 Oct Wed to Sun 13:00-17:30. 6 Nov to 5 Dec Sat & Sun only 13:00-16:30. Open BH Mons. Admission: Adult £6.00, Child £3.50, Family £17.00. Garden only: Adult £3.00, Child £1.50, Family £9.00. NT Members Free. Location: On north bank of the Mersey, one mile off A561 on west side of Liverpool Airport. Map Ref: 13

Sudley House

Mossley Hill Road, Mossley Hill, Liverpool L18 8BX Tel: 0151 724 3245 Fax: 0151 724 4729 Web: www.sudleyhouse.org.uk

The former home of Victorian ship builder George Holt, housing his personal collection of 18th and 19th century British art. A charming gallery with works by Turner, Gainsborough, Lord Leighton and Holman Hunt. Many of the original Victorian features of the building survive, including tiles, ceramics, stained glass and wallpaper.

Opening Times: Mon to Sat 10:00-17:00, Sun 12:00-17:00. Closed 24-26 Dec & 1 Jan. Admission: Free. Location: Mossley Hill train and bus stop ten minute walk. Map Ref: 13

Cheshire, Manchester & Merseyside

Tate Liverpool

Albert Dock, Liverpool L3 4BB
Tel: 0151 702 7400 Fax: 0151 702 7401
Email: liverpoolinfo@tate.org.uk Web: www.tate.org.uk/liverpool/

Tate Liverpool is one of the largest galleries of modern and contemporary art outside London and is housed in a beautiful converted warehouse in the historic Albert Dock. Home of the National Collection of Modern Art in the North, Tate Liverpool displays work selected from the Tate Collection, and special exhibitions which bring together artwork loaned from around the world.

Exterior of Tate Liverpool,
Photo Roger Sinek

Opening Times: Tue to Sun 10:00-17:50. Closed Mon (except BH), 24-26 Dec, 1 Jan & Good Friday. Admission: Free to Tate Collection; charges for special exhibitions. Location: Five minute walk from city centre, ten minute walk from Lime Street Station.

Map Ref: 13

University of Liverpool Art Gallery

3 Abercromby Square, Liverpool L69 3BX Tel: 0151 794 2347/8 Fax: 0151 794 2343
Email: artgall@liv.ac.uk Web: www.liv.ac.uk/artgall/

Fine and decorative art from the University collections is displayed in an elegant Georgian house. Works by JMW Turner, Wright of Derby, Burne-Jones, Augustus John, Epstein, Freud and Frink.

Opening Times: Mon to Fri 12:00-16:00. Closed Aug BH & weekends. Admission: Free.
Location: Ten minute walk from city centre.

Map Ref: 13

The Walker

NATIONAL MUSEUMS LIVERPOOL

William Brown Street, Liverpool L3 8EL Tel: 0151 478 4199 Fax: 0151 478 4190
Web: www.thewalker.org.uk

The national gallery of the North, the Walker is one of the finest art galleries in Europe housing outstanding collections spanning from 1300 to the present day. Especially rich in European Old Masters, Victorian and Pre-Raphaelite pictures and modern British works. A major refurbishment in 2002 has enabled the Walker to host must-see exhibitions in the new temporary exhibition galleries.

Opening Times: Mon to Sat 10:00-17:00, Sun 12:00-17:00. Closed 24-26 Dec & 1 Jan. Admission: Free.
Location: Lime Street Railway Station and Queen Square bus station - five minute walk.
Exhibitions & Events 2004 : 16 Oct to 18 Jan: Rossetti, 26 Feb to 3 May: Art Behind Barbed Wire, 27 May to 22 Aug: Heath Robinson, 27 May to 22 Aug: Tim Lewis, 18 Sep to 28 Nov: The Stuckists Punk Victoria, 18 Sep to 28 Nov: John Moores 23 Exhibition of Contemporary Painting.

Map Ref: 13

Capesthorne Hall

Siddington, Macclesfield SK11 9JY Tel: 01625 861221 Fax: 01625 861619
Email: info@capesthorne.com

Home of the Bromley-Davenport family since Doomsday times. The hall was rebuilt in Victorian times around the core of an 18th century house in grand Jacobean revival style. Collections include paintings, sculpture, family muniments and Americana. There are extensive gardens, a landscaped park and lake.

Opening Times: Apr to Oct Location: Five miles west of Macclesfield

Map Ref: 14

Cheshire, Manchester & Merseyside

Manchester Jewish Museum

190 Cheetham Hill Road, Manchester M8 8LW   Tel: 0161 834 9879
Fax: 0161 834 9801   Email: info@manchesterjewishmuseum.com
Web: www.manchesterjewishmuseum.com

The Museum, set in a beautifully restored Grade II* listed Spanish and Portuguese synagogue building, tells the history of the Jewish community in Manchester and Salford over the past 250 years. Our education and outreach programme won the 1998 Sandford Award and is much in demand. The shop sells educational materials, books and gifts.

Opening Times: Mon to Thu 10:30-16:00, Sun 10:30-17:00. Closed 1 Jan, 6, 7, 12 & 13 Apr, 26 & 27 May, 16 & 30 Sep, 7 Oct, 24 to 27 Dec and at 13:00 on 5 Apr & 15 Sep.
Admission: Adult £3.95, Concession £2.95, Family £9.50.   Location: Half a mile from
Manchester Victoria and Metrolink Station.   Map Ref: 17

The Manchester Museum

The University of Manchester, Oxford Road, Manchester M13 9PL
Tel: 0161 275 2634   Fax: 0161 275 2676

The Manchester Museum has just undergone a major £19.5 million refurbishment which has created new galleries with hundreds of fascinating displays, a temporary exhibition programme, a new Discovery Centre with hands-on exhibits, a café, shop and disabled access to all areas. It amazing collections, containing six million items, provide a window on the world from Peru to Japan, from Egypt to North America.

Opening Times: Mon to Sat 10:00-17:00, Sun & BH 11:00-16:00. Please ring for Christmas opening.
Admission: Free.   Location: One mile south of
Manchester City Centre on the campus of the University of Manchester.   Map Ref: 17

Manchester United Museum & Tour Centre

Sir Matt Busby Way, Old Trafford, Manchester M16 0RA   Tel: 0870 442 1994   Fax: 0161 868 8861   Email: tours@manutd.co.uk   Web: www.manutd.com

Manchester United's new museum was opened by the legendary Pele in April 1998. Filling three floors of Old Trafford's massive North Stand, the museum outlines Manchester United's history from 1878 to the present day. Displays include the magnificent Trophy Room, the history of United, a special display on the Munich Air Disaster, kit and equipment, fans, the Legends Gallery and the new Treble Exhibition. There is also a changing programme of temporary exhibitions throughout the year. Explore the interactive Man-U-Net and find out about every player to

Ryan Giggs - one of our
regular temporary exhibitions

have made a first team appearance for the club. Add your own distinctive style of commentary to match action as Martin Tyler gives you tips in our commentary booth. Visit our audio-visual theatre. Pop into our Legends Cafe for a quick snack or into the Red Cafe for something more substantial. After visiting the Museum, why not go on a tour and see the pitch, sit in the dugout, enter the changing rooms and walk down the players' tunnel?

Ruud van Nistelrooy
A British record transfer to United

Opening Times: Daily 09:30-17:00, tours daily 09:40-16:30.   Admission: Museum - Adult £5.50, Child/OAP £3.75, Family £15.50. Museum & Tour - Adult £8.50, Child/OAP £5.75, Family £23.50, Under 5s Free.   Location: Five minute walk from Old Trafford Metro Station, which is accessible from Piccadilly Train Station in Manchester.
Exhibitions & Events 2004 : Ring for details.   Map Ref: 17

Cheshire, Manchester & Merseyside

The Museum of Science and Industry in Manchester

Liverpool Road, Castlefield, Manchester M3 4FP   Tel: 0161 832 2244   Fax: 0161 833 1471
Email: marketing@msim.org.uk   Web: www.msim.org.uk

The Museum of Science and Industry in Manchester is one of the world's biggest and most impressive science museums. Bursting with entertaining galleries and amazing exhibits, the Museum tells the compelling story of Manchester. Highlights include: historic locomotives and incredible aircraft, thunderous cotton machinery and huge steam mill engines, interactive exhibits and Special Exhibitions, including Dan Dare Pilot of the Future, Destination Mars and Blackfoot Indians.

Based in the building of the world's oldest passenger railway station

Opening Times: Daily 10:00-17:00. Closed 24-26 Dec.
Admission: Free entry to permanent collections, charge for Special Exhibitions.   Location: City centre location, nearest railway station, Deansgate is five minutes walk. Nearest Metrolink station, G-Mex is five minutes walk.

Map Ref: 17

Museum of Transport - Greater Manchester

Boyle Street, Cheetham, Manchester M8 8UW
Tel / Fax: 0161 205 2122   Web: www.gmts.co.uk

Over 85 vehicles mainly buses relating to over a century of road public transport in Greater Manchester. Small exhibits and archives.

Opening Times: Wed, Sat, Sun & BH 10:00-17:00.
Admission: Adult £3.00, Concession £1.75, Under 5s Free.   Location: One and a half miles north of Victoria Station, five minute walk from Woodlands Road Metrolink.

Map Ref: 17

Peoples History Museum

Bridge Street, Manchester M3 3ER   Tel: 0161 839 6061   Fax: 0161 839 6027   Email: info@peopleshistorymuseum.org.uk
Web: www.peopleshistorymuseum.org.uk

The People's History Museum is the only national museum in Britain dedicated to people's history, it celebrates the triumphs and struggles of everyday people. Watch the first Match of the Day, visit the Co-op shop, play your favourite vinyl on the jukebox and try your hand at sweated labour. The Head Office of the museum houses the Textile Conservation Centre which specializes in the conservation of banners in both the museums own collection nationally.

National Union of Railwaymen banner, Wakefield branch, about 1920

Opening Times: Tue to Sun 11:00-16:30. Closed Mon (except BH) & Good Fridays.   Admission: Adult £1.00, Child/OAP/Student/Concession Free, Free to all on Fri.   Location: Easy walking distance from city centre.
Gartside Street multi-storey car park next door. Ten minute walk from Deansgate Train Station.

Map Ref: 17

The Whitworth Art Gallery

The Whitworth Art Gallery

The University of Manchester, Oxford Road, Manchester M15 6ER
Tel: 0161 275 7450   Fax: 0161 275 7451   Email: whitworth@man.ac.uk
Web: www.whitworth.man.ac.uk

Situated in Whitworth Park to the south of Manchester city centre, the Whitworth Art Gallery is internationally famous for its collections of art and design. The Whitworth's collection includes an outstanding range of prints and drawings, one of the great collections of British watercolours, and excellent work by modern and contemporary artists. In addition to this, the Whitworth is home to the finest collections of textiles and wallpapers outside the Victoria and Albert Museum in London.
(continued over the page)

Cheshire, Manchester & Merseyside

A changing programme of special exhibitions designed to complement the permanent collection runs throughout the year.
Opening Times: Mon to Sat 10:00-17:00, Sun 14:00-17:00.
Admission: Free. Location: Approx one and a half miles south of Manchester City Centre, in Whitworth Park (Oxford Road), opposite Manchester Royal Infirmary. Exhibitions & Events 2004 : 14 Nov to 15 Feb: Flexible 4: Identities (Textiles), 3 Oct to 11 Jan 04: Under Heaven (sculpture & drawings), 28 Jun to Mar 04: Revivals (textiles & wallpapers), 18 Oct to May 04: Walter Crane, 27 Feb to 18 Apr: Landscapes from the Whitworth, 4 Apr to Dec: William Morris 1834-1896, 7 May to 18 Jul: Blasting the Future: British Avant-garde Art, Oct to Dec: Walter Sickert (1860-1942), Sep to Dec: Shirley Diamond (sculpture). Map Ref: 17

'Sudden Shower at Ohashi Bridge' Utagawa Hiroshige 1797-1858

NANTWICH *Cheshire*

Nantwich Museum
Pillory Street, Nantwich CW5 5BQ Tel: 01270 627104 Email: nantwich.museum@virgin.net

A fascinating insight into the history of the ancient market town of Nantwich together with a cheese making room and a modern Millennium Gallery for temporary exhibition.

Opening Times: Apr to Sep Mon to Sat 10:30-16:30, Oct to Mar Tue to Sat 10:30-16:30.
Admission: Free. Location: Near town centre. Map Ref: 18

NORTHWICH *Cheshire*

Arley Hall
Northwich CW9 6NA Tel: 01565 777353 Fax: 01565 777465
Email: enquiries@arleyhallandgardens.com Web: www.arleyhallandgardens.com

An early Victorian Jacobean-style mansion with fine plasterwork, panelling and a grand staircase. Egerton Warburton painting collection. Plant collections in Grade II listed gardens.

Opening Times: Gardens 3 Apr to 26 Sept Tue to Sun & BH 11:00-17:00, Hall 11 Apr to 26 Sep Tue & Sun only 12:00-17:00. Admission: Adult £4.50, OAP £3.90, Child £2.00. Additional charge for the hall. Location: Five miles north west of Northwich, five miles from Knutsford. Five miles from M6 and M56. Map Ref: 19

OLDHAM *Gtr Man*

Gallery Oldham
Greaves Street, Oldham OL1 1AL Tel: 0161 911 4653 Fax: 0161 911 4669
Email: ecs.galleryoldham@oldham.gov.uk Web: www.galleryoldham.org.uk

This fine and decorative art collection of mainly British artists was first established by Victorian industrial philanthropists and now includes work by modern and contempory artists. Large collection of objects representing Oldham people's lives from the industrial era of cotton and engineering. Extensive natural history collection of mainly local plants, geology, insects and birds reflects historic local passion for scientific study.

Opening Times: Mon to Sat 10:00-17:00.
Admission: Free. Location: In Oldham Town Centre behind library. Five minutes from Oldham Mumps Station.
Map Ref: 20

www.mghh.co.uk

For current information on the outstanding Collections in over 1600 Museums, Galleries & Historic Houses in England, Scotland, Wales and Ireland

Saddleworth Museum & Art Gallery

High Street, Uppermill, Oldham OL3 6HS   Tel: 01457 874093   Fax: 01457 870336
Email: curator@saddleworthmuseum.co.uk   Web: www.saddleworthmuseum.co.uk

Set in a beautiful location beside the Huddersfield narrow canal, Saddleworth Museum charts 3000 years of history in this ancient Yorkshire parish, set in the foothills of the Pennines. Refreshments for tours by arrangement.

Opening Times: Mar to Oct Mon to Sat 10:00-17:00, Sun 12:00-17:00. Nov to Feb Mon to Sun 13:00-16:00.   Admission: Adult £2.00, Child/OAP £1.00, Family £4.00.   Location: In the centre of Uppermill village, eight miles from Oldham on A670.   Map Ref: 21

Rochdale Pioneers Museum or Toad Lane Museum

31 Toad Lane, Rochdale OL12 0NU   Tel: 01706 524920   Email: museum@co-op.ac.uk
Web: http://museum.co-op.ac.uk

The home of the worldwide co-operative movement. In 1844 the Rochdale Pioneers opened their store selling pure food at fair prices and honest weights and measures. See how your ancestors did their shopping.

Opening Times: Tue to Sat 10:00-16:00, Sun 14:00-16:00.   Admission: Adult £1.00, OAP/Student 50p, Family £2.00.   Location: Situated in the Toad Lane Conservation Area at the rear of the Rochdale Exchange Shopping Precinct on Hunters Lane.   Map Ref: 22

Norton Priory Museum & Gardens

Tudor Road, Manor Park, Runcorn WA7 1SX   Tel: 01928 569895   Fax: 01928 589743
Email: info@nortonpriory.org   Web: www.nortonpriory.org

Unique and beautiful site incorporating atmospheric museum, excavated Priory remains, sculpture trail, peaceful and relaxing two and a half acre walled garden and the awe inspiring St Christopher statue, now housed in its own gallery.

Opening Times: Apr to Oct Mon to Fri 12:00-17:00, Sat, Sun & BH 12:00-18:00. Nov to Mar daily 12:00-16:00. Closed Xmas & New Year.   Admission: Adult £3.95, Concession £2.75, Family £10.00, Under 5s Free.   Location: Less than 30 minutes by car from Chester, Liverpool and Manchester. Close to junction 11 of M56.   Map Ref: 23

The World of Glass

Chalon Way East, St Helens WA10 1BX   Tel: 08700 114 466   Fax: 01744 616 966
Email: info@worldofglass.com   Web: www.worldofglass.com

The World of Glass is constructed on an historic site, which incorporates a Victorian glassmaking furnace which is a scheduled ancient monument and Grade II* listed building. The Centre also houses the Pilkington Glass Collection and St Helens Council's Social History Collection.

Opening Times: Tue to Sun 10:00-17:00 & BH. Closed Xmas & New Year.   Admission: Adult £5.30, Child & Concessions £3.80, Under 5s Free. Group rates available.   Location: Situated in the heart of St Helens, just a five minute walk from the bus and railway stations. Excellent access by road from Junction 7 on M62 & Junction 23 on M6.   Map Ref: 24

Ordsall Hall Museum

332 Ordsall Lane, Ordsall, Salford M5 3AN   Tel: 0161 872 0251   Fax: 0161 872 4951
Email: ordsall@btopenworld.com   Web: www.salford.gov.uk

Grade I listed Tudor Manor House with black and white timbers, and 600 years of history, including a part in the gunpowder plot. Educational visits, guided tours and temporary exhibitions.

Opening Times: Mon to Fri 10:00-16:00, Sun 13:00-16:00.   Admission: Free.   Location: Five minutes walk from Exchange Quay Metrolink.   Map Ref: 25

Salford Museum & Art Gallery

Peel Park, Crescent, Salford M5 4WU   Tel: 0161 736 2649   Fax: 0161 745 9490
Email: salford.museum@salford.gov.uk   Web: www.salford.gov.uk

A traditional reconstructed Victorian Street with shops, workshops and houses - plus a Victorian

Cheshire, Manchester & Merseyside

Gallery. Most exhibitions here look forward rather than back, showcasing the work of both young British artists and international culture.

Opening Times: Mon to Fri 10:00-16:45, Sat & Sun 13:00-17:00. Admission: Free.
Location: Situated on the A6 near the Greater Manchester motorway network, five minutes.

Map Ref: 25

Atkinson Art Gallery

Lord Street, Southport PR8 1DH   Tel: 01704 533133   Fax: 0151 934 2109
Web: www.seftonarts.co.uk

Permanent collection of 19th and 20th century works, including LS Lowry, John Piper and Henry Moore. Temporary exhibition programme, including contemporary artists.

Opening Times: Mon to Wed & Fri 10:00-17:00, Thu & Sat 10:00-13:00. Closed BH.   Admission: Free.
Location: In town centre, next to library.   Map Ref: 26

Breton Dining Room by Sir William Russell Flint (1880-1969)

Botanic Gardens Museum

Churchtown, Southport PR9 7NB   Tel: 01704 227547   Fax: 01704 224112
Web: www.seftonarts.co.uk

Local history galleries, Victorian room with toy display and costume, natural history gallery. Temporary exhibition programme.

Opening Times: Tue to Fri 11:00-15:00, Sat & Sun 14:00-17:00, BH 12:00-16:00, closed following Fri.   Admission: Free.   Location: In Churchtown to north of Southport.   Map Ref: 26

Astley Cheetham Art Gallery

Trinity Street, Stalybridge SK15 2BN   Tel: 0161 338 2708

Astley Cheetham Art Gallery originally operated as a lecture hall but developed into an art gallery when J F Cheetham bequeathed his collection of paintings to the town in 1932. The collection includes Italian paintings from the 14th and 15th centuries and works from British masters such as Cox and Burne-Jones.

Opening Times: Mon to Wed & Fri 10:00-12:30 & 13:00-17:00 Sat 09:00-12:30 & 13:00-17:00.
Admission: Free.   Location: Two minutes from bus station.   Map Ref: 27

Bramall Hall

Bramhall Park, Bramhall, Stockport SK7 3NX   Tel: 0161 485 3708
Web: www.stockport.gov.uk/heritageattractions

Magnificent black and white timber-framed Tudor manor house with Victorian additions, set in 70 acres of beautiful parkland. Tour the beautiful period rooms and glimpse into the Hall's fascinating history spanning over six centuries.

Opening Times: Good Friday to Sep 13:00-17:00, Sun & BH 11:00-17:00. Oct to 1 Jan Tue to Sat 13:00-16:00 Sun & BH 11:00-16:00. 2 Jan to Good Friday Sat & Sun 13:00-16:00.
Admission: Park, Gardens & Shop - Free. Hall: Adult £3.95, Concession £2.50, Family £10.00.

Map Ref: 28

Hat Works - The Museum of Hatting

Wellington Mill, Wellington Road South, Stockport SK3 0EU   Tel: 0161 355 7770   Fax: 0161 480 8735   Web: www.hatworks.org

The UK's only museum dedicated to the hatting industry and headwear. Guides reveal the art of hat making with working machinery. The gallery houses a fantastic collection of hats which date back to the 18th century.

Opening Times: Mon to Sat 10:00-17:00, Sun 11:00-17:00.   Admission: Adult £3.95, Concession £2.50, Family £11.00. Free entry to top level, cafe, internet access and community room. Location: Centre of Stockport, five minute walk from bus and railway stations.   Map Ref: 29

Lyme Park

Disley, Stockport SK12 2NX   Tel: 01663 762023   Fax: 01663 765035
Email: lymepark@nationaltrust.org.uk   Web: www.nationaltrust.org.uk

Lyme Hall

Originally a Tudor house, Lyme was transformed by the Venetian architect Leoni into an Italianate palace. Some of the Elizabethan interiors survive and contrast dramatically with later rooms. The state rooms are adorned with Mortlake tapestries, Grinling Gibbons wood-carvings and an important collection of English clocks. The 17 acre Victorian garden boasts impressive bedding schemes, a sunken parterre, an Edwardian rose garden, Jekyll-style herbaceous borders, reflection lake, a ravine garden and Wyatt conservatory. The garden is surrounded by a medieval deer park of almost 1400 acres of moorland, woodland and parkland, containing an early 18th century hunting tower. Lyme appeared as 'Pemberley' in the BBC's adaptation of the Jane Austen novel Pride and Prejudice.

A Clock Collection
in the Clock Room

Opening Times: House: 29 Mar to 30 Oct Fri to Tue 13:00-17:00. BH Mon 11:00-17:00.   Admission: House: Adult £5.80, Family £12.50. House only: £4.20. Garden only: £2.70. NT Members Free. Park Admission £3.80 (Refunded on purchase of adult ticket).   Location: Entrance on A6, six and a half miles south east of Stockport, 17 miles north west of Buxton. Disley Station half a mile from park entrance.   Exhibitions & Events 2004 : Please telephone for details.   Map Ref: 30

Stockport Art Gallery & War Memorial

Wellington Road South, Stockport SK3 8AB   Tel: 0161 474 4453   Fax: 0161 480 4960
Email: stockport.art.gallery@stockport.gov.uk

Three galleries showing a changing programme of exhibitions of local, regional and national significance. Small permanent collection of 19th and 20th century works and local community based exhibitions and events.

Opening Times: Mon to Fri 11:00-17:00, Sat 10:00-17:00. Closed Wed & Sun.
Admission: Free.   Location: Next door to Stockport College. One minute from railway station, five minutes from bus station on A6.   Map Ref: 29

Stockport Museum

Vernon Park, Turncroft Lane, Stockport SK1 4AR   Tel: 0161 474 4460
Web: www.stockport.gov.uk

Set in beautiful surroundings of Vernon Park, Stockport Museum houses a fascinating collection of objects dating back to the Stone Ages and is home to 'One Round Hill' - the story of the history of Stockport.

Opening Times: Apr to Oct daily 13:00-17:00, winter months Sat & Sun 13:00-17:00.
Admission: Free.   Location: Located in the glorious Vernon Park, five minute drive from Stockport.   Map Ref: 29

Beeston Castle

Tarporley CW6 9TX   Tel: 01829 260464

The history of this castle goes back more than 4,000 years to when it was a Bronze age fort. It was built in 1226 and became a royal stronghold only falling centuries later in the civil war. Situated on sheer rocky crags it has some of the most stunning views of any castle in England. There is a display of every element of Bronze age working from Neolithic times to the 20th century.

Opening Times: 1 Apr to 30 Sep daily 10:00-18:00, 1-31 Oct daily 10:00-17:00, 1 Nov to 31 Mar daily 10:00-16-00   Admission: Adult £3.20, Concession £2.40, Child £1.60, Family £8.00.
Location: 11 Miles south east of Chester, on a minor road off A49.   Map Ref: 31

Cornwall & Isles of Scilly

Bodmin Town Museum

Mount Folly Square, Bodmin PL31 2DQ   Tel: 01208 77067   Fax: 01208 79268
Email: bodmin.museum@ukonline.co.uk

Local history museum with exhibits and text from medieval times to the 1950s, featuring Bodmin Moor, agriculture, law and order, trades and occupations, transport, Victorian domestic life and costume, World Wars I & II.

Opening Times: Apr to Sep daily 10:30-16:30, Oct 10:30-14:30. Closed Sun & BH.
Admission: Free.   Location: Town centre, two minute walk from car parks.   Map Ref: 1

Duke of Cornwalls Light Infantry Regimental Museum
(Military Museum Bodmin)

The Keep, Bodmin PL31 1EG   Tel / Fax: 01208 72810   Email: dclimus@talk21.com

Covers military history from the capture of Gibraltar in 1704 up to World War II. Fascinating displays of weapons, pictures, uniforms and documents - including General George Washington's Bible 'taken' by the Regiment in 1777.

Opening Times: Mon to Fri (and Sun in Jul & Aug) 09:00-17:00.   Admission: Adult £2.50, Child 50p.   Location: Bodmin.   Map Ref: 1

Lanhydrock

Lanhydrock, Bodmin PL30 5AD   Tel: 01208 73320   Fax: 01208 74084
Email: lanhydrock@nationaltrust.org.uk   Web: www.nationaltrust.org.uk

One of the most fascinating late 19th century houses in England. Although the gatehouse and north wing survive from the 17th century, the rest of the house was rebuilt following a disastrous fire in 1881. It houses a large collection of theological books and family portraits. The garden features a stunning collection of flowering shrubs.

Opening Times: 27 Mar to 30 Sep Tue to Sun 11:00-17:30, 1 Oct to 31 Oct Tue to Sun 11:00-17:00. Open BH Mons.   Admission: Adult £7.50, Child £3.75, Family £18.75. Group Adult £6.50, Child £3.25. NT Members Free.   Location: Two and half miles south east of Bodmin; follow signposts from either A30, A38 Bodmin-Liskeard or B3268 Bodmin-Lostwithiel roads.
Map Ref: 2

Pencarrow

Bodmin PL30 3AG   Tel / Fax: 01208 841369   Email: pencarrow@aol.com
Web: www.pencarrow.co.uk

Historic Georgian house and Grade II star listed garden; still owned and lived in by the family. Superb collection of paintings, furniture, porcelain and some antique dolls. Gold Award for Best Property in UK.

Opening Times: End Mar to end Oct Sun to Thu 11:00-17:00.   Admission: Adult £7.00, Child £3.50, Family ticket £20.00.   Location: Four miles north west of Bodmin, signed off A389 and B3266 at Washaway.   Map Ref: 1

The Museum of Witchcraft

The Harbour, Boscastle PL35 0HD   Tel: 01840 250111   Email: museumwitchcraft@aol.com
Web: www.museumofwitchcraft.com

The world's largest collection of Witchcraft related artefacts. This unique museum (over 50 years old) is one of the most popular in Cornwall.

Opening Times: Easter to Halloween Mon to Sat 10:30-18:00, Sun 11:30-18:00.
Admission: Adult £2.50, Child/OAP £1.50.   Location: Boscastle Harbour.   Map Ref: 3

Bude-Stratton Museum

The Castle, Bude EX23 8LG   Tel / Fax: 01288 353576   Email: museum@bude-stratton.gov.uk
Web: www.bude-stratton.gov.uk

Old photographs, models and an audio-visual presentation tell the story of Bude and Stratton.

Opening Times: Good Friday to Oct daily 12:00-17:00.   Admission: Adult 50p, Child Free, OAP 25p.   Location: On Bude's canalside.   Map Ref: 4

Cornwall & Isles of Scilly

Camborne Public Library & Museum

The Cross, Camborne TR14 8HA   Tel: 01209 713544
Email: enquiries@helstonmuseum.org.uk

A history of Camborne and the immediate area. Trades inventions, archaeology, mining, Roman villa.

Opening Times: Mon & Wed to Fri 15:00-17:00, Sat 10:00-12:00. Closed Sun & Tue.
Admission: Free. Location: Town centre location, above the public library.   Map Ref: 5

British Cycling Museum   📧 ♿ 🏛 🚂

The Old Station, Camelford PL32 9TZ   Tel / Fax: 01840 212811   Web: www.chycor.co.uk/

The British Cycling Museum is the largest and foremost display of cycling history from 1818 to present day with over 400 various machines and the largest display of cycling memorabilia on show.

Opening Times: Sun to Thu 10:00-17:00. Admission: Adult £2.50, Child £1.50.
Location: One mile north of Camelford on B3266.   Map Ref: 6

North Cornwall Museum & Gallery   🏛

The Clease, Camelford PL32 9PL   Tel / Fax: 01840 212954
Email: camelfordtlc@eurobell.co.uk

The museum shows many aspects of life in North Cornwall from 50-100 years ago. The gallery has monthly changing exhibitions by artists and craftsmen.

Opening Times: Apr to Sep Mon to Sat 10:00-17:00. Closed Sun. Admission: Adult £2.00,
Child £1.00, OAP/Concession £1.50. Location: Just off the A39 in Camelford at southern end
of town, opposite free car park.   Map Ref: 6

Falmouth Art Gallery   📧 ♿ 🏛

Muncipal Buildings, The Moor, Falmouth TR11 2RT   Tel: 01326 313863   Fax: 01326
318608   Email: info@falmouthartgallery.com   Web: www.falmouthartgallery.com

Falmouth Art Gallery is one of the leading art galleries in the South West. Its permanent collection features works by major British artists including Sir Frank Brangwyn, Sir Edward Coley Burne-Jones, Sir Alfred Munnings, Henry Scott Tuke and Dame Laura Knight. The gallery's most famous work is 'The Lady of Shallot' by John William Waterhouse, which is known throughout the world. The gallery also puts on a varied temporary exhibitions programme, showing major one person shows, touring and mixed themed exhibitions.

John T Richardson, The Bar Pool, Falmouth
signed and dated 1912, oil on canvas

Opening Times: Mon to Sat 10:00-17:00.
Admission: Free. Location: On the Moor, above the
library.   Map Ref: 7

Key to Classifications
see Classifications Index on page 423

Anthropology	Horticultural	Police, Prisons
Archaeological	Jewellery	& Dungeons
Art Galleries	Literature & Libraries	Railways
Arts, Crafts & Textiles	Maritime	Religion
China, Glass & Ceramics	Military & Defence	Roman
Communications	Multicultural	Science - Earth & Planetary
Egyptian	Music & Theatre	Sculpture
Fashion	Natural History	Sporting History
Geology	Oriental	Toy & Childhood
Health & Medicine	Palaces	Transport
Historic Houses	Photography	Victoriana

Cornwall & Isles of Scilly

John Southern Wildlife Art Gallery

Dobwalls, Liskeard PL14 6HB   Tel: 01579 320325   Fax: 01579 321345

Original watercolours and limited edition prints by Steven Townsend - Artist of the Year 1999. Also the largest and most comprehensive permanent display of limited edition prints by Carl Brenders in the world.

Opening Times: Daily 10:30-16:00. Closed Xmas Day & New Year's Day.   Admission: Free.   Location: Adjacent to Dobwalls Adventure Park.   Map Ref: 12

'Roger' Watercolour by Steven Townsend - Artist of the Year 1999

Mevagissey Folk Museum

East Quay, Mevagissey PL26 6PP   Tel: 01726 843568

Located in an 18th century boat builders (1745) with the original lath insitu. Three floors of artefacts, with an excellent display of photos taken throughout the last century. Also on display are larger exhibits such as the apple crusher the cider press and a Cornish kitchen complete with clome oven.

Opening Times: Good Friday to end Oct Mon to Fri 10:00-17:00, Sat 10:00-13:30, Sun 13:00-16:00.   Admission: Adult £1.50, Child 50p.   Location: Town Quay.   Map Ref: 13

Trerice

Kestle Mill, Newquay TR8 4PG   Tel: 01637 875404
Email: trerice@nationaltrust.org.uk   Web: www.nationaltrust.org.uk

This is a small Elizabethan manor house in a secluded setting. The highlight of the interior is the magnificient great chamber with its barrel ceiling. It houses fine fireplaces, oak and walnut furniture, interesting clocks, needlework and Stuart portraits. The garden has some unusual plants and the orchard has old varieties of fruit trees.

Opening Times: 28 Mar to 18 Jul, closed Tue & Sat 11:00-17:30, 19 Jul to 12 Sep, Sun to Fri 11:00-17:30, 13 Sep to 30 Sep closed Tue & Sat 11:00-17:30, 1 Oct to 31 Oct closed Tue & Sat 11:00-17:00.   Admission: Adult £4.70, Child £2.30, Family £11.70. Group £3.90. NT Members Free.   Location: Three miles south east of Newquay via A392 and A3058 (turn right at Kestle Mill).   Map Ref: 14

Prideaux Place

Padstow PL28 8RP   Tel: 01841 532411   Fax: 01841 532945
Email: office@prideauxplace.fsnet.co.uk

Beautiful Home of the Prideaux-Brune family for over 400 years. Surrounded by gardens, wooded grounds and overlooking the deer park. An international film and television location in recent years.

Opening Times: House: 11 Apr to 15 Apr inc, re-open 16 May to 7 Oct inc, 13:30-16:00 (last tour). Closed Fri & Sat. Grounds & Tearoom: 12:30-17:00.   Admission: House & Grounds: Adult £6.00, Child £2.00. Grounds: Adult £2.00, Child £1.00.   Location: Just off main B3276 Padstow to Newquay Road.   Map Ref: 15

Geevor Tin Mine

Pendeen, Penzance TR19 7EW   Tel: 01736 788662   Fax: 01736 786059
Email: pch@geevor.com   Web: www.geevor.com

Mining museum, largest preserved mining site in UK. Guided underground tour, spectacular coastal setting. Support for educational/study groups.

Opening Times: Apr to Sep 09:00-17:00, Nov to Feb 09:00-16:00. Closed Sat (unless a BH) & Sun in winter season.   Admission: Adult £6.00, Student £3.50, OAP £5.50, Family £16.00.   Location: In Pendeen, on B3066 road from St Ives to Lands End, six miles from Penzance (bus/railway station).   Map Ref: 16

Cornwall & Isles of Scilly

Newlyn Art Gallery

New Road, Newlyn, Penzance TR18 5PZ   Tel: 01736 363715
Fax: 01736 331578   Email: mail@newlynartgallery.co.uk
Web: www.newlynartgallery.co.uk

Newlyn Art Gallery is one of the South West's leading contemporary art organisations, showing work by local, national and international artists. As an educational charity the gallery's education programme encourages a better understanding and enjoyment of the work on show. The programme includes talks, discussion sessions, workshops and projects for the widest cross section of the community as possible.

Opening Times: Mon to Sat 10:00-17:00 (including BH).
Admission: Free. Exhibitions & Events 2004 : 17 Jan to 21 Feb: Kurt Jackson 'Porth', 15 May to 12 Jun: Ian McKeever, 19 Jun to 17 Jul: Tanya Kovats.   Map Ref: 17

Penlee House Gallery & Museum

PENLEE HOUSE
Gallery & Museum

Penlee Park, Morrab Road, Penzance TR18 4HE   Tel: 01736 363625
Fax: 01736 361312 Email: info@penlee-house.demon.co.uk Web: www.penleehouse.org.uk

Penlee House Gallery & Museum, Penzance, is an elegant gallery set within a Victorian house and park. Changing exhibitions mainly feature famous 'Newlyn School' artists (1880-1930), including Stanhope and Elizabeth Forbes, Walter Langley, Harold Harvey and 'Lamorna' Birch. The museum features 5,000 years of the history of Penwith. There is an excellent café and shop.

Opening Times: May to Sep Mon to Sat 10:00-17:00, Oct to Apr Mon to Sat 10:30-16:30. Admission: Adult £2.00, Child Free, Concession £1.00. Location: Situated in Penlee Park, a short walk from town centre and seafront.   Map Ref: 17

The Pilchard Works

Tolcarne, Newlyn, Penzance TR18 5QH   Tel: 01736 332112   Fax: 01736 332442
Email: nick@pilchardworks.co.uk   Web: www.pilchardworks.co.uk

Text, photographs and artefacts combine in this 'working museum'. Sole producers of salted, pressed pilchards using traditional methods. Visitors can taste the product, draw their own stencils and talk to production staff.

Opening Times: Apr to Oct Mon to Fri 10:00-18:00. Last admission 17:00. Admission: Adult £3.25, Child £1.95, OAP £2.95, Family £10.00. Location: 50 yards upstream from Newlyn Bridge.   Map Ref: 17

The Chevy Chase room

St Michael's Mount

Marazion, Penzance TR17 0EF   Tel: 01736 710507,
01736 710265 (Tide & Ferry info) Fax: 01736 711544
Email: godolphin@manor-office.co.uk
Web: www.nationaltrust.org.uk

Approached by a causeway at low tide and ferry at high tide, this was originally the site of a Benedictine priory. It was converted into a private house in the 17th century and contains an armoury and rococo Gothic drawing room with a good collection of portraits and a small collection of silver. At the highest point is a 14th century church and there is an 18th century walled garden, terraces and magnificient views.

Opening Times: Castle: 31 Mar to 20 Jun Sun to Fri 10:30-17:30, 21 Jun to 5 Sep daily 10:30-17:30, 6 Sep to 31 Oct Sun to Fri 10:30-17:30. Also open Easter Sat. Admission: Adult £5.20, Family £13.00. Groups (20+) £4.70. NT Members Free. Location: Half mile south of A394 at Marazion. Tide and ferry information only: (01736) 710507/710265   Map Ref: 18

Cornwall & Isles of Scilly

REDRUTH

Camborne School of Mines Geological Museum & Art Gallery

University of Exeter, Redruth TR15 3SE   Tel: 01209 714866   Fax: 01209 716977
Email: scamm@csm.ex.ac.uk   Web: www.geo-server.ex.ac.uk

The museum features an extensive collection of rocks which is continuously updated by international geological research at CSM. There are also displays on the history and future of mining in Cornwall.

Opening Times: Mon to Fri 10:00-16:00.   Admission: Free.   Location: Next to Camborne Pool, Redruth College, 20 minutes walk from Camborne or Redruth station.   Map Ref: 19

ST AUSTELL

Cornwall's Museum of The Clay Country

Carthew, Wheal Martyn, St Austell PL26 8XG   Tel / Fax: 01726 850362

26 acre museum of the china clay industry. Comprises industrial and social history items. Photographic collections. Features two water wheels, sand and mica drags, settling pits, pan kiln, transport etc.

Opening Times: Apr to Oct daily 10:00-17:00, Nov to Mar daily 11:00-16:00.   Admission: Adult £5.00, Child £3.00, OAP £4.00, Family £13.00. Group rates available.   Location: Two miles north of St Austell B3274.   Map Ref: 20

ST IVES

Penwith Galleries

Back Road West, St Ives TR26 1NL   Tel: 01736 795579

Mixed exhibitions and one man shows all year.

Opening Times: Tue to Sat 10:00-13:00 14:30-17:00.   Admission: Adult 50p.   Location: Near town centre.   Map Ref: 21

St Ives Museum

Wheal Dream, St Ives TR26 1PR   Tel: 01736 796005

A 'real' museum, in which every facet of St Ives' fascinating history is represented in its many collections, from which old and young can glean and learn of the past. These include: art, blacksmith, boat building, Cornish kitchen, Cryséde, farming, fire brigade, fishing, geology, Hain Steamship Company, lifeboat, lighthouses, mining, photographs, police, railway, shipwrecks, toys, Victorian clothes, wartime memorabilia.

Opening Times: 5 Apr to 30 Oct, Mon to Fri 10:00-17:00, Sat 10:00-16:00. Closed Sun & Good Friday.   Location: Near harbour quay.   Map Ref: 21

St Ives Society of Artists

Norway Gallery, Norway Sq, St Ives TR26 1NA   Tel: 01736 795582   Email: gallery@stisa.co.uk
Web: www.stisa.co.uk

Art works in this gallery are largely traditional and representational. Members submit new work each year for inclusion in the Exhibition. Paintings sold are replaced by others, therefore the Exhibition is continuous but changing.

Opening Times: Mid Mar to Mid Nov Mon to Sat & BH Sun 10:00-16:30.   Admission: Free. Location: Close to harbour - behind The Sloop Inn car park. In the Old Mariners Church.   Map Ref: 21

Cornwall & Isles of Scilly

Tate St Ives

St IVES

TATE

Porthmeor Beach, St Ives TR26 1TG Tel: 01736 796226 Fax: 01736 794480
Web: www.tate.org.uk

Alfred Wallis, The Blue Ship c. 1934

Tate St Ives opened in 1993 and offers a unique introduction to modern art, where paintings and sculpture can be seen in the surroundings which inspired many of them. The gallery presents changing displays from the Tate Collection focusing on the post-war modern movement for which St Ives is famous. There are also major exhibitions of work by contemporary artists. Tate St Ives manages the Barbara Hepworth Museum and Sculpture Garden in St Ives, which offers a remarkable insight into the work and outlook of one of Britain's most important 20th century sculptors.

Barbara Hepworth, Sea Form (Porthmeor) 1958

Opening Times: Mar to Oct daily 10:00-17:30, Nov to Feb Tue to Sun 10:00-16:30. Admission: Adult £4.75, Under 18's Free, Concession £2.50, OAP Free.
Location: Situated by Porthmeor Beach close to town centre. Map Ref: 22

SALTASH

Cotehele

St Dominick, Saltash PL12 6TA Tel: 01579 352739
Email: cotehele@nationaltrust.org.uk Web: www.nationaltrust.org.uk

Tapestry entitled 'The Liberal Arts' from Antwerp, 1660s-1670s

Set in the heart of this riverside estate, the house was mainly built between 1485 and 1627 and contains a remarkable collection of tapestries and textiles. There is the original furniture and the great hall is hung with arms and armour. The formal gardens overlook the richly planted green valley below.

Opening Times: 20 Mar to 30 Sep Sat to Thu 11:00-17:00, 2 Oct to 31 Oct Sat to Thu 11:00-16.30. Open Good Friday. Admission: Adult £7.00, Child £3.50, Family £17.50. Group £6.00. NT Members Free.
Location: Eight miles south west of Tavistock, 14 miles from Plymputh via Saltash Bridge; two miles east of St Dominick. Map Ref: 23

TORPOINT

Antony

Torpoint, Plymouth PL11 2QA Tel: 01752 812 191
Email: antony@nationaltrust.org.uk Web: www.nationaltrust.org.uk

The Library

One of Cornwall's finest early 18th century houses, faced in Pentewan stone. The house contains furniture, tapestries, and an extensive collection of family portraits and memorabilia. The formal garden has the National Collection of Day Lilies, fine summer borders and outstanding displays of flowering shrubs.

Opening Times: 30 Mar-27 May Tue to Thu 13:30-17:30, 1 Jun-29 Aug Sun,Tue-Thu 13:30-17:30, 31 Aug to 28 Oct Tue to Thu 13:30-17:30. Open BH Mons.
Admission: Adult £4.80, Child £2.40, Family £12.00. Group Adult £4.00, Child £2.00. NT Members Free.
Location: Five miles west of Plymouth via Torpoint car ferry,two miles north west of Torpoint,north of A376, sixteen miles south east of Liskeard. Map Ref: 24

Cornwall & Isles of Scilly

Mount Edgcumbe House & Country Park

Mount Edgcumbe House, Cremyll, Torpoint PL10 1HZ   Tel: 01752 822236
Fax: 01752 822199   Email: mt.edgecumbe@plymouth.gov.uk
Web: www.cornwalltouristboard.co.uk/mountedgcumbe

Mount Edgcumbe House, Cornwall

Sir Richard Edgcumbe of Cotehele built a new home in his deer park at Mount Edgcumbe in 1547-53. It is now beautifully furnished with family possessions, including paintings by Sir Joshua Reynolds, Gerard Edema and William van de Velde, Irish bronze age horns, 16th century tapestries and 18th century Chinese and Plymouth porcelain.

Opening Times: Apr to end Sep Sun to Thu 11:00-16:30.
Admission: Adult £4.50, Child £2.25, Concession £3.50.
Group advanced booking (min 10) £3.50.
Location: Across the river from Plymouth by passenger ferry (10 mins). By car - Torpoint Ferry or Tamar Bridge
(A374, B3247 follow brown signs).   Exhibitions & Events 2004 : For 2004: Rame Connection with World War II: Commemorating 60th Anniversary of Normandy Landings. Plus local artist's exhibitons.   Map Ref: 24

Royal Cornwall Museum

River Street, Truro TR1 2SJ   Tel: 01872 272205   Fax: 01872 240514
Email: enquiries@royal-cornwall-museum.freeserve.co.uk
Web: www.royalcornwallmuseum.org.uk

Nationally important collection of Cornish minerals, Cornish archaeology and local history, paintings, ceramics, Greek, Roman and Egyptian archaeology, and a regular temporary exhibition progamme. Many activities for children and families, especially in holidays.

Opening Times: Mon to Sat 10:00-17:00, closed Sun and BH. Admission: Adult £4.00, Child free, OAP/Student £2.50. (Free admission from 01/04/04). Location: Near town centre on A390 past the railway station. Map Ref: 25

Cumbria

To many, Cumbria is synonymous with the Lake District, with its amazing variety of scenery contained within a relatively small area. South Cumbria, sandwiched between the Lake District and the Yorkshire Dales has its history recorded in the art and literature of William Turner and John Ruskin. On the west coast a succession of ports once exported coal and in the north the county town, Carlisle, stands guard over the flat lands leading to the Scottish boarder, its castle for centuries a bastion against the marauding Scots.

Cumbria lays claim to some outstanding museums including collections of its literary, artistic, boating and military history.

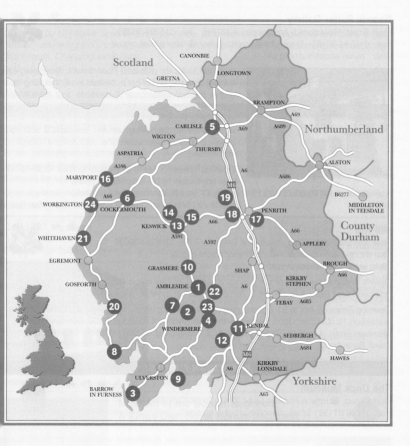

The Red Map References should be used to locate Museums etc on the pages that follow

Cumbria

The Bishops Stone,
Border Reiver Pathway

Tullie House
Museum & Art Gallery

Castle Street, Carlisle CA3 8TP
Tel: 01228 534781 Fax: 01228 810249
Email: enquiries@tullie-house.co.uk Web: www.tulliehouse.co.uk

Tullie House combines the features of historic house and modern Museum. Old Tullie House is a 17th century town house of character, with a fine classical façade overlooking a herb garden. Inside are some early features - including Jacobean staircase and panelled Drawing Room. The latter displays key artworks by the pre-Raphaelites; other rooms feature portraits and fine paintings and a childhood gallery. The modern Border Galleries show Carlisle's exciting history and wildlife. There is a wealth of objects from prehistoric and Roman times (complete with reconstruction of Hadrian's Wall). Inter-actives include Roman writing and artillery. The spectacular Reivers audio-visual presentation brings to life the lawless Borders of the Middle Ages; the railway story is told by the 'station announcer'. Local wildlife - complete with badger sett - is seen under a domed ceiling with changing light and sound. The exciting, and innovative Millennium Gallery celebrates unique aspects of Carlisle's collections and includes a stunning display of minerals from Cumbria/N Pennines, set on cast glass; rare archaeology with transforming 'Peppers Ghost' interactive; local paintings and costume. The walls feature Carlisle building styles and also tell stories. A rotunda viewing platform affords striking views of Carlisle Castle. Tullie House was the winner of Cumbria Tourist Boards best website of the year and special gold award for large tourist attraction (over 200,000 visitors).

Railway Area, Border Gallery

Opening Times: Nov to Mar Mon to Sat 10:00-16:00, Sun 12:00-16:00. Apr to Jun & Sep to Oct Mon to Sat 10:00-17:00, Sun 12:00-17:00. Jul & Aug Mon to Sat 10:00-17:00, Sun 11:00-17:00. Closed 25 & 26 Dec and 1 Jan. Admission: Adult £5.20, Child (16 and under) £2.60 - under 5's go free. Group rate (10 people +) £3.10, Family £14.50. Exhibitions & Events 2004 : 22 Nov to 11 Jan: Northern Potters, 17 Jan to 7 Mar: Mariele Neudecker: Between Us, 13 Mar to 8 May: 2D>3D: Design for Theatre and Performance, 15 May to 4 Jul: Jim Partridge: Burning Bridges, 18 Sep to 8 Jan 05: Quilts, 12 Nov to Apr 05: Christopher Dresser Special Exhibitions Gallery & Carlisle Millenium Gallery, To 15 Mar: Carlisle Artists, 3 Apr to 3 Oct: Special Exhibitions Gallery Into the hands of the shades - Death in Roman Cumbria For further info call (01228) 534781
Map Ref: 5

Cumberland Toy & Model Museum

Banks Court, Market Place, Cockermouth CA13 9NG Tel: 01900 827606
Email: rod@toymuseum.co.uk Web: www.toymuseum.co.uk

This national award winning museum has many visitor operated exhibits including Hornby Trains, Scalextric Cars and Lego. Come and re-live your childhood.

Opening Times: Feb to Nov 10:00-17:00. Dec to Jan times vary, please phone.
Admission: Adult £3.00, Child £1.50, OAP £2.60, Group rates for parties of 10+.
Location: Market Place. Follow signs from car parks.
Map Ref: 6

Wordsworth House

Cockermouth CA13 9RX Tel: 01900 824805
Email: wordsworthhouse@ntrust.org.uk Web: www.nationaltrust.org.uk

The Georgian town house where William Wordsworth was born in 1770. There is a good collection of engravings, and some of the poets personal effects. His childhood garden has been attractively restored. Re-opens Jun 2004, imaginatively presented as the home of William Wordsworth. Costumed Tours.

Opening Times: Jun to 5 Nov Mon to Sat 10:30-16:30. Admission by timed ticket.
Admission: Adult £4.50, Child £2.50, Family £13.00. Group (15+) Adult £3.50, Child £1.50. NT Members Free. Location: Main Street, Cockermouth.
Map Ref: 6

Cumbria

Brantwood

🦽 🎁 📷 🐾 🚗

Coniston LA21 8AD   Tel: 015394 41396   Fax: 015394 41263
Email: enquiries@brantwood.org.uk   Web: www.brantwood.org.uk

The former home of John Ruskin, Brantwood presents and explores the various themes that interested him throughout his life - art, the environment, geology, architecture and society.

Opening Times: Mid Mar to mid Nov daily 11:00-17:30, mid Nov to mid Mar Wed to Sun 11:00-16:30.   Admission: Adult £5.50, Child £1.00, Student £4.00, Family £11.00. Garden only £3.75.
Location: On the east side of Coniston Water, two and a half miles from the village of Coniston.

Map Ref: 7

The Ruskin Museum

📷 🦽 🎁 🚗

Yewdale Road, Coniston LA21 8DU   Tel: 015394 41164   Fax: 015394 41132
Email: vmj@ruskinmuseum.com   Web: www.ruskinmuseum.com

The Ruskin Museum, Coniston's award-winning 'cabinet of curiosities' introduces a local story as old as the hills which copper-bottomed the fleet and slate-roofed the world; celebrates the life, art and radical ideas of John Ruskin, 'one of those rare men who think with their hearts'; honours heroic Speed Ace Donald Campbell and Bluebird.

Opening Times: Easter/1 Apr to Oct daily 10:00-17:30, Nov to Mar Wed to Sun 10:30-15:30.   Admission: Adult £3.50, Child £1.75, Family £9.00. Group rates available.
Location: Near village centre, on Yewdale Road, three minute walk from main car park and Tourist Information

Sunset at Herne Hill through the smoke of London, 1886, watercolour John Ruskin

Centre.   Exhibitions & Events 2004 : 3/4 Apr, 8/9 May, 9/10 Jun, 8/9 Sep, 9/10 Oct: Each two-day, non-residential, practical courses - How to Make Ruskin Lace - taught by world expert, Elizabeth Prickett. Please phone for details.   Map Ref: 7

Dalton Castle

🦽 🚗

Market Place, Dalton-in-Furness LA15 8AX   Tel / Fax: 01524 701178
Web: www.nationaltrust.org.uk

A 14th century tower with gothic windows in the main street of town. It contains displays of armour and local artifacts.

Opening Times: 10 Apr to 25 Sep Sat only 14:00-17-00   Admission: Free. Donations welcome.
Location: In main street of Dalton.

Map Ref: 8

Holker Hall

📷 🦽 📷 🐾 🚗 🏛

Cark-in-Cartmel, Grange-over-Sands LA11 7PL   Tel: 015395 58328   Fax: 015395 58378   Email: publicopening@holker.co.uk   Web: www.holker-hall.co.uk

Discover the beauty and elegance of Holker Hall without the confines of ropes or barriers to restrict your viewing. Relax in 25 acres of National Award Winning Garden. Stroll through the formal gardens and thrill at the unique and rare treasures they offer. Treat yourself to a special lunch or afternoon tea in the Courtyard Café or picnic in the grounds. Children will delight at the adventure playground. Plants from our nursery, unique gifts and specialty products all hand selected by Lady Cavendish are available in our gift shop. Shops, Cafe and Motor Museum open in winter - please telephone for details.

Opening Times: 28 Mar to 31 Oct Sun to Fri 10:00-18:00, last admission 16:30.
Admission: Adult £9.25. Child £5.25, Family £25.75.   Location: Follow brown tourism signs from A590 from Barrow or junction 36 of M6.

Map Ref: 9

Lakeland Motor Museum

🎁 📷 🚗

Holker Hall and Gardens, Cark-in-Cartmel, Grange-over-Sands LA11 7PL   Tel / Fax: 015395 58509   Email: info@lakelandmotormuseum.co.uk   Web: www.lakelandmotormuseum.co.uk

A nostalgic reminder of transport and horticultural bygones appealing to all ages and offering a

Cumbria

truly astonishing insight into our forefathers' inventiveness and dexterity. Over 30,000 exhibits including The Campbell Legend Bluebird Exhibition.

Opening Times: 1 Mar to 19 Dec daily from 10:30. Admission: Please telephone for details.
Location: On B5278 near Grange-over-Sands. Map Ref: 9

GRASMERE

Dove Cottage & the Wordsworth Museum

The Wordsworth Trust
Centre for British Romanticism

The Wordsworth Trust, Dove Cottage, Grasmere LA22 9SH Tel: 015394 35544 Fax: 015394 35748 Email: enquiries@wordsworth.org.uk
Web: www.wordsworth.org.uk

Dove Cottage was the poet, William Wordsworth's home from 1799-1808. Visitors are offered guided tours of this atmospheric cottage. The award-winning museum displays The Wordsworth Trust's unique collections of manuscripts, books and paintings interpreting the life and work of William Wordsworth, his family and circle. There is a major special exhibition every year.

Opening Times: Daily 09:30-17:30. Last entry 5pm. Closed Xmas and Jan. Admission: Adult £5.80, Child £2.60, Groups £4.70 (pre booked). Museum only: Adult £3.00, Child £1.30.
Location: South of Grasmere village, on the main A591 Kendal to Keswick road. Map Ref: 10

KENDAL

Abbot Hall Art Gallery

Abbot Hall, Kendal LA9 5AL Tel: 01539 722464 Fax: 01539 722494
Email: info@abbothall.org.uk Web: www.abbothall.org.uk ·

A fine Georgian house containing a growing collection of modern art. The ground floor rooms contain furniture by Gillows of Lancaster and painting by Kendal born artist George Romney. Changing exhibitions.

Opening Times: 20 Jan to 23 Dec Mon to Sat 10:30-17:00. Winter closing 16:00.
Admission: Please phone for details. Location: Junction 36 of M6, Kendal is ten minutes drive. Nearest station: Oxenholme. Map Ref: 11

Kendal Museum

Station Road, Kendal LA9 6BT Tel: 01539 721374 Fax: 01539 737976
Email: info@kendalmuseum.org.uk Web: www.kendalmuseum.org.uk

Displays of archaeology and natural history, both local and global. With examples of lakeland flora and fauna, the museum charts developments from pre-historic times through Roman, Medieval and Victorian and into the 21st century.

Opening Times: Feb to Dec Mon to Sat 10:30-17:00. Winter closing 16:00. Location: Junction 36 on M6, ten minutes drive. Nearest station: Kendal. Map Ref: 11

Levens Hall

Kendal LA8 0PD Tel: 015395 60321 Fax: 015395 60669
Email: email@levenshall.fsnet.co.uk Web: www.levenshall.co.uk

Levens Hall is an Elizabethan mansion, home of the Bapot family, containing fine panelling, plasterwork and period furniture. World famous topiary gardens laid out by Monsieur Beaumont in 1694.

Opening Times: 4 Apr to mid Oct. Gardens: Sun to Thu 10:00-17:00, House: Sun to Thu 12:00-17:00. Closed Fri & Sat. Guided tours available by arrangement. Map Ref: 11

Museum of Lakeland Life

Abbot Hall, Kendal LA9 5AL Tel: 01539 722464 Fax: 01539 722494
Email: info@lakelandmuseum.org.uk Web: www.lakelandmuseum.org.uk

Real objects and displays tell the story of Cumbria's history - from the age of 18th century yeoman farmers, through Georgian and Victorian periods and into living memory.

Opening Times: 20 Jan to 23 Dec Mon to Sat 10:30-17:00. Winter closing 16:00.
Admission: Please phone for details. Location: Junction 36 of M6, ten minutes drive to Kendal. Nearest station: Oxenholme. Map Ref: 11

Cumbria

Sizergh Castle and Garden

Sizergh, Kendal LA8 8AE   Tel: 015395 60070   Fax: 015395 61621
Web: www.nationaltrust.org.uk

This medieval castle was the home of the Strickland family for over 750 years. It has an exceptional series of oak-panelled interiors with intricately carved chimneypieces and early oak furniture, culminating in the magnificent Inlaid Chamber. The castle is surrounded by handsome gardens and a particularly imposing rock garden.

The Drawing Room

Opening Times: Castle: 3 Apr to 27 Oct Sun to Thu 13:30-17:30. Garden: 3 Apr to 27 Oct Sun to Thu 12:30-17:30. Admission: Adult £5.50, Child £2.70, Family £13.70. Group (15+) £4.50. Garden only: Adult £3.00, Child £1.50. NT Members Free. Location: Three and a half miles south of Kendal, signposted off A590.   Map Ref: 12

KESWICK

Cars of The Stars Motor Museum

Standish Street, Keswick CA12 5HH   Tel: 0176787 73757   Fax: 0176787 72090
Web: www.carsofthestars.com

This world famous museum features vehicles from television and film, including Chitty Chitty Bang Bang, Batmobiles, Herbie, A-Team van, Del Boy's yellow Reliant, FAB 1, Back to the Future, James Bond's Aston Martin and many more. A souvenir shop and famous autographs. Definitely not to be missed! New this year: Harry Potter's Ford Anglia and the car from Dukes of Hazzard.

Delorean - Back to the Future

Opening Times: Easter to end Nov daily 10:00-17:00. Also open Feb half term and weekends in Dec. Admission: Adult £3.50, Child £2.50 (3-14 years). Discount of 10% on parties of 20+. Location: In town centre. 100 yards from car park, five minutes walk from bus station.   Map Ref: 13

Cumberland Pencil Museum

Southey Works, Greta Bridge, Keswick CA12 5NG   Tel: 017687 73626   Fax: 017687 74679
Email: museum@acco-uk.co.uk   Web: www.pencils.co.uk/

The pencil story; from the discovery of graphite to the present day method of pencil manufacture. Told through exhibitions and a video presentation. Including a techniques video, world's longest pencil, gift shop.

Opening Times: 09:30-16:00. Closed Xmas & New Year. Admission: Adult £2.50, Child/OAP £1.25, Family £6.25. Location: 300 yards west of town centre.   Map Ref: 13

Keswick Museum & Art Gallery

Fitz Park, Station Road, Keswick CA12 4NF   Tel: 017687 73263   Fax: 017687 80390
Email: keswick.museum@allerdale.gov.uk   Web: www.allerdale.gov.uk

Keswick's Victorian museum is full of surprises: the amazing musical stones played by Royal Command, the 500 year old cat and a stunning collection of crystals. Art exhibitions monthly.

Opening Times: 1 Apr to 31 Oct daily 10:00-16:00. Admission: Adult £1.50, Child/Concession 50p, Groups 10% discount on 10 or more. Location: In Fitz Park, on Station Road, five minutes walk from town centre, follow brown and white signs for 'Museum & Art Gallery'.   Map Ref: 13

Mirehouse

Underskiddaw, Keswick CA12 4QE   Tel / Fax: 017687 72287
Email: info@mirehouse.com   Web: www.mirehouse.com

Living family home which has passed by descent for three hundred years. Remarkable group of 19th century friendships illustrated by manuscripts and portraits: Tennyson, Wordsworth, Southey,

Cumbria

Carlyle, Fitzgerald, Constable. Also Francis Bacon Collection from his biographer James Spedding.

Opening Times: Gardens & Tearoom: Apr to Oct daily 10:00-17:30. House: Apr to Oct Sun & Wed 14:00-17:00 (last entry 16:30), also Fri in Aug. Groups by appointment throughout year. Admission: Gardens & Lakeside Walk: Adult £2.20. House & Gardens: Adult £4.60. Child 1/2 price, Family ticket £13.80 (2 adults and up to 4 children). Location: Three and a half miles north of Keswick on A591. Excellent rural bus service. Map Ref: 14

Threlkeld Quarry & Mining Museum

Threlkeld Quarry, Threlkeld, Keswick CA12 4TT Tel: 017687 79747
Email: coppermaid@aol.com Web: www.golakes.co.uk www.earthlines.com

The finest mining museum in the north of England - realistic mine tour of 45 minutes pure history and adventure. Excavators and locomotives, we have the 'lot'.

Opening Times: Mar to Oct daily 10:00-17:00. Admission: Museum: Adult £2.50. Mine Tour: £3.00. Location: Keswick - four miles on A66 Penrith/Keswick Road. Map Ref: 15

Maryport Maritime Museum
1 Senhouse Street, Shipping Brow, Maryport CA15 6AB Tel: 01900 813738

Comprehensive display on the maritime traditions of Maryport including the origins of the famous White Star Line.

Opening Times: Mon to Sat 10:00-13:00 & 14:00-16:30. Closed Sun. Location: Listed building on the edge of harbour. Map Ref: 16

The Senhouse Roman Museum

Sea Brows, Maryport CA15 6JD Tel / Fax: 01900 816168
Email: romans@senhouse.freeserve.co.uk Web: www.senhousemuseum.co.uk

The museum houses the Netherhall Collection, one of the largest collections of Roman altars from a single site in Britain. Also many fine religious sculptures, including the mysterious 'Serpent Stone'.

Opening Times: Apr to end Jun Tue, Thu, Fri to Sun 10:00-17:00, Jul to end Oct daily 10:00-17:00. Nov to end Mar Fri to Sun 10:30-16:00. Admission: Adult £2.50, Child 75p. Group rates available. Location: Set on low lying cliffs overlooking Maryport harbour. Map Ref: 16

Brougham Castle

Penrith CA10 2AA Tel: 01768 862488

Built in 1092 on the site of a Roman fort, it was destroyed in 1172 and rebuilt by Henry 11. His tower survives, but later buildings were destroyed by fire in 1521. It was restored in the 17th century by Lady Anne Clifford. There is a collection of gravestones associated with the Roman cemetery. Also medieval pottery and everyday objects.

Opening Times: 1 Apr to 30 Sep daily 10:00-18:00, 1-31 Oct daily 10:00-17:00.
Admission: Adult £2.50, Concession £2.00, Child £1.50. Location: One and a half miles south east of Penrith off A66. Map Ref: 17

Dalemain Historic House & Garden

Penrith CA11 0HB Tel: 01768 486450 Fax: 01768 486223
Email: admin@dalemain.com Web: www.dalemain.com

Mediaeval Tudor and Georgian house, home to Hasell family since 1679. Fascinating interiors, delightful gardens, rare plants, old fashioned roses, free parking, restaurant and tearoom, gift shop - plant sales.

Opening Times: 28 Mar to 14 Oct Sun to Thu. House: 11:00-16:00, Garden, Tearoom & Gift Shop: 10:30-17:00. Admission: House & Garden: £5.50, Garden: £3.50. Location: Between Penrith and Ullswater. Map Ref: 18

Hutton-In-The-Forest
Penrith CA11 9TH Tel: 017684 84449 Fax: 017684 84571
Email: hutton-in-the-forest@talk21.com

Historic house and gardens, based on a medieval pole tower, with substantial additions in 17th,

Cumbria

18th and 19th centuries; collections of portraits, tapestries, ceramics and furniture. Surrounded by beautiful gardens and woodland.

Opening Times: 9 to 18 Apr, 2 May to 3 Oct Thu, Fri, Sun & BH 12:30-16:00. Admission: Adult £4.50, Child £2.50, Family £12.00. Location: On B5305, two and a half miles north west of M6 junction 41. Map Ref: 19

RAVENGLASS

Muncaster Castle Gardens & Owl Centre

Muncaster Castle, Ravenglass CA18 1RQ Tel: 01229 717614
Fax: 01229 717010 Email: info@muncaster.co.uk Web: www.muncaster.co.uk

Home to the Pennington family for 800 years. Muncaster is a genuine treasure trove of art and antiques including Henry VI's drinking bowl. The rich furnishings and decor include some fine Elizabethan furniture and embroidery. A walk through the castle brings you seven centuries of glorious history including portraits by famous artists and beautiful tapestries.

Opening Times: Mar to Nov daily 10:30-18:00. Castle open Sun to Fri 12:00-17:00. Admission: Please telephone for prices. Location: One mile south of Ravenglass on the A595. Map Ref: 20

WHITEHAVEN

The Beacon

West Strand, Whitehaven CA28 7LY Tel: 01946 592302 Fax: 01946 598150
Email: thebeacon@copelandbc.gov.uk Web: copelandbc.gov.uk

Home to Whitehaven's museum, The Beacon also offers the world's first Met Office Weather Gallery and an attractive programme of exhibitions throughout the year.

Opening Times: Easter to Oct Tue to Sun 10:00-17:30. Nov to Mar 10:00-16:30. School & BH open Mon. Admission: Adult £4.25, Child/Concession £2.80, OAP £3.50, Family £12.70. Group rates available. Location: On harbourside. Map Ref: 21

WINDERMERE

Townend

Troutbeck, Windermere LA23 1LB Tel: 015394 32628 Web: www.nationaltrust.org.uk

A yeoman farmhouse dating mainly from the 17th century. The solid stone and slate house belonged to a wealthy farming family and houses carved oak furniture and a collection of books. The small garden is planted with flowers known to have grown in Edwardian times.

Opening Times: 1 Apr to 31 Oct Tue to Fri & Sun 13:00-17:00. Open BH Mons.
Admission: Adult £3.20, Child £1.50, Family £8.00. NT Members Free. Location: Three miles south east of Ambleside at south end of Troutbeck village. Map Ref: 22

Windermere Steamboats & Museum

Rayrigg Road, Windermere LA23 1BN Tel: 015394 45565 Fax: 015394 48769
Email: steamboat@ecosse.net Web: www.steamboat.co.uk

Large collection of Victorian/Edwardian launches and motor boats in spectacular lakeside setting. Cruises on steam launches. Swallows & Amazons exhibition. 'Model Boats - You Too Can Do It!' exhibition.

Opening Times: 15 Mar to 26 Oct daily 10:00-17:00. Admission: Adult £3.50, Child £2.00, Family £8.50. Group rates available. Location: Half a mile north of Bowness-on-Windermere on A592. Map Ref: 23

WORKINGTON

Helena Thompson Museum

Park End Road, Workington CA14 4DE Tel: 01900 326255

Costume, ceramics of 18th and 19th century. Social history and photographic archive of Workington town and industries.

Opening Times: Mon to Sat 10:00-16:00. Admission: Free. Location: Opposite Workington Hall and Curwen Park overlooking the Irish Sea. Map Ref: 24

Derbyshire & Staffordshire

BUXTON *Derbys*

Buxton Museum & Art Gallery

Terrace Road, Buxton SK17 6DA   Tel: 01298 24658   Fax: 01298 79394
Email: buxton.museum@derbyshire.gov.uk   Web: www.derbyshire.gov.uk

Explore the wonders of the Peak through seven time zones revealing the geology, archaeology and history of the Peak District. Enjoy our busy programme of temporary art and craft exhibition.

Opening Times: Tue to Fri 09:30-17:30, Sat 09:30-17:00. Also from Easter to 30 Sep Sun & BH Mon 10:30-17:00. Closed Mon.   Admission: Free.   Location: Near Town Hall, ten minutes from train station.   Map Ref: 5

CANNOCK *Staffs*

Museum of Cannock Chase

Valley Road, Hednesford, Cannock WS12 1TD   Tel: 01543 877666   Fax: 01543 428272
Email: museum@cannockchasedc.gov.uk   Web: www.museumofcannockchase.co.uk

Small museum occupying ex-colliery site. Illustrates history of Cannock Chase from medieval hunting forest to coalfield community. Collections comprise social history, domestic and industrial artefacts.

Opening Times: Easter to Sep daily 11:00-17:00. Oct to Easter Mon to Fri 11:00-16:00.
Admission: Free except for guided parties.   Location: Near Hednesford centre on A460 to Rugeley, ten minutes from station.   Map Ref: 6

CHESTERFIELD *Derbys*

Chesterfield Museum & Art Gallery

St Marys Gate, Chesterfield S41 7TD   Tel: 01246 345727
Email: museum@chesterfieldbc.gov.uk

Taking the 'Story of Chesterfield' as its theme the museum shows how the town has become the place it is today, by looking at different aspects of its history.

Opening Times: Mon, Tue, Thu, Fri, Sat 10:00-16:00. Closed Wed & Sun and Xmas & New Year.
Admission: Free.   Location: The museum is located on St Mary's Gate close to the parish church (Crooked Spire), easy walking distance of car parks and railway station.   Map Ref: 7

Hardwick Hall, Gardens & Park

Doe Lea, Chesterfield S44 5QJ   Tel: 01246 850430   Fax: 01246 854200
Email: hardwickhall@nationaltrust.org.uk   Web: www.nationaltrust.org.uk

Set high on a hill in North East Derbyshire, spectacular 405 year old Hardwick, the home of Bess of Hardwick is one of the greatest Elizabethan houses, surviving almost unchanged to date. The Hall contains one of Europe's best collections of furniture, embroideries and tapestries.

Surrounded by four walled courtyards, aromatic garden and famous herb garden. Enjoy great walks around the ponds.

The Long Gallery containing
the famous Gideon Tapestries

Opening Times: Hall: 31 Mar to 31 Oct Wed, Thu, Sat, Sun plus BH Mons & Good Friday 12:00-16:30.
Admission: Adult £6.80, Child £3.40, Family £17.00. NT Members Free.   Location: Access via Stainsby Mill near junction 29 on the M1, follow Brown Tourist Signs. Map Ref: 8

The Blue Bedroom

Revolution House

High Street, Old Whittington, Chesterfield   Tel: 01246 345727
Email: museum@chesterfieldbc.gov.uk

Originally an alehouse, this 17th century thatched cottage was the site of a meeting between local noblemen involved in the Revolution of 1688.

Opening Times: Good Friday to end Sep 11:00-16:00 open daily except Tue. 18 Dec to 24 Dec & 27 Dec to 31 Dec.   Admission: Free.   Location: In the centre of Old Whittington village near the 'Cock & Magpie'. Regular bus service from Chesterfield.   Map Ref: 9

Derbyshire & Staffordshire

Calke Abbey

Ticknall, Derby DE73 1LE   Tel: 01332 863822   Fax: 01332 865272
Email: calkeabbey@nationaltrust.org.uk   Web: www.nationaltrust.org.uk

The School Room

This baroque mansion was built in the early 18th century. It contains family portraits and sporting pictures. The baroque state bed with Chinese embroidered silk hangings are unchanged since the 1880s. The attractive grounds feature a walled garden.

Opening Times: 27 Mar to 31 Oct Sat to Wed 13:00-17:30. Admission: Adult £5.90, Child £2.90, Family £14.50. Group (15+) Adult £4.90, Child £2.40. NT Members Free.   Location: Ten miles south of Derby, on A514 at Ticknall between Swadlincote and Melbourne.

Exhibitions & Events 2004 : 13 & 14 Aug: Open air concerts. Events to celebrate 300th anniversary throughout 2004.   Map Ref: 10

Derby Industrial Museum

The Silk Mill, Silk Mill Lane, off Full Street, Derby DE1 3AF   Tel: 01332 255308   Fax: 01332 716670   Email: david.fraser@derby.gov.uk   Web: www.derby.gov.uk/museums

The museum is housed in Derby's historic Silk Mill. Built circa 1720 as one of Britain's first factories. Displays feature local industries, including railway engineering and Rolls Royce aero engines.

Opening Times: Mon 11:00-17:00, Tue to Sat 10:00-17:00, Sun & BH 14:00-17:00. Closed Xmas & New Year break.   Admission: Free.   Location: Beside the River Derwent, five minutes walk from bus station, 25 minutes walk from railway station.   Map Ref: 11

Derby Museum & Art Gallery

The Strand, Derby DE1 1BS   Tel: 01332 716659   Fax: 01332 716670
Email: david.fraser@derby.gov.uk   Web: www.derby.gov.uk/museums

The Ceramics Gallery

The museum houses internationally important collections of Derby porcelain and major paintings by Joseph Wright of Derby (1734-97). Derbyshire wildlife and geology feature in a splendid series of natural settings and hands-on exhibits. Other galleries are devoted to local regiments, local archaeology, Bonnie Prince Charlie's visit to Derby during the 1745 uprising, and to exciting temporary exhibitions.

Opening Times: Mon 11:00-17:00, Tue to Sat 10:00-17:00, Sun & BH 14:00-17:00. Closed Xmas & New Year break.   Admission: Free.   Location: In city centre, ten minutes walk from bus station, 25 minutes walk from railway station.   Map Ref: 11

Donington Grand Prix Collection

Donington Park, Castle Donington, Derby DE74 2RP   Tel: 01332 811027
Fax: 01332 812829   Email: enquiries@doningtoncollection.co.uk
Web: www.doningtoncollection.com

The Mclaren Hall, featuring the World's largest collecion of McLaren F1 cars

Take a lap around the Donington Grand Prix Collection, which is the world's largest collection of Grand Prix racing cars. Featuring over 130 cars within five halls and described by a number of visitors as 'a gold mine to motor racing heritage'. The collection features the world's largest collection of McLaren Formula One cars on public display and also cars such as Ferrari, Jordan, Williams, BRM and Vanwalls. Driven by such famous names as Senna, Nuvolari, Moss, Hill and Fangio. Also there are drivers' helmets and memorabilia covering every wall within the collection.

Opening Times: Daily 10:00-17:00, last admission 16:00.   Admission: Adult £7.00, Child £2.50, Student/OAP £5.00, Family (2 adults and 3 children) £14.00, Group discount available.
Location: Two miles from junction 23A M1/M42.   Exhibitions & Events 2004 : A number of anniversaries are celebrated to commemorate racing drivers and cars.   Map Ref: 12

Derbyshire & Staffordshire

Cheddleton Flint Mill
Leek Road, Cheddleton, Leek ST13 7HL   Tel: 01782 502907
Web: www.ex.ac.uk/~akoutram/cheddleton-mill/index.htm

Two water mills, complete with wheels. Shows the process of grinding flint for the pottery industry. Panels tell the story of the materials used in pottery manufacture. Allow an hour.

Opening Times: Sat & Sun 13:00-17:00. Open some weekdays (phone first) 14:00-17:00.
Closed Xmas & New Year.   Admission: Free, but donations most welcome.
Location: Cheddleton village on A520, three miles south of Leek.   Map Ref: 17

Lichfield Heritage Centre

Market Square, Lichfield WS13 6LG   Tel: 01543 256611   Fax: 01543 414749
Email: info@lichfieldheritage.org.uk   Web: www.lichfieldheritage.org.uk

The 'Lichfield Story' exhibition gives a vivid account of 2000 years of Lichfield's rich and varied history. It is home to the unique, historically important Staffordshire Millennium Embroideries. Two A.V. presentations, a fine Treasury plus a Family Trail and for younger children a Mousehole Trail complete the exhibition. Magnificent views from the Spire Viewing Platform (please check as limited opening times).

Opening Times: Mon to Sat 10:00-17:00, Sun 10:30-17:00, last admission 16:00. Closed 25-26 Dec & New Year's Day.
Admission: Adult £3.50, Child (5-15yrs) £1.00, Under 5s Free, Concession £2.50, Booked Groups £2.50, Family £8.00. Prices are for 2003 and may be subject to change.   Location: Inside historic church building on main Market Square in city centre.   Exhibitions & Events 2004 : For up to date details contact the Administrator's Office or visit the website.   Map Ref: 18

Stafford Millennium Embroidery

Samuel Johnson Birthplace Museum

Breadmarket Street, Lichfield WS13 6LG   Tel: 01543 264972   Fax: 01543 414779
Email: sjmuseum@lichfield.gov.uk   Web: www.lichfield.gov.uk/sjmuseum

The birthplace of Dr Samuel Johnson now houses a splendid museum dedicated to the life, work and personality of one of England's greatest writers and most fascinating characters.

Opening Times: Apr to Sep daily 10:30-16:30. Oct to Mar daily 12:00-16:30.   Admission: Adult £2.20, Child/Concession £1.30, Family £5.80.   Location: City centre, location overlooking Market Place.   Map Ref: 18

Staffordshire Regiment Museum

Whittington Barracks, Lichfield WS14 9PY   Tel: 01543 4308/4229   Fax: 01543 434205
Email: museum@rhqstaffords.fsnet.co.uk   Web: www.armymuseums.org.uk

History of the Regiment and its forebears since 1705. Good collections of medals (including British & Victoria Cross sets), uniforms and weapons. Hands on area and quizzes for children. 100 metres of outdoor World War I trench, two World War II Anderson shelters. Key stage 2 and 3 education, archive (booking only).

Opening Times: Year round Tue to Fri 10:00-16:30. Apr to Oct Sat, Sun & BH 12:30-16:30.
Closed Xmas & New Year.   Admission: Adult £2.00, Concession £1.50, Under 5s Free, Family £5.00, Group £1.00. Members of Regiment & Association Free.   Location: On A51 between Lichfield and Tamworth. Between main barracks and golf club.   Map Ref: 19

Wall Roman Site & Museum (Letocetum)
Watling Street, Wall, Lichfield WS14 0AW   Tel: 01543 480768

Wall was once a staging-post on Watling Street, with a bath house and guest house where travellers could stay overnight. The museum houses a display of Romano-British finds from the site including pottery, jewellery, coins and metalwork.

Opening Times: Apr to Sep daily 10:00-18:00, Oct daily 10:00-17:00. Times & prices may change.   Admission: Adult £2.60, Child £1.30, Concession £2.00. EH & NT Members Free.
Location: Off A5 at Wall near Lichfield.   Map Ref: 20

Derbyshire & Staffordshire

Peak District Mining Museum & Temple Mine

The Pavilion, Matlock Bath, Matlock DE4 3NR   Tel: 01629 583834
Email: mail@peakmines.co.uk   Web: www.peakmines.co.uk

Depicting mining in Derbyshire since Roman times, Wills founder engine, Howie mineral collection, rag and chain pump, informative displays. Temple mine shows insight into mineral mining with spacious well lit tunnels.

Opening Times: Apr to Oct daily 10:00-17:00, Nov to Mar daily 11:00-15:00. Closed Xmas.
Admission: Museum or Mine: Adult £2.50, Child/OAP £1.50, Family £6.00. Joint Ticket: Adult £4.00, Child/OAP £2.50, Family £9.00. Group rates available.   Location: Adjacent A6 Matlock Bath.   Map Ref: 21

Sir Richard Arkwrights Cromford Mill

Cromford Mill, Mill Lane, Cromford, Matlock DE4 3RQ   Tel / Fax: 01629 823256

Visit the world's first successful water powered cotton spinning mill. Tours available daily and exhibitions. Part of the Derwent Valley Mills, having reached World Heritage status in December 2000.

Opening Times: Daily 9:00-17:00. Closed Xmas.   Admission: No charge to the site. Tours - Adult £2.00, Concession £1.50.   Location: Off the A6 Derby to Buxton Road, located on the outside of the village of Cromford.   Map Ref: 22

Borough Museum & Art Gallery

Brampton Park, Newcastle-under-Lyme ST5 0QP   Tel: 01782 619705
Fax: 01782 626857   Email: nulmuseum@newcastle-staffs.gov.uk
Web: www.newcastle-staffs.gov.uk/museum.htm

Newcastle's long history can be traced through the Roman period, its medieval castle, Royal Charters and industries. All of these and more are represented in the museum's permanent displays. The art gallery includes local artists, travelling exhibitions and a frequently changing programme of exhibitions, which means that there is always something new to see in both the main art gallery and the small gallery.

Chemist, Victorian Street Scene

Opening Times: Mon to Sat 10:00-17:30, Sun 14:00-17:30.   Admission: Free.   Location: In Brampton Park on Brampton Road (A527), just 1/2 mile from Newcastle Town Centre and three miles from junction 15 of the M6.   Map Ref: 23

Midland Railway - Butterley

Butterley Station, Ripley DE5 3QZ   Tel: 01773 747674   Fax: 01773 510721
Email: info@midlandrailwaycentre.co.uk

Large collection of railway locomotives and rolling stock. Operating standard gauge railway (three and a half miles) and narrow gauge railway (one mile). Farm Park, Country Park, Demonstration Signal Box, Victorian Railwayman's Church and much more.

Opening Times: Daily 10:00-16:00. Trains run weekends throughout the year, Wed Apr to Oct & school holidays. Admission: Adult £7.50, OAP £6.50, Child £3.50, under 3s free.   Location: On B6179, one mile north of Ripley, signposted from A38.   Map Ref: 24
'Midday Midlander' Sunday lunch train departs from Butterley Station

Guided or Private Tours	Disabled Access	Gift Shop or Sales Point	Café or Refreshments	Restaurant	Car Parking

Derbyshire & Staffordshire

in the Art Gallery and Changing Fashions displays. From ancient Roman pots to a Mark XVI Spitfire; from a Staffordshire Wallaby to our famous slipware owl jug; from a Rodin bronze to a popular dolls' house - there is something here for everyone! Enjoy hands-on exhibits, touch-screen computers and a lively programme of holiday activities, talks, tours and workshops. Expert opinion is available through our public enquiry service.

Opening Times: Mar to Oct Mon to Sat 10:00-17:00, Sun 14:00-17:00. Nov to Feb Mon To Sat 10:00-16:00, Sun 13:00-16:00. Admission: Free. Location: In the city centre, within the cultural quarter, one mile from railway station, four miles from junction 15, M6. Map Ref: 27

Spode Museum & Visitor Centre

Church Street, Stoke-on-Trent ST4 1BX Tel: 01782 744011 Fax: 01782 744220
Email: visitorcentre@spode.co.uk Web: www.spode.co.uk

Museum Gallery part of Visitor Centre housing a selection of items produced by Spode from 1770 up to the present day. Contact the Visitor Centre for special exhibitions and more details.

Opening Times: Jan to Dec Mon to Sat 09:00-17:00, Sun 10:00-16:00. Closed 25-26 Dec & New Year. Admission: Adult £2.75, Child/OAP £2.25, Under 5s Free. Location: Town centre, ten minute walk from Stoke-on-Trent railway station. Map Ref: 27

Izaak Walton's Cottage

Worston Lane, Shallowford, Stone ST15 0PA Tel: 01785 760278/619619
Fax: 01785 760278 Email: izaakwaltonscottage@staffordbc.gov.uk
Web: www.staffordbc.gov.uk/heritage

izaak
waLton's
cottage

Izaak Walton, author of 'The Compleat Angler' once owned this charming cottage. There is an Anglers Museum in this 16th century half timbered building, and the splendid rose and herb gardens are a delight to visit.

Opening Times: Apr to Oct Wed to Sun 13:00-17:00. Admission: Free, charges may apply for events. Location: Ten minutes by car from Stafford. Map Ref: 28

Tamworth Castle

The Holloway, Ladybank, Tamworth B79 7NA Tel: 01827 709629 Fax: 01827 709630
Email: heritage@tamworth.gov.uk Web: www.tamworth.gov.uk/tamworthleisure

Dramatic Norman castle with later additions houses furnished room displays plus 'Tamworth Story' and Norman exhibitions. Reputedly haunted by two lady ghosts. With clothes to try on, rubbings and free quizzes, there's lots to interest children.

Opening Times: 15 Feb to 31 Oct Tue to Sun 12:00-17:15. Last admission 16:30. Please telephone for winter opening times. Admission: Admission charge. Location: In town centre, five minute walk from central bus stops, ten minutes from the railway station. Map Ref: 29

Moseley Old Hall

Moseley Old Hall Lane, Fordhouses, Wolverhampton WV10 7HY Tel/Fax: 01902
782808 Email: moseleyoldhall@nationaltrust.org.uk Web: www.nationaltrust.org.uk

This Elizabethan house was built in 1600, and is famous for its association with Charles 11, who hid here after the Battle of Worcester in 1651. There is good collection of 17th century oak furniture. The garden is full of 17th century plants.

Opening Times: 20 Mar to 31 Oct Sat, Sun & Wed 13:00-17:00, 7 Nov to 19 Dec Sun only (guided tours only) 13:00-16:00, Open BH Mons 11:00-17:00 and following Tue. Closed Good Friday. Admission: Adult £4.60, Child £2.30, Family £11.50. Group (15+) £3.90. NT Members £0

Location: 4 miles north of Wolverhampton; south of M54 between A449 and A460. Map Ref: 30

Devon

Devon is a county of great seafarers. It was from the fine natural harbour of Plymouth that the Pilgrim Fathers sailed to the New World, and it was from here that Sir Francis Drake and Sir John Hawkins sailed to confront the mighty Spanish Armada. Between the coasts the county is dominated by lofty brooding Dartmoor and the north of the county includes a part of Exmoor where moorland meets the sea. Exeter, the county town has a magnificent Norman cathedral holding the remarkable Anglo-Saxon Exeter book.

Devon's many excellent museums, mills and historic houses cover all aspects of the regions maritime history, its local industries and social history including 'Dartmoor Life'.

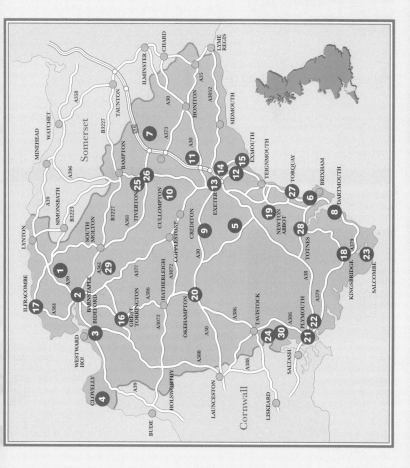

The Red Map References should be used to locate Museums etc on the pages that follow

Devon

Arlington Court

Arlington, Barnstaple EX31 4LP   Tel: 01271 850296   Web: www.nationaltrust.org.uk

The Craven Coach

This Regency house is crowded with treasures amassed by Miss Rosalie Chichester on her travels. The collections include model ships, porcelain, pewter, musical instruments and shells. In the stable block is one of the best collections of 19th century horse-drawn vehicles in the country. The gardens are largely formal with an ornamental pond.

Opening Times: 28 Mar to 31 Oct Sun to Fri 11:00-17:00. Open Good Friday.   Admission: Adult £6.20, Child £3.00, Family £15.00. Group (15+) £5.10. NT Members Free.   Location: On A39, eight miles north of Barnstaple.

Map Ref: 1

Museum of Barnstaple & North Devon

The Square, Barnstaple EX32 8LN   Tel: 01271 346747

Story of North Devon from pre-history to 1930s. Tarka Centre depicting river life and woodland life. Undersea room with replica mammals and fish around North Devon coast. Temporary exhibitions, seven centuries of pottery.

Opening Times: Mon to Sat 09:30-17:00. Closed Sun.   Admission: Free.   Location: By the Long Bridge and Clock Tower.

Map Ref: 2

The Burton Art Gallery & Museum

Kingsley Road, Bideford EX39 2QQ   Tel: 01237 471455
Fax: 01237 473813   Web: www.burtonartgallery.co.uk

MUSEUM ART GALLERY

North Devon Slipware Jugs 19th century

North Devon Slipware, model of Bideford Long Bridge (1280-1925), 17th/18th century coin hoard, Napoleonic bone ship models, Richard Grenville's Elizabethan Charter, 1573; paintings by Coop, Clausen, Fisher, Reynolds, Ackland/Edwards, etc. Exhibitions all year by national & local artists. Craft gallery selling area for regional artists.

Opening Times: Easter to end Oct Tue to Sat 10:00-17:00, Sun 14:00-17:00. Nov to Easter Tue to Sat 10:00-16:00 Sun 14:00-16:00. BH 10:00-17:00. Closed Mon.   Admission: Free.   Location: Near town centre, in Victoria Park, opposite coach park.   Exhibitions & Events 2004 : Jun: 100 Devon Potters, May, Jun & Jul: The Glass Aquarium.

Map Ref: 3

Hartland Abbey

Hartland, Bideford EX39 6DT   Tel: 01237 441264/(01884) 860225
Fax: 01237 441264/(01884) 861134   Web: www.hartlandabbey.com

Hartland Abbey was built 1157. Given by Henry VIII to Sergeant of his Wine Cellar whose descendants live here today. Fascinating collections and architecture, beautiful walled and woodland gardens. Walk to the beach.

Opening Times: Wed, Thu, Sun & BH, plus Tue in Jul & Aug. 14:00-17:30. Gardens open daily except Sat.   Admission: Adult £6.00, OAP £5.50, Child over 9 £1.50. Garden: Adult £4.00, Child 50p.   Location: 15 miles West of Bideford, off A39.

Map Ref: 4

Devon

Devon Guild of Craftsmen

Riverside Mill, Bovey Tracey TQ13 9AF Tel: 01626 832223 Fax: 01626 834220
Email: devonguild@crafts.org.uk Web: www.crafts.org.uk

The South West's leading gallery and craft showrooms with work selected from around 240 designer/makers. Top touring and themed shows in Grade II listed Riverside Mill. Major refurbishment in 2004 to include new gallery, roof terrace café, extended craft shop & lift. Open throughout.

Opening Times: Daily 10:00-17:30. Closed Xmas Day & New Years Day. Admission: Free admission to all exhibitions and facilities.
Location: In the centre of Bovey Tracey, only two miles off A38, Exeter to Plymouth road.   Map Ref: 5

Craft Shop, Devon Guild of Craftsmen

Brixham Heritage Museum & History Society

Bolton Cross, Brixham TQ5 8LZ Tel: 01803 856267 Email: mail@brixhamheritage.org.uk
Web: www.brixhamheritage.org.uk

The museum exhibits Brixham's heritage: the fishing industry, Reverend Lyte (Abide With Me), Victorian Life, World War II, interactive displays, model of former town railway, Napoleonic forts at Berry Head with exhibits of museum's archeological 'digs'.

Opening Times: Mid Feb to Easter 10:00-13:00. Easter to end Oct Mon to Fri 10:00-17:00, Sat 10:00-13:00. Admission: Adult £1.50, Child 75p, OAP £1.25, Family £4.00. Location: Near town centre, one minute walk from central bus station.   Map Ref: 6

Coldharbour Mill Working Wool Museum

Coldharbour Mill, Uffculme, Cullompton EX15 3EE Tel: 01884 840960 Fax: 01884 840858
Email: info@coldharbourmill.org.uk Web: www.coldharbourmill.org.uk

The 200 year old waterside mill houses working spinning and weaving machines, and steam engines restored to their former glory. Picnic areas and gardens.

Opening Times: Mar to Dec daily 10:30-17:00, Feb Mon to Fri, please telephone for details.
Admission: Adult £5.50, Child £2.50, Family £15.00. Location: Five minutes drive off junction 27 of M5, in village of Uffculme.   Map Ref: 7

Dartmouth Museum

The Butterwalk, Duke Street, Dartmouth TQ6 9PZ Tel: 01803 832923
Email: curator@dartmouthmuseum.org.uk Web: www.devonmuseum.net/dartmouth

Local history and maritime museum set in old merchants' house (1640).

Opening Times: Mar to Oct Mon to Sat 10:00-16:30. Nov to Feb Mon to Sat 11:00-15:00.
Admission: Adult £1.50, Child 50p, OAP £1.00. Location: In the town centre.   Map Ref: 8

Castle Drogo

Drewsteignton, Exeter EX6 6PB Tel: 01647 433306 Fax: 01647 433186
Web: www.nationaltrust.org.uk

This granite castle was built in the early 20th century for millionaire Julius Drewe. The interior includes family portraits, oak fittings and furniture by Lutyens. There is a delightful formal garden and many fine walks.

Opening Times: 20 Mar to 31 Oct Wed to Mon 11:00-17:00, 1 Nov to 7 Nov Wed to Mon 11:00-16:00. Admission: Adult £6.20, Child £3.00, Family £15.00. Group Adult £5.25, Child £2.60. NT Members Free. Location: Five miles south of A30 Exeter-Okehampton road via Crockernwell or A382 Moretonhampstead-Whiddon Down road.   Map Ref: 9

Devon

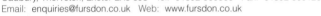

Fursdon House

Cadbury, Thorveton, Exeter EX5 5JS Tel: 01392 860860 Fax: 01392 860126
Email: enquiries@fursdon.co.uk Web: www.fursdon.co.uk

The home of the Fursdons for more than seven hundred years. Tour reflects this long association with Devon. A small museum has family momentoes & costumes.

Opening Times: Easter 10 to 16 Apr. May BH 1 to 8 May. 29 May to 5 Jun. Aug BH 28 Aug to 3 Sep. Tours at 14:30 & 15:30. Admission: Adult £4.00, Under 10 Free, 10 to 16 £2.00.

Map Ref: 10

Killerton House

Broadclyst, Exeter EX5 3LE Tel: 01392 881345
Web: www.nationaltrust.org.uk

The house was rebuilt in 1778 to the design of John Johnson. It houses the Paulise de Bush costume collection displayed in period rooms. The hillside garden features an ice house and an early 19th century rustic-style summer house.

Opening Times: 13 Mar to 31 Mar Wed to Sun 11:00-17:30, 1 Apr to 31 Jul Wed to Mon 11:00-17:30, 1 Aug to 31 Aug daily 11:00-17:30, 1 Sep to 30 Sep Wed to Mon 11:00-17:30, 1 Oct to 31 Oct Wed to Sun 11:00-17:30, 11 Dec to 23 Dec daily 14:00-16:00.
Admission: Adult £5.80, Child £2.85, Family £14.30. Groups £4.80.
NT Members Free. Location: Six miles from Exeter off B3181.

View of a printed cotton dress, 1837, with muslin pelerine and net cap   Map Ref: 11

Powderham Castle

Kenton, Exeter EX6 8LQ Tel: 01626 890243 Fax: 01626 890729
Email: castle@powderham.co.uk Web: www.powderham.co.uk

POWDERHAM CASTLE

Family home of the Earl of Devon. Castle dates back to 1391 and has been in the family for over 600 years. Magnificent state rooms, 17th and 18th century fine furniture, china, paintings. Guided tours throughout the day. Beautiful location in ancient deer park overlooking the Exe Estuary, with tranquil gardens and woodland walks to enjoy.

Opening Times: 4 Apr to 2 Oct Sun to Fri 10:00-17:30.
Admission: Adult £6.90, Child £3.90, OAP £6.45.
Location: Kenton village on A379, eight miles outside Exeter.

Map Ref: 12

Royal Albert Memorial Museum & Art Gallery

Queen Street, Exeter EX4 3RX Tel: 01392 665858

Exeter City Council

From archaeology to zoology this fine building holds outstanding collections of local and national importance and presents a range of exciting displays. Archaeology and Local History Galleries present finds from c.500,000 years ago to the end of the Middle Ages, including a Roman mosaic a reproduction of a Roman bathhouse. Superlactives abound in the Natural History displays, animals from all around the globe including the largest and tallest land mammals - elephant and giraffe - as well as exotic birds and butterflies, sea urchins and starfish. The effect geology has had on the landscape and people of Devon is explored in the Geology at Work Gallery. Three galleries of world cultures present thousands of amazing objects from all around the globe including exceptional Pacific and North West Coast material from the early voyages of Captain Cook. The museum also presents regular themed exhibitions of works

96

Devon

from the Fine Art collection. The Museum shop stocks fascinating items from all over the world and the friendly, licensed café serves snacks, simple meals and a delicious selection of cakes and biscuits.

Opening Times: Mon to Sat 10:00-17:00. Closed BH. Admission: Free. Location: In Queen Street, just off high street in Exeter City Centre. Central Station is 100m away. St David's Station is ten minutes walk or short bus/taxi ride. Exhibitions & Events 2004 : 24 Jan to 26 Apr: Second Skin: everyday and sacred uses of bark worldwide, 31 Jan to 17 Apr: Circled with Stone, 7 Feb to 5 Jun: In Nature's Instant, 12 Jun to 17 Jul: SW Academy of Fine and Applied Arts Open Exhibition, 24 Jul to 11 Sep: A Passion for Plants, 25 Sep to 13 Nov: BP Portrait Award 2004 and BP Travel Award 2003, Oct to Dec: Myth and Legend. Map Ref: 13

Topsham Museum

25 The Strand, Topsham, Exeter EX3 0AX Tel: 01392 873244 Email: museum@topsham.org
Web: www.devonmuseums.net/topsham

Museum situated in 17th century furnished house overlooking Exe Estuary. Exhibits include history of maritime and wildlife around Topsham with multi-media presentations. 2003 Exhibition - Topsham's Burning. The story of the Topsham Fire Service.

Opening Times: Apr to Oct Mon, Wed, Sat & Sun 14:00-17:00. Admission: Free. Annual membership subscription £7.00 per person or £13.00 for two people at the same address. Location: 300 yards from Topsham Quay - terminus of the 'T' bus from centre of Exeter.
Map Ref: 14

A La Ronde

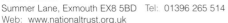

Summer Lane, Exmouth EX8 5BD Tel: 01396 265 514
Web: www.nationaltrust.org.uk

A unique 16-sided house built in the late 18th century. The fascinating interior includes a feather frieze and a shell-encrusted gallery.

Opening Times: 31 Mar to 31 Oct Sun to Thu 11:00-17:30. Admission: Adult £4.20, Child £2.10. NT Members Free. Location: Two miles north of Exmouth on A376. Map Ref: 15

Shell picture of a house, 18th-century

Torrington Museum & Archive

Town Hall Building, The Square, Great Torrington EX38 8HN Tel: 01805 624324

Local bygones, local industries and personalities, 17th to 20th century portrait collection, extensive family archive, domestic and agricultural equipment, features on Thomas Fowler (inventor of Thermosyphon and calculator) and Keble Martin of Concise British Flora fame.

Opening Times: May to Sep daily 11:00-16:00, Sat 11:00-13:30. Admission: Free. Location: In Town Hall building, The Square. Map Ref: 16

Ilfracombe Museum

Runnymede Gardens, Wilder Road, Ilfracombe EX34 8AF Tel: 01271 863541
Email: ilfracombe@devonmuseums.net Web: www.devonmuseums.net

A fascinating collection started in 1932 by Mervyn G Palmer who collected in South America for the British Museum. Be amazed by the variety of displays, some slightly old fashioned but popular: Granny's attic, childhood memories, butterflies, beetles, bats, ethnography, Lundy Island, ship to shore radio, yesterday's domestic luxuries, Victorian costume and trinkets, Ilfracombe railway and paddle steamer history and lots more.

Opening Times: Apr to Oct daily 10:00-17:00, Nov to Mar Mon to Fri 10:00-13:00. Admission: Adults £1.50, Child 50p, OAP/Concessions £1.00. Location: Next to Landmark Theatre on sea front. Map Ref: 17

Devon

Cookworthy Museum

The Old Grammar School, 108 Fore Street, Kingsbridge TQ7 1AW   Tel: 01548 853235
Email: wcookworthy@talk21.com

Discover the story of Kingsbridge in our 17th century school room, complete walk in Victorian kitchen, Edwardian pharmacy, large farm gallery in walled garden. With everything from costumes to carts this lively museum provides something for all the family.

Opening Times: 29 Mar to Sep Mon to Sat 10:30-17:00, Oct 10:30-16:00. Local Heritage Resource Centre open throughout the year. Admission: Adult £2.00, Child 90p, OAP £1.50, Family £5.00, Group £1.50 per person, child 45p. Location: 100 metres up Fore Street from Cookworthy Road car park.
Map Ref: 18

Bradley

Newton Abbot TQ12 6BN   Tel: 01626 354 513   Web: www.nationaltrust.org.uk

A small medieval manor house set in woodland. The house contains Tudor wall paintings, oak furniture and a fine carved wooden screen in the hall. There is also a collection of family memorabilia.

Opening Times: 1 Apr-30 Sep Tue to Thu. Admission: Adult £3.00, Child £1.50. NT Members Free. Location: Half a mile from town centre on Totnes road A381.
Map Ref: 19

Museum of Dartmoor Life

Museum Courtyard, 3 West Street,
Okehampton EX20 1HQ
Tel: 01837 52295   Fax: 01837 659330
Email: dartmoormuseum@eclipse.co.uk
Web: museumofdartmoorlife.eclipse.co.uk

Housed on three floors in an early 19th century mill, this lively museum tells the story of how people have lived, worked and played on and around Dartmoor through the centuries. It shows how the moorland has shaped their lives just as their work has shaped the moorland. In the Cranmere Gallery, temporary exhibitions feature local history, art and crafts. Closed for refurbishment, re-opens May 2004.

Opening Times: Easter to Oct Mon to Sat 10:00-17:00, plus Sun Jun to Sep 10:00-16:30. Admission: Adult £2.00, Child/Student £1.00, OAP £1.80, Family £5.60. Group/School rates available.
Location: Centre of Okehampton, next door to The White Hart Hotel.
Map Ref: 20

Elizabethan House

32 New Street, Plymouth PL1 2NA   Tel: 01752 304774

This rare survival of a sea captain's or merchant's house in the centre of Elizabethan Plymouth is 400 years old. The house retains most of its original architectural features and the rooms contain period furniture.

Opening Times: Easter to end of Sep Wed to Sun & BH 10:00-17:00. Admission: Adult £1.25, Child 75p. Location: Situated in the historic Barbican, follow brown tourism signs from city centre.
Map Ref: 21

Merchants House

33 St Andrews Street, Plymouth   Tel: 01752 304774

The largest and finest merchant's house of the 16th and 17th centuries left in Plymouth. Recently restored, it contains fascinating displays that bring the city's history to life. The exhibits include a Victorian schoolroom, a Plymouth Blitz exhibition, photographs of old Plymouth and the Park Pharmacy Shop.

Opening Times: Easter to end of Sep Tue to Fri 10:00-17:30, Sat & BH 10:00-17:00.
Admission: Adult £1.25, Child 75p. Location: Off Royal Parade near St Andrew's Church. Follow signs.
Map Ref: 21

Devon

Plymouth City Museum & Art Gallery   ♿ ❂

Drake Circus, Plymouth PL4 8AJ Tel: 01752 304774 Fax: 01752 304775
Email: plymouth.museum@plymouth.gov.uk Web: www.plymouthmuseum.gov.uk

The building has been a focal point of the city since 1910, and miraculously survived the Second World War Blitz. It holds important works of art including the Cottonian Collection, featuring paintings by Joshua Reynolds, the Plymouth artist, works by the Newlyn School, Maritime Paintings, Plymouth Silver and Porcelain. Redisplayed Natural History Gallery opening May 2004. Exciting programme of changing exhibitions and events. Tales from the City is a special exhibition involving 1000 people telling the story of 20th century Plymouth in their own words.

Opening Times: Tue to Fri 10:00-17:30, Sat & BH Mon 10:00-17:00. Admission: Free. Location: Near the city centre, opposite the university. Five minutes walk from the railway station.   Map Ref: 21

Porcelain fiigures of Chelse
fiishermen, after Meissen b
Chelsea c. 1755

Saltram House   ♿ ❂ ☕

Plympton, Plymouth PL7 1UH
Tel: 01752 333500 Fax: 01752 336474
Email: saltram@nationaltrust.org.uk
Web: www.nationaltrust.org.uk

A remarkable George II mansion with magnificient state rooms. There are exquisite plasterwork ceilings and four rooms are decorated with 18th century Chinese wallpaper. The house contains fine period furniture, china, pictures and a doll's house. The superb 18th century gardens have an orangery and several follies.

Opening Times: 27 Mar to 30 Sep Sat to Thu 12:00-16:30, 2 Oct to 31 Oct Sat to Thu 11:30-15:30. Open Good Friday.
Admission: House: Adult £6.60, Child £3.20, Family £16.30. Group (15+) £5.80. NT Members Free. Location: Three and half miles east of Plymouth city centre, between Plymouth-Exeter road (A38) and Plymouth-Kingsbridge road (A379); take Plympton turn at Marsh Mills roundabout.   Map Ref: 22

Smeatons Tower

The Hoe, Plymouth PL1 2PA Tel: 01752 600608

The former Eddystone Lighthouse built in 1759. Recently conserved and redisplayed as the lighthouse would have been around the mid-19th century.

Opening Times: Tue to Sat 10:00-16:00. Admission: Adult £2.00, Child £1.00. Location: On Plymouth Hoe, five minutes walk from city centre.   Map Ref: 21

Overbecks Museum & Garden   ☜ ♿ ❂ ☕ ⚓

Sharpitor, Salcombe TQ8 8LW Tel: 01548 842 893 Web: www.nationaltrust.org.uk

This elegant Edwardian house contains the eclectic collections of the scientist Otto Overbeck. Among the items are late 19th century photographs of the area, shipbuilding tools, model boats, toys, shells, and a nautical collection. There is also a collection of dolls and doll's furniture. The garden overlooks the sea and is home to many rare plants.

Opening Times: 29 Mar to 30 Jul Sun to Fri 11:00-17:30, 1 Aug to 31 Aug daily,11:00-17:30, 1 Sep to 30 Sep Sun to Fri 11:00-17:30, 3 Oct to 31 Oct Sun to Thu 11:00-17:00.
Admission: Adult £4.60, Child £2.30, Family £11.50. NT Members Free. Location: One and half miles south west of Salcombe, signposted from Marlborough and Salcombe. Map Ref: 23

Morwellham Quay Museum   ☜ ♿ ❂ ☕ ◉ ⚓

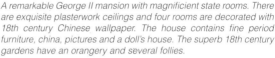

Morwellham, Tavistock PL19 8JL Tel: 01822 832766 Fax: 01822 833808
Email: enquiries@morwellham-quay.co.uk Web: www.morwellham-quay.co.uk

MORWELLHAM
—QUAY—
HISTORIC PORT & COPPER MINE

The greatest copper port in Queen Victoria's empire lies 23 miles inland. The Tamar ketch 'Garlandstone' is moored at the quay; original cottages, shops and hostelry. 1860s costumed staff

Devon

welcome visitors and host guided tours. Explore one of the copper mines travelling by tram deep underground. In grounds extending to 150 acres enjoy carriage rides; a visit to the farm; the wildlife reserve. Live the history - wear Victorian fashion. Activities throughout the day.

Opening Times: 25 Mar to 3 Nov daily 10:00-17:30. 4 Nov to 29 Mar daily 10:00-16:30. Admission: Main Season: Adult £8.90, Child £6.00, Family £26.00, Senior £7.80. Winter: Adult £5.00, Child £3.00, Senior £4.00. Location: Valley adjacent River Tamar, approx two miles from railway, four miles from Tavistock. Map Ref: 24

TIVERTON

Knightshayes Court
Bolham, Tiverton EX16 7RQ Tel: 01884 254665
Fax: 01884 243050 Web: www.nationaltrust.org.uk

Designed by William Burges, building began in 1869 and is a rare survival of his domestic work. There is a collection of family portraits, furniture and 17th-century majolica. The garden features a lily pond, topiary and rare shrubs.

Opening Times: 27 Mar to 30 Sep Sat to Thu 11:00-17:30, 2 Oct to 31 Oct Sat to Thu 11:00-16:00. Open Good Friday.
Admission: Adult £6.20, Child £3.10, Family £14.80. Group Adult £5.20, Child £2.60. NT Members Free. Location: Two miles north of Tiverton; turn right off Tiverton-Bampton road (A396) at Bolham.
'A Lady in a White Cap', artist unknown, in the Drawing Room Map Ref: 25

Tiverton Castle
Tiverton EX16 6RP Tel: 01884 253200/255200 Fax: 01884 254200
Email: tiverton.castle@ukf.net Web: www.tivertoncastle.com

Historic medieval Castle with fascinating history, home of Princess Katherine Plantagenet, and later besieged by Fairfax in the Civil War, now contains important armoury - try some on. Interesting furniture, pictures. Beautiful garden.

Opening Times: Easter Sun to end June & Sep Sun, Thu & BH Mon. Jul & Aug Sun to Thu. 14:30-17:30. Admission: Adult £4.00, Child (7-16) £2.00, Under 7 Free. Map Ref: 26

Tiverton Museum of Mid-Devon Life
Beck's Square, Tiverton EX16 6PJ Tel: 01884 256295 Email: tivertonmus@eclipse.uk
Web: www.tivertonmuseum.org.uk

Large regional museum with collections of mid-Devon social history including agriculture, farm equipment, wagons and carts and GWR memorabilia, including Loco 1442 'Tivvy Bumper'. 15 galleries and display areas.

Opening Times: Feb to Xmas Mon to Fri 10:30-16:30, Sat 10:00-13:00. Admission: Adult £3.50, Child £1.00, OAP £2.50, Family £8.00. Group rates available. Location: Near to the town centre and bus station. Map Ref: 26

Key to Classifications
see Classifications Index on page 423

Anthropology	Horticultural	Police, Prisons
Archaeological	Jewellery	& Dungeons
Art Galleries	Literature & Libraries	Railways
Arts, Crafts & Textiles	Maritime	Religion
China, Glass & Ceramics	Military & Defence	Roman
Communications	Multicultural	Science - Earth & Planetary
Egyptian	Music & Theatre	Sculpture
Fashion	Natural History	Sporting History
Geology	Oriental	Toy & Childhood
Health & Medicine	Palaces	Transport
Historic Houses	Photography	Victoriana

Devon

Torquay Museum

529 Babbacombe Road, Torquay TQ1 1HG   Tel: 01803 293975
Fax: 01803 294186

Torquay Museum re-opened after extensive lottery funded improvements. New galleries include the Devon Farmhouse, re-designed Agatha Christie Exhibition celebrating Torquay's most famous daughter and the exciting and innovative Time Ark Gallery with interactives for children. See the giant replica of a Japanese man-flying kite in the entance hall.

Also archaeology, including Kents Cevern material, natural history, geology, local history, Victoriana, world adornment, ancient Egyptians and wartime photography of Torquay. New local studies centre is open two days per week for local history research. Holiday activities and events.

Schoolgroup viewing the Japanese man-fllying kite

Opening Times: Mon to Sat 10:00-17:00, Sun (Easter to Oct) 13:30-17:00.   Admission: Adult £3.00, Child £1.50, OAP £2.00, Family £7.50.   Location: Six minutes walking from clocktower at bottom of Torwood Street (near harbour). 32 bus stop outside.   Map Ref: 27

Torre Abbey Historic House & Gallery

TORRE ABBEY

The Kings Drive, Torquay TQ2 5JE   Tel: 01803 293593
Fax: 01803 215948   Email: torre-abbey@torbay.gov.uk   Web: www.torre-abbey.org.uk

Founded as a monastery in 1196, the present appearance of Torre Abbey dates from 1741-3, when it was remodelled by the Cary family. As well as nationally important monastic remains, today's visitors can see over 20 historic rooms, which contain Devon's largest art gallery together with room settings and mementoes of crime writer Agatha Christie. Teas are served in the Victorian kitchen.

Opening Times: 1 Apr to 1 Nov daily 09:30-18:00. 2 Nov to Easter open to Groups by appointment only.
Admission: Adult £3.50, Child £1.70, OAP/Student £3.00, Family £7.75.   Location: On Torquay sea front, next to the Riviera Centre.   Map Ref: 27

Torre Abbey, West Wing

Totnes Costume Museum

Bogan House, 43 High Street, Totnes TQ9 5NP

Themed costume exhibition, changed annually. Collection holds examples of fashionable clothing for men, women and children - 18th, 19th and 20th century. Displayed in one of the most interesting Tudor merchants' houses in Totnes.

Opening Times: 27 May to end Sep Tue to Fri 11:00-17:00. Oct by appointment.
Admission: Adult £2.00, Child 80p, Concession £1.50, Family £4.00.   Location: Centre of town, opposite Market Square.   Map Ref: 28

Totnes Elizabethan House Museum

70 Fore Street, Totnes TQ9 5RU   Tel: 01803 863821   Email: totnesmuseum@btconnect.com

Grade I Elizabethan Merchant's House c.1575. Collections cover local history, archaeology, crafts, industries, clocks, costumes etc. Also room devoted to computer pioneer Charles Babbage and his inventions.

Opening Times: Apr to Oct Mon to Fri 10:30-17:00. Other times by appointment.
Admission: Adult £1.50, accompanied Child 25p, OAP/Student/Concession £1.00, Totnes residents (with proof) Free.   Location: In main street, very central.   Map Ref: 28

Devon

Cobbaton Combat Collection

Chittlehampton, Umberleigh EX37 9RZ   Tel: 01769 540 740   Fax: 01769 540 141
Email: info@cobbatoncombat.co.uk   Web: www.cobbatoncombat.co.uk

Over 60 mainly World War II vehicles and artillery pieces, plus thousands of smaller items. All undercover, including Home Front building. Militaria and souvenir shop, NAAFI wagon, disabled facilities, picnic area.

Opening Times: 1 Apr to 31 Oct 10:00-17:00 except Sat. Winter most weekdays, please phone.
Admission: 2003 - Adult £4.50, Child £3.00, OAP £4.00.   Location: Six miles south east of
Barnstaple, eight miles west of South Molton.   Map Ref: 29

The cider press in the Great Barn

Buckland Abbey

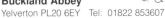

Yelverton PL20 6EY   Tel: 01822 853607
Fax: 01822 855448
Email: bucklandabbey@nationaltrust.org.uk
Web: www.nationaltrust.org.uk

Tucked away in its own secluded valley above the River Tavy, Buckland was originally a small but influential Cistercian monastery. The house has rich associations with Sir Francis Drake and contains much interesting memorabilia. There are exhibitions of seven centuries of history at Buckland, as well as a magnificent monastic barn, craft workshop, herb garden and delightful estate walks.

Opening Times: 14 Apr to 21 Mar Sat & Sun 14:00-17:00, 27 Mar
to 31 Oct Fri to Wed 10:30-17:30, 6 Nov to 19 Dec Sat & Sun 14:00-
17:00, 19 Feb to 27 Mar Sat & Sun14:00- 17:00, 19 Feb to 27 Mar
Sat & Sun 14:00-17:00.   Admission: House & Estate: Adult £5.30,
Child £2.60, Family £13.52. Group (15+) £4.40.Garden only: Adult £2.90, Child £1.40. NT
Members Free.   Location: Six miles south of Tavistock, 11 miles north of Plymouth. Map Ref: 30

Dorset

Dorset has great literary connections, there being few parts of the county that Thomas Hardy has not lovingly written about. It is renowned for its beautiful countryside, but can also lay claim to some delightful seaside towns. Poole, once the haunt of pirates and smugglers, was developed as a major port in the 13th century.

The county is rich in history and has a wonderfully wide and comprehensive selection of exhibitions, displays and demonstrations portraying its diverse heritage as well as subjects from Dinosaurs to Tutankhamun.

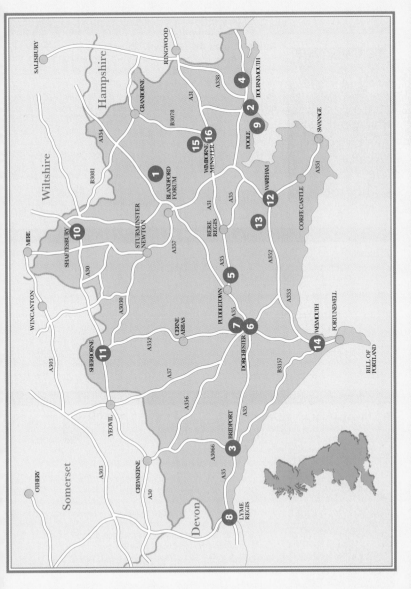

The Red Map References should be used to locate Museums etc on the pages that follow

Dorset

Royal Signals Museum

Blandford Camp DT11 8RH   Tel: 01258 482248   Fax: 01258 482084   Email: royalsignals
Web: www.royalsignals.army.org.uk/museum

Interactive communications, science and technology. Plus a unique series of hands-on exhibitions featuring Enigma, SOE and Elite Special Forces. Prize winning Fun and Discovery trails for children.

Opening Times: All year Mon to Fri 10:00-17:00, end of Feb to Oct also Sat & Sun 10:00-16:00. Closed 2 weeks Xmas.   Admission: Adult £4.50, Child £2.50, OAP £3.50, Family £11.00.
Location: On Blandford Camp, follow the signs from A354 Bypass and bring some form of ID.

Map Ref: 1

Russell-Cotes Art Gallery & Museum

East Cliff, Bournemouth BH1 3AA   Tel: 01202 451858
Fax: 01202 451851   Email: kathy.walker@bournemouth.gov.uk
Web: www.russell-cotes.bournemouth.gov.uk

The Art Gallery and Museum is a Victorian villa, built and furnished by Sir Merton and Lady Annie Russell-Cotes and gifted to the town in 1908. The Victorian house is of architectural and historic importance with a remarkable interior, which houses a diverse collection of British fine art and ethnographic objects. Additional art galleries were built in the 1920s to house more of the founder's collections.

Opening Times: Tue to Sun 10:00-17:00. Closed Mon, Good Friday and 25 Dec.   Admission: Free.   Location: On the cliff top overlooking the sea. Five minute walk from the town centre to the east.

Map Ref: 2

Bridport

South Street, Bridport DT6 3NR   Tel: 01308 458703/422116   Fax: 01308 458704
Email: sh-bridportmus@btconnect.com

From Romans to ropemaking. The development of Bridport is told from its Saxon origins to the present day. The history of the world-famous rope and net industry is covered, along with stories of local people and events. Finds from a nearby Roman hillfort are on display. Temporary exhibitions show the extensive fine art and photograph collections. Local History Centre open year round - call for details.

Opening Times: Apr to Oct Mon to Sat 10:00-17:00. Closed Sun.   Admission: Adult £2.00, accompanied Child Free, unaccompanied Child 50p.   Location: In town centre.   Exhibitions & Events 2004 : For details please telephone.

Map Ref: 3

Red House Museum & Gardens

Hampshire
County
Council

Quay Road, Christchurch BH23 1BU   Tel: 01202 482860
Fax: 01202 481924
Email: jim.hunter@hants.gov.uk
Web: www.hants.gov.uk/museum/redhouse

The Red House Museum and Gardens (once a Georgian Workhouse) is the setting for outstanding displays of local social and natural history. Highlights include an interactive archaeology gallery, a display of Arthur Romney Green furniture in a 1930s room setting and a reconstruction of a local 19th century High Street taxidermist. Special exhibitions of contemporary and traditional art and an ever changing garden make every visit a new one.

Opening Times: Tue to Sat 10:00-17:00, Sun 14:00-17:00. Open spring and summer BH Mon.   Admission: Adult £1.50, Concession 80p, Family £3.50. Free to residents of Hants & Dorset C.C. and Christchurch Borough.   Location: Near town centre and

Dorset

Christchurch Priory, close to Quay. Exhibitions & Events 2004 : 10 Jan to 27 Apr: Marvellous Meals - A Potted History of Food, May/Jun: Roses, Jul/Aug: Christchurch Arts Guild exhibition of members work, Sep/Dec: Invaders - Solve the Ancient Mystery in this interactive exhibition.

Map Ref: 4

DORCHESTER

Athelhampton House & Gardens

Athelhampton, Dorchester DT2 7LG Tel: 01305 848363 Fax: 01305 848135
Email: enquiry@athelhampton.co.uk Web: www.athelhampton.co.uk

One of the finest 15th century manor houses with its Great Hall and fine collection of English furniture. Grade 1 listed gardens with famous topiary pyramids, fountains and the River Piddle.

Opening Times: Mar to Oct Daily except Fri & Sat, Nov to Feb Sun only 10:30-17:00.
Admission: Adult £7.75, OAP £7.00, Child Free, Student/Disabled £5.50.
Location: Athelhampton

Map Ref: 5

Tyrannosaurus rex

Dinosaur Museum

Icen Way, Dorchester DT1 1EW Tel: 01305 269880 Fax: 01305 268885
Email: info@thedinosaurmuseum.com
Web: www.thedinosaurmuseum.com

Explore the enthralling pre-historic world of dinosaurs through actual fossils, skeletons, and life-size dinosaur reconstructions combined with hands-on, video and computer displays at this award-winning museum. The museum's innovative and friendly approach mean it was voted one of Britain's top ten Hands-On Museums and make it a must for all families. It's frequently featured on national television.

Opening Times: Apr to Oct daily 09:30-17:30, Nov to Mar daily 10:00-16:30. Closed 24-26 Dec. Admission: Adult £5.50, Child £3.95, Under 4s Free, OAP/Student £4.75, Family £15.95.
Location: In centre of town - follow pedestrian signposts from car parks.

Map Ref: 6

Dorset County Museum

High West Street, Dorchester DT1 1XA Tel: 01305 262735 Fax: 01305 257180
Email: dorsetcountymuseum@dor-mus.demon.co.uk Web: www.dorsetcountymuseum.org

Roman Mosaic Floors

Free audio-guides cover 60 key exhibits. Enjoy walking on the royal mosaic floors in the magnificent Victorian Hall. Visit the Dorchester Gallery depicting Dorchester's history from six thousand years ago to today. Other galleries include Archaeology (illustrating the life of Maiden Castle), Geology, Natural History and The Dorset Writers Gallery. This houses the largest collection of Thomas Hardy memorabilia in the world, and includes a reconstruction of the Max Gate Study. There is a variety of children's trails and interactives, making it a museum for all the family.

Opening Times: 1 Jul to 30 Sep daily 10:00-17:00, 1 Oct to 30 Jun Mon to Sat 10:00-17:00. Admission: Adult £4.20, Child Free (up to 2 children), Concession £3.20. Location: In middle of town centre.

Map Ref: 6

Dorset Teddy Bear Museum

Antelope Walk, Dorchester DT1 1BE Tel: 01305 263200 Fax: 01305 268885
Email: info@teddybearhouse.co.uk Web: www.teddybearhouse.co.uk

Visit Edward Bear and his extended family of human-sized teddy bears in their Edwardian style home, then marvel at bears from throughout the last century displayed in atmospheric settings.

Opening Times: Daily 09:30-17:00. Closed 25-26 Dec. Admission: Adult £2.95, Child £1.95, Family £8.95. Location: In centre of Dorchester, pedestrian signposted from car parks.

Map Ref: 6

Dorset

DORCHESTER (continued)

The Keep Military Museum

1 Bridport Road, Dorchester DT1 1RN   Tel: 01305 264066   Fax: 01305 250373
Email: keep.museum@talk21.com   Web: www.keepmilitarymuseum.org

A military museum housing the artefacts of the Infantry and Yeomanry regiments of Devon and Dorset, housed in a Grade II listed building.

Opening Times: Apr to Sep Mon to Sat 09:30-17:00, Sun (Jul to Aug) 10:00-16:00. Oct to Mar Tue to Sat 09:30-17:00.   Admission: Adult £3.00, Child/OAP £2.00. Group/Family rates available.   Location: On the junction of Bridport Road and High West Street at the top of the town.   Map Ref: 6

Old Crown Court & Cells

58/60 High West Street, Dorchester DT1 1UZ   Tel: 01305 252241   Fax: 01305 257039   Email: tourism@westdorset-dc.gov.uk   Web: www.westdorset.com

1. Old Crown Court, Dorchester.
©West Dorset District Council

The Court is famous for the trial of the Tolpuddle Martyrs in 1834. Experience four centuries of gruesome crime and punishment in a setting little changed over the years. Stand in the dock and sit in the dimly lit Cells where prisoners waited for their appearance before the judge.

Opening Times: Court Room & Cells: 19 Jul to 10 Sep Mon to Fri 14:00-16:00, (excluding BH) & Wed 10:00-12:00. Court Room only at other times during office hours. Admission: Charge for Adults, accompanied Under 16s Free.   Location: Town centre approx. 300 metres from Top o' Town coach/car park.   Exhibitions & Events 2004 : 17 & 18 Jul: Tolpuddle Martyrs Festival, 11 & 12 Sep: Civic Trust Heritage.   Map Ref: 6

Terracotta Warriors Museum

High East Street, Dorchester DT1 1JU   Tel: 01305 266040   Fax: 01305 268885
Email: info@terracottawarriors.co.uk   Web: www.terracottawarriors.co.uk

The only museum devoted to the terracotta warriors - 8th Wonder of the Ancient World - outside of China. See unique museum replicas from China, costumes and armour recreated, and multimedia presentations.

Opening Times: Daily 10:00-17:30. Please phone for winter hours. Closed 25-26 Dec.
Admission: Adult £4.75, Child £2.95, Under 5s Free, OAP/Student £3.75, Family £13.95.
Location: In centre of Dorchester.   Map Ref: 6

The Golden Funerary Mask

Tutankhamun Exhibition

High West Street, Dorchester DT1 1UW
Tel: 01305 269571   Fax: 01305 268885
Email: info@tutankhamun-exhibition.co.uk
Web: www.tutankhamun-exhibition.co.uk

Experience the mystery and the wonder of the world's greatest discovery of ancient treasure. Tutankhamun's tomb, treasures, jewels and mummified body are exquisitely recreated through sight, sound and smell. Be at the discovery, explore the ante-chamber and the burial chamber. Finally marvel at the superb facsimilies of Tutankhamun's greatest golden treasures including the golden Funerary Mask and the Harpooner.

Opening Times: Apr to Oct daily 09:30-17:30, Nov to Mar Mon to Fri 09:30-17:00, Sat & Sun 10:00-17:00. Closed 24-26 Dec.
Admission: Adult £5.50, Child £3.95, Under 5s Free, OAP/Student £4.75, Family £15.95.   Location: In centre of Dorchester, pedestrian signposted from car parks.
Map Ref: 6

Guided or Private Tours	Disabled Access	Gift Shop or Sales Point	Café or Refreshments	Restaurant	Car Parking

Dorset

Wolfeton House

Dorchester DT2 9QN   Tel: 01305 263500   Fax: 01305 265090
Email: kthimbleby@wolfeton.freeserve.co.uk

Grade 1 Medieval and Elizabethan House. Carved oak panelling, plaster ceilings, grand fireplaces, unique stone great stairs. 17th Century pictures & furniture, medieval Gatehouse and Cider House.

Opening Times: Jun to Sep Mon, Wed & Thu 14:00-18:00. Groups by appointment all year.
Admission: £4.00.   Location: One and a half miles from Dorchester on A37 towards Yeovil.
Map Ref: 7

LYME REGIS

Lyme Regis Philpot Museum

Bridge Street, Lyme Regis DT7 3QA   Tel: 01297 443370
Email: info@lymeregismuseum.co.uk   Web: www.lymeregismuseum.co.uk

THE AWARD-WINNING
LYME REGIS
MUSEUM

The museum tells the story of Lyme Regis and its landscape, with award winning displays featuring: early history from prehistoric to civil war; the Cobb harbour and Lyme's involvement with the sea; fossils and geology, and the importance of local personalities such as Mary Anning; Lyme's literary connections from Henry Fielding and Jane Austen to John Fowles.

Opening Times: Apr to Oct Mon to Sat 10:00-17:00, Sun 11:00-17:00. Nov to Mar Sat 10:00-17:00, Sun 11:00-17:00, weekdays in school holidays.   Admission: Adult £2.00, Child Free, Concession £1.50.   Location: In the centre of town facing the sea and beside the Guildhall and tourist information centre.
Map Ref: 8

POOLE

Scaplen's Court Museum

High Street, Poole BH15 1BW   Tel: 01202 262600   Fax: 01202 262622
Email: museums@poole.gov.uk   Web: www.poole.com

Scaplen's Court is part of the museum's education service. It is only open to the general public during the month of August or for special events, which are advertised locally.

Opening Times: Aug Mon to Sat 10:00-17:00, Sun 12:00-17:00.   Admission: Free.
Location: Adjacent to Waterfront Museum, off Poole Quay.
Map Ref: 9

Waterfront Museum
&

4 High Street, Poole BH15 1BW   Tel: 01202 262600   Fax: 01202 262622
Email: museums@poole.gov.uk   Web: www.poole.com

Waterfront Museum tells of Poole's history. Displays include a street scene, Roman occupation, trade with Newfoundland, the Studland Bay Wreck and more. Poole Local History Centre offers research facilities on the history of the town.

Opening Times: Museum: Apr to Oct Mon to Sat 10:00-17:00, Sun 12:00-17:00. Nov to Mar Mon to Sat 10:00-15:00, Sun 12:00-15:00. Local History Centre: All year Tue to Sat 10:00-15:00.
Admission: Free.   Location: Adjacent to Poole Quay
Map Ref: 9

SHAFTESBURY

Shaftesbury Town Museum

Gold Hill, Shaftesbury SP7 8JW   Tel: 01747 852157

Special items reflecting life in Shaftesbury, domestically and agriculturally with some civic items. Two floors with special displays each year.

Opening Times: Easter to end Oct daily 10:30-16:30.   Admission: Adult £1.00, Child Free.
Location: Top of Gold Hill, behind Town Hall, centre of town.
Map Ref: 10

www.mghh.co.uk

For current information on the outstanding Collections in over 1600 Museums, Galleries & Historic Houses in England, Scotland, Wales and Ireland

Dorset

Sherborne Castle

New Road, Sherborne DT9 5NR   Tel: 01935 813182   Fax: 01935 816727
Email: enquiries@sherbornecastle.com   Web: www.sherbornecastle.com

Historic country house built by Sir Walter Raleigh in 1594 and extended by the Digby family who's home it has been since 1617. Fine collections of pictures, English furniture, Oriental and European ceramics representing four hundred years of collecting. Delightful setting with lakeside gardens and parkland landscaped by Capability Brown. Walks round the lake give views of the deer park and ruined Old Castle.

Opening Times: Apr to Oct daily except Mon & Fri 11:00-16:30. Also open BH. Guided tours by arrangement.
Admission: Gardens: Adult £3.50, Child Free. Castle &
Gardens: Adult £7.00, Child Free, OAP £6.50.   Location: Near town centre, five minute walk from London/Waterloo to Exeter mainline railway.   Map Ref: 11

Clouds Hill

Wareham BH20 7NQ   Tel: 01929 405616   Web: www.nationaltrust.org.uk

A tiny isolated brick and tile cottage, bought in 1925 by T.E.Lawrence as a retreat. There is a good collection of Lawrence memorabilia and furniture designed by him.

Opening Times: 1 Apr to 31 Oct Thu to Sun 12:00-17:00. Open BH Mons.   Admission: Adult £3.10, no reduction for children. NT Members Free.   Location: Nine miles east of Dorchester, one and a half miles east of Waddock crossroads, (B3390), four miles south of A35 Poole-Dorchester road.   Map Ref: 12

Tank Museum

Bovington, near Wool, Wareham BH20 6JG   Tel: 01929 405096   Fax: 01929 405360   Email: davidb@tankmuseum.co.uk   Web: www.tankmuseum.co.uk

The Tank Museum houses the world's finest international indoor collection of Armoured Fighting Vehicles; there are 150 vehicles from 26 different countries. Free audio guides available, large car park, outdoor children's play area, large specialist gift and model shop and licensed restaurant. During school holidays the exhibits are brought to life with live demonstrations and Tanks in Action displays throughout the summer.

Opening Times: Daily 10:00-17:00. Closed Xmas.
Admission: Please phone for prices.   Location: In the village of Bovington, near Wool which is a main-line station from Waterloo.   Map Ref: 13

The famous Bovington Tiger

Nothe Fort

Barrack Road, Weymouth DT4 8UF   Tel: 01305 766626

A dramatically restored Victorian fort with ramparts, gun floors and magazines furnished as a museum of coastal defence. 70 rooms of guns, equipment, displays, models, artefact and military memorabilia.

Opening Times: 4 Apr to 18 Apr, 1 May to 30 Sep, 24 Oct to 31 Oct, Sun all year 10:30-17:30 (16:30 winters).   Admission: Adult £3.50, Concessions £2.50.   Location: 15 minute walk from town centre or rowboat ferry from Pavilion.   Map Ref: 14

Guided or Private Tours	Disabled Access	Gift Shop or Sales Point	Café or Refreshments	Restaurant	Car Parking

Dorset

Weymouth Museum & Exhibition Gallery

   ♿ ▯ 🚐

Brewers' Quay, Hope Square, Weymouth DT4 8TR Tel: 01305 777622 Fax: 01305 761680

Collections of local and social history, costumes, prints and paintings - including The Russell Collection, and Borough Archives. Regular Exhibitions during the year.

Opening Times: Daily 10:00-17:00, except second two weeks in Jan. Admission: Free. Location: Situated at the Brewers Quay Complex. Follow brown signs. Map Ref: 14

Statue of George III, stands on a fine Georgian Esplanade

Kingston Lacy

Wimborne Minster BH21 4EA Tel: 01202 883402/842913 Fax: 01202 882402
Email: kingstonlacy@nationaltrust.org.uk

This 17th century house was the home of the Bankes family for over 300 years, and replaced the ruined family seat at Corfe Castle. The house contains an outstanding collection of paintings and other works of art. There is the dramatic Spanish Room, with walls hung in magnificent gilded leather. There is also furniture, books, Italian sculptures and bronzes. The garden is set in a wooded park with attractive walks.

The Library with a selection of portraits by Sir Peter Lely

Opening Times: House: 20 Mar to 31 Oct Wed to Sun 11:00-17:00. Open BH Mons. Garden & Park: 20 Mar to 31 Oct Daily 10:30-18:00, 5 Nov to 19 Dec Fri to Sun 10:30-16:00, 5 Feb to 20 Mar Sat & Sun 10:30-16:00.
Admission: Adult £7.20, Child £3.60, Family £19.00. Group (15+) Adult £5.80, Child £2.90. Park & garden only: Adult £3.60, Child £1.80, Family £9.50. NT Members Free. Admission by timed ticket.
Location: On B3082 Blandford-Wimbourne road, one and a half miles west of Wimbourne.

Savorgnan Della Torre by Titian

Map Ref: 15

Priest's House Museum & Garden

   📖 ♿ 🔵 ▯

23/27 High Street, Wimborne Minster BH21 1HR Tel / Fax: 01202 882533
Email: priestshouse@eastdorset.gov.uk

The Priest's House is set in an historic town house. A series of period rooms take the visitor back through the centuries. The Museum tells the story of East Dorset from ancient to modern times. With hands-on activities in the the Victorian schoolroom and Galleries of Childhood and Archaeology - there is plenty to do. The walled garden behind the house is a tranquil retreat in the centre of town. Costume & Textile Gallery.

The Victorian Kitchen

opposite the Minster.

Opening Times: 1 Apr to 30 Oct Mon to Sat 10:00-16:30.
Admission: Adult £2.70, Child £1.00, OAP/Student £2.00, Family £7.00. Location: Centre of Wimborne town,

Map Ref: 16

Essex is well endowed with interesting towns. Colchester, claiming to be Britain's oldest recorded town, has Europe's biggest Norman keep. Ancient Chelmsford is Essex's county town, once a New Town planned in 1199 by the Bishop of London. All of these towns have their stories to tell in a plethora of splendid museums.

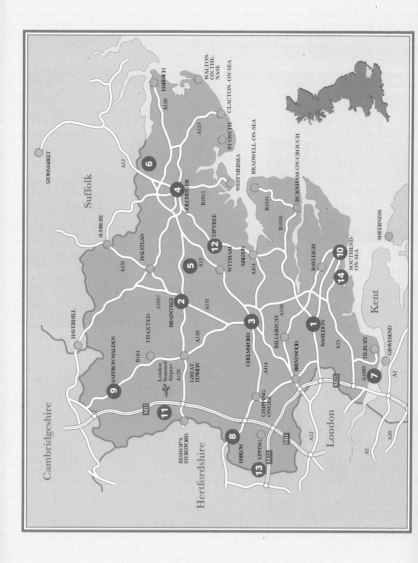

The Red Map References should be used to locate Museums etc on the pages that follow

Essex

The Haven Plotlands Museum

Langdon Visitor Centre, Third Avenue, Lower Dunton Road, Basildon SS16 6EB Tel: 01268 419103 Fax: 01268 546137 Email: langdon@essexwt.org.uk Web: www.essexwt.org.uk

Original 1930s Plotland home has been restored. Fully furnished with 1930s style furnishings, memorabilia, kitchen/garden implements. The Haven offers people the chance to enjoy their memories.

Opening Times: Mar to Oct Tue to Sun 13:30-16:30. Other times by arrangement.
Admission: Free; donations appreciated. Location: On a nature reserve. Access by public transport limited.

Map Ref: 1

Braintree District Museum

Town Hall Centre, Market Square, Braintree CM7 3YG Tel: 01376 325266 Fax: 01376 344345
Email: jean@bdcmuseum.demon.co.uk

The Museum's Gallery exhibits interpret the diverse local industrial heritage of this area which has a major influence on 20th century life in England and the world, particularly in silks, man-made textiles and metal window design. The natural historian John Ray, who was born in the district, has a gallery devoted to his life and work.

Opening Times: Mon to Sat & BH 10:00-17:00 all year round, Nov/Dec Sun 13:00-16:00. Admission: District visitors: Adult £1.00, Concession 50p. All other visitors Adult £2.00, Concession £1.00. Location: Town centre, five minutes from railway station and one minute from bus station.

The Victorian Schoolroom

Map Ref: 2

Chelmsford Museum & the Essex Regiment Museum

Oaklands Park, Moulsham Street, Chelmsford CM2 9AQ Tel: 01245 615100 Fax: 01245 268545 Email: oaklands@chelmsfordbc.gov.uk Web: www.chelmsfordmuseums.co.uk

Local history museum featuring 'The Story of Chelmsford' exhibition, natural history, social history, costume, ceramics, early English drinking glasses, coins. The Essex Regiment Museum tells the story of the local county regiment.

Opening Times: Mon to Sat 10:00-17:00. Sun 14:00-17:00 in Summertime, 13:00-16:00 in Wintertime. Closed Good Friday & Xmas. Admission: Free. Location: Three quarters of a mile from town centre.

Map Ref: 3

Castle Museum

Castle Park, Colchester CO1 1TJ Tel: 01206 282939 Fax: 01206 282925
Web: www.colchestermuseums.org.uk

A visit to Colchester Castle Museum takes you through 2000 years of some of the most important events in British history. The Castle is the largest keep ever built by the Normans and is constructed on the foundations of Roman Temple of Claudius. An award winning museum featuring hands-on displays and lively events programme.

Opening Times: Mon to Sat 10:00-17:00, Sun 11:00-17:00. Admission: Adult £4.25, Child £2.80, OAP/Concession £2.80, Family £11.00. Location: Central off high street, Castle park. Five mins walk from bus station and town railway station.

Colchester Castle

Map Ref: 4

Hollytrees Museum

High Street, Colchester CO1 1UG Tel: 01206 282940 Fax: 01206 282925
Web: www.colchestermuseums.org.uk

Hollytrees Museum is in a beautiful Georgian town house built in 1718 interpreting 300 years of

Essex

domestic life with fun and humour in mind. Highlights are the Childhood Gallery and interactive displays.

Opening Times: Mon to Sat 10:00-17:00, Sun 11:00-17:00. Admission: Free. Location: Off high street, in Castle Park five minutes from bus and railway station. Map Ref: 4

Natural History Museum

All Saint's Church, High Street, Colchester CO1 1DN Tel: 01206 282941
Fax: 01206 282925 Web: www.colchestermuseums.org.uk

The Natural History Museum offers an interesting perspective on the natural history of Essex from the ice age to the present day, with many hands-on displays, and summer events programme.

Opening Times: Mon to Sat 10:00-17:00, Sun 11:00-17:00. Admission: Free. Location: End of high street five minutes from bus and train station. Map Ref: 4

Paycocke's
West Street, Coggeshall, Colchester CO6 1NS Tel / Fax: 01376 561305
Web: www.nationaltrust.org.uk

An early sixteenth century town house containing unusually rich panelling and wood carving. There is a display of local Coggeshall lace and an attractive cottage garden.

Opening Times: 4 Apr to 10 Oct Tue, Thu, Sun only 14:00-17:30. Open BH Mons.
Admission: Adult £2.30, Child £1.15. NT Members Free. Location: Signposted off A120, on south side of West Street, 300 yards from centre of Coggeshall, on road to Braintree next to the Fleece Inn. Map Ref: 5

Tymperleys Clock Museum

Trinity Street, Colchester CO1 1JN Tel: 01206 282943 Fax: 01206 282925
Web: www.colchestermuseums.org.uk

Tymperleys has a fine display of Colchester made clocks from the outstanding Mason collection. It is situated in a beautiful restored 15th century timber-framed house with medieval herb garden in the grounds.

Opening Times: May to Oct Tue to Sat 10:00-13:00 & 14:00-17:00. Admission: Free.
Location: Town centre. Map Ref: 4

Sir Alfred Munnings Art Museum

Castle House, Dedham CO7 6AZ Tel: 01206 322127

The home, studios and grounds where Sir Alfred Munnings KCVO PRA lived and worked for 40 years until his death in 1959. A large collection of his works shown in his former home. Annual special exhibition.

Opening Times: Easter Sun to 1st Sun in Oct Wed & Sun 14:00-17:00, also Aug Thu & Sat 14:00-17:00. Groups by appointment. Admission: Adult £4.00, Child £1.00p, Concession £3.00. Location: Three quarters of a mile from centre of Dedham. Map Ref: 6

Thurrock Museum
Thameside Complex, Orsett Road, Grays RM17 5DX Tel: 01375 382555 Fax: 01375 392666
Email: jcatton@thurrock.gov.uk Web: www.thurrock.gov.uk/museum

Local history collection from archaeology to social history collections covering the history of Thurrock.

Opening Times: Mon to Sat 09:00-17:00. Closed Sun. Admission: Free. Location: Near town centre, five minutes walk from Grays Railway Station. Map Ref: 7

---

www.mghh.co.uk

For current information on the outstanding Collections in over 1600 Museums, Galleries & Historic Houses in England, Scotland, Wales and Ireland

Essex

The Museum of Harlow

Muskham Road, Off First Avenue, Harlow CM20 2LF Tel: 01279 454959 Fax: 01279 626094
Email: tmoh@harlow.gov.uk Web: www.tmoh.com

The museum, set within its own walled gardens, tells the story of the development of Harlow from its earliest origins 7000 years ago through to the present day.

Opening Times: Tue to Fri 10:00-17:00, Sat 10:00-12:30 & 13:30-17:00. Admission: Free.
Location: Located at Muskham Road, off First Avenue. Approx one kilometre from Harlow Mill Station.
Map Ref: 8

Audley End House & Gardens

Audley End, Saffron Walden CB11 4JF Tel: 01799 522399

The Chapel

Audley End was one of the great wonders of the nation when it was built by the first Earl of Suffolk, Lord Treasurer to James I. Some interiors were remodelled in the 18th century by Robert Adam, and the grounds were landscaped by Capability Brown. Picture collections, comprising family portraits and Old Master paintings, furniture, silver, mounted birds and animals, and more.

Opening Times: Please phone for details.
Admission: House & Grounds: Adult £8.00, Child £4.00, Concession £6.00, Family £20.00. Grounds only: Adult £4.00, Child £2.00, Concession £3.00, Family £10.00. EH Members Free. Prices may change. Location: One mile west of Saffron Walden on B1383.
Map Ref: 9

Fry Public Art Gallery

Bridge End Gardens, Castle Street, Saffron Walden CB10 1BD Tel: 01799 513779
Web: www.fryartgallery.org

A unique collection of work by Edward Bawden, Michael Rothenstein, Eric Ravizious & other artists who have links with 20th century North West Essex. Significant contemporary works are aslo included.

Opening Times: Easter Sun to last Sun in Oct Tue, Sat, Sun & BH 14:00-17:00.
Admission: Free. Location: Castle Street is off The High Street.
Map Ref: 9

Saffron Walden Museum

Museum Street, Saffron Walden CB10 1JL Tel / Fax: 01799 510333
Email: museum@uttlesford.gov.uk

Friendly, family-size museum. Winner Best Museum of Social History. Good disabled access. Moccasins, mummy cases, woolly mammoths and 'Wallace The Lion' - something for all ages.

Opening Times: Mar to Oct Mon to Sat 10:00-17:00 Sun & BH 14:00-17:00. Nov to Feb Mon to Sat 10:00-16:30 Sun & BH 14:00-16:30. Closed 24-25 Dec. Admission: Adult £1.00, Child Free, Concession 50p. Location: Close to Parish Church, castle ruins in grounds. Map Ref: 9

Prittlewell Priory

Priory Park, Victoria Avenue, Southend-on-Sea Tel: 01702 342878 Fax: 01702 349806
Email: southendmuseum@hotmail.com Web: www.southendmuseums.co.uk

Prittlewell Priory from the Old World Gardens

12th century Cluniac Priory with later additions, extensively restored in the 1920s, set in an attractive park. Displays focus on the history of the Priory itself and on the museum's fine collection of radios and televisions (Ekco was a local firm). A fine series of recently restored panel paintings by artist Alan Sorrell are also on show.

Opening Times: Tue to Sat 10:00-13:00 & 14:00-17:00.
Closed Sun, Mon and BH. Admission: Free.
Location: In Priory Park, 1 kilometre north of town centre.
Exhibitions & Events 2004 : 17 to 24 Feb: Activity Week 'Ancient & Traditional Crafts'.
Map Ref: 10

Essex

Southchurch Hall

Southchurch Hall Close, Southchurch, Southend-on-Sea SS1 2TE Tel: 01702 467671
Fax: 01702 439806 Email: southendmuseums@hotmail.com
Web: www.southendmuseums.co.uk

Southchurch Hall from the South

A moated early 14th century timber framed manor house set in gardens. It has rooms furnished in medieval, Tudor and Victorian styles. An exhibition room tells the story of the Hall and there are exhibits from excavations near the moat. The museum specialises in historic presentations to school children and also hosts various events, such as open days, during the year.

Opening Times: Tue to Sat 10:00-13:00 & 14:00-17:00 (mornings reserved for schools during term time). Closed Sun, Mon and BH. Admission: Free. Location: One kilometre east of town centre, five minutes walk from Southend East Railway Station. Exhibitions & Events 2004 : 6 Jun: Family Fun Day, 1 Aug: Tudor Day, 4 Dec: Christmas Fair.

Map Ref: 10

Southend Central Museum & Planetarium

Victoria Avenue, Southend-on-Sea SS2 6EW Tel: 01702 434449 Fax: 01702 349806
Email: southendmuseums@hotmail.com Web: www.southendmuseums.co.uk

The new Discovery Centre

The museum has displays of local history, geology and wildlife with special sections on the Thames Estuary and Victorian Life. An imposing feature, dominating the main hall, is the late medieval 'Reynolds' fireplace, originally part of a building in nearby Prittlewell. The museum's Discovery Centre, opened in 2000, is an interactive centre where visitors can handle exhibits. Video microscopes allow visitors to examine a range of specimens, from London Clay fossils to coins and garden pests, in amazing detail. In addition, they can try and solve problems on topic tables and refer to SID, a rapidly growing database of historic local photographs

which has a particularly fine selection of views of Southend from Victorian times to the 1960s. Upstairs, Southend Planetarium allows visitors to sit back and enjoy a forty minute tour of the Universe presented by a guide lecturer. Investigate the scale of Space, details of the Sun and the planets or take a look at the myths and legends of the skies. (Please note that under 5s are not admitted to the planetarium).

A demonstration in the Discovery Centre

Opening Times: Tue to Sat 10:00-17:00, closed Sun, Mon and BH. Planetarium open Wed to Sat at 11:00, 14:00 and 16:00. Admission: Museum Free. Planetarium Adult £2.40, Child £1.70, OAP £1.70, Group rates on request. Location: In town centre, next to Southend Victoria Railway Station.

Map Ref: 10

House on the Hill Museums Adventure

Stansted CM24 8SP Tel: 01279 813237 Fax: 01279 816391
Web: www.mountfitchetcastle.com

A huge range of toys and games from later Victorian times up to the 1970s - about 75,000 exhibits in total.

Opening Times: Daily 10:00-17:00. Closed Xmas & New Year. Admission: Adult £4.00, Child £3.20, OAP £3.50. 10% off admissions when visiting the Toy Museum and Mountfitchet Castle (next door) in the same day. Location: Adjacent to Mountfitchet Castle, in the centre of Stansted village.

Map Ref: 11

Essex

Tiptree Museum

   ♿ ◆ ☕ 🚚

Wilkin & Sons Ltd, Tiptree CO5 0RF Tel: 01621 815407 Fax: 01621 814555 Email: tiptree@tiptree.com Web: www.tiptree.com

Over 50 years ago John Wilkin grandson of the founder Arthur Charles Wilkin began collecting the paraphernalia of preserve making and Essex village life, storing away pictures, documents and redundant machines. With the opening of the museum in a renovated farm building in 1995, John Wilkin's foresight was at last rewarded and visitors can now see how life was and how the art of jam making has advanced over the years.

Opening Times: Mon to Fri 10:00-17:00. During May, Jun, Jul & Aug also open Sun 12:00-17:00. Closed Xmas week. Admission: Free. Location: Tiptree is 15

Renovated Farm Building at Tiptree

minutes from Colchester and the Jam Factory & Museum is along the B1023 heading towards Tollesbury.   Map Ref: 12

Epping Forest District Museum

   ♿ ◆

39/41 Sun Street, Waltham Abbey EN9 1EL Tel: 01992 716882 Fax: 01992 700427
Email: museum@efdc.fsnet.co.uk Web: www.eppingforestdistrictmuseum.org.uk

The museum tells the story of the people who have lived and worked in this part of West Essex, from the earliest inhabitants to the present. Housed in a building dating to 1520, with a changing programme of temporary exhibitions.

Opening Times: Mon & Fri 14:00-17:00, Sun (1 May to 30 Sep) 14:00-17:00, Tue 12:00-17:00, Sat 10:00-17:00. Wed & Thu Group bookings available. Admission: Free. Location: Near town centre.   Map Ref: 13

Beecroft Art Gallery

   ♿

Station Road, Westcliff-on-Sea, Westcliff-on-Sea SS0 7RA Tel: 01702 347418 Fax: 01702 347681 Web: www.beecroft-art-gallery.co.uk

The gallery's fine collection of over 2,000 works includes a selection of Dutch and Flemish 17th century paintings by artists such as Molenaer, Ruisdael and Berchem. Also represented is a fair selection of 19th century artists including Rossetti, with a fine pencil drawing of model Fanny Cornforth, Constable with an early oil sketch of the Stour valley and Edward Lear with a watercolour of Egypt, 20th century works including paintings by Carel Weight,

Edward B Seago (1910-1974).
The Doge's Palace, Venice

the Great Bardfield Group and a fine bronze by Jacob Epstein. The local artist Alan Sorrell is well represented by

his 'Drawings of Nubia' series depicting a visit to Egypt prior to the building of the Aswan Dam. Of particular interest is the Thorpe Smith Collection of local landscape views, containing paintings, drawings and prints from as early as 1803. A selection of the finest works is always on show. There is a range of temporary exhibitions. Particularly popular are the summer 'Essex Open Exhibition', a selected show open to artists working and living in Essex, and the annual Christmas Show with a range of items suitable for presents.

Opening Times: Tue to Sat 10:00-13:00 & 14:00-17:00. Closed Sun and Mon, but open at least one Sun during exhibitions.
Admission: Free. Location: Ten minute walk from town centre, opposite Cliffs Pavilion. Exhibitions & Events 2004 : 10 Jan to 28

Dante Gabriel Rossetti (1828-1882).
Fanny Cornforth

Feb: Works by Alan Sorrell (1904-1974), 6 Mar to 24 Apr: Southend Art Club, 1 May to 19 Jun: Victorian Costume from the Smart Collection plus work by Christian Figg, 10 Jul to 11 Sep: 46th Essex Open Exhibition, 18 Sep to 30 Oct: 'At the Sign of the Rainbow' - Margaret Calkin-James (1895-1985), plus works by Ian Glazier, 6 Nov to 18 Dec: Christmas Exhibition.   Map Ref: 14

Gloucestershire

Cheltenham, the small spa village, was transformed into an elegant fashionable town in 1788 through the visit of George III and the consequent patronage. Gloucester with its magnificent cathedral, the nave of which is dominated by the largest stained glass window in Britain created in 1349, was once a commercially important port.

The county's museums tell the story of its Arts and Crafts, its Roman occupation, its waterways, railways, the Forest of Dean and its heritage.

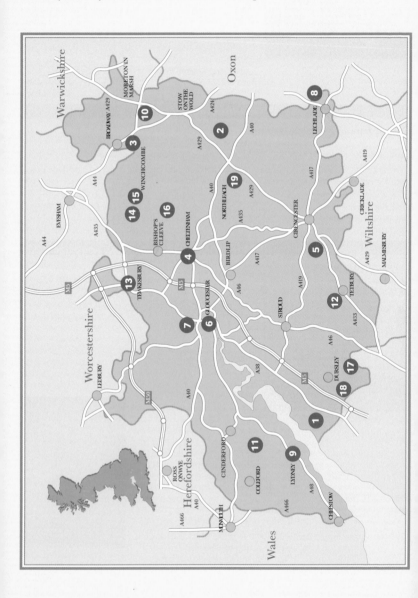

The Red Map References should be used to locate Museums etc on the pages that follow

Gloucestershire

Berkeley Castle

Berkeley GL13 9BQ   Tel: 01453 810332   Fax: 01453 512995
Email: info@berkeley-castle.com   Web: www.berkeley-castle.com

A romantic Medieval castle full of history and treasures, surrounded by Elizabethan terraced gardens and overlooking rolling countryside towards the Severn Estuary. Berkeley Castle has been in possession of the same family for over 800 years, celebrated by Shakespeare, the scene of murder - of a king, breached by the Roundheads in the Civil War, host to Francis Drake, Elizabeth I, and more English kings and queens than we care to count, and is still home to the Berkeley family today.

Berkeley Castle from Queen Elizabeth 1st's
Bowling Green. © Jason Ingran

Opening Times: Apr to Sep Wed to Sat 11:00-16:00, Sun 14:00-17:00. Oct Sun 14:00-17:00. Admission: Adult £6.25, Child £3.25, OAP £5.00. Garden & Butterfly House only: Adult £3.00, Child £1.00. Location: South Gloucestershire, just off A38 (half way between Bristol and Gloucester), between junction 13 & 14 of M5. Exhibitions & Events 2004 : Joust - A weekend of Medieval mayhem, never before has a festival of this scale taken place in the UK, not only will there be full contact jousting but you can also witness daring display of weaponary, falconry and archery. www.joust.info. Map Ref: 1

Jenner Museum

Church Lane, Berkeley GL13 9BH   Tel: 01453 810631   Fax: 01453 811690
Email: manager@jennermuseum.com   Web: www.jennermuseum.com

Georgian country home of Edward Jenner, discoverer of vaccination against smallpox. Portraits, personal possessions and reconstruction of study, vaccination equipment and computerised display explaining modern immunology.

Opening Times: Apr to Sep Tue to Sat 12:30-17:30, Sun 13:00-17:30. Oct Sun only 13:00-17:30. Groups at other times by appointment. Admission: Adult £3.00, Child £1.50, OAP £2.30. Group discounts available. Location: Near Berkeley Town Centre, beside church and castle, one mile from A38 - use junction 14 or 15 of M5. Map Ref: 1

Cotswold Motoring Museum & Toy Collection

The Old Mill, Bourton-on-the-Water GL54 2BY   Tel: 01451 821255
Email: michelle.blackmore@csma.uk.com

Full of exciting memorabilia including classic cars, motorcycles, model aeroplanes, pedal cars and one of the largest collections of metal motoring signs. The museum is also home to Brum, the little yellow car from the children's TV series.

Opening Times: Feb to Nov 10:00-18:00. Admission: Adult £2.95, Child £1.95, Family £8.95. Location: Just off High Street, a short walk from The Green. Map Ref: 2

Snowshill Manor

Snowshill, Broadway WR12 7JU   Tel: 01386 852410   Fax: 01386 842822
Email: snowshill@nationaltrust.org.uk   Web: www.nationaltrust.org.uk

The Manor is closed for 2004 for essential repairs and reopens in 2005. There is a delightful organic garden, together with shop and restaurant.

Opening Times: Garden only: 19 Mar to 31 Oct Wed to Sun 11:00-17:30. Admission: Garden only: Adult: £3.80, Child £1.90, Family £9.50 (2 adults and 3 children), NT Members Free. Location: Two and a half miles south west of Broadway: turn from A44 Broadway bypass into Broadway village and by village green turn uphill to Snowshill. Map Ref: 3

Guided or Private Tours	Disabled Access	Gift Shop or Sales Point	Café or Refreshments	Restaurant	Car Parking

Gloucestershire

Voysey Display in Arts and Crafts Movement Gallery

Cheltenham Art Gallery & Museum

Clarence Street, Cheltenham GL50 3JT   Tel: 01242 237431   Fax: 01242 262334
Email: artgallery@cheltenham.gov.uk
Web: www.cheltenham.artgallery.museum

Cheltenham's Arts and Craft Movement collection of furniture, textiles, ceramics, carvings, silver and jewellery is recognised as an outstanding collection of international importance. Cheltenham's history is also well represented, and in addition there are paintings spanning four centuries, oriental collections of pottery and costume, archaeological treasures from the neighbouring Cotswolds, as well as a programme of special exhibitions changing regularly throughout the year.

Opening Times: Mon to Sat 10:00-17:20, Sun 14:00-16:20. Closed Easter and BH. Admission: Free.
Location: Town centre. Exhibitions & Events 2004 : 17 Jan to 29 Feb: Scenes in Passing: Watercolours from the Art Gallery & Museum's collections, 24 Jan to 28 Mar: Spring Sensations: Dress from the Art Gallery & Museum's collections, 8 May to 18 Jul: Playing Away, 24 July to 5 Sep: A Collector's Vision: 20th-century art from Osbert Sitwell's home, 4 Dec to mid Jan: Fusion.   Map Ref: 4

Holst Birthplace Museum

4 Clarence Road, Pittville, Cheltenham GL52 2AY   Tel: 01242 524846   Fax: 01242 580182
Email: holstmuseum@btconnect.com   Web: www.holstmuseum.org.uk

Birthplace of the composer of The Planets, displaying personal memorabilia including his piano. Also a fine period house with rooms illustrating the 'upstairs-downstairs' way of Victorian life. Holst's music is played.

Opening Times: Tue to Sat 10:00-16:00, closed Sun, Mon and some BH. Closed Dec to Jan, except for pre-booked groups. Admission: Adult £2.50, Concessions £2.00, Family £7.00, special rate for schools. Location: Ten minute walk from town centre. Near Portland Street car park. Opposite Gateway of Pittville Park.   Map Ref: 4

Rodmarton Manor

Rodmarton, Cirencester GL7 6PF   Tel: 01285 841253   Fax: 01285 841298
Email: simon.biddulph@farming.co.uk   Web: www.rodmarton-manor.co.uk

One of the last country houses to be built and furnished by hand (1909-1929). Cotswold Arts and Crafts furniture, metalwork, hand painted furniture and pottery, wall hangings. Contemporary 8 acre garden off many outdoor rooms.

Opening Times: House & Garden: 3 May to 30 Aug Wed, Sat & BH 14:00-17:00. Garden: Jun & Jul Mon 14:00-17:00. Groups (20+) at other times. Admission: House & Garden: Adult £7.00, Age 5-15yrs £3.50. Garden only: Adult £4.00, Age 5-15yrs £1.00. Location: Off A433 between Cirencester and Tetbury.   Map Ref: 5

City Museum & Art Gallery

Brunswick Road, Gloucester GL1 1HP   Tel: 01452 396131   Fax: 01452 410898
Email: city.museum@gloucester.gov.uk   Web: www.gloucester.gov.uk &
www.livinggloucester.co.uk

The Museum's collections include dinosaurs, fossils, unique Roman remains, stunning Birdlip mirrors, antique furniture, painting and decorative arts. Temporary exhibitions, hands-on displays, children's holiday activities and regular special events.

Opening Times: Tue to Sat 10:00-17:00 Admission: Adults £2.00, Free for all Gloucester City Residents and under 18s. Location: Five minutes walk from Central Bus Station, near Town Centre   Map Ref: 6

Gloucestershire

Gloucester Folk Museum

99/103 Westgate Street, Gloucester GL1 2PG   Tel: 01452 396467   Fax: 01452 330495
Email: folk.museum@gloucester.gov.uk   Web: www.gloucester.gov.uk &
www.livinggloucester.co.uk

Grade II Listed Tudor and Jacobean timber-framed buildings with new extensions housing displays on social history, crafts, trades and industries of Gloucester City and County. Regular special exibitions, activities, crafts and an interactive ICT gallery.

Opening Times: Tue to Sat 10:00-17:00   Admission: Adults £2.00, Free for all Gloucester City Residents and under 18s.   Location: Ten minutes walk from Central Bus Station, near Town Centre   Map Ref: 6

National Waterways Museum

Llanthony Warehouse, The Docks, Gloucester GL1 2EH   Tel: 01452 318200
Fax: 01452 318202

Museum Entrance and Shop

The collection is designated as being 'of national importance' and includes many artefacts and historic floating exhibits that chart the fascinating 300 year story of our inland waterways. Interactives and touch-screen computers bring history to life as does our working blacksmith forge. From Easter to October you can even take a 45 minute boat trip along the Gloucester and Sharpness Canal.

Opening Times: Daily 10:00-17:00. Closed Xmas Day.
Admission: Adult £5.00, Child/OAP £4.00, Family £12.00-£16.00.   Location: Situated in historic docks five minutes from city centre, 15 minutes walk from Gloucester Bus Station and Railway Station.   Map Ref: 6

Nature in Art

Wallsworth Hall, Twigworth, Gloucester GL2 9PA   Tel: 01452 731422   Fax: 01452 730937
Email: ninart@globalnet.co.uk   Web: www.nature-in-art.org.uk

World's first museum dedicated exclusively to art inspired by nature. Fine, decorative and applied art spanning 1500 years from 60 countries in all styles and media. Situated in a fine Georgian mansion.

Opening Times: Tue to Sun & BH 10:00-17:00. Closed Xmas.   Admission: Adult £3.60, Child/OAP/Concession £3.00, Under 8s Free. Group rates available.   Location: Two miles north of Gloucester on main A38.   Map Ref: 7

Kelmscott Manor

Kelmscott, Lechlade GL7 3HJ   Tel: 01367 252486   Fax: 01367 253754
Email: admin@kelmscottmanor.co.uk   Web: www.kelmscottmanor.co.uk

A gabled Cotswold manor house of 1570 with a taller block added in the 17th century.Famouse as the country house of William Morris from 1871 until his death in 1896. There is an interesting collection of furniture, textiles, carpets and ceramics.

Opening Times: 1 Apr to Sep Wed 11:00-17:00.   Admission: Manor & Gardens: Adult £7.00, Student £3.50, Child £3.50.   Location: Two miles east of Lechlade, off Lechlade/Faringdon road.   Map Ref: 8

Dean Forest Railway Museum

Norchard Railway Centre, Forest Road, New Mills, Lydney GL15 4ET   Tel / Fax: 01594 845840
Web: www.deanforestrailway.co.uk

General railway artefacts with emphasis on local Forest of Dean area. Also includes working telephone exchange (old restored BT system) for railway system. Story of Severn and Wye railway since 1809. Information (24 hrs) 01594 843423.

Opening Times: Summer daily 11:00-17:00. Winter Wed, Sat & Sun 11:00-16:00. Closed Xmas. Admission: Free on non-operational days. Operational Days: Rover ticket for train travel. Adult £6.00, Child £4.00, OAP £5.50. Group rates available. Prices subject to change.
Location: Road: one mile north of Lydney Town Centre on B4234 - off A48, follow brown tourist signs. Rail: 300 yards from Lydney mainline to DFR Lydney Junction.   Map Ref: 9

Gloucestershire

MORETON-IN-MARSH

Sezincote

Sezincote, Moreton-in-Marsh GL56 9AW   Tel: 01386 700444   Fax: 01386 700422

The house, garden and orangery form an exotic Indian fantasy with Hindu and Muslim architecture.

Opening Times: May to Jul & Sep 14:30-18:00.   Admission: House: Adult £5.00, Garden: Adult £3.50, Child £1.00 (under 5's Free).   Location: Two and a half miles south west of Morton-in-Marsh. Map Ref: 10

ROYAL FOREST OF DEAN

Dean Heritage Centre

Camp Mill, Soudley, Royal Forest of Dean GL14 2UB   Tel: 01594 824024   Fax: 01594 823711
Email: deanmuse@btinternet.com

Restored mill and pond in a wooded valley. The collection covers the period from pre-history to the present day, reflecting life in the Forest of Dean and rural skills.

Opening Times: Summer: 10:00-17:30. Winter: 11:00-16:30. Closed 24-26 Dec & 1 Jan.
Admission: Adult £4.00, Child £2.50, OAP £3.50, Family £12.00. Group rates & season tickets available.   Location: Pretty woodland setting. Map Ref: 11

TETBURY

Chavenage House

Chavenage, Tetbury GL8 8XP   Tel: 01666 502329   Fax: 01453 836778
Email: info@chavenage.com   Web: www.chavenage.com

Lived in Elizabethan Manor House, with Cromwellian associations. Guided tours by the owner or his family. Chavenage house has been used for several film and TV productions.

Opening Times: Easter Sun & Mon, BH Mon, May to Sep Thu & Sun 14:00-17:00.
Admission: Adult £5.00, Child £2.50. Map Ref: 12

TEWKESBURY

John Moore Countryside Museum

41 Church Street, Tewkesbury GL20 5SN   Tel: 01684 297174
Email: simonlawton@btconnect.com
Web: www.gloster.demon.co.uk/JMCM/index.html

A natural history collection exhibited in a 15th century house and honouring the prophetic writings on nature conservation of John Moore the writer. Displays of British woodland and wetland wildlife. The impact of people on the natural environment and the need for conservation are explored.

Opening Times: Apr to Oct & BH Tue to Sat 10:00-13:00 & 14:00-17:00. Nov to Mar most Sat plus special Xmas & spring half term 11:00-13:00 & 14:00-16:00.   Admission: Adult £1.25, Child 75p, OAP £1.00p, Group £1.00p.   Location: In the precincts of Tewkesbury Abbey, three minute walk from town centre. Map Ref: 13

WINCHCOMBE

Gloucestershire Warwickshire Railway

The Railway Station, Toddington GL54 5DT   Tel: 01242 621405   Email: enquiries@gwsr.plc.uk
Web: www.gwsr.plc.uk

'Raveningham Hall' and 'Bahamas'
Dixton Cutting, Glos/Warks Railway

The 'Friendly Line in the Cotswolds' operates a round trip of 20 miles from Toddington via Winchcombe to Gotherington (Cheltenham Racecourse), including the 693 yard Greet Tunnel, one of the longest on a preserved railway. Superb views of the Cotswolds, Malverns and Vale of Evesham. Steam and diesel locomotives. Restored carriages and stations. Locomotives under restoration.

Opening Times: Mar to Nov, Sat & Sun. BH, Apr, Jul & Aug, selected weekdays 10:00-17:00. Dec Sat & Sun Santa Specials.   Admission: Adult £9.00, Child £5.50, Under 5s Free, OAP £7.50, Family £24.00. Group rates available.   Location: Ten miles east of junction 9 on M5, near the junction of B4077 and B4632. Map Ref: 14

Gloucestershire

Hales Abbey

Winchcombe, near Cheltenham GL54 5PB   Tel: 01242 602398

This Cistercian abbey was built by Richard, Earl of Cornwall in the 13th century, in gratitude for surviving a perilous sea journey. The museum contains an important collection of floor tiles, including early inlaid tiles.

Opening Times: Apr to Sep daily 10:00-18:00, Oct daily 10:00-17:00. Closed in winter. Times & prices may change.   Admission: Adult £3.00, Child £1.50, Concession £2.30. EH & NT Members Free.   Location: Two miles north east of Winchcombe off B4632.   Map Ref: 15

Sudeley Castle

Winchcombe GL54 5JD   Tel: 01242 604357/602308   Fax: 01242 602959
Email: marketing@sudeley.org.uk   Web: www.sudeleycastle.co.uk

Set against the beautiful backdrop of the Cotswold Hills, Sudeley Castle is steeped in history. With Royal connections spanning thousands of years, it has played an important role in the turbulent and changing times of England's past.

Opening Times: Gardens, Grounds, Shop, Exhibition & Plant Centre: 6 Mar to 31 Oct 10:30-17:30. Castle Apartments and St Mary's Church: 27 Mar to 31 Oct 11:00-17:00.   Admission: Castle & Gardens: Adult £6.85, Child £3.85, Family £18.50 Concession £5.85. Gardens: Adult £5.50, Child £3.25, Concession £4.50.   Location: Near Winchcombe, eight miles north east of Cheltenham on the B4632 (A46) or ten miles from junction 9 off the M5.

Aerial view of Sudeley Castle and Gardens

Map Ref: 16

Newark Park

Ozleworth, Wotton-under-Edge GL12 7PZ   Tel / Fax: 01453 842644
Email: michael@newark98.freeserve.co.uk   Web: www.nationaltrust.org.uk

This unusual property is a Tudor hunting Lodge. It contains a collection of Far Eastern artefacts, toys and costume designs. The property is in a marvellous position overlooking the Cotswolds.

Opening Times: 31 Jan to 15 Feb Sat & Sun 11:00-17:00, 1 Apr to 27 May Wed & Thu 11:00-17:00, 2 Jun to 31 Oct Wed, Thu, Sat & Sun 11:00-17:00. Open BH Mons.   Admission: Adult £4.50, Child £2.20, Family £11.00 (2 adults and 3 children). NT Members Free.   Location: One and a half miles east of Wotton-under-Edge, one and three quarter miles south of junction of A4135 & B4058 follow signs for Ozleworth.   Map Ref: 17

Wotton Heritage Centre

The Chipping, Wotton-under-Edge GL12 7AD   Tel: 01453 521541
Web: www.wottonheritage.com

Local and family history, artefacts from Wotton's crafts and industries, with photographs, postcards, documents, maps and books. Also includes, research facilities, Tourist Information Point and a small shop.

Opening Times: Tue to Fri 10:00-13:00, 14:00-17:00 (16:00 in winter), Sat 10:00-13:00. Some Sun afternoons in summer 14:30-17:00.   Admission: Free, small charge for research facilities.   Location: In main car park.   Map Ref: 18

Chedworth Roman Villa

Yanworth GL54 3LJ   Tel: 01242 890256   Fax: 01425 890544
Email: chedworth@nationaltrust.org.uk   Web: www.nationaltrust.org.uk

Discovered in 1864, this is the remains of one of the largest Romano-British villas in the country. Over one mile of the walls survive. There are several fine mosaics, two bathhouses, hypocausts, a water shrine and latrine. The site museum houses objects from the villa.

Opening Times: 28 Feb to 26 Mar & 26 Oct to 14 Nov Tue to Sun 11:00-16:00, 27 Mar to 24 Oct Tue to Sun 10:00-17:00. Open BH Mons.   Admission: Adult £4.10, Child £2.00, Family £10.20 (2 adults and 3 children). NT Members Free.   Location: Three miles north west of Fossebridge on Cirencester-Northleach road (A429),approach from A429 via Yarnworth or from A436 via Withington.   Map Ref: 19

Hampshire & Isle of Wight

Nursery Rhyme tiles
in the ceramics collection

Allen Gallery

Church Street, Alton GU34 2BW Tel: 01420 82802 Fax: 01420 84227
Email: tony.cross@hants.gov.uk
Web: www.hants.gov.uk/museum/allen

The Allen Gallery houses an outstanding collection of ceramics, nearly 1900 items dating from 1250 to the present day. Highlights include the unique Elizabethan Tichborne spoons. A range of delightful watercolours and oil paintings by local artist William Herbert Allen are also on display. There is an exciting programme of temporary exhibitions, a comfortable coffee lounge and a delightful walled garden behind the gallery.

Opening Times: Tue to Sat 10:00-17:00. Admission: Free.
Location: Town centre. Exhibitions & Events 2004 : 10 Jan to 6 Mar: The Crimean War - 150th Anniversary Exhibition, 20 Mar to 1 May: The Chosen Letter - Created and Creative Shapes, 15 May to 19 Jun: A Natural View - Wildlife Illustrations by Cecilia Fitzsimons, 3 Jul to 28 Aug: Richard Farrington Sculptures.

Map Ref: 3

Curtis Museum

High Street, Alton GU34 1BA Tel: 01420 82802 Fax: 01420 84227
Email: tony.cross@hants.gov.uk Web: www.hants.gov.uk/museum/curtis

One of the finest local history collections in Hampshire, exploring 100 million years of history. The wonderful array of objects includes the celebrated Roman cup found near Selborne and the impressive Anglo Saxon Alton buckle. The Gallery of Childhood is packed with toys, children's books and dolls dating back to the 18th century. Displays include prehistoric tools, local Roman pottery, Saxon burials, hop picking and brewing and local celebrities.

The renowned Anglo-Saxon Alton Buckle

Opening Times: Tue to Sat 10:00-17:00.
Admission: Free. Location: Town centre. Map Ref: 3

Jane Austen's House

Chawton, Alton GU34 1SD Tel: 01420 83262

17th century house where Jane Austen lived between 1809-17. She wrote and revised her novels here. Memorabilia of Jane Austen and her family. Donkey carriage and pretty garden.

Opening Times: Mar to Nov daily 11:00-16:30, Admission: Fee charged. Location: One and a half miles south west of Alton.

Map Ref: 3

Andover Museum

6 Church Close, Andover SP10 1DP Tel: 01264 366283 Fax: 01264 339152 Email: david.allen@hants.gov.uk
Web: www.hants.gov.uk/museum/andoverm

Flints, fossils, freshwater fish and natural habitats introduce the Andover area - detailed archaeology displays depict the rich story of human activity from the Stone Age to Saxon times. Local history episodes involve the reading of the Riot Act and an infamous Work House Scandal. The gallery has regularly changing exhibitions and the museum hosts numerous clubs and societies with a busy calendar.

Opening Times: Tue to Sat 10:00-17:00. Apr to Sep Sun and BH 14:00-17:00. Admission: Free. Location: Near St Mary's Church, three minutes walk from town centre.

Children's workshop in action

Exhibitions & Events 2004 : 10 Jan to 23 Feb: Other Lives, Distant Lands - Photography by Harshad Mistry, Jul/Aug: Paddy Killer Textile Artist, Sep/Dec: Marvellous Meals - A Potted History of Food.

Map Ref: 4

ANDOVER (continued)

Museum of the Iron Age

Hampshire County Council

6 Church Close, Andover SP10 1DP   Tel: 01264 366283   Fax: 01264 339152   Email: david.allen@hants.gov.uk
Web: www.hants.gov.uk/museum/ironagem

Discover a way of life destroyed by the Romans. Life-sized models of weaver and warrior, reconstructed rampart and roundhouse, miniature street scene, recently excavated objects, replicas of tools, a plough, grave pits and more.

Opening Times: Tue to Sat 10:00-17:00, Apr to Sep Sun and BH 14:00-17:00.
Admission: Free.   Location: Near St Mary's Church, three minutes walk from town centre.

Map Ref: 4

BASINGSTOKE

Basing House

Hampshire County Council

Redbridge Lane, Basing, Basingstoke RG24 7HB   Tel: 01256 467294
Fax: 01256 326283   Email: alan.turton@hants.gov.uk
Web: www.hants.gov.uk/museum/basingho

Exploring the ruins of the Old House

Hampshire's most exciting historic ruin was once England's largest private palace, home of the Marquess of Winchester, Treasurer of Elizabeth I. His immense building covered eight acres and replaced a great Norman Castle. Civil war brought disaster to Basing which fell to the forces of Cromwell after a two year siege. Today the site, with its dovecote towers, secret tunnel, restored garden, museum and spectacular barn make an attraction of beauty and great historic interest.

Opening Times: Apr to Sep Wed to Sun and BH 14:00-16:00.   Admission: Adult £2.00, Child £1.00, Concessions £1.00.   Location: Entrance in centre of Old Basing, short drive from Basingstoke Town Centre and junction 6 of the M3.

Map Ref: 5

Milestones - Hampshire's Living History Museum

Hampshire County Council

Leisure Park, Churchill Way, Basingstoke RG21 6YR
Tel: 01256 477766   Fax: 01256 477784   Email: ivan.preston@hants.gov.uk
Web: www.milestones-museum.com

Winner of the Social and Industrial History Award under the National Heritage Museum of the Year scheme. Atmospheric street scenes with shops from the late Victorian period to early 1940s bring Hampshire's recent history to life. An amazing 20,000 objects, including the Tasker and Thornycroft historic vehicles, are supported by easily accessible information and free audio-guide tours. Working demonstrations by costumed staff. Regular programme of events and hands-on holiday activities for children. 'Edwardian' pub open at lunchtime and refreshments in the Speedwell Cafe served until 16:30 each day; outdoor picnic area; well stocked gift shop. To book our award winning programme for schools or for details of facilities to hire and group visits please telephone 01256 477766 or email: linda.owen@hants.gov.uk.

Jubilee Street, Milestones Museum

Opening Times: Tue to Fri 10:00-17:00, Sat & Sun 11:00-17:00.
Admission: Adult £6.50, Child £3.50, Concession £5.25, Family £16.50, (valid until 31/03/04). To book our award winning programme for schools or for details of facilities to hire and group visits please telephone 01256 477766 or email: linda.owen@hants.gov.uk.

Map Ref: 5

☞ Guided or Private Tours	♿ Disabled Access	🎁 Gift Shop or Sales Point	☕ Café or Refreshments	🍴 Restaurant	🚜 Car Parking

Hampshire & Isle of Wight

Stratfield Saye House & Wellington Exhibition

Stratfield Saye House, Stratfield Saye, Basingstoke RG27 0AS   Tel: 01256 882882
Fax: 01256 881466   Email: info@stratfield-saye.co.uk
Web: www.stratfield-saye.co.uk

Given to the Duke of Wellington by a grateful nation after the Battle of Waterloo in 1817. Filled with memorabilia of the Great Duke and his adversary Napoleon.

Opening Times: 9 Apr to 1 Aug, Mon to Fri open 11:30, Sat & Sun open 10:30. Guided tour only.   Location: One and a half miles west of A33.   Map Ref: 6

Soho tapestry detail
in the Tapestry Room

The Vyne

Sherborne St John, Basingstoke RG24 9HL
Tel: 01256 883858, (01256) 881337 (info line)
Fax: 01256 881720   Email: thevyne@nationaltrust.org.uk
Web: www.nationaltrust.org.uk/thevyne

At the forefront of country house architecture, interior design and taste for over 400 years, this fascinating country house is set within attractive gardens with lakeside and woodland walks. It contains a Tudor chapel with Renaissance glass, a Palladian staircase and a wealth of old panelling and fine furniture.

Opening Times: House: 20 Mar to 31 Oct Sat & Sun 11:00-17:00, 22 Mar to 27 Oct Mon to Wed 13:00-17.00. Open Good Friday 11:00-17:00.   Admission: Adult £7.00, Child £3.50, Family £17.50. Group (15+) £5.50. Grounds only: Adult £4.00, Child £2.00. NT Members Free.   Location: Four miles north of Basingstoke between Bramley & Sherbourne St John.   Map Ref: 7

Willis Museum

Hampshire County Council

Old Town Hall, Market Place, Basingstoke RG21 7QD   Tel: 01256 465902   Fax: 01256 471455
Email: sue.tapliss@hants.gov.uk
Web: www.hants.gov.uk/museum/willis

Discover Basingstoke's past from the rich archaeological heritage beneath our feet to a tour through the last 200 years. Meet Pickaxe, a 19th century scavenger scraping a living from the streets, and revisit the days of twin-tubs and teddy boys in the 1960s sitting room. There is always something new to see with a regularly changing programme of Special Exhibitions, children's quizzes, cafe and gifts.

The 1960s kitchen

Opening Times: Mon to Fri 10:00-17:00, Sat 10:00-16:00.
Admission: Free.   Location: Top of town, ten minutes walk from bus/train station. Follow signs for tourist information centre.
Exhibitions & Events 2004 : 17 Jan to 5 Mar: The Chosen Letter - Created and Creative Shapes, Mar/Apr: Basingstoke Camera Club - Four of a Kind, May/Aug: Marvellous Meals - A Potted History of Food, Sep/Oct: Other Lives, Distant Lands - Photography by Harshad Mistry, Nov/Dec: The Bicycle - A Free-wheeling journey through history.   Map Ref: 5

Beaulieu Abbey & Display of Monastic Life

John Montage Building, Beaulieu SO42 7ZN   Tel: 01590 612345
Fax: 01590 612624   Email: info@beaulieu.co.uk   Web: www.beaulieu.co.uk

Palace House, once the Great Gatehouse of Beaulieu Abbey, is the family home of Lord Montagu of Beaulieu. The house contains splendid rooms full of fine portraits, pictures, furniture, family memorabilia and photographs. The surviving monastic buildings house an absorbing exhibition about its history and the life of worship lived there by the monks. Beaulieu 800 in 2004 will celebrate the founding of the Abbey in 1204 by King John.

Opening Times: May to Sep 10:00-18:00, Oct to Apr 10:00-17:00. Closed Xmas.   Admission: Please phone for latest prices.   Location: Beaulieu is in the heart of the New Forest.   Map Ref: 8

Hampshire & Isle of Wight

Bucklers Hard Village

Maritime Museum, Bucklers Hard, Beaulieu SO42 7XB   Tel: 01590 616203
Fax: 01590 616283   Email: info@bucklershard.co.uk
Web: www.bucklershard.co.uk

The historic and picturesque shipbuilding village of Bucklers Hard. After setting a course for its Maritime Museum and Historic Cottages savour the sight and sounds of the countryside on a ramble along the Riverside Walk.

Opening Times: Easter to Sep 10:30-17:00, Oct to Easter 11:00-16;00. Closed Xmas.
Admission: Please phone for latest prices.   Location: Five minutes from the world famous National Motor Museum at Beaulieu.   Map Ref: 9

National Motor Museum

John Montagu Building, Beaulieu SO42 7ZN   Tel: 01590 612345
Fax: 01590 612624   Email: info@beaulieu.co.uk   Web: www.beaulieu.co.uk

This world renowned collection features 250 vehicles as well as memorabilia and displays. From some of the earliest examples of motoring in the 1890s to legendary World Record Breakers, 'film star' cars to family cars from the 30s, 40s and 50s. There is also a stunning James Bond Experience and a sensational Motorsport Gallery.

Opening Times: May to Sep 10:00-18:00, Oct to Apr 10:00-17:00. Closed Xmas. Admission: Please phone for latest prices.   Location: Beaulieu is in the heart of the New Forest.   Map Ref: 8

Bishop's Waltham Palace

Bishops Waltham SO32 1DH   Tel: 01489 892460

This medieval seat of the Bishops of Winchester once stood in an enormous park. Wooded grounds surround the mainly 12th and 14th century remains. Much was destroyed in fire during the Civil War, but the Dower House is intact and furnished as an 1860s farmhouse.

Opening Times: Apr to Sep daily 10:00-18:00, Oct daily 10:00-17:00. Times & prices may change. Admission: Adult £2.50, Child £1.30, Concession £1.90. EH Members Free.
Location: In Bishop's Waltham, five miles from junction 8 of M27.   Map Ref: 10

Eastleigh Museum

Hampshire County Council

The Citadel, 25 High Street, Eastleigh SO50 5LF   Tel: 023 8064 3026
Fax: 023 8065 3582   Email: alan.johnston@hants.gov.uk
Web: www.hants.gov.uk/museum/eastlmus

Take a tour through Eastleigh's past and discover what life was like during the 1930s. Meet Mr & Mrs Brown, a local engine driver and his wife. Visit our recreation of their home, a Victorian terraced house for which Eastleigh is well known. The museum has also recreated part of the Southern Railway Locomotive Works, and a steam engine footplate. Special exhibitions, Local Studies Area, Whistle Stop Café and Gift Shop.

Local historians undertake research for the Museum

Opening Times: Tue to Fri 10:00-17:00, Sat 10:00-16:00.
Admission: Free. Location: Town centre location, five minutes walk from bus and train station.   Exhibitions & Events 2004 : 17 Jan to 6 Mar: A Natural View - Wildlife illustrations by Cecilia Fitzsimons, May/Aug: Invaders - Solve the Ancient Mystery in this interactive exhibition, Sep/Oct: The Bicycle - A free-wheeling journey through history.   Map Ref: 11

www.mghh.co.uk

For current information on the outstanding Collections in over 1600 Museums, Galleries & Historic Houses in England, Scotland, Wales and Ireland

FAREHAM

Royal Armouries at Fort Nelson

Fort Nelson, Down End Road, Fareham PO17 6AN   Tel: 01329 233734
Fax: 01329 822092   Email: fnenquiries@armouries.org.uk
Web: www.armouries.org.uk

ROYAL
ARMOURIES
FORT NELSON

Victorian Kitchen

Fort Nelson is a wonderfully restored Victorian fort overlooking Portsmouth Harbour and houses the Royal Armouries national artillery collection. There are 19 acres to explore with secret underground chambers and tunnels. Daily big gun salutes, live costumed performances, professional guided tours, café and gift shop. All year there are regular special events including our action-packed Grand Military Tattoo.

Opening Times: Apr to Oct daily 10:00-17:00, Nov to Mar 10:30-16:00. Closed 25-26 Dec. Admission: Free.
Location: Junction 11 of M27, follow brown tourist signs for Royal Armouries.   Map Ref: 12

The Strawberry Story

Westbury Manor Museum

84 West Street, Fareham PO16 0JJ
Tel: 01329 824895   Fax: 01329 825917
Email: julie.biddle-combe@hants.gov.uk
Web: www.hants.gov.uk/museum/westbury

Hampshire
County
Council

Westbury Manor Museum is housed in an impressive 18th century building in the heart of town. It unravels the history of the ancient borough of Fareham with displays on the natural, social and industrial history of the area. Highlights include The Strawberry Story, The Poor Law and the local brick industry. Exhibitions are shown in the temporary exhibitions gallery with topics ranging from contemporary art to photography and local history.

Opening Times: Mon to Fri 10:00-17:00, Sat 10:00-16:00.
Admission: Free. Location: Town centre, opposite Fareham Shopping Centre. Exhibitions & Events 2004 : 17 Jan to 1 May:
Invaders - Solve the Ancient Mystery in this interactive exhibition, Jul/Aug: The Bicycle - A free-wheeling journey through history.   Map Ref: 12

FORDINGBRIDGE

Breamore House & Museum

Breamore, Fordingbridge SP6 2DF   Tel: 01725 512233   Fax: 01725 512858
Email: breamore@ukonline.co.uk   Web: www.breamorehouse.com

Breamore remains a family home and is an Elizabethan Manor House completed in 1583 with a fine collection of pictures and furniture. The museum takes visitors back to when a village was self-sufficient with many full size 'shops'.

Opening Times: May to Sep 14:00-17:30. Admission: £6.00. Location: Nine miles south of Salisbury.   Map Ref: 13

Rockbourne Roman Villa

Rockbourne, Fordingbridge SP6 3PG   Tel: 01725 518541
Email: jim.hunter@hants.gov.uk
Web: www.hants.gov.uk/museum/rockbourne

Hampshire
County
Council

The remains of the largest known Roman villa in the area. Mosaics, remains of underfloor heating system and outline of 40 rooms in original positions. Museum, special events and facilities for schools.

Opening Times: Apr to Sep daily 10:30-18:00. Admission: Adult £1.95, Concession £1.10, Family £5.00. Location: Three miles west of Fordingbridge off the B3079.   Map Ref: 14

| Guided or Private Tours | Disabled Access | Gift Shop or Sales Point | Café or Refreshments | Restaurant | Car Parking |

Hampshire & Isle of Wight

Gosport Museum and Gosport Gallery

Walpole Road, Gosport PO12 1NS   Tel: 023 9258 8035   Fax: 023 9250 1951   Email: oonagh.palmer@hants.gov.uk
Web: www.hants.gov.uk/museum/gosport

The Local History Gallery tells the story of the Borough from the earliest times, with fascinating objects, old photographs, archive film and life-sized costume figures. Discover more about the ground beneath your feet in the Geology Gallery, containing rare fossils and even a dinosaur footprint. The Gosport Gallery, housed in a separate building, hosts a regular programme of exhibitions from costume and textiles to photography and contemporary art.

Opening Times: Tue to Sat 10:00-17:00.
Admission: Free.   Location: In town centre, a few minutes walk from ferry and bus station.   Map Ref: 15

A 200 million year old ammonite in the Geology Gallery

Royal Navy Submarine Museum

Haslar Jetty Road, Gosport PO12 2AS
Tel: 023 92 529217/510354   Fax: 023 92 511349
Email: rnsubs@rnsubmus.co.uk
Web: www.rnsubmus.co.uk

Celebrate a hundred years of submarines at The Royal Navy Submarine Museum, Gosport's Premier Waterfront Tourist Attraction on Portsmouth Harbour. Step on board for a guided tour of the UK's only walk on submarine HMS Alliance. This unique attraction offers you the chance to discover stories of undersea adventure and vividly brings the heroic story of the Royal Navy's Submarine Service to life.

Opening Times: Apr to Oct 10:00-17:30, Nov to Mar 10:00-16:30. Closed Xmas & New Year.   Admission: Adult £4.00, Child £2.75, OAP £2.75, Family (2 adults and 2 children) £11.00.
Location: From junction 11 on M27 follow A32. Pass the Gosport Ferry and turn left at Haslar Road. Over Haslar Bridge, the Museum is second left.   Map Ref: 15

SEARCH

50 Clarence Road, Gosport PO12 1BU   Tel: 023 9250 1957
Fax: 023 9250 1921   Email: janet.wildman@hants.gov.uk
Web: www.hants.gov.uk/museum/search

Hampshire Museums' hands-on education centre using real museum collections for lifelong learning. Superb facilities for schools and other groups. Open days and summer holiday workshops for families.

Opening Times: Pre-booked groups only, apart from special open days. Enquiries Mon to Fri 09:00-17:30.   Admission: Special open days free, small charge for family workshops, school groups and other groups. Please telephone.   Location: In town centre, a few minutes walk from ferry and bus station.   Map Ref: 15

Havant Museum

56 East Street, Havant PO9 1BS   Tel: 023 9245 1155   Fax: 023 9249 8707
Email: oonagh.palmer@hants.gov.uk   Web: www.hants.gov.uk/museum/havant

The museum houses local history displays including Scalextric, Bronze Age and Roman hoards and local transport. It is the home of the nationally important Vokes Collection of Firearms. The Local Studies Collection contains an impressive range of resources and the special exhibition gallery hosts a wide range of shows from contemporary art and craft to photography and natural history.

(further details over the page)

The contents of an old chemist's shop

Hampshire & Isle of Wight

Opening Times: Tue to Sat 10:00-17:00. Admission: Free. Location: Short walk from town centre, next to Arts Centre. Exhibitions & Events 2004 : 10 Jan to 21 Feb: The Bicycle - A free-wheeling journey through history, Mar/Apr: A Natural View - Wildlife illustrations by Cecilia Fitzsimons, May/Aug: Pattern in Textiles, Sep/Oct: Richard Farrington Sculptures. Map Ref: 16
Photo Caption:

HIGHCLERE

Highclere Castle

Highclere, near Newbury RG20 9RN
Tel: 01635 253210 Fax: 01635 255315
Email: theoffice@highclerecastle.co.uk
Web: www.highclerecastle.co.uk

Some of the old cellars in the Castle now house the impressive private museum of ancient Egyptian finds amassed from excavations in Thebes by the 5th Earl of Carnarvon and Howard Carter between 1907 and 1913. An additional gallery of photographs recalls their discovery, in 1922, of the tomb of Tutankhamun, probably the greatest archaeological story ever.

Opening Times: 6 Jul to 5 Sep Tue to Fri & Sun. Also BH 11/12 Apr, 2/3 & 30/31 May and 30 Aug. 11:00-17:00 daily, last admission one hour before closing. (As the house may be subject to closure during this period - please call 01635 253210 to check before

Bronze figure of Harpocrates from the Egyptian Centre.

travelling). Admission: Adult £7.00, Concession £5.50, Wheelchair pushers Free, Child £3.50, Family (2 adults and 2 children or 1 adult and 3 children). Grounds & Garden only: Adult £4.00, Child £1.50. Group rates, private guided tours, school groups and annual VIP season tickets available. Location: Seven miles from Newbury on A34 towards Winchester. Map Ref: 17

ISLE OF WIGHT

Bembridge Maritime Museum & Shipwreck Centre
Providence House, Sherbourne Street, Bembridge, Isle of Wight PO35 5SB Tel: 01983 872223
Web: www.isle-of-wight.uk.com/shipwrecks

Local history and story of Bembridge Lifeboats - past and present. Countless artefacts recovered from local shipwrecks, unique collection of ship models and much more.

Opening Times: Apr to Oct daily 10:00-17:00. Admission: Please phone for details.
Location: Centre of Bembridge village. Map Ref: 18

Carisbrooke Castle Museum
Newport, Isle of Wight PO30 1XY Tel: 01983 523112 Fax: 01983 536126 Email: carismus@lineone.net
Web: www.carisbrookecastlemuseum.org.uk

Accommodated inside the Castle's Great Hall, this independent museum exhibits material relating to the Castle and the history of the Isle of Wight. The Castle exhibition includes items connected with the imprisonment of King Charles I. Local history displays are changed regularly, and may feature Island places and people, and aspects of social history.

Opening Times: Apr to Sep daily 10:00-18:00, Oct 10:00-17:00, Nov to Mar 10:00-16:00. Closed Xmas & New Year.
Admission: Adult £5.00, Child £2.50, Concession £3.80, Family £12.50. (2003 charges). Location: One mile south west of Newport. Map Ref: 19

400-year-old Chamber Organ, presented to Princess Beatrice

Cowes Maritime Museum
Branch Library & Maritime Museum, Beckford Road, Cowes, Isle of Wight PO31 7SG
Tel: 01983 823433 Fax: 01983 823841 Email: rachel.silverson@iow.gov.uk

Ship models, photographs and real boats reflect Cowes' yachting and shipbuilding heritage. The museum holds photographs and archives from Samuel White Shipyard.

Opening Times: Mon to Wed, Fri 09:30-18:00, Sat 09:30-16:00. Admission: Free.
Location: Just off High Street, five minutes from bus and ferry terminal. Map Ref: 20

Hampshire & Isle of Wight

Dinosaur Isle

Culver Parade, Sandown, Isle of Wight PO36 8QA   Tel: 01983 404344   Fax: 01983 407502
Web: www.dinosaurisle.com

Resurrects dinosaurs which lived 125 million years ago, along with their ancient habitat. Unlocks the rocky tombs of fossils and brings them together in the first ever, purpose built dinosaur attraction in Britain.

Opening Times: Apr to Oct daily 10:00-18:00, Nov to Mar daily 10:00-16:00.   Admission: Adult £4.60, Child £2.60, Family £12.00.   Location: Situated on the B3395 coast road at Culver Parade.   Map Ref: 21

Isle of Wight Steam Railway

The Railway Station, Havenstreet, Isle of Wight PO33 4DS   Tel: 01983 882204   Fax: 01983 884515   Email: hugh@iwsteamrailway.co.uk   Web: www.iwsteamrailway.co.uk

A working museum of the island's railway history. A ten mile round trip in Victorian and Edwardian carriages, often hauled by a Victorian locomotive. Museum artefacts on display.

Opening Times: Apr Thu & Sun 10:00-16:00, May Wed, Thur & Sun 10:00-16:00, Jun Tue to Thu, Sat & Sun 10:00-16:00, Jul to Sep daily 10:00-16:00, Oct Thu & Sun 10:00-16:00. Admission: Admission & Train: Adult £7.50, Child £4.00, OAP £7.00.   Location: Havenstreet Village Station, rail served on open days.   Map Ref: 22

Lilliput Antique Doll and Toy Museum

High Street, Brading, Isle of Wight PO36 0DJ   Tel: 01983 407231
Email: lilliput.museum@btconnect.com   Web: www.lilliputmuseum.com

One of Britain's finest and most comprehensive collections of antique dolls and toys with over 2000 exhibits dating from c2000 BC to c1945. All are genuine, there are no modern reproductions.

Opening Times: Daily 10:00-17:00. Closed Xmas.   Admission: Adult £1.95, Child/Concession £1.15.   Location: In Brading Town Centre.   Map Ref: 23

Museum of Island History

The Guildhall, High Street, Newport, Isle of Wight PO30 1TY   Tel / Fax: 01983 823841
Email: rachel.silverson@iow.gov.uk

Discover the history of the Isle of Wight from the dinosaurs to the present day, through the latest hands-on exhibits, computers and interactives. The museum also houses the Island's central Tourist Information Centre.

Opening Times: Mon to Sat 10:00-17:00 and Sun 11:00-15:30.   Admission: Adult £1.80, Child/OAP £1.00, Families £4.00.   Location: In the Guildhall, town centre of Newport. Two minute walk from bus station.   Map Ref: 19

National Wireless Museum

Puckpool Park, Seaview, Isle of Wight PO34 5AR   Tel: 01983 567665   Fax: 01983 563730

A collection of radio, television and sound reproduction, for educational, historical and cultural purposes.

Opening Times: 14:00-17:00.   Admission: Free.   Map Ref: 24

Newport Roman Villa

Cypress Road, Newport, Isle of Wight PO30 1HE   Tel: 01983 529720   Fax: 01983 823841
Email: rachel.silverson@iow.gov.uk

Discover the luxuries of third century Roman British life. The Villa has a wonderfully preserved bath suite and reconstructed living room, kitchen and charming herb garden. Hands on activities.

Opening Times: Apr to Oct Mon to Sat 10:00-16:30, also Sun in Jul & Aug 12:00-16:00. Open for group bookings only Nov to Mar.   Admission: Adult £2.00 Child/OAP/Concession £1.20 Families £5. Group bookings (01983) 823847.   Location: The villa is ten minute walk from central bus station.   Map Ref: 19

Nunwell House (Aylmer Military Collection)

Brading, Isle of Wight PO36 0JQ   Tel: 01983 407240

A historic and beautifully furnished house - a family home since 1522. Special collection of one family's militaria.

Hampshire & Isle of Wight

Opening Times: End May to early Sep Mon to Wed 13:00-17:00. Tours at 13:30, 14:30 & 15:30.
Admission: Adult £4.00, Child (under 10) £1.00, OAP £3.50. Location: Signed on A3055.
Short walk from Brading Station or bus stop. Map Ref: 23

Osborne House

East Cowes, Isle of Wight PO32 6JY Tel: 01983 200022

Osborne House was built for Queen Victoria and Prince Albert as a private home. The house was built by Thomas Cubitt in Italianate style and is set among terraced gardens and filled with treasured mementoes.

Opening Times: Apr to Sep daily 10:00-18:00, Oct daily 10:00-17:00 last admission 16:00.
Please phone to check winter opening/pre-booked guided tours of house only. Times & prices
may change. Admission: House & Grounds: Adult £8.00, Child £4.00, Concession £6.00,
Family £20.00. Grounds only: Adult £4.50, Child £2.30, Concession £3.40. Tour rates available.
EH Members Free. Location: One mile south east of East Cowes. Map Ref: 25

St Barbe Museum & Art Gallery

New Street, Lymington SO41 9BH Tel: 01590 676969 Fax: 01590 679997
Email: office@stbarbe-museum.org.uk Web: www.stbarbe-museum.org.uk

The Museum tells the story of the New Forest coastal area, with chronological and themed displays which include boat building, smuggling and the Barton Fossils. The Art Galleries feature changing art exhibitions.

Opening Times: Mon to Sat 10:00-16:00. Admission: Adult £3.00, Concession £2.00, Family
£6.00. Group rates available. Location: In town centre, only one minute walk from High Street.
Map Ref: 26

Sammy Miller Motorcycle Museum

Bashley Manor, Bashley Cross Road, New Milton BH25 5SZ Tel: 01425 620777 Fax: 01425
619696 Web: www.sammymiller.co.uk

Sammy Miller is a legend in his own lifetime, winning competitions for 46 years. The museum houses the finest collection of fully restored motorcyles in Europe, including factory racers and exotic prototypes.

Opening Times: Daily 10:00-16:30. Closed Xmas. Admission: Adult £4.50, Child £2.00.
Location: New Milton Hampshire off A35 at Hinton Church. Map Ref: 27

Flora Twort Gallery

Church Path, Petersfield GU32 1HS Tel: 01730 260756
Web: www.hants.gov.uk/museum/floratwo

Hampshire
County
Council

A charming gallery, once the home and studio of local artist Flora Twort. It is now devoted to the display of her delightful paintings and drawings, which form a very personal record of Petersfield between the wars. The ground floor of the building has been transformed into a restaurant serving coffee, lunch and afternoon teas. It is also open for dinner on two evenings each week.

Opening Times: Tue to Sat 09:45-17:00. Admission:
Free. Location: Town centre location. Map Ref: 28

The Flora Twort Gallery

Portchester Castle

Castle Street, Portchester PO16 9QW Tel: 023 9237 8291

A residence for kings, this castle has a history stretching back nearly 2000 years. Built by the Romans as a defence against barbarian attacks, Porchester became a royal castle in the medieval period. The collection includes extensive excavation material.

Hampshire & Isle of Wight

Opening Times: Apr to Sep daily 10:00-18:00, Oct daily 10:00-17:00, Nov to Mar Wed to Sun 10:00-16:00. Closed Xmas & New Year. Times & prices may change. Admission: Adult £3.50, Child £1.80, Concession £2.60. EH Members Free. Location: On south side of Portchester off A27, junction 11 on M27. Map Ref: 29

PORTSMOUTH

Charles Dickens Birthplace Museum

393 Old Commercial Road, Portsmouth PO1 4QL Tel: 023 9282 7261

Born in this modest house in 1812. Beautifully restored room settings recreate Regency life. With memorabilia, illustrations from Charles Dickens' published works, portraits of the Dickens family and the couch on which he died.

Opening Times: Apr to Sep daily 10:00-17:30, Oct daily 10:00-17:00. Admission: Adult £2.50, Child £1.50, OAP £1.80, Family £6.50. Location: Ten minute walk from town centre/Portsmouth & Southsea Railway Station. Map Ref: 30

City Museum & Records Office

Museum Road, Old Portsmouth, Portsmouth PO1 2LJ Tel: 023 9282 7261

Dedicated to local history and fine and decorative art. 'The Story of Portsmouth' displays room settings showing life in Portsmouth from the 17th century to the 1950s using modern audio-visual techniques. Experience the different life-styles of the Victorian working poor in the 'Dockyard Workers Cottage' and the affluent 'Victorian Parlour'. A 1930s kitchen with everything including the kitchen sink! A 1930s 'Art Deco' dining room and a 1950s front-room complete with flying ducks on the wall and early television showing 'Listen With Mother'. The 'Portsmouth at Play' exhibition looks at all aspects of leisure pursuits from the Victorian period to the 1970s. The museum has a fine and decorative art gallery and temporary exhibition gallery with regular changing exhibitions. The Record Office contains the official records of the City of Portsmouth from the 14th century and private and commercial records. Collections and Exhibits of consequence: 17th Century Furniture; Art Deco Furniture - Frank Dobson Sculptures (Terracottage & Bronze), Ceri Richards Relief Work 'Le Piano', Ronald Ossory Dunlop Painting 'Still Life with Black Bottle'; JMW Turner RA watercolour 'Gosport, the Entrance to Portsmouth Harbour' c.1829. Local History: Sir Alec Rose (Round the World Yachtsman - artefacts), Verrecahias Ice Cream Parlour and artefacts.

Opening Times: Apr to Sep daily 10:00-17:30, Oct to Mar daily 10:00-17:00. Closed 24-26 Dec. Admission: Free. Location: Ten minute walk from the town centre/Portsmouth and Southsea Railway Station. Seven minute walk from Harbour Railway/Bus Station Exhibitions & Events 2004 : For Exhibition and Events please telephone for details. Map Ref: 30

D-Day Museum and Overlord Embroidery

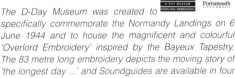

Clarence Esplanade, Portsmouth PO5 3NT Tel: 023 9282 7261

The D-Day Museum was created to specifically commemorate the Normandy Landings on 6 June 1944 and to house the magnificent and colourful 'Overlord Embroidery' inspired by the Bayeux Tapestry. The 83 metre long embroidery depicts the moving story of 'the longest day ...' and Soundguides are available in four languages. An archive film show (in five languages) includes original footage and brings this period of the Second World War alive to the visitor. The exciting displays and exhibits recreate what it must have been like to live through this period and the events of that day. The

D-Day Museum Overlord Embroidery

equipment, the men who took part... it's all here at the D-Day Museum. Experience life in the Anderson Shelter and the period front room of the ARP Warden. 'Listen While You Work' in the factory scene, keep vigil with the troops camped in the forest waiting their time to embark. Eavesdrop on communications in 'The Map Room', Southwick House. Board a 'Dakota' and be the

Hampshire & Isle of Wight

first to land in a field in France and hear the story behind the crashed Horsa Glider, pass through the German pill-box and see the armada approaching the beaches and, finally, board an original landing craft of the period.

Opening Times: Apr to Sep daily 10:00-17:30, Oct to Mar daily 10:00-17:00. Closed 24-26 Dec. Admission: Adult £5.00, Child £3.00, OAP £3.75, Family £13.00. Group rates: Adult £4.25, Child £2.50, OAP £3.20, Student £2.30. Exhibitions & Events 2004 : For Exhibitions and Events please telephone for details.
Map Ref: 30

Natural History Museum & Butterfly House

Cumberland House, Eastern Parade, Southsea, Portsmouth PO4 9RF
Tel: 023 9282 7261

Wildlife dioramas and geology of the Portsmouth area, it has a full size reconstruction of Dinosaur 'Iguanodon' and other fossil remains. During the summer months, British and European butterflies flying free.

Opening Times: Apr to Sep daily 10:00-17:30, Oct to Mar daily 10:00-17:00. Closed 24-26 Dec. Admission: Apr to Oct: Adult £2.50, Child £1.50, OAP £1.80, Family £6.50. Nov to Mar: Adult £2.00, Child £1.20, OAP £1.50, Family £5.20. Location: Situated Canoe Lake area, nearest bus stop - Festing Road.
Map Ref: 30

Portsmouth Historic Dockyard

portsmouth HISTORIC DOCKYARD

Building 1/7 College Road, Portsmouth   Tel: 023 9286 1533
Fax: 023 9229 5252   Email: mail@historicdockyard.co.uk   Web: www.historicdockyard.co.uk

HMS Victory

No visit to Southern England is complete without a trip to Portsmouth Historic Dockyard. The Historic Dockyard is the leading attraction on the South Coast and is home to the world famous historic ships, Mary Rose, HMS Victory, HMS Warrior 1860 and the stunning new interactive attraction, Action Stations. Together with the Dockyard Apprentice Exhibition and Harbour Tours around the modern fleet, it is without doubt one of the most exciting, entertaining and educational days out for all the family in the country. Action Stations is the Historic Dockyard latest major attraction. It is a show-case for the modern day Navy and simulates what it is like to go to sea on a Type 23 Frigate. Mary Rose is the only recovered 16th century warship on display in the world and was a favourite of Henry VIII. She sank in the Solent in 1545, watched by the horrified king. In 1805, HMS Victory gained her immortality at the Battle of Trafalgar along with Nelson, Britain's greatest naval hero. The world's oldest commissioned warship, her gun-decks vividly depict the harsh conditions in which ordinary sailors lived, worked and fought. Opposite HMS Victory is the award-winning Royal Naval Museum and its four exciting galleries. One of them is devoted to The History of HMS Victory exhibition, focussing on the admirals, crews and craftsmen who have worked on board her. Just 55 years separate

HMS Warrior

Trafalgar and the launch of the mighty HMS Warrior 1860, pride of Queen Victoria's Black Battlefleet. Explore her four huge decks and discover why she was the ultimate deterrent being the first warship powered by steam and sail, the largest and fastest of her day.

Opening Times: Nov to Mar 10:00-17:00, Apr to Oct 10:00-17:30. Admission: Adult £14.85, Child/OAP £11.90, Family £47.55. Location: Portsmouth.
Map Ref: 30

Royal Marines Museum

Eastney Esplanade, Southsea, Portsmouth PO4 9PX   Tel: 023 9281 9385   Fax: 023 9283 8420
Email: info@royalmarinesmuseum.co.uk   Web: www.royalmarinesmuseum.co.uk

An award winning museum that helps you discover the exciting 330 year story of the Royal Marines through dramatic and interactive displays. Visit the Museum at what was one of the most stately Officers' Messes in England and tour its world famous medal collection.

Opening Times: Jun to Aug daily 10:00-17:00, Sep to May daily 10:00-16:30. Admission: Adult £4.75, OAP £3.50, Child £2.25 - Kids Go Free (under 16) 1 Apr to 31 Mar 05, Family £12.00. Location: On the seafront, about one mile east of South Parade Pier.
Map Ref: 30

Hampshire & Isle of Wight

Southsea Castle

Clarence Esplanade, Southsea, Portsmouth PO5 3PA   Tel: 023 9282 7261

Built by Henry VIII in 1544 to protect Portsmouth Harbour. Military history from Tudor times to the Victorians. 'Time Tunnel Experience' showing 'Life in the Castle', underground passages and audio-visual presentation.

Opening Times: Apr to Sep daily 10:00-17:30, Oct daily 10:00-17:00.   Admission: Adult £2.50, Child £1.50, OAP £1.80, Family £6.50.   Location: Situated on Southsea Seafront. Nearest bus stop - Palmerston Road.   Map Ref: 30

Treadgold Industrial Heritage Museum

Hampshire County Council

1 Bishop Street, Portsea, Portsmouth PO1 3DA   Tel: 023 9282 4745
Fax: 023 9283 7310   Email: peter.lawton@hants.gov.uk
Web: www.hants.gov.uk/museum/treadgold

This 'Victorian time capsule' comprises an ironmonger's shop and storerooms, offices, stable, workshop with forges and a reconstructed tenement c1810. A rare industrial archaeological site, it houses an entire collection of tools, machinery, office paperwork and shop stock at its original location. The listed collection of buildings dates to 1706.

Opening Times: Apr to Sep Wed to Thu 10:00-16:00. Schools and other groups, by appointment, weekdays throughout the year. Admission: Free.   Location: Near Portsmouth historic dockyard, ten minute walk from rail and bus station.   Exhibitions & Events 2004 : Events

The forge workshop

2004: Free opening 11 & 12 Sep as part of The Civic Trust's Heritage Open Days.   Map Ref: 30

Mottisfont Abbey Garden, House and Estate

Mottisfont, Romsey SO51 0LP   Tel: 01794 340757   Fax: 01794 341492
Email: mottisfontabbey@nationaltrust.org.uk   Web: www.nationaltrust.org.uk

This 12th century Augustinian priory was converted into a private house after the Dissolution. The Abbey contains a drawing room decorated with Rex Whistler's murals.In the grounds are magnificent trees, walled gardens and the National Collection of Old-fashioned Roses.

Opening Times: House & Garden: 6 Mar to 21 Mar Sat & Sun 11:00-16:00, 22 Mar to 2 Jun Sat to Wed 11:00-18:00, 28 Jun to 31 Aug Sat to Thu 11:00-18:00, 1 Sep to 31 Oct 11:00-18:00 Sat to Wed. Open Good Friday 11:00-18:00.   Admission: Adult £6.50, Child £3.00, Family £16.00. NT Members Free.   Location: Four and a half miles north west of Romsey, one mile west of A3057.   Map Ref: 31

Bursledon Windmill

Hampshire County Council

Windmill Lane, Bursledon, Southampton SO31 8BG   Tel: 023 8040 4999
Email: gavin.bowie@hants.gov.uk
Web: www.hants.gov.uk/museum/windmill

Hampshire's only working windmill, built in 1813 and lovingly restored. Wooden machinery, traditional timber-framed barn and granary. Stoneground flour made and sold to visitors. Nature trail and special events. Teachers pack.

Opening Times: May to Sep Sat & Sun 10:00-16:00, Oct to Apr Sun 10:00-16:00.
Admission: Adult £1.50, Concession 75p, Family £3.75.   Location: Short drive from junction 8 of the M27.   Map Ref: 32

John Hansard Gallery

University of Southampton, Highfield, Southampton SO17 1BJ   Tel: 023 8059 2158   Fax: 023 8059 4192   Email: info@hansardgallery.org.uk   Web: www.hansardgallery.org.uk

Around six contemporary visual art exhibitions per year lasting approximately seven weeks each. University collection. Sculpture trail.

Opening Times: Tue to Fri 11:00-17:00, Sat 11:00-16:00. Please contact Gallery for Easter & Xmas closures.   Admission: Free.   Location: On the west side of the University of Southampton, next to the Turner Sims Concert Hall and Student Health Centre.   Map Ref: 32

Hampshire & Isle of Wight

Museum of Archaeology

Gods House Tower, Winkle Street, Southampton SO14 2NY Tel: 023 8063 5904
Fax: 023 8033 9601 Email: k.wardley@southampton.gov.uk
Web: www.southampton.gov.uk/leisure/museums

One of the top designated archaeology collections in the country. The displays use finds from excavations within the city. Highlights include colourful imported pottery and glass from the medieval port, evidence of international trade and local industry from Saxon Hamwic and objects from everyday life in Roman Clausentum. Activities for children include 'try on a toga', mosaic making and interactive CD-Rom.

Opening Times: Tue to Fri 10:00-12:00 & 13:00-17:00, Sat 10:00-12:00 & 13:00-16:00, Sun 14:00-17:00.

Gods House Tower Museum, main hall

Admission: Free. Location: In old town area, near Isle of Wight ferry terminal, five minutes walk from West Quay Shopping Centre. Exhibitions & Events 2004 : Until 15 Feb: Pots, Brooms and Hurdles from the Heathlands, 17 Jan: Family Trails, 18 Feb: Half Term Activity for kids, Feb to Jul (tbc): Clues From Clay. Map Ref: 32

Southampton City Art Gallery

Civic Centre, Southampton SO14 7LP Tel: 023 8083 2277 Fax: 023 8083 2153
Email: art.gallery@southampton.gov.uk Web: www.southampton.gov.uk/art

The most outstanding gallery in the south of England, internationally renowned for its collection of contemporary works by British artists. The collection numbers over 3500 works and spans six centuries of European art history. The gallery presents four major temporary exhibitions a year, which range from historic to contemporary art.

Opening Times: Tue to Sat 10:00-17:00, Sun 13:00-16:00. Closed Mon. Admission: Free. Location: City centre, five minute walk from railway station, opposite Watts Park, in Commercial Road. Exhibitions & Events 2004 : Until

Galley 3, Southampton City Art Gallery

7 Mar: The Hidden Hand: John Salt, 25 Mar to 22 May: Immaterial: Brancusi, Gabo, Moholy-Nagy, Jun to Sep: Ben Hartley, Jul to Sep: Alice Kettle. Map Ref: 32

Southampton Maritime Museum

Wool House, Bugle Street, Southampton SO14 2AR
Tel: 023 8022 3941 Fax: 023 8033 9601
Email: historic.sites@southampton.gov.uk
Web: www.southampton.gov.uk/leisure/museums

The Wool House was built as a Warehouse for the medieval wool trade. It is now a museum telling the story of the port of Southampton and the great liners that sailed from here to all parts of the world. Highlights include Titanic Voices Exhibition, telling the real story of the Titanic through original artefacts and the voices of local people whose lives were affected by the tragedy.

Opening Times: Tue to Fri 10:00-13:00 & 14:00-17:00, Sat 10:00-13:00 & 14:00-16:00, Sun 14:00-17:00. Admission: Free. Location:

Enjoy a memorable day at the Southampton Maritime Museum

Corner of Bugle Street and Town Quay Road, five minutes walk from West Quay Shopping Centre. Exhibitions & Events 2004

: Titanic - The 90th Anniversary - see new artefacts never before on public display. Map Ref: 32

Tudor House Museum & Garden

Bugle Street, Southampton SO14 2AD Tel: 023 8063 5904 Fax: 023 8033 9601
Email: historic.sites@southampton.gov.uk
Web: www.southampton.gov.uk/leisure/museums

Tudor House is closed while a full building survey and photographic record are made, prior to restoration. Group visits are available to see this work in progress.

Opening Times: Closed for refurbishment. Admission: Free. Location: Bugle Street, five minutes walk from West Quay Shopping Centre. Map Ref: 32

Hampshire & Isle of Wight

STOCKBRIDGE

Museum of Army Flying

Middle Wallop, Stockbridge SO20 8DY   Tel: 01980 674421   Fax: 01264 781694
Email: enquiries@flying-museum.org.uk   Web: www.flying-museum.org.uk

Sopwith Pup 1916 with World War I military cycle

This award winning museum celebrates over 100 years of Army Aviation and is home to one of the country's finest historical collections of military kites, gliders, aeroplanes and helicopters. Imaginative tableaux trace the developments of Army flying from pre World War I to today's modern Army Air Corps. The museum includes a children's Science and Education centre.

Opening Times: Daily 10:00-16:30. Admission: Adult £5.00, Child £3.50, Concession £4.00. Group rates available. Location: On the A343 between Andover and Salisbury.
Map Ref: 33

WATERLOOVILLE

Goss & Crested China Centre

62 Murray Road, Horndean, Waterlooville PO8 9JL   Tel: 023 925 97440   Fax: 023 925 91975
Email: info@gosschinaclub.demon.co.uk   Web: www.gosscrestedchina.co.uk

A vast display of Victorian and Edwardian crested china souvenir ware made in the Staffordshire Potteries between 1860 and 1939. These include World War I, animals, miniatures, cottages, Parian busts of royalty, politicians etc.

Opening Times: Mon to Sat 09:00-17:00. Closed Sun & BH.   Admission: Free.   Location: Nine miles from Portsmouth, nine miles from Petersfield.
Map Ref: 34

WHITCHURCH

Whitchurch Silk Mill

28 Winchester Street, Whitchurch RG28 7AL   Tel: 01256 892065   Fax: 01256 893882   Email: silkmill@btinternet.com   Web: www.whitchurchsilkmill.org.uk

Traditional Silk Making at Whitchurch Silk Mill

This delightful Grade II* watermill built on the river Test in 1800 has produced silk continuously since the 1820s. Now a working museum it keeps alive the art of making silk on machinery installed between 1890 and 1950. It used to produce silk for lining Burberry raincoats and for legal and academic gowns and weaves short runs for theatrical costume and historic houses.

Opening Times: Tue to Sun 10:30-17:00, also BH Mon. Last admission 16:15. Closed 24 Dec to 2 Jan.
Admission: Adult £3.50, Child £1.75, OAP/Student £3.00, Family (2 adults and 3 children) £8.75.   Location: Near town centre, 15 minute walk from rail station.
Map Ref: 35

WINCHESTER

City of Winchester Museum

The Square, Winchester   Tel: 01962 848269
Email: museums@winchester.gov.uk
Web: www.winchester.gov.uk

Tells Winchester's nationally important story, as a major Roman centre and afterwards as the principal city of Alfred and later Anglo-Saxon and Norman kings. The story continues through the centuries with Winchester's revival as a fashionable county town in the 18th century and displays include reconstructed Victorian & Edwardian shops. Lift to all floors.

Opening Times: Apr to Oct Mon to Sat 10:00-17:00, Sun 12:00-17:00. Nov to Mar Tue to Sat 10:00-16:00, Sun 12:00-16:00.
Admission: Free.   Location: The Square, between High Street and the Cathedral.
Map Ref: 36

Guildhall Gallery

Broadway, Winchester SO23 9LJ   Tel: 01962 848289
Email: museums@winchester.gov.uk   Web: www.winchester.gov.uk

Frequently changing exciting exhibitions of paintings, craft, photography, ceramics and sculpture.

Opening Times: During exhibitions: Apr to Oct Mon to Sat 10:00-17:00, Sun 12:00-17:00. Nov to Mar Tue to Sat 10:00-16:00, Sun 12:00-16:00. Admission: Free. Location: The Broadway, situated in the Victorian Guildhall above the Tourist Information Centre.   Map Ref: 36

The Gurkha Museum

Peninsula Barracks, Romsey Road, Winchester SO23 8TS   Tel: 01962 842832/843657
Fax: 01962 877597   Email: curator@thegurkhamuseum.co.uk
Web: www.the gurkhamuseum.co.uk

A unique commemoration of Gurkha service to the British Crown and people spanning 190 years, two world wars and numerous smaller campaigns. There is much about Nepal, its people, culture, arts and customs.

Opening Times: Mon to Sat 10:00-17:00, Sun 12:00-16:00. Closed Xmas & New Year. Admission: Adult £1.50, Child/OAP 75p. Group 50p per person. Location: Town centre, near Great Hall.
Map Ref: 36

The King's Royal Hussars Museum in Winchester

Peninsula Barracks, Romsey Road, Winchester SO23 8TS   Tel: 01962 828541/828539
Fax: 01962 828538   Email: beresford@krhmuseum.freeserve.co.uk   Web: www.krh.org.uk

Story of famous cavalry regiments; 10th Royal Hussars (Prince of Wales' Own) and 11th Hussars (Prince Albert's Own) 'The Cherry Pickers' raised in 1715. The Royal Hussars 1969-1992 and today's regiment, The King's Royal Hussars from 1992. See the Charge of the Light Brigade, experience World War I trench, and see the cupboard in which Private Fowler was hidden in a French farm for three years during World War I.

The diary of The Charge of The Light Brigade by RSM Loy Smith

Opening Times: Tue to Fri 10:00-12:45 & 13:15-16:00 Sat, Sun, BH and 1/2 term Mon 12:00-16:00. Admission: Free.
Location: Beside Great Hall/Law Courts. Exhibitions & Events 2004 : May to Jun: Winchester Military Museums Exhibition 60th Anniversary of D-Day in the New Visitor Centre.   Map Ref: 36

Light Infantry Museum

Peninsula Barracks, Romsey Rd, Winchester SO23 8TS   Tel: 01962 828550   Fax: 01962 828534

A collection which depicts the Light Infantry Regiment, its origins, soldiers and operations.

Opening Times: Tue to Sat and holiday Mon 10:00-16:00 (closed for lunch). Sun 12:00-16:00. Admission: Free, but donations welcome. Location: Top of town, behind the Great Hall and five minutes from railway station.   Map Ref: 36

Royal Hampshire Regiment Museum & Memorial Garden

Serle's House, Southgate Street, Winchester SO23 9EG   Tel / Fax: 01962 863658

Re-opening May 2004. History of the regiment 1702 to 1992. Medals, uniforms, colours, weapons and many personal artefacts. Covers regulars, Volunteers, Territorials and Militia.

Opening Times: Mon to Fri 11:00-15:30. Closed 2 wks Xmas & New Year. Wkends & BH Apr to Oct only 12:00-16:00. Admission: Free. Location: Town ctr, 2 mins walk from high st. Map Ref: 36

Westgate

High Street, Winchester   Tel: 01962 848269
Email: museums@winchester.gov.uk   Web: www.winchester.gov.uk

New displays in the medieval gateway tell the story of Tudor and Stuart Winchester, its role as a debtor's prison and as a store for unique civic weights and measures. Brass rubbing. Hand-on activities. Rooftop city views.

Opening Times: Apr to Oct Mon to Sat 10:00-17:00, Sun 12:00-17:00. Feb to Mar Tue to Sat 10:00-16:00, Sun 12:00-16:00. Closed Nov to Jan. Admission: Free. Location: High Street, close to Great Hall.   Map Ref: 36

The region boasts some singularly handsome towns including Hereford, once the capital of the powerful Anglo-Saxon kingdom of Mercia and now home to the magnificent twelfth century cathedral which towers over the banks of the River Wye. Worcester too has its proud history, being an important centre during the Civil War. The Cotswolds in the east offer magnificent views and inspired much of the music of Sir Edward Edgar.

There are a number of excellent museums and galleries dealing with this rich region.

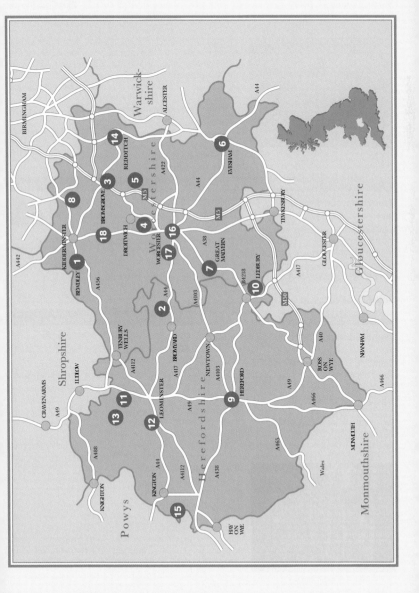

The Red Map References should be used to locate Museums etc on the pages that follow

Herefordshire & Worcestershire

BEWDLEY *Worcs*

Bewdley Museum
     ♿ ⬤ ▱

The Shambles, Load Street, Bewdley DY12 2AE   Tel: 01299 403573   Fax: 01299 404740
Email: museum_wfdc@online.rednet.co.uk   Web: http://bewdleymuseum.tripod.com

Housed in the town's old Butchers Shambles, the museum provides a fascinating insight into the growth and trades of the town. Displays feature the work of basket and besom makers, charcoal burners, pewterers and brass founders. Daily craft demonstrations.

Opening Times: Apr to Sep daily 10:00-16:30, Oct daily 11:00-16:00.   Admission: Free. Group charges apply.   Location: Bewdley - off the A456 Leominster Road, on the B4190.   Map Ref: 1

Severn Valley Railway
    🚂 ♿ ⬤ ▱ ♿

The Railway Station, Bewdley DY12 1BG   Tel: 01299 403816
Fax: 01299 400839   Web: www.svr.co.uk

A standard-gauge steam railway running between Kidderminster and Bridgnorth, 16 miles. The journey provides fine views of the River Severn and visitors can alight at any of the four intermediate stations. Refreshments at main stations and on most trains. Special events throughout the year. The railway is home to one of the largest collections of pre-nationalisation locomotives, coaches and wagons.

Opening Times: Every Sat & Sun. May to Sep daily and local school holidays.   Admission: Prices depend on journey taken.   Location: On A448 Comberton Hill. Signposted from all major roads.   Map Ref: 1

Loco 3442 crossing
River Severn on Victoria Bridge

BRINGSTY *Worcs*

Brockhampton Estate
    ♿ ⬤ ▱ ♿

Greenfields, Bringsty WR6 5TB   Tel: 01885 482077   Web: www.nationaltrust.org.uk

A moated manor house built in the late 14th century. An unusual timber framed gatehouse straddles the moat. There is a small collection of family portraits. The extensive woodland contains many ancient trees.

Opening Times: Estate; All year, daylight. House; 3 to 31 Mar Wed to Sat 12:00-16:00, 1 Apr to 30 Sep Wed to Sat 12:00-17:00, 1 Oct to 31 Oct Wed to Sat 12:00-16:00. Open BH Mons. Admission: House; Adult £3.50, Child £1.75, Family £8.50. Estate; Free to pedestrians. NT Members Free.   Location: Two miles east of Bromyard on Worcester road (A44).   Map Ref: 2

BROMSGROVE *Worcs*

Avoncroft Museum of Historic Buildings
    🚂 ♿ ⬤ ▱ ♿

Stoke Heath, Bromsgrove B60 4JR   Tel: 01527 831363   Fax: 01527 876934
Email: avoncrofteducation@compuserve.com   Web: www.avoncroft.org.uk

Collection of over 25 historic buildings, including windmill, prefab and church. Includes the National Telephone Kiosk collection.

Opening Times: Mar & Oct Tue to Thu, Sat & Sun 10:30-16:00. Nov Sat & Sun only 10:30 to 16:00. Apr to Jun, Sep to Oct Tue to Fri 10:30-16:30. Jul & Aug Mon to Fri 10:30-17:00, Sat & Sun 10:30-17:30.   Admission: Adult £5.50, Child £2.75, Concession £4.50, Family £14.50. Party rates available.   Location: Three miles north of junction 5, M5, three miles south of junction 1, M42. Off A38, south of Bromsgrove.   Map Ref: 3

Reconstruction of Victorian
and Edwardian shop windows

Bromsgrove Museum
    🚂 ⬤ ♿

26 Birmingham Road, Bromsgrove B61 0DD   Tel / Fax: 01527 831809

Bromsgrove Museum gives an insight into local history with displays of past craft and industries such as nail, glass, lead, button and salt making. Also incorporated into the Museum is a street of Victorian and Edwardian shops, including a chemists, stationers and cobblers. There are also displays on The Bromsgrove Guild and AE Housman.

Opening Times: Mon to Sat 10:30-12:30 13:00-16:30. Admission: Free.   Location: Near town centre, on Birmingham Road.   Map Ref: 3

Herefordshire & Worcestershire

Droitwich Heritage Centre

St Richard's House, Victoria Square, Droitwich Spa WR9 8DS   Tel: 01905 774312
Fax: 01905 794226

See the fascinating history of Droitwich from prehistoric settlement to luxury Spa. BBC Radio room with hands-on display. Brass rubbing, Tourist Information Centre and souvenirs.

Opening Times: Mon to Sat 10:00-16:00. Close Sun and BH.   Admission: Free.
Location: Town centre location, ten minute walk from rail station.   Map Ref: 4

Hanbury Hall & Gardens

School Road, Hanbury, Droitwich Spa WR9 7EA   Tel: 01527 821214
Fax: 01527 821251   Email: hanburyhall@nationaltrust.org.uk
Web: www.ntrustsevern.org.uk

Beautiful English country house with tranquil reconstructed 18th century gardens and parkland. Many unusual features including outstanding staircase murals, working mushroom house and orangery, Watney Collection of fine porcelain and Dutch flower paintings.

Opening Times: 1 Mar to 31 Oct Sat to Wed 13:00-15:00. House tours: 6 Mar to 31 Oct Sat & Sun 11:00-13:00. Open Good Friday.   Admission: House: Adult £5.40, Child £2.70, Family £13.00. Group £4.60. Garden only: Adult £3.50, Child £1.80, Family £8.50. NT Members Free. House & Garden closed on 12, 13, 14 Mar 2004 for Homes & Gardens Exhibition.
Location: Near junction 5 of M5, four and a half miles east of Droitwich, one mile north of B4090, six miles south of Bromsgrove.   Exhibitions & Events 2004 : 12-14 Mar: Homes & Garden Exhibition (house and garden closed).   Map Ref: 5

The Almonry Heritage Centre

Abbey Gate, Evesham WR11 4BG   Tel: 01386 446944   Fax: 01386 442348
Email: tic@almonry.ndo.co.uk   Web: www.evesham.uk.com   .

Exhibits relating to Evesham Abbey 709-1540, Battle of Evesham 1265. Agricultural and social history - Anglo Saxon treasure, archaeology, children's activities.

Opening Times: Mon to Sat 10:00-17:00, Sun 14:00-17:00. Closed Sun Nov, Dec, Jan & Feb. Closed two weeks Xmas & New Year.   Admission: Adult £2.50, Child Free, OAP/Concession £1.50.   Map Ref: 6

Malvern Museum

Priory Gatehouse, Abbey Road, Great Malvern WR14 3ES   Tel: 01684 567811

The museum is located in the ancient Priory Gatehouse. It takes visitors from the earliest Iron Age settlements, through to the medieval community, the arrival of the Water Cure, Victorian enterprise and the scientific advances made by radar research.

Opening Times: Easter to Oct daily 10:30-17:00. Closed Wed in term time.   Admission: Adult £1.00, Under 7s Free, Student 20p. Audio Guide 50p.   Location: In town centre, close to Tourist Office and main Post Office.   Map Ref: 7

Hagley Hall

Hagley DY9 9LG   Tel: 01562 882408   Fax: 01562 882632
Email: enquiries@hagleyhall.info   Web: www.hagleyhall.com

Grade I Georgian House set in Grade I Park. Containing a fine collection of 18th century portraits and furniture. Hagley Hall is the home of Viscount and Viscountess Cobham.

Opening Times: 5 to 30 Jan, 1 to 27 Feb, 12 to 16 Apr, 31 May to 4 Jun, 30 Aug to 3 Sep 14:00-17:00. Closed all Sat.   Admission: Adult £4.00, Child £1.50, Concession £2.50.   Location: One mile from Hagley Station.   Map Ref: 8

Guided or Private Tours	Disabled Access	Gift Shop or Sales Point	Café or Refreshments	Restaurant	Car Parking

Herefordshire & Worcestershire

Hereford Museum & Art Gallery

Broad Street, Hereford HR4 9AU   Tel: 01432 260692
Fax: 01432 342492
Web: www.museumsherefordshire.gov.uk

Hereford Museum displays 'A Sense of Place', a changing exhibition which gives an insight into the county of Herefordshire. Included are objects from collections on agriculture, landscape, folklore, schooldays and laundering. Included are community cases with changing displays, an observation beehive and hands-on displays for all ages. The Art Gallery houses a varied programme of temporary exhibitions on art, craft, photography and other themes.

Opening Times: Tue to Sat 10:00-17:00, Sun (Apr to Sep) 10:00-16:00, BH Mon 10:00-16:00. Closed Mon, Xmas & New Year and Good Friday. Admission: Free. Location: In the town centre, opposite Hereford Cathedral.   Map Ref: 9

Mappa Mundi & Chained Library

5 College Cloisters, Cathedral Close, Hereford HR1 2NG   Tel: 01432 374202   Fax: 01432 374220

The Mappa Mundi and Chained Library Exhibition is open all year round and is famous for housing both the spectacular medieval map of the world and the cathedral's unique Chained Library. Here the stories of these national treasures are told through models, original artefacts and the latest interactive computer technology.

Opening Times: Summer: Mon to Sat 10:00-16:15, Sun 11:00-15:15. Winter: Mon to Sat 11:00-15:15, closed Sun. Admission: Adult £4.00, Under 5s Free, Concession £3.50, Family £10.00.
Location: Town centre.   Map Ref: 9

Old House

High Town, Hereford HR1 2AA   Tel: 01432 260694   Fax: 01432 342492
Web: www.museums.herefordshire.gov.uk

Built in 1621, one of Hereford's finest timber-framed buildings, the last remaining from Butcher's Row. Furnished in 17th century style on three floors, the house includes a kitchen, hall and bedrooms. There is a play area for children with period dressing-up clothes and hands-on activities. There is a computer generated virtual tour on the ground floor for visitors who cannot take the stairs.

Opening Times: Tue to Sat 10:00-17:00, Sun (Apr to Sep) 10:00-16:00, BH Mon 10:00-16:00. Closed Mon, Xmas & New Year and Good Friday. Admission: Free. Location: In the pedestrian area of the High Town at the heart of the city.   Map Ref: 9

Eastnor Castle

Ledbury HR8 1RL   Tel: 01531 633160   Fax: 01531 631776
Email: enquiries@eastnorcastle.com

A towered symetrical 'fairytale' castle facing the Malvern Hills, designed in 1812.It contains an unrivalled collection of armour, British and Italian paintings and Italian furniture.

Opening Times: Castle & grounds: 11 Apr to 3 Oct Sun & BH Mons. Jul & Aug daily except Sat 11:00-17:00. Deer Park: 2 Apr to 3 Oct. Admission: Adult £6.50, OAP £6.00, Child £4.00. Family £17.00. Location: Two and a half miles east of Ledbury on A438 Tewkesbury road.
                                                                     Map Ref: 10

Herefordshire & Worcestershire

Berrington Hall

near Leominster HR6 0DW   Tel: 01568 615721   Fax: 01568 613263
Email: berrington@nationaltrust.org.uk   Web: www.nationaltrust.org.uk

This elegant Henry Holland house was built in the late 18th century and is set in parkland designed by 'Capability Brown'. The fiine interior has beautifully ecorated ceilings and a spectacular staircase hall. There are collections of furniture, paintings, clocks and small objets d'art. The walled garden contains an historic collection of local apple trees.

Opening Times: 6 Mar to 4 Apr Sat & Sun 12:00-16:30, 10 Apr to 26 Sep Sat & Sun, 5 Apr to 29 Sep Mon to Wed 13:00-16:30, 2 Oct to 31 Oct Sat to Wed 13:00-16:30. Open Good Friday. Between 6 Mar & 30 Sep access from

The Drawing Room, view of a c18th kidney table   12:00-13:00 is by guided tour only.   Admission: Adult £4.80, Child £2.40, Family £12.00. Group (15+) Adult £4.20, Child £1.95. Grounds only: £3.40. NT Members Free. Location: Three miles north of Leominster, seven miles south of Ludlow on west side of A49.   Map Ref: 11

Burton Court

Eardisland, Leominster HR6 9DN   Tel: 01544 388231   Email: helenjsimpson@hotmail.com
Web: www.burtoncourt.com

14th century Great Hall, European and Oriental costumes, ship models, natural history specimens, working model fairground. Archaeology dig.

Opening Times: Spring BH to end Sep Wed, Thu, Sat, Sun & BH 14:30-18:00.
Admission: Adult £3.50, Child £2.00, Groups £3.00.   Location: Near Leominster, five miles on A44.   Map Ref: 12

Croft Castle

Leominster HR6 9PW   Tel: 01568 780246   Fax: 01568 780462
Email: croftcastle@nationaltrust.org.uk   Web: www.nationaltrust.org.uk

This 15th century castle has recently had a major refurbishment. There are fine period furnishings and paintings, including works by Gainsborough and Lawrence. Many of the books are by members of the Croft family. There are pleasant walks in the gardens and park.

Opening Times: 6 Mar to 28 Mar Sat & Sun 13:00-17:00, 1 Apr to 30 Sep Wed to Sun 13:00-17:00, 2 Oct to 31 Oct Sat & Sun 13:00-17:00. Open BH Mons.
Admission: Adult £4.40, Child £2.20, Family £11.00. Group (15+) £4.00. NT Members Free. Location: Five miles north west of Leominster, nine miles soth west of Ludlow; approach from B4362, turning north at Cock Gate between Bircher and Mortimer's Cross.   Map Ref: 13

Forge Mill Museum & Bordesley Abbey

Needle Mill Lane, Riverside, Redditch B98 8HY   Tel: 01527 62509
Email: museum@redditchbc.gov.uk   Web: www.redditchbc.gov.uk

Industrial museum with unique displays and collections telling the fascinating story of how needles are made. Also archaeological site museum with children's activities showing finds from the adjacent Cistercian Abbey of Bordesley.

Opening Times: Easter to Sep Mon to Fri 11:00-16:30, Sat & Sun 14:00-17:00. Feb to Easter & Oct to Nov Mon to Thu 11:00-16:00, Sun 14:00-17:00.   Admission: Adult £3.50, Child 50p, OAP £2.50. Pre-booked Group rates available.   Location: Off A441 Birmingham to Evesham road; junction 2 on M42. Located just north of Redditch Town Centre.   Map Ref: 14

Cwmmau Farmhouse

Brilley, Whitney-On-Wye HR3 6JP   Tel: 01885 483075
Web: www.nationaltrust.org.uk

This is a superb example of an early 17th century timber framed and stone tiled farmhouse. There is a collection of antique and modern furnishings including embroidery.

Herefordshire & Worcestershire

Opening Times: 9 Apr to 12 Apr Fri to Mon 14:00-17:00, 29 May to 31 May Sat to Mon 14:00-17:00, 28 Aug to 30 Aug Sat To Mon 14:00-17:00. Admission: Adult £3.00, Child £1.50, Family £7.00. NT Members Free. Location: Four miles south west of Kington between A4111 and B438; approach by narrow lane leading south from Kington to Whitney road at Brilley Mountain.

Map Ref: 15

WORCESTER *Worcs*

Commandery

Sidbury, Worcester WR1 2HU   Tel: 01905 361821   Fax: 01905 361822
Email: thecommandery@cityofworcester.gov.uk
Web: www.worcestercitymuseums.org.uk

The commandery is the most important secular building in Worcester dating back nearly 1000 years. As well as period rooms such as the Great Hall and Painted Chamber there are exhibitions on the building's past and the English Civil War, when the building served as the Royalist Headquarters at the Battle of Worcester in 1651.

Opening Times: Mon to Sat 10:00-17:00, Sun 13:30-17:00. Admission: Charges apply. Location: Two minute walk from Worcester Cathedral.   Map Ref: 16

King Charles II at the Commandery's Oak Apple Day

The Elgar Birthplace Museum

Crown East Lane, Lower Broadheath, Worcester WR2 6RH   Tel: 01905 333224   Fax: 01905 333426   Email: birthplace@elgar.org   Web: www.elgar.org

A fascinating insight into the life and music, family and friends, inspirations and musical development of one of Britain's greatest composers, Sir Edward Elgar. Historic birthplace cottage in pretty garden. New exhibition and special events in the Elgar Centre, opened in 2000.

Opening Times: Daily 11:00-17:00. Closed Xmas to end Jan. Admission: Adult £3.50, Child £1.75, Concession £3.00, Family £8.75. Reduction for pre-booked groups. Location: Three miles west of Worcester, signposted off Worcester/Leominster road.   Map Ref: 17

The Greyfriars

Friar Street, Worcester WR1 2LZ   Tel: 01905 23571
Email: greyfriars@nationaltrust.org.uk   Web: www.nationaltrust.org.uk

A fine timber framed merchant's house built in 1480. The panelled interior contains an interesting collection of furniture, textiles and antiquarian books. There is a delightful small walled garden.

Opening Times: 3 Mar to 18 Dec Wed to Sat 13:00-17:00, 4 Jul to 29 Aug Sat 13:00-17:00. Open BH Mons. Admission: Adult £3.20, Child £1.60, Family £8.00. Group £2.75. NT Members Free. Location: In centre of Worcester.   Map Ref: 16

Museum of Worcester Porcelain

Severn Street, Worcester WR1 2NE   Tel: 01905 746000   Fax: 01905 617807
Email: museum@royal-worcester.co.uk   Web: www.worcesterporcelainmuseum.org

Travel on a design journey through time and see rare porcelain sumptuously displayed in period room settings and dining scenes in the Georgian, Victorian and 20th Century galleries.

Opening Times: Mon to Sat 09:00-17:30, Sun 11:00-17:00. Admission: Adult £3.50, Concession £2.75. Location: Two minute walk from Worcester Cathedral and town centre.

Map Ref: 16

Herefordshire & Worcestershire

Worcester City Museum & Art Gallery

Foregate Street, Worcester WR1 1DT

Tel: 01905 25371   Fax: 01905 616979
Email: artgalleryandmuseum@cityofworcester.gov.uk
Web: www.worcestercitymuseums.org.uk

Housed in a beautiful Victorian building, the City Museum & Art Gallery runs a lively programme of exhibitions, activities and events for all the family. Explore the fascinating historic displays or drop in and see one of our contemporary art exhibitions. Visit our award winning café, gallery shop, children's activity area and the newly refurbished Worcestershire Soldier exhibition, dedicated to the Soldiers of the Worcestershire Regiment and the Worcestershire Yeomanry Cavalry.

'The Yellow Dress',
by Dame Laura Knight (1877-1970)

Opening Times: Mon to Fri 09:30-17:30, Sat 09:30-17:00. Closed Sun. Admission: Free. Location: Town centre, 150 yards from Foregate Street Railway Station. Map Ref: 16

Worcestershire County Museum

Hartlebury Castle, Hartlebury, Worcester DY11 7XZ

Tel: 01299 250416   Fax: 01299 251890
Email: museum@worcestershire.gov.uk

Housed in the sandstone home of the Bishops of Worcester for over a thousand years, the County Museum illustrates local life from the Roman period until the 20th century. Particular exhibits include reconstructed cider mill, horse-drawn transport, female costume and social history from the Victorian and Edwardian eras.

Opening Times: Feb to Sep Mon to Thu 10:00-17:00, Fri & Sun 14:00-17:00. Closed Sat & Good Friday. Other BH in season 11:00-17:00. Admission: Adult £3.00, Child/Concession £1.50, Family £8.00. Location: Four miles south of Kidderminster, signed from A449 Worcester Road. Map Ref: 18

Hartlebury Castle, home of the WCM and Bishops of Worcester

Kent

Kent, the closest county to the continent, through which a host of armies poured including the Roman armies of Julius Caesar, the Saxon hordes of Horsa and Hengist and on a quieter note, missionaries from Rome on their way to Canterbury, the spiritual capital of England. Long known as the 'Garden of England', this pleasant region has always attracted the powerful and wealthy to build their manors and mansions here.

Splendid and varied museums together with historic houses cover Roman occupation, naval history through to the Second World War, and encompass Charles Darwin to Charles Dickens

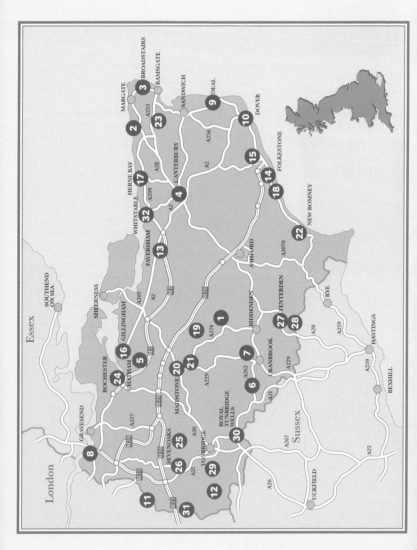

The Red Map References should be used to locate Museums etc on the pages that follow

Kent

Lashenden Air Warfare Museum

Headcorn Aerodrome, Headcorn, Ashford TN27 9HX Tel: 01622 890226/206783 Fax: 01622 206783 Email: lashairwar@aol.com

The museum preserves the aviation heritage of Kent, with particular emphasis on World War II. There is a separate building housing a First World War display, including various uniforms, tunics etc.

Opening Times: Easter Sun to end Oct 10:30-18:00. Nov to Easter 10:30-15:30. Closed Xmas & New Year. Admission: Free. Location: Nine miles south of Maidstone on A274, one mile from Headcorn. Map Ref: 1

Powell-Cotton Museum & Quex House & Gardens

Quex Park, Birchington CT7 0BH Tel: 01843 842168 Fax: 01843 846661 Email: powell-cotton.museum@virgin.net Web: www.powell-cottonmuseum.co.uk

An extraordinary collection, within a museum, stately home and garden setting, of African and Asian animal displays, tribal artefacts, weapons, cannons, archeology, chinese porcelain and much more.

Opening Times: Apr to Oct Tue to Thu, Sun & BH 11:00-17:00, Nov & Mar Sun 11:00-16:00. Quex House: 14:00-17:00, closed Dec, Jan and Feb. Admission: Adult £4.00, Child/OAP £3.00, Student £2.50, Family £12.00. Location: Coastal location, near town centre, 20 minute walk from railway station. Map Ref: 2

Dickens House Museum, Broadstairs

2 Victoria Parade, Broadstairs CT10 1QS Tel / Fax: 01843 863453 Email: aleeault@aol.com

This lovely old house, once the home of Miss Mary Pearson Strong on whom Dickens based much of the character of Miss Betsey Trotwood ('David Copperfield'), is now a museum to commemorate the novelist's association with Broadstairs.

Opening Times: Easter to Oct daily 14:00-17:00. Except school summer hol 11:00-17:00. Admission: Adult £2.00, Child £1.00, Student £1.00, Family discount. Location: On the main seafront. Map Ref: 3

Canterbury Roman Museum

Butchery Lane, Canterbury Tel: 01227 785575 Fax: 01227 455047
Email: museums@canterbury.gov.uk Web: www.canterbury-museum.co.uk

Step below today's Canterbury to discover an exciting part of the Roman town including the real remains of a house with fine mosaics. Experience everyday life in the reconstructed market place and see exquisite silver and glass. Try your skill on the touch-screen computer, and in the hands-on area with actual finds. Use the computer animation of Roman Canterbury to join the search for the lost temple.

Acclaimed Hands-On area

Opening Times: Mon to Sat 10:00-17:00 plus Jun to end Oct on Sun 13:30-17:00. Closed Good Friday and Xmas. Last admission 16:00 Admission: Adult £2.70, Concession £1.70, Family £7.00 (until 31.3.2004). Location: Town centre, part of the Long Market, near the Cathedral. Map Ref: 4

Kent

Canterbury Royal Museum & Art Gallery
with Buffs Regimental Museum

18 High Street, Canterbury CT1 2RA   Tel: 01227 452747   Fax: 01227 455047
Email: museums@canterbury.gov.uk   Web: www.canterbury-artgallery.co.uk

A splendid Victorian building, houses decorative arts and the city's picture collections - including a gallery for TS Cooper, England's finest cattle painter. The art gallery is the major space in the area for the visual arts with a varied exhibitions programme. Here too is the Buffs Museum, which tells the story of one of England's oldest infantry regiments and its worldwide service.

Opening Times: Mon to Sat 10:00-17:00. Closed Good Friday and Xmas. Admission: Free. Location: Situated on the first floor of the Beaney Institute in the High Street, almost opposite the Post Office.   Map Ref: 4

The Art Gallery

Canterbury West Gate Towers

St Peter's Street, Canterbury   Tel: 01227 789576
Fax: 01227 455047   Email: museums@canterbury.gov.uk
Web: www.canterbury-museum.co.uk

Medieval West Gate is one of England's finest city gates. Built in about 1380, it has a guard chamber with its 'murder holes' and battlement cells on view. On display are arms and armours from the Civil War to the Second World War. Displays also tell the story of the city defenders. There are fine panoramic views over the city from the battlements.

Opening Times: Mon to Sat 11:00-12:30 13:30-15;30. Closed Good Friday & Xmas. Admission: Adult £1.00, Concession 65p, Family £2.50 (until 31.3.2004). Location: West Gate stands at the end of the main street beside the river. The entrance is under the arch.
Map Ref: 4

View from the Battlements

Museum of Canterbury with Rupert Bear Museum

Poor Priests' Hospital, Stour Street, Canterbury   Tel: 01227 475202
Fax: 01227 452747   Email: museums@canterbury.gov.uk
Web: www.canterbury-museum.co.uk

Discover the story of Canterbury in a beautiful medieval building. See the city's treasures including the famous Canterbury Cross. Try the fun activities in the Medieval Discovery Gallery. Find out about the mysteries surrounding Christopher Marlowe's life and death. Spot friend or foe planes in the WW2 Blitz Gallery. Meet favourite children's TV character Bagpuss and friends. Enjoy the Rupert Bear Museum - full of adventure and surprises.

Opening Times: Mon to Sat 10:30-17:00 plus Jun to end Sep Sun 13:30-17:00 (last admission 16:00). Closed Xmas & Good Friday. Admission: Adult £3.00, Concession £2.00, Family £8.00 (until 31.3.2004). Location: In town centre, situated in the Medieval Poor Priests' Hospital, just off St Margaret's Street or High Street and within easy walking distance of Cathedral.   Map Ref: 4

Rupert Bear Museum, Rupert Characters TM & © Express Newspapers

---

St Augustines Abbey

Longport, Canterbury CT1 1TF   Tel: 01227 767345

This great shrine, founded by St Augustine in 597, the year he arrived in England from Rome, marks the birthplace of Christianity in this country. St Augustine himself is buried here.

Opening Times: Apr to Sep daily 10:00-18:00, Oct daily 10:00-17:00, Nov to Mar daily 10:00-16:00. Closed Xmas & New Year. Times & prices may change. Admission: Adult £3.00, Child £1.50, Concession £2.30. EH Members Free. Location: In Longport, quarter of a mile east of Cathedral Close.   Map Ref: 4

Kent

The Historic Dockyard Chatham
The Historic Dockyard, Chatham ME4 4TZ
Tel: 01634 823800   Fax: 01634 823801
Email: info@chdt.org.uk   Web: www.chdt.org.uk

Maritime and naval heritage site covering 80 acres. Displays include Britain's last operational WWII destroyer and submarine Ocelot. Wooden Walls is an 18th century dockyard adventure and in Lifeboat! 16 of the RNLI's most historic craft are displayed. The Ropewalk is the last ropewalk from the age of sail and the Museum of The Royal Dockyard details Chatham's naval history.

Opening Times: 14 Feb to 31 Oct Daily 10:00-18:00 (or dusk if earlier). Last entry 15:00 until 27 Mar, 16:00 thereafter. Closed Dec, Jan and until 13 Feb. Admission: Adult £9.50, Child £6.00,

HMS Gannet

Concession £7.00, Family £25.00 (2 adults and 2 children) additional Family Child £3.00. Location: Regular buses to Main Gate and Main Visitor Entrance from Chatham Rail Station and Pentagon Shopping Centre. Exhibitions & Events 2004 : 11 & 12 Apr: Medway Festival of Steam and Transport. Various Events throughout the year - please refer to website for details.
Map Ref: 5

Kent Police Museum
The Historic Dockyard, Dock Road, Chatham ME4 4TZ   Tel / Fax: 01634 403260
Email: info@kent_police_museum.co.uk   Web: www.kent-police-museum.co.uk

Museum showing the history of the Kent County Constabulary from 1857 to current day. The collection consists of Police artefacts of uniform, equipment, vehicles and photographs.

Opening Times: Please phone for opening times. Admission: No entry fee to Police Museum.
Location: Within the Historic Dockyard, Chatham next to Rochester north of M2.   Map Ref: 5

The Royal National Lifeboat Collection
The Historic Dockyard, Chatham ME4 4TZ   Tel: 01634 823800   Web: www.lifeboats.org.uk

'Lifeboat!, The Royal National Lifeboat Collection'. The gallery has been created around a collection of 17 historic lifeboats.

Opening Times: 14 Feb to 31 Oct daily 10:00-18:00. Nov Sat & Sun 10:00-18:00.   Map Ref: 5

Finchcocks Living Museum of Music
Goudhurst, Cranbrook TN17 1HH   Tel: 01580 211702   Fax: 01580 211007
Email: katrina@finchcocks.co.uk   Web: www.finchcocks.co.uk

Celebrated collection of 100 period keyboard instruments; 40 in concert condition. Housed in fine Georgian manor in beautiful gardens. Pictures and prints on musical themes. Recitals/Demonstrations for all visitors. Festive and many special events.

Opening Times: Open Days: Easter to Sep Sun & BH Mon, also Aug Wed & Thu 14:00-18:00.
By appointment Mar to Dec most days. Admission: Open Days: Adult £7.50, Child £4.00.
Group rates available. Location: One mile off A262.   Map Ref: 6

Sissinghurst Castle & Garden

Sissinghurst, Cranbrook TN17 2AB   Tel: 01580 710700   Fax: 01580 710702
Email: sissinghurst@nationaltrust.org.uk   Web: www.nationaltrust.org.uk

One of the world's most celebrated gardens, the creation of Vita Sackville-West and her husband Sir Harold Nicolson. It was developed around the surviving parts of an Elizabethan mansion. The study and library where Vita worked contain a mixed collection of furniture.

Opening Times: 20 Mar to 31 Oct Mon, Tue, Fri, Sat & Sun 11:00-18:30. Open BH.
Admission: Adult £7.00, Child £3.50, Family £17.50. NT Members Free. Location: Two miles north east of Cranbrook, one mile east of Sissinghurst village (A262).   Map Ref: 7

Dartford Borough Museum
Market Street, Dartford DA1 1EU   Tel: 01322 224739   Fax: 01322 343209

The museum presents the history and archaeology of the Borough of Dartford through permanent

Kent

displays together with temporary exhibitions which draw upon the extensive reserve collections.

Opening Times: Mon to Fri 12:30-17:30, Sat 09:00-13:00 & 14:00-17:00. Closed Wed & Sun.
Admission: Free. Location: In town centre, adjacent to library and Central Park. Map Ref: 8

DEAL

Walmer Castle
Kingsdown Road, Walmer, Deal CT14 7LJ Tel: 01304 364288

Walmer Castle was one of a chain of coastal artillery forts built by Henry VIII to protect the Downs. Walmer was transformed when it became the official residence of the Lords Warden of the Cinque Ports.

Opening Times: Apr to Sep daily 10:00-18:00, Oct daily 10:00-17:00, Nov to Dec & Mar Wed to Sun 10:00-16:00, Jan to Feb Sat & Sun 10:00-16:00. Closed Xmas & New Year. Times & prices may change. Admission: Adult £5.50, Child £2.80, Concession £4.10, Family £13.80. EH Members Free. Location: On coast south of Walmer on A258. Junction 13 off M20 or from M2 to Deal. Map Ref: 9

DOVER

View of the Anti-aircraft Control Room. © English Heritage

Dover Castle
Dover CT16 1HN Tel: 01304 201628/211067

For over 2000 years, the site of Dover Castle has protected the stretch of English coast closest to Europe. From the Iron Age to the Atomic Age, the castle's defences have grown to meet the changing demands of warfare. Hidden inside the White Cliffs of Dover is a fascinating and secret world: below, deep underground, are miles of tunnels. The keeps, built in the 1180s, contain displays devoted to the siege of 1216 and the arrival of the Court of Henry VIII in 1539.

Opening Times: Apr to Sep daily 10:00-18:00, Oct daily 10:00-17:00, Nov to Mar daily 10:00-16:00. Closed Xmas & New Year. Times & prices may change. Admission: Adult £8.00, Child £4.00, Concession £6.00, Family £20.00. EH Members Free.
Location: On east side of Dover. Map Ref: 10

Discovering archaeology, the interactive lab at Dover Museum

Dover Museum & The Bronze Age Boat Gallery
Market Square, Dover CT16 Tel: 01304 201066
Fax: 01304 241186 Email: museum@dover.gov.uk
Web: www.dovermuseum.co.uk

Dover Museum tells the story of the town and port since prehistoric times, a town that for centuries has been the Gateway to England. Displays include Dover's history as a Roman port and Saxon town, Cinque Ports, Napoleonic Wars, Victorian Dover, and the two World Wars. Also on display is the world's oldest sea-going boat. Found in Dover in 1992, it is 3,550 years old, older than Tutankhamun and from the same age as Stonehenge.

Opening Times: Mon to Sat 10:00-17:30. Closed Xmas & New Year.
Admission: Adults £2.00, Child/OAP £1.25. Group discount 10%.
Location: In Town Centre, three minutes from main Bus Station,
10 minutes from Dover Priory Railway Station. Map Ref: 10

Regimental Museum, Princess of Wales's
Royal Regiment & Queen's Regiment
Inner Bailey, Dover Castle CT16 1HU Tel / Fax: 01304 240121
Email: pwrrqueensmuseum@tinyworld.co.uk Web: www.123pwrr.co.uk

The story of the 12 forebear regiments of the PWRR, as well as exhibitions & interactive displays on WWI & WWII and the 56 Victorian Crosses war by regimental members.

Opening Times: Summer 10:00-18:00. Winter 10:00-16:00. Open daily except Xmas & New Year. Admission: As per entrance fee for Dover Castle. Museum entrance free. Map Ref: 10

Kent

Down House

Luxted Road, Downe BR6 7JT Tel: 01689 859119

From his study at Down House, Charles Darwin worked on the scientific theories that first scandalised and then revolutionised the Victorian world, culminating in the publication of 'On the Origin of Species by means of Natural Selection'. 3,500 objects relating to Darwin's work remain including portraits, photographs, family furniture, memorabilia from the Beagle voyage and manuscripts, including his Beagle Journal.

Opening Times: Please telephone to check times and pre-book for the month of Aug. Groups over 11 must pre-book at all times. Times & prices may change. Admission: Adult £6.00, Child £3.00, Concession £4.50. EH Members Free. Location: In Luxted Road, Downe, off A21 near Biggin Hill. Map Ref: 11

The Old Study © English Heritage

EDENBRIDGE

Hever Castle & Gardens

Edenbridge TN8 7NG Tel: 01732 865224 Fax: 01732 866796
Email: mail@hevercastle.co.uk Web: www.hevercastle.co.uk

Romantic 13th century Moated Castle, once childhood home of Anne Boleyn. Hever Castle contains Tudor portraits, furniture & other Objets d'Art. Set in award winning gardens including lake, yew & water mazes, Tudor & Italian gardens.

Opening Times: 1 Mar to 30 Nov Daily Garden: 11:00-18:00 Castle: 12:00-18:00. Last admission 5:00. Map Ref: 12

Kent & Sharpshooters Yeomanry Museum

Hever Castle, Edenbridge TN8 7NG Tel: 01732 865224 Email: ksymuseum@aol.com
Web: www.ksymuseum.org.uk

Includes pictures, uniforms, badges, medals, flags, weapons of the East Kent Yeomanry, West Kent Yeomanry, 3rd/4th County of London Yeomanry (Sharpshooters).

Opening Times: Mar to Nov 12:00-18:00, during winter time (GMT) 12:00-16:00.
Admission: Adult £8.00, Child £4.40, OAP £6.80, Family £20.40. Location: Three miles south east of Edenbridge off the B2026. Map Ref: 12

FAVERSHAM

Fleur de Lis Museum

13 Preston Street, Faversham ME13 8NS Tel: 01795 590726/534542 Fax: 01795 533261
Email: faversham@btinternet.com Web: www.faversham.org

Recently expanded and updated, and housed in 16th century premises, the centre's colourful displays tell the story of 2,000 years of life in one of Britain's most historic ports. Also to see in Faversham - the Chart Gunpowder Mills and the Maison Dieu Museum.

Opening Times: Mon to Sat 10:00-16:00, Sun 10:00-13:00. Admission: Adult £2.00, Child/OAP/Disabled £1.00. Location: In town centre, four minute walk from mainline station. Map Ref: 13

FOLKESTONE

Folkestone Museum & Gallery

Grace Hill, Folkestone CT20 1HD Tel / Fax: 01303 256710
Email: folkstonelibrary@kent.gov.uk

Story of Folkestone, important Victorian seaside resort and Channel Port. Audio and film, hands-on activities. Programme of events for Museum and Gallery. New Craft Gallery, research facilities.

Opening Times: Mon, Tues & Thu 09:30-18:00, Fri 09:30-19:00, Wed & Sat 09:30-17:00, Sun 10:00-16:00. Closed BH. Admission: Free. Location: Two minutes walk from bus station and pay car parks. Map Ref: 14

Kent

Kent Battle of Britain Museum

Aerodrome Road, Hawkinge, Folkestone CT18 7AG   Tel: 01303 893140
Email: kentbattleofbritainmuseum@btinternet.com   Web: www.kbobm.org.uk or
www.kentbattleofbritainmuseum.org.uk

Most important collection of Battle of Britain artefacts on show in the country - aircraft, vehicles, weapons, flying equipment, prints, relics from over 600 crashed Battle of Britain aircraft.

Opening Times: Good Friday to 30 Sep Tue to Sun 10:00-17:00. Closed Mon except BH. Closed Oct to Easter.   Admission: Adult £3.50, Child £2.00, OAP £3.00. Group discounts available.   Location: Three miles north of Folkestone. Off Aerodrome Road, Hawkinge.

Map Ref: 15

GILLINGHAM

Royal Engineers Museum

Prince Arthur Road, Gillingham ME4 4UG   Tel: 01634 822839   Fax: 01634 822371
Email: remuseum.rhqre@gnet.gov.uk   Web: www.royalengineers.org.uk

Displays of engineering equipment, working models, superb medal galleries with 25 VCs and the regalia of four Field Marshalls including Kitchener. Costumes and curios from around the world.

Opening Times: Mon to Thu 10:00-17:00, Sat, Sun & BH 11:30-17:00. Closed Fri, Xmas & New Year. Guided Tours by arrangement.   Admission: Adult £5.00, Concession £2.50, Family £12.50.   Location: Prince Arthur Road, Gillingham, 20 minute walk from Gillingham Station.

Map Ref: 16

HERNE BAY

Herne Bay Museum & Gallery

12 William Street, Herne Bay CT6 5EJ   Tel: 01227 367368
Email: museums@canterbury.gov.uk   Web: www.hernebay-museum.co.uk

Lancaster dropping a prototype
Bouncing Bomb off Reculver

The museum highlights the history of the Victorian seaside resort of Herne Bay. Find out about the town's famous piers. See exciting finds from the nearby Roman fort and Saxon church of Reculver, as well as fossils including mammoth tusks and fossilised sharks teeth. Also on display is a famous 'bouncing bomb' from World War II. The art gallery has regularly changing temporary exhibitions.

Opening Times: Mon to Sat 10:00-16:00 plus Jul & Aug on Sun 13:00-16:00. Closed Good Friday & Xmas.
Admission: Free. Location: Town centre, 12 William Street, near the seafront at the Clock Tower end.

Exhibitions & Events 2004 : 20 Mar to 24 Apr: Wildlife Photographer of the Year. Prize-winning images from the prestigious annual international competition organised by BBC Wildlife Magazine and the Natural History Museum: a split-site exhibition showing at Herne Bay and Whitstable Museum & Gallery.

Map Ref: 17

HYTHE

Hythe Local History Room

Oaklands, 1 Stade Street, Hythe CT21 6BG   Tel: 01303 266152   Fax: 01303 262912
Email: admin@hythe-kent.com   Web: www.hythe-kent.com

Three rooms depicting history of the town and cinque port of Hythe - social and military history.

Opening Times: Mon 09:30-18:00, Tue to Thu 09:30-17:00, Fri 09:30-19:00, Sat 09:30-16:00.
Admission: Free. Location: Hythe, in Oaklands Park, entrance to via Public Library.

Map Ref: 18

MAIDSTONE

Dog Collar Museum

Leeds Castle, Maidstone ME17 1PL   Tel: 01622 765400   Fax: 01622 735616
Email: enquiries@leeds-castle.co.uk   Web: www.leeds-castle.com

The Dog Collar Museum at Leeds Castle is home to the world's finest collection of historic dog collars with some of the exhibits dating back over 500 years.

Kent

Opening Times: Mar to Oct 10:00-17:00, Nov to Feb 10:00-15:00. Closed Xmas, 26 Jun, 3 Jul & 6 Nov. Admission: Mar to Jun, Sep & Oct: Adult £11.00, Child £7.50, OAP/Student £9.50. Jul & Aug: Adult £12.00, Child £8.50, OAP/Student £10.50, Nov to Feb Adult £9.50, Child £6.00, OAP/Student £8.00. Location: Seven miles east of Maidstone at junction 8 of M20.

Map Ref: 19

Maidstone Museum & Bentlif Art Gallery

St Faiths Street, Maidstone ME14 1LH   Tel: 01622 602838

One of the finest general collections in the south east. Galleries include Dinosaurs/ Natural History, Japanese Art, Costume and Natural History. Programme of temporary exhibitions.

Opening Times: Mon to Sat 10:00-17:15, Sun 11:00-16:00. Closed Xmas Day.
Admission: Free. Location: Nr town centre, five minutes walk from Maidstone East Railway Station.

Map Ref: 20

Museum of Kent Life

Lock Lane, Sandling, Maidstone ME14 3AU   Tel: 01622 763936
Fax: 01622 662024   Email: enquiries@museum-kentlife.co.uk
Web: www.museum-kentlife.co.uk

Kent's award-winning open air museum is home to an outstanding collection of historical buildings which house exhibitions on life in Kent over the last 150 years. A Chapel of 1897, a Farmhouse of 1554 and reconstruction of cottages from the 17th & 20th centuries are more recent buildings to be viewed.

Opening Times: Feb to Nov daily 10:00-17:30. Admission: Adult £6.00, Child/Student £4.00, OAP £4.50. Location: Five minutes from Maidstone.

Map Ref: 20

The Museum Oast House

Stoneacre

Otham, Maidstone ME15 8RS   Tel: 01622 862157
Email: stoneacrent@aol.com   Web: www.nationaltrust.org.uk

A half-timbered yeoman's house dating from the late 15th century. It has a great hall and crownpost, and a staircase of solid oak blocks. The house is surrounded by a beautiful garden and wild meadows.

Opening Times: 20 Mar to 13 Oct Wed & Sat 14:00-18:00. Open BH Mons. Admission: Adult £2.60, Child £1.30, Family £6.50. Group £2.20. NT Members Free. Location: At north end of Otham village, three miles south east of Maidstone, one mile south of A20.

Map Ref: 21

Tyrwhitt-Drake Museum of Carriages

Archbishops Stables, Mill Street, Maidstone ME15 6YE   Tel: 01622 602838

Major collection of carriages, items include private and state vehicles, some items belonging to Queen Victoria. Housed in historic medieval stables.

Opening Times: Daily 10:00-15:45. Admission: Adult £2.00, Child £1.05, Under 5s Free, Family £4.00. Location: Town centre, two minutes walk from High Street.

Map Ref: 20

Romney Hythe & Dymchurch Railway

New Romney TN28 8PL   Tel: 01797 362353   Fax: 01797 363591

Email: rhdr@romneyrail.fsnet.co.uk
Web: www.rhdr.org.uk

Most complete collection of one-third full size steam engines in the world (11 in all). Also toy and model museum on site.

Opening Times: Feb half term, Easter to end Sep and Oct half term daily, also in Mar & Oct Sat & Sun 09:00-18:00. Admission: Please phone for details. Location: Most stations within five minutes of A259. Hythe Station is three miles from junction 11 of M20.

Map Ref: 22

Kent

Spitfire & Hurricane Memorial Building

The Airfield, Manston Road, Ramsgate CT12 5DF   Tel / Fax: 01843 821940
Email: pete@spitfire752.freeserve.co.uk   Web: www.spitfire-museum.com

The Memorial Building houses wartime Spitfire & Hurricane fighter aircraft together with an ever expanding display of original and emotive memorabilia from the 1939-1945 war periods. Battle of Britain Tapestry. 'Dambusters' and 'Channel Dash' displays. The Merlin Cafeteria has superb views across London (Manston) Airport. Study/research room and Allied Air Forces Memorial Garden.

Opening Times: Apr to Sep 10:00-17:00, Oct to Mar 10:00-16:00. Closed Xmas & New Year. Admission: Free.
Location: On B2050 road, adjacent to London (Manston) Airport. Follow brown tourism signs.   Map Ref: 23

Spitfiire MK XVI - TB752 on displa

Guildhall Museum

High Street, Rochester ME1 1PY
Tel: 01634 848717   Fax: 01634 832919
Email: guildhall.museum@medway.gov.uk
Web: www.medway.gov.uk

A museum for all the family. Colourful and attractive displays in two historic buildings feature the archaeology, local and social history of the Medway towns. The 'Hulks Experience' highlights the cramped, insanitary and harsh conditions forced upon Napoleonic prisoners-of-war and convicts incarcerated on the Medway Hulks. The museum also features everyday life in Victorian and Edwardian times.

Opening Times: Daily 10:00-16:30. Closed Xmas & New Year.
Admission: Free.   Location: In Rochester High Street, 15 minutes walk from Rochester Railway Station.   Map Ref: 24

Reconstruction of
17th Century Militia

Restoration House

17/19 Crow Lane, Rochester ME1 1RF   Tel: 01634 848520   Fax: 01634 880058
Web: www.restorationhouse.co.uk

Historic and Poetic City Mansion, stayed in by Charles II. Satis House of 'Great Expectations'. Wonderful collection of English furniture and pictures including Gheerarts, Mytens, Kneller, Dahl, Mercier, Reynolds and six Gainsboroughs. Privately owned gem.

Opening Times: 3 Jun to 1 Oct Thu & Fri 10:00-17:00.   Map Ref: 24

Ightham Mote

Ivy Hatch, Sevenoaks TN15 0NT   Tel: 01732 810378   Fax: 01732 811029
Web: www.nationaltrust.org.uk

A superb moated manor house dating from the early 14th century. The main features of the house span many centuries and include the Great Hall, Old Chapel, crypt and Tudor chapel with painted ceiling. There are collections of furniture, tapestries and stained glass. The extensive gardens have interesting walks in the surrounding woodland.

Opening Times: House: 28 Mar to 7 Nov Wed, Thu, Fri, Sun & Mon 10:30-17:30. Garden: 28 Mar to7 Nov Mon, Wed, Thu, Fri & Sun 10:00-17:30. Admission: Adult £6.50, Child £3.25, Family £16.50. Group (15+) Adult

The Great Hall

£5.50, Child £3.00.NT Members Free.   Location: Six miles east of Sevenoaks, off A25, and two and a half miles south of Ightham, off A227.   Map Ref: 25

Kent

Knole

Sevenoaks TN15 0RP   Tel: 01732 462100/450608   Fax: 01732 465528
Email: knole@nationaltrust.org.uk   Web: www.nationaltrust.org.uk

Table and gueridons (torcheres)
in the Cartoon Gallery

The original 15th century house was enlarged and embellished in 1603 by Thomas Sackville, the 1st Earl of Dorset, and has remained essentially unaltered ever since. There are thirteen state rooms open to the public which contain magnificient collections of royal Stuart furniture, including state beds, silver furniture and the prototype of the famous Knole Settee. There are outstanding tapestries, textiles, porcelain and important portraits. The house is set in a magnificent deer park.

Part of a Worcester porcelain dessert service

Opening Times: 27 Mar to 31 Oct Wed to Sun 11:00-16:00. Open BH Mons.   Admission: Adult £6.00, Child £3.00, Family £15.00. Group (15+) Adult £5.00, Child £2.50,NT Members Free.   Location: Park entrance in Sevenoaks town centre off A225 Tonbridge Road, leave M25 at Junction 5.

Map Ref: 26

Colonel Stephens Railway Museum

Tenterden Town Station, Station Road, Tenterden TN30 6HE   Tel: 01580 765350   Fax: 01580 765654   Email: kesroffice@aol.com   Web: www.hfstephens-museum.org.uk

Displays depicting the career of light railway promoter and engineer Lt Colonel Holman F Stephens, his pre-Raphaelite childhood, military career and involvement in 17 railways are covered with pictures, models, tableaux and relics.

Opening Times: Apr to Oct when trains run on Kent & East Sussex Railway 12:30-16:30 (hours extended for special events). Train times: tel. 01580 765155   Admission: Adult £1.00, Child 50p, Under 8s Free. Special rates for pre-booked groups of 10 or more.   Location: Adjacent to Tenterden Town Station, Station Road. 300 yards from High Street.   Map Ref: 27

A full length, side on view of a
dress worn by Ellen Terry
in her role as Mrs Page

Smallhythe Place

Smallhythe, Tenterden TN30 7NG   Tel: 01580 762334
Fax: 01580 761960
Email: smallhytheplace@nationaltrust.org.uk
Web: www.nationaltrust.org.uk

This early 16th century half timbered house was the home of the Victorian actress Ellen Terry from 1899 until her death in 1928. It contains many personal and theatrical mementoes, and beautiful stage costumes from her partnership with Sir Henry Irving at the Lyceum Theatre. The charming garden includes her rose garden, orchard and nuttery. The Barn Theatre is also open for viewing.

Opening Times: 6-21 Mar Sat & Sun only, 27 Mar to 3 Nov Sat to Wed 11:00-17:00. Open Good Friday.   Admission: Adult £3.75, Child £1.80, Family £9.30. NT Members Free.   Location: Two miles south of Tenterden, on east side of the Rye road (B2082).
Exhibitions & Events 2004: Please telephone for details. Map Ref: 28

Guided or Private Tours	Disabled Access	Gift Shop or Sales Point	Café or Refreshments	Restaurant	Car Parking

155

Kent

Penshurst Place & Gardens

Penshurst, Tonbridge TN11 8DG   Tel: 01892 870307   Fax: 01892 870866
Email: enquiries@penshurstplace.com   Web: www.penshurstplace.com

Penshurst Place is one of Kent's loveliest historic houses with 10 acres of walled Tudor gardens, set in a peaceful rural setting in the medieval village of Penshurst. The oldest part of the house is the Barons Hall, built in 1342 it is regarded as one of the best preserved examples of medieval domestic architecture in England. A series of Staterooms contain a wonderful collection of portraits, tapestries, furniture, porcelain and armour from the past five centuries. Modern facilities include a Toy Museum, a Garden Tea Room, Gift Shop, Plant Centre, Venture Playground, and a Woodland Trail with plenty of free parking for cars and coaches.

Opening Times: Sat & Sun from 1 Mar, daily from 29 Mar to 2 Nov. House: 12:00-17:00, Grounds: 10:30-18:00. Admission: Adult £6.50, Child £4.50, Concession £6.00. Location: Six miles from Tunbridge Wells and Tonbridge. Exhibitions & Events 2004 : Special events at Penshurst Palace include an exciting variety of shows in Home Park, drama, falconry, music, historic entertainment and storytelling in the house and grounds.   Map Ref: 29

Tunbridge Wells Museum and Art Gallery

Civic Centre, Mount Pleasant, Tunbridge Wells TN1 1JN
Tel: 01892 554171
Web: www.tunbridgewells.gov.uk/museum

From Tunbridge ware caskets to Pantiles paintings and Minnie the LuLu terrier to an 18th century polonaise, there are displays to fascinate everyone at Tunbridge Wells Museum. The Art Gallery has varied and frequently changing art and craft exhibitions. Educational workshops and other events for all ages are held linked to the exhibit collections and Tunbridge Wells history.

Opening Times: Mon to Sat 09:30-17:00. Closed Sun & BH.
Admission: Free.   Location: In the Library and Museum building, next to the Town Hall, just off the A264.   Map Ref: 30
The Art Gallery

Chartwell

Westerham TN16 1PS   Tel: 01732 868381   Fax: 01732 868193
Email: chartwell@nationaltrust.org.uk   Web: www.nationaltrust.org.uk

The family home where Britain's wartime prime minister lived for more than 40 years. The rooms, which are kept as they were in Sir Winston Churchill's lifetime, offer an insight into both his domestic and political life. Photographs, books and personal possessions, including his famous cigars, evoke his career, personality and family. Museum and exhibition rooms contain displays, sound recordings

Dining Room

and collections of memorabilia including many gifts from other world leaders, uniforms

The Studio

and correspondence. The house contains several of Sir Winston's own paintings and more are on view in his studio, together with his easel and paint box. Many features created by Sir Winston survive in the garden including the walls he built himself, the swimming pool and lake and ponds stocked with the golden orfe he loved to feed.

Opening Times: 20 Mar to 30 Jun, 1 Sep to 7 Nov Wed to Sun 11:00-17:00. 1 Jul to 31 Aug Tue

Kent

to Sun 11:00-17:00. Open BH Mons. Admission: Adult £7.00, Child £3.50, Family £17.50, Garden & Studio only: Adult £3.50, Child £1.75, Family £8.75. NT Members Free.
Location: Two miles south of Westerham, fork left off B2026 after one and a half miles.
Exhibitions & Events 2004 : Please telephone for details, 2-6 Jun: Programme of events and displays to commemorate the 60th anniversary of D-Day. Map Ref: 31

Quebec House

Quebec Square, Westerham TN16 1TD
Tel: 01732 868381 (Chartwell Office) Web: www.nationaltrust.org.uk

This 16th century gabled, red brick house was the early home of General James Wolfe. The low ceilinged panelled rooms contain memorabilia relating to his family and career, and the Tudor stable block houses an exhibition about the Battle of Quebec in 1759.

Opening Times: 4 Apr to 31 Oct Tue & Sun 14:00-17:30. Admission: Adult £3.00, Child £1.50, Family £7.50. Group £2.50. NT Members Free. Location: At east end of village, on north side of A25, facing junction with B2026 Edenbridge road. Map Ref: 31

Squerryes Court

Westerham TN16 1SJ Tel: 01959 562345/563118 Fax: 01959 565949
Email: squerryes.court@squerryes.co.uk Web: www.squerryes.co.uk

17th century manor house. Paintings collected by the Warde family 1747-1774, including 17th and 18th century Italian, Dutch and English schools. 18th century Soho tapestries. Items connected with General Wolfe. Pre-booked guided tours.

Opening Times: Apr to Sep Wed, Thu, Sun and BH Mon House: 13:30-17:30, Garden: 12:00-17:30. (Last entry 17:00) Admission: House & Gardens: Adult £5.00, Child £2.70, OAP £4.40, Family £12.50. Group rates available. Garden only: Adult £3.40, Child £1.70, OAP £2.90, Family £7.50. Location: Half a mile west of Westerham, just off A25. Map Ref: 31

Whitstable Museum & Gallery

Oxford Street, Whitstable CT5 1DB Tel: 01227 276998
Fax: 01227 772379 Email: museums@canterbury.gov.uk
Web: www.whitstable-museum.co.uk

The museum explores Whitstable's unique coastal community and its seafaring traditions with special features on oyster fishery, diving and shipping for which the town was famous. Ship portraits, archaeology and an early piece of silent film showing the oyster fishers dredging for oysters can be seen as well as an original horse drawn fire engine. The art gallery has a range of changing exhibitions.

Opening Times: Mon to Sat 10:00-16:00 plus Jul & Aug Sun 13:00-16:00. Closed Good Friday and Xmas. Admission: Free.
Location: Town centre, in Oxford Street, close to the theatre, library and St Mary's Hall. Easy walking distance of car parks and railway station. Exhibitions & Events 2004 : 20 Mar to 24 Apr: Wildlife Photographer of the Year. Prize-winning images from the prestigious annual international competition organised by BBC Wildlife Magazine and the Natural History Museum: a split-site exhibition showing at Whitstable and Herne Bay Museum & Gallery. Map Ref: 32

Oyster dredge used to scrape
the seabed for oysters

The cities and towns of the county reflect in their buildings the prosperity brought to the area by the Industrial Revolution. The seaside resorts still retain their well-deserved popularity. Blackpool, with its spectacular illuminations, piers and golden beaches, remains arguably Britain's most popular.

The cities of Lancashire, proud of their industrial heritage, present through their museums and galleries a quite remarkably comprehensive history of the Industrial Revolution and Lancashire's rich cultural, historical and natural heritage.

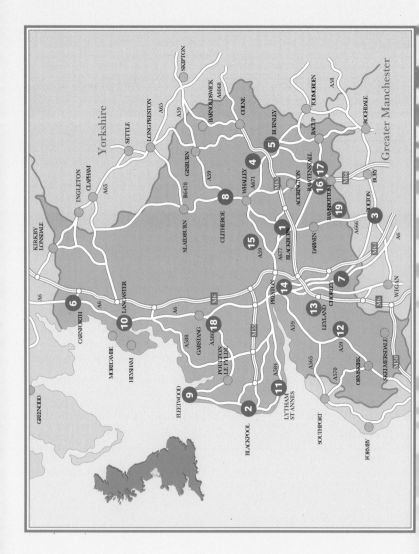

The Red Map References should be used to locate Museums etc on the pages that follow

Lancashire

Blackburn Museum & Art Gallery

Museum Street, Blackburn BB1 7AJ Tel: 01254 667130 Fax: 01254 685541
Email: paul.flintoff@blackburn.gov.uk Web: www.blackburn.gov.uk/museum

Collections of medieval manuscripts and early printed books, large collections of coins, Japanese prints, Greek and Russian icons. Extensive collections of local social history and textile history in the adjoining Lewis Textile Museum. Other attractions include Victorian paintings and sculpture, ceramics, Egyptology and contemporary art exhibitions.

Opening Times: Tue to Sat 10:00-16:45. Closed Sun, Mon & BH. Admission: Free. Location: Town centre, five minute walk from railway and central bus station.

HoKusai Lightning over Mount Fuji

Map Ref: 1

BLACKPOOL

Blackpool Lifeboat Station & Visitor Centre

The Promenade, Adjacent New Bonney Street, Blackpool FY1 5YA Tel: 01253 290816
Web: www.lifeboats.org.uk

Viewing gallery above lifeboats with displays, exhibits and videos portraying the RNLI in Blackpool.

Opening Times: All year. Admission: Free. Map Ref: 2

The Grundy Art Gallery

Queen Street, Blackpool FY1 1PX Tel: 01253 478170 Fax: 01253 478172
Email: grundyartgallery@blackpool.gov.uk

A selection of works from The Grundy collection, including painting and sculpture mainly from the 19th & 20th century, are always on display. A varied programme of temporary exhibitions.

Opening Times: Mon to Sat 10:00-17:00, closed Sun and BH. Admission: Free. Location: In the town centre near Talbot Road Bus Station and Blackpool North Railway Station and North Pier tramstops. Map Ref: 2

BOLTON

Smithills Hall Museum

Smithills Dean Road, Bolton BL1 7NP Tel / Fax: 01204 332377
Email: office@smithills.org Web: www.smithills.org

Unique Grade 1 listed Manor, one of the oldest in the North West. Over 600 years of family history under one roof. Medieval/Tudor/Victorian in a stunning location. Guided tours available throughout the day.

Admission: Adult £3.00, Child/Concession £1.75, Family £7.75 (2 adults and 3 children).

Map Ref: 3

BURNLEY

Gawthorpe Hall

Padiham, Burnley BB12 8UA Tel: 01282 771004 Fax: 01282 770178
Email: gawthorpe.hall@mus.lancscc.gov.uk Web: www.bringinghistoryalive.co.uk

A magnificent Jacobean house restored in the Victorian period by Sir Charles Barry. The hall houses the internationally important Rachel Kay-Shuttleworth textile collection and has an exciting programme of events.

Opening Times: 1 Apr to 2 Nov Tue to Thu & Sat to Sun, 13:00-17:00. Open BH Mons & Good Friday. Admission: Adult £3.00, Child Free when accompanied by an adult. Concession £1.50. Garden free. NT Members Free. Location: On east outskirts of Padiham; M65 junction 8 towards Clitheroe, then signposted from second traffic light junction to Padiham. Map Ref: 4

Guided or Private Tours	Disabled Access	Gift Shop or Sales Point	Café or Refreshments	Restaurant	Car Parking

Lancashire

Towneley Hall Art Gallery & Museum

Towneley Holmes Road, off Todmorden Road, Burnley BB11 3RQ   Tel: 01282 424213
Fax: 01282 436138   Email: townleyhall@burnley.gov.uk   Web: www.towneleyhall.org.uk

18th and 19th century oil and watercolour paintings; studio pottery; Royal Lancastrian Pilkington Pottery; 17th and 18th century oak furniture; 18th century glass; 18th and 19th century clocks and watches.

Opening Times: Mon to Thu 10:00-17:00 Sat & Sun 12:00-17:00.   Admission: Free. Charge for tours.
Location: One and a half miles south east of town centre, one mile from Park entrance on Todmarden Road (A671).
Map Ref: 5

Leighton Hall

Carnforth LA5 9ST   Tel: 01524 734474   Fax: 01524 720357
Email: info@leightonhall.co.uk   Web: www.leightonhall.co.uk

Set in beautiful parkland against a backdrop of the Lakeland Fells, award winning neo Gothic Leighton Hall is the lived-in home of the Gillow furniture-making family

Opening Times: 1 May to 30 Sep Tue to Fri & Sun 14:00-17:00 (open 12:30 in Aug). Open BH Mons.   Admission: Adult £5.00, Child £3.50, OAP £4.50. Family £15.00. Grounds only (after 16:30) £1.50.   Location: A few miles from Lancaster, just outside Carnforth.   Map Ref: 6

Astley Hall Museum & Art Gallery

Astley Park, Chorley PR7 1NP   Tel: 01257 515555   Fax: 01257 515556
Email: astleyhall@lineone.net   Web: www.astleyhall.co.uk

A furnished house dating back to the 1580s, including fine oak furniture of the 16th and 17th centuries. Also, a collection of 18th century creamware and fine art from 17th century portraits to contemporary art.

Opening Times: Apr to Oct Tue to Sun 12:00-17:00 and BH. Nov to Mar Sat & Sun 12:00-16:00.
Admission: Adult £2.95, Concession £1.95. Group rates available.   Location: One mile west of Chorley, off A581 Southport Road.   Map Ref: 7

Clitheroe Castle Museum

Castle Hill, Clitheroe BB7 1BA   Tel / Fax: 01200 424568
Email: hannah.chalk@mus.lancscc.gov.uk   Web: tourism@ribblevalley.gov.uk

We hold and display a range of local history and geology collections, which focus on Clitheroe and surrounding areas. Please ring for details of events.

Opening Times: 31 Jan to 16 Feb Sat & Sun, 17 Feb to 20 Feb daily, 21 Feb to 4 Apr Sat to Wed, 5 Apr to 30 Oct daily, 31 Oct to 19 Dec Sat & Sun 11:00-16:30.   Admission: Adult £1.70, Child £0.25, OAP £0.85, Family £3.6 0.   Location: Near town centre, ten minute walk from bus and railway stations.   Map Ref: 8

Fleetwood Museum

Queens Terrace, Fleetwood FY7 6BT   Tel: 01253 876621   Fax: 01253 878088
Email: fleetwood.museum@mus.lancscc.gov.uk   Web: www.nettingthebay.org.uk

Situated in the Decimus Burton designed Custom House building, the museum covers the history of Fleetwood and the fishing and maritime collections of Morecambe Bay. The museum also includes a full size dolls' boarding house and an interactive gallery.

Opening Times: Apr to early Nov & BH throughout the season.   Admission: Adult £2.00, Child/Concessions £1.00, Family £5.00.   Location: On Queens Terrace, opposite P&O Ferry Booth - between the market and Knott End Ferry. Within easy walking distance of buses and trams.
Map Ref: 9

Lancashire

Cottage Museum

15 Castle Hill, Lancaster   Tel: 01524 64637   Fax: 01524 841692   .
Email: lancaster.citymuseum@mus.lancscc.gov.uk
Web: www.lancaster.gov.uk/council/museums

A cottage of 1739, refitted and divided c.1820, and furnished in the style of that date.

Opening Times: Easter to Sep daily 14:00-17:00.   Admission: Adult 75p, Concession 25p.
Location: Near city centre, close to Castle.   Map Ref: 10

Judges Lodgings Museum

Church Street, Lancaster LA1 1YS   Tel: 01524 32808
Email: judges.lodgings@mus.lancscc.go.uk   Web: www.bringinghistoryalive.co.uk

Lancaster's oldest town house, The Judges' Lodgings, displays an impressive collection of Gillow furniture in period rooms. Also includes porcelain, silver and paintings and a Museum of Childhood with dolls, toys and games.

Opening Times: Good Friday to end of Oct.   Admission: Adult £2.00, Child Free, Concessions £1.00, Family season ticket £8.00.   Location: Town centre, five minutes from bus station and ten minutes from railway station.   Map Ref: 10

Lancaster City Museum

Market Square, Lancaster LA1 1HT   Tel: 01524 64637   Fax: 01524 841692

Email: lancaster.citymuseum@mus.lancscc.gov.uk
Web: www.lancaster.gov.uk/council/museums

Collections illustrate history and archaeology of Lancaster and North Lancashire. Paintings, decorative arts and a series of changing exhibitions.

Opening Times: Mon to Sat 10:00-17:00. Closed Xmas.
Admission: Free.   Location: City centre, five minutes from main rail and bus stations.

Medieval Fish Stall   Map Ref: 10

Lancaster Maritime Museum

Custom House, St Georges Quay, Lancaster LA1 1RB   Tel: 01524 64637   Fax: 01524 841692
Email: lancaster.citymuseum@mus.lancscc.gov.uk   Web: www.lancaster.gov.uk/council/museums

Collections illustrate the history of the Port of Lancaster, fishing in Morecombe Bay, slaving and the West Indies trade. Changing exhibitions. ·

Opening Times: Easter to Oct daily 11:00-17:00, Nov to Easter daily 12:30-16:00.
Admission: Adult £2.00, Concession £1.00.   Location: On St George's Quay, five minutes from city centre.   Map Ref: 10

Museum of The Kings Own Regiment (Lancaster)

City Museum, Market Square, Lancaster LA1 1HT   Tel: 01524 64637   Fax: 01524 841692 .
Email: kingsownmuseum@iname.com   Web: www.lancaster.gov.uk/council/museums

Collections illustrate the history and actions of the King's Own Royal Regiment (Lancaster) (4th of Foot) from its raising in 1680 to the present day. Uniforms, medals, archives and photographs.

Opening Times: Mon to Sat 10:00-17:00. Closed Xmas.   Admission: Free.   Location: City centre, five minutes from main rail and bus station.   Map Ref: 10

Peter Scott Gallery

Lancaster University, Lancaster LA1 4YW

Tel: 01524 593057   Fax: 01524 592603
Email: m.p.gavagan@lancaster.ac.uk
Web: www.peterscottgallery.com

The gallery presents temporary exhibitions and associated talks and houses the University's Art Collection. The Collection includes works by significant European artists Joan Miró, Pablo Picasso, Victor Vasarely and Max Ernst, and British artists Barbara Hepworth, Sir Terry Frost and Andy Goldsworthy. The University's stunning collection of Royal Lancastrian Pottery is on permanent display in the John Chambers Ceramics Room.

Scottie Wilson, Flowering Thoughts
©Peter Scott Gallery, Lancaster University

Lancashire

Opening Times: Mon to Fri 11:00-16:00 & late Thu 18:00-20:30, during exhibitions. Please telephone for details. Group bookings welcome. Admission: Free. Location: On Lancaster University Campus. Accessible by road, leave junction 33 on M6; A6 to Lancaster. Public transport Lancaster Railway Station, Bus to University from city centre. Exhibitions & Events 2004 : 19 Jan to 19 Mar: Prints and Paintings from the Irene Manton International Collection (Main Gallery); Eduardo Chillida - Prints and Ink Drawings (Manton Room), 26 Apr to 2 Jun: Alan Davie (Main Gallery); Reginald Farrer - Plant Explorer and Botanist (Manton Room), Jun: Degree Show, Sep: MA Show.	Map Ref: 10

Roman Bath House

Castle Hill, Vicarage Field, Lancaster   Tel: 01524 64637

Conserved ruin forming bath wing of important Roman house just outside the fort walls. Demolished c.340 AD to build new walls and ditch, but preserved in upcast.

Opening Times: Open all daylight hours. Admission: Free. Location: Near Castle and Priory Church, two minutes from rail station.	Map Ref: 10

Ruskin Library

Lancaster University, Lancaster LA1 4YH   Tel: 01524 593587   Fax: 01524 593580
Email: ruskin.library@lancaster.ac.uk   Web: www.lancs.ac.uk/users/ruslinlib/

Largest collection of books, manuscripts and drawings by and relating to the writer and artist John Ruskin (1819-1900), in an award-winning new building. Public gallery with at least three exhibitions a year.

Opening Times: Mon to Sat 11:00-16:00, Sun 13:00-16:00. Admission: Free. Location: South of Lancaster, on A6 just off junction 33 of M6.	Map Ref: 10

Lytham Heritage Centre

2 Henry Street, Lytham FY8 5LE   Tel / Fax: 01253 730767
Email: thecentre@lythamheritage.fsnet.co.uk   Web: www.lythamheritage.fsnet.co.uk

A Grade II Listed building built in 1899, formerly the Manchester and County Bank. Acquired by Lytham Heritage Group in 1996 and converted into an exhibition centre and gallery in a Victorian style. A variety of exhibitions include Lytham Heritage and local community arts and crafts.

Opening Times: Tue to Sun & BH 10:00-16:00. Admission: Free. Location: In Lytham Town Centre, at the corner of the Piazza.	Map Ref: 11

'Lytham Heritage Centre' from a Watercolour by Tom Eccles

Lytham Windmill Museum

East Beach, Lytham FY8 4HZ   Tel / Fax: 01253 730767
Email: thecentre@lythamheritage.fsnet.co.uk
Web: www.lythamheritage.fsnet.co.uk

Built in 1805 and worked as a corn mill until 1919, the Windmill Museum, housed in a restored Grade II listed building, is now a permanent heritage exhibition. Displays record the 200 years history of the mill and explain its machinery, with models and memorabilia. The basement includes many tableaux of Victorian life in Lytham. The museum was awarded National Museum status in 2001 and won an Award from Northwest Tourist Board as a Visitor Attraction.

Lytham Windmill Museum on Lytham Green

Opening Times: May to Sep Tue to Thu, Sat & Sun 10:30-13:00 & 14:00-16:30. Admission: Free. Location: Near town centre on Lytham Green overlooking River Ribble.	Map Ref: 11

Lancashire

Rufford Old Hall

Rufford, Ormskirk L40 1SG   Tel: 01704 821254
Email: ruffordoldhall@nationaltrust.org.uk   Web: www.nationaltrust.org.uk

One of Lancashire's finest 16th century buildings, famed for its Great Hall with an intricately carved 'moveable' wooden screen and dramatic hammerbeam roof. There is a collection of arms and armour from various European countries, and heraldic decoration. Also various other collections including Japanese and Chinese ceramics, a mixed collection of stained glass from various periods, prints and watercolours of local interest and oak furniture.

Opening Times: House: 3 Apr to 27 Oct Sat to Wed 13:00-17:00. Garden: 3 Apr to 27 Oct Sat to Wed 11:00-

South east corner of The Old Hall

17:30. Admission: Adult £4.50, Child £2.00, Family £11.00. Group Adult £2.75, Child £1.00. NT Members Free. Location: Seven miles north of Ormskirk, in village of Rufford on east side of A59.   Map Ref: 12

British Commercial Vehicle Museum

King Street, Leyland, Preston PR25 2LE   Tel: 01772 451011   Fax: 01772 623404
Web: www.thevehicleworks.com

Britain's premier collection of fully restored commercial and passenger vehicles tracing the history of road transport over the last 100 years.

Opening Times: Apr to Sep Sun, Tue, Wed, Thu and BH Mon 10:00-16:30. Oct Sun only 10:00-16:30. Admission: Adult £4.00, Child/OAP £2.00, Family £10.00. Location: Exit M6 at junction 28, one mile from exit.   Map Ref: 13

Harris Museum & Art Gallery

Market Square, Preston PR1 2PP   Tel: 01722 258248   Fax: 01772 886764
Email: harris.museum@preston.gov.uk   Web: www.visitpreston.com/harris

The Harris offers the best of Preston's heritage in a beautiful Grade I listed building, with its collections of paintings, sculpture, textiles, costume, glass and ceramics, as well as The Story of Preston Gallery. The museum shows an exciting programme of exhibitions and has a national reputation for contemporary art shows. The programme also includes local history, fine and decorative art and contemporary craft.

Opening Times: Mon to Sat 10:00-17:00, Sun 11:00-16:00. Closed BH. Admission: Free. Location: Market

Harris Museum and Art Gallery, Preston

Square, Preston, one minute from bus station, five minutes from railway station.   Map Ref: 14

Museum of Lancashire

Stanley Street, Preston PR1 4YP   Tel: 01772 534075   Fax: 01772 534079
Web: www.bringinghistoryalive.co.uk

Housed in Preston's Old Court House, the museum brings to life aspects of Lancashire's exciting past. Discover our exciting events and exhibitions programme.

Opening Times: Daily 10:30-17:00, closed Thursdays, Sundays and BH. Admission: Adult £2.00, Concession £1.00, Child Free. Location: Town centre, five minutes walk from bus station.   Map Ref: 14

The National Football Museum

Sir Tom Finney Way, Deepdale, Preston PR1 6RU   Tel: 01772 908442   Fax: 01772 908433
Email: enquiries@nationalfootballmuseum.com   Web: www.nationalfootballmuseum.com

The world's largest collection of football memorabilia including the FIFA, FA, Football League and Wembley Collections. Inter-active gallery and children's education trail.

Opening Times: Tue to Sat 10:00-17:00, Sun 11:00-17:00, Midweek Match Day 10:00-19:30. Closed Mon except BH. Admission: Free. Location: One mile from town centre. Map Ref: 14

Lancashire

Queens Lancashire Regiment

Fulwood Barracks, Preston PR2 8AA   Tel: 01772 260362   Fax: 01772 260583

Extensive museum, archive and library, containing material relating to 30th, 40th, 47th, 59th, 81st and 82nd Regiments of Foot, The East Lancashire, South Lancashire, Loyal (North Lancashire), Lancashire and Queen's Lancashire Regiment.

Opening Times: Tue to Thu 10:00-16:00 or by appointment.   Admission: Free. Guided groups £2.00 per person.   Location: Two miles north of town centre.   Map Ref: 14

Ribchester Roman Museum

Riverside, Ribchester, Preston PR3 3XS   Tel: 01254 878261
Email: ribchestermuseum@btconnect.com   Web: www.ribchestermuseum.org

This museum contains displays of military life at Roman Ribchester. New exhibitions include many exciting finds from the site.

Opening Times: Mon to Fri 09:00-17:00, Sat to Sun 11:00-17:30.   Admission: Adult £2.00, Child £1.00.   Location: On B6245 off A59. Bus routes from Blackburn and Preston.
                                                                                     Map Ref: 15

Rossendale Museum

Whitaker Park, Rawtenstall, Rossendale BB4 6RE   Tel: 01706 244682   Fax: 01706 250037

19th century mill owner's residence set in a park, now a museum with varied collections, including local history, fine decorative arts, natural history. Features - William Bullock's tiger and python, small collection of late Victorian wallpapers.

Opening Times: Please telephone for times.   Admission: Free.   Location: Quarter of a mile from Rawtenstall centre; off A681; on main Accrington to Rochdale bus route.   Map Ref: 16

Helmshore Mills Textile Museum

Holcombe Road, Helmshore, Rossendale BB4 4NP   Tel: 01706 226459   Fax: 01706 218554
Email: helmshore.museum@mus.lancscc.gov.uk   Web: www.bringinghistoryalive.co.uk

Two of Lancashire's original textile mills. View international treasures including an Arkwright Water Frame and an improved Spinning Jenny. Enjoy live demonstrations of traditional textile techniques, plus new Revolution Gallery.

Opening Times: Apr to Oct.   Admission: Adult £3.00, Child Free, Concession £1.50, Family & Friends Season Ticket £8.00.   Location: Rural location, approximately 15 minutes from junction 5 on M65.   Map Ref: 17

Meols Hall

Churchtown, Southport PR9 7LZ   Tel: 01704 228326   Fax: 01704 507185
Email: events@meolshall.com   Web: www.meolshall.com

17th Century House with subsequent additions. Interesting collection of pictures, furniture and objects of local interest.

Opening Times: 14 Aug to 14 Sep Daily 14:00-17:00.   Admission: Adult £3.00, Child £1.00.
Location: Three miles NE of Southport town centre in Churchtown. SE off A565.   Map Ref: 18

Turton Tower

Chapletown Road, Turton BL7 0HG   Tel: 01204 852203   Fax: 01204 853759
Email: turtontower.lcc@btinternet.com   Web: www.bringinghistoryalive.co.uk

A distinctive English country house with period rooms displaying a magnificent collection of decorative woodwork, paintings and furniture, including items loaned from the Victoria and Albert Museum.

Opening Times: Feb to Nov.   Admission: Adult £3.00, Concessions £1.50, Child Free.
Location: Suburban location, nearest railway station one and a half miles - Bromley Cross.
Buses stop outside.   Map Ref: 19

Leicestershire, Rutland & Nottinghamshire

Leicestershire is the home of the famous Quorn, Belvoir and Cottesmore hunts. However to the west of the county many of the towns belong to the industrial east Midlands. Nottinghamshire, lying in the low ground of the Trent basin, is the county of Robin Hood and Sherwood Forest.

The social history of these counties is preserved in some of the most comprehensive and attractive Museums in the land, catering for all interests and tastes.

The Red Map References should be used to locate Museums etc on the pages that follow

Leicestershire, Rutland & Nottinghamshire

The Manor House

Manor Road, Donington-le-Heath, Coalville LE67 2FW   Tel / Fax: 01530 831259
Email: museums@leics.gov.uk   Web: www.leics.gov.uk/museums

Medieval manor house dating back to 1280, with a fascinating history. The surrounding grounds have scented herb gardens, and the adjoining stone barn is home to a tempting restaurant.

Opening Times: Apr to Sep daily 11:30-17:00. Oct to Mar daily 11:30-15:00. Dec, Jan & Feb only open weekends 11.30-17.00.   Admission: Free.   Location: Southern outskirts of Coalville.

Map Ref: 1

Snibston Discovery Park

Ashby Road, Coalville LE67 3LN   Tel: 01530 278444   Fax: 01530 813301
Email: snibston@leics.gov.uk   Web: www.leics.gov.uk/museums

One of the largest and most dynamic museums in the Midlands, Snibston is Leicestershire's all-weather science and industry museum. Visitors can get their hands-on loads of fun in the popular 'Science Alive!' Gallery or explore the county's rich heritage in the Transport, Extractives, Engineering, Textiles and Fashion Galleries, and The Toybox, an area for under 5's and 8's. Other attractions include guided colliery tours, outdoor science and water playgrounds, sculptures and nature reserve.

An interactive exhibit in the Science Alive! Gallery

Opening Times:Daily 10:00-17:00. Admission:Adult £5.50, Child £3.50, Concession £3.75. Group rates available.

Map Ref: 1

Belvoir Castle

Belvoir, Grantham NG32 1PD   Tel: 01476 870262   Email: info@belvoircastle.co.uk

Home of the Duke & Duchess of Rutland. Stunning views over the Vale of Belvoir. One of the finest collections of 18th and 19th century pictures, furniture and tapestry in a private collection. Home of the Queen's Royal Lancers Museum, attractive gardens and grounds.

Opening Times: Easter to end Sep daily. Sun only in Oct. Closed Mon & Fri except BH.
Admission: Adult £8.00, Child £5.00, OAP £7.00, Family (2 adults and 2 children) £22.00.
Location: Six miles from the A1 at Grantham and 12 miles from Melton Mowbray. Nottingham and Stamford are within half an hours drive. Follow brown heritage signs.   Map Ref: 2

The Queens Royal Lancers

Belvoir Castle, Belvoir, Grantham NG31 7TJ   Tel: 01159 573295   Fax: 01159 573195
Email: mickandterry@qrl.uk.com   Web: www.qrl.uk.com

The museum traces the military and social history of the 16th/5th Lancers, the 17th/21st Lancers and The Queen's Royal Lancers from their formation to the present day. Weapons, uniforms, paintings, silver and personal artefacts form part of this fine collection.

Opening Times: Apr to Sep Sat, Sun, Tue, Wed, Thu, Good Fri & BH Mon. Sun only in Mar & Oct. 11:00-17:00.   Admission: As Belvoir Castle.   Location: As Belvoir Castle.   Map Ref: 2

Abbey Pumping Station Museum

Corporation Road, Off Abbey Lane, Leicester LE4 5PX   Tel: 0116 299 5111   Fax: 0116 299 5125   Web: www.leicester.gov.uk/museums

Home to Gimson beam engines, exhibits include cinema equipment, vehicles, an interactive loo and public health and sanitation displays. The museum is also home to an impressive historic vehicle collection, including a coal-fired fish and chip van!

Opening Times: Please contact the site for seasonal opening hours.   Admission: Free (except for certain special events).   Map Ref: 3

Leicestershire, Rutland & Nottinghamshire

Belgrave Hall and Gardens

Church Road, off Thurcaston Road, Belgrave, Leicester LE4 5PE   Tel: 0116 266 6590
Web: www.leicester.gov.uk/museums

Belgrave Hall is an 18th century Queen Anne house furnished in both Edwardian and Victorian room settings. There are several separate gardens and a glasshouse containing permanent collections of tropical, sub-tropical and alpine plants.

Opening Times: Please contact the site for seasonal opening hours.   Admission: Free.
Map Ref: 3

Guildhall

Guildhall Lane, Leicester LE1 5FQ   Tel: 0116 253 2569   Web: www.leicester.gov.uk/museums

The Guildhall is one of Leicester's most famous buildings, dating back to the 14th century. Visitors can step back in time and see the Victorian police cells and maybe even a few ghosts!

Opening Times: Please contact the site for seasonal opening hours.   Admission: Free.
Map Ref: 3

Jewry Wall Museum

St Nicholas Circle, Leicester LE1 4LB   Tel: 0116 225 4971
Web: www.leicester.gov.uk/museums

Local pre-historic, Roman and medieval artefacts. The museum houses several exhibitions including a series of illustrations showing street scenes from Iron Age, Roman, Saxon, Medieval and 18th century Leicester.

Opening Times: Please contact the site for seasonal opening hours.   Admission: Free.
Map Ref: 3

Leicestershire CCC Museum

County Ground, Grace Road, Leicester LE2 8AD   Tel: 0116 283 1727

Collections of cricket memorabilia; bats, trophies, photographs. Themed showcases eg Ball-making, many archives from 1870 onwards, caps, blazers, medals etc.

Opening Times: Mon to Fri 09:30-15:30, winter by appointment.   Admission: Free.
Location: Two miles from town centre, access from M1/M69.
Map Ref: 3

New Walk Museum & Art Gallery

53 New Walk, Leicester LE1 7EA   Tel: 0116 225 4900   Web: www.leicester.gov.uk/museums

Visitors of all ages will be fascinated by the Ancient Egypt gallery with its mummies, coffins and other treasures, and by the dinosaurs, rock and fossils collection in the Natural History section. The museum is a major regional Art Gallery with a notable collection of German Expressionist and European art dating from the 15th century to the present day. Wild Space, the interactive natural sciences exhibition, is a must-see for anyone interested in the natural world.

The Dinosaurs at New Walk Museum

Opening Times: Please contact the site for seasonal opening hours.   Admission: Free.   Location: Situated in the historic New Walk area of the City of Leicester.   Exhibitions & Events 2004 : Summer 2004: The Amazing Music Studio.
Map Ref: 3

Newarke Houses Museum

The Newarke, Leicester LE2 7BY   Tel: 0116 225 4980   Web: www.leicester.gov.uk/museums

Newarke Houses Museum is composed of two historic houses, Wygston's Chantry House and Skeffington House. The Museum houses many fine collections including clocks, toys, greeting cards and coins.

Opening Times: Please contact us for seasonal opening hours.   Admission: Free.   Map Ref: 3

Leicestershire, Rutland & Nottinghamshire

Bellfoundry Museum

Freehold Street, Loughborough LE11 1AR   Tel: 01509 233414   Fax: 01509 263305
Email: museum@taylorbells.co.uk   Web: www.taylorbells.co.uk

Exhibits showing how bells are made and tuned. Material relating to history of Taylor Family and Company. Examples of bells, many of which can be rung by visitors. Only Bell Museum in the UK.

Opening Times: Tue to Fri & summer Sat 10:00-12:30 & 13:30-16:30. Winter Sat - please call for dates & times. Sun - tour on first Sun in month at 14:00.   Admission: Adult £1.50, Child 75p. Tour of Works (inc Museum): Adult £3.80, Child £1.90.   Location: 15 minute walk from town centre, ten minute walk from railway station. Map Ref: 4

Charnwood Museum

Queen's Hall, Granby Street, Loughborough LE11 3DU   Tel: 01509 233754   Fax: 01509 268140   Email: museums@leics.gov.uk   Web: www.leics.gov.uk/museums

Charnwood Museum features a wide range of exhibits, which reflect local history and industries. Permanent exhibitions are in four areas: 'Coming to Charnwood', 'The Natural World of Charnwood', 'Living off the Land' and 'Earning a Living'.

Opening Times: Mon to Fri 10:00-16:30, Sun 14:00-17:00.   Admission: Free.   Location: Within town centre. Map Ref: 4

Great Central Railway Museum

Great Central Road, Loughborough LE11 1RW   Tel: 01509 230726

GREAT CENTRAL RAILWAY

Fax: 01509 239791   Email: booking-office@gcrailway.co.uk   Web: www.gcrailway.co.uk

Main Line Steam trains - every weekend throughout the year. Recreating the experience of famous expresses of the steam age. Passenger trains also on weekdays, June to September. See one of our classic demonstration freight or parcel trains. Relax in the comfort of our classic corridor trains - steam heated in winter. Just like British Railways in the great years of steam.

Opening Times: Weekend and BH all year, daily Jul, Aug and school hols.   Admission: Platform ticket at Loughborough Station £3.00.   Location: Located south east of Loughborough Town Centre. 15 minute walk from Loughborough Railway Station.

'Green Arrow' on Great Central Railway

Map Ref: 4

Stanford Hall

Lutterworth LE17 6DH   Tel: 01788 860250   Fax: 01788 860870
Email: enquiries@stanfordhall.co.uk   Web: www.stanfordhall.co.uk

Stanford Hall, built in the 1690's for Sir Roger Cave, is still home to his descendants and is one of the most exquisite examples of architecture of the period.

Opening Times: Mid Apr to end Sep Sun & BH Mon 13:30-17:00. Grounds open 12:00 on BH & earlier on event days.   Admission: House & Grounds: Adult £5.00, Child £2.00. Grounds only: Adult £3.00, Child £1.00. Museum: Adult £1.00, Child 35p. Map Ref: 5

Mansfield Museum & Art Gallery

Leeming Street, Mansfield NG18 1NG   Tel: 01623 463088   Fax: 01623 412922
Email: mansfield_museum@hotmail.com

Permanent display galleries showing local, natural and social history of Mansfield and district, along with fine and decorative arts from days gone by. Always something new to see due to the varied programme of temporary exhibitions.

Opening Times:Mon to Sat 10:00-17:00. Admission:Free. Location: In the town centre.Map Ref: 6

Foxton Canal Museum

Middle Lock, Foxton, Market Harborough LE16 7RA   Tel: 0116 279 2657
Email: mike@foxcm.freeserve.co.uk   Web: www.foxcanal.fsnet.co.uk

The story of canals, locks and boat lifts with models, interactive displays and artefacts. There is a

Leicestershire, Rutland & Nottinghamshire

play boat and working lock model for younger visitors. High tech touch-screen display, and lots of artefacts.

Opening Times: Easter to Oct daily 10:00-17:00, Oct to Easter Sat to Wed 11:00-16:00. Admission: Adult £2.50, Child Free (up to three children free with each full paying adult), Concession £2.00. Location: Five miles from Market Harborough at Foxton Locks. Follow brown signs. Map Ref: 7

Harborough Museum

Adam & Eve Street, Market Harborough LE16 7AG Tel: 01858 821085 Fax: 01858 821086 Email: museums@leics.gov.uk Web: www.leics.gov.uk/museums

Displays include the Symington Collection of Corsetry and reconstruction of a local shoemaker's workshop.

Opening Times: Mon to Fri 10:00-16:30, Sun 14:00-17:00. Admission: Free. Location: Within town centre. Map Ref: 8

Melton Carnegie Museum

Thorpe End, Melton Mowbray LE13 1RB Tel: 01664 569946 Fax: 01664 564060 Email: museums@leics.gov.uk Web: www.leics.gov.uk/museums

Permanent displays feature local and natural history of the area and include work by British sporting artist John Ferneley as well as collections featuring foxhunting, the Stilton cheese and pork pie industries and the famous two-headed calf.

Opening Times: Daily 10:00-16:30. Admission: Free. Map Ref: 9

Upton Hall

Upton, Newark NG23 5TE Tel: 01636 813795 Fax: 01636 812258 Email: clocks@bhi.co.uk Web: www.bhi.co.uk

Upton Hall, a lovely late Georgian House, is surrounded by beautiful gardens and houses The British Horological Institutes intriguing clock and watch collection.

Opening Times: Apr to Oct Sat & BH Mon 11:00-17:00 & Sun 14:00-17:00. Admission: £3.50. Location: Newark. Map Ref: 10

British Horological Institute

Upton Hall, Upton, Newark-on-Trent NG23 5TE Tel: 01636 813795 Fax: 01636 812258

A fascinating collection of clocks, watches and tools in a fine country house with beautiful grounds. Includes some beautiful grandfather clocks and the original Speaking Clock.

Opening Times: Apr to Oct Sat 11:00-17:00, Sun 14:00-17:00. Guided tours all year by appointment (w/ends only). Admission: Adult £3.50, Child £2.00, OAP £3.00. Location: In the centre of Upton village, ten minutes drive from Newark. Map Ref: 10

Millgate Museum

48 Millgate, Newark-on-Trent NG24 4TS Tel: 01636 655730 Fax: 01636 655735 Email: museums@nsdc.info

Re-created streets, shops and rooms showing the commercial, social and domestic life of Newark. New 20th Century Gallery. Also Mezzanine Gallery displaying work of local artists.

Opening Times: Mon to Fri 10:00-17:00 Sat, Sun & BH 13:00-17:00. Admission: Free. Location: On the riverside walk, five minutes from Newark Town Centre. Map Ref: 11

Newark Air Museum

Winthorpe Showground, Newark-on-Trent NG24 2NY Tel / Fax: 01636 707170 Email: newarkair@lineone.net Web: www.newarkairmuseum.co.uk

UK's largest volunteer managed aviation museum displaying 65 aircraft and cockpit sections from across the history of aviation. Large under cover display areas, artefact displays, souvenir shop and cafe.

Opening Times: Mar to Oct daily 10:00-17:00. Nov to Feb daily 10:00-16:00. Admission: Adult £4.50, Child £2.75, OAP £3.75. Location: Easy access from A1, A17, A46 and A1133, follow brown/white signs. Map Ref: 12

Newark Museum

Appletongate, Newark-on-Trent NG24 1JY   Tel: 01636 655740   Fax: 01636 655745
Email: museums@nsdc.info

Ever wondered about Newark's early history? Find out more from the fine archaeology collections. Also look out for Newark's Civil War Heritage. Free fun trails link all the displays.

Opening Times: Mon to Sat 10:00-13:00, 14:00-17:00, closed Thu. Apr to Sep also open Sun 14:00-17:00, BH 13:00-17:00. Admission: Free. Location: Town centre, close to parish church.   Map Ref: 11

Newark Town Treasures & Art Gallery

Town Hall, Market Place, Newark-on-Trent NG24 1DU   Tel: 01636 680333   Fax: 01636 680350
Email: post@newark.gov.uk   Web: www.newarktowntreasures.co.uk

Museum housed in Grade I listed Georgian Town Hall designed by John Carr in 1776. Collection consists of sumptuous civic gifts and paintings from 17th and 18th centuries. Temporary exhibitions in the Spotlight Gallery.

Opening Times: Mon to Fri 11:00-16:00, Sat 12:00-16:00 all year. Closed Sun & BH.
Admission: Free. Location: Town centre.   Map Ref: 11

Vina Cooke Museum of Dolls & Bygone Childhood

The Old Rectory, Cromwell, Newark-on-Trent NG23 6JE   Tel: 01636 821364

Large collection of dolls, toys, prams, dolls houses, books, games and costumes. Handmade dolls by Vina Cooke depicting royalty, stage, screen and historical characters. Also various christening robes, children's clothing and accessories. Attractively displayed in late 17th century Dower House and former rectory. An Easter Monday Extravaganza takes place every year, with Morris dancers and fascinating craft displays.

Opening Times: Daily except Fri 10:30-12:00, 14:00-17:00. Fri, evenings and other hours by appointment. Admission: Adult £3.00, Child £1.50, OAP £2.50. Location: Five miles north of Newark, easy access from A1. Next to church in village of Cromwell.   Map Ref: 10

Angel Row Gallery

Central Library Building, 3 Angel Row, Nottingham NG1 6HP   Tel: 0115 915 2869   Fax: 0115 915 2860   Email: deborah.dean@nottinghamcity.gov.uk

A varied and constantly changing programme of contemporary art.

Opening Times: Mon to Sat 10:00-17:00, Wed 10:00-19:00. Admission: Free. Location: City centre, one minute walk from Market Square.   Map Ref: 13

Brewhouse Yard Museum

Castle Boulevard, Nottingham NG7 1FB   Tel: 0115 915 3600   Fax: 0115 915 3601
Email: alisonb@ncmg.demon.co.uk

Nestled in the rock below Nottingham Castle and housed in a row of 17th century cottages, Brewhouse Yard provides a realistic glimpse of life in Nottingham over the last 300 years. Discover the dug out caves behind the museum and get a glimpse of old Nottingham as you peer into 1920's shop window. Visit the World War II air raid shelter, imagine being in a Victorian home or revisit your childhood in the Kaleidoscope Galleries.

Opening Times: Daily 10:00-17:00. Admission: Adult £1.50, Child/Concession 80p, Family £3.80.
Location: Ten minutes walk from city centre. Map Ref: 13

Leicestershire, Rutland & Nottinghamshire

Castle Museum & Art Gallery

Nottingham NG1 6EL   Tel: 0115 915 3700   Fax: 0115 915 3653
Email: davidg@ncmg.demon.co.uk   Web: www.nottinghamcity.gov.uk

Situated high above the city on the Castle Rock, Nottingham Castle has had a turbulent 1000 year history. Nottingham Castle is a 17th century Ducal Mansion built over 300 years ago on the site of a medieval castle originally built by William the Conqueror that was in turn demolished during the civil war. Housed within the Castle are collections of historic and contemporary fine art, china and silverware as well as a programme of touring exhibitions. There are detailed displays about the history of Nottingham, a children's gallery and a medieval themed playground. Tours are available of the network of caves and hidden passageways underneath the Castle. The Castle is surrounded by beautiful Victorian gardens and provides scenic views across the city and countryside beyond. Within the grounds are remains of the original Castle enabling you to imagine how it would have looked.

Opening Times: Daily 10:00-17:00.   Admission: Free Mon to Fri. Sat, Sun & BH - Adult £2.00, Child/Concession £1.00, Family (2 adult and 4 children) £5.00.   Location: Five minutes walk from Nottingham City Centre, easy access from train and bus station.   Map Ref: 13

Djanogly Art Gallery

Lakeside Arts Centre, University Park, Nottingham NG7 2RD   Tel: 0115 846 7777
Email: neil.walker@nottingham.ac.uk   Web: www.lakesidearts.org.uk

Temporary exhibition galleries offering a year-round programme of contemporary and historic fine art exhibitions with education activities and events targeted at general public and schools/colleges.

Opening Times: Mon to Sat 11:00-17:00, Sun & BH 14:00-17:00.   Admission: Free.
Location: One and a half miles outside city centre, on major bus route. Easy access by car from motorway.   Map Ref: 13

Galleries of Justice

Shire Hall, High Pavement, Nottingham NG1 1HN   Tel: 0115 952 0555
Fax: 0115 993 9828   Email: info@galleriesofjustice.org.uk
Web: www.galleriesofjustice.org.uk

Journey with us through 300 years of Crime and Punishment on this historic site, where your senses are bombarded with the sounds, sights and smells of justice and injustice, the guilty and the innocent. Witness a real trial in the authentic Victorian courtroom before being sentenced and 'sent down' to the original cells and medieval caves.

Opening Times: Tue to Sun & BH 10:00-17:00. Closed Xmas & New Year.   Admission: Adult £6.95, Child £5.25, Concession £5.95, Family £19.95.   Location: Midland Railway Station and Victoria Bus Station ten minute walk.   Map Ref: 13

Holme Pierrepont Hall

Holme Pierrepont, Nottingham NG12 2LD   Tel / Fax: 0115 933 2371
Web: www.holmepierreponthall.com

Private Tudor Manor House open to the public. Also available for weddings and business functions.

Opening Times: June Thu. Jul Wed & Thu. Aug Tue, Wed & Thu.   Map Ref: 14

Industrial Museum

Courtyard Buildings, Wollaton Park, Nottingham NG8 2AE   Tel: 0115 915 3900
Email: carolb@ncmg.demon.co.uk

The Museum is housed in the 18th century stable block for Wollaton Hall. It tells the story of the industries of Nottingham and its environs, from heavy industries such as coal mining and engineering to its famous lace.

Opening Times: Apr to Sep daily 11:00-17:00. Oct to Apr daily 11:00-16:00.
Admission: Weekdays Free. Weekends and BH Adult £1.50, Child/Concession 80p, Family £3.80.   Location: Four miles from Nottingham City Centre off the A6514.   Map Ref: 15

Leicestershire, Rutland & Nottinghamshire

D H Lawrence Heritage

Durban House Heritage Centre, Mansfield Road, Eastwood, Nottingham NG16 3DZ   Tel: 01773 717 353   Fax: 01773 713 509

A twin site, the D H Lawrence Birhtplace Museum and Durban House Heritage Centre, based around the working class Victorian upbringing and hometown of the famous writer D H Lawrence.

Opening Times: Apr to Oct daily 10:00-17:00. Nov to Mar daily 10:00-16:00. Admission: Adult £3.50, Child/Concession £1.80 for both sites. Location: Coveniently located just off M1 Junction 26, follow the A610, and Junction 27, follow the A608 through Brinsley.   Map Ref: 16

Long Eaton Town Hall

Derby Road, Long Eaton, Nottingham   Tel: 0115 907 1141   Fax: 0115 932 9264
Email: museum@erewash.gov.uk   Web: www.erewash.gov.uk

Temporary exhibitions of art, local and social history. Plus Howitt bequest of paintings.

Opening Times: Mon to Fri 10:00-16:00. Admission: Free. Location: Near town centre.
Map Ref: 17

Natural History Museum, Wollaton Park

Wollaton Park, Nottingham NG8 2AE   Tel: 0115 915 3900   Fax: 0115 915 3932
Email: carolb@ncmg.demon.co.uk

Nottingham's natural history collection housed in an Elizabethan mansion, set in 500 acres of natural parkland.

Opening Times: Apr to Sep daily 11:00-17:00. Oct to Mar daily 11:00-16:00. Admission: Free, except Sat, Sun & BH Adults £1.50, Child/Concession 80p, Family £3.80. Location: Three miles from Nottingham City Centre. Follow signs off the A52.   Map Ref: 15

Oakham Castle

Market Place, Oakham   Tel: 01572 758440   Fax: 01572 758445
Email: museum@rutland.gov.uk   Web: www.rutnet.co.uk/rcc/rutlandmuseums

The 12th century Great Hall of Oakham Castle is an important monument of Norman England. Over 200 presentation horseshoes, given by lords and royalty to the lord of the manor, hang inside. The Hall has been a court for over 800 years, but today the fine arcitecture and sculptures of medieval musicians make it a popular venue for civil marriages.

Opening Times: Mon to Sat (all year) 10:30-17:00, closed 13:00-13:30 for lunch, Sun 14:00-16:00. Closed Good Friday & Xmas. Admission: Free. Location: Off Market Place.   Map Ref: 18

The 12th century Great Hall of Oakham Castle

Rutland County Museum

Catmose Street, Oakham LE15 6HW   Tel: 01572 758440   Fax: 01572 758445
Email: museum@rutland.gov.uk   Web: www.rutnet.co.uk/rcc/rutlandmuseums

Rutland County Museum is the perfect introduction to England's smallest county. The new 'Welcome to Rutland' gallery is a guide to the history of Rutland and leads into displays of local archaeology, history and an extensive rural life collection. The site itself is also remarkable as the Museum is set in the old riding school of the Rutland Fencible Cavalry.

Opening Times: Mon to Sat (all year) 10:30-17:00, Sun 14:00-16:00. Closed Good Friday & Xmas.
Admission: Free. Location: On A6003 just south of town centre.   Map Ref: 18

The Rutland County Museum's
1794 riding school building

Leicestershire, Rutland & Nottinghamshire

Newstead Abbey

Newstead Abbey Park, Ravenshead NG15 8NA   Tel: 01623 455900   Fax: 01623 455904
Email: enquiries@newsteadabbey.org.uk   Web: www.newsteadabbey.org.uk

A beautiful historic house set in scenic gardens and parkland. Founded as a monastic house in the late 12th century, Newstead Abbey became the Byron family seat in 1540.

Opening Times: Apr to Sep daily 12:00-17:00.   Admission: House & Park: Adult £5.00, Concession £2.50, Family £12.00, Group rate £2.50.   Location: 12 miles north of Nottingham on the A60, close to junction 27 of the M1.   Map Ref: 19

Papplewick Pumping Station

off Longdale Lane, Ravenshead NG15 9AJ   Tel: 0115 963 2938   Fax: 0115 955 7172
Email: secretary@papplewickpumpingstation.co.uk
Web: www.papplewickpumpingstation.co.uk

Late Victorian working waterworks in landscaped grounds. One of Europe's great industrial monuments. Original engines/boilers in magnificent Temple of Steam.

Opening Times: BH and other weekends operational.   Admission: Adult £3.00, Child £1.50, Concession/Group £2.50.   Location: Signposted off A60/A614 seven miles north of Nottingham.
                                                                                         Map Ref: 19

Bassetlaw Museum & Percy Laws Memorial Gallery

Amcott House, Grove Street, Retford DN22 6JU   Tel / Fax: 01777 713749

Collections relating to the history and archaeology of North Nottinghamshire. Continuous programme of short-term exhibitions. Permanent display of the Retford civic plate. In restored Georgian town house setting.

Opening Times: Mon to Sat 10:00-17:00. Closed Sun & BH.   Admission: Free.   Location: 200 metres from town centre (Market Square), three minutes from bus station.   Map Ref: 20

Harley Gallery

Welbeck, Worksop S80 3LW   Tel: 01909 501700   Fax: 01909 488747   Email: ssherrit@harley-welbeck.co.uk   Web: www.harleygallery.co.uk

A changing display of contemporary arts and crafts exhibitions. Craft shop selling work from eminent British artists, a museum showing fine/decorative arts from The Portland Collection and a range of events/workshops exploring the arts.

Opening Times: Feb to Dec Tue to Sun 10:00-17:00.   Admission: Free.   Location: Situated on the A60 Mansfield Road, five miles south of Worksop.   Map Ref: 21

Mr Straw's House

7 Blyth Road, Worksop S81 0JG   Tel: 01909 482380
Email: mrstrawshouse@nationaltrust.org.uk   Web: www.nationaltrust.org

A semi-detached house where time stood still in the 1930s and nothing was thrown away. Letters, photos, furniture, household objects all shown exactly as the family left them.

Opening Times: 1 Apr to 30 Oct Tue to Sat 11:00-16:30. Due to the domestic scale of the property pre-booking is essential for all visitors.   Admission: Adult £4.40, Child £2.20, Family £11.00. NT Members Free.   Location: Follow signs to Bassetlaw General Hospital, House signposted from Blyth Road (B6045).   Map Ref: 22

Lincolnshire

The county town Lincoln dominates the old county of Lincolnshire, standing on the central chalk ridge, the Lincolnshire Edge. The impressive triple towered cathedral overlooks the ancient historic city with its beautiful stained glass windows and the famous Lincoln Imp. Skegness, Lincolnshire's seaside resort, was developed during the nineteenth century and flourished with the coming of the railway in 1873. The Holland region of drained Fen is the commercial bulb-growing centre, ablaze with colour during the Spring months leading to Spalding's spectacular Tulip Parade in May.

A fine selection of museums and historic houses encapsulate the local and social history of Lincolnshire.

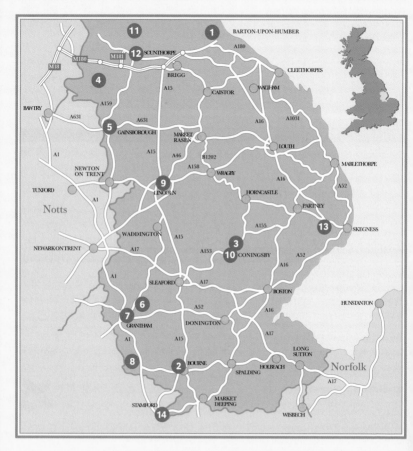

The Red Map References should be used to locate Museums etc on the pages that follow

Lincolnshire

Baysgarth House Museum

Baysgarth Leisure Park, Caistor Road, Barton-upon-Humber DN18 6AH   Tel: 01652 632318

An 18th century mansion house with fine period rooms, a collection of 18th and 19th century English and Oriental pottery and an industrial museum in the stable block.

Opening Times: Tue to Sun & BH 10:00-16:00. Closed Mon and Xmas & New Year.
Admission: Free.   Location: Near town centre, three minutes walk from Market Place.
Map Ref: 1

Grimsthorpe Castle

Bourne PE10 0LY   Tel: 01778 591205   Fax: 01778 591259
Email: ray@grimsthorpe.co.uk   Web: www.grimsthorpe.co.uk

Dating from 13th century. Stunning treasure house with beautiful contents including paintings, furniture, tapestries. Surrounded by parkland, lakes, gardens, deer herd and woodland walks.

Opening Times: Apr to Sep Thu & Sun, Aug Thu to Sun 11:00-18:00 (castle open 13:00).
Admission: Adult £7.00, Child £3.50, Concession £6.00.   Location: On the A151, ten minutes drive from the A1.
Map Ref: 2

Battle of Britain Memorial Flight Visitor Centre

RAF Coningsby, Coningsby LN4 4SY   Tel: 01526 344041   Fax: 01526 342330
Email: bbmf@lincolnshire.gov.uk   Web: www.lincolnshire.gov.uk/bbmf

Unique opportunity to view the historic aircraft of BBMF at their home base at RAF Coningsby. Visitors are shown around the hangar by knowledgeable volunteers.

Opening Times: Mon to Fri 10:00-17:00. Closed Sat, Sun, BH and two weeks at Xmas.
Admission: Adult £3.50, Child £1.50, OAP £2.00, Groups £2.00.   Location: Half mile from Coningsby Village.
Map Ref: 3

Epworth Old Rectory

1 Rectory Street, Epworth DN9 1HX   Tel: 01427 872268
Email: curator@epwortholdrectory.org.uk   Web: www.epwortholdrectory.org.uk

1709 Queen Anne House, boyhood home of John and Charles Wesley. Set in large grounds, with portraits, period furniture, prints, memorabilia.

Opening Times: Mar to Oct daily. Mar, Apr & Oct 10:00-12:00 & 14:00-16:00. May, Jun, Jul, Aug & Sep Mon to Sat 10:00-16:30, Sun 14:00-16:30.   Admission: Adult £3.00, Child £1.00, OAP £2.50, Family £7.00.   Location: 200 yards from Epworth Town Centre.
Map Ref: 4

Gainsborough Old Hall

Parnell Street, Gainsbrorough DN21 2NB   Tel: 01427 612669   Fax: 01427 612779
Email: gainsborougholdhall@lincolnshire.gov.uk   Web: www.lincolnshire.gov.uk

Gainsborough's own medieval manor house. Principally a timber-framed building with a brick tower, magnificent Great Hall and one of the best preserved medieval kitchens in the country.

Opening Times: Mon to Sat 10:00-17:00, Sun 14:00-17:30. Closed Sun from end of Oct to Easter, Xmas & New Year.   Admission: Adult £2.50 Child £1.00 OAP £1.50.   Location: In the centre of Gainsborough.
Map Ref: 5

www.mghh.co.uk

For current information on the outstanding Collections in over 1600 Museums, Galleries & Historic Houses in England, Scotland, Wales and Ireland

Lincolnshire

Belton House

Belton, Grantham NG32 2LS Tel: 01476 566116 Fax: 01476 579071
Email: belton@nationaltrust.org.uk Web: www.nationaltrust.org.uk

Built in the 17th century this is a crowning achievement of Restoration architecture. The stunning interiors of this restored country house contain exceptionally fine plasterwork and wood carving, as well as important collections of paintings, furniture, tapestries and silverware. There are formal gardens, an orangery and a landscaped park.

Opening Times: 31 Mar to 31 Oct Wed to Sun 12:30-17:00. Open BH Mons. Admission: Adult £6.50, Child £3.00, Family £15.00. Group (15+) Adult £5.00, Child £2.50. NT Members Free. Location: Three miles north east of Grantham on A607 Grantham to Lincoln Road.

Saloon at Belton with Brownlow family portraits and Grinling Gibbons carving

Exhibitions & Events 2004 : 17 Jul: 'The Spitfire Prom' open air concert. Map Ref: 6

Grantham Museum

St Peters Hill, Grantham NG31 6PY Tel: 01476 568783 Fax: 01476 592457
Email: grantham.museum@lincolnshire.gov.uk

Grantham Museum is the interpretation centre of the town with displays from its earliest archaeological remains, to displays on Isaac Newton, the Dambusters and Margaret Thatcher. Regular temporary exhibitions and events. Please contact the Museum for further details.

Opening Times: Mon to Sat 10:00-17:00, also BH & Good Friday. Closed Xmas & New Year.
Admission: Free. Location: Situated in the centre of Grantham next to the Guildhall.
Map Ref: 7

Woolsthorpe Manor

23 Newton Way, Woolsthorpe-by-Colsterworth, Grantham NG33 5NR
Tel: 01476 860338 Email: woolsthorpemanor@nationaltrust.org.uk
Web: www.nationaltrust.org.uk

A small 17th century manor house, the birthplace and family home of Sir Isaac Newton. There is an early edition of Principia on display, along with prints and artefacts relating to Newton. The orchard includes a descendant of the famous apple tree.

Opening Times: Mar 6 to 28 Mar Sat & Sun Only 13:00-17:00, 1 Apr to 30 Jun Wed to Sun 13:00-17:00, 1 Jul to 29 Aug Wed to Sun 13:00-18:00, 1 Sep to 30 Sep Wed to Sun 13:00-17:00. 2 Oct to 31 Oct Sat & Sun only 13:00-17:00. Open BH Mons. Admission: Adult £4.00, Child £2.00, Family £10.00. NT Members Free. Location: Seven miles south of Grantham, half mile north west of Colsterworth, one mile west of A1. Map Ref: 8

Doddington Hall

Lincoln LN6 4RU Tel: 01522 694308 Fax: 01522 685259
Email: fionawatson@doddingtonhall.free-online.co.uk
Web: www.doddingtonhall.free-online.co.uk

The Hall stands today in its walled courtyard as it was built in 1600. The elegant Georgian interior contains a fascinating collection of pictures, textiles, porcelain and furniture that reflect four centuries of unbroken occupation.

Opening Times: House & Gardens: May to Sep Sun, Wed & BH. Gardens only: Feb to May Sun, Wed & BH. Admission: House & Gardens: Adult £4.60, Child £2.30, Family £12.75. Gardens: Adult £3.10, Child £1.55. Location: Clearly signposted off the A46 Lincoln by-pass on the B1190. Map Ref: 9

Greyfriars

Broadgate, Lincoln LN2 1HQ Tel: 01522 530401 Fax: 01522 530724
Email: hollandk@lincolnshire.gov.uk

Greyfriars is a beautiful 13th century building located in the lower part of Lincoln. Greyfriars is used to display annual themed exhibitions drawn from the collections of the City and County Museum, which range from pre-history to 1750. A lively programme of events throughout the year.

Lincolnshire

Opening Times: Tue to Sat 10:00-13:00 & 14:00-16:00. Closed 25-26 Dec and New Years Day. Admission: Free. Location: Located in the lower part of Lincoln between St Swithin's Church and central library. Map Ref: 9

Museum of Lincolnshire Life

The Old Barracks, Burton Road, Lincoln LN1 3LY Tel: 01522 528448 Fax: 01522 521264
Email: lincolnshire.museum@lincolnshire.gov.uk

The largest community museum in Lincolnshire boasting a nationally renowned agricultural collection; richly represented industrial and social history displays, and incorporating the newly refurbished Royal Lincolnshire Regimental Museum and an 18th century working windmill nearby.

Opening Times: May to Oct 10:00-17:30. Nov to Apr Mon to Sat 10:00-17:30, Sun 14:00-17:30. Closed Xmas & New Year. Admission: Adult £2.00, Child 60p, Family £4.50, Groups of 10 or over £1.60 per adult. Location: Within five minutes walk of Lincoln Cathedral and Castle sites. Map Ref: 9

Royal Lincolnshire Regiment Museum

Museum of Lincolnshire Life, Burton Road, Lincoln LN1 3LY Tel: 01522 528448

The newly refurbished Regimental Galleries display over 300 years of the regiment's history from its inception to its amalgamation with the Royal Anglian Regiment. It uses objects and text to portray life as a soldier from 1685 to 1960.

Opening Times: May to Oct 10:00-17:00. Nov to Apr Mon to Sat 10:00-17:30, Sun 14:00-17:30. Admission: Adult £2.00, Child 60p, Family £4.50, Group of 10 or more £1.60 per adult. Location: Within five minutes walk of Lincoln Cathedral and Castle sites. Map Ref: 9

Tattershall Castle

Tattershall, Lincoln LN4 4LR Tel: 01526 342543
Email: tattershallcastle@nationaltrust.org.uk Web: www.nationaltrust.org.uk

A vast fortified and moated red brick tower, built in medieval times. The building was restored in the early 20th century by Lord Curzon. It contains four great chambers with Gothic fireplaces and tapestries.

Opening Times: 6 Mar to 28 Mar Sat & Sun only 12:00-16:00, 3 Apr to 29 Sep Sat to Wed 11:00-17:30, 2 Oct to 31 Oct Sat to Wed 11:00-16:00, 6 Nov to 12 Dec Sat & Sun Only 12:00-16:00. Open Good Friday. Admission: Adult £3.50, Child £1.80, Family £8.80. Group (15+) Adult £3.10, Child £1.50. Free audio guide. NT Members Free. Location: On south side of A153, 15 miles north east of Sleaford; ten miles south west of Horncastle. Map Ref: 10

Usher Gallery

Lindum Road, Lincoln LN2 1NN Tel: 01522 527980 Fax: 01522 560165
Email: usher.gallery@lincolnshire.gov-uk

Major Lincolnshire venue for fine and decorative arts including the Peter de Wint Collection. A lively programme of temporary exhibitions throughout the year.

Opening Times: Tue to Sat 10:00-17:30, Sun 14:30-17:00. Closed 24-31 Dec, Mon except BH. Admission: Adult £2.00, Child/Concession 50p. Free day Fri. Location: Situated on the slope below the Cathedral, five minutes from the town centre. Map Ref: 9

Normanby Hall

Normanby Hall Country Park, Normanby, Scunthorpe DN15 9HU Tel: 01724 720588
Fax: 01724 721248

Normanby Hall is a Regency country house designed by Sir Robert Smirke and furnished in period style. It also contains a costume gallery in which annually changing exhibitions are held.

Opening Times: 31 Mar to 28 Sep daily 13:00-17:00. Other times by appointment. Admission: Adult £4.00, Concession £3.00, Family £11.00 (2003 prices). Special Rates for North Lincolnshire residents & Groups. Location: Four miles north of Scunthorpe off the B1430. Map Ref: 11

Normanby Park Farming Museum

Normanby Hall Country Park, Normanby, Scunthorpe DN15 9HU Tel: 01724 720588
Fax: 01724 721248

Lincolnshire

The Normanby Park Farming Museum shows the history of farming and rural crafts in the late 19th and early 20th centuries. Holding regular activities for children.

Opening Times: 31 Mar to 28 Sep daily 13:00-17:00. Other times by appointment. Admission: Adult £4.00, Concession £3.00, Family £11.00 (2003 prices). Special Rates for North Lincolnshire residents & Groups. Location: Four miles north of Scunthorpe off the B1430. Map Ref: 11

North Lincolnshire Museum

Oswald Road, Scunthorpe DN15 7BD Tel: 01724 843533

The museum housed in a Victorian vicarage, depicts North Lincolnshire's early and later history, through displays of geology, archaeology and social history.

Opening Times: Tue to Sat & BH 10:00-16:00, Sun 13:00-16:00. Closed Mon and Xmas & New Year. Admission: Free. Location: Near town centre, two minute walk from railway station, bus stop outside. Map Ref: 12

SPILSBY *Lincs*

Gunby Hall

Gunby, Spilsby PE23 5SS Tel: 01909 486411 (Regional Off)
Web: www.nationaltrust.org.uk

A fine red brick house, dating from 1700 and situated in one of England's most remote corners. Many of the rooms are panelled and there is a beautiful oak staircase. The house contains collections of family portraits, furniture and china. The exquisite walled garden is planted with traditional English vegetables, fruit and flowers.

Opening Times: 31 Mar to 29 Sep Wed only 14:00-18:00. Admission: Adult £4.00, Child £2.00, Family £10.00. NT Members Free. Location: Two and half miles north west of Burgh le Marsh, seven miles west of Skegness on south side of A158. Map Ref: 13

'Thomas William Coke Esq, MP for Norfolk Inspecting Sheep', by Thomas Weaver (1774 - 1843)

STAMFORD *Lincs*

Burghley House

Stamford PE9 3JY Tel: 01780 752451 Fax: 01780 480125
Email: burghley@burghley.co.uk Web: www.burghley.co.uk

Burghley House

18 state rooms including one of the most important private collections of 17th century Italian paintings, the earliest inventoried collection of Japanese ceramics in the west and wood carving by Grinling Gibbons and his followers. There are also four magnificent state beds, fine examples of English and continental furniture and important tapestries and textiles.

Opening Times: 27 Mar to 31 Oct 11:00-17:00. Admission: Adult £7.80, Child £3.50, OAP £6.90. Location: One mile east of Stamford on B1443, close to A1 clearly signposted. Map Ref: 14

Stamford Museum

Broad Street, Stamford PE9 1PJ Tel: 01780 766317 Fax: 01780 480363
Email: stamford_museum@lincolnshire.gov.uk Web: www.lincolnshire.gov.uk/stamfordmuseum

Displays illustrate the history of this fine stone town and include Stamford Ware pottery, the visit of Daniel Lambert and the town's more recent industrial past. Temporary exhibitions and holiday activities.

Opening Times: Apr to Sep Mon to Sat 10:00-17:00, Sun 14:00-17:00. Oct to Mar Mon to Sat 10:00-17:00. Closed 24-26 Dec & New Years Eve & Day. Admission: Free. Location: Town centre. Map Ref: 14

Central London

In a sense London is one enormous museum: from the first century AD when the Romans settled here through the early medieval period of the building of the first St Paul's Cathedral, the Norman period of the construction of the White Tower, the prosperous years of the Livery Companies, through plague, fire and pestilence and the gracious years of Wren's building, to the London of today, this city has drawn to itself the nation's talent and expertise. This great city of history and pageantry has become the treasure house of Britain's skills where everything is recorded in a vast selection of the finest, and certainly the most fascinating, museums and galleries of the world.

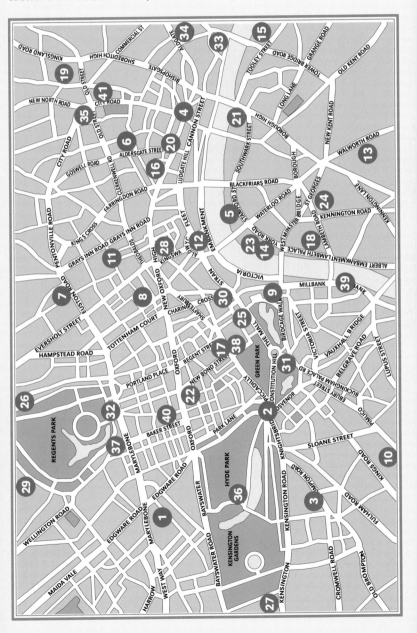

The Red Map References should be used to locate Museums etc on the pages that follow

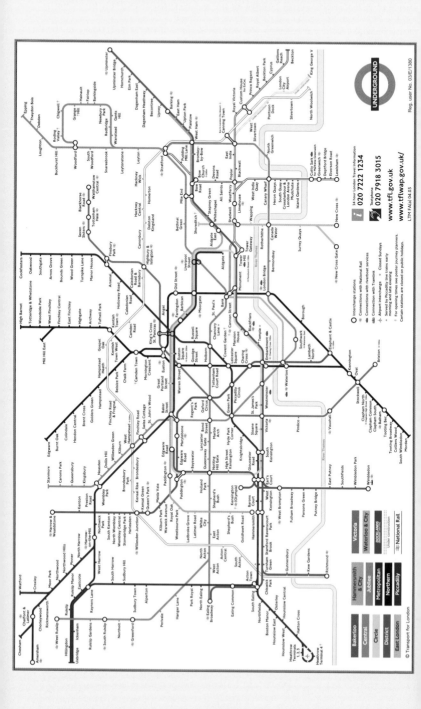

Central London

Alexander Fleming Laboratory Museum

St Marys Hospital, Praed Street, London W2 1NY   Tel: 020 7886 6528   Fax: 020 7886 6739
Email: kevin.brown@st-marys.nhs.uk

In situ reconstruction of Fleming's laboratory as it was in 1928 when he discovered penicillin there, with video and exhibition telling the story of the man, the mould and its impact on mankind.

Opening Times: Mon to Thu 10:00-13:00 (other times by appointment). Admission: Adult £2.00, Concession £1.00. Location: A two minute walk from Paddington Station.   Map Ref: 1

Apsley House

Hyde Park Corner, London W1J 7NT   Tel: 020 7499 5676   Fax: 020 7493 6576

Apsley House, famously known as No. 1 London, is one of the capital's finest residences. Ancestral home of the Dukes of Wellington since 1815, its sumptuous interiors house the first Duke's outstanding collection of paintings, silver, porcelain and sculpture. Visitor Attraction of the Year 2003 (Visit London: Under 100,000 visitors).

Opening Times: Tue to Sun 11:00-17:00. Admission: Adult £4.50, Under 18s/OAP Free, Concession £3.00, Group £2.50. Price includes free sound guide. Location: Hyde Park Corner.

Apsley House, The Waterloo Gallery   Map Ref: 2

Baden Powell House

Suite 210, 28 Old Brompton Road, South Kensington, London SW7 3SS   Tel: 020 7584 7031
Fax: 020 7590 6902   Email: conferences.bphhostel@scout.org.uk   Web: www.scouts.org.uk

Welcomed by the only granite statue in London - Lord Robert Baden-Powell (founder of the Scouting Movement) welcomes you to a memorial to his life-time achievements. It hosts a display, which depicts his life story and boasts memorabilia given to him by world delegations. As an artist Baden-Powell produced some magnificent paintings and sketches, which are also on display.

Opening Times: 4 Jan to 21 Dec daily 07:00-23:00. Admission: Free. Location: Central London, South Kensington - five minute walk from Gloucester Road and South Kensington tube stations.   Map Ref: 3

The Granite Statue welcoming
you to Baden Powell House

Bank of England Museum

Bank of England, Threadneedle Street, London EC2R 8AH   Tel: 020 7601 5491   Fax: 020 7601 5808
Email: june.greenhalf@bankofengland.co.uk
Web: www.bankofengland.co.uk

The Museum is housed within the Bank of England itself, right at the heart of the City of London. It traces the history of the Bank from its foundation by Royal Charter in 1694 to its role today as the nation's central bank. There are gold bars dating from ancient times to the modern market bar, coins and a unique collection of bank notes.

Opening Times: Mon to Fri 10:00-17:00, also day of Lord Mayor's Show. Closed Sat & Sun & BH. Admission: Free. Location: One minute walk from Bank underground, ten minutes from Liverpool Street, Fenchurch Street and Cannon Street.   Map Ref: 4

Bankside Gallery

48 Hopton Street, London SE1 9JH   Tel: 020 7928 7521   Fax: 020 7928 2820
Email: info@banksidegallery.com   Web: www.banksidegallery.com

Bankside Gallery is home to the Royal Watercolour Society and the Royal Society of Painter-Printmakers, and stages an annual programme of exhibitions of members' work.

Opening Times: Tue to Fri 10:00-17:00, Sat, Sun & BH Mon 11:00-17:00. Admission: Adult £3.50, Concession £2.00. Group rates available. Some exhibitions free. Location: Situated on riverside, near Blackfriars Bridge and adjacent to Tate Modern.   Map Ref: 5

Central London

Barbican Art Gallery

Barbican Centre, Silk Street, London EC2Y 8DS   Tel: 0845 120 7520
Email: artinfo@barbican.org.uk
Web: www.barbican.org.uk/art

Changing exhibitions of photography, art and design.
Opening Times: Mon, Tue & Thu 10:00-18:00, Wed 10:00-21:00, Sun & BH 10:00-18:00. Admission: Adult £8.00, Child/OAP/Student £6.00. Location: In the heart of the city centre. Nearest underground stations are Barbican & Moorgate.   Map Ref: 6

Photo by wyndavies.com

The British Library

96 Euston Road, London NW1 2DB   Tel: 020 7412 7332
Email: visitor-services@bl.uk   Web: www.bl.uk

On display are hundreds of items from the world's greatest collection of books, manuscripts, music, stamps, sound recordings and maps. The Library's collections span over three millennia and contain items from all continents of the world. The John Ritblat Gallery is home to a permanent exhibition of over 200 of the Library's Treasures. It includes documents which made and recorded history, sacred texts from the world's religions, masterpieces of illumination, landmarks of printing, great works of literature and music and major advances in science and mapmaking. Items on display include Codex Sinaiticus (c350), Magna Carta (1215), the Gutenberg Bible (1455), Shakespeare's First Folio (1623), as well as works in the handwriting

The Lindisfarne Gospels:
Opening page of St Luke's Gospel

of Leonardo da Vinci, Lord Nelson, Lewis Carroll, Handel, Sir Paul McCartney and many others. It also features the Library's award winning Turning the Pages computer interactive, which allows you to turn pages or unroll a scroll simply by touching a screen. The Pearson Gallery is home to special thematic exhibitions. The Workshop of Words, Sounds and Images traces the story of book production and offers regular free demonstrations. There is also an extensive display of philatelic material, which is probably the best permanent display of stamps in the world, and National Sound Archive Jukeboxes offering a changing selection of sounds from their extensive collection of recordings. Visitors can also see the Kings Library, housed in a 17 metre glass-walled tower at the heart of the building, plus a number of other major works of art.

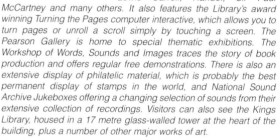

Early copy of The Canterbury
Tales at the British Library

Opening Times: Galleries: Mon 09:30-18:00, Tue 09:30-20:00, Wed to Fri 09:30-18:00, Sat 09:30-17:00, Sun & BH 11:00-17:00. Closed 1 Jan, 9-11 Apr. The Reading Room times differ. Please phone for Xmas & New Year 2005 closures. Admission: Free. Location: Next door to St Pancras mainline station, five minutes from both Euston and Kings Cross.   Map Ref: 7

British Museum

THE BRITISH MUSEUM

Great Russell Street, London WC1B 3DG   Tel: 020 7323 8000
Email: information@thebritishmuseum.ac.uk
Web: www.thebritishmuseum.ac.uk

Permanent display and special exhibitions of the works of man from prehistory to the present day. Permanent displays of antiquities from Egypt, the ancient Near East, Greece and Rome as well as Prehistory, Roman Britain, Medieval, Renaissance, Modern and Oriental collection. Also the national collection of prints and drawings, coins and banknotes. The Great Court houses the Clore Education Centre, galleries and exhibition space and improved visitor facilities.

Opening Times: Galleries: Sat to Wed 10:00-17:30, Thu &

The South Facade of the British Museum, London

Fri 10:00-20:30. Great Court: Sun to Wed 09:00-18:00, Thu to Sat 09:00-23:00. Admission: Free. Location: Nearest underground stations: Tottenham Court Road, Holborn, Russell Square.   Map Ref: 8

Central London

Cabinet War Rooms

Clive Steps, King Charles Street, London SW1A 2AQ   Tel: 020 7930 6961   Fax: 020 7839 5897   Email: cwr@iwm.org.uk   Web: www.iwm.org.uk

The secret headquarters of Winston Churchill and his Cabinet. Step back in time and view the original complex just as it was left at the end of six years of war, when the lights were finally extinguished.

Opening Times: Apr to Sep daily 09:30-18:00, Oct to Mar daily 10:00-18:00. Last admission 17:15. Closed 24-26 Dec. Admission: Adult £7.00, Child Free, OAP/Student £5.50. Group rates available. Location: Two minutes from Westminster Underground Station.   Map Ref: 9

Carlyle's House

National Trust, 24 Cheyne Row, London SW3 5HL   Tel: 020 7352 7087
Fax: 020 7352 5108   Web: www.nationaltrust.org.uk

This Chelsea Queen Anne house was the home of historian, social writer, ethical thinker and powerful public speaker Thomas Carlyle for some 47 years until his death in 1881. The skilful Scottish home making of his wife Jane is much in evidence, the furniture, pictures, portraits and books are are still in place Their academic and domestic lives can be experienced today in the atmosphere of the house.

Opening Times: 31 Mar to 29 Oct Wed to Fri 14:00-17:00, 3 Apr to 31 Oct Sat & Sun 11:00-17:00. Open BH Mons & Good Friday. Admission: Adult £3.80, Child

The Library, or Drawing Room

£1.80. NT Members Free. Location: Off Chelsea Embankment between Albert & Battersea bridges, or via Kings Road and Oakley Street.   Map Ref: 10

The Charles Dickens Museum

48 Doughty Street, London WC1N 2LX   Tel: 020 7405 2127   Fax: 020 7831 5175
Email: info@dickensmuseum.com   Web: www.dickensmuseum.com

The only surviving London home of Charles Dickens. Here, between 1837 and 1839 he completed Pickwick Papers, Oliver Twist, Nicholas Nickleby and Barnaby Rudge.

Opening Times: Mon to Sat 10:00-17:00, Sun 11:00-17:00. Admission: Adult £4.00, Child £2.00, Concession £3.00, Family £9.00. Location: Central London, near Russell Square.
        Map Ref: 11

Courtauld Institute Gallery

Somerset House, Strand, London WC2R 1LA   Tel: 020 7848 2526
Fax: 020 7848 2589   Email: galleryinfo@courtauld.ac.uk
Web: www.courtauld.ac.uk

The Gallery has one of the most important and best-loved small collections in the country, including world-famous Impressionist and post-Impressionist paintings. It is an integral part of the Courtauld Institute of Art, the oldest centre for the teaching of history of art in England and is housed at Somerset House, one of the finest 18th century buildings in London.

Opening Times: Daily 10:00-18:00. Admission: Adult £5.00, Concessions £4.00. Location: Central London. Nearest Undergrounds: Temple, Charing Cross, Holborn and Covent Garden.

Vincent Van Gogh, Self-Portrait with Bandaged Ear 1889

        Map Ref: 12

183

Central London

Cuming Museum

155/157 Walworth Road, London SE17 1RS Tel: 020 7701 1342
Fax: 020 7703 7415 Email: cuming.museum@southwark.gov.uk

Home of the rich and unusual Cuming Collection and museum of Southwark's history. Between 1780 and 1900 the Cuming family collected objects from all over the world. In 1900 the unique collection of everyday and extraordinary objects was left to the people of Southwark and the gallery was opened in 1906. The museum has an active programme of events and activities, a changing temporary exhibition space and hands-on family area.

Opening Times: Tue to Sat 10:00-17:00. Admission: Free.
Location: Near Elephant & Castle Shopping Centre, five minutes walk on the Walworth Road.   Map Ref: 13

Dali Universe

County Hall Gallery, Riverside Building, County Hall,
London SE1 7PB
Tel: 0870 744 7485 Fax: 020 7620 3120
Email: info@daliuniverse.com Web: www.daliuniverse.com

Celebrate 100 years of surreal success with the Dali Centenary in 2004. The Dali Universe is a conceptual art space housing Europe's most important collection by the master Surrealist, Salvador Dali. Arranged thematically to cover the major influences of Dali's life and work, the Dali Universe features more than 500 original works of art, from sculpture to rare etchings, furniture to gold jewellery. Among the highlights are the Mae West Lips sofa, the Lobster Telephone and The Divine Comedy. The Dali Universe boasts three themed areas - Sensuality and Feminity;

Space Venus next to the
London Eye © Richard Price

includes the world-renowned Mae West Lips sofa and the famous sculpture Buste de Femme Retrospectif, which remains one of the defining classics of Surrealism from the 1930s. Graphics illustrating the major themes of literature are also featured, including ten rare lithographs from the Romeo and Juliet series and twelve erotic Casanova images. Religion and Mythology; reflects Salvador Dali's tempestuous and ambiguous relationship with the church. Two of Dali's most famous masterpieces - the epic illustrations of the Bible and Dante's Divine Comedy number well over 100 graphics in this area. In Dreams and

The Mae West Lips Sofa © Galerie du Dragon

Fantasy; Dali's enduring fascination with the subconscious as the true canvas for expression of personality comes into vivid focus via his sculptural works such as the Persistence of Memory and the Profile of Time. Other works that refer to a life lived through dreams and distorted visions of reality include the enchanting Alice in Wonderland and Don Quichotte. Since opening its doors in June 2000, the Dali Universe has proved to be a phenomenal success for domestic visitors and overseas ones alike. With more than 250,000 entrances per year, Dalimania has decidedly swept over London.

Opening Times: Daily 10:00-17:30. Admission: Adult £8.50, Child (10-16 yrs) £4.95, Under 10s £1.00, OAP/Student £6.50. Location: Next to the London Eye.   Map Ref: 14

Design Museum

28 Shad Thames, London SE1 2YD Tel: 0870 909 9009
Fax: 0870 909 1909 Web: www.designmuseum.org

The Design Museum is the world's first museum of industrial design, fashion and architecture. Concerned as much with the future as the past, a changing exhibition programme captures the excitement and ingenuity of design's evolution through the 20th and 21st centuries.

Opening Times: Daily 10:00-17:45 (last entry 17:15).
Admission: Adult £6.00, Concession £4.00, Family (2 adults and 2 children) £16.00. Location: London, ten minutes from Tower Hill and London Bridge Tubes.
Design Museum, London, © Jefferson Smith   Map Ref: 15

Central London

Dr Johnsons House

17 Gough Square, London EC4A 3DE   Tel / Fax: 020 7353 3745
Email: curator@drjh.dircon.co.uk   Web: www.drjh.dircon.co.uk

This House can be described as a shrine to the English language, for it was here that Dr Samuel Johnson worked for many years to compile the first comprehensive English Dictionary which was published in 1755.

Opening Times: May to Sep Mon to Sat 11:00-17:30, Oct to Apr Mon to Sat 11:00-17:00. Closed BH. Admission: Adult £4.00, Child £1.00, Under 10s Free, Concession £3.00. Group rate £3.00. Location: Near two underground lines (Blackfriars, Chancery Lane) and many bus routes.   Map Ref: 16

Dunhill Museum & Archive

48 Jermyn Street, London SW1Y 6DL   Tel: 020 7838 8233

A cross-section of the company's history, its products and famous customers, from motoring accessories in the 1890s, to pipes in 1910, lighters and other related products from the 1920s up to the 1950s.

Opening Times: Mon to Fri 09:30-18:00, Sat 10:00-18:00. Admission: Free. Location: Just below Piccadilly, a minutes walk from the Royal Academy.   Map Ref: 17

Florence Nightingale Museum

St Thomas Hospital, 2 Lambeth Palace Road, London SE1 7EW
Tel: 020 7620 0374   Fax: 020 7928 1760
Email: info@florence-nightingale.co.uk   Web: www.florence-nightingale.co.uk

Large collection of Florence Nightingale personal items including childhood souvenirs, her dress, furniture from her houses and Harley Street Hospital and honours awarded to Nightingale in old age. There is a small military history collection of souvenirs from the Crimean War, including military medals and military nursing uniforms from Scutari Hospital. There is also a small nursing history collection.

Opening Times: Mon to Fri 10:00-17:00. Sat, Sun & BH 11:30-16:30. Closed Good Friday, Easter Sunday and Xmas. Last admission 1 hour before closing.

Lifesize reconstruction of a Crimean wardscene

Admission: Adult £4.80, Child/OAP/Student £3.80, Family (2 adults and 2 children) £12.00. Location: Car park level of St Thomas' Hospital, opposite Houses of Parliament. Nearest tube station - Westminster, Waterloo and Lambeth North. Exhibitions & Events 2004 : 2004: 150th Anniversary of Florence Nightingale's entry into the Crimea.   Map Ref: 18

Geffrye Museum

Kingsland Road, London E2 8EA
Tel: 020 7739 9893   Fax: 020 7729 5647
Email: info@geffrye-museum.org.uk
Web: www.geffrye-museum.org.uk

The Geffrye Museum presents the changing style of the English domestic interior through a series of period rooms from 1600 to the present day. Fine collections of furniture, paintings and decorative arts. Attractive gardens including an award-winning walled herb garden and a series of period gardens.

Opening Times: Tue to Sat 10:00-17:00, Sun 12:00-17:00. Closed Mon (except BH), Good Friday and Xmas & New Year. Admission: Free. Location: Liverpool Street Tube, then bus 149 or 242. Old Street Tube exit 2, then bus 243.   Map Ref: 19

Regency Room, 1800-1830

Guided or Private Tours	Disabled Access	Gift Shop or Sales Point	Café or Refreshments	Restaurant	Car Parking

Central London

Gilbert Collection
see Page opposite
Map Ref: 12

Gilbert Collection

Guildhall Art Gallery & Roman London's Amphitheatre ♿ ◈
Guildhall Yard, London EC2P 2EJ   Tel: 020 7606 3030   Fax: 020 7332 3342

Pleading 1876,
Sir Lawrence Alma-Tadema oil on panel

The Corporation of London's renowned collection of works of art is now on view in a new gallery opened in 1999. The display includes Victorian art, including famous Pre-Raphaelite works, London subjects from the 17th century to the present, portraits from the 16th century onwards and one of Britain's largest oil paintings. There is also a programme of temporary exhibitions. The remains of Roman London's Amphitheatre are on view as well.

Opening Times: Mon to Sat 10:00-17:00, Sun 12:00-16:00.   Admission: Adult £2.50, Child Free, Concession £1.00.   Location: Follow street signs in the City of London for Guildhall Art Gallery and Guildhall.   Map Ref: 20

HMS Belfast launch 17 March 1938

HMS Belfast ♿ ◈ ▱ ⚓
Morgan's Lane, Tooley Street, London SE1 2JH
Tel: 020 7940 6300   Fax: 020 7403 0719
Email: jwilson@iwm.org.uk   Web: www.iwm.org.uk

HMS Belfast is a cruiser that was launched in 1938 and served throughout the Second World War, playing a leading role. After the war, she supported United Nations forces in Korea and remained in service with the Royal Navy until 1965. In 1971 she was saved for the nation as a unique and historic reminder of Britain's naval heritage in the first half of the 20th century.

Opening Times: 1 Mar to 31 Oct 10:00-18:00. 1 Nov to 28 Feb 10:00-17:00. Closed 24-26 Dec.   Admission: Adult £6.00, Child Free, OAP/Student/Concession £4.40, Groups (10+): Adult £4.80, OAP/Student/Concession £3.80.   Location: The ship is three minutes walk from London Bridge Station.   Map Ref: 21

Handel House Museum ▱ ♿ ◈
25 Brook Street, London W1K 4HB   Tel: 020 7495 1685   Fax: 020 7495 1759
Email: mail@handelhouse.org   Web: www.handelhouse.org

Located in the house where G F Handel lived from 1723 until his death in 1759. Portraits, furniture, manuscripts, special exhibitions, live music, family events, study days, all in beautiful 18th century interiors.

Opening Times: Tue to Sat 10:00-18:00 (Thu until 20:00), Sun 12:00-18:00.   Admission: Adult £4.50, Child £2.00, Concession £3.50.   Location: Mayfair, London.   Map Ref: 22

Key to Classifications
see Classifications Index on page 423

Anthropology	Horticultural	Police, Prisons
Archaeological	Jewellery	& Dungeons
Art Galleries	Literature & Libraries	Railways
Arts, Crafts & Textiles	Maritime	Religion
China, Glass & Ceramics	Military & Defence	Roman
Communications	Multicultural	Science - Earth & Planetary
Egyptian	Music & Theatre	Sculpture
Fashion	Natural History	Sporting History
Geology	Oriental	Toy & Childhood
Health & Medicine	Palaces	Transport
Historic Houses	Photography	Victoriana

Gilbert Collection

Somerset House, Strand, London, WC2R 1LA
Tel: 020 7420 9400   Fax: 020 7420 9440
Email: info@gilbert-collection.org.uk   Web: www.gilbert-collection.org.uk

The Gilbert Collection is London's newest museum of decorative arts. The collection was formed over four decades by Sir Arthur Gilbert, a Londoner who moved to California in 1949 and made this extraordinary gift to the nation in 1996, "I felt it should return to the country of my birth." Thanks to Sir Arthur and the Heritage Lottery Fund, today this pre-eminent collection is beautifully housed in the vaulted spaces of the Embankment Building of the newly restored Somerset House, overlooking the Thames. The sequences of 17 galleries creates an impressive setting for treasure of English and Continental gold and silver, precious snuffboxes, miniature portraits in enamel and Italian cabinets and tables.

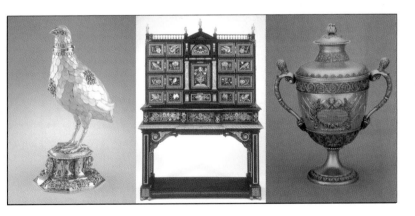

Opening Times: Daily 10:00-18:00. Closed 24-26 Dec.
Admission: Adult £5.00, Child/Student Free, Concession £4.00
Location: Located in the Embankment Building at Somerset House, between Covent Garden and the South Bank.
Events for 2004: For up to date details of special exhibitions, tours, talks, workshops and seminars call Gilbert Collection or visit the website.

Central London

Hayward Gallery

South Bank Centre, Belvedere Road, London SE1 8XZ Tel: 020 7960 4242 Fax: 020 7401 2664 Email: hgenquiries@hayward.org.uk Web: www.hayward.org.uk

As part of London's South Bank Centre, the Hayward Gallery is one of London's finest venues for temporary exhibitions of contemporary and historical art. The Hayward Gallery provides a prominent platform for emerging art and artists and new perspectives on internationally acclaimed artists. With every exhibition the Hayward runs a lively programme of educational activities including tours, lectures and workshops. The Hayward has an artist designed Glass Pavilion housing six touch sensitive monitors showing artists videos and new media commissions. The gallery also has a café and shop. The Hayward administers the Arts Council Collection and National touring Exhibitions on behalf of the Arts Council England.

Opening Times: Daily 10:00-18:00, Tue & Wed until 20:00. Location: South Bank, one minute walk from Waterloo Station. Exhibitions & Events 2004 : For Exhibitions and Events please telephone for details.

Map Ref: 23

Hermitage Rooms at Somerset House

Somerset House, Strand, London WC2R 1LA Tel: 020 7845 4630 Fax: 020 7845 4637 Email: info@hermitagerooms.org.uk Web: www.hermitagerooms.org.uk

The Hermitage Rooms recreate, in miniature, the imperial splendour of the Winter Palace and its various wings, which now make up The State Hermitage Museum in St Petersburg and creates a backdrop of rotating exhibitions.

Opening Times: Daily 10:00-18:00 during exhibitions.
Admission: Adult £5.00, Concession £4.00, Child/Student Free.

Map Ref: 12

Imperial War Museum

Lambeth Road, London SE1 6HZ Tel: 020 7416 5320

The Imperial War Museum traces the history of 20th century conflict from 1914, covering both World Wars and conflicts involving Britain and the Commonwealth post 1945. The museum has permanent exhibitions illustrating military, social, scientific and artistic aspects of war. Also a permanent exhibition dedicated to the Holocaust, art galleries, interactive displays and a changing programme of temporary exhibitions, including the 1940s House. Women and War closing Apr 2004. The Museum will be commemorating the 60th anniversary of D-Day opening an exhibition in May 2004.

The Large Exhibits Gallery

Opening Times: Daily 10:00-18:00. Closed 24-26 Dec.
Admission: Free Location: Central London, 15 minute walk from Waterloo Station, 5 minutes from Lambeth North.

Map Ref: 24

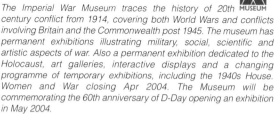

www.mghh.co.uk

For current information on the outstanding Collections in over 1600 Museums, Galleries & Historic Houses in England, Scotland, Wales and Ireland

Central London

Institute of Contemporary Arts

♿ ⬤ ▯ ◊

The Mall, London SW1Y 5AH   Tel: 020 7930 3647   Fax: 020 7930 9851
Email: info@ica.org.uk   Web: www.ica.org.uk

See art from contemporary artists like Damien Hirst, Steve McQueen and Tracey Emin. Watch fascinating world cinema from directors like Wong Kar Wai, Jan Svankmajer and Jane Campion. Listen to talks by philosopher Anthony Grayling, Professor Stuart Hall and journalist Rosie Millard and attend dance, music and theatrical performances. The ICA houses art galleries, two cinemas, a bar and café, a new media centre, a theatre and a bookshop.

Opening Times: Mon 12:00-23:00, Tue to Sat 12:00-01:00, Sun 12:00-22:30. Admission: ICA Members Free. Annual Membership Adult £30.00, Concession £20.00.
Day Membership Weekdays £1.50, Weekends £2.50. Location: Five minute walk from Trafalgar Square. Nearest tubes - Charing Cross and Piccadilly Circus.   Map Ref: 25

Jewish Museum - Camden Town, The Museum of Jewish Life

≋ ♿ ⬤ ▯

Raymond Burton House, 129/131 Albert Street,Camden Town, London NW1 7NB

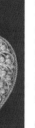

Tel: 020 7284 1977   Fax: 020 7267 9008
Email: admin@jmus.org.uk   Web: www.jewishmuseum.org.uk

Visit the Jewish Museum with its world's finest collection of Jewish ceremonial art - awarded designated status in recognition of its outstanding national importance. Housed in the lively area of Camden Town, the Museum features a History Gallery tracing Jewish immigration and settlement in Britain and a Ceremonial Art Gallery illustrating Jewish religious life with object of rarity and beauty. Special exhibition, family activities and events are held throughout the year.

Opening Times: Mon to Thu 10:00-16:00, Sun 10:00-17:00. Closed Fri, Sat, Jewish Festivals and Public Holidays. Admission: Adult £3.50, Child £1.50, OAP £2.50, Family £8.00. Location: Three minute walk from Camden Town Underground Station. Map Ref: 26

Gold Birth Amulet, English, mid 19th century

Kensington Palace, State Apartments & Royal Ceremonial Dress Collection

⬤ ▯ ◊

London W8 4PX   Tel: 0870 751 5170/751 5176   Web: www.kensington-palace.org.uk

Featuring dresses from the Royal Ceremonial Dress Collection, HM Queen Elizabeth I and Diana, Princess of Wales, this elegant palace truly is the home of royal fashion. Birthplace of Queen Victoria and designed by Sir Christopher Wren, the magnificent State Apartments provide a tranquil setting for the impressive display of paintings from the Royal Collection.

Opening Times: Mar to Oct daily 10:00-17:00. Nov to Feb 10:00-16:00. Closed 24-26 Dec and 1 Jan.
Admission: Adult £10.50, Child £7.00, OAP/Student £8.00, Family £31.00. Location: Five minutes from High

A Court Occasion at Kensington Palace

Street Kensington Underground.   Map Ref: 27

Leighton House Museum

≋ ⬤

12 Holland Park Road, London W14 8LZ   Tel: 020 7602 3316 ext 302   Fax: 020 7371 2467
Email: leightonhousemuseum@rbkc.gov.uk   Web: www.rbkc.gov.uk/leightonhousemuseum

Leighton House was the home of Frederic, Lord Leighton (1830-1896), the great classical painter and President of The Royal Academy. The house was built between 1864-79 to designs by George Aitchison and is the expression of Leighton's vision of a private palace devoted to art.

Opening Times: 11:00-17:30 daily. Closed Tue. Admission: Adults £3.00, Concession £1.00.
Location: Ten minutes from High Street Kensington Underground.   Map Ref: 27

Central London

The Library & Museum of Freemasonry

Freemasons Hall, 60 Great Queen Street, London WC2B 5AZ   Tel: 020 7395 9250   Fax: 020 7404 7418

One of the finest collections of Masonic material in the world: pottery and porcelain, glassware, silver, furniture and clocks, Masonic jewels and regalia, portraits, prints, photographs and social history items.

Opening Times: Mon to Fri 10:00-17:00.   Admission: Free.   Location: Close to Covent Garden/Holborn Tube Station.
Map Ref: 28

London's Transport Museum

Covent Garden, London WC2E 7BB

London's Transport Museum
Covent Garden Piazza

Tel: 020 7379 6344   Fax: 020 7565 7253
Email: resourcec@ltmuseum.co.uk   Web: www.ltmuseum.co.uk

Located in the heart of London's Covent Garden, the Museum is housed in the original Victorian Flower Market. The Museum is bright and airy with upper levels and a glass walkway, offering visitors a unique perspective of the historic buses, trams and trains. Complementing the display of vehicles are galleries housing originals of the famous Underground map and vibrant posters from the Museum's extensive collection. Designed to appeal to Londoners and tourists alike, the Museum invites visitors to take a journey through time, telling the story of interaction between transport, the capital and its people from 1800 to the present day. Hands-on exhibits, special Kidzones, working models and the latest

'Knifeboard' horse bus circa 1875

technology, including videos and touch-screen displays in several languages, contribute to the story. For visitors wanting to delve further into transport history, one innovative feature of the Museum is its new Learning Centre. This drop-in information space contains a wealth of resources including books, journals, on-line databases and the Museum's website. Facilities include a shop, café, baby changing and disabled toilets. A lift and ramps provide wheelchair and pushchair access throughout the Museum.

West Ham Electric Tram 1910, LCC Tramways Class E1 1907/8, Metropolitan 1931

Opening Times: Sat to Thu 10:00-18:00, Fri 11:00-18:00. Closed 24-26 Dec.   Admission: Adult £5.95, Child Free, Concession £4.50. Group rates available.   Location: Nearest Underground: Covent Garden, Holborn, Leicester Square.
Map Ref: 28

Lord's Tour & MCC Museum

Lord's Ground, London NW8 8QN   Tel: 020 7616 8595/6   Fax: 020 7266 3825
Email: tours@mcc.org.uk   Web: www.lords.org

A fully guided tour of 'The Home of Cricket' including the Pavilion, MCC Museum and many other places of interest. The collection includes fine art, portraits, memorabilia and other items such as the world renowned Ashes urn.

Opening Times: Guided Tours Apr to Sep 10:00, 12:00 & 14:00, Oct to Mar 12:00 & 14:00. No tours on major Match Days/restrictions other Match Days. Check for Xmas opening
Admission: Adult £7.00, Child £4.50, Concession £5.50, Family £20.00. Group rates available.
Location: Located in St John's Wood in central London, 15 minute walk from St John's Wood tube station.
Map Ref: 29

Museum of Garden History

Lambeth Palace Road, London SE1 7LB   Tel: 020 7401 8865   Fax: 020 7401 8869
Email: info@museumgardenhistory.org   Web: www.museumgardenhistory.org

Fine collection of historic garden tools and information about the history of gardening in Britain. Replica 17th century knot garden and art exhibitions. Housed in an historic church building.

Opening Times: Feb to mid Dec daily 10:30-17:00.   Admission: Voluntary admission charge £3.00, Concession £2.50.   Location: Next to Lambeth Palace, at the end of Lambeth Bridge. A ten minute walk Vauxhall, Lambeth North. 15 minutes Waterloo.
Map Ref: 18

Central London

Museum of London

MUSEUM OF LONDON

150 London Wall, London EC2Y 5HN   Tel: 020 7600 3699   Fax: 020 7600 1058
Email: info@museumoflondon.org.uk   Web: www.museumoflondon.org.uk

1920s: the decade that changed London

The Museum of London is the world's largest urban history museum. With a collection of more than a million objects, the museum aims to inspire a passion for London in all visitors. The collections cover every aspect of social life from pre-historic times to the present through material ranging from archaeological finds to contemporary photographs and the magnificent Lord Mayor's coach.

Opening Times: Mon to Sat 10:00-17:50, Sun 12:00-17:50. Closed 24-26 Dec, 1 Jan. Admission: Free.
Location: Near St Paul's tube station. Exhibitions & Events 2004 : Until 18th July: 1920s - the decade that changed London. 1920s London embraced new ideas from American jazz to Russian ballet. This exhibition offers a panorama of the 1920s, including: Pavlova's ballet costumes; Gandhi's spinning wheel; and original Woolworth's merchandise (everything cost 6d!) Adult £5.00, Concession £3.00, Under 16s Free.

Map Ref: 6

Museum of The Royal Hospital Chelsea

Royal Hospital Road, Chelsea, London SW3 4SR   Tel: 020 7881 5203   Fax: 020 7881 5463
Email: eventsao@chelsea-pensioners.org.uk   Web: www.chelsea-pensioners.org.uk

View of The Royal Hospital from the north

Illustrated panels covering the history of the Royal Hospital, a large diorama of the Hospital estate c. 1742, documents, uniforms, cap badges and a replica of a modern Pensioners cubicle. A recent addition is the Sovereign's Mace presented to the Royal Hospital in 2002 by HM The Queen together with the Parade Chair which was the Royal Hospital's gift to Her Majesty.

Opening Times: Mon to Sat 10:00-12:00 & 14:00-16:00, Sun 14:00-16:00 (only Apr to Sep). Closed BH.
Admission: Free. Location: Five minutes from Sloane Square Underground.

Map Ref: 10

National Army Museum

Royal Hospital Road, Chelsea, London SW3 4HT   Tel: 020 7730 0717   Fax: 020 7823 6573
Email: info@national-army-museum.ac.uk   Web: www.national-army-museum.ac.uk

Rifleman of the 95th Regiment, c1809

'Tommy' goes to War c1914

Discover the colourful story of the British Army and how the men and women who have served in it have lived and fought, from the middle ages, through two world wars, to the present day. Find out the facts behind some of the most remarkable episodes in Britain's history and the experiences of the people involved. Interactive displays enable visitors to try on helmets and kit from different eras, feel the weight of a Tudor cannonball, survey the opposing forces on a huge model of the Battle of Waterloo, explore a reproduction First World War trench and even test modern 'military' skills in exciting computer challenges. There's so much to see, from portraits by Reynolds and Gainsborough, to a lamp used by Florence Nightingale, the frostbitten fingers of Everest Conqueror Major Michael 'Bronco' Lane, and even the skeleton of Napoleon's horse. Life-like models range from an Agincourt archer to an SAS trooper, and together with videos, photos, amazing anecdotes and a host of unusual personal relics, the ordinary soldier's story is brought vividly to life. Affording your trip won't be a battle - admission is free! New this year - newly refurbished Art Gallery features paintings not previously displayed at the Museum.

Opening Times: Daily 10:00-17:30. Closed 24-26 Dec, 1 Jan, Good Friday, early May BH.
Admission: Free. Location: Ten minutes from Sloane Square Tube (Circle/District lines); 20 minutes from Victoria Station.

Map Ref: 10

Central London

National Gallery

Trafalgar Square, London WC2N 5DN   Tel: 020 7747 2885   Fax: 020 7747 2423
Email: information@ng-london.org.uk   Web: www.nationalgallery.org.uk

The National Gallery, London

The National Gallery possesses one of the greatest collections of European paintings in the world, housed in a building that is an internationally recognised landmark. Its permanent collection spans the period from about 1250 to 1900 and consists of over 2,300 works by many of the world's most famous artists. Admission to the permanent collection is free. The National Gallery also organises and hosts major temporary loan exhibitions, often in close collaboration with other national and international museums and galleries. Admission may be charged for some of these exhibitions. The gallery also offers a wide variety of free talks, guided tours and lectures. There are also courses, practical workshops and family days on the second Saturday and Sunday of each month. The National Gallery also has shops selling products inspired by the collection, Crivelli's Garden restaurant in the Sainsbury Wing and a café for light snacks and refreshments.

Titian: Bacchus and Ariadne

Opening Times: Daily 10:00-18:00, Wed until 21:00. Closed 24-26 Dec & 1 Jan.
Admission: Free.   Location: North side of Trafalgar Square.   Map Ref: 30

National Portrait Gallery

St Martin's Place, London WC2H 0HE
Tel: 020 7306 0055   Fax: 020 7306 0056
Web: www.npg.org.uk

The National Portrait Gallery is home to the largest collection of portraiture in the world featuring famous British men and women who have created history from the middle ages until the present day. Over one thousand portraits are on display across three floors with sitters from Shakespeare to the Rolling Stones. The Ondaatje Wing, including new Tudor Galleries and Twentieth Century Galleries, also has a roof-top restaurant with spectacular views across London and a state-of-the-art lecture theatre. The Portrait Cafe serves a selection of refreshments and the gift/book shop offers a wide range of goods based on the Gallery's collection.

Early 20th Century Galleries
© Andrew Putler

Opening Times: Mon to Wed, Sat & Sun 10:00-18:00. Thu & Fri 10:00-21:00.   Admission: Free, although a fee is charged for some exhibitions - Adult £7.00, Concession £4.50.   Location: Nearest tube station - Leicester Square, Charing Cross. Mainline service - Charing Cross. Buses to Trafalgar Square. Map Ref: 30

The World's most life like robotic 'T.rex:
The Killer Question' (closes May 04)

Natural History Museum

Cromwell Road, London SW7 5BD
Tel: 020 7942 5000   Fax: 020 7942 5075

Arguably the finest museum of nature in the world. Highlights include 'Dinosaurs', 'The Power Within' offering an 'earthquake experience' and the beautiful 'Earths Treasury' displaying a unique collection of gems and minerals. Find out more about the important research work undertaken at the Museum in phase one of the Darwin Centre, a major new life sciences complex providing unprecedented access to the Museum's amazing specimen collections.

Opening Times: Mon to Sat 10:00-17:50, Sun 11:00-17:50.
Admission: Free.   Location: Five minutes walk from South Kensington Tube Station.   Map Ref: 3

Central London

Old Operating Theatre, Museum & Herb Garret

9A St Thomas Street, Southwark, London SE1 9RY   Tel: 020 7955 4791   Fax: 020 7378 8383
Email: curator@thegarret.org.uk   Web: www.thegarret.org.uk

The museum houses a Victorian operating theatre. It has displays on surgery and herbal medicine. A secret, atmospheric space situated in the roof of a 300 year old church. Spiral staircase access.

Opening Times: Daily 10:30-17:00. Closed 15 Dec to 5 Jan.   Admission: Adult £4.00, Child £2.50, Concession £3.00, Family £10.00. Group Visit Service (pre-booked) also available (2003 prices).   Location: Five minute walk from London Bridge station.   Map Ref: 21

Percival David Foundation of Chinese Art

53 Gordon Square, London WC1H 0PD   Tel: 020 7387 3909   Fax: 020 7383 5163
Email: ej4@soas.ac.uk   Web: www.pdfmuseum.org.uk

The Percival David Foundation houses the finest collection of Chinese ceramics outside China. There are approximately 1700 items in the collection dating mainly to the period 10th-18th century. Guided Tours by prior arrangement only.

Opening Times: Mon to Fri 10:30-17:00. Closed Sat, Sun & BH.   Admission: Free, donations welcome.   Location: Ten minute walk Russell Square, Euston Square, Euston and Goodge St Underground Stations.   Map Ref: 7

Pollocks Toy Museum

1 Scala Street, London W1T 2HL   Tel: 020 7636 3452   Email: info@pollocksmuseum.co.uk
Web: www.pollocksmuseum.co.uk

A delightful museum occupying adjoining Georgian and Victorian houses. Exhibits include optical toys, teddies, dolls houses, toy theatres, tin toys and dolls. Toy theatre performances are given during school holidays.

Opening Times: Mon to Sat, 10:00-17:00. Closed Sun and BH.   Admission: Adult £3.00, Child/Student £1.50.   Location: 2 minutes from Goodge Street Underground Station. Map Ref: 7

The Queen's Gallery

Buckingham Palace, London SW1A 1AA
Tel: 020 7766 7301   Fax: 020 7930 9625
Email: information@royalcollection.org.uk   Web: www.royal.gov.uk

Exhibitions in 2004 will include Fabergé, (21 Nov 2003 - 7 Mar 2004) which brings together more than 300 of Carl Fabergé's finest works. George III and Queen Charlotte: Patronàge, Collecting and Court Taste, (26 Mar 2004 to 9 Jan 2005). This major exhibition is the first ever to focus on both George III and Queen Charlotte, as collectors.

Opening Times: Daily 10:00-17:30 (last admission 16:30). Entry by timed ticket.   Admission: Adult £6.50, Child £3.00, OAP £5.00, Under 5s Free, Family (2 adults and 3 children) £16.00.
Location: Buckingham Palace Road, next to Buckingham Palace. Five minute walk from Victoria Station.   Map Ref: 31

The Queen's Gallery, Buckingham Palace - exterior. Photo by EZM. The Royal Collection © 2003

Royal Academy of Arts

Burlington House, Piccadilly, London W1J 0BD   Tel: 020 7300 8000   Fax: 020 7300 8001   Email: webmaster@royalacademy.org.uk   Web: www.royalacademy.org.uk

The Royal Academy of Arts is world famous for its programme of outstanding exhibitions all year round. Highlights of 2004 include the exhibition Giorgio Armani: A Retrospective in the Royal Academy's new space at Burlington Gardens, The Art of Philip Guston (1913-1980), a major show celebrating his work. The Royal Academy will also present the work of Edouard Vuillard the French post-impressionist painter renowned for his paintings of domestic interiors, Tamara de Lempicka: Art Deco Icon,

Spectacular new courtyard, opened in 2002 by the Queen, houses modern sculpture

Central London

who painted some of the most recognisable paintings of the Art Deco age and the ever popular Summer Exhibition 2004.

Opening Times: Daily 10:00-18:00, Fri until 22:00. Admission: Prices vary for each exhibition, concessions available. Location: In the centre of the West End of London. Two minutes walk from Green Park and Piccadilly Circus Underground Stations. Map Ref: 17
Photo Caption:

Royal Academy of Music
Marylebone Road, London NW1 5HT   Tel: 020 7873 7373   Web: www.ram.ac.uk

A museum displaying many fine and rare items from the Academy Collection. Regular events take place in the galleries, including performances and demonstrations on some of the instruments on display.

Opening Times: Mon to Fri 12:30-18:00. Sat & Sun 14:00-17:30. Admission: Free. Map Ref: 32

20th Battalion, Flanders 1916

Royal Fusiliers Museum
HM Tower of London, London EC3N 4AB
Tel: 020 7488 5610/5612 Fax: 020 7481 1093
Email: royalfusiliers@124.com

The collection depicts the history of the Royal Fusiliers (the seventh regiment of foot) from 1685 when it was raised in the Tower of London. The numerous campaigns of the regiment are carried from Namur to the Gulf War and Bosnia. 11 of the 19 Victoria Crosses won are displayed, as are several fine portraits, and many items of memorabilia.

Royal Fusiliers on parade.Brantford Canada 1866

Opening Times: Mar to Oct daily 09:30-18:00, Oct to Mar daily 09:30-17:00.
Admission: Adults 50p, Child Free. Location: Within HM Tower of London. Map Ref: 33

Royal Institution's Michael Faraday Museum
The Royal Institution, 21 Albemarle Street, London W1S 4BS   Tel: 020 7409 2992   Fax: 020 7629 3569   Email: ri@ri.ac.uk   Web: www.ri.ac.uk

The museum contains a reconstruction of Faraday's laboratory as it was in the 1850s with original apparatus and furniture. Also on display is the first electric transformer and electric generator both made by Faraday in 1831.

Opening Times: Mon-Fri 10:00-17:00, closed BH. Admission: Adult £1.00, Concession 50p.
Location: Close to Green Park Underground Station. Map Ref: 17

Royal London Hospital Archives & Museum
Royal London Hospital, Whitechapel, London E1 1BB   Tel: 020 7377 7608
Email: jonathan.evans@bartsandthelondon.nhs.uk   Web: www.brlcf.org.uk

The London (founded 1740) became Britain's largest voluntary hospital. Its story is told in the crypt of the former hospital church. Exhibits feature surgery, nursing, children and health, x-rays, dentistry, nursing, uniforms and videos. The lives and works of individuals like Dr Barnardo, Edith Cavell, Joseph Merrick and Lord Knutsford also feature.

Opening Times: Mon to Fri 10:00-16:30. Closed Sat, Sun & BH. Admission: Free.
Location: Three minute walk from Whitechapel Underground Station. Map Ref: 34

Central London

The Saatchi Gallery

The Riverside Gallery, County Hall, London SE1 7PB Tel: 020 7823 2363 Fax: 020 7823 2334
Email: office@saatchi-gallery.co.uk Web: www.saatchi-gallery.co.uk

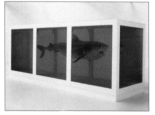

The Saatchi Gallery opened in March 1985. Max Gordon, a leading British architect, was commissioned by Charles Saatchi to convert 30,000 square feet of warehousing into a contemporary art museum. Its aim is to introduce new art, or art largely unseen in the UK to a wider audience. The Gallery draws from a collection of over 2000 paintings, sculptures and installations.

Opening Times: Sun to Thu 10:00-20:00, Fri & Sat 10:00-22:00. Admission: Adult £8.50, Concession £6.50, Family £25.00. Group £5.00. Location: Next to the London Eye. Entrances on Riverside & Belvedere Road.

The Physical Impossibility of Death in the Mind of Someone Living, by D Hirst

Map Ref: 14

St John's Gate

Museum of the Order of St John, St Johns Lane, Clerkenwell, London EC1M 4DA Tel: 020 7253 6644 Fax: 020 7336 0587

St John's Gate, Museum of the Order of St John, St John Ambulance. The Priory of Clerkenwell was built by the Knights Hospitaller in the 1140s and it is their remarkable story that lies behind the modern work of today's St John Ambulance. The Knights' surprising tale is revealed through collections including furniture, paintings, silver, armour, stained glass and other items, housed in the Gate, 500 years old this year. It contains one of the country's few remaining wooden Tudor spiral staircases. Also given to Mary Tudor as her palace after the Dissolution. Royalty, authors and artists, Shakespeare, Hogarth, Edward Cave, Dr Johnson, Dickens and David Garrick were just a few of its notable visitors. Guided tours at 11:00 and 14:30 on Tuesday, Fridays and Saturdays, take visitors through upstairs rooms inside the Gate and over to the Priory Church and 12th century Crypt. The four ground floor exhibition rooms are open daily 10:00-17:00, 10:00-16:00 on Saturday (closed Sunday and bank holiday weekends). Two reference libraries are housed in the Gate, open by appointment only, one with specialist collections relating to the Knights of St John, the Knights Templar, the Crusades and related subjects; the other, the St John Ambulance reference collection.

Opening Times: Mon to Fri 10:00-17:00, Sat 10:00-16:00. Closed Sun & BH weekend. Tours: Tue, Fri & Sat 11:00 & 14:30. Admission: Free, donations requested for tours: Adult £5.00, Concession £3.50. Location: Four minute walk from Farringdon Station.
Exhibitions & Events 2004 : For Exhibitions and Events please telephone for details. Map Ref: 35

Science Museum

Exhibition Road, London SW7 2DD
Tel: 0870 870 4868 Web: www.sciencemuseum.org.uk

See, touch and experience the major scientific advances of the last 300 years at the largest museum of its kind in the world with a state of the art IMAX cinema and a virtual reality simulator it really is something to entertain and inspire all.

Opening Times: Daily 10:00-18:00. Closed Xmas.
Admission: Free. Location: Five minute walk from South Kensington Tube Station.

The Science Museum's Welcome Wing

Map Ref: 3

Central London

Serpentine Gallery

     ♿ 🏛 🚌 Serpentine Gallery

Kensington Gardens, London W2 3XA   Tel: 020 7402 6075
Fax: 020 7402 4103   Email: information@serpentinegallery.org
Web: www.serpentinegallery.org

The Serpentine Gallery, situated in the heart of Kensington Gardens in a 1934 tea pavilion, was founded in 1970 by the Arts Council of Great Britain. Attracting over 400,000 visitors a year it is one of London's most loved galleries for modern and contemporary arts.

Opening Times: Daily 10:00-18:00. During exhibitions.
Admission: Free.   Location: Underground: Knightsbridge, South Kensington or Lancaster Gate. Buses: 9, 10, 12, 52, 94.
Serpentine Gallery, ó Peter Durant/ arcblue.com   Map Ref: 36

Sherlock Holmes Museum

221b Baker Street, London NW1 6XE
Tel: 020 7935 8866   Fax: 020 7738 1269
Web: www.sherlock-holmes.co.uk

The Museum has already had over 2 million visitors since opening 12 years ago. It is unique. It is in a Georgian building dating from 1815. It is totally unspoiled (by which is meant unmodernised!) and is identical to the lodging house described in the stories. The rooms in Mr Holmes's apartment on the first floor are maintained just as he would have left them nearly 100 years ago! The Museum has entertainment, cultural and educational value. Sherlock Holmes is very much a part of England's

The Sherlock Homes Museum

literary heritage and visitors flock to Baker Street to see how we are perpetuating this great legend. There is a large and attractive souvenir shop on the ground floor of the Museum, containing the world's largest and most varied range of Sherlockian memorabilia, which is of tremendous interest to the collector.

The Sitting Room at The Sherlock Holmes Museum

Opening Times: Daily 09:30-18:00. Closed Xmas Day.   Admission: Adult £6.00, Child £4.00. Groups of Under 16s one free for every 8, 10% Group Discount for over 16s.   Location: One minute walk from Baker Street Underground Station.   Map Ref: 37

Sir John Soane's Museum

    🏛

13 Lincolns Inn Fields, London WC2A 3BP   Tel: 020 7405 2107
Fax: 020 7831 3957   Email: jbrock@soane.org.uk
Web: www.soane.org

Collection of antique fragments, sculpture, painting, models, books and drawings amassed by the architect Sir John Soane (1753-1837) in three linked houses built by him between 1793 and 1824. The interiors and collection were preserved by an Act of Parliament on his death in 1837.

Opening Times: Tue to Sat 10:00-17:00, open late on first Tue of each month 18:00-21:00. Admission: Free. Location: Central London, two minutes from Holborn Tube Station. Exhibitions & Events 2004 : 16 Jan to 27 Mar: William West & the Regency Toy Theatre, 16 Apr to 19 Jun: Maggie's at the Soane, 25 Jun to

The Dome Area.
Photo: Martin Charles

28 Aug: Wotton: The Story of a Soane Country House, 8 Oct to
31 Dec: Raymond Erith, Architect (1904-73) Progressive Classicist.   Map Ref: 28

---

www.mghh.co.uk

For current information on the outstanding Collections in over 1600 Museums,
Galleries & Historic Houses in England, Scotland, Wales and Ireland

---

Central London

Spencer House

27 St James's Place, London SW1A 1NR   Tel: 020 7499 8620   Fax: 020 7409 2952
Web: www.spencerhouse.co.uk

Spencer House, built in 1756-66 for the first Earl Spencer, an ancestor of Diana, Princess of Wales (1961-97), is London's finest surviving eighteenth-century town house situated in the heart of St James's. Designed by John Vardy and James 'Athenian' Stuart and housing a fine collection of furniture and paintings, the spectacular neoclassical interiors reflect the period's passion for classical Greece and Rome.

Opening Times: Sun 10:30-17:30 (last tour 16:45). Closed Jan & Aug. Mon a.m. pre-booked groups only. Admission: Adult £6.00, Child £5.00 (Under 16. No Children under ten admitted), Concession £5.00.   Map Ref: 38

Tate Britain

Millbank, London SW1P 4RG   Tel: 020 7887 8008   Fax: 020 7887 8729   Web: www.tate.org.uk

The national gallery of British art from 1500 to the present day, from the Tudors to the Turner Prize. Tate holds the greatest collection of British art in the world, including works by Blake, Constable, Epstein, Gainsborough, Hockney, Moore, Stubbs and Turner. The gallery is the world centre for the understanding and enjoyment of British art and it runs an excellent programme of special exhibitions and events throughout the year.

Giovanna Baccelli, Oil on canvas by Thomas Gainsborough 1782

Opening Times: Daily 10:00-17:50.   Admission: Free, but charges apply for special exhibitions.   Location: On the North bank of the Thames by Vauxhall Bridge, five minutes walk from Pimlico Tube Station.   Map Ref: 39

Tate Modern

Bankside, London SE1 9TG   Tel: 020 7887 8000   Fax: 020 7887 8729   Web: www.tate.org.uk

Tate Modern displays the Tate collection of international modern art from 1900 to present day, including major works by artists such as Bacon, Dali, Duchamp, Giacometti, Matisse, Picasso, Rothko and Warhol.

Opening Times: Sun to Thu 10:00-18:00, Fri & Sat 10:00-22:00.   Admission: Free.   Location: Situated opposite St Paul's Cathedral on banks of River Thames, close to both Southwark and Blackfriars Tube.   Map Ref: 5

Art of Commitment, Tate Modern, Photocredit Marcus Leith

Theatre Museum: National Museum of the Performing Arts

Russell Street, Covent Garden, London WC2E 7PR
Tel: 020 7943 4700   Fax: 020 7943 4777   Web: www.theatremuseum.org

The Theatre Museum, situated in the heart of London's Theatreland, celebrates performance in Britain through imaginative exhibitions, workshops and events based on the world's most exciting performing arts collections. The galleries, charting the British stage from today back to Shakespeare's time, are brought to life by tour guides who explore the work of star performers, practitioners and their audiences using videos, photographs, costumes, designs and other memorabilia. Hands-on demonstrations reveal the secrets and skills of stage make-up and costume.

Make-up demonstrations daily at Theatre Museum

Opening Times: Daily 10:00-18:00. Closed Mon & BH. Admission: Free.   Location: One minute walk from Covent Garden Underground.   Map Ref: 8

Central London

Tower Bridge Exhibition

Tower Bridge, London SE1 2UP
Tel: 020 7403 3761   Fax: 020 7357 7935
Email: enquiries@towerbridge.org.uk
Web: www.towerbridge.org.uk

See inside London's most famous landmark. Discover the history of Tower Bridge and find out how it works. Experience the breathtaking views and be amazed by the unique architecture.

Opening Times: Daily 09:30-18:00. (Last admission 17:00).
Admission: Adult £4.50, Child £3.00, OAP £3.00.   Location: Rail stations: London Bridge and Fenchurch Street. Underground Stations: Tower Hill and London Bridge.   Map Ref: 33

H M Tower of London

Tower Hill, London EC3N 4AB   Tel: 0870 756 6060/751 5177
Web: www.tower-of-london.org.uk

Founded by William the Conqueror, this fortress and royal palace now displays armour including items worn by Henry VIII and Charles I, and houses an impressive collection of 17th century weapons. Marvel at the breathtaking Crown Jewels and enjoy the tales of over 900 years of history and intrigue as your attention is captured on a Yeoman Warder 'Beefeater' tour.

Opening Times: Mar to Oct Mon to Sat 09:00-17:00, Sun 10:00-17:00. Nov to Feb Tue to Sat 09:00-16:00, Sun to Mon 10:00-16:00. Closed 24-26 Dec & 1 Jan.   Admission: Adult £13.50, Child £9.00, OAP/Student £9.00, Family £36.00. Prices subject to change April 2003.   Map Ref: 33

Armour of Henry VIII (1540) displayed in the Royal Armour Gallery

Victoria and Albert Museum

Cromwell Road, South Kensington, London SW7 2RL   Tel: 020 7942 2000
Web: www.vam.ac.uk

The V&A is the world's greatest museum of art and design. More than seven miles of galleries are filled with outstanding collections of objects dating from 3000BC to the present day, including glass, textiles, ceramics, photography, jewellery and fashion. Highlights include the breathtaking Cast Courts, paintings by Constable and the largest collection of Italian Renaissance sculpture outside Italy. In addition, there is an exciting programme of exhibitions, displays, activities and contemporary events.

The British Galleries tell the story of British design from 1500-1900. From Chippendale to Morris and Adam to Mackintosh, all of the top British designers of the times feature in the beautiful sequence of 15 galleries. The

The V&A Dome

wealth of exhibits is enhanced by computer interactives, objects to handle, video screens and audio programmes, offering an entirely new visitor experience in a stunning and innovative setting. A must see for your visit to London.

Opening Times: Daily 10:00-17:45, on Wed & last Fri of month 10:00-22:00. Admission: Free. A separate charge may apply to some special exhibitions and events. Location: Close to South Kensington Underground. A short walk from Harrods.   Map Ref: 3

The breathtaking V&A Cast Courts

Guided or Private Tours	Disabled Access	Gift Shop or Sales Point	Café or Refreshments	Restaurant	Car Parking

Central London

Wallace Collection

Hertford House, Manchester Square, London W1U 3BN
Tel: 020 7563 9500   Fax: 020 7224 2155

Room 3, Dining Room. © The Wallace Collection

The Wallace Collection is both a national museum and the finest private art collection ever assembled by one family. The collection was acquired principally in the 19th century by the third and fourth Marquesses of Hertford and Sir Richard Wallace, the illegitimate son of the 4th Marquess. It was bequeathed to the nation by Sir Richard's widow in 1897 and is displayed on three floors of Hertford House, the family's main London residence. The 26 rooms present unsurpassed collections of French 18th century painting, furniture and porcelain together with Old Master paintings by, among others, Titian, Canaletto, Rembrandt, Hals, Rubens, Velázquex and Gainsborough. The magnificent collection of princely arms and armour is shown in four galleries and there are further important displays of gold boxes, miniatures, French and Italian sculpture and fine medieval and Renaissance works of art, including maiolica, glass, Limoges enamels, silver and jewellery. By the terms of Lady Wallace's bequest nothing must be added or loaned to the Collection. This provision has preserved the remarkable character of one of the greatest collections ever made by an English family.

Gallery 5, The Front State Room.
© The Wallace Collection

Opening Times: Mon to Sat 10:00-17:00, Sun 12:00-17:00. Admission: Free. Location: On a garden square just off Oxford Street, behind Selfridges department store.
Map Ref: 40

Wesley's Chapel, Museum of Methodism & John Wesley's House

49 City Road, London EC1Y 1AU   Tel: 020 7253 2262   Fax: 020 7608 3825
Web: www.wesleyschapel.org.uk

John Wesley's House, Library and personal belongings. Collections relating to the history of Methodism including paintings, ceramics and manuscript letters. An 18th century Georgian House furnished with Wesley's personal belongings.

Opening Times: Mon to Sat 10:00-16:00. Sun 12:30-13:45. Admission: Free. Donations welcome. Location: One minute walk from Old Street Underground Station. Exit No.4.
Map Ref: 41

Whitechapel Art Gallery

80/82 Whitechapel High Street, London E1 7QX   Tel: 020 7522 7888   Fax: 020 7522 7887   Email: info@whitechapel.org
Web: www.whitechapel.org

Situated in London's East End, the Whitechapel has always aimed to bring the best visual arts to the widest possible public. The Gallery has no permanent collection, but mounts a diverse programme of international modern and contemporary art.

Opening Times: Tue to Sun 11:00-18:00 (Wed until 20:00).
Admission: Free, (one paying exhibition per year).
Location: Aldgate East Underground.
Map Ref: 34

Within a bus ride or a short underground journey from Central London, there are many exceptional museums, galleries and historic houses covering subjects as diverse as Rugby, Lawn Tennis, Botany, Artillery, Keats, Palaces, Clipper Ships and also housing important collections of paintings and furniture.

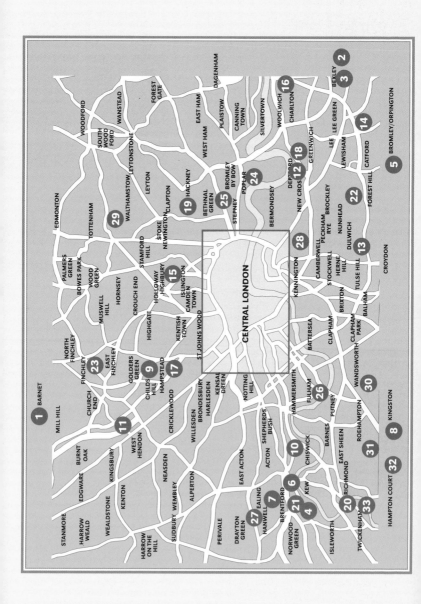

The Red Map References should be used to locate Museums etc on the pages that follow

Outer London

The Practical Householder,
Cover Oct 1957

Museum of Domestic Design & Architecture (MoDA)

Middlesex University, Cat Hill, Barnet EN4 8HT   Tel: 020 8411 5244   Fax: 020 8411 6639   Email: moda@mdx.ac.uk   Web: www.moda.ac.uk

The Museum of Domestic Design & Architecture (MoDA) houses one of the most important and comprehensive collections of late 19th and 20th century decorative design for the home, including the world-renowned Silver Studio Collection. Located in north London, MoDA offers a wide-ranging exhibition and events programme throughout the year alongside its permanent exhibition, 'Exploring Interiors: Decoration of the Home 1900-1960'.

Opening Times: Tue to Sat 10:00-17:00, Sun 14:00-17:00. Closed Mon, Easter, BH & Xmas. Admission: Free. Location: Tube: Piccadilly line to Oakwood or Cockfosters. Car: from junction 24 of M25 follow A111 signposed Cockfosters to MoDA.   Map Ref: 1

Hall Place

Hall Place, Bourne Road, Bexley DA5 1PQ   Tel: 01322 526574   Fax: 01322 522921   Email: museum@bexleyheritagetrust.freeserve.co.uk

Grade I listed Tudor/Stewart country house with panelled Great Hall and Ministrels' Gallery. Set in award winning gardens. Numerous historical and artistic exhibitions throughout the year. Rooms available for hire.

Opening Times: 1 Nov to end Mar Tue to Sat 10:00-16:15. Closed Sun & Mon. Apr to Oct Mon to Sat 10:00-17:00, Sun & BH 11:00-17:00. Admission: Free. Location: Between Bexley and Bexley Heath, nearest railway station Bexley.   Map Ref: 2

Red House

Red House Lane, Bexleyheath DA6 8JF   Tel: 01494 559799 (Info), 01494 755588 (Booking)   Email: red.house@nationaltrust.org.uk   Web: www.nationaltrust.org.uk

The home of William Morris, artist, craftsman and designer. The house (acquired by the National Trust in 2003) contains original features and fixed items of furniture designed by Morris and Philip Webb, as well as wall paintings and stained glass by Burne-Jones.

Opening Times: 3 Mar to 30 Sep Wed to Sun 11:00-17:00, 1 Oct to 27 Feb Wed to Sun 11:00-16:15. Closed 25-26 Dec & 1 Jan. Advance booking is essential Admission: Adult £5.00, Child £2.50, Family £12.50, NT Members Free Location: Off A221 Bexleyheath.   Map Ref: 3

Kew Bridge Steam Museum

Green Dragon Lane, Brentford TW8 0EN   Tel: 020 8568 4757   Fax: 020 8569 9978   Email: info@kbsm.org   Web: www.kbsm.org

Magnificent 19th century steam powered pumping station used to supply London's water. Also Water For Life Gallery exploring social use of water. Engines work every weekend.

Opening Times: Daily 11:00-17:00. Closed Good Friday and week prior to Xmas. Admission: Adult £5.20, Child £3.00, OAP £4.20, Family £15.95. Location: Junction 2 of M4, A205 to Kew Bridge, museum on north side of river. Two minutes from Kew Bridge Station.   Map Ref: 6

Outer London

Long Gallery

Syon Park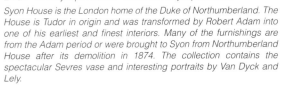

Brentford TW8 8JF   Tel: 020 8560 0882
Fax: 020 8568 0936
Email: info@syonpark.co.uk   Web: www.syonpark.co.uk

Syon House is the London home of the Duke of Northumberland. The House is Tudor in origin and was transformed by Robert Adam into one of his earliest and finest interiors. Many of the furnishings are from the Adam period or were brought to Syon from Northumberland House after its demolition in 1874. The collection contains the spectacular Sevres vase and interesting portraits by Van Dyck and Lely.

Opening Times: 24 Mar to 31 Oct Wed, Thu, Sun & BH 11:00-17:00.   Admission: Adult £7.25, Concession £5.95, Family £16.00.

Map Ref: 4

Bromley Museum

The Priory, Church Hill, Orpington BR6 0HH   Tel: 01689 873826
Email: bromley.museum@bromley.gov.uk   Web: www.bromley.gov.uk/museums

Archaeology of London Borough of Bromley from earliest times to Domesday. Life and work of Sir John Lubbock, First Lord of Avebury, the man responsible for giving this country its Bank Holidays. 20th century Social History displays.

Opening Times: 1 Apr to 31 Oct Sun to Fri 13:00-17:00, Sat 10:00-17:00. 1 Nov to 31 Mar Mon to Fri 13:00-17:00, Sat 10:00-17:00. Closed BH.   Admission: Free.   Location: Near town centre, 20 minutes walk from Orpington Railway Station.

Map Ref: 5

Crofton Roman Villa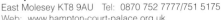

Crofton Road, Orpington BR6 8AD   Tel: 01689 873826/020 8462 4737   Fax: 020 8462 4737
Web: www.bromley.gov.uk/museums

Remains of ten rooms of a Roman villa can be seen within a modern cover building. Details of the central heating system and tessellated floors. Activities for visitors.

Opening Times: 2 Apr to 31 Oct Wed, Fri & BH 10:00-13:00 14:00-17:00, Sun 14:00 -17:00.
Admission: Adult 80p Concession 50p.   Location: Adjacent to Orpington Railway Station.

Map Ref: 5

Kings Staircase,
Hampton Court Palace

Hampton Court Palace

East Molesey KT8 9AU   Tel: 0870 752 7777/751 5175
Web: www.hampton-court-palace.org.uk

Over 500 years of royal history is brought together to create Britain's greatest palace. Immaculately restored gardens, stunnning architecture and one of the finest collections of Renaissance paintings in Europe are complemented by costumed performances and the world famous maze. Enjoy one of our guided or audio tours and come face to face with the life of a royal court.

Opening Times: Daily mid Mar to mid Oct Mon 10:15-17:15, Tue to Sun 09:30-17:15. Mid Oct to mid Mar Mon 10:15-17:45, Tue to Sun 09:30-17:45. Closed 24-26 Dec.   Admission: Adult £11.50, Child £7.50 OAP/Student £8.50, Family £34.00. Subject to change April 2003.   Location: Two minute walk from Hampton Court Station.

Map Ref: 32

Guided or Private Tours	Disabled Access	Gift Shop or Sales Point	Café or Refreshments	Restaurant	Car Parking

Outer London

Osterley Park House

Jersey Road, Isleworth TW7 4RB   Tel: 020 8232 5050   Fax: 020 8232 5080
Email: osterley@nationaltrust.org.uk   Web: www.nationaltrust.org.uk

A Robert Adam Villa, commissioned in 1761. Spectacular interiors contain one of Britain's most complete examples of Adam's work. There is a fine collection of Adam furniture and an important set of Gobelins Tapestries. The magnificent 16th century stables are largely intact and still in use. There is extensive parkland and neo-classical garden buildings.

Opening Times: 6 Mar to 28 Mar Sat & Sun 13:00-16:30, 31 Mar to 31 Oct Wed to Sun 13:00-16:30. Open BH Mons & Good Friday.   Admission: Adult £4.70, Child £2.30, Family £11.70. Group £3.80. NT Members Free.

The Long Gallery

Location: On A4 between Gillette Corner and Osterley underground station. M4, junction 3 follow A312/A4 towards central London.   Map Ref: 7

Kingston Museum

Wheatfield Way, Kingston upon Thames KT1 2PS   Tel: 020 8546 5386   Fax: 020 8547 6747
Email: king.mus@rbk.kingston.gov.uk

The Museum has two permanent galleries telling the story of Kingston, ancient origins and Town of Kings. The Eadweard Muybridge Gallery describes the life and work of this internationally renowned pioneer photographer.

Opening Times: 10:00-17:00, closed Wed & Sun.   Map Ref: 8

Camden Arts Centre

Arkwright Road, London NW3 6DG   Tel: 020 7472 5500   Fax: 020 7794 3371
Email: info@camdenartscentre.org   Web: www.camdenartscentre.org

The centre is a venue for contemporary visual art and education. A changing programme of exhibitions, artists' residencies, offsite projects and artist-led activities offers you an opportunity to look, to make and to discuss.

Opening Times: Tue to Thu 11:00-19:00, Fri to Sun 11:00-17:30. Closed Mon and BH.
Admission: Free.   Location: On Finchley Road/Arkwright Road, ten minutes walk from Finchley Road Tube.   Map Ref: 9

Chiswick House

Burlington Lane, London W4 2RP   Tel: 020 8995 0508

Surrounded by beautiful gardens, close to the centre of London lies one of England's finest Palladian villas, designed by the third Earl of Burlington. Collections include 19 paintings from Lord Burlington's original collection.

Opening Times: Apr to Sep Wed to Sun & BH 10:00-17:30, Oct Wed to Sun 10:00-17:00, every Sat 10:00-14:00. Closed Nov to Mar. Times & prices may change.   Admission: Adult £3.50, Child £2.00, Concession £3.00. EH Members Free.   Location: Burlington Lane, Chiswick Railway station half a mile, Turnham Green Tube three quarters of a mile.   Map Ref: 10

Church Farmhouse Museum

Greyhound Hill, Hendon, London NW4 4JR   Tel: 020 8203 0130   Fax: 0870 889 6804
Email: gerrard.roots@barnet.gov.uk   Web: www.barnet.gov.uk/cultural_services

17th century farmhouse with reconstructed Victorian period dining room, kitchen and laundry room. Four temporary exhibitions on local and social history and the decorative arts each year. Small public garden.

Opening Times: Mon to Thu 10:00-13:00 & 14:00-17:00, Sat 10:00-13:00 & 14:00-17:30, Sun 14:00-17:30. Closed Fri.   Admission: Free.   Location: Next to St Mary's Church, Hendon. One minute walk from bus stop.

Outer London

Cutty Sark the world's sole
surviving tea clipper

Cutty Sark Trust

2 Church Street, Greenwich, London SE10 9BG
Tel: 020 8858 3445 Fax: 020 8853 3589
Email: info@cutttysark.org.uk Web: www.cuttysark.org.uk

Cutty Sark was built in 1869 to be the fastest clipper in the annual race to bring the first of the season's crop of tea home to Britain. She is the world's sole surviving tea clipper, and since being opened to the public in 1957, has welcomed over 15 million visitors across her gangplank. Visitors 'come aboard' via an entrance to the 'Tween Deck', so called because it is between the Main Deck and the Lower Hold. This is the main museum display area telling Cutty Sark's history and details of merchant trade, together with displays of original artefacts and models. The new children's interpretive panels give the same information but in a fun and colourful way. The souvenir shop is also on deck. The Main Deck houses the crew and officers' accommodation, restored to 1870s condition - a real insight to life on board a Victorian tea clipper. The Gallery, Carpenter's workshop and the masts can also be seen, complete with their 11 miles of rigging. The Lower Hold houses one of the world's largest collections of colourful merchant ships' figureheads, as well as our new children's 'hands-on' activities.

'Masters Saloon', Cutty Sark

Opening Times: Daily 10:00-17:00. Closed Xmas. Admission: Adult £3.90, Child/Student £2.90, OAP £2.90, Family £9.70. Location: Greenwich Town Centre, seven minutes from railway station, one minute from tube and ferry links. Map Ref: 12

Dulwich Picture Gallery

Gallery Road, London SE21 7AD Tel: 020 8693 5254
Fax: 020 8299 8700 Email: i.evans@dulwichpicturegallery.org.uk
Web: www.dulwichpicturegallery.org.uk

DULWICH PICTURE GALLERY

Dulwich Picture Gallery is the greatest find in London; a magnificent collection of masterpieces by Rembrandt, Poussin, Watteau, Rubens, Canaletto, Gainsborough and many more. The critically-acclaimed international loan exhibitions and its setting in the beautiful 18th century village of Dulwich, make the Gallery a must for all art lovers. The building has been described as the most perfect small art gallery in the world.

Opening Times: Tue to Fri 10:00-17:00, Sat, Sun & BH 11:00-17:00.
Admission: Adult £4.00, OAP £3.00, Concession Free.
Location: Dulwich is in south east London, 12 minutes by train from Victoria to West Dulwich. Exhibitions & Events 2004 : 4 Feb to 18 Apr: Crystal Palace at Sydenham, 12 May to 19 Sep: Henry Moore.
The enfilade of galleries designed in 1811 by Sir John Soane Map Ref: 13

Eltham Palace

Courtyard, Eltham, London SE9 5QE Tel: 020 8294 2548

Completed in 1936 this is the only English Art Deco house open to the public. It was built on a site of great antiquity and joined to a medieval hall. The house is an eclectic mix of high style French influenced Art Deco, ultra-smart ocean liner style and Swedish design. The Great Hall, incorporated into the house, was built for Edward 1V in the 1470s. There are 19 acres of beautiful gardens including herbaceous borders, a rock garden and a formal sunken rose garden.

204

Outer London

LONDON POSTCODES (continued)

Opening Times: 1 Apr to 30 Sep Wed to Fri, Sun & BH 10:00-18-:00, 1-31 Oct Wed to Fri & Sun 10:00-17:00, 1 Nov to 31 Mar Wed to Fri & Sun 10:00-16:00. Closed 22 Dec to 31 Jan 2004. Admission: House & Gardens; Adult £6.50, Concession £5.00, Child £3.50, Family £16.50. Location: Junction 3 on the M25, then A20 to Eltham, off Court Road SE9.   Map Ref: 14

Estorick Collection of Modern Italian Art

39A Canonbury Square, Islington, London N1 2AN   Tel: 020 7704 9522   Fax: 020 7704 9531
Email: curator@estorickcollection.com   Web: www.estorickcollection.com

The permanent collection has at its core powerful images by early 20th century Futurists housed in the intimate setting of a large Georgian villa. Also on display are works by figurative artists and regular temporary exhibitions.

Opening Times: Wed to Sat 11:00-18:00, Sun 12:00-17:00. Closed Mon, Tue, Xmas & New Year. Admission: Adult £3.50, Concession £2.50.   Location: A five minute walk from Highbury and Islington Underground Stations.   Map Ref: 15

The Fan Museum

12 Crooms Hill, Greenwich, London SE10 8ER   Tel: 0208 3051441   Fax: 0208 2931889
Email: admin@fan-museum.org   Web: www.fan-museum.org

The only museum in the world entirely dedicated to the history of fans and to the art and craft of fan-making. Situated within Maritime Greenwich, a World Heritage site.

Opening Times: Tue to Sat 11:00-17:00, Sun 12:00-17:00. Admission: Adult £3.50, Concession £2.50, Under 7s Free. OAP Free on Tue after 14:00 (except for Groups).   Location: Greenwich Town Centre, five minute walk from Greenwich BR and Cutty Sark DLR Station.   Map Ref: 12

Fenton House

Windmill Hill, Hampstead, London NW3 6RT   Tel / Fax: 0207 435 3471
Email: fentonhouse@nationaltrust.org.uk   Web: www.nationaltrust.org.uk

Charming William and Mary Merchants' House with fine collections of Georgian furniture, porcelain and needlework and the Benton Fletcher Collection of early keyboard instruments. Walled gardens include a kitchen garden and apple orchard.

Opening Times: 6 Mar to 28 Mar Sat & Sun 14:00-17:00, 7 Apr to 29 Oct Wed to Fri 14:00-17:00, 3 Apr to 31 Oct Sat & Sun 11:00-17:00. Open BH Mons & Good Friday 11:00-17:00. Admission: Adult £4.60, Child £2.30, Family £11.50. Group (15+) £3.90. NT Members Free.

Ceramic Court Dancers from the Drawing Room

Location: Visitors'entrance on west side of Hampstead

Grove. Hampstead Tube 300yards.   Map Ref: 9

Firepower - The Royal Artillery Museum

Royal Arsenal, Woolwich, London SE18 6ST   Tel: 020 8855 7755
Fax: 020 8855 7100   Email: info@firepower.org.uk   Web: www.firepower.org.uk

In the historically secret Royal Arsenal at Woolwich, artillery from slingshot to shell. Alongside the huge guns see gunners' uniforms, artwork and medals. The dramatic Field of Fire presentation using big screens and surround sound tells the story of 20th century gunners in their own words, from Burma to Bosnia.

Opening Times: Nov to Mar Fri to Sun 11:00-17:00, Apr to Oct Wed to Sun 11:00-17:30 & BH. Booked groups Thu 11:00-17:00   Admission: Adult £6.50, Child £4.50, OAP £5.50, Concession £5.50, Family £18.00, Group discount

Visit the Monster Bits Gallery

available.   Location: Royal Arsenal, Woolwich. Five minutes from Woolwich Arsenal Railway Station.   Map Ref: 16

Freud Museum

20 Maresfield Gardens, Hampstead, London NW3 5SX   Tel: 020 7435 2002/5167   Fax: 020 7431 5452   Email: freud@gn.apc.org   Web: www.freud.org.uk

Home of Sigmund Freud and his family when they came to London as refugees from Nazi

persecution, the family recreated their Vienna home in London. Displays include his extensive library and collection of 2000 antiquities.

Opening Times: Wed to Sun 12:00-17:00. Admission: Adult £5.00, Concession £2.00.

Map Ref: 17

Greenwich Borough Museum

232 Plumstead High Street, London SE18 1JT Tel: 020 8854 2452 Fax: 020 8854 2490
Email: beverley.burford@greenwich.gov.uk

Permanent displays of local history including social history, archaeology and natural history. A temporary exhibition programme, an education service for schools, a children's Saturday Club and an adult lecture and workshop programme.

Opening Times: Mon 14:00-19:00, Tue, Thu, Fri & Sat 10:00-13:00 & 14:00-17:00. Closed Wed, Sun & BH. Admission: Free. Location: First floor Plumstead Library in High Street. Ten minutes walk or five minutes by bus from Plumstead Railway Station. Map Ref: 18

Gunnersbury Park Museum

Gunnersbury Park, London W3 8LQ Tel: 020 8992 1612
Fax: 020 8752 0686 Email: gp-museum@cip.org.uk

A beautiful 19th century mansion, Gunnersbury Park Museum was formerly home to the Rothschild family. It is now the community museum for Ealing and Hounslow. In contrast to the grand house, see where the servants lived and worked, in our original 19th century kitchens. View the horse drawn vehicles of Gunnersbury, including the Rothschilds' State and travelling carriages.

Opening Times: Apr to Oct daily 13:00-17:00. Nov to Mar daily 13:00-16:00. Victorian Kitchens: Apr to Oct Sat, Sun & BH 13:00-17:00. Admission: Free. Location: In park, on bus route (E3), near tube station (Acton Town).

Exhibitions & Events 2004 : Apr to Oct: The History of Questors Theatre, Ealing, May to Oct: Lace in Costume, Sep to Spring 05: Griffin Park and Brentford Football, Oct to Jan: The Polish Community in West London. Map Ref: 6

Hackney Museum

Hackney Tech & Learning Centre, 1 Reading Lane, London E8 1GQ Tel: 020 8356 3500
Fax: 020 8356 2563 Email: hmuseum@hackney.gov.uk
Web: www.hackney.gov.uk/hackneymuseum

This exciting new museum investigates why people have come to Hackney from all over the world for 1000 years. There are also two temporary exhibition galleries with constantly changing displays.

Opening Times: Tue, Wed, Fri 09:30-17:30, Thu 09:30-20:00, Sat 10:00-17:00. Closed Sun, Mon & BH. Admission: Free. Location: In the heart of Central Hackney, two minute walk from Hackney Central Railway Station. Exhibitions & Events 2004 : 16 Mar to 19 Jun: Matchbox Memories. Map Ref: 19

The entrance to Hackney Museum

Outer London

Hampstead Museum

🖼 🏛 📷

Burgh House, New End Square, London NW3 1LT   Tel: 020 7431 0144   Fax: 020 7435 8817
Email: hampsteadmuseum@talk21.com   Web: www.burghhouse.org.uk

Queen Anne House containing a collection tracing the history of Hampstead from pre-historic times to the present day. Notable is the Helen Allingham collection and 'Isokon' furniture.

Opening Times: Wed to Sun 12:00-17:00, Sat by appointment. BH 14:00-17:00. Closed Good Friday, Easter Monday, Xmas to New Year.   Admission: Free.   Location: Near central Hampstead, a five minute walk from Hampstead Tube Station.   Map Ref: 17

Hogarth's House

🏛

Hogarth Lane, Great West Road, London W4 2QN   Tel: 020 8994 6757

Early 18th century house which was the country home of William Hogarth (1697-1764) during the last 15 years of his life. Displays of his prints, information on the life of this 'Father of English Painting', and a secluded garden containing Hogarth's mulberry tree.

Opening Times: Apr to Oct Tue to Fri 13:00-17:00, Sat, Sun & BH 13:00-18:00. Nov to Mar Tue to Fri 13:00-16:00, Sat, Sun & BH 13:00-17:00. Closed Mon except BH, Good Friday, 25-26 Dec and all Jan. Admission: Free.   Location: On A4 (Great West Road) near Hogarth Roundabout, Chiswick. Nearest tube station - Turnham Green (15 minutes walk).   Map Ref: 21

Horniman Museum & Gardens

🖼 ♿ 🏛 📷 � HORNIMAN MUSEUM

100 London Road, Forest Hill, London SE23 3PQ

Tel: 020 8699 1872   Fax: 020 8291 5506
Email: enquiry@horniman.ac.uk   Web: www.horniman.ac.uk

Set in 16 acres of beautiful gardens, this fascinating, free museum has unique exhibitions, events and activities to delight adults and children alike. Housed in Townsend's stunning Arts and Crafts building, the museum has outstanding collections which illustrate the natural and cultural world. A new centenary development opened in 2002 doubling the public space and dramatically transforming the Museum for the future. With a new entrance linking the Museum and Gardens the development includes four new galleries, a new café and shop, plus a lift to all gallery spaces. The new Horniman has masses more to see and

Sri Lankan Mask,
photo H Scheebeli

Horniman Clock Tower, photo M Harding

to explore: Sound out the Music Gallery with Britain's largest collection of musical instruments from around the world in a dynamic new environment, celebrate world cultures in the Centenary Gallery, discover African Worlds featuring the largest African mask, experience the Natural History Gallery with many original specimens from the Victorian age, observe aquatic life up close in the Aquarium, explore the Hands On Base with masses of exhibits to touch and handle, find out more about the collections in the Library, and relax with a picnic in the beautiful Gardens. From Febuary 2004 explore the prehistoric world in Dinomites.

Opening Times: Daily 10:30-17:30. Closed 24-26 Dec. Admission: Free. A charge is made for Dinomites.   Location: South Circular Road (A205), free parking in surrounding streets. Forest Hill BR, 13 mins from London Bridge.   Exhibitions & Events 2004 : 12 Feb to 31 Oct: Dinomites: The A-Z of Baby Dinosaurs, Apr to Oct: Savu: Textiles from Indonesia, May: Spring Concert Series.   Map Ref: 22

Jewish Museum - Finchley,
London's Museum of Jewish Life

🖼 ♿ 🏛 📷 ⬧

The Sternberg Centre, 80 East End Road, Finchley, London N3 2SY   Tel: 020 8349 1143   Fax: 020 8343 2162   Email: jml.finchley@lineone.net   Web: www.jewishmuseum.org.uk

Lively social history displays tracing Jewish immigration and settlement in London with reconstructions of tailoring and furniture workshops and hands-on activities for children. Moving

Outer London

exhibition on British born Holocaust survivor Leon Greenman OBE. Group visits and education programmes by arrangement.

Opening Times: Mon to Thu 10:30-17:00, Sun 10:30-16:30. Closed Fri, Sat, Jewish Festivals and Public Holidays. Also closed Sun in month of Aug and BH weekends. Admission: Adult £2.00, Child Free, OAP £1.00. Location: Nearest underground station Finchley Central (via Station Road and Manor View). Located on A504. Map Ref: 23

Keats House

Keats Grove, Hampstead, London NW3 2RR Tel: 020 7435 2062
Email: keatshouse@corpoflondon.gov.uk Web: www.cityoflondon.gov.uk/keats

The house where John Keats lived from 1818 to 1820. Here he wrote his most intensely moving poems and fell in love.

Opening Times: Nov to Mar Tue to Sun 12:00-16:00, from April open until 17:00. Closed Xmas, New Year and Good Friday. Admission: Adult £3.00, Child Free, Concession £1.50. Tickets are valid for one year. Location: On the edge of Hampstead Heath close to mainline and underground stations and bus routes. Map Ref: 17

Kenwood House

Hampstead Lane, London NW3 7JR
Tel: 020 8348 1286

Kenwood houses one of the most important collections of paintings, given to the nation by Lord Iveagh - including works by Rembrandt, Gainsborough, Turner, Van Dyck to name but a few. The house was remodelled by Robert Adam for the great judge, Lord Mansfield, and the richly decorated library is one of his masterpieces.

Opening Times: Apr to Sep daily 10:00-17:30, Oct daily 10:00-17:00, Nov to Mar daily 10:00-16:00. Wed & Fri opens 10:30. Closed Xmas & New Year. Times may change. Admission: Free, donations welcome. Location: Hampstead Lane. Map Ref: 17

Mirrored recess in the Library © English Heritage

Museum in Docklands

No 1 Warehouse, West India Quay, Hertsmere Road, London E14 4AL
Tel: 0870 444 3856 Fax: 0870 444 3858
Email: info@museumindocklands.org.uk Web: www.museumindocklands.org.uk

The Museum in Docklands unlocks the history of London's river, port and people in the 19th century warehouse at West India Quay. Originally used to house imports of exotic spices, rum and cotton, it now holds a wealth of objects from whale bones to ship models. There is also a dedicated gallery and play area for children, Mudlarks.

Opening Times: Daily 10:00-18:00 Admission: Adult £5.00, Concession £3.00, Under 16s Free.
Location: Near West India Quay (Docklands Light Railway). Map Ref: 24

Museum of Childhood at Bethnal Green

Cambridge Heath Road, London E2 9PA Tel: 020 8983 5200 Fax: 020 8983 5225
Email: bgmc@vam.ac.uk Web: www.museumofchildhood.org.uk

One of the best collection of toys and games in the world, dating from the 16th century to the present day.

Opening Times: Mon to Thu, Sat & Sun 10:00-17:50. Closed Fri, Xmas & New Year.
Admission: Free. Location: One minute walk from Bethnal Green Tube Station. Map Ref: 25

Guided or Private Tours	Disabled Access	Gift Shop or Sales Point	Café or Refreshments	Restaurant	Car Parking

Norfolk

The jewel of the county is undoubtedly Norwich, the county town with its superb cathedral built in Caen stone and its impressive Norman Castle. To the east of Norwich are the Norfolk Broads, an area of glorious reedy lakes and meandering waterways. Norfolk, a highly efficient farming county was largely bypassed by the Industrial Revolution and its consequent urban development.

A quarter of Norfolk's museums lie within the surrounds of Norwich and as one would expect in a county with such a pastoral background there are many excellent rural life museums.

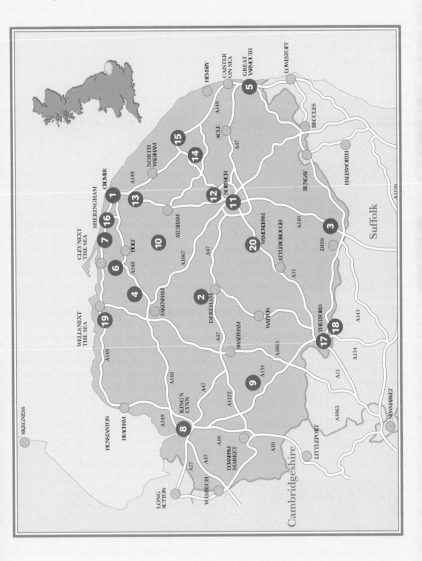

The Red Map References should be used to locate Museums etc on the pages that follow

Norfolk

Cromer Museum

East Cottages, Tucker Street, Cromer NR27 9HB   Tel: 01263 513543   Fax: 01263 511651
Email: cromer.museum@norfolk.gov.uk   Web: www.norfolk.gov.uk/tourism/museums

Enter the Victorian fisherman's cottage illuminated by gaslight and imagine what it was like to live in Cromer at the end of the 19th century. Find out about Henry Blogg's famous lifeboat rescues and much more.

Opening Times: Mon to Sat 10:00-17:00, Sun 14:00-17:00.   Admission: Adult £1.80, Child 90p, Concession £1.40.   Location: In Tucker Street, opposite the East end of Cromer Parish Church.
Map Ref: 1

RNLI Henry Blogg Lifeboat Museum

No 2 Boathouse, The Promenade, Cromer NR27 9HE   Tel: 01263 511294
Web: www.lifeboats.org.uk

Display on the life of Coxwain Henry Blogg, winner of three RNLI Gold Medals for bravery. Also displays relating to Cromer Lifeboats and the Royal National Lifeboat Institution.

Opening Times: Easter to Sep daily 10:00-16:00. By appointment in winter.   Admission: Free.
Location: Near town centre.
Map Ref: 1

Roots of Norfolk at Gressenhall

Gressenhall, Dereham NR20 4DR   Tel: 01362 860563
Fax: 01362 860385   Email: gressenhall.museum@norfolk.gov.uk
Web: www.norfolk.gov.uk/tourism/museums

A museum of rural life housed in a former workhouse, with displays on village and rural life and a farm worked with horses and stocked with rare breeds, all in an idyllic rural setting with farm woodland and riverside trails, gardens, a children's play area and the Mardlers Rest Café. A perfect day out for all the family, whatever the weather.

Opening Times: Telephone for details.   Admission: Adult £5.45, Child £4.35, Concession £4.95, Saver ticket £17.00.   Location: On B1146, three miles north west of Dereham. Follow brown signs from A47 and Dereham Town Centre.
Map Ref: 2

Playing the Game of Life in the Workhouse Experience

100th Bomb Group Memorial Museum

Common Road, Dickleburgh, Diss IP21 4PH   Tel: 01379 740708

A fine collection of USAAF uniforms, decorations, combat records, equipment, memorabilia and wartime photographs.

Opening Times: Sat, Sun & BH 10:00-17:00, May to Sep also open Wed. Also by appointment. Closed Nov, Dec & Jan.   Admission: Free.   Location: Turn off the A140 at Dickleburgh by pass (to Thorpe Abbotts), 17 miles south of Norwich, 26 miles north of Ipswich.   Map Ref: 3

Thursford Collection

Thursford, Fakenham NR21 0AS   Tel: 01328 878477   Fax: 01328 878415
Email: admin@thursfordcollection.co.uk

A glittering Aladdin's cave of majestic old road engines and mechanical organs of magical variety all gleaming with colour. Robert Wolfe stars live in the mighty Wurlitzer show, and there's a programme of music too from Thursford's nine very different mechanical pipe organs. Old farm buildings have been transformed into a small village with a touch of Charles Dickens' England.

Opening Times: Good Friday to last Sun in Sep daily 12:00-17:00. Closed Sat   Admission: Adult £5.30, Child £2.80 (4 to 14 yrs), Under 4s Free, OAP £5.00, Student £4.55. Group rates available.   Location: One mile off

Savages Venetian Gondola Ride

A148 between Fakenham and Holt.
Map Ref: 4

Norfolk

GREAT YARMOUTH

Elizabethan House

4 South Street, Great Yarmouth NR30 2QH   Tel: 01493 855746   Fax: 01493 745526
Web: www.norfolk.gov.uk/tourism/museums

A Tudor merchant's house hidden behind a Georgian street front, with furnished rooms and displays of home life through the ages. Visit the panelled parlour where the death of King Charles I was decided.

Opening Times: 5 Apr to 29 Oct Mon to Fri 10:00-17:00, 10 Apr to 31 Oct Sat & Sun 13:15-17:00.   Admission: Adult £2.70, Child £2.00, Concession £2.00, Family group: Adult £2.20, Child £1.80. Map Ref: 5

Old Merchants House & Row 111 Houses

South Quay, Great Yarmouth NR30 2RQ   Tel: 01493 857900

These two 17th century houses are a type of building unique to Great Yarmouth. They are two of the earliest surviving merchants' houses in England, and contain original fixtures and displays of local architectural fittings.

Opening Times: Admission by escorted tours only, 1 Apr to 31 Oct 12:00, 14:00 & 16:00. Closed 1 Nov to 31 Mar. Times & prices may change.   Admission: Adult £3.00, Child £1.50, Concession £2.00. EH Members Free. Map Ref: 5

HOLT

Glandford Shell Museum

Glandford, Holt NR25 7JR   Tel: 01263 740081

Sir Alfred Jodrell built this charming Victorian museum for his unique collection of sea shells and artefacts. Also see the evocative John Craske tapestry. This year the museum has been beautifully restored.

Opening Times: Easter Sat to 31 Oct Tue to Sat 10:00-12:30 & 14:00-16:30.   Admission: Adult £1.75, Child 75p, OAP £1.25.   Location: Situated midway between Letheringsett and Blakeney on the north Norfolk coast. Map Ref: 6

Muckleburgh Collection

Weybourne, Holt NR25 7EG   Tel: 01263 588210/608

The Museum is housed in the former Ack-Ack NAAFI. Since the Museum's inception 13 years ago it has carefully restored tanks and other military vehicles; to date there are 16 working tanks and other guns and vehicles.

Opening Times: Feb to Good Friday Sun 10:00-17:00, Good Friday to 2 Nov daily 10:00-17:00, Feb Half Term 10:00-17:00   Admission: Adult £5.50, Child £3.00, OAP £4.50.   Location: Four miles west of Sheringham. Map Ref: 7

KING'S LYNN

Houghton Hall

Kings Lynn PE31 6UE   Tel: 01485 528569   Fax: 01485 528167
Email: enquiries@houghtonhall.com   Web: www.houghtonhall.com

18th century Palladian Mansion built by Britain's first Prime Minister, Sir Robert Walpole. Model soldier collection with over 20,000 model soldiers and militaria. Five acre walled garden.

Opening Times: 11 Apr to 30 Sep Wed, Thu, Sun & BH.   Admission: Adult £6.50, Child £3.00. Excluding House Adult £4.00, Child £2.00.   Location: Just off the A148 King's Lynn to Cromer road. Map Ref: 8

Lynn Museum

Market Street, King's Lynn PE30 1NL   Tel: 01553 775001   Email: lynn.museum@norfolk.gov.uk
Web: www.norfolk.gov.uk/tourism/museums

Tells the story of the people and places of King's Lynn and West Norfolk. Travel back through history and explore the changing local landscape from the earliest farmers, through Roman, Saxon and medieval times.

Opening Times: Tue to Sat. Closed BH, Xmas & New Year. Please ring for times. Admission: Adult £1.00, Child 60p, Concession 80p.   Location: Entrance off King's Lynn Bus Station, adjacent to the shopping precinct. Map Ref: 8

Norfolk

Oxburgh Hall, Garden and Estate

Oxborough, Kings Lynn PE33 9PS   Tel: 01366 328258   Fax: 01366 328066
Web: www.nationaltrust.org.uk

The Old Drawing Room

A moated manor house, with magnificent Tudor gatehouse and accessible Priests Hole built in 1482. It houses an outstanding display of embroidery by Mary, Queen of Scots and Bess of Hardwick. There are attractive gardens and delightful woodland walks.

Opening Times: 20 Mar to 7 Nov Sat to Wed 13:00-17:00. Open BH Mons. Admission: Adult £5.75, Child £2.90, Family £15.00. Group £4.65. NT Members Free. Location: At Oxborough, seven miles south west of Swaffham on south side of Stoke Ferry road.   Exhibitions & Events 2004 : Please telephone for details. Map Ref: 9

Tales of the Old Gaol House

Saturday Market Place, King's Lynn PE30 5DQ   Tel: 01553 774297   Fax: 01553 772361
Email: gaolhouse@west-norfolk.gov.uk   Web: www.west-norfolk.gov.uk

Set in the town's old cells, visitors have the chance to hear the stories and experience the sights (and smells) of Lynn's criminal past. Also housed there are some of Britain's finest civic treasures, including the priceless King John Cup.

Opening Times: Please telephone. Admission: Prices on application. Location: Town centre, ten minutes walk from bus station, in the heart of the medieval part of King's Lynn.   Map Ref: 8

Town House Museum of Lynn Life

46 Queen Street, King's Lynn PE30 5DQ   Tel: 01553 773450
Email: townhouse.museum@norfolk.gov.uk   Web: www.norfolk.gov.uk/tourism/museums

Housed in a 19th century town house and former inn. Displays focus on the everyday life of Lynn people through the ages and take you through a series of carefully reconstructed rooms.

Opening Times: May to Sep Mon to Sat 10:00-17:00 Sun 14:00-17:00. Oct to Apr Mon to Sat 10:00-16:00. Admission: Adult £1.80, Child 90p, Concession £1.40. Location: Queen Street in the heart of historic 'Old Lynn' and close to the medieval Guildhall and St Margaret's Church.
Map Ref: 8

Blickling Hall

Blickling, Norwich NR11 6NF   Tel: 01263 738030   Fax: 01263 731660
Web: www.nationaltrust.org.uk

Room view of the Long Gallery

Built in the seventeenth century, it is one of England's great Jacobean houses. It is famed for its spectacular long gallery and collection of fine furniture, pictures and tapestries set in magnificent State Rooms. The Peter the Great Room is dominated by its massive tapestry of Peter the Great at the Battle of Poltawa. Close to the Hall you will find a delightful secret garden, an eighteenth century orangery and a dry moat. The gardens are full of colour all year and there is extensive parkland

Opening Times: 20 Mar to 3 Oct Wed to Sun 13:00-17:00, 6 Oct to 31 Oct Wed to Sun 13:00-16:00 Park: All year dawn to dusk. Admission: Adult £7.00. Garden only: Adult £4.00. NT Members Free.
Location: One and half miles northwest of Aylsham on B1354.   Exhibitions & Events 2004 : For Exhibitions and Events please telephone for details.   Map Ref: 10

Bridewell Museum

Bridewell Alley, Norwich NR2 1AQ   Tel: 01603 667228   Email: museums@norfolk.gov.uk
Web: www.norfolk.gov.uk/tourism/museums

This former merchant's house, part of which dates from 1325, became an 'open' prison for vagrants, children and women (a Bridewell), before becoming a museum focusing on Norwich life and industry.

Norfolk

Opening Times: 21 Jul to 1 Nov, 1 Apr to 30 Oct School terms Tue to Fri 10:00-16:30, Sat 10:00-17:00 Closed Sun & Mon. School half-term Easter & Summer Hol Mon to Sat 10:00-17:00 Closed Sun. Admission: Adult £2.00, Child £1.20, Concession £1.60, Family £5.00. Location: In city centre. Map Ref: 11

City of Norwich Aviation Museum

Aviation Museum

Old Norwich Road, Horsham St Faith, Norwich NR10 3JF
Tel: 01603 893080 Web: www.cnam.co.uk

Aircraft on display include a massive Vulcan Bomber and Civil and Military aeroplanes which have flown from Norfolk over the past 40 years. Inside displays feature the achievement and sacrifces of the heroes and pioneers who have formed the aviation history of Norfolk.

Opening Times: Apr to Oct Tue to Sat 10:00-17:00, Sun & BH 12:00-17:00. Nov to Mar Wed & Sat 10:00-16:00 Sun 12:00-16:00. Closed Xmas & New Year. Admission: Adult £2.50, Child/Concession £1.50, OAP £2.00, Family £7.00. Location: One mile from A140 Norwich to Cromer road, follow brown tourist signs. Map Ref: 12

Felbrigg Hall

Felbrigg, Norwich NR11 8PR Tel: 01263 837444 Web: www.nationaltrust.org.uk

One of the finest seventeenth century houses in East Anglia.It contains a mixed collection of furniture, mainly English and French. There is one of the largest collections of Grand Tour paintings and an outstanding library. The park is well known for its magnificent and aged trees.

Opening Times: House: 20 Mar to 31 Oct Sat to Wed 13:00-17:00. Gardens: 20 Mar to 31 Oct Sat to Wed 11:00-17:00, 22 Jul to 3 Sep Daily 11:00-17:00. Open BH Mons. Admission: Adult £6.30, Child £3.00, Family £15.50. Groups: Adult £5.10, Child £2.50. NT Members

Still life of books in the Library

Free. Location: Two miles south west of Cromer: entrance off B1436, signposted from A148 and A140. Exhibitions & Events 2004 : Please telephone for details. Map Ref: 13

Inspire Hands on Science Centre

St Michaels Church, Coslany Street, Norwich NR3 3DT Tel: 01603 612612 Fax: 01603 616721 Email: inspire@science-project.org Web: www.science-project.org

Hands-on exhibits, shows and special events. Science shop and light refreshments, perfect for families, parties and schools.

Opening Times: Daily 10:00-17:30 (last admission 16:30). Admission: Adult £4.20, Child £3.60, Under 3s Free, Saver (2 adults and 2 children) £12.00. Location: Norwich City Centre, five minutes walk from market. Map Ref: 11

Norwich Castle Museum & Art Gallery

Shirehall, Market Avenue, Norwich NR1 3TQ Tel: 01603 493625 Fax: 01603 493623
Email: museum@norfolk.gov.uk Web: www.norfolk.gov.uk/tourism/museum

Norwich Castle has outstanding archaeology, natural history and fine art collections and is placed with treasures as diverse as ancient gold jewellery, silver, delicate porcelain and Roman pottery. See the best collections anywhere of the Norwich School of Artists, Norwich Silver, Lowestoft Porcelain, ceramic teapots and regular exhibitions from Tate.

Opening Times: Mon to Fri 10:00-16:30 Sat 10:00-17:00 Sun 13:00-17:00. School Half-Term Easter & Summer Hol Mon to Sat 10:00-18:00 Sun 13:00-17:00. Closed 23-26 Dec & 1 Jan. Admission: From £2.15-£4.95 Prices

subject to change. Location: In city centre. Map Ref: 11

Norfolk

Royal Air Force Air Defence Radar Museum

RAF Neatishead, Norwich NR12 8YB   Tel: 01692 633309   Fax: 01692 633214
Email: curator@radarmuseum.co.uk   Web: www.radarmuseum.co.uk

History of radar and air defence from 1935 to date. Housed in original 1942 building. Features Battle of Britain, 1942 operations, Cold War Operations Room and Space Defence. Radar convoy vehicles.

Opening Times: Apr to Oct second Sat each month, BH Mon, Tue & Thu 10:00-17:00. Nov to Mar second Sat each month.   Admission: Adult £4.00, Concessions £3.50, Teens £3.00, Child under 12 Free. Free two hour guided Tour.   Location: Near Horning, Norfolk.   Map Ref: 14

Royal Norfolk Regimental Museum

Shirehall, Market Avenue, Norwich NR1 3JQ   Tel: 01603 493649   Fax: 01603 630214
Email: museum@norfolk.gov.uk   Web: www.norfolk.gov.uk/tourism/museums

Situated in the Shirehall, which dates from the early 1830s. The displays are themed and set out chronologically with excellent interpretative panels, designed for those with no military knowledge as well as the military historian.

Opening Times: School Terms & Xmas Hol Tue to Fri 10:00-16:30, Sat 10:00-17:00. Closed Sun & Mon. School Half-Term Easter & Summer Hol Mon to Sat 10:00-17:00 Closed Sun.
Admission: Adult £2.00, Child £1.20, Concession £1.60.   Location: In the Shirehall buildings at the base of Norwich Castle opposite Anglia TV.   Map Ref: 11

Strangers Hall Museum

Charing Cross, Norwich NR2 4AL   Tel: 01603 667229   Email: museums@norfolk.gov.uk
Web: www.norfolk.gov.uk/tourism/museums

One of the oldest and most fascinating buildings in Norwich. It is typical of houses occupied by the well-to-do city merchants when Norwich was in its heyday.

Opening Times: Open Sat 10:30 to 16:30. Guided tours only on Wed. Tel (01603) 493636 for details and tickets.   Admission: Adult £2.50, Child £1.50, Concession £2.00.   Map Ref: 11

Sutton Windmill & Broads Museum

Sutton, Stalham, Norwich NR12 9RZ   Tel: 01692 581195   Fax: 01692
583214   Email: broadsmuseum@btinternet.com

Windmill with nine floors. Museum has seven buildings, 1880s pharmacy, Tobacco Museum, kitchen items, animal traps, veterinary, TVs, radios, large engines, razors, banknotes, farm and trade tools, leathertrades, camera, soaps, polish, trade tricycles and coopers display.

Opening Times: Apr to Sep daily 10:00-17:30.   Admission: Child £1.50, OAP £3.50.
Location: One mile off A149, nr Stalham. Brown tourism signs on A149.   Map Ref: 15

North Norfolk (M & GN) Railway Museum

The Station, Station Approach, Sheringham NR26 8RA   Tel: 01263 822045   Fax: 01263 820801   Email: enquiries@mandgn.co.uk   Web: www.mandgn.co.uk

The Midland & Great Northern joint railway society is the support charity behind the North Norfolk Railway. The society is dedicated to preserving our railway heritage in East Anglia, especially that of the M & GN Railway. Displays of smaller artefacts are currently on view in the Sheringham Museum Coach and the model railway facilities at Weybourne and Holt. The society's collection of locomotives and rolling stock is also based on the railway.

Opening Times: Feb to Oct & Dec each day of timetable railway service.   Admission: Free.
Location: Museum coach is on platform three at the North Norfolk Railway's Sheringham Station.   Map Ref: 16

Ancient House Museum

White Hart Street, Thetford IP24 1AA   Tel: 01842 752599
Email: ancient.house.museum@norfolk.gov.uk   Web: www.norfolk.gov.uk/tourism/museums

This magnificent timber-framed Tudor merchant's house was built about 1490, with an extension added about 1590. The house is jetted and timber-framed, using oak with wattle and daub in-fill with fine carved ceiling and fireplace timbers.

Norfolk

Opening Times: Mon to Sat 10:00-12:30, 13:00-17:00. Also open 1 Jun to 31 Aug Sun 14:00-17:00. Admission: Sep to Jun free, Adult £1.00, Child 60p, OAP/Student/Concession 80p.

Map Ref: 17

Euston

Euston, Thetford IP24 2QP   Tel: 01842 766366   Fax: 01842 766764
Web: www.eustonhall.co.uk

Georgian country house in brick, one wing of a larger house which suffered fire in 1902. The Dukes of Grafton are descended from Charles 11, and the collection of royal Stuart portraits here is rivalled only by those at Windsor Castle.

Opening Times: June to Sep   Location: 12 Miles north of Bury St Edmunds on A1088.

Map Ref: 18

WELLS-NEXT-THE-SEA

The Bygones Museum at Holkham

Holkham Park, Wells-next-the-Sea NR23 1AB   Tel: 01328 711383   Fax: 01328 711707
Email: s.harvey@holkham.co.uk   Web: www.holkham.co.uk

Over 5000 items of domestic and agricultural memorabilia, carriages and vintage cars. Working steam engines, kitchen, dairy, laundry. Music and money boxes. Typewriters and sewing machines.

Opening Times: 10-12 Apr, early May to end Oct daily 10:00-17:30. Closed Wed.
Admission: Holkham Hall & Bygones Museum: Adult £10.00, Child £5.00, Family £25.00.
Museum: Adult £5.00, Child £2.50.   Location: Two miles west of Wells-next-the-Sea, off A149
coast road.

Map Ref: 19

Thomas William Coke, First Earl of Leicester of the second creation

Holkham

Wells-next-the-Sea NR23 1AB
Tel: 01328 710227 Fax: 01328 711707
Email: l.herrieven@holkham.co.uk
Web: www.holkham.co.uk

This classic Palladian mansion was built in the mid 1700s by Thomas Coke, the first Earl of Leicester and is home to his descendants. It has a magnificent alabaster entrance hall and the sumptuous state rooms house Roman Statues, fine furniture and paintings by Rubens, Van Dyck, Gainsborough and many others. The Bygones Museum, housed in the Hall's original stable block, has more than 5,000 items of domestic and agricultural memorabilia on display from gramophones to fire engines.

Opening Times: May to end of Sept, please call (01328) 710227 before you travel. Admission: Holkham Hall: Adult £6.50, Child £3.25. Bygones Museum: Adult £5.00, Child £2.50. Combined ticket (Hall & Bygones): Adult £10.00, Child £5.00, Family £25.00. Location: Holkham is two miles west of Wells-next-the-Sea on the main A149, within easy reach of Norwich on the A1067, Kings Lynn on the A148 and London and Cambridge from the M11 and the A10.

Map Ref: 19

WYMONDHAM

Wymondham Heritage Museum

10 The Bridewell, Norwich Road, Wymondham NR18 0NS   Tel: 01953 600205
Web: www.wymondham-norfolk.co.uk

Award-winning museum in 18th century model prison built 1785, later serving as a police station and courthouse. Dungeon and original cell. Displays about history of the building and town including Kett's rebellion, agriculture and brushmaking.

Opening Times: Mar to Nov Mon to Sat 10:00-16:00, Sun 14:00-16:00.   Admission: Adult £2.00, Child 50p, Concession £1.50. Groups by prior arrangement.   Location: Near town centre, two minutes walk from Market Cross and central car park.

Map Ref: 20

Northumberland, Tyne & Wear, Durham

Never was such an area blessed with so many museums, exhibitions, shows, galleries and festivals. It is not surprising considering that this northern region (comprising Northumberland, Cleveland, County Durham and Tyne & Wear) is simply steeped in history, social, industrial and military and all minutely recorded in some of the finest museums in Britain. Added to this there are four hundred square miles of National Park telling its own story of the majestic beauty of the extreme north from Hadrian's Wall to the Cheviots and the Scottish Border. Hadrian's Wall, of course, boasts a string of museums telling their story of the Roman occupation of these lands, and most cities and towns of the region have their own museums.

The Red Map References should be used to locate Museums etc on the pages that follow

Northumberland, Tyne & Wear, Durham

ALNWICK *N'land*

Alnwick Castle

Alnwick NE66 1NQ   Tel: 01665 510777/511100   Fax: 01665 510876
Email: enquires@alnwickcastle.com   Web: www.alnwickcastle.com

Set in magnificent Capability Brown landscape, Alnwick Castle is the home of the Duke of Northumberland. Owned by his family, the Percies, since 1309, the castle was a major stronghold during the Scottish wars. Restorations by the First and Fourth Dukes have transformed the massive fortress into a comfortable family home. The Italian Renaissance style State Rooms are filled with fine furniture, porcelain and paintings by Canaletto, Van Dyck and Titian. Within the grounds are the recently refurbished museums of the Northumberland Fusiliers (1674 to present day), Northumberland Archaeology and the Percy Tenantry Volunteers (1798-1814). Quizzes and a location for the Harry Potter film make it a magical place for the whole family. Events include: birds of prey demonstrations, live music, open-air theatre and Wellington's Redcoat camp.

Opening Times: 1 Apr to 31 Oct daily 11:00-17:00 (last admission at 16:15).   Admission: Adult £7.50, Child (under 16) Free, Concession £6.50.   Exhibitions & Events 2004 : For details of events visit the website or telephone 01665 510777.   Map Ref: 1

Bondgate Gallery

22 Narrowgate, Alnwick NE66 1JG   Tel: 01665 576450

Eight exhibitions per year, also craft work including wood and glass.

Opening Times: Mon to Sat 10:30-16:00.   Admission: Free.   Location: 22 Narrowgate.
                                                                                       Map Ref: 1

BAMBURGH *N'land*

Bamburgh Castle

Bamburgh NE69 7DF   Tel: 01668 214515   Fax: 01668 214060
Email: bamburghcastle@aol.com   Web: www.bamburghcastle.com

Magnificent coastal castle overlooking Lindisfarne and miles of sandy beach. Ten viewing rooms with collections of china, paintings, furniture, armour. Site of major archaelogical dig.

Opening Times: 13 Mar to 31 Oct 11:00-16:30.   Admission: Adult £5.00, OAP £4.00, Child (6-15 yrs) £2.00.   Location: Bamburgh Northumberland.   Map Ref: 2

The RNLI Grace Darling Museum

2 Radcliffe Road, Bamburgh NE69 7AE   Tel: 01668 214465   Web: www.lifeboats.org.uk

Items relating to the life of Grace Darling, including the original coble used for rescue.

Opening Times: Easter to Oct Mon to Sat 10:00-17:00, Sun 12:00-17:00.   Admission: Free.
                                                                                       Map Ref: 2

Key to Classifications

see Classifications Index on page 423

Anthropology	Horticultural	Police, Prisons
Archaeological	Jewellery	& Dungeons
Art Galleries	Literature & Libraries	Railways
Arts, Crafts & Textiles	Maritime	Religion
China, Glass & Ceramics	Military & Defence	Roman
Communications	Multicultural	Science - Earth & Planetary
Egyptian	Music & Theatre	Sculpture
Fashion	Natural History	Sporting History
Geology	Oriental	Toy & Childhood
Health & Medicine	Palaces	Transport
Historic Houses	Photography	Victoriana

Northumberland, Tyne & Wear, Durham

The Bowes Museum

Newgate, Barnard Castle DL12 8NP   Tel: 01833 690606   Fax: 01833 637163
Email: info@bowesmuseum.org.uk   Web: www.bowesmuseum.org.uk

The Bowes Museum has 30 public galleries.
Set in formal gardens and parkland

A world-class visitor attraction, housed in a magnificent château in the picturesque market town of Barnard Castle. Opened in 1892, the Museum contains one of Britain's finest collections of art, textiles, ceramics and furniture. Host to a series of outstanding internationally significant exhibitions throughout the year. The wonderful building is set in 23 acres of parkland with a parterre garden.

Opening Times: Jan to Dec daily 11:00-17:00. Closed 25 to 26 Dec & 1 Jan. Admission: Adult £6.00, OAP/Concession £5.00, Under 16s Free. Group rates available. Location: Barnard Castle. Exhibitions & Events 2004 : 4 Jul to 11 Jan: The Tim Rice Collection, 24 May to 18 Apr: Wedding Belles, 11 Oct to 29 Feb: William Morris and the Arts and Crafts Movement in the North East, 15 Dec to 11 Jan: Lindisfarne Gospels, 17 Jan to 21 Mar: After Life, 27 Feb ongoing: The John & Joséphine Bowes Story, 3 Apr to 30 May: Northumbria Gardens Trust, 3 Apr to 27 Jun: Braids and Beyond, Spring onwards: The Lady Ludlow Collection, 29 to 30 Aug: Monet and Boudin on the Normandy Coast, 12 Jun to 12 Sep: Anthony Clark, 11 Sep to 9 Jan: Toulouse Lautrec and the Art Nouveau poster, 25 Sep to Jan: Lubaina Himid and Friends.

Map Ref: 3

Berwick-upon-Tweed Borough Museum & Art Gallery

The Clock Block, Berwick Barracks, Ravensdowne, Berwick-upon-Tweed TD15 1DQ
Tel: 01289 301869   Fax: 01289 330540

Berwick Museum, housed within Ravensdowne Barracks, explores local social history in 'Window on Berwick'. Also on display are many of the paintings and artefacts given to the town by Sir William Burrell.

Opening Times: 1 Nov to 29 Mar Wed to Sun 10:00-16:00, 30 Mar to 31 Oct daily 10:00-18:00. Admission: Adult £3.00, Child £1.50, Concession £2.30. Location: Near town centre.
Map Ref: 4

The King's Own Scottish Borderers Regimental Museum

The Barracks, Berwick-upon-Tweed TD15 1DG   Tel: 01289 307426   Fax: 01289 331928
Email: kosbmus@milnet.uk.net   Web: www.kosb.co.uk

The history of the Regiment from 1689 to the present day is traced through displays of uniforms, badges, medals, weapons, paintings and relics from the various campaigns in which it has been involved. Tableaux and dioramas dramatically bring to life the Regiment's battles and aspects of the soldier's profession.

Opening Times: Mon to Sat 09:30-16:30. Closed certain public holidays, Xmas & New Year. Admission: Adult £2.70, Child £1.40, Under 5s Free, Concession £2.00. Members of English Heritage Free. Members of Historic Scotland and CADW Free or half price. Location: Within Berwick Barracks, beside the town of Ramparts, two minutes walk from the town centre.

Map Ref: 4

Lady Waterford Gallery

Ford Village, Berwick-upon-Tweed TD15 2QA   Tel: 01890 820524

A Victorian Hall, formerly Ford village school, houses the Waterford Murals created by Louisa Marchioness of Waterford from 1862 to 1883. The murals depict well known stories from the Bible, using children from the school and other local people as the subjects.

Opening Times: 13 Mar to 31 Oct, daily 10:30-12:30 & 13:30-17:30   Admission: Adult £1.75,

www.mghh.co.uk

For current information on the outstanding Collections in over 1600 Museums, Galleries & Historic Houses in England, Scotland, Wales and Ireland

Northumberland, Tyne & Wear, Durham

Child over 12s £0.75, OAP/Concession £1.25.   Location: Approx 12 miles south west from Berwick-upon-Tweed, Signposted from the A1 and A697.   Map Ref: 5

Lindisfarne Castle
Holy Island, Berwick-upon-Tweed TD15 2SH   Tel: 01289 389244   Fax: 01289 389349   Web: www.nationaltrust.org.uk

Originally a Tudor fort, it was converted into a private house in 1903 by the young Edwin Lutyens. The small rooms are full of intimate decoration and design, the windows looking down upon the charming walled garden planned by Gertrude Jekyll.

Opening Times: Castle; 14 Feb to 22 Feb Tue to Sun times vary, 15 Mar to 2 Nov Tue to Sun times vary. Open BH Mons. Admission: Adult £5.00, Child £2.50, Family £12.50. NT Members Free.   Location: On Holy Island, six miles east of A1 across causeway.   Map Ref: 6

Lindisfarne Priory
Holy Island, Berwick-upon-Tweed TD15 2RX   Tel: 01289 389200

One of the holiest sites of Anglo-Saxon England, Lindisfarne was renowned as the original burial place of St Cuthbert. Founded in 635 by St Aidan who came from Iona, it was the centre of Christianity in Scotland. Lindisfarne was a treasure house of jewels and manuscripts, including incomparable illuminated Gospels (now in British Library), and is still a holy site and place of pilgrimage today. In the award winning museum one of the most important collections of Anglo-Saxon stonework is on display.

Lindisfarne Priory © English Heritage

Opening Times: Apr to Sep daily 10:00-18:00, Oct daily 10:00-17:00, Nov to Mar daily 10:00-16:00. Closed Xmas & New Year. Times & prices may change. Admission: Adult £3.00, Child £1.50, Concession £2.30. EH Members Free.   Location: On Holy Island, only reached at low tide across causeway. For details of tides telephone Berwick Tourist Information 01289 330733.   Map Ref: 6

Billingham Art Gallery
Queensway, Billingham TS23 2LN   Tel: 01642 397590   Fax: 01642 397594

Offers an exciting selection of art to suit all tastes, providing a lively forum for local artists to exhibit their work.

Opening Times: Mon to Sat 09:00-17:00. Closed Sun & BH. Admission: Free.
Location: Town centre.   Map Ref: 7

Binchester Roman Fort
Bishop Auckland   Tel: 01388 663089   Web: www.durham.gov.uk/bincester

Once the largest Roman Fort in County Durham. Now carefully excavated and displayed for you to enjoy to the full.

Opening Times: 18 to 21 Apr and 28 Apr to 28 Sept. Admission: Adult £1.60,
Child/Concession 80p.   Map Ref: 8

Killhope, the North of England Lead Mining Museum
near Cowshill, Upper Weardale, Bishop Auckland DL13 1AR   Tel: 01388 537505   Fax: 01388 537617   Email: killhope@durham.gov.uk   Web: www.durham.gov.uk/killhope

Explores the life of North Pennine lead mining families. Visitors walk down the original mine tunnel and discover the working conditions of Victorian miners. See how miners lived and worked. Woodland walk & picnic site.

Opening Times: Apr to Sep 10:30-17:00, Oct Sat & Sun 10:30-17:00. Admission: Without Mine: Adult £3.40 Child £1.70 Family £8.50. With Mine: Adult £5.00, Child £2.50, Family £12.50.
Location: On A689, 20 minutes from Stanhope and ten minutes from Alston.   Map Ref: 9

Beamish, The North of England Open Air Museum

Beamish, Co. Durham DH9 0RG   Tel: 0191 370 4000   Fax: 0191 370 4001
Email: museum@beamish.org.uk   Web: www.beamish.org.uk

Beamish is unique, a living, working, experience of life as it was in the Great North. Buildings from throughout the region have been rebuilt and furnished as they once were to create a Town, Colliery Village and working Farm of 1913. Pockerley Manor and The 1825 Railway portray life in the early 1800's. Photographic archive and library. Designated museum.

Opening Times: Apr to Oct daily 10:00-17:00. Nov to Mar Tue to Thu, Sat & Sun 10:00-16:00. Closed Mon & Fri. Check for Xmas & New Year opening. Last adm 15:00.
Admission: (2003 rates) Summer Adult £12.00, Child £7.00, OAP £10.00. Group & educational rates available.

Recreation of The 1825 Railway at Beamish

Winter £4.00 per person.   Location: 12 miles north west of Durham, signposted from junction 63 of A1M.   Exhibitions & Events 2004 : 16 May: Morgan Car Meet, 5 & 6 Jun: North Country Quilting Weekend, 21 & 22 Aug: North Country Quilting Weekend.   Map Ref: 10

Corbridge Roman Site Museum

Corbridge NE45 5NT   Tel: 01434 632349

Originally the site of a fort on the former patrol road, Corbridge evolved into a principal town of the Roman era, flourishing until the fifth century. The large granaries are among its most impressive remains. The museum contains a vast selection of finds from the area, illustrating the history of Hadrian's Wall.

Opening Times: Apr to Sep daily 10:00-18:00, Oct daily 10:00-17:00, Nov to Mar Wed to Sun 10:00-13:00 & 14:00-16:00. Closed Xmas & New Year. Times & prices may change.
Admission: Adult £3.10, Child £1.60, Concession £2.30. EH Members Free.   Location: Half a mile north west of Corbridge - signed Corbridge Roman Site.   Map Ref: 11

Darlington Railway Centre & Museum

North Road Station, Darlington DL3 6ST   Tel: 01325 460532   Fax: 01325 287746
Email: museum@darlington.gov.uk   Web: www.drcm.org.uk

Experience the atmosphere of the steam railway in the historic North Road Station of 1842. See Stephenson's 'Locomotion' and explore the railway heritage of the North East through a collection of engines, carriages/wagons and railway ephemera.

Opening Times: Daily 10:00-17:00. Closed Xmas & New Year.   Admission: Adult £2.20, Child £1.10, Concession £1.50.   Location: 15 minute walk from town centre, frequent bus service.
                    Map Ref: 12

Raby Castle

Staindrop, Darlington DL2 3AH   Tel: 01833 660202   Fax: 01833 660169
Email: admin@rabycastle.com   Web: www.rabycastle.com

The dramatic 14th century castle, built by the mighty Nevills has been home to Lord Barnard's family since 1626. In the well-preserved halls and chambers history comes vibrantly to life. Rooms display fine furniture, impressive artworks and elaborate architecture. Set within a 200 acre deer park, with large walled gardens and a coach and carriage collection.

Opening Times: Jun, Jul & Aug Daily except Sat. May & Sep Wed & Sun. BH Sat to following Wed. Castle: 13:00-17:00. Park & Gardens: 11:00-17:30.   Admission: Castle, Park & Gardens: Adult £7.00, Child £3.00, OAP/Student £6.00. Park & Gardens: £4.00, Child £2.50, OAP/Student £3.50. Family ticket £16.00 (2 adults and three children).   Location: Near Barnard Castle, Co Durham.   Exhibitions & Events 2004 : 1 to 3 May: Raby Cashe Orchid Show, 30 May: Raby Cashe 10K Race (Teesdale Athletics Club), 6 Jun: Plant Fair, 27 Jun: Vintage Car Rally, 24 Jul: As You Like It (Outdoor Theatre), 5 Sep: Autumn Plant Fair. Map Ref: 13

Northumberland, Tyne & Wear, Durham

DLI - Durham Light Infantry Museum & Durham Art Gallery

Aykley Heads, Durham DH1 5TU   Tel: 0191 384 2214   Fax: 0191 386 1770
Web: www.durham.gov.uk/dli

Interactive museum for all ages, telling the story of DLI soldiers and life on the 'home front'. Art Gallery - Exhibitions and events all year. Beautiful grounds with new nature walk.

Opening Times: Apr to Oct 10:00-17:00. Nov to Mar 10:00-16:00. Closed Xmas Day.
Admission: Adult £2.50, Concession £1.25, Family £6.25.   Location: Ten minute walk from city centre.   Map Ref: 14

Durham Art Gallery

Aykley Heads, Durham DH1 5TU
Tel: 0191 384 2214
Web: www.durham.gov.uk/dli

Featuring a changing programme of artistic exhibitions and events. Details available in our Events Brochure and on our website.

Opening Times: 1 Apr to 31 Oct 10:00-17:00, 1 Nov to 31 Mar 10:00-16:00.   Admission: Charges, family ticket available.   Map Ref: 14

Durham City Young Embroiderers Workshop

Durham University Oriental Museum

Elvet Hill, Durham DH1 3TH   Tel: 0191 334 5694   Fax: 0191 374 7911
Email: oriental.museum@durham.ac.uk   Web: www.dur.ac.uk/oriental.museum

The Oriental Museum is the only museum in the North East devoted solely to Oriental art and archaeology. Here you can explore cultures that range from Ancient Egypt to Imperial China and modern Japan.

Opening Times: Mon to Fri 10:00-17:00, Sat to Sun 12:00-17:00. Closed Xmas & New Year.
Admission: Adult £1.50, Concessions 75p, Family £3.50.   Location: Five minute from bus stop. 15 minute walk from town centre.   Map Ref: 14

The Monks Dormitory, Durham Cathedral

The College, Durham DH1 3EH   Tel: 0191 386 4266   Fax: 0191 386 4267
Email: enquiries@durhamcathedral.co.uk   Web: www.durhamcathedral.co.uk

Magnificent beamed roof and collection of pre-conquest stones. During August facsimile of Lindisfarne Gospels.

Opening Times: 7 Apr to 28 Sep Mon to Sat 10:00-15:30, Sun 12:30-15:15.   Admission: Adult 80p, Child 20p, Family £1.50.   Location: In cloisters of Durham Cathedral.   Map Ref: 14

Museum of Archaeology, University of Durham

The Old Fulling Mill, The Banks, Durham DH1 3EB   Tel: 0191 334 1823/5695   Fax: 0191 334 1824   Web: www.dur.ac.uk/archaeology

The Old Fulling Mill is a 16th century mill originally part of the Cathedral estates. It houses an archaeology museum tracing the history of Durham City from prehistoric to post-medieval times.

Opening Times: Apr to Oct daily 11:00-16:00. Nov to Mar Fri to Mon 11:30-15:30.
Admission: Adult £1.00, Concession 50p, Family £2.50.   Location: Five minutes from city centre on riverbank below Cathedral.   Map Ref: 14

Treasures of St Cuthbert Exhibition

The Chapter Office, The College, Durham DH1 3EH   Tel: 0191 386 4266   Fax: 0191 386 4267
Email: enquiries@durhamcathedral.co.uk   Web: www.durhamcathedral.co.uk

St Cuthbert's Coffin and Pectoral Cross, Anglo Saxon embroideries, silverware, seals, manuscripts. 'Turning the pages' electronic version of Lindisfarne Gospels.

Opening Times: Mon to Sat 10:00-16:00, Sun 14:00-16:30 (Dec & Jan 16.15). Closed Xmas & Good Friday.   Admission: Adult £2.00, Child 50p, Concession £1.50, Family £5.00.
Location: In cloisters of Durham Cathedral.   Map Ref: 14

Northumberland, Tyne & Wear, Durham

Shipley Art Gallery

Prince Consort Road, Gateshead NE8 4JB
Tel: 0191 477 1495 Fax: 0191 478 7917
Web: www.twmuseums.org.uk

The Shipley Art Gallery combines a dazzling display of the latest glass, jewellery, ceramics, textiles and furniture alongside stunning historical artworks. The Craft Gallery features over 700 breathtaking pieces by the county's leading makers and paintings including Dutch and Flemish Old Masters. The fascinating history of the town is told in 'Made in Gateshead' and the Gallery stages superb temporary exhibitions.

Opening Times: Mon to Sat 10:00-17:00, Sun 14:00-17:00.
Admission: Free. Location: Ten minute walk from town centre and metro station. Map Ref: 15

HMS Trincomalee Trust

Jackson Dock, Hartlepool TS24 0SQ
Tel: 01429 223193

HMS Trincomalee was built in 1817 and is the oldest ship afloat in Britain. This classic British frigate has been fully and sensitively restored and interpreted in an award-winning scheme. There are disabled lifts between three decks. The ship provides a unique opportunity to experience life aboard a British warship two centuries ago. There are audio guides with guided tours available for groups.

Opening Times: Apr to Oct 10:30-17:00, Nov to Mar 11:00-16:00. Closed Xmas & New Year. Admission: Adult £4.25, Concession £3.25, Family (2 adults and 3 children) £11.75. Education Groups £1.70. Location: Located at Hartlepool Historic Quay. Follow the brown tourist signs for the Quay and look for the masts!

HMS Trincomalee Map Ref: 16

Hartlepool Art Gallery

Church Square, Hartlepool TS24 8EQ
Tel: 01429 869706 Fax: 01429 523408
Email: arts-museums@hartlepool.gov.uk
Web: www.destinationhartlepool.com

Programme of changing exhibitions feature the best of contemporary art and craft and a varied and innovative selection from Hartlepool's collection. Also views from tower of Hartlepool (small charge).

Opening Times: Tue to Sat 10:00-17:30, Sun 14:00-17:00. Closed Mon, Xmas & New Year. Admission: Free.
Location: In magnificent converted Victorian Church, one minute walk from Hartlepool Railway Station. Map Ref: 16

Key to Classifications
see Classifications Index on page 423

Anthropology	Horticultural	Police, Prisons
Archaeological	Jewellery	& Dungeons
Art Galleries	Literature & Libraries	Railways
Arts, Crafts & Textiles	Maritime	Religion
China, Glass & Ceramics	Military & Defence	Roman
Communications	Multicultural	Science - Earth & Planetary
Egyptian	Music & Theatre	Sculpture
Fashion	Natural History	Sporting History
Geology	Oriental	Toy & Childhood
Health & Medicine	Palaces	Transport
Historic Houses	Photography	Victoriana

Northumberland, Tyne & Wear, Durham

Museum of Hartlepool

Jackson Dock, Hartlepool   Tel: 01429 860006
Fax: 01429 867332   Email: historic.quay@hartlepool.gov.uk
Web: www.destinationhartlepool.com

The museum of Hartlepool tells the story of Hartlepool from prehistoric times to the present day using many original artefacts, photographs, models, hands-on and interactive displays.
Fascinating archaeological finds from the stone age and the time of the Saxons give way to the engineering and shipbuilding achievements of the Victorians. The constant presence of the sea has influenced the development of the town throughout its history and this is reflected in many of the objects on display. Toys and games, sport and education provide a picture of social conditions. The paddle steamer 'Wingfield Castle' is moored alongside the museum quay and has a café on board.

Opening Times: Daily 10:00-17:00. Closed 25-26 Dec & New Year's Day. Admission: Free. Location: At Hartlepool Marina, ten minutes walk from Hartlepool Railway Station.

Map Ref: 16

Housesteads Roman Fort & Museum

Haydon Bridge NE47 6NN   Tel: 01434 344363

Housesteads is the most complete example of a Roman fort in Britain and is one of the twelve permanent forts built by Emperor Hadrian in around 124 AD. The museum houses a range of objects found at the site, including flat-bottomed pottery and larger cooking pots which are Friesian in origin. Some of the Wall has been partially reconstructed to give one of the most vivid pictures of the Romans and their works in Britain.

Opening Times: Apr to Sep daily 10:00-18:00, Oct daily 10:00-17:00, Nov to Mar daily 10:00-16:00. Closed Xmas & New Year. Times & prices may change.

Housesteads Fort © English Heritage

Admission: Adult £3.10, Child £1.60, Concession £2.30. EH & NT Members Free.
Location: Nearly three miles north east of Bardon Mill on B6318.

Map Ref: 17

Chesterholm Museum - Vindolanda

Bardon Mill, Hexham NE47 7JN   Tel: 01434 344 277   Fax: 01434 344 060   Email: info@vindolanda.com
Web: www.vindolanda.com

Vindolanda is a Roman Frontier military and civilian site, with archaeologists on site April to August, Sunday to Thursday, weather permitting. Vindolanda also offers an Open Air Museum featuring a Roman Temple, Shop and House, and an extensive museum housing finds from the site such as Roman boots, shoes, jewellery, textiles and special photographs of the rare ink on wood tablets written nearly 2000 years ago.

Opening Times: Feb, March, Oct & Nov daily 10:00-17:00, Apr to Sep daily 10:00-18:00. Admission: Adult £4.50, Child £2.90, OAP/Student £3.80, Family (2 Adults, 2 Children) £13.00.

Aerial View of Roman Vindolanda

Discounted joint saver tickets available with the Roman Army Museum. Location: One mile north of the A69, near Bardon Mill, Northumberland.

Map Ref: 18

Chesters Fort & Museum

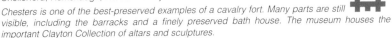

Chollerford, Humshaugh, Hexham-on-Tyne NE46 4EP   Tel: 01434 681379

Chesters is one of the best-preserved examples of a cavalry fort. Many parts are still visible, including the barracks and a finely preserved bath house. The museum houses the important Clayton Collection of altars and sculptures.

Opening Times: Apr to Sep daily 09:30-18:00, Oct daily 10:00-17:00, Nov to Mar daily 10:00-16:00. Closed Xmas & New Year. Times & prices may change.   Admission: Adult £3.10, Child £1.60, Concession £2.30. EH Members Free.   Location: Quarter mile west of Chollerford on B6318.   Map Ref: 19

Captain Cook Birthplace Museum

Stewart Park, Marton, Middlesbrough TS7 8AT   Tel: 01642 515658   Fax: 01642 515659
Email: captcookmuseum@middlesbrough.gov.uk

Discover why Captain Cook is the world's most famous explorer with a unique insight into his early life, seafaring career and legacy of his voyages. Experience life below decks for a sailor of the 18th century. Audio-visual presentations, hands-on, interactive displays and original objects interesting and fun for all ages. Temporary exhibition gallery and regular programme of events. Fully accessible.

Exploring the wonders of life in the 18th century, when Cook was a lad

Opening Times: Mar to Oct Tue to Sun 10:00-17:30, Nov to Feb Tue to Sun 09:00-15:30. Admission: Adult £2.40, Child £1.20, OAP £1.20, Family £6.00. Location: Within Stewart Park. Five minutes from Marton Railway Station.

Exhibitions & Events 2004 : Oct 2004: Captain Cook Festival.   Map Ref: 20

Ormesby Hall

Ormesby, Middlesbrough TS7 9AS   Tel: 01642 324188   Fax: 01642 300937
Web: www.nationaltrust.org.uk

A mid-18th century Palladian mansion, notable for its fine plasterwork and carved wood decoration. The Victorian laundry and kitchen with scullery and game larder are especially interesting, and there is a particularly beautiful stable block.

Opening Times: 30 Mar to 2 Nov Tue, Wed, Thu & Sun 13:30-16:30. Open BH Mons & Good Friday. Admission: Adult £3.90, Child £1.90, Family £9.50. Group (15+) £3.30. NT Members Free. Location: Three miles south east of Middlesborough, west of A171. From the A19 take the A174 to the A172. Follow signs.   Map Ref: 21

Morpeth Chantry Bagpipe Museum

Bridge Street, Morpeth NE61 1PJ   Tel: 01670 500717   Fax: 01670 500710
Email: amoore@castlemorpeth.gov.uk

A unique museum, specialising in the Northumbrian small pipes, which are set in the context of bagpipes from around the world, from India to Inverness.

Opening Times: Jan to Dec Mon to Sat 10:00-17:00. Admission: Free. Location: Town centre, one minute from bus station, five minutes from railway station.   Map Ref: 22

Wallington

Cambo, Morpeth NE61 4AR   Tel: 01670 773600   Fax: 01670 774420
Email: nwaplr@smtp.ntrust.org.uk
Web: www.nationaltrust.org.uk

The Wallington estate was laid out in the 18th-century by Sir Walter Blackett. It houses very good Rococo plasterwork in the main rooms and a Victorian painted and galleried 2-storey hall.The house has a collection of ceramics, curiosities, stuffed birds and geological specimens. There is a 17th-century formal garden and parkland.
View of the Dining Room at Wallington

Northumberland, Tyne & Wear, Durham

MORPETH *N'land (continued)*

Opening Times: 1 Apr to 5 Sep Wed to Mon 13:00-17:30, 6 Sep to 31 Oct Wed to Mon 13:00-16:30. Admission: Adult £7.00, Child £3.50, Family £17.50. Group (15+) £6.50. NT Members Free. Location: 12 miles west of Morpeth (B6343), six miles north west of Belsay (A696), take B6342 to Cambo.

Map Ref: 23

NEWCASTLE UPON TYNE *Tyne & Wear*

Castle Keep Museum

The Castle Keep, Castle Garth, Newcastle upon Tyne NE1 1RQ   Tel: 0191 2327938
Web: thekeep-newcastle.org.uk

Built in 1168-1178 one of the finest surviving examples of a Norman keep. Panoramic views of the city, the Tyne and its bridges (overlooks central railway station and main rail lines) from its roof. Small museum with artefacts relevant to site.

Opening Times: Apr to Sep daily 09:30-17:30, Oct to Mar daily 09:30-16:30. Closed Good Friday, 25-26 Dec & New Year. Admission: Adult £1.50, Child/OAP 50p. Special rates for parties of 12 or more. Location: Near town centre, three minutes walk from central railway station.

Map Ref: 24

Hancock Museum

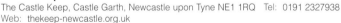

Barras Bridge, Newcastle upon Tyne NE2 4PT   Tel: 0191 222 6765
Fax: 0191 222 6753 Web: www.twmuseums.org.uk

The North of England's premier Natural History Museum unravels the secrets of the natural world through sensational galleries. For more than one hundred years visitors have gained an insight into the animal kingdom and the powerful and sometimes destructive forces of Nature. From the Dinosaurs to live animals, the Hancock is home to creatures past and present and even the odd Egyptian mummy or two.

Opening Times: Mon to Sat 10:00-17:00, Sun 14:00-17:00.
Admission: Charges vary in accordance with temporary exhibitions. Location: Five minutes walk from city centre.
Exhibitions & Events 2004 : Please telephone for details or visit the website.

Map Ref: 24

Hatton Gallery

The Quadrangle, University of Newcastle, Newcastle upon Tyne NE1 7RU   Tel: 0191 222 6059
Fax: 0191 222 3454 Email: hatton-gallery@ncl.ac.uk Web: www.ncl.ac.uk/hatton

Permanent collections on display - African art and the Kurt Schwitters Merzbarn. In addition the gallery presents a series of prestigious and stimulating temporary exhibitions.

Opening Times: Mon to Sat 10:00-17:00. Closed Sun, BH, Xmas & New Year.
Admission: Free. Location: City centre, two minutes walk from Haymarket Metro Station and Haymarket Bus Station.

Map Ref: 24

Laing Art Gallery

New Bridge Street, Newcastle upon Tyne NE1 8AG   Tel: 0191 232 7734
Fax: 0191 222 0952 Web: www.twmuseums.org.uk

The North of England's premier art gallery displays a stunning array of watercolours, costume, silver, glass, pottery and sculpture alongside a striking programme of historical and contemporary exhibitions. Major works by leading Pre-Raphaelite artists including Willian Holman Hunt and Edward Burne-Jones by L S Lowry. Younger visitors can let their artistic skills run riot in the P & G Children's Gallery which includes soft play, puzzles and books. Art on Tyneside looks about the rich history of art and craft on Tyneside, including paintings, silver, ceramic, glass and

textiles. Using sound, interactive games and open exhibits, the exhibitions also features a re-creation of an 18th century coffee shop, a Victorian art gallery and Tyne Bridge. The hugely popular and high profile temporary exhibition programme of both historical and contemporary art has made the Laing Art Gallery one of the most popular art galleries in the UK. The gallery also offers a café and new craft shop that sells everything from art history books to the latest contemporary craft.

Opening Times: Mon to Sat 10:00-17:00, Sun 14:00-17:00. Admission: Free. Location: One minute walk from city centre. Exhibitions & Events 2004 : Please telephone for details or visit the website. Map Ref: 24

Military Vehicle Museum

Exhibition Park Pavillion, Newcastle upon Tyne NE2 4PZ Tel: 0191 281 7222
Email: miltmuseum@aol.com Web: www.military.museum.org.uk

Over 50 vehicles, 60 cabinets depicting a soliders life from 1900 to date. World War I trench, Anderson Shelter and Home Front display.

Opening Times: Mar to Nov daily 10:00-16:00, closed Aug BH. Nov to Mar Sat, Sun and school holidays 10:00-16:00. Closed 25-26 Dec & New Years Day. Admission: Adult £2.00, Child/Concession £1.00, Under 5s Free. Map Ref: 24

Museum of Antiquities

University of Newcastle upon Tyne, Newcastle upon Tyne NE1 7RU Tel: 0191 222 7849
Fax: 0191 222 8561 Email: l.allason-jones@ncl.ac.uk Web: www.ncl.ac.uk/antiquities

Ideal place to start visit to Hadrian's Wall. Artefacts from 8000BC to 1600AD give the visitor a unique insight into the history of the north of England.

Opening Times: Mon to Sat 10:00-17:00. Closed Sun, Xmas & New Year and Good Friday.
Admission: Free. Location: In town centre. One minute walk from Haymarket. Map Ref: 24

Newcastle Discovery Museum

Blandford Square, Newcastle upon Tyne NE1 4JA Tel: 0191 232 6789
Fax: 0191 233 1088 Web: www.twmuseums.org.uk

Explore Newcastle's past from Romans to the present day. Tyneside inventions that changed the world, a fun approach to science, a soldier's life, and take a walk through fashion. The museum is currently undergoing an exciting £12.25 million transformation to introduce spectacular new displays, including a whole floor of galleries devoted to life on the River Tyne.

Opening Times: Mon to Sat 10:00-17:00, Sun 14:00-17:00. Admission: Free. Location: Ten minutes from city centre and central station. Map Ref: 24

Shefton Museum of Greek Art & Archaeology

The Armstrong Building, University of Newcastle upon Tyne, Newcastle upon Tyne NE1 7RU
Tel: 0191 222 8996 Fax: 0191 222 8561 Email: l.allason-jones@ncl.ac.uk
Web: www.ncl.ac.uk/shefton-museum

The most important collection of archaeological material from the Greek world in the north of England.

Opening Times: Mon to Fri 10:00-16:00. Closed Sat, Sun and BH. Admission: Free.
Location: In town centre, one minute walk from Haymarket. Map Ref: 24

Northumberland, Tyne & Wear, Durham

Stephenson Railway Museum

Middle Engine Lane, West Chirton, North Shields NE29 8DX   Tel /
Fax: 0191 200 7145   Web: www.twmuseums.org.uk

Relive the glorious days of the steam railway at Stephenson Railway Museum. The Museum is home to George Stephenson's 'Billy', a forerunner of the world-famous Rocket and many other engines from the great age of steam including 'Jackie Milburn', named after the Newcastle United legend. A ride on a real steam train can be taken and the story of coal and electricity is also told.

Opening Times: Seasonal - call for details.
Admission: Free.   Map Ref: 25

Kirkleatham Old Hall Museum

Kirkleatham, Redcar TS10 5NW   Tel: 01642 479500

Local history collection reflecting life in Redcar and Cleveland: archaeology; social history (working and domestic life - ironstone mining; iron and steel making; fishing; shipbuilding; sea rescue); paintings; photographs. Permanent Galleries, temporary exhibitions, associated activities and events. Programme for schools and other groups. Housed in early 18th century listed building in important conservation area.

Opening Times: Apr to Sep Tue to Sun 10:00-17:00, Oct to Mar Tue to Sun 10:00-16:00. Closed Mon (except BH) and Xmas to New Year. Admission: Free. Location: Kirkleatham Village, near Redcar.   Map Ref: 26

Zetland Lifeboat Museum

The Esplanade, Redcar TS10 3AH   Tel: 01642 471813   Web: www.lifeboats.org.uk

Displays relating to Zetland Lifeboat, the oldest surviving lifeboat, and the Royal National Lifeboat Institution.

Opening Times: Daily during summer. Closed Nov to Mar. Admission: Free.   Map Ref: 26

Cragside

Rothbury NE65 7PX   Tel: 01669 620150   Fax: 01669 620066
Email: ncrvmx@smtp.ntrust.org.uk   Web: www.nationaltrust.org.uk

Built on a bare and rugged hillside above Rothbury by the 1st Lord Armstrong, Cragside was one of the most modern and surprising houses for its time in the country. In the 1880s the house had hot and cold running water, central heating, fire alarms, telephones, a Turkish bath suite and a passenger lift. There is a collection of early light fittings, sculpture, pottery and family portraits, also stained glass and wallpaper by Morris & Co. Most remarkable of all it was the first house in the world to be lit by hydroelectricity. Around and below the house is one of Europe's largest rock gardens.

The Butler's Pantry

Opening Times: House: 1 Apr to 28 Sep Tue to Sun 13:00-17:30, 30 Sep to 2 Nov Tue to Sun 13:00-16:30. Open BH Mons. Admission: Adult £8.00, Child £4.00, Family £20.00. Group (15+) £6.10. Garden & estate; Adult £4.80, Child £2.40, Family £12.00. NT Members Free. Location: Entrance one mile north of Rothbury on B6341, 15 miles north west of Morpeth, 13 miles south west of Alnwick.   Map Ref: 27

Shildon Railway Village

Soho Cottages, Shildon DL4 1PQ   Tel: 01388 772000
Email: awarren.srv@lycos.uk   Web: www.srv.org.uk

In Autumn 2004 the northwest will become home to a premier new railway museum, Shildon Railway Village. Shildon Railway Village is a partnership venture between Sedgefield Borough

Council and the National Railway Museum and will become the first branch of a national museum in the region. The popular Timothy Hackworth Museum, currently based onsite, will be revamped and incorporated into the railway village to form a single six-hectare site. As well as an enhanced Timothy Hackworth Museum, the Village will feature a 6000 sq metre single-storey collections centre capable of housing up to 60 vehicles from the National Railway Museum's collection, making it the first-ever 'out-station' for the NRM. There will be modern, interactive interpretation of the exhibits plus a workshop where apprentices will be trained in the skills needed to restore and conserve railway vehicles. An education centre, offices, retail and catering space and landscaped parkland will also feature at this first class visitor attraction.

Opening Times: From end Sep 2004. 1 Apr to 31 Oct Daily 10:00-17:00. 1 Nov to 31 Mar Wed to Sun 10:00-16:00. Admission: Free. Location: South east of Shildon town centre, 2 mins from railway station. Events 2004 : Monthly programme available on request.　　Map Ref: 28

Arbeia Roman Fort & Museum

Baring Street, South Shields NE33 2BB
Tel: 0191 456 1369　Fax: 0191 427 6862　Web: www.twmuseums.org.uk

Situated four miles east of the end of Hadrian's Wall at South Shields, Arbeia Roman Fort guarded the entrance to the River Tyne. Built about AD160 the stone fort played an essential role in the mighty frontier system. Originally built to house a garrison Arbeia soon became the military supply base for the 17 forts along the Wall. Today, the excavated remains, stunning reconstructions of original buildings and finds from the fort show what life was like in Roman Britain. Arbeia combines the excavated remains of this Roman military supply base with reconstructions of the fort's buildings and stunning finds unearthed from the site to show what life was like on Hadrian's Wall. The fort's West Gate

has been reconstructed and work is currently under way to reconstruct the Commanding Officer's house and a soldiers' barrack block. Nowhere else on Hadrian's Wall can the sheer scale of the Romans' achievements be better understood than here at Arbeia. The museum displays feature finds excavated at Arbeia, which are amongst the most impressive found along the World Heritage Site. TimeQuest gives visitors the chance to find out what it's like to be an archaeologist.

Opening Times: Easter to Sep Mon to Sat 10:00-17:30, Sun 13:00-17:00. Oct to Easter Mon to Sat 10:00-16:00, closed Sun. Admission: Free. Location: Near town centre 10-15 minutes walk from metro and bus. Exhibitions & Events 2004 : Please telephone for details or visit the website.　　Map Ref: 29

South Shields Museum & Art Gallery

Ocean Road, South Shields NE33 2TA　Tel: 0191 456 8740
Fax: 0191 456 7850　Web: www.twmuseums.org.uk

Famous for its gallery dedicated to the world famous author Catherine Cookson, which features reconstructions of her childhood home and key objects from her life, from the desk on which she penned her greatest novels to her 'Big Red Book' from 'This is your Life'. The Museum also takes a look at the history of South Tyneside and how the land, sea and river have all played a part in shaping its story over the years.

Opening Times: Easter to Sep Mon to Sat 10:00-17:30, Sun 14:00-17:00. Oct to Easter Mon to Sat 10:00-16:00, closed Sun. Admission: Free. Location: In centre of town.　　Map Ref: 29

Northumberland, Tyne & Wear, Durham

STOCKSFIELD *N'land*

Cherryburn

Station Bank, Mickley, Stocksfield NE43 7DD
Tel: 01661 843276 Web: www.nationaltrust.org.uk

The birthplace of Thomas Bewick (1753-1828), Northumberland's greatest artist, wood-engraver and naturalist. A 19th century farmhouse, the later home of the Bewick family, houses an exhibition on Bewick's life and work. Splendid views over the Tyne valley.

Opening Times: 29 Mar to 31 Oct Thu to Mon 13:00-17:30.
Admission: Adult £3.20, Child £1.60. Group (15+) Adult £2.80, Child £1.40. NT Members Free except for some events.
Location: 11 miles west of Newcastle, 11 miles east of Hexham.
Thomas Bewick's Press Room   Map Ref: 30

STOCKTON-ON-TEES *Teesside*

Green Dragon Museum

Theatre Yard, off High Street, Stockton-on-Tees TS18 1AT Tel: 01642 393938 Fax: 01642 393936

Incorporating the focus at photography gallery. The museum offers a lively mix of the best in contemporary photography and history as told through photography.

Opening Times: Mon to Sat 09:00-17:00. Closed Sun & BH. Admission: Free.
Location: Town centre off High Street.   Map Ref: 31

Preston Hall Museum

Yarm Road, Stockton-on-Tees TS18 3RH Tel: 01642 781184

The museum illistrates Victorian social history with reconstructions of period rooms and a street with working craftsmen; collection includes costume, toys, arms, armour. There are 112 acres of parkland with riverside walks.

Opening Times: Easter to Sep daily 10:00-17:30, Oct to Easter Mon to Sat 10:00-16:30, Sun 14:00-16:30. Closed Good Friday, Xmas & New Year. Admission: Adult £1.30, Child/Concession 60p. Location: Set in 112 acres of parkland, between Stockton and Yarm on A135.   Map Ref: 32

SUNDERLAND *Tyne & Wear*

Monkwearmouth Station Museum

North Bridge Street, Sunderland SR5 1AP

Tel: 0191 567 7075
Fax: 0191 510 9415
Web: www.twmuseums.org.uk

This splendid Victorian railway station recreates a sense of rail travel in times past. Explore the ticket office as it would have looked in Victorian times, see the guard's van and goods wagon in the railway sidings and watch today's trains zoom past Platform Gallery. The Children's Gallery has a range of toys, books and dressing-up clothes.

Opening Times: Mon 10:00-15:45, Tue to Sat 10:00-17:00, Sun 14:00-17:00. Admission: Free. Location: Ten minute walk from city centre.   Map Ref: 33

North East Aircraft Museum

Washington Road, Sunderland SR5 3HZ Tel: 0191 5190662
Web: www/members.tripod.com/~BDaugherty/neam.html

A collection of 35 aircraft including the Vulcan Bomber and Pucara from the Falkland Islands. Aero engines, aeronautica and a large display of models from the early days of flight to the present day.

Opening Times: Apr to Sep daily 10:00-17:00, Oct to Mar 10:00-16:00. Closed Xmas & New Year. Admission: Adult £3.00, Child/OAP £1.50. Please phone for Family and Group Concessions. Location: Brown signposted off the A19 west of Sunderland, near to the Nissan Car Assembly Plant.   Map Ref: 33

Sunderland Museum & Winter Gardens

Mowbray Gardens, Burdon Road, Sunderland SR1 1PP   Tel: 0191 553 2323
Fax: 0191 553 7828   Web: www.twmuseums.org.uk

11 exciting hands-on exhibits and interactive displays tell the story of Sunderland from its prehistoric past through to the present day. The Art Gallery features paintings by L S Lowry alongside Victorian masterpieces and artefacts from the four corners of the world. The displays look at traditional industries including shipbuilding coal mining, pottery, glass and textile crafts through to the prehistoric, medieval and 20th century history of the City. The natural world is also explored through stunning wildlife displays and live animals. The newly

refurbished museum features a striking new glazed entrance; visitor facilities such as a large shop, a brasserie, toilets and lifts to all floors form a significant part of the scheme. The stunning new Winter Gardens is home to over 1,000 of the world's most exotic flowers, plants and trees. Some of the amazing plants include an 80 year old Sicilian olive tree, a 3.5 metre-high Palm tree and a 6.5 metre-high Yucca elaphanties from Honduras, the world's largest type of Yucca. The Gardens also feature sculptures, a waterfall, Koi carp and a stunning treetop walkway, from which visitors can look on to the displays.

Opening Times: Mon to Sat 10:00-17:00, Sun 14:00-17:00.   Admission: Free.   Location: In town centre.   Exhibitions & Events 2004 : Please telephone for details or visit the website.

Map Ref: 33

Segedunum Roman Fort, Baths & Museum

Buddle Street, Wallsend NE28 8HR   Tel: 0191 236 9347   Fax: 0191 295 5858   Web: www.twmuseums.org.uk

In AD122 the Emperor Hadrian ordered a mighty frontier system to be built across Britain to defend the Roman Empire from the barbarians to the north. Segedunum Roman Fort stood on the banks of the River Tyne and was the last outpost of Hadrian's Wall. Today, Segedunum is once again the gateway to this world-famous heritage site. The excavated remains of the fort with spectacular reconstructions and exciting, hands-on museum displays show what life was like in Roman Britain. The remains

represent the most extensively excavated site in the Empire and the reconstructed bath-house is the only one of its kind in Britain. No other site on Hadrian's Wall can match the views from the 100 feet-high tower. The museum features finds excavated from the fort with the latest technology to show what life was like for the soldiers who lived at the fort. The history of the fort and Wallsend after the decline of the Roman Empire is also explored.

Opening Times: 1 Apr to 31 Oct daily 10:00-17:00. 1 Nov to 31 May daily 10:00-15:30.   Admission: Adult £3.50, Child/Concession £2.95.   Location: One minute walk from Wallsend Metro.
Exhibitions & Events 2004 : Please telephone for details or visit the website.

Map Ref: 34

Guided or Private Tours	Disabled Access	Gift Shop or Sales Point	Café or Refreshments	Restaurant	Car Parking

Northumberland, Tyne & Wear, Durham

Washington Old Hall

The Avenue, District 4, Washington NE38 7LE
Tel: 0191 416 6879   Fax: 0191 419 2065   Web: www.nationaltrust.org.uk

A delightful stone built 17th century manor house, which incorporates parts of the original medieval home of George Washington's direct ancestors. There are displays on George Washington, and the recent history of the Hall. There is also a fine collection of oil paintings, delftware and heavily carved oak furniture.

Opening Times: 1 Apr to 31 Oct Sun to Wed 11:00-17:00. Open Good Friday.
Admission: Adult £3.50, Child £2.00, Family £9.00. Group (10+) Adult £3.00, Child £1.50. NT Members Free.   Location: Seven miles south of Newcastle, five miles from The Angel of the North. In Washington Village next to church on the hill.   Map Ref: 35

Chillingham Castle

Near Wooler NE66 5NJ   Tel: 01668 215359   Fax: 01668 215463
Email: enquiries@chillingham-castle.com   Web: www.chillingham-castle.com

Chillingham Castle has been owned by Earls Grey and relations since the twelve-hundreds. You will see active restoration of complex masonry, metalwork and ornamental plaster as the great halls and state rooms are gradually brought back to life with antique furniture, tapesteries, arms and armour.

Opening Times: 1 May to 30 Sep Grounds & Garden 12:00-17:00. Castle 13:00-17:00 last admission 16:30. Groups (by appointment) all year.   Admission: Adult £6.00, OAP £5.50, Child £2.50, Under 5 70p.   Map Ref: 36

Wylam Railway Museum

The Falcon Centre, Falcon Terrace, Wylam NE41 8EE   Tel: 01661 852174/853520
Email: wylampc@btinternet.com

George Stephenson 'The Father of Railways' was born in Wylam and historic locomotive 'Puffing Billy' worked on Wylam Colliery waggonway. Displays in this attractive small museum illustrate Wylam's unique place in railway history.

Opening Times: Tue & Thu 14:00-17:00 & 17:30-19:30, Sat 09:00-12:00.   Admission: Free.
Donations welcome.   Location: The Falcon Centre, off Main Street at Fox & Hounds Inn.
Map Ref: 37

The county is not renowned for its large cities and towns with Oxford, the county town, being the largest. However, the city is an important commercial, residential and industrial centre dominated by its university, the colleges of which, both ancient and modern, have their own particular character and treasures.

Oxford boasts museums and galleries of international fame and there are interesting collections to be found in Banbury, Henley and Woodstock.

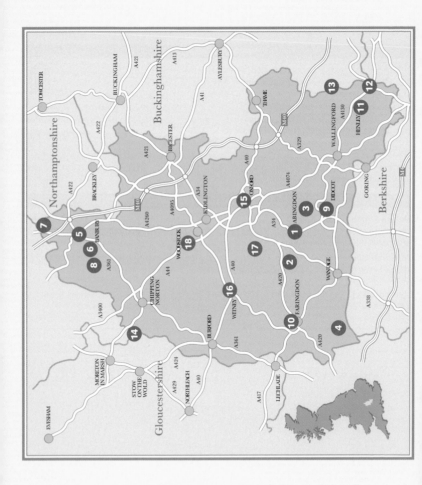

The Red Map References should be used to locate Museums etc on the pages that follow

Oxfordshire

Abingdon Museum
County Hall, Market Place, Abingdon OX14 3HG   Tel: 01235 523703   Fax: 01235 536814

The County Hall was built between 1678-1682 by Christopher Kempster, master mason who worked with Christopher Wren on St Paul's Cathedral. The museum contains local history from 'England's oldest town'.

Opening Times: Daily 10:30-16:00. Please telephone to check BH. Roof top closed during winter.   Admission: Free. (Roof top: Adult £1.00, Child (over 6) 50p).   Location: In town centre.
Map Ref: 1

Kingston Bagpuize House
Kingston Bagpuize, Abingdon OX13 5AX   Tel: 01865 820259   Fax: 01865 821659
Email: kingstonbagpuizehouse

A beautiful 1660s manor house remodelled in the early 1770s in red brick with stone facings. Canterlevered staircase and finely proportioned panelled rooms. Set in mature parkland and gardens containing a collection of plants, rare trees and shrubs.

Opening Times: Feb to Oct 14:30-16:30. Please phone for details of open days.
Admission: Adult £4.00, OAP £3.50, Child £2.50.   Location: Off A415, south of A415/A420 intersection.
Map Ref: 2

Pendon Museum
Long Wittenham, Abingdon OX14 4QD   Tel: 01865 407365   Web: www.pendonmuseum.com

Rural life in the Vale of the White Horse in the 1930s, recreated in miniature, together with the railways that ran through the Vale.

Opening Times: Sat & Sun 14:00-17:00, also Wed during Jul & Aug. Open from 11:00 on all Bank Holiday weekends except Xmas.   Admission: Adult £4.00, Child £2.00, Under 7s Free, OAP £3.50, Family £12.00.
Map Ref: 3

Ashdown House
Lambourn RG16 7RE   Tel: 01488 72584   Web: www.nationaltrust.org.uk

An extraordinary Dutch-style 17th century house, perched on the Berkshire Downs. The interior has an impressive great staircase rising from hall to attic. There is an important group of paintings contemporary with the house.

Opening Times: House & Garden: 31 Mar to 30 Oct 14:00-17:00 Wed & Sat. Woodland: All year, daylight, Sat to Thu.   Admission: Adult £2.20. NT Members Free. Admission by guided tour.
Location: Two and a half miles south of Ashbury, three and a half miles north of Lambourn, on west side of B4000.
Map Ref: 4

Banbury Museum
Spiceball Park Road, Banbury OX16 2PQ   Tel: 01295 259855   Fax: 01295 269469
Web: www.cherwell-dc.gov.uk/banburymuseum

Banbury's new canal-side museum is open. The stunning new displays illustrate Banbury's history, beginning with some of the stories and events that have made Banbury famous, such as the nursery rhyme 'ride a cock horse to Banbury Cross'. The principal displays tell four stories: the English Civil War and how it affected Banbury; the development of the plush weaving industry (plush is a velvet like fabric); the Victorian Town;

and Banbury in the 20th century. Also on display is a rare collection of costume dating from the 17th century. A separate gallery interprets the Tooley's Boatyard and the Oxford Canal. Tooley's Boatyard is a scheduled ancient monument that is attached to the museum and can be visited on a guided tour. Excellent visitor facilities are

Oxfordshire

available including a canal-side café.

Opening Times: Mon to Sat 09:30-17:00, Sun 10:30-16:00. Admission: Free. Location: Town centre, main entrance Castle Quay Shopping Centre. Exhibitions & Events 2004 : The Museum has a lively programme. For furthur information visit our website. Map Ref: 5

Broughton Castle

Banbury OX15 5EB   Tel / Fax: 01295 276070
Email: admin@broughtoncastle.demon.co.uk
Web: www.broughtoncastle.demon.co.uk

Historic 14th century and 16th century moated manor house owned by Lords Saye and Sele for over 600 years. Fine panelling and plasterwork. Civil war connections and memorabilia. Lovely walled gardens.

Opening Times: 1 May to 15 Sep Wed & Sun 14:00-17:00. Also Thu in Jul & Aug and all BH Sun & Mon. Admission: Adult £5.50, OAP £4.50, Child £2.50. Location: Two and a half miles SW of Banbury on B4035. Map Ref: 6

Bygones Museum

Butlin Farm, Claydon, Banbury OX17 1EP   Tel: 01295 690258
Email: bygonesmuseum@yahoo.com

Local Banbury shops, display centre. Victorian kitchen and work shops. Traction engine, steam roller, stationary engines, tractors etc. War and craft memorabilia, typewriters, sewing machines, jars, bottles and lots more.

Opening Times: Apr to Oct Wed to Sun 10:30-16:30. Closed Mon & Tue. Admission: Adult £2.50, Child £1.75, OAP £2.00, Family £7.50. Location: In the centre of a small village, six miles north of Banbury. Map Ref: 7

Swalcliffe Barn

Shipston Road, Swalcliffe, Banbury
Tel: 01295 788278
Email: jcdemmar@btinternet.com
Web: www.oxfordshire.gov.uk

A magnificent 15th century barn with an original half-cruck timber roof structure. It was built in 1401 for the Rectorial Manor of Swalcliffe by New College, Oxford. The barn houses a collection of trade vehicles and agricultural machinery from Oxfordshire used in the 19th & 20th centuries.

Opening Times: Easter to Oct Sun 14:00-17:00 or by appointment. Admission: Free. Location: In village centre. Map Ref: 8

Bread delivery hand cart, Headington, Oxford

Didcot Railway Centre

Didcot OX11 7NJ   Tel: 01235 817200   Fax: 01235 510621   Email: didrlyc@globalnet.co.uk
Web: didcotrailwaycentre.org.uk

See the steam trains of the Great Western Railway, the original engine shed and a recreation of Brunel's broad gauge railway. Programme of Steamdays and special events including 'Day out with Thomas' during the year.

Opening Times: 25 May to 5 Sep daily 10:00-17:00, rest of the year Sat & Sun 10:00-16:00. Admission: Adult £4.00-£8.00, Child £3.00-£5.00, OAP £3.50-£6.50, Family £12.00-£22.00. Location: At Didcot Parkway rail station, signed from M4 junction 13 and A34. Map Ref: 9

---

www.mghh.co.uk

For current information on the outstanding Collections in over 1600 Museums, Galleries & Historic Houses in England, Scotland, Wales and Ireland

Oxfordshire

The Hall, with 'Egyptian' furniture, by Thomas Hope

Buscot Park

Estate Office, Faringdon SN7 8BU
Tel: 01367 240786, 0845 345 3387 (Infoline)
Fax: 01367 241794 Email: estbuscot@aol.com
Web: www.buscot-park.com

The 18th century house houses the Faringdon Collection of fine paintings, including works by Rembrandt, Murillo, Reynolds, Rossetti and the famous Briar Rose series by Burne-Jones. Also furniture with important pieces by Adam, Thomas Hope and others, together with porcelain and objets d'art. It is set in attractive parkland with lakes, a water garden by Peto and a walled garden. A tea room serves home-made cream teas and cakes from 14:30-17:30.

Opening Times: 1 Apr to 30 Sep Wed to Fri 14:00-18:00 (last entry 17:30). Open BH Mons. Admission: Adult £6.50, Child £3.25. NT Members Free. Location: On A417 between Faringdon & Lechlade. Map Ref: 10

Greys Court

Rotherfield Greys, Henley-on-Thames RG9 4PG
Tel: 01491 628529 Fax: 01491 628935
Email: greyscourt@nationaltrust.org.uk Web: www.nationaltrust.org.uk

A picturesque 14th century house that was much added to, with one surviving tower dating from 1347. There is some fine 18th century plasterwork and early English furniture, in mahogany, walnut and oak. A plain pine staircase with a window at the top contains panels of Swiss stained glass. There are beautiful walled gardens full of old-fashioned roses.

Opening Times: House: 7 Apr to 24 Sep Wed to Fri 14:00-17:00. Open BH Mons. Closed Good Friday. Open 1st Sat of the month 7 Apr to 24 Sep. Admission: Adult £5.00, Child £2.50, Family £12.50. Garden only: Adult £3.50, Child £1.70,Family £8.70. NT Members Free.
Location: West of Henley-on-Thames. Map Ref: 11

River & Rowing Museum

Mill Meadows, Henley-on-Thames RG9 1BF Tel: 01491 415600
Fax: 01491 415601 Email: museum@rrm.co.uk Web: www.rrm.co.uk

The Rowing Gallery

Visit the award winning River & Rowing Museum with its stunning architecture and unique interpretation of the River Thames from its source to sea, the riverside town of Henley-on-Thames with its famous Royal Regatta and the sport of Rowing from the days of the Ancient Greek Trireme to the recent success of the Sydney Coxless Four. History is brought to life with interactive displays and fascinating exhibits for all the family. Special exhibitions, family activities and events are held throughout the year and its Riverside Café offers excellent food in distinctive surroundings.

Henley Gallery

Opening Times: Sep to Apr daily 10:00-17:00, May to Aug daily 10:00-17:30. Closed 24-25 Dec & 31 Dec-1 Jan. Admission: Adult £4.95, Concession £3.75, Family £13.95. Location: Off A4130, signposted to Mill Meadows. A short walk from Henley Town Centre, five minutes from Henley on Thames Railway Station. Map Ref: 12

Stonor Park

Henley-on-Thames RG9 6HF Tel: 01491 638587 Fax: 01491 639348
Email: jweaver@stonor.com Web: www.stonor.com

Historic family home of the Stonor Family, set it a wooded deer park in the Chiltern Hills. The house contains rare furnishings, paintings, bronzes, silhouettes and sculptures. Peaceful hillside gardens overlook the house and parkland.

Oxfordshire

Opening Times: 1 Apr to 30 Sep Sun, BH Mon. Jul, Aug & Sep also Wed. 14:00-17:30.
Admission: Adult £6.00, Child (Under 14) Free. Location: Five miles North of Henley-on-Thames on B480.   Map Ref: 13

MORETON-IN-MARSH

Chastleton House

Chastleton, Moreton-in-Marsh GL56 0SU Tel: 01608 674355, 01494 755585
(Advance Bookings) Fax: 01608 674355 Email: chastleton@nationaltrust.org.uk
Web: www.nationaltrust.org.uk/regions/thameschilterns

One of England's finest and most complete Jacobean houses. It is filled with a mixture of rare and everyday objects. There are furniture and textiles collected since its completion in 1612, by the continuous occupation of one family. The gardens have a typical Elizabethan and Jacobean layout with a ring of fascinating topiary at their heart.

Opening Times: 31 Mar to 2 Oct Wed to Sat 13:00-17:00, 6 Oct to 30 Oct Wed to Sat 13:00-16:00.

The Fettiplace Room showing the tapestries and carved bed

Admission: Adult £5.80, Child £2.90, Family £14.50. NT Members Free. Location: Six miles from Stow-on-the-Wold. Approach only from A436 between A44 (west of Chipping Norton) and Stow-on-the-Wold.   Map Ref: 14

OXFORD

Ashmolean Museum of Art & Archaeology

Beaumont Street, Oxford OX1 2PH Tel: 01865 278000
Fax: 01865 278018 Web: www.ashmol.ox.ac.uk

The Ashmolean houses the Oxford University's collections of art and antiquities. They range over four millennia - from Ancient Egypt, Greece and Rome to Renaissance Europe and the 20th century, plus an extensive Far Eastern collection. Sculpture, paintings, ceramics, glass, coins and musical instruments are all on show.

Opening Times: Tue to Sat 10:00-17:00, Sun 14:00-17:00. Admission: Free. Location: Town centre, five minutes walk from bus station, ten minutes walk from Railway Station. Exhibitions & Events 2004 : 11 Feb to 23 May:

Uccello, The Hunt in the Forest

Paul Drury and the Pastoral Landscape, 10 Mar to 9 May:
Chinese Silk, 16 Jun to 19 Sep: A Treasured Inheritance: 600 years of College Silver. Map Ref: 15

Bate Collection of Musical Instruments

Faculty of Music, St Aldate's, Oxford OX1 1DB Tel: 01865 276139 Fax: 01865 276128
Email: bate.collection@music.ox.ac.uk Web: www.ashmol.ox.ac.uk/bcmipage.html

A collection of over a thousand historic woodwind, brass and percussion instruments, a dozen historic keyboards including what may have been Handel's harpsichord; a unique bow-maker's workshop and fine collection of bows.

Opening Times: Mon to Fri 14:00-17:00, Sat 10:00-12:00. (During Oxford full term only)
Admission: Free. Location: Near town centre, next to Christ Church College.   Map Ref: 15

Christ Church Picture Gallery

Christ Church, Oxford OX1 1DP Tel: 01865 276172 Fax: 01865 202429
Email: picturegallery@chch.ox.ac.uk Web: www.chch.ox.ac.uk

Christ Church Picture Gallery was designed in 1968 by Powell and Moya and holds 300 paintings and 2000 drawings by famous artists such as Van Dyck, Leonardo and Michelangelo.

Opening Times: Oct to Mar Mon to Sat 10:30-13:00 & 14:00-16:30, Sun 14:00-16:30. Easter to Sep daily 10:30-17:30. Admission: Adult £2.00, OAP/Student/Concession £1.00. Free on Mon.
Location: Near the town centre.   Map Ref: 15

Oxfordshire

Modern Art Oxford

30 Pembroke Street, Oxford OX1 1BP   Tel: 01865 722733   Fax: 01865 722573
Web: www.modernartoxford.org.uk

Located in the heart of historic Oxford, the Modern Art Oxford presents outstanding exhibitions of modern and contemporary art from all over the world. Exhibitions include painting, sculpture, photography, video, film and architecture. It's a great place to add to your 'must see' list in Oxford. The Café serves delicious, freshly cooked food and is child and baby friendly.

Opening Times: Tue to Sat 10:00-17:00, Sun 12:00-17:00, Closed Mon. Late openings on event nights.
Admission: Free.   Location: City centre, ten minutes walk from railway station, five minutes from High Street.   Map Ref: 15

Museum of Oxford

St Aldates, Oxford OX1 1DZ   Tel: 01865 252761   Fax: 01865 202447
Email: museum@oxford.gov.uk   Web: www.oxford.gov.uk/museum

Discover Oxford's history by visiting the Museum of Oxford, the only museum in Oxford to tell the story of the city and its people from

A Victorian Kitchen c.1880

prehistoric times to the present day. The exhibits range from a mammoth's tooth to a 'Morris Motor' car engine.   Archaeological treasures including a preserved Roman pottery kiln and a whole pavement made of cattle bones. There are six Oxford rooms recreated inside the museum from an Elizabethan inn to a Victorian kitchen. A full programme of workshops and activities for schools and families is available - term time, school holiday and weekends.

Hythe Bridge/Oxford Castle
by Michael Angelo Rooker c.1790

Opening Times: Tue to Fri 10:00-16:00, Sat 10:00-17:00, Sun 12:00-16:00.   Admission: Adult £2.00, Child 50p, Concession £1.50.   Location: Centre of town, five minute walk from bus station, ten minutes walk from train station.   Map Ref: 15

Museum of the History of Science

Broad Street, Oxford OX1 3AZ   Tel: 01865 277280
Fax: 01865 277288   Email: museum@mhs.ox.ac.uk
Web: www.mhs.ox.ac.uk

Outstanding collection of early scientific instruments, astrolabes, sundials, telescopes, microscopes, etc. Displayed in Britain's first museum building includes globes, navigation, physics, chemistry and some of the earliest surviving instruments from a range of countries and cultures.

Opening Times: Tue to Sat 12:00-16:00, Sun 14:00-17:00. Closed Xmas. Admission: Free.   Location: Broad Street, next to Sheldonian Theatre.   Map Ref: 15

Islamic Astrolabe

OXFORD (continued)

Oxford University Museum of Natural History

 ♿ ◈

Parks Road, Oxford OX1 3PW

Tel: 01865 272950
Fax: 01865 272970
Email: info@oum.ox.ac.uk
Web: www.oum.ox.ac.uk

The Oxford University Museum of Natural History houses Oxford University's extensive collection of entomological, geological, mineralogical and zoological material of international importance. Current displays include the remains of Alice's Dodo Bird and a splendid display of Dinosaurs.

Opening Times: Daily 12:00-17:00. Closed Xmas and Easter.
Admission: Free. Location: Central Oxford on Parks Road immediately opposite Keble College. Map Ref: 15

T-rex in Victorian Court

Pitt Rivers Museum

♿ ◈  PittRivers MUSEUM

Parks Road, Oxford OX1 3PP Tel: 01865 270927 Fax: 01865 270943
Web: www.prm.ox.ac.uk

This unique museum is one of Oxford's most popular attractions, famous for its period atmosphere and outstanding collections. Founded in 1884, the displays still retain much of the original layout and appearance; cases are crowded with amulets, beads, pots, masks, shrunken heads, textiles, toys and more, from many cultures around the world past and present. Many objects still carry their first tiny hand-printed label.

Opening Times: Mon to Sat 12:00-16:30, Sun 14:00-16:30. Admission: Free. Location: Ten minutes walk

The Pitt Rivers Museum from the Upper Gallery

from city centre. Entrance through Oxford University Museum of Natural History. Map Ref: 15

WITNEY

Bishop's Palace Site

♿ 🚜

Mount House, Church Green, Witney Tel: 01993 814114 Fax: 01993 813239
Email: martyn.brown@oxfordshire.gov.uk Web: www.oxfordshire.gov.uk

The archaelogical site of the Bishop of Winchester's Palace at Witney.

Opening Times: Easter to Sep Sat & Sun 14:00-16:00. Admission: Free. Location: East of the church on the Green. Map Ref: 16

Oxfordshire Museums Store

✍ ♿ 🚜

Witney Road, Standlake, Witney OX28 7QG Tel: 01865 300972 Fax: 01865
300519 Email: martyn.brown@oxfordshire.gov.uk Web: www.oxfordshire.gov.uk

Purpose built store and collections centre for conservation and museum support services. Contains natural science, archaeology, social history, transport, agricultural, crafts, textiles, arts - all relating to Oxfordshire.

Opening Times: Mon to Fri 9:00-17:00 by appointment. Public open days in May & Sep.
Admission: Free. Location: A415 four miles south of Witney. Map Ref: 17

Guided or Private Tours	Disabled Access	Gift Shop or Sales Point	Café or Refreshments	Restaurant	Car Parking

Oxfordshire

Blenheim Palace
Woodstock OX20 1PX

Tel: 08700 602080
Fax: 01993 810570
Email: administrator@blenheimpalace.com
Web: www.blenheimpalace.com

Blenheim Palace, home of the 11th Duke of Marlborough and birthplace of Sir Winston Churchill, is an English Baroque masterpiece, with a collection including tapestries, paintings, sculptures and fine furniture displayed in magnificent gilded state rooms. It is a World Heritage site, reflecting the importance of both the house and the 2,100 acre park, landscaped by 'Capability' Brown.

Opening Times: Mid Feb to end Oct daily 10:30-16:45, 1 Nov to mid Dec Wed to Sun 10:30-16:45. Admission: Off-peak: Adult £11.00, Child £5.50, OAP/Student £8.50. Peak: Adult £12.50, Child £7.00, OAP/Student £10.00. Location: A44, eight miles from

Blenheim Palace, South Front

Oxford (M40 J9). Exhibitions & Events 2004 : 1704-2004 Battle of Blenheim Tercentenary Year, May Day: Battle re-enactments, Whitsun to Sep: Battle of Blenheim Exhibition, 10 to 13 Jun: Blenheim Palace Flower Show, 1 to 3 Jul: Blenheim Music Festival, 11 Jul: Fly to the Past, 9 to 12 Sep: Blenheim Petplan International Horse Trials, Nov: Living Crafts at Christmas. Map Ref: 18

Oxfordshire Museum
Fletchers House, Park Street, Woodstock OX20 1SN

Tel: 01993 811456 Fax: 01993 813239 Email: oxonmuseum@oxfordshire.gov.uk
Web: www.oxfordshire.gov.uk

The museum provides a window on Oxfordshire's rich history. The new displays celebrate Oxfordshire in all its diversity. Collections reflect the archaeology, local history, landscape and wildlife of the county as well as providing an introduction to the astonishing range of ideas and technologies developed in Oxfordshire. Gallery interactives provide hands-on enjoyment for children and new computer programmes enable visitors to explore a variey of information about the objects on display.

Opening Times: Tue to Sat 10:00-17:00, Sun 14:00-17:00. Last admission 16:30. Admission: Free. Location: In town centre, adjacent gates to Blenheim Palace.

The Ark - one of the new galleries
at the Oxfordshire Museum

Exhibitions & Events 2004 : 10 Jan to 14 Mar: Slices of Life: the history of food, 23 Mar to 3 May: Crossing Boundaries: John Piper Centenary exhibition, 15 Jun to 10 Jul: British Society of Enamellers. Map Ref: 18

Shropshire

Shrewsbury, the county town, almost encircled by the River Severn, was from Norman times strategically important as the gateway to Wales. In the eighteenth century it became a popular centre of fashionable society and boasts a wealth of fine Georgian buildings. Despite being primarily a rural agricultural county, it was here in the eighteenth century that the Industrial Revolution was born, in the Ironbridge Gorge of the Severn.

Shropshire can be justifiably proud of its first class museums concerned with the archaeology, natural history, social and industrial history of the region.

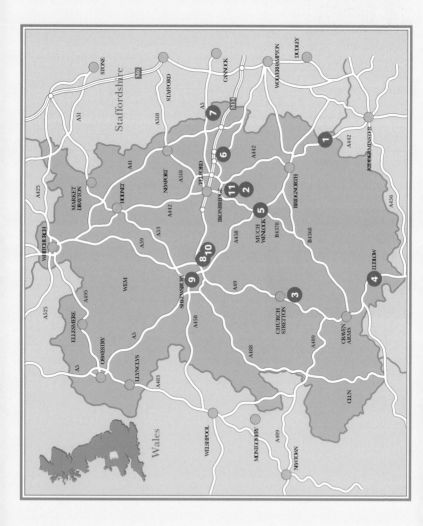

The Red Map References should be used to locate Museums etc on the pages that follow

Shropshire

Dudmaston

Quatt, Bridgnorth WV15 6QN   Tel: 01746 780866   Fax: 01746 780744
Email: dudmaston@nationaltrust.org.uk   Web: www.nationaltrust.org.uk

A late 17th century house with intimate family rooms containing fine furniture. Dutch oil paintings, as well as interesting contemporary paintings and sculpture. The gardens are a mass of colour in spring and include a walk in the Dingle, a wooded valley.

Opening Times: 4 Apr to 29 Sep Sun, Tue, & Wed 14:00-17:30. Open BH Mons.   Admission: Adult £4.50, Child £2.20, Family £10.50. Group (15+) £3.50. Garden only: Adult £3.20, Child £1.40, Family £7.50. NT Members Free.
Location: Four miles south east of Bridgnorth on A442.

Dutch 17th century portrait of two girls holding hands

Map Ref: 1

Benthall Hall

Broseley TF12 5RX   Tel: 01952 882159   Email: benthall@nationaltrust.org.uk
Web: www.nationaltrust.org.uk

This small stone manor house was built in the 16th century. The stunning interior has a carved oak staircase, decorated plaster ceilings and oak panelling. There is a small garden which has been carefully restored.

Opening Times: 6 Apr to 30 Jun Tue & Wed 14:00-17:30, 4 Jul to 26 Sep Sun, Tue & Wed 14:00-17:30. Open BH Suns & Mons.   Admission: Adult £4.00, Child £2.00. Garden only: Adult £2.50 Child £1.25. NT Members Free.   Location: One mile north west of Broseley (B4375), four miles north east of Much Wenlock, one mile south west of Ironbridge.   Map Ref: 2

Acton Scott Historic Working Farm Museum

Wenlock Lodge, Acton Scott, Church Stretton SY6 6QN   Tel: 01694 781306/7   Fax: 01694 781569   Email: acton.scott.museum@shropshire-cc.gov.uk
Web: www.actonscottmuseum.co.uk

Acton Scott Historic Working Farm demonstrates farming and rural life in South Shropshire at the close of the 19th century. This is achieved not only by collecting, renovating and exhibiting implements and other agricultural items, but also by farming as it would have been farmed in the period from about 1875 to the 1920s.

Opening Times: 26 Mar to 27 Oct Tue to Sun & BH 10:00-17:00. Closed Mon except BH.
Admission: Adult £3.95, Child £1.50, Under 5s Free, OAP £3.50. Groups: Adult £3.00, Child £1.25, Under 5s Free, OAP £2.50.   Location: Four miles south of Church Stretton off A49, 17 miles south of Shrewsbury of A49, 14 miles north of Ludlow off A49 at Marshbrook.   Map Ref: 3

Ludlow Museum

11/13 Castle Street, Ludlow SY8 1AS   Tel: 01584 875384   Email: ludlow.museum@shropshire-cc.gov.uk   Web: www.shropshiremuseums.co.uk

Make a visit to Ludlow Museum and unlock the natural and social history of this fascinating planned town and the surrounding region.

Opening Times: Apr to Oct Mon to Sat 10:30-13:00 14:00-17:00. Jun, Jul & Aug also open Sun.
Admission: Free.   Location: In town centre.   Map Ref: 4

Much Wenlock Museum

High Street, Much Wenlock TF13 6HR   Tel: 01952 727773
Email: much.wenlock.museum@shropshire-cc.gov.uk   Web: www.shropshiremuseums.co.uk

Displays of archaeology, natural history, social history, Wenlock Olympian Society, Wenlock Edge Geology.

Opening Times: Apr to Sep Mon to Sat 10:30-13:00 & 14:00-17:00. Jun, Jul & Aug also open Sun.   Admission: Free.   Location: In the centre of town.   Map Ref: 5

Shropshire

Royal Air Force Museum Cosford

Cosford, Shifnal TF11 8UP   Tel: 01902 376200   Fax: 01902 376211
Email: cosford@rafmuseum.org   Web: www.rafmuseum.org

Soar through an outstanding collection of aircraft and associated memorabilia. The Royal Air Force Museum Cosford includes both indoor and outdoor exhibits of commercial aircraft, warplanes, research and development aircraft, military transport, aero engines, rockets and missiles. The museum also features an art gallery, hands-on interactives, special exhibitions and 1940's room. New to Cosford is the exciting Black Hawk simulator, which lets visitors take a flight with the Red Arrows. Free admission means free fun for all the family at this award winning museum.

Opening Times: Daily 10:00-18:00 (last entry 16:00). Closed 24 to 26 Dec & 1 Jan.
Admission: Free admission. Location: On A41, less than one mile from junction 3 on M54.
From the South, leave M6 at Junction 10a. From the North leave M6 at Junction 12 & follow A5
West. By train, Cosford Halt is on the Wolverhampton to Shrewsbury line. Exhibitions & Events
2004 : 13 June: RAF Cosford Air Show. Call 0870 606 2014 for Air Show info, 10 & 11 Jul:
International large model Aircraft Rally.   Map Ref: 6

Weston Park

Weston-under-Lizard, Shifnal TF11 8LE   Tel: 01952 852100   Fax: 01952 850430
Email: enquiries@weston-park.com   Web: www.weston-park.com

Weston Park is a magnificent Stately Home set in 1000 acres of Parkland. Built in 1671 the house boasts a superb collection of paintings including works by Van Dyck, Constable and Stubbs, furniture and objets d'art. Outside, visitors can explore the glorious parkland, meander through the formal gardens, take a variety of woodland walks before relaxing for lunch in The Stables Restaurant.

Opening Times: Easter, Apr, May, Jun & Sep weekends,
Jul & Aug daily. Admission: Adult £5.50, Child £3.50,
OAP £4.50. Location: Situated on A5 at Weston-under-
Lizard, three miles off junction 3 on M54 and eight miles off junction 12 on M6.   Map Ref: 7

Attingham Park

Shrewsbury SY4 4TP   Tel: 01743 708162/708123
Fax: 01743 708175
Email: attingham@nationaltrust.org.uk
Web: www.nationaltrust.org.uk

This elegant mansion built in 1785 for the 1st Lord Bewick, is one of the great houses of the Midlands. The magnificent Regency interiors

contain collections of
ambassadorial silver and
Italian furniture. There is a
purpose built John Nash
gallery which houses the
Grand Tour collection of
paintings. The landscaped
park has attractive walks
along the River Tern.

Dining room at Attingham Park,
(1783-5)

Hereford Bull, signed W H Davis, dated 1853

Opening Times: 19 Mar to 31 Oct Fri to Tue 12:00-17:00.
Open BH Mons 11:00-17:00. Closed 25 Dec.
Admission: Adult £5.50, Child £2.70, Family £13.50.
Group: (15+) £4.50. NT Members Free. Location: Four
miles south east of Shrewsbury, on north side of B4380 in Atcham village.

Map Ref: 8

Shropshire

Shrewsbury Museum & Art Gallery

Rowley's House, Barker Street, Shrewsbury SY1 1QH   Tel: 01743 361196   Fax: 01743 358411
Email: museums@shrewsbury-atcham.gov.uk   Web: www.shrewsburymuseums.com

Major regional museum; archaeology, geology, Shropshire ceramics, costume and social history, special exhibition programme linking historic collections and contemporary artists, including national and international names.

Opening Times: May BH to end of Sep Tue to Sat 10:00-17:00, Sun & Mon 10:00-16:00. Oct to May Tue to Sat 10:00-16:00.   Admission: Free.   Location: Town centre, five minutes from bus and railway stations.   Map Ref: 9

Wroxeter Roman City

Wroxeter Roman Site, Wroxeter, Shrewsbury SY5 6PH   Tel: 01743 761330

Wroxeter was once the fourth largest city in Roman Britain, with an impressive bath house, the remains of which are still visible today. The museum includes a column capital carved in the shape of a hare.

Opening Times: Apr to Sep daily 10:00-18:00, Oct daily 10:00-17:00, Nov to Mar daily 10:00-13:00 & 14:00-16:00. Closed Xmas & New Year. Times & prices may change.   Admission: Adult £3.70, Child £1.90, Concession £2.80, Family £9.00. EH Members Free.   Location: At Wroxeter, five miles east of Shrewsbury on B4380.   Map Ref: 10

Blists Hill Victorian Town

Telford   Tel: 01952 586063/583003
Email: info@ironbridge.org.uk   Web: www.ironbridge.org.uk

Working factories, shops and cottages in a beautiful wooded landscape where life is lived - and demonstrated - as it was in Victorian times. Victorian industry, crafts and traditions are brought to life by the townsfolk who illustrate Britain's fascinating industrial history and social life in the streets and buildings of the town.

Opening Times: Apr to Nov daily 10:00-17:00, Nov to Mar 10:00-16:00.   Admission: Please call for details. Group rates available.
Location: Situated five miles from Telford Central.   Map Ref: 11

Broseley Pipe Works

Duke Street, Broseley, Telford   Tel: 01952 882445
Email: info@ironbridge.org.uk   Web: www.ironbridge.org.uk

Once home to one of the most prolific clay tobacco pipe factories in Britain. Production ceased in the 1950s when the works were abandoned and left untouched until reopened as a museum in 1996. During its restoration little has been changed since the workers left, a wonderfully preserved 'time capsule' of an ancient local industry.

Opening Times: Apr to Nov daily 13:00-17:00. Closed Nov to Mar.   Admission: Please call for details. Group rates available.   Location: Five miles from Telford Central.   Map Ref: 11

Coalport China Museum

Coalport, Telford   Tel: 01952 580650   Email: info@ironbridge.org.uk
Web: www.ironbridge.org.uk

The national collections of Caughley and Coalport china are displayed in the restored factory buildings and bottle kilns of the old Coalport China Works. Galleries show the beautiful china and explore the hardships of factory life. Enjoy the children's gallery, workshops and speciality shop.

Opening Times: Daily 10:00-17:00. Closed Xmas.   Admission: Please call for details. Group rates available.   Location: Five miles from Telford Central.   Map Ref: 11

Darby Houses & Quaker Burial Ground

Darby Road, Coalbrookdale, Telford   Email: info@ironbridge.org.uk
Web: www.ironbridge.org.uk

Rosehill and Dale House are restored Quaker Ironmasters' homes, built overlooking the Darby

Shropshire

Furnace in Coalbrookdale. Rosehill is fully restored as it would have been when the Darby family lived there, housing personal belongings of the family.

Opening Times: Apr to Nov daily 10:00-17:00. Closed Nov to Mar. Admission: Please call for details. Group rates available. Location: Five miles from Telford Central. Map Ref: 11

Iron Bridge & Tollhouse

Ironbridge, Telford Tel: 01952 884391 Email: tic@ironbridge.org.uk
Web: www.ironbridge.org.uk

The great symbol of success for the iron industry is the Iron Bridge, located in the heart of the designated world heritage site. The Toll House houses an exhibition about the Bridge and its fascinating history.

Opening Times: Iron Bridge: open year round. Toll House: Daily 10:00-17:00. Admission: Please call for details. Location: Located in Ironbridge Town Centre - five miles from Telford Central. Map Ref: 11

Jackfield Tile Museum
Jackfield, Telford Tel: 01952 882030 Email: info@ironbridge.org.uk
Web: www.ironbridge.org.uk

Jackfield boasts magnificent displays of decorative tiles and ceramics throughout its gas-lit galleries within the restored Victorian factory buildings. Witness modern tile making combining drop-in workshops to make this a fascinating visit.

Opening Times: Closed for refurbishment until Spring 2004. Admission: Please call for details. Group rates available. Location: Five miles from Telford Central. Map Ref: 11

Museum of Iron & Darby Furnace
Coalbrookdale, Telford Tel: 01952 433418
Email: info@ironbridge.org.uk Web: www.ironbridge.org.uk

The museum interprets the beginnings of industry and the lives of those who lived and worked in Coalbrookdale. The galleries now house an exhibition dedicated to the Great Exhibition of 1851. There is also a chance to see the original iron smelting furnace of Abraham Darby I.

Opening Times: Daily 10:00-17:00. Closed Xmas.
Admission: Please call for details. Group rates available.
Location: Five miles from Telford Central. Map Ref: 11

Museum of the Gorge
Ironbridge, Telford Tel: 01952 432405 Email: info@ironbridge.org.uk
Web: www.ironbridge.org.uk

The Old Severn Warehouse is a short walk alongside the River Severn from the Iron Bridge. Built in the 1830s it was used as a riverside warehouse by the Coalbrookdale Company. Inside is an exhibition covering the whole history of the Gorge including a scaled model of the River Valley as it was in 1796.

Opening Times: Daily 10:00-17:00. Closed Xmas. Admission: Please call for details. Group rates available. Location: Five miles from Telford Central. Map Ref: 11

Tar Tunnel
Coalport Road, Coalport, Telford Tel: 01952 580827
Email: info@ironbridge.org.uk Web: www.ironbridge.org.uk

A feature that presents the first natural source of bitumen that was discovered over 200 years ago. Visitors can don a hard hat to witness this spectacular monument.

Opening Times: Apr to Nov daily 10:00-17:00. Closed Nov to Mar. Admission: Please call for details. Group rates available. Map Ref: 11

Somerset

Taunton, the county town, has been the centre of county life since Saxon times and it was here in 1685 that the Duke of Monmouth was declared King of England. Glastonbury is closely associated with the Arthurian legends and stories of the Holy Grail and the miraculous Christmas flowering Glastonbury Thorn.

Somerset is an intriguing county of strange places and strange happenings, well reflected in its excellent museums.

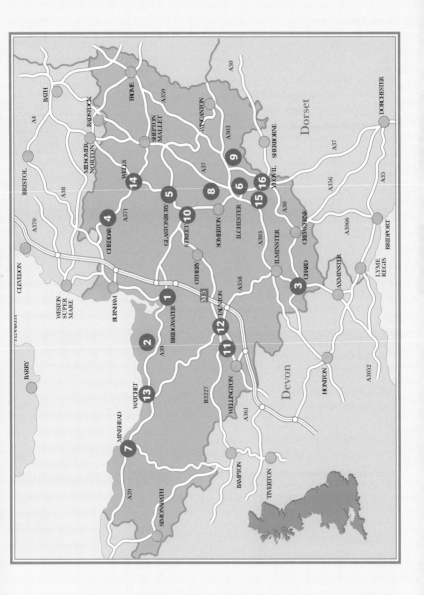

The Red Map References should be used to locate Museums etc on the pages that follow

Somerset

BRIDGWATER

Blake Museum

Blake Street, Bridgwater TA6 3NB   Tel: 01278 456127   Fax: 01278 446412
Email: museums@sedgemoor.gov.uk   Web: www.sedgemoor.gov.uk

Bridgwater's museum of local history and archaeology. Special features include Robert Blake (1598-1657), The Monmouth Rebellion (1685). Bridgwater's colourful and exciting carnival, maritime history and the brick and tile industry.

Opening Times: Tue to Sat 10:00-16:00.   Admission: Free.   Location: In the town centre.

Map Ref: 1

Coleridge Cottage

35 Lime Street, Nether Stowey, Bridgwater TA5 1NQ   Tel: 01278 732662
Web: www.nationaltrust.org.uk

The home of Samuel Taylor Coleridge for three years from 1797. There are mementoes of the poet on display. It was here that he wrote The Rime of the Ancient Mariner.

Opening Times: 1 Apr to 26 Sep Thu to Sun 14:00-17:00. Open BH Mons.   Admission: Adult £3.20, Child £1.60. NT Members Free.   Location: At west end of Nether Stowey, on south side of A39, eight miles west of Bridgwater.

Map Ref: 2

Somerset Brick & Tile Museum

East Quay, Bridgwater TA6 3NB   Tel: 01278 426088

The only remaining tile kiln in Bridgwater and an impressive survivor of a major Somerset industry. Visitors can enter the kiln and see some of the many varied patterns of bricks, tiles and other wares made here.

Opening Times: Thu & Fri 09:00-16:00 or by arrangement.   Admission: Free.   Location: In East Quay, ten minutes from town centre.

Map Ref: 1

CHARD

Forde Abbey & Gardens

Chard TA20 4LU   Tel: 01460 220231

A Cistercian monastery, founded mid-12th century. The buildings seen today almost all existed in the Middle Ages when the monks departed. The interior was substantially remodelled in 1649-58 and there are important Mortlake tapestries. The large 30 acre garden has herbaceous borders, a bog garden and rockery.

Opening Times: Apr to Oct   Location: Just off the B3167 four miles south of Chard.

Map Ref: 3

CHEDDAR

Cheddar Caves & Gorge

Cheddar BS27 3QF   Tel: 01934 742343   Fax: 01934 744637
Email: caves@cheddarcaves.co.uk   Web: www.cheddarcaves.co.uk

'Cheddar Man' Museum connected with show caves and other attractions. Museum features Britain's oldest complete skeleton (9000 years old) and evidence of late upper palaeolithic life in Gough's Cave. Come and see how your ancestors lived in our caves. Ticket includes entry to all attractions.

Opening Times: Daily May to mid Sep 10:00-17:00, mid Sep to Apr 10:30-16:30.
Admission: Adult £8.90, Child £5.90, Under 5s Free.   Location: In Britain's biggest gorge, one mile from Cheddar village centre.

Map Ref: 4

GLASTONBURY

Repairing a wagon wheel

Somerset Rural Life Museum

Abbey Farm, Chilkwell Street, Glastonbury BA6 8DB

Tel: 01458 831197

In the Abbey Farmhouse the social and domestic life of Victorian Somerset is described in reconstructed rooms and an exhibition which tells the life story of a farm worker, John Hodges. The magnificent 14th century Abbey barn is the centrepiece of the Museum. The barn and farm buildings surrounding the courtyard contain displays

Somerset

illustrating the tools and techniques of farming in Somerset until the 1940s.

Opening Times: Apr to Oct Tue to Fri & BH Mon 10:00-17:00, Sat & Sun 14:00-18:00. Closed Good Friday. Nov to Mar Tue to Sat 10:00-17:00. Admission: Free. Location: In Glastonbury, follow signs to the Tor and Shepton Mallet A361. Map Ref: 5

ILCHESTER

Fleet Air Arm Museum

FLEET AIR ARM MUSEUM
YEOVILTON

RNAS Yeovilton, Ilchester BA22 8HT Tel: 01935 840565
Fax: 01935 842630 Email: info@fleetairarm.com Web: www.fleetairarm.com

The Fleet Air Arm Museum is a national museum in a rural setting with an area the size of four football pitches under cover. It is the only British Museum sited next to an operational military airfield. From the viewing galleries you may see some of the Royal Navy's aircraft flying. The Museum shows over 40 aircraft within the many exhibitions throughout the four large halls. 'Leading edge' tells the story of aircraft from early biplane to Concorde and the Sea Harrier. Innovative touch screen displays show how aircraft fly and tell the stories of the aircraft and the men who flew them. 'Fly on board' the Museum's own aircraft carrier. The incredible 'Carrier' Exhibition allows visitors to 'go to sea'
on dry land by travelling to an aircraft carrier via a simulated helicopter ride that never actually leaves the ground. Explore the flight deck and see some historic jet aircraft drawn up 'ready for take off'. You can even tour the inside of the ship and 'meet' the captain.

Opening Times: Apr to Oct daily 10:00-17:30, Nov to Mar daily 10:00-16:30. Closed 24-26 Dec. Admission: Adult £8.50, Child (5 to 16 yrs) £5.75, Child (under 5 yrs) Free, Concession £6.75, Family (2 adults and 3 children) £27.00. Location: On the B3151, just off the A303 near Ilchester. Map Ref: 6

MINEHEAD

Dunster Castle

Dunster, Minehead TA24 6SL
Tel: 01643 821314 Fax: 01643 823000
Email: dunstercastle@nationaltrust.org.uk
Web: www.nationaltrust.org.uk

The present castle was remodelled in the late 19th century for the Luttrell family, who lived here for 600 years. There are family pictures, mahogany furniture and an important series of leather hangings. The large wooded garden houses Britain's oldest lemon tree.

Opening Times: 20 Mar to 23 Oct Sat to Wed 11:00-17:00, 24 Oct to 31 Oct Sat to Wed 11:00-16:00. Open Good Friday. Admission: Adult £6.80, Child £3.40, Family £16.80 (2 adults and 3 children). Group (15+) £5.80. Garden & park only: Adult £3.70, Child £1.60, Family £9.00. NT Members Free. Location: In Dunster, three miles south east of Minehead. Map Ref: 7

Thomas Luttrell, portrait in the Inner Hall

West Somerset Railway

The Railway Station, Minehead TA24 5BG Tel: 01643 704996
Fax: 01643 706349 Email: info@west-somerset-railway.co.uk
Web: www.west-somerset-railway.co.uk

Britain's longest Heritage Railway running 20 miles between Bishop's Lydeard (near Taunton) and Minehead, through the Quantock Hills and along the Exmoor Coast. Ten stations serving a variety of destinations.

Opening Times: Mar to Dec (selected dates) 09:30-17:30. Admission: Adult £12.00, Child £6.00, OAP £11.00. Party rates on application. Location: Four miles from Taunton (junction 25 on M5). Nearest main line railway station - Taunton. Map Ref: 7

7828 'Odney Manor' arrives at Minehead Station

Somerset

Lytes Cary Manor

Charlton Mackrell, Somerton TA11 7HU
Tel: 01458 224471
Email: lytescarymanor@nationaltrust.org.uk
Web: www.nationaltrust.org.uk

A small medieval manor house which was rescued from dereliction in the 20th century. It is furnished in period style and houses a display of 17th century Flemish tapestries. There is an attractive hedged garden with mixed borders.

Opening Times: 5 Apr to 31 Oct Mon, Wed, Fri & Sun 11:00-17:00. Admission: Adult £5.00, Child £2.00. Garden only: Adult £3.00, Child £1.00. NT Members Free. Location: Signposted from Podimore roundabout at junction of A303, A37 take A372. Map Ref: 8

The Great Hall showing stained glass windows attributed to John Lyte early C16th

Haynes Motor Museum

Sparkford BA22 7LH   Tel: 01963 440804   Fax: 01963 441004
Email: info@haynesmotormuseum.co.uk   Web: www.haynesmotormuseum.co.uk

300 historic cars, over 50 motorcycles, military and commerical vehicles plus memorabilia displayed in spectacular style. Exhibits include Schumacher's F1 Ferrari and a Jaguar XJ220 supercar. Awarded 'Motor Museum of the Year'.

Opening Times: Mar to Oct 09:30-17:30, Nov to Feb 10:00-16:30. Open 09:30-18:00 during summer school holidays. Closed Xmas Day and New Year's Day. Admission: Adult £6.50, Child £3.50, Concession £5.00, Family from £8.50. Location: Conveniently located just off A303 at Sparkford in Somerset. Map Ref: 9

The Shoe Museum

40 High Street, Street BA16 0YA   Tel: 01458 842169   Email: janet.targett@clarks.com

Contains shoes from Roman times to the present, buckles, fashion plates, machinery, hand tools and advertising material. Early history of Clarks Shoes and its role in the town. Disabled access weekdays only.

Opening Times: Mon to Fri 10:00-16:45, Sat 10:00-17:00, Sun 11:00-17:00. Admission: Free. Location: Close to Clarks Village. Map Ref: 10

Sheppy's Farm & Cider Museum

Three Bridges Farm, Bradford-on-Tone, Taunton TA4 1ER   Tel: 01823 461233   Fax: 01823 461712   Email: info@sheppyscider.com   Web: www.sheppyscider.com

A small private collection of agricultural and cider-making artefacts and machinery. Includes a video of the cider-maker's year.

Opening Times: Mon to Sat (all year) 08:30-18:00, Sun (Easter to Xmas) 11:00-13:00. Admission: Adult £2.00, Child £1.50, OAP £1.75. Location: A38 half way between Taunton and Wellington, Junction 26 of M5. Map Ref: 11

Somerset County Museum

The Castle, Castle Green, Taunton TA1 4AA
Tel: 01823 320201

There is a rich variety of objects on show at the Museum relating to the County of Somerset to intrigue and stir the imagination. There are toys and dolls, fossils, fine silver and pottery, and a rich collection of archaeological items from pre-historic and Roman Somerset. You can follow the fortunes of the Somerset Light Infantry in part of the Somerset Military Museum.

Opening Times: Tue to Sat & BH Mon 10:00-17:00. Closed Good Friday. Admission: Free. Location: Five minute walk from Taunton Town Centre. Map Ref: 12

Somerset

Somerset Military Museum

County Museum, The Castle, Taunton TA1 4AA   Tel: 01823 320201

The history of the County Regiments, especially the Somerset Light Infantry (Prince Albert's) from the 18th to the 20th century, illustrated through their uniforms, equipment, medals and memorabilia.

Opening Times: Tue to Sat & BH Mon 10:00-17:00. Closed Good Friday.   Admission: Free.
Location: Within the Somerset County Museum, five minute walk from Taunton Town Centre.
Map Ref: 12

WATCHET

Watchet Market House Museum

Market Street, Watchet TA23 0AN   Tel: 01984 631345

Watchet from pre-history to present day. Fossils and Saxon Mint, iron ore mines, railways and harbour trade and industries. Maritime paintings, photographs and models.

Opening Times: Easter to Oct daily 10:30-16:30.   Admission: Free.   Location: Close to harbour.
Map Ref: 13

WELLS

Wells & Mendip Museum

8 Cathedral Green, Wells BA5 2UE   Tel: 01749 673477   Email: wellsmuseum@ukonline.co.uk

Wells Museum exhibits Medieval Cathedral statuary at close quarters, an insight into the social and natural history of Wells and the Mendip area and the varied artefacts excavated from the archaeological dig in the museum gardens. Also a valuable sampler collection.

Opening Times: Easter to Oct 10:00-17:30. Oct to Easter 11:00-16:00. Aug open until 20:00.
Closed Tue (in winter) and Xmas Day.   Admission: Adult £2.50, Child £1.00, Concession £2.00,
Family £6.00.   Location: Adjacent to Wells Cathedral.
Map Ref: 14

YEOVIL

Montacute House

Montacute, Yeovil TA15 6XP
Tel: 01935 823289   Fax: 01935 826921
Email: montacute@nationaltrust.org.uk
Web: www.nationaltrust.org.uk

An Elizabethan house, adorned with elegant chimneys, carved parapets and other Renaissance features. The magnificent state rooms, including a long gallery which is the largest of its type in Britain, are full of furniture and portraits on loan from the National Portrait Gallery. There are also tapestries, hangings and an exhibition of 17th century samplers. The formal garden with its mixed borders and old roses is surrounded by parkland.

Opening Times: House: 19 Mar to 31 Oct Wed to Mon 11:00-17:00.
Garden: 1 Jan to 18 May Wed to Sun 11:00-16:00, 19 Mar to 31 Oct
Wed to Mon 11:00-18:00, 3 Nov to 25 Mar Wed to Sun 11:00-16:00.

The Millefleurs Tapestry
from the Dining Room

Admission: Adult £6.90, Child £3.40, Family £16.00. Group (15+) Adult £5.80, Child £2.90. NT
Members Free.   Location: In Montacute village, four miles west of Yeovil, on south side of
A3088, three miles east of A303.
Map Ref: 15

Museum of South Somerset

Hendford, Yeovil BA20 1UN   Tel: 01935 424774

Pre-historic and Roman occupation through to agricultural and industrial revolutions, South Somerset's association with leather and glove manufacturing. You can also see the Linotype setter which was in use for newspaper production.

Opening Times: Apr to Sep Tue to Sat 10:00-16:00, Oct to Mar Tue to Fri 10:00-16:00.
Admission: Free.   Location: Near town centre.
Map Ref: 16

Suffolk

The superb landscape of this county has been immortalised in the paintings of John Constable who delighted in painting the lovely Stour Valley. The county is also renowned for the work of another great painter, Thomas Gainsborough.

The Suffolk museums and galleries are mostly concerned with local history and indeed the beauty of the county but other subjects include horseracing, transport, mechanical music, historic aircraft, and clocks and watches.

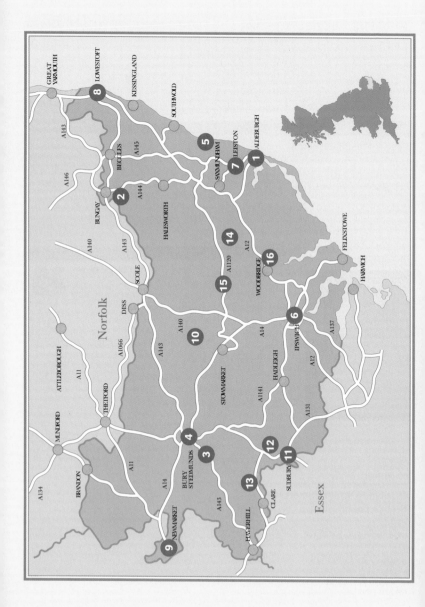

The Red Map References should be used to locate Museums etc on the pages that follow

Suffolk

ALDEBURGH

The Aldeburgh Museum
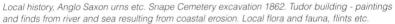

The Moot Hall, Aldeburgh IP15 5LE   Tel: 01728 454666
Email: aldeburgh@museum.freeserve.co.uk

Local history, Anglo Saxon urns etc. Snape Cemetery excavation 1862. Tudor building - paintings and finds from river and sea resulting from coastal erosion. Local flora and fauna, flints etc.

Opening Times: Easter to May Sat & Sun 14:30-17:00, Jun, Sep & Oct daily 14:30-17:00, Jul & Aug 10:30-12:30 14:30-17:00. Closed Nov to Easter.   Admission: Adult £1.00, Child Free.
Location: Near centre of town.   Map Ref: 1

BUNGAY

Norfolk & Suffolk Aviation Museum:
East Anglia's Aviation Heritage Centre
Buckeroo Way, The Street, Flixton, Bungay NR35 1NZ   Tel: 01986 896644
Email: nsam.flixton@virgin.net   Web: ww.aviationmuseum.net

Historic aircraft, indoor exhibitions - both civil and military, from the pioneer years through World War I to the present day. Special displays on Boulton & Paul, World War II Decoy Sites & Nature Walk.

Opening Times: Apr to Oct Sun to Thu 10:00-17:00, Nov to Mar Sun, Tue & Wed 10:00-16:00. Closed 15 Dec to 15 Jan.   Admission: Free.   Location: On B1062 off A143, one mile west of Bungay.   Map Ref: 2

BURY ST EDMUNDS

Ickworth House, Park & Gardens

The Rotunda, Horringer, Bury St Edmunds IP29 5QE   Tel: 01284 735270
Fax: 01284 735175   Email: ickworth@nationaltrust.org.uk
Web: www.nationaltrust.org.uk/ickworth

The eccentric Earl of Bristol created this equally eccentric house, with its central Rotunda and curved corridors, to house his collections. These include paintings by Titian, Gainsborough and Velasquez and a magnificent Georgian silver collection. The house is surrounded by an Italianate garden and set in a 'Capability' Brown park with woodland walks, deer enclosure, vineyard, church, canal and lake.

Opening Times: House: 19 Mar to 30 Sep Fri to Tue 13:00-17:00, 1 Oct to 31 Oct Fri to Tue 13:00-16:30. Park: daily 07:00-19:00. Admission: Adult £6.40, Child £2.90. Group: Adult £5.40, Child £2.40. NT Members Free. Location: Located in the village of Horringer, three miles

Collection of Silver Fish used as scent containers and ornamental pendants

south west of Bury St Edmunds on west side of A143.   Exhibitions & Events 2004 : For full events list, call 01284 735961.   Map Ref: 3

Manor House Museum
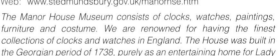

Honey Hill, Bury St Edmunds IP33 1RT

Tel: 01284 757076
Fax: 01284 747231
Email: saskia.stent@stedsbc.gov.uk
Web: www.stedmundsbury.gov.uk/manorhse.htm

The Manor House Museum consists of clocks, watches, paintings, furniture and costume. We are renowned for having the finest collections of clocks and watches in England. The House was built in the Georgian period of 1738, purely as an entertaining home for Lady Elizabeth Hervey, the wife of the first Earl of Bristol.

Opening Times: Wed to Sun 11:00-16:00. Admission: Adult £2.50, Child/OAP £2.00, Free to residents of St Edmundsbury. Location: Five minute walk from the Town Centre, through the Abbey gardens and churchyard.   Map Ref: 4

Suffolk

Moyses Hall Museum

Cornhill, Bury St Edmunds IP33 1DX   Tel: 01284 706183   Fax: 01284 765373
Email: moyses.hall@stedsbc.gov.uk   Web: www.stedmundsbury.gov.uk/moyses.htm

Recently extended and refurbished local history museum includes Suffolk Regiment Gallery, history of Bury St Edmunds display in a wonderful 800 year old building.

Opening Times: Daily 10:30-16:30, Sat & Sun 11:00-16:00   Admission: Free for residents of Bury St Edmunds, non-residents £2.50 Adult, Concessions £2.00   Location: Town centre.
Map Ref: 4

DUNWICH

The Museum

St James Street, Dunwich IP17 3EA   Tel: 01728 648796

History of town of Dunwich from Roman times with local wildlife and social history.

Opening Times: Mar Sat & Sun 14:00-16:30, Apr to Sep daily 11:30-16:30, Oct daily 12:00-16:00. Closed Nov to Feb.   Admission: Free. Donations welcome.   Location: In centre of village.
Map Ref: 5

IPSWICH

Christchurch Mansion

Christchurch Park, Ipswich IP4 2BE   Tel: 01473 433554

Period rooms from Tudor to Victorian. Wolsey Art Gallery has contemporary art exhibitions work by Constable, Gainsborough and other Suffolk artists.

Opening Times: Tue to Sat 10:00-17:00, Sun 14:30-16:30. Closes at dusk during winter.
Admission: Free.   Location: Town centre, one mile from railway station.   Map Ref: 6

Ipswich Museum

High Street, Ipswich IP1 3QH   Tel: 01473 433550   Fax: 01473 433568

IPSWICH

Romans in Suffolk; Anglo-Saxons in Ipswich; mankind galleries; local and world geology; Victorian natural history gallery; Suffolk wildlife; British birds.

Opening Times: Tue to Sat 10:00-17:00.
Admission: Free.   Location: Town centre, one mile from railway station.   Map Ref: 6

Anglo-Saxon Gallery

Ipswich Transport Museum

Cobham Road, Ipswich IP3 9JD   Tel: 01473 715666
Web: www.ipswichtransportmuseum.co.uk

Believed the largest collection in the UK devoted to the transport and engineering heritage of one town - Ipswich. Includes bicycles, cranes, prams, fire engines, buses etc.

Opening Times: Apr to Nov Sun & BH 11:00-16:30. School holidays, Mon to Fri 13:00-16:00.
Admission: Adult £2.50, Child £1.50, Concession £2.00, Family £7.00.   Location: South east Ipswich, close to A14.
Map Ref: 6

LEISTON

Long Shop Museum

Main Street, Leiston IP16 4ES   Tel / Fax: 01728 832189   Email: longshop@care4free.net
Web: www.longshop.care4free.net

Two hundred years of the Garrett family history from the first production line to the first woman doctor. Housed in original Garrett Works buildings including Grade II* long shop.

Opening Times: Apr to Oct Mon to Sat 10:00-17:00, Sun 11:00-17:00.   Admission: Adult £3.50, Child £1.00, Under 5s Free, Concession £3.00.   Location: Near town centre.   Map Ref: 7

Suffolk

LOWESTOFT

Lowestoft & East Suffolk Maritime Museum

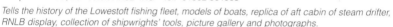

Whapload Road, Lowestoft NR32 1XG   Tel: 01502 561963

Tells the history of the Lowestoft fishing fleet, models of boats, replica of aft cabin of steam drifter, RNLB display, collection of shipwrights' tools, picture gallery and photographs.

Opening Times: Easter 9 to 17 Apr, 1 May to 10 Oct daily 10:00-16:30.   Admission: Adult 75p, Child 25p, OAP 50p.   Location: 30 minute walk from railway station, 25 minute walk from bus station.   Map Ref: 8

Lowestoft Museum

Broad House, Nicholas Everitt Park, Lowestoft NR33 9JR   Tel: 01502 511457

Third largest collection in the world of Lowestoft porcelain as well as the history of the area going back to the Stone Age and beyond.

Opening Times: End Mar to early Oct Mon to Fri 10:30-17:00, Sat/Sun 14:00-17:00. 12 Oct to 3 Nov Sat & Sun 14:00-16:00. Half term week Mon to Fri 10:30-16:00. Admission: Free.
Location: In Nicholas Everitt Park in Oulton Broad, one mile inland from town centre. Map Ref: 8

NEWMARKET

British Sporting Art Trust

BSAT Gallery, 99 High Street, Newmarket CB8 8LU   Tel: 01264 710344   Fax: 01264 710114
Email: BSATrust@aol.co.uk   Web: www.bsatrust.co.uk

Annually changing exhibition of sporting paintings. Library of books relating to sporting art and field sports.

Opening Times: Easter to end Oct Tue to Sun 10:00-17:00. Admission: Adult £3.00. Location: Near town centre, above National Horseracing Museum, next door to Jockey Club.   Map Ref: 9

National Horseracing Museum

99 High Street, Newmarket CB8 8JH   Tel: 01638 667333   Fax: 01638 665600
Web: www.nhrm.co.uk

The story of racing told through the museum's permanent collections, featuring the horses, people, events and scandals that made it so colourful. New: At the Races Gallery, hands on fun with Channel 4.

Opening Times: 6 Apr to 31 Oct Tue to Sun 11:00-17:00, also open Mon in Jul, Aug & BH. Admission: Adult £4.50, Child £2.50, Concession £3.50, Family ticket £10.00.   Location: In town centre. Bus stop opposite, 15 minute walk from station.   Map Ref: 9

STOWMARKET

Mechanical Music Museum & Bygones

Blacksmiths Road, Cotton, Stowmarket IP14 4QN   Tel: 01449 613876
Email: museum@davidivory.co.uk   Web: www.davidivory.co.uk

Unique collection of music-boxes, gramophones, polyphons, organettes, street pianos, barrel organs, fair organs, Wurlitzer Theatre Pipe Organ, many unusual items all played, plus large collection of teapots and memorabilia.

Opening Times: Jun to Sep Sun only 14:30-17:30. Groups by arrangement during the week. Fair Organ Enthusiasts Day 3 Oct 10:00-17:00. Admission: Adult £4.00, Child £1.00. Location: Six miles north of Stowmarket, just off B1113 road. Nearest railway station: Stowmarket.   Map Ref: 10

Limonaire Fairground Organ circa 1850

Gainsborough's House

46 Gainsborough Street, Sudbury CO10 2EU   Tel: 01787 372958   Fax: 01787 376991
Email: mail@gainsborough.org   Web: www.gainsborough.org

Georgian fronted townhouse, birthplace of Thomas Gainsborough RA, displaying much of his

Suffolk

work, together with 18th century furniture and memorabilia. Varied programme of contemporary exhibitions throughout the year. Attractive walled garden.

Opening Times: Mon to Sat 10:00-17:00, BH Sun & Mon 14:00-17:00. Closed Sun, Good Fri & Xmas to New Year. Admission: Adult £3.50, Child £1.50, Concessions £2.80, Family £8.00.
Location: In the heart of Sudbury. Map Ref: 11

Melford Hall

Long Melford, Sudbury CO10 9AA Tel: 01787 880286
Email: melford@nationaltrust.org.uk Web: www.nationaltrust.org.uk

One of East Anglia's most celebrated Elizabethan houses. There is a Regency library, Victorian bedrooms and good collections of furniture and porcelain. Also a small collection of Beatrix Potter memorabilia. The garden contains some spectacular specimen trees.

Opening Times: 3 Apr to 25 Apr Sat & Sun only 14:00-17:30, 1 May to 30 Sep Wed to Sun 14:00-17:30, 2 Oct to 31 Oct Sat & Sun only 14:00-17:30. Admission: Adult £4.50, Child £2.25, Family £11.25. Group (15+) Adult £3.40, Child £1.70. NT Members Free. Location: In Long Melford off A134,14 miles south of Bury St Edmunds, three miles north of Sudbury. Map Ref: 12

Sue Ryder Museum

PO Box 5736, Cavendish, Sudbury CO10 8AY Tel: 01787 282591 Fax: 01787 282991

Includes original exhibits from Nazi Concentration Camps. Also embroidery and handicrafts made by patients in Sue Ryder homes.

Opening Times: Daily 10:00-17:00. Closed Xmas. Admission: Adult £1.00, Child/OAP 40p.
Location: On A1092 between Clare and Long Melford; Sudbury eight miles; Bury St Edmunds 16 miles; Cambridge 29 miles. Map Ref: 13

Lanman Museum

Framlingham Castle, Framlingham, Woodbridge IP13 9BP Tel: 01728 724189

Part of a visit to the castle and telling the social history of Framlingham, this museum has all the copies of the Framlingham Weekly News (1859-1938) recording fascinating local happenings.

Opening Times: Winter 10:00-16:00. Summer 10:00-18:00. Admission: Part of admission ticket to the castle. Map Ref: 14

Saxstead Green Post Mill

The Mill House, Saxtead Green, Framlingham, Woodbridge IP13 9QQ
Tel: 01728 685789

This is a fine example of a post mill, where the superstructure turns on a great post to face the wind. There has been a mill here since 1287, as Framlingham was a thriving farming community.

Opening Times: Apr to Sep Mon to Sat 10:00-13:00 & 14:00-18:00, Oct Mon to Sat 10:00-13:00 & 14:00-17:00. Please check times before visiting in early part of season. Admission: Adult £2.50, Child £1.50, Concession £2.00. EH Members Free. Location: Two and a half miles north west of Framlingham on A1120. Map Ref: 15

Helmet of war

Sutton Hoo

Tranmer House, Sutton Hoo, Woodbridge IP12 3DJ
Tel: 01394 389700 Fax: 01394 389702
Email: suttonhoo@nationaltrust.org.uk
Web: www.nationaltrust.org.uk

Sutton Hoo is the burial ground of the pagan Anglo Saxon kings of East Anglia. It is the site of the famous excavations and discovery of treasure in 1939. The site has a large visitor centre and exhibition hall displaying some of the stunning original artefacts. There are peaceful walks to the burial mounds and around the 250 acre estate.

Opening Times: Exhibition Hall: 20 Mar to 30 Sep daily 10:00-17:00, 1 Oct to 31 Oct Wed to Sun 10:00-17:00, 1 Nov to 31 Dec Fri to Sun 10:00-16:00, 1 Jan to 28 Feb Sat & Sun only 10:00-16:00. Closed 25/26 Dec & 1 Jan. Estate open daily. Admission: Adult £4.00, Child £2.00, Group £3.50, NT Members Free.
Location: Signed from A12, near Woodbridge, the site is located off B1083 Bawdsey Road.
Exhibitions & Events 2004 : Please telephone for details. Map Ref: 16

Surrey

Britain's most wooded county can still claim countryside of outstanding beauty. The magnificent North Downs cross the county from east to west and include Box Hill, a famous beauty spot for over 200 years. To the south is the fertile Surrey Weald, while to the north is the low-lying belt of the Thames Valley.

The museums and galleries of Surrey are extremely varied in topics ranging from local history, geology and archaeology, to rural life and local crafts.

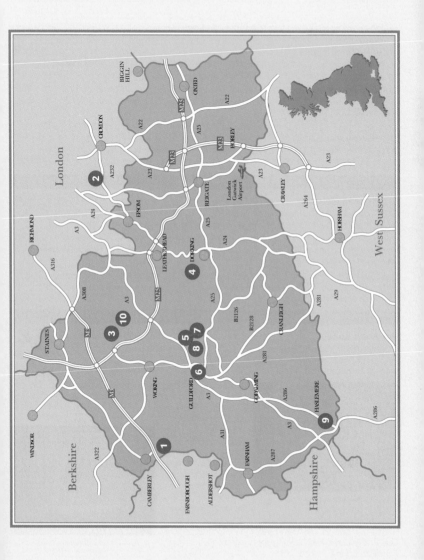

The Red Map References should be used to locate Museums etc on the pages that follow

Surrey

Royal Logistic Corps Museum

Princess Royal Barracks, Deepcut, Camberley GU16 6RW   Tel: 01252 833371   Fax: 01252 833484   Email: rlcmuseum@btconnect.com

Formed in 1993, the museum houses the collection of The Royal Logistics Corps, Royal Corps of Transport, Royal Army Ordnance Corps, Royal Pioneer Corps, Army Catering Corps and Royal Engineers' Postal & Courier Service.

Opening Times: Apr to Dec Tue to Fri 10:00-16:00, Apr to Sep Sat 12:00-16:00 (please telephone 01252 388371).   Admission: Free.   Location: Deepcut village near Frimley Green.

Map Ref: 1

Little Holland House

40 Beeches Avenue, Carshalton SM5 3LW   Tel: 020 8770 4781   Fax: 020 8770 4777   Email: valary.murphy@sutton.gov.uk   Web: www.sutton.gov.uk/lfl/heritage/lhh

Built between 1902-04 by Frank Dickinson, an ardent devotee of the Arts & Crafts Movement, the Grade II* interior contains Dickinson's paintings, hand-made furniture, carvings and metal work in an eclectic style which is unique.

Opening Times: First Sun every month plus Sun & Mon of BH weekends 13:30-17:30. Closed Xmas & New Year.   Admission: Free. Group visits outside opening times by prior arrangement only - include talks and guided tour £3.00 per person.   Location: On B278 four minute walk south of Carshalton Beeches Station.

Map Ref: 2

Chertsey Museum

The Cedars, 33 Windsor Street, Chertsey KT16 8AT   Tel: 01932 565764   Fax: 01932 571118   Email: curator@chertseymuseum.org.uk   Web: www.chertseymuseum.org.uk

Collection displays explore the history of the Runnymede area and British fashion, including Thames Valley archaeology, clocks, social history, decorative art, Greek pottery, Chertsey Abbey and 'The Matthews Dress Collection'.

Opening Times: Tue to Fri 12:30-16:30, Sat 11:00-16:00. Closed Xmas & New Year and Good Friday.   Admission: Free.   Location: Near town centre, one minute walk from bus stop, 15 minute walk from train station.

Map Ref: 3

Polesden Lacey

Great Bookham, Dorking RH5 6BD   Tel: 01372 452048/458203   Fax: 01372 452023   Email: polesdenlacey@ntrust.org.uk   Web: www.nationaltrust.org.uk

A Collection of pill boxes

In an exceptional setting on the North Downs, this originally Regency house was extensively remodelled in 1906-9 by the Hon Mrs Ronald Greville, a well known Edwardian hostess. Her collection of fine paintings, furniture, porcelain and silver are displayed in the reception rooms and galleries, as they were at the time of her cele-brated house parties. There are extensive grounds, a walled rose garden, lawns and walks. King George VI and Queen Elizabeth The Queen Mother spent part of their honeymoon here in 1923.

Chinese porcelain goose-tureen by Qianlong, c.1780

Opening Times: House: 24 Mar to 7 Nov Wed to Sun 11:00-17:00. Open BH Mons. Garden: daily 11:00-18:00 or dusk if earlier.   Admission: House: Adult £8.00, Child £4.00, Family £20.00. Group (15+) £6.50. Grounds only: Adult £5.00, Child £2.50, Family £12.50. NT Members Free. Location: Five miles north west of Dorking, two miles south of Great Bookham, off A246 Leatherhead-Guildford road.

Map Ref: 4

Surrey

Clandon Park

West Clandon, Guildford GU4 7RQ   Tel: 01483 222482   Fax: 01483 223479
Email: clandonpark@nationaltrust.org.uk
Web: www.nationaltrust.org.uk/clandonpark

Clandon Park was built by the Venetian architect Leoni in the 1730s and is considered to have one of the finest Marble Halls in Europe. The house is filled with an amazing collection of 18th century furniture, porcelain, textiles and carpets acquired in the 1920s by the connoisseur Mrs Gubbay. The attractive gardens contain a grotto, sunken Dutch garden and a fascinating Maori Meeting House.

Opening Times: 28 Mar to 31 Oct Tue, Wed, Thu, Sun 11:00-17:00. Open BH Mons, Good Friday & Easter Sat. Admission: Adult £6.00, Child £3.00, Family £15.00. Group £5.00. NT Members Free. Location: At West Clandon on A247, three miles east of Guildford: if using A3 follow signposts to Ripley to join A247.

The conductor of the Meissen Monkey Band, c.1753-1755

Map Ref: 5

Guildford Cathedral Treasury

Stag Hill, Guildford GU2 7UP   Tel: 01483 547860   Fax: 01482 303350
Email: visits@guildford-cathedral.org   Web: www.guildford-cathedral.org

Out of 215 parishes, 35 Churches have lent 135 different artefacts to the Cathedral. The display represents nearly 450 years of ecclesiastical history and wonderful examples of art and craftmanship.

Opening Times: Daily 08:30-17:30. Admission: Free - donation welcome. Small fee for Groups.   Location: Ten minute walk from mainline station.

Map Ref: 6

Guildford House Gallery

155 High Street, Guildford GU1 3AJ   Tel / Fax: 01483 444742
Email: guildfordhouse@guildford.gov.uk   Web: www.guildfordhouse.co.uk

Fascinating 17th century Grade I listed building. Original features include a finely carved staircase, panelled rooms, decorative plaster ceilings and wrought iron window fittings. Varied temporary exhibition programme throughout the year.

Opening Times: Tue to Sat 10:00-16:45. Closed Mon. Admission: Free.   Location: Guildford Town Centre.

Map Ref: 6

Guildford Museum

Castle Arch, Guildford GU1 3SX   Tel: 01483 444751   Fax: 01483 532391
Email: museum@guildford.gov.uk   Web: www.guildfordmuseum.co.uk

The Museum was founded in 1898. It now houses the largest collection of archaeology, local history and needlework in Surrey. The archaeology collection contains objects from the Palaeolithic to the post-medieval period, including flint hand axes, Roman priests' head dresses, Saxon grave goods, medieval floor tiles and Wealden glass. The needlework collection includes patchwork, samplers and smocks. Objects and pictures cover local trades and industries, social life, childhood and the home, and two local characters: Lewis Carroll and Gertrude Jekyll. A recreated Victorian schoolroom is available for daily 'role-play' sessions for pre-booked Key Stage 2 school groups during term-time.

Opening Times: Mon to Sat 11:00-17:00. Closed Sun. Admission: Free. Victorian Schoolroom sessions (Tue, Wed & Thu) - £5.00 per child (Adults free) Teacher's Pack included.   Exhibitions & Events 2004 : Easter 2004: Re-opening of Guildford Castle Keep, 19 Jun to 4 Sep: Glorious Gardens: a celebration of local gardens and gardeners, 2-31 Aug: Breweries Exhibition

Map Ref: 6

Surrey

Hatchlands Park

East Clandon, Guildford GU4 7RT   Tel: 01483 222482   Fax: 01483 223176
Email: hatchlands@nationaltrust.org.uk   Web: www.nationaltrust.org.uk/hatchlands

Hatchlands is set in a beautiful 430 acre Repton Park offering a variety of walks. The house was built for the naval hero Admiral Boscawen in 1756 and can boast the earliest surviving interiors by Robert Adam. Inside explore the world's largest collection of composer related keyboards upon which J C Bach, Chopin, Mahler and Elgar (to mention but a few) have played.

Opening Times: 1 Apr to 29 Jul & 1 Sep to 31 Oct Tue, Wed, Thu, & Sun 14:00-17:30. 1 Aug to 31 Aug Tue, Wed, Thu, Fri, & Sun 14:00-17:30. Open BH Mons.
Admission: House: Adult £6.00, Child £3.00, Family £15.00. Park: Adult £2.50, Child £1.25. NT Members Free.   Location: East of East Clandon, north of A246 Guildford-Leatherhead road.   Map Ref: 6

Loseley Park

Guildford GU3 1HS   Tel: 01483 304440   Fax: 01483 302036
Email: enquiries@loseley-park.com   Web: www.loseley-park.com

Loseley House is a fine example of Elizabethan Architecture featuring many fine works of art including paintings, tapestries, chalk fireplace and panelling from Henry VIII's Nonsuch Palace.

Opening Times: Walled Garden: 3 May to 30 Sep Wed to Sun 11:00-17:00. Loseley House: 2 Jun to 30 Aug Wed to Sun 13:00-17:00. (Guided tours) Admission: Garden: Adult £3.00, Child £1.50, OAP £2.50. House & Garden: Adult £6.00, Child £3.00, OAP £5.00.
Location: Three miles from Guildford Town Centre, five minutes drive from A3.   Map Ref: 7

Queen's Royal Surrey Regiment Museum

Clandon Park, Guildford GU4 7RQ   Tel / Fax: 01483 223419
Email: queenssurrey@care4free.net   Web: www.queensroyalsurreys.org.uk

Set in the National Trust mansion, Clandon Park, this museum tell the story of the long and distinguished service of the Infantry Regiments of Surrey. Spectacular medal display. Exhibitions refurbished in 2002.

Opening Times: Apr to Oct Tue to Thu, Sun & BH Mon 12:00-17:00.   Admission: Free.
Location: West Clandon, four miles from Guildford Town Centre.   Map Ref: 8

Haslemere Educational Museum

78 High Street, Haslemere GU27 2LA   Tel: 01428 642112   Fax: 01428 645234
Email: haslemeremuseum@aol.com   Web: www.haslemeremuseum.co.uk

Permanent exhibitions in refurbished galleries include geology, natural history, archaeology and human history. Popular features are Egyptian mummy, stuffed bear, wild flower table, and observation beehive. Attractive grounds with ha-ha, gazebo, pond and some unusual trees.

Opening Times: Tue to Sat 10:00-17:00.   Admission: Free.   Location: High Street location - ten minutes walk from station.   Map Ref: 9

Brooklands Museum Trust Ltd

Brooklands Road, Weybridge KT13 0QN   Tel: 01932 857381   Fax: 01932 855465
Email: info@brooklandsmuseum.com   Web: www.brooklandsmuseum.com

The birthplace of British motorsport and aviation, features a fine collection of historic racing and sports cars and aircraft. Including the Loch Ness Wellington bomber 'R' for 'Robert' and the Napier-Railton built for John Cobb.

Opening Times: Tue to Sun 10:00-17:00 (summer), 10:00-16:00 (winter). Last entry one hour before closing.   Admission: Adult £7.00, Child £5.00, OAP/Student £6.00, Family £18.00. NB. Extra charges may be levied on events.   Location: A 20 minute walk from Weybridge station and ten minutes from Cobham/Painshill A3, exit M25 J10.   Map Ref: 10

Sussex

Much has been said and written about 'Sussex by the Sea', ever since Rudyard Kipling praised its glories. Brighton, the queen of Sussex seaside towns and the largest town in East Sussex, was mentioned in Domesday Book. The county town of West Sussex is Chichester, a Roman town retaining something of its Roman grid-iron street plan.

The cream of Sussex's museums and galleries and palaces are located in the coastal towns and have outstanding collections as well as covering the county's social and archaeological history.

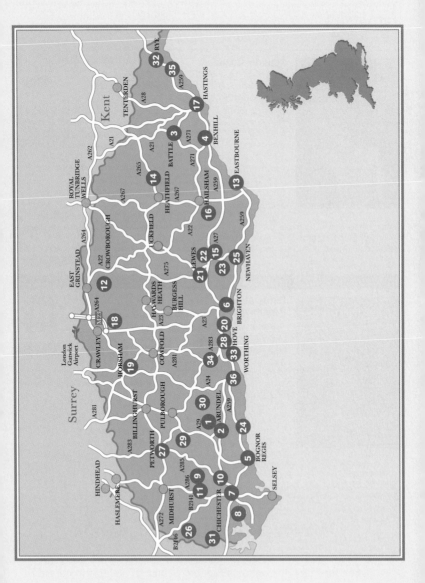

The Red Map References should be used to locate Museums etc on the pages that follow

Sussex

Amberley Working Museum

Amberley, Arundel BN18 9LT   Tel: 01798 831370   Fax: 01798 831831
Email: office@amberleymuseum.co.uk   Web: www.amberleymuseum.co.uk

Amberley Working Museum is a 36 acre open-air site dedicated to preserving the industrial heritage of the south-east. Exhibits include a narrow-gauge railway and vintage bus collection (both of which provide free travel around site). Besides the SEEBOARD electricity hall, a printing workshop and a roadmarker's exhibition, the museum is also home to traditional craftspeople, such as a blacksmith, potter and broom-maker.

Opening Times: 20 Mar to 3 Nov Wed to Sun 10:00-17:00. Open BH and daily through school holidays.   Admission: Adult £6.75, Child £3.75, OAP/Student £6.00, Group rates available.
Location: On the B2139, between Arundel and Storrington. Adjacent to Amberley Railway Station.
Map Ref: 1

Arundel Castle

Arundel BN18 9AB   Tel: 01903 883136
Fax: 01903 884581   Email: info@arundelcastle.org
Web: www.arundelcastle.org

Towering fortified castle and stately home overlooking the River Arun. Seat of the Dukes of Norfolk since 1067. Medieval Keep. Containing fine collections of furniture, paintings, armour, tapestries, clocks and the personal possessions of Mary, Queen of Scots. Renovated Victorian bedrooms. Restored Victorian tropical greenhouses, flower and kitchen gardens. Licensed restaurant, gift shop and free parking.

Opening Times: 1 Apr to 31 Oct. Grounds, Gardens, Restaurant, Shop & Keep: 11:00-17:00. Castle 12:00-17:00. Last entry 16:00. Closed Sat.   Admission: Adult £9.50, Child £6.00, OAP/Student £7.50, Family £26.50 (2 adults and up to 5 children).   Exhibitions & Events 2004 : 13-16 May: Antiques & Audacity Fair, 30-31 May: Medieval Festival, Sep: Fanfare for Food, 31 Oct: Halloween Firewords Spooktacular. Medieval re-enactments most Sun during the season.
Map Ref: 2

Battle Abbey

Battle TN33 0AD   Tel: 01424 773792

Battle Abbey was founded around 1070 by William the Conqueror, on the site of the Battle of Hastings. The best-preserved and most impressive part of the abbey is the great gate-house, the finest of all surviving Medieval abbey entrances, which was built around 1338. There is an exhibition on the build-up to the Battle of Hastings. Collections include architectural stonework and archaeological finds.

Opening Times: Apr to Sep daily 10:00-18:00, Oct daily 10:00-17:00, Nov to Mar daily 10:00-16:00. Closed Xmas & New Year. Times & prices may change.   Admission: Adult £5.00, Child £2.50, Concession £3.80, Family £12.50. EH Members Free.   Location: In Battle, at south end of High Street.
Map Ref: 3

Great Gatehouse from South
© English Heritage

Sussex

Buckleys Yesterdays World

Next to Battle Abbey, 89/90 High Street, Battle TN33 0AQ
Tel: 01424 775378   Fax: 01424 775174
Email: info@yesterdaysworld.co.uk   Web: www.yesterdaysworld.co.uk

Meet colourful lifesized
characters from 1850 onwards

Step into the world of yesterday - today! Journey through a hundred glorious years of shopping and social history at one of the South East's top-award winning visitor attractions. Discover colourful life-sized characters in the interactive displays, with push-button commentaries, and evocative smells. Enjoy the country garden, children's play village, toddlers' activity area, miniature golf (£1), summer tea terrace and fudge-fayre.

Opening Times: Daily 09:30-18:00 (17:00 in winter). Admission: Adult £5.25, Child £3.75, OAP/Student £4.75, Family £16.75. Location: Battle High Street, opposite Battle Abbey Gatehouse.   Exhibitions & Events 2004 : 8 to 18 Apr: Easter Egg Hunt, 23 to 31 Oct: Halloween Hunt, 27 Dec to 4 Jan: Santa Search.

Map Ref: 3

Bexhill Museum

Egerton Road, Bexhill TN39 3HL   Tel / Fax: 01424 787950   Email: museum@rother.gov.uk
Web: bexhillmuseum.co.uk

Housed in an Edwardian Park Pavilion, collections reflect the fascinating history of Bexhill - important collections include local dinosaur remains, architect's model of De La Pavilion and much more. New access centre.

Opening Times: Feb to Dec Tue to Fri 10:00-17:00. Sat & Sun & BH 14:00-17:00. Admission: Adult £1.00, Child Free, Concession 50p, Group 50p. School Groups Free. Location: Just off Bexhill Seafront (B2182) by the Clock Tower, quarter mile railway station.   Map Ref: 4

Bognor Regis Museum/Bognor Regis Wireless Museum

69 High Street, Bognor Regis PO21 1RY   Tel: 01243 865636

The main museum houses displays of local history, also included is an independent wireless museum.

Opening Times: Tue to Sun 10:30-16:30. Closed Mon (except BH). Admission: Free.
Location: In the town centre.   Map Ref: 5

Booth Museum of Natural History

194 Dyke Road, Brighton BN1 5AA   Tel: 01273 292777   Fax: 01273 292778
Web: www.booth.virtualmuseum.info

Over half a million specimens and natural history literature and data extending back over three centuries are housed in this fascinating museum, including hundreds of British birds, butterflies, skeletons, whale and dinosaur bones.

Opening Times: Mon, Tue, Wed, Fri & Sat 10:00-17:00, Sun 14:00-17:00. Closed Thu, Good Friday, 25-26 Dec, 1 Jan. Admission: Free. Location: 15 minute bus ride from town centre, ten minute walk from Brighton Station. Buses 27 & 27A.   Map Ref: 6

Spine Chair (des.1986) by Andre Dubreuil

Brighton Museum & Art Gallery

Royal Pavilion Gardens, Brighton BN1 1EE
Tel: 01273 290900   Fax: 01273 292871
Web: www.virtualmuseum.info

A state-of-the-art visitor attraction, dynamic and innovative new galleries feature exciting interactive displays appealing to all ages. Brighton Museum is famous for its collection of 20th century furniture, glass, textiles and jewellery, including examples by leading designers. The

Sussex

extensive ceramics collection includes the famous Willett Gallery, exploring 18th and 19th century British social history through earthenware. The museum's spectacular collection of non-western arts is of national importance and it also boasts stunning collections of fashion and fascinating local history collections. The museum also has an extensive collection of fine art, ranging from the 15th to the 20th century.

Frank Stella (1936) Red Scramble, 1977, Oil on Canvas

Opening Times: Tue 10:00-19:00, Wed, Thu, Fri & Sat 10:00-17:00. Sun 14:00-17:00. Closed Mon (except Bank Holidays), 24-26 Dec & 1 Jan.
Admission: Free.   Location: Royal Pavilion Gardens, Town Centre, Brighton.   Map Ref: 6

Preston Manor

Preston Drove, Brighton BN1 6SD   Tel: 01273 292770   Fax: 01273 292771
Email: visitor.services@brighton-hove.gov.uk
Web: www.prestonmanor.virtualmuseum.info

Delightful manor house, powerfully evoking the atmosphere of an Edwardian gentry home both upstairs and downstairs. Explore over 20 rooms on four floors from superbly renovated servant's quarters to the attic bedrooms.

Opening Times: Mon 13:00-17:00, Tue to Sat 10:00-17:00, Sun 14:00-17:00 and Bank Holidays 10:00-17:00. Closed Good Friday, 25 & 26 Dec. Admission: Please phone for details.
Location: 10 minute bus ride from town centre. Buses 5 & 5A   Map Ref: 6

Royal Pavilion

4/5 Pavilion Buildings, Brighton BN1 1EE
Tel: 01273 290900   Fax: 01273 292871
Email: visitor.services@brighton-hove.gov.uk
Web: www.royalpavilion.org.uk

The Royal Pavilion, Brighton

The Royal Pavilion, the famous seaside palace of King George IV, is one of the most exotically beautiful buildings in the British Isles. Originally a simple farmhouse, in 1787 architect Henry Holland created a neoclassical villa on the site. From 1815-1822, the Pavilion was transformed by John Nash into its current distinctive Indian style complete with Chinese inspired interiors. Magnificent decorations and fantastic furnishings have been re-created in an extensive restoration programme. From the opulence of the main State rooms to the charm of the first floor bedroom suites, the Royal Pavilion is filled with astonishing colours and superb craftsmanship. Witness the magnificence of the Music Room with a domed ceiling of gilded shell shapes, and the dramatic Banqueting Room lit by a huge crystal chandelier held by a silvered dragon. Visitors can discover more about life behind the scenes at the Palace during the last 200 years with an interactive multimedia visitor interpretation programme and join public guided tours daily at 11:30 and 14:30 (for a small extra charge). The Royal Pavilion is an ideal location for filming and photography, from fashion shoots to corporate videos. Rooms are also available for hire for corporate and private functions and civil wedding ceremonies.

Opening Times: Daily Oct to May 10:00-17:15, Jun to Sep 09:30-17:45. Closed 25-26 Dec. Admission: Please phone for details.
Location: Situated in town centre.   Exhibitions & Events 2004

The Music Room at the Royal Pavilion, Brighton

: Family days, special interest talks and tours based on the collection and history of the Royal Pavilion.   Map Ref: 6

Chichester District Museum

29 Little London, Chichester PO19 1PB   Tel: 01243 784683   Fax: 01243 776766
Email: districtmuseum@chichester.gov.uk   Web: www.chichester.gov.uk/museum

Find out about the archaeology and local history of the Chichester district through displays and

Sussex

hands-on activities. Changing exhibitions and events for all ages.

Opening Times: Tue to Sat 10:00-17:30. Closed Sun, Mon and all Public Holidays.
Admission: Free. Location: Off East Street, Chichester. 15 minutes from Bus and Train
Stations. Map Ref: 7

Fishbourne Roman Palace
Salthill Road, Fishbourne, Chichester PO19 3QR Tel: 01243 785859 Fax: 01243
539266 Email: adminfish@sussexpast.co.uk Web: www.sussexpast.co.uk

Britain's finest collection of in situ Roman mosaics are on display at Fishbourne Roman Palace along with a museum of finds from this internationally important site, and a Roman garden replanted to its original plan. An audio-visual presentation helps bring the site back to life.

Opening Times: Jan & 16 Dec to 31 Dec Sat & Sun 10:00-16:00, Feb & Nov to 15 Dec daily 10:00-16:00, Mar to Jul & Sep to Oct daily 10:00-17:00, Aug daily 10:00-18:00. Closed Xmas. Admission: Adult £5.20, Child £2.70, Concession £4.50, Family £13.40, Disabled £4.00.
Location: Five minutes walk from Fishbourne Railway

Trajan's Column

Station. North of A259 off Salthill Road in Fishbourne village. Bus services stop near end of
Salthill Road. Map Ref: 8

Goodwood House
Goodwood, Chichester PO18 0PD Tel: 01243 755000 Fax: 01243 755005
Email: curator@goodwood.co.uk Web: www.goodwood.co.uk

Goodwood House has been the home of the Dukes of Richmond for over three hundred years, and has an unrivalled collection of art, and French furniture, tapestries and Sévres porcelain.

Opening Times: Apr to Sep Sun & Mon, Aug Sun to Thurs 13:00-17:00. Admission: Adult
£7.00, OAP £6.00, Child (12 to 18) & Student £3.00, Family ticket (2 adults and 4 children)
£15.00. Location: Three miles NE of Chichester, off A285 & A286. Map Ref: 9

Guildhall Museum
Priory Park, Chichester Tel: 01243 784683 Fax: 01243 776766
Email: districtmuseum@chichester.gov.uk Web: www.chichester.gov.uk/museum

Medieval (1282) Greyfriars Church that became a town hall and court house. Poet William Blake was brought to trial here in 1804.

Opening Times: Please contact number above. Admission: Free. Location: In Priory Park,
located to the north-east of the City. Map Ref: 7

Pallant House Gallery
9 North Pallant, Chichester PO19 1TJ Tel: 01243 774557
Fax: 01243 536038 Email: info@pallant.org.uk Web: www.pallant.org.uk

Predominantly British 20th century paintings. Superb collection in Queen Anne townhouse and contemporary building. Regular temporary exhibitions throughout the year.

Opening Times: Gallery closed for new wing building. Please telephone for opening date.
Admission: Please telephone for details. Location: Near city centre, take East Street from City
Cross and turn right at Marks & Spencer. Map Ref: 7

Royal Military Police Museum
Roussillon Barracks, Broyle Road, Chichester PO19 4BN Tel: 01243 534225 Fax: 01243
534288 Email: museum@rhqrmp.freeserve.co.uk Web: www.rhqrmp.freeserve.co.uk

Tracing military police history from Tudor origins, the museum displays artefacts from conflicts including World War I and World War II, Northern Ireland, the Gulf and NATO operations in the former Yugoslavia. Uniforms, badges, medals, videos.

Opening Times: Apr to Sep Tue to Fri 10:30-12:30 & 13:30-16:30, Sat & Sun 14:00-17:00. Oct to
Mar Tue to Fri 10:30-12:30 & 13:30-16:30. Closed Xmas to end Jan. Admission: Free. Groups
by appointment only. Location: 15 minute walk from bus and railway station, on A286
Chichester to Midhurst road. Map Ref: 7

Sussex

Tangmere Military Aviation Museum

Tangmere, Chichester PO20 2ES   Tel: 01243 775223   Fax: 01243 789490
Email: admin@tangmere-museum.org.uk   Web: www.tangmere-museum.org.uk

The museum tells the story of military flying from the earliest days to the present time with special emphasis on the air war over southern England 1939-45.

Opening Times: Feb & Nov daily 10:00-16:30, Mar to Oct daily 10:00-17:30.   Admission: Adult £4.00, Child £1.50, OAP £3.00, Family £9.50.   Location: Three miles east of Chichester off A27.

Map Ref: 10

Weald & Downland Open Air Museum

Singleton, Chichester PO18 0EU   Tel: 01243 811348/811363
Fax: 01243 811475   Email: office@wealddown.co.uk   Web: www.wealddown.co.uk

The Weald & Downland Open Air Museum is home to over 45 historic buildings which have been rescued from destruction and rebuilt in a beautiful 50-acre setting in the South Downs, bringing to life the homes, farms and workplaces of the south east over the past 500 years. Exhibits include a medieval farmstead; a working 17th century watermill; exhibitions of traditional countryside skills; a working Tudor kitchen, historic gardens and farm animals. Special events are held throughout the year.

Opening Times: Winter Weekends only 10:30-16:00, 26 Dec to 2 Jan daily & Feb half term daily. Summer daily 10:30-18:00.   Admission: Adult £7.50, OAP £6.50, Child/Student £4.00, Under 5s Free, Family £20.00 (2 adults and 3 children).   Location: Off A286 in Singleton, on Chichester to Midhurst Road.   Exhibitions & Events 2004 : 11 & 12 Apr: Celebrate the Taste: Easter Food Fair, May: Sustainable Building Event, 6 Jun: Heavy Horse Spectacular, 25 Jul: Rare and Traditional Breeds Show, 2 & 3 Oct: Autumn Countryside Celebration, 26 Dec to 2 Jan 05: Tastes of a Tudor Christmas.

Map Ref: 11

Standen

East Grinstead RH19 4NE   Tel: 01342 323029
Fax: 01342 316424
Email: standen@nationaltrust.org.uk
Web: www.nationaltrust.org.uk/standen

A family house built in the 1890s, a showpiece of the Arts & Crafts Movement. It is decorated throughout with William Morris carpets, fabrics and wallpapers. There are contemporary paintings, tapestries, furniture and many of the original light fittings. The hillside terraced garden has fine views over the Sussex countryside.

Opening Times: End Mar to end Oct Wed to Sun 11:00-17-00. Open BH Mons. Admission: Adult £6.00, Child £3.00, Family £15.00. Group (15) £5.00. Garden only: Adult £3.20, Child £1.60. NT Members Free. Location: Two miles south of East Grinstead, signposted from B2110 (Turners Hill road).

Red Lustre Vase in the hall by De Morgan, chameleon design

Map Ref: 12

Filching Manor & Motor Museum
& Karting Track Campbell Circuit

Filching Manor, Filching Nr Polegate, Eastbourne BN26 5QA   Tel: 01323 487838
Fax: 01323 486331   Email: campbellcurcuit@aol.com   Web: www.campbellcurcuit.co.uk

Set in 15th century Wealden Hall House. 100 top historic cars, motorcycles, boats and aircraft, including Sir Malcolm Campbell's 1937 Bluebird and many classics.

Opening Times: Easter to end of Sep Sat & Sun 11:00-14:30. Guided tours BH 14:30 only.
Admission: Adult £5.00, Child/OAP £3.50.   Location: One mile from A22 and A27 at Polegate.
Brown tourist board signs A22 and A259 Friston.

Map Ref: 13

Sussex

Museum of the Royal National Lifeboat Institution

King Edward Parade, Eastbourne BN21 4BY Tel: 01323 730717

Showing the history of Eastbourne lifeboats from 1824. Many photos of past crews and of epic rescues. Various items of lifeboat memorabilia. A small selection of lifeboat models.

Opening Times: 25 Mar to 28 Apr & 30 Sep to end Dec daily 10:00-16:00. 29 Apr to 29 Sep daily 10:00-17:00. Admission: Free. Location: On seafront, at The Wish Tower. Map Ref: 13

Queens Royal Irish Hussars Museum

c/o Sussex Combined Services Msum, Redoubt Fortress,Royal Parade, Eastbourne BN22 7AQ
Tel: 01323 410300

Tracing history of cavalry regiments who took part in the Charge of the Light Brigade, up to their involvement in the Gulf War. Collections include rare uniforms.

Opening Times: Apr to 5 Nov 09:45-17:30. Admission: £3.50. Location: Half a mile east of pier on seafront. Map Ref: 13

Royal Sussex Regiment Museum

c/o Sussex Combined Services Musm, Redoubt Fortress, Royal Parade, Eastbourne BN22 7AQ
Tel: 01323 410300

Collections of local infantry regiment, including uniforms, medals, regimental silver and a German General's staff car.

Opening Times: Apr to 5 Nov 09:45-17:30. Admission: £3.50. Location: Half a mile east of pier on seafront. Map Ref: 13

Sussex Combined Services Museums & Redoubt Fortress

Royal Parade, Eastbourne BN22 7AQ Tel: 01323 410300

The history of the Army, Navy and RAF in the Sussex area. Displays include uniforms and medals, set in a Napoleonic fortress.

Opening Times: Apr to 5 Nov 09:45-17:30. Admission: £3.50. Location: e Map Ref: 13

Bateman's (Kiplings House)

Burwash, Etchingham TN19 7DS
Tel: 01435 882302 Fax: 01435 882811
Email: batemans@nationaltrust.org.uk
Web: www.nationaltrust.org.uk

A 17th century Ironmaster's house, which was the former home of Rudyard Kipling. This family house with plenty of atmosphere nestles in the beautiful Sussex countryside. A working water mill, gardens and Kipling's Rolls Royce all enhance this house's appeal. Each season this house hosts concerts and events, one of the most popular being 'Last Night of the Proms', when over 4000 people gather.

Kipling's Nobel Prize Medallion

Opening Times: 3 Apr to 31 Oct Sat to Wed 11:00-17:00. Open Good Friday. Admission: Adult £5.50, Child £2.70, Family £13.70. Group (15+) Adult £4.60, Child £2.30. NT Members Free.

Location: Half a mile south of Burwash. Map Ref: 14

Firle Place

Firle BN8 6LP Tel: 01273 858567 Fax: 01273 858570

The house contains a magnificent collection of Old Master paintings, fine English and European furniture and an impressive collection of Sèvres porcelain.

Opening Times: Mid May to end Sep Wed, Thu, Sun & BH 13:45-16:15. Admission: Adult £5.00, Child £2.50, OAP £4.50. Location: Four miles south of Lewes. Map Ref: 15

Sussex

Michelham Priory & Gardens

Upper Dicker, Hailsham BN27 3QS Tel: 01323 844224 Fax: 01323 844030
Email: adminmich@sussexpast.co.uk Web: www.sussexpast.co.uk

With nearly 800 years of history on display, Michelham Priory offers visitors a wealth of fascinating exhibits inside and out. Of particular interest are the remains of a former Augustinian Priory that evolved into a splendid Tudor mansion, a 14th century gatehouse, a rope museum, a working watermill and England's longest water-filled Medieval moat, surrounding more than seven acres of beautiful gardens.

Opening Times: 1 Mar to 31 Oct, Tue to Sun. Times: Mar & Oct 10:30-16:00, Apr to Jul & Sep 10:30-17:00, Aug 10:30-17:30. Admission: Adult £5.20, Child £2.70, Concession £4.50, Family £13.40, Disabled & Carer £2.60 each. Location: At Upper Dicker, approx two miles west of Hailsham and eight miles north-west of Eastbourne. Map Ref: 16

Fishermans Museum

Rock-a-Nore Road, Hastings TN34 3DW Tel: 01424 461446

Model of a Hastings Lugger

Opened as a museum in 1956, the centrepiece is the 'Enterprise' one of the last Hastings sailing luggers (worked 1912-1954). Exhibits also include model ships and boats, fishing gear, historic paintings and photographs illustrating the local fishing industry. Outside are four other types of Hastings fishing boats and some examples of the unique net shops.

Opening Times: Apr to Oct daily 10:00-17:00. Nov to Mar daily 11:00-16:00. Closed Xmas. Admission: Free. Donations welcome. Location: In and around Old Fishermen's Church, on beach at eastern end of Hastings Old Town. Map Ref: 17

Hastings Museum & Art Gallery

Bohemia Road, Hastings TN34 1ET Tel: 01424 781155 Fax: 01424 781165
Email: museum@hastings.gov.uk Web: www.hmag.org.uk

Paintings, ceramics, fossils, native Americans, special features on John Logie Baird, Robert Tressell and Grey Owl, exhibitions of contemporary art. The Durbar Hall was built as part of an Indian Palace in 1886.

Opening Times: Mon to Sat 10:00-17:00, Sun 14:00-17:00. Admission: Free. Location: Ten minute walk from town centre and railway station. Map Ref: 17

Museum of Local History

Old Town Hall, High Street, Hastings TN34 1EW Tel: 01424 781166
Email: oldtownmuseum@hastings.gov.uk Web: www.hmag.org.uk

A walk back in time through the history of Hastings Old Town from the 1960s to pre-history. Subjects covered include seaside entertainment, the Napoleonic Garrison, smuggling, the Armada and the Cinque Ports.

Opening Times: Apr to Sep Mon to Sun 10:00-17:00, Oct to Mar Mon to Sun 11:00-16:00.
Admission: Free. Map Ref: 17

Shipwreck Heritage Centre

Rock-a-Nore Road, Hastings TN34 3DW Tel / Fax: 01424 437452

Displayed are the remains of a Roman ship, the complete hull of a Victorian river barge and many relics from a 1749 Dutch merchant ship whose wreck is visible off St Leonards at low tide.

Opening Times: Mar to Oct daily 10:30-17:00, Nov to Feb daily 11:00-16:00.
Admission: Suggested donation Adult £1.00. Guided Tours for Groups £1.00 per person.
Map Ref: 17

Sussex

Nymans

Handcross, Haywards Heath RH17 6EB
Tel: 01444 400321 Web: www.nationaltrust.org.uk

This is one of the great gardens of the Sussex Weald, with an historic collection of plants, shrubs and trees. The Messel family have also shown their creativity in the library, drawing room, and dining room.

Opening Times: Garden: 18 Feb to 31 Oct Wed to Sun 11:00-18:00. 6 Nov to 20 Feb Sat & Sun only 11:00-16:00. House: 24 Mar to 31 Oct Wed to Sun 11:00-18:00. Open BH Mons.
Admission: Adult £6.50, Child £3.25, Family £16.25. Group (15+) £5.50. NT Members Free.
Location: On B2114 at Handcross, four and a half miles south of Crawley, just off London-Brighton M23/A23.   Map Ref: 18

Horsham Museum

9 Causeway, Horsham RH12 1HE Tel: 01403 254959 Fax: 01403 217581
Email: museum@horsham.gov.uk

Set in a timber framed Medieval house with over 20 galleries, two walled gardens, the museum displays costume, dinosaur bones, bicycles, toys, packaging, art and crafts as well as books by Shelley, the poet.

Opening Times: Mon to Sat (excluding BH & Sun) 10:00-17:00. Admission: Free.
Location: Near town centre, in historic street leading to Parish Church.   Map Ref: 19

Hove Museum & Art Gallery

19 New Church Road, Hove BN3 4AB Tel: 01273 290200 Fax: 01273 292827
Web: www.hove.virtualmuseum.info

Hove Museum & Art Gallery has re-opened following major re-development works. New features include the installation of a lift and new displays of the craft, toy, film and fine art collections.

Opening Times: Tue to Sat 10:00-17:00, Sun 14:00-17:00. Closed Mon (inc Bank Holidays), Good Friday, 25-26 Dec & 1 Jan. Admission: Free. Location: Five minute walk from Hove Station.   Map Ref: 20

West Blatchington Windmill

Holmes Avenue, Hove BN3 7LE Tel: 01273 776017
Web: www.blatchington.virtualmuseum.info

Dating from the 1820s, this grade II listed building still has the original mill workings in place over five floors. Discover how grain is turned into flour in a traditional windmill.

Opening Times: May to Sep Sun & BH only 14:30-17:00, groups can be taken around at other times of the year by arrangement. Admission: Please phone for details. Location: Ten minute walk from Aldrington Station, 30 minutes bus ride from town centre. Buses 5A & 5B Map Ref: 20

Anne of Cleves Museum

52 Southover High Street, Lewes BN7 1JA Tel: 01273 474610
Email: anne@sussexpast.co.uk Web: www.sussexpast.co.uk

The house given to Anne by Henry VIII as part of their divorce settlement. See the old kitchen and the oak furnished main chamber, and investigate the history of the Sussex iron industry.

Opening Times: Jan & Feb, Nov & Dec Tue to Sat 10:00-17:00. Mar to Oct Tue to Sat 10:00-17:00, Sun & Mon 11:00-17:00. Closed Xmas. Admission: Adult £2.90, Child £1.45, Concession £2.60, Family (2 adults and 2 children) £7.35 or (1 adult and 4 children) £5.90.
Location: Near town centre, about ten minutes walk from Lewes Castle and eight minutes walk from Lewes Railway Station. Bus stops nearby.   Map Ref: 21

Sussex

Charleston

near Firle, Lewes BN8 6LL   Tel: 01323 811265   Fax: 01323 811628
Email: info@charleston.org.uk   Web: www.charleston.org.uk

Virginia Woolf's sister, Vanessa Bell, moved to Charleston in 1916 with fellow artist Duncan Grant and their unconventional household. They transformed the house with decorations, painting the walls, doors and furniture in their own unique and inspirational style and collecting paintings and works of art. Charleston became the country meeting place for the group of writers and artists known as Bloomsbury.

Opening Times: 1 Apr to 31 Oct Wed to Sun & BH Mon, 14:00-18:00 (last entry 17:00). Jul & Aug Wed to Sat 11:30-18:00, Sun & BH Mon 14:00-18:00 (last entry 17:00).   Admission: Adult £6.00, Concession £4.50, Special tours.   Location: Seven miles east of Lewes, between villages of Firle and Selmeston.   Exhibitions & Events 2004 : 15-23 May: Charleston Festival.   Map Ref: 15

Glynde Place

Glynde, Lewes BN8 6SX   Tel / Fax: 01273 858224
Email: hampden@glyndeplace.co.uk

A magnificent Elizabethan manor house set in the heart of the South Downs. Glynde Place was built in 1569 from local flint and stone from Normandy and extensively added to in the 18th century. There is a collection of Old Masters, family portraits, furniture, embroidery and silver all belonging to the family who had lived there for over 400 years.

Opening Times: Jun to Sep Sun & Wed & Aug BH 14:00-17:00.   Admission: Adult £5.50, Child £2.75, Groups (25+) £4.00.   Location: Three miles to the east of Lewes. Follow the brown tourist board signs off the A27 or the B2192.   Map Ref: 22

Lewes Castle & Barbican House Museum

169 High Street, Lewes BN7 1YE   Tel: 01273 486290   Fax: 01273 486990
Email: castle@sussexpast.co.uk   Web: www.sussexpast.co.uk

Explore the Castle built soon after the Conquest of 1066 and see the spectacular views from the top. Next door Barbican House Museum displays a range of exhibitions plotting the history of the area along with a sound and light show based around a scale town model, and an interactive touch-screen computer.

Opening Times: Tue to Sat 10:00-17:30 Sun, Mon BH 11:00-17:30. Closed Mon in Jan & Xmas.
Admission: Adult £4.30, Child £2.15, Concession £3.80, Family (2 adults and 2 children) £11.00 or (1 adult and 4 children) £8.75.   Location: In town centre, ten minutes walk from bus and railway stations.   Map Ref: 21

Monks House

Rodmell, Lewes BN7 3HF   Tel: 01372 453401 (Regional Off)
Web: www.nationaltrust.org.uk

This small weather boarded house was the home of Leonard and Virginia Woolf until Leonard's death in 1969. The rooms reflect the life and times of the literary circle in which they moved.

Opening Times: 31 Mar to 30 Oct Wed & Sat 14:00-17:30.   Admission: Adult £2.80, Child £1.40, Family £7.00. NT Members Free.   Location: From A27 south west of Lewes, follow signs for Kingston and then Rodmell village, turn left at Abergavenny Arms pub, then half a mile.   Map Ref: 23

Guided or Private Tours	Disabled Access	Gift Shop or Sales Point	Café or Refreshments	Restaurant	Car Parking

272

Sussex

LITTLEHAMPTON *W Sussex*

Littlehampton Museum

Manor House, Church Street, Littlehampton BN17 5EW   Tel: 01903 738100
Fax: 01903 731690   Email: littlehamptonmuseum@arun.gov.uk

Varied collection of archaeology, social history artefacts and art relating to the Littlehampton area. Also, special displays of photographic and maritime history - over 200 ship models on show!

Opening Times: Tue to Sat 10:30-16:30.   Admission: Free.   Location: 50 metres from High Street, seven minutes walk from train.   Map Ref: 24

NEWHAVEN *E Sussex*

Planet Earth Museum & Sussex History Trail

Paradise Park, Avis Road, Newhaven BN9 0DH   Tel: 01273 512123
Fax: 01273 616005   Email: enquiries@paradisepark.co.uk   Web: paradisepark.co.uk

Planet Earth is one of the finest museums of its type in the country with life size moving dinosaurs, interactive displays and a spectacular collection of fossils, minerals and crystals. Handcrafted models of Sussex landmarks are the setting for the Sussex History Trail.

Opening Times: Daily 10:00-18:00.   Admission: Adult £4.99, Child £3.99, Family £16.99. Group rates available.   Location: Signposted from A26 and A259. Short walk from Newhaven Railway Station and Denton Corner bus stop.   Map Ref: 25

PETERSFIELD *W Sussex*

Uppark

South Harting, Petersfield GU31 5QR   Tel: 01730 825415   Fax: 01730 825873
Email: uppark@nationaltrust.org.uk   Web: www.nationaltrust.org.uk

The dining room with stained glass designed by Repton, 1813

A fine late 17th century house set high on the South Downs. The drama of the 1989 fire and restoration adds to the magic of this romantic house. The elegant Georgian interior houses a famous Grand Tour collection that includes paintings, furniture and ceramics. An 18th century dolls' house with original contents is one of the star items in the collection. The garden is now fully restored in the early 19th century 'picturesque' style.

Opening Times: 28 Mar to 28 Oct Sun to Thu 13:00-17:00. Open BH Mons 11:00-17:00.   Admission: Adult £5.50, Child £2.75, Family £13.75. Group (15+) £4.50. NT Members Free.
Location: Five miles south east of Petersfield on B2146, one and a half miles south of South Harting.   Map Ref: 26

'Meekness' by Pompeo Batoni (1708-87)

PETWORTH *W Sussex*

Lord Seymour attributed to the English School

Petworth House & Park

Petworth GU28 0AE   Tel: 01798 342207
Fax: 01798 342963   Email: petworth@ntrust.org.uk
Web: www.nationaltrust.org.uk/petworth

This magnificient late 17th century mansion set in a beautiful park was landscaped by 'Capability Brown'. It houses one of the finest and largest collection of pictures, with numerous works by Turner, Van Dyck, Reynolds and Blake. There is a large collection of sculpture, furniture and Chinese porcelain. The Servants' Quarters contain interesting kitchens with over 1,000 pieces on display. There is a 650-acre deer park which was severely damaged in the great storm of 1987, but has now been replanted.

Very rare examples of black and gold sgabello hall chairs, c.1615-35

Sussex

Opening Times: 27 Mar to 31 Oct Sat to Wed 11:00-17:30. Admission: Adult £7.00, Child £4.00, Family £18.00. NT Members Free. Location: Located in the centre of Petworth.

Map Ref: 27

PORTSLADE-BY-SEA E Sussex

Foredown Tower

Foredown Road, Portslade-by-Sea BN41 2EW Tel: 01273 292092
Web: www.foredown.virtualmuseum.info

A converted Edwardian water tower, home to the only operational 'camera obscura' in the south east with outstanding views over the surrounding countryside.

Opening Times: Feb to Oct Sat to Sun, Jul to Aug Thu to Fri, inc Bank Holidays 10:00-17:00. Closed Nov to Jan. Available for group visits by appointment only Mon to Fri throughout the year. Please phone for details. Location: 30 minute bus ride from town centre. Buses 6 & 6A.

Map Ref: 28

PULBOROUGH W Sussex

Bignor Roman Villa

Bignor, Pulborough RH20 1PH Tel / Fax: 01798 869259
Email: bignorromanvilla@care4free.net

All under cover. Discovered 1811. Some of the finest mosaics in Great Britain including Venus and Cupid Gladiators, Medusa and Ganymede. Remains of Hypocaust system. Guided tours must be pre-booked.

Opening Times: Mar to Apr Tue to Sun & BH 10:00-17:00, May daily 10:00-17:00, Jun to Sep daily 10:00-18:00, Oct daily 10:00-17:00. Admission: 2004 Prices. Adult £4.00, Child £1.70, OAP £2.85. Party Rate (10+) Adult £3.20, Child £1.35, Senior £2.30. Guided Tour (max 30 per tour) £18.50. Location: Six miles north of Arundel on A29. Six miles from Petworth A285.

Map Ref: 29

Parham House and Gardens

Parham Park, Pulborough RH20 4HS

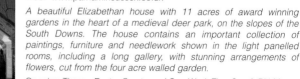

Tel: 01903 742021 Fax: 01903 746557
Email: enquiries@parhaminsussex.co.uk
Web: www.parhaminsussex.co.uk

A beautiful Elizabethan house with 11 acres of award winning gardens in the heart of a medieval deer park, on the slopes of the South Downs. The house contains an important collection of paintings, furniture and needlework shown in the light panelled rooms, including a long gallery, with stunning arrangements of flowers, cut from the four acre walled garden.

Opening Times: Easter Sun to end Sep Wed, Thu, Sun & BH Mon, also Tue & Fri in Aug. Admission: House & Garden: Adult £6.00, Child £2.00, OAP £5.50, Family (2 adult and 2 children) £14.00. Garden only: Adult/OAP £4.00, Child £1.00, Family £9.00.

Map Ref: 30

ROWLANDS CASTLE W Sussex

Stansted Park

Rowlands Castle PO9 6DX Tel: 023 9241 2265 Fax: 023 9241 3773
Email: enquiry@stanstedpark.co.uk Web: www.stanstedpark.co.uk

An Edwardian Country House in its heyday with elegant state rooms and a collection of bird paintings. The servants quarters holds a fascinating collection of household items from a byegone era.

Opening Times: 11 Apr to 27 Sep Sun & Mon. Jul & Aug Sun to Wed. 13:00-17:00.
Admission: Adult £5.50, OAP/Student £4.50, Child £3.50, Family £14.50.

Map Ref: 31

Lamb House

West Street, Rye TN31 7ES Tel: 01372 453401 Web: www.nationaltrust.org.uk

This 18th-century brick fronted house was the home of writer Henry James. A collection of memorabilia and his writing desk can be seen. There is a charming walled garden.

Opening Times: 27 Mar to 30 Oct Wed & Sat only 14:00-18:00. Admission: Adult £2.75, Child £1.30, Family £6.90. Group £2.35. NT Members Free. Location: In West Street, facing west end of church.

Map Ref: 32

Sussex

Rye Art Gallery

Ockman Lane, East Street, Rye TN31 7JY   Tel: 01797 223218/222433   Fax: 01797 225376

Two buildings linked by a courtyard. Easton Rooms holds a programme of exhibitions by contemporary artists and craftsmen. Stormant Studio holds the permanent collection of over 400 pieces shown in rotation together with in-house exhibitions.

Opening Times: Daily 10:30-13:00 & 14:00-17:00. Admission: Free. Location: High Street location.   Map Ref: 32

Rye Castle Museum

3 East Street, Rye TN31 7JY   Tel: 01797 226728

Rye 18th century fire engine, Rye Pottery, maritime history, smuggling items, paintings, etc. All about Rye's long and illustrious history.

Opening Times: Both sites: Apr to Oct Thu to Mon 10:30-13:00 & 14:00-17:00. Ypres Tower: Nov to Mar Sat & Sun 10:30-13:00 & 14:00-15:30. Closed 13:00-14:00. Admission: Both sites Adult £2.90, Child £1.50, Concession £2.00, Family £5.90. Single site Adult £1.90, Child £1.00, Concession £1.50, Family £4.50. Location: In town centre.   Map Ref: 32

Marlipins Museum

High Street, Shoreham-by-Sea BN43 5DA   Tel: 01273 462994   Fax: 01273 486990
Email: smomich@sussexpast.co.uk   Web: www.sussexpast.co.uk

The growth of Shoreham and its importance as a Channel Port are on view at Marlipins, itself an important Norman building, believed to have once been used as a Customs House.

Opening Times: 1 May to 30 Sep Tue to Sat 10:30-16:30. Admission: Adult £2.00, Child £1.00, Concession £1.50. Location: On Shoreham-by-Sea High Street, five minutes walk from Shoreham railway station.   Map Ref: 33

Steyning Museum

Church Street, Steyning BN44 3YB   Tel: 01903 813333

The museum charts the fluctuations in Steyning's fortunes over 2000 years. Its people, buildings, railway and 400 year old school occupy centre stage in the displays. Temporary exhibitions, displays for children and research facilities.

Opening Times: Tue, Wed, Fri, Sat & Sun PM only. Summer: 10:30-12:30 14:30-16:30, winter: 10:30-12:30 14:30-16:00. BH & other days by appointment. Admission: Free. Location: Near town centre, four minute walk.   Map Ref: 34

The Priest House

North Lane, West Hoathly RH19 4PP   Tel: 01342 810479
Email: priest@sussexpast.co.uk   Web: www.sussexpast.co.uk

Built in the 15th century, The Priest House has been open as a museum since 1908. Its furnished rooms contain a fascinating array of 17th and 18th century domestic furniture, needlework and household items. Outside a formal herb garden contains over 150 culinary, medicinal and household herbs.

Opening Times: Mar to Oct Tue to Sat and BH Mon 10:30-17:30, Sun 12:00-17:30.
Admission: Adult £2.70, Child £1.35, Concession £2.40. Location: In centre of village of West Hoathly.   Map Ref: 35

Worthing Museum & Art Gallery

Chapel Road, Worthing BN11 1HP   Tel: 01903 239999   Fax: 01903 236277
Email: museum@worthing.gov.uk   Web: www.worthing.gov.uk

This beautiful building is home to a fascinating collection of toys, costume, art and decorative art, local history and archaeology. There's so much to see that one visit just won't be enough. The Studio, Art Gallery, Norwood Gallery and Sculpture Garden feature work by local, national and international artists.

Opening Times: Mon to Sat 10:00-17:00. Closed Sun & some BH. Admission: Free.
Location: In town centre, ten minute walk from Worthing Central Railway Station.   Map Ref: 36

Warwickshire & West Midlands

Warwickshire is the quintessential English county in a region rich in history and blessed with some of the country's loveliest scenery. Warwick was rebuilt following a disastrous fire in 1694 and possesses a wondrous castle and some fine buildings. Stratford-upon-Avon is a magnet to the thousands who flock to see Shakespeare's birthplace. Birmingham dominates the West Midlands.

There is an interesting selection of quality museums and galleries throughout the region.

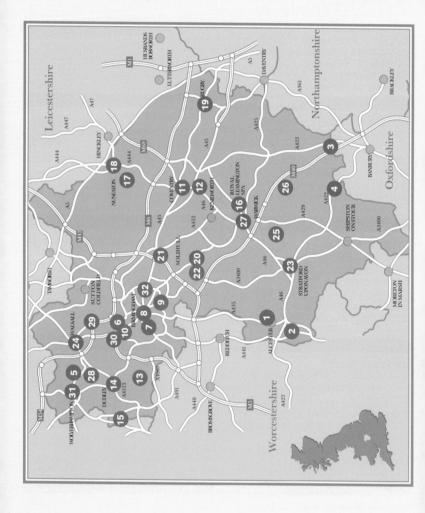

The Red Map References should be used to locate Museums etc on the pages that follow

Warwickshire & West Midlands

Coughton Court

Alcester B49 5JA   Tel: 01789 400777   Fax: 01789 765544
Email: secretary@throckmortons.co.uk
Web: www.coughtoncourt.co.uk

The home of the Throckmorton family since 1530, and with close connections to the Gunpowder Plot - still of Roman Catholic faith with exhibitions/material on recusancy and Catholic emancipation. Excellent collection of family portraits from Tudor times to present day plus family memorabilia, furniture, porcelain, books and tapestries.

Opening Times: 6 Mar to 28 Mar, 2 Oct to 31 Oct 11:30-17:00 Sat & Sun only, 1 Apr to 30 Jun, 1 Sep to 30 Sep Wed to Sun 11:30-17:00, 1 Jul to 31 Aug 11:30-17:00 Tue to Sun. Open BH Mons. Closed Good Friday and Sat 26 Jun. May close early some Sats - check the visitor info line: 01789 762435. Admission: House & Garden: Adult £8.25, Child £4.15, Family (2 Adults and 2 Children) £23.90, Family (2 adults and 3 children) £27.65, Groups 15+ £7.00.

Detail of the family coat of arms in the turret window

Location: Two miles north of Alcester on A435.   Map Ref: 1

Ragley Hall

Alcester B49 5NJ   Tel: 01789 762090   Fax: 01789 764791
Email: info@ragleyhall.com   Web: www.ragleyhall.com

Designed in 1680 by Robert Hooke, Ragley has England's finest Baroque plasterwork by James Gibbs, 1750. Wood carvings by Grinling Gibbons, family portraits by Sir Joshua Reynolds. Sheraton and Louis XVI furniture and Minton, Copeland and Meissen china amongst others. 20th century mural by Graham Rust completed 1969-1983.

Opening Times: 3 Apr to 26 Sept Thu to Sun & BH Mondays 10:00-18:00 (House 12:00-17:30). Last admission 16:30.   Admission: Please visit our website or telephone for details.   Location: Two miles south west of Alcester, off the A46/A435.   Map Ref: 2

Ragley Hall - The Great Hall

Farnborough Hall

Banbury OX17 1DU   Tel: 01295 690002   Web: www.nationaltrust.org.uk

A beautiful stone house, richly decorated in the mid 18th century which as been the home of the Holbech family for over 300 years. The interior plasterwork is quite outstanding. There is a collection of paintings, furniture and sculptures. The grounds contain 18th century temples, a terrace walk and an obelisk.

Opening Times: 7 Apr to 25 Sep Wed & Sun, 2 & 3 May Sun & Mon 14:00-18:00.   Admission: Adult £3.80, Child £1.90, Family £ 9.50. NT Members Free.   Location: Six miles north of Banbury, half a mile west of A423.   Map Ref: 3

The Entrance Hall with classical busts in wall niches

Warwickshire & West Midlands

Chelsea porcelain figure of Una
and the Lion, depicting Truth

Upton House 🎲 🜂 🚃

Banbury OX15 6HT   Tel / Fax: 01295 670266
Email: uptonhouse@nationaltrust.org.uk
Web: www.nationaltrust.org.uk

This impressive 17th century house was remodelled in the late 1920s. There is an outstanding collection of English and Old Master paintings including works by Hogarth, Stubbs and Canaletto. English 18th century furniture, French porcelain, German stained glass and Brussels tapestries are also on display. The garden has terraces, herbaceous borders, ornamental pools and an interesting 1930s water garden.

Brussels tapestry showing border
pattern of flowers and fruit

Opening Times: 3 Apr to 31 Oct Sat to Wed 13:00-17:00. Open Good Friday. Closed Wed 7 Jul. Admission: Adult £6.50, Child £3.50, Family £16.00, Group (15+) £5.20. NT Members Free.
Location: On A422 seven miles north west of Banbury, 12 miles south east of Statford-on-Avon. Follow signs from junction 12 on M40.   Map Ref: 4

Bilston Craft Gallery ♿ 🎲 🚃

Mount Pleasant, Bilston WV14 7LU   Tel: 01902 552507   Fax: 01902 552504
Web: www.wolverhamptonart.org.uk

The gallery hosts an exciting programme of contemporary craft exhibitions with workshops and events. Craftplay, an activity room for pre-school children is open for groups by appointment. Coming in 2004 - Craftscense.

Opening Times: Tue to Fri 10:00-16:00, Sat 11:00-16:00. Admission: Free. Location: Four miles from Wolverhampton and five minutes from Bilston Metro Stop.   Map Ref: 5

Aston Hall 🖎 🗇 🚃   BM&AG

Birmingham Museums & Art Gallery

Trinity Road, Aston, Birmingham B6 6JD   Tel: 0121 327 0062
Web: www.bmag.org.uk

One of the last great houses to be built in a Jacobean style, Aston Hall hosts a fine collection of paintings, textiles and furniture and a 136ft Long Gallery.

Opening Times: Apr to Oct Tue to Sun 11:30-16:00. Closed Mon except BH. Admission: Free.
Location: Three miles from city centre, near junction 6 off M6.   Map Ref: 6

Barber Institute of Fine Arts 🖎 ♿ 🎲 🗇 🚃

University of Birmingham, Edgbaston, Birmingham B15 2TS   Tel: 0121 4147333   Fax: 0121 4143370   Email: info@barber.org.uk   Web: www.barber.org.uk

One of the finest small art galleries in the world housing an outstanding collection of Old Master and Modern paintings, including masterpieces by Rubens, Murillo, Rossetti, Monet and Magritte.

Opening Times: Mon to Sat 10:00-17:00, Sun 12:00-17:00. Admission: Free. Location: On University of Birmingham Campus, three miles south of city centre.   Map Ref: 7

Birmingham Museum and Art Gallery 🖎 ♿ 🎲 🜂

Chamberlain Square, Birmingham B3 3DH   Tel: 0121 303 2834   Fax: 0121 303 1394
Email: bmag_enquiries@birmingham.gov.uk   Web: www.bmag.org.uk

Home to the largest collection of Pre-Raphaelite art in Europe, Birmingham Museum & Art Gallery also host a fine collection of 18th and 19th century art, silver, sculpture, ceramics and archeology. Also houses the Waterhall Gallery of modern art and local history galleries. Gas Hall has a range of temporary exhibitions across the year.

Opening Times: Mon to Thur & Sat 10:00-17:00, Fri 10:30-17:00, Sun 12:30-17:00. Closed Xmas & New Year. Admission: Free - voluntary contribution. Location: Five minutes from New Street and Snow Hill Stations. Short walk from any city centre bus stop.   Map Ref: 8

Warwickshire & West Midlands

Museum of the Jewellery Quarter

75/79 Vyse Street, Hockley, Birmingham B18 6HA   Tel: 0121 554 3598
Email: bmag_enquiries@birmingham.gov.uk   Web: www.bmag.org.uk

A perfectly preserved jewellery workshop little changed since the early part of this century. The Museum tells the story of jewellery making in Birmingham, through guided tours and demonstrations.

Opening Times: Apr to Oct 11:30-16:00. Closed Mon except BH.   Admission: Free.
Location: Short bus ride from city centre. Jewellery Quarter Railway Station five minutes away.
Map Ref: 8

Sarehole Mill

Cole bank Road, Hall Green, Birmingham B13 0BD   Tel: 0121 777 6612
Email: bmag_enquiries@birmingham.gov.uk   Web: www.bmag.org.uk

Sarehole is the only surviving example of the 60 or so watermills that once existed in Birmingham. It was also the childhood haunt of JRR Tolkien and inspiration for the mill in 'The Hobbit'.

Opening Times: Easter to Oct 11:30-16:00. Closed Mon except BH.   Admission: Free.
Location: Five miles from city centre off A34. 15 minutes from Hall Green Station or a short walk from the 11A/11C bus stop.
Map Ref: 9

Soho House
Soho Avenue, Handsworth, Birmingham B18 5LB   Tel: 0121 554 9122
Fax: 0121 554 5929   Email: bmag_enquiries@birmingham.co.uk   Web: www.bmag.org.uk

Soho House was Matthew Boulton's 18th century home, restored with original items from the house. You can find out about this fascinating inventor and the great thinkers that met at the house - the Lunar Society.

Opening Times: 11:30-16:00. Closes Mon except BH.   Admission: Free.   Location: Ten minutes from city centre by bus or train. Ring for more details.
Map Ref: 10

Coventry Toy Museum
Whitfriars Gate, Much Park Street, Coventry CV1 2LT   Tel: 024 7622 7560

A collection of toys of every description housed in a 14th century monastery gatehouse.

Opening Times: Daily 13:00-17:00   Admission: Adult £1.50, Child/OAP £1.00.
Location: Coventry City Centre.
Map Ref: 11

Coventry Transport Museum
Hales Street, Coventry CV1 1PN   Tel: 024 7683 2425   Fax: 024 7683 2465
Email: museum@mbrt.co.uk   Web: www.mbrt.co.uk

Largest collection of British road transport in the world. Designated as a collection of National Importance with 200 cars and commercial vehicles, 200 cycles and 90 motorcycles and Thrust 2 and Thrust SSC land speed record cars.

Opening Times: Daily 10:00-17:00. Closed 24-26 Dec.   Admission: Free.   Location: Town centre, one minute walk from bus station, ten minutes from train station.
Map Ref: 11

Herbert Art Gallery & Museum

Jordan Well, Coventry CV1 5QP
Tel: 024 7683 2565   Fax: 024 7683 2410

Email: artsandheritage@coventry.gov.uk
Web: www.coventrymuseum.org.uk
The Herbert Art Gallery and Museum is situated in the heart of Coventry City Centre a couple of minutes walk away from Coventry Cathedral. The award winning Godiva City exhibition tells the story of the city from before Lady Godiva to the present. The rest of the Gallery is used for temporary exhibitions using objects from the museum collections and provided by other organisations and individuals. (continued over page)

Jacquard Loom dating from 1845 in Godiva City Exhibition

Warwickshire & West Midlands

Items from the Museum's permanent collection of Lady Godiva paintings and drawings and sketches forGraham Sutherland's Cathedral tapestry are invariably on display. The collections cover visual arts, natural history, archaeology, industrial and social history.

Opening Times: Mon to Sat 10:00-17:30, Sun 12:00-17:00. Admission: Free. Location: City centre near Tourist Information Centre and Coventry Cathedral.
'Lady Godiva' by Hon. John Collier   Map Ref: 11

Jaguar Daimler Heritage Trust
Jaguar Cars, Browns Lane, Coventry CV5 9DR   Tel: 024 76402121

Display of 30+ Jaguars, collection totals 130+ available to view if required. Archive housing original factory records and photographic collection and picture gallery.

Opening Times: Mon to Fri 08:30-16:45 and last Sun of month 10:00-16:00. Admission: Free.
Location: On bus route from city centre, good access to motorways.   Map Ref: 11

Lunt Roman Fort
Coventry Road, Baginton, Coventry   Tel: 024 7683 2381   Fax: 024 7683 2410   Email: artsandheritage@coventry.gov.uk
Web: www.coventrymuseum.org.uk

Coventry City Council

Once inhabited by the Roman Army, this ancient site includes the Granary building which contains a museum of Roman Life with archaelogical finds.

Opening Times: Pre booked parties 31 Jan to 1 Dec. 1 Apr to 31 Oct Sat, Sun & BH Mon 10:00-17:00. 17 Jul to 30 Aug Daily except Wed 10:00-17:00. 31 May to 4 Jun Daily 10:00-17:00.
Admission: Adult £2.00, Concession £1.00. Location: Baginton Village is on the south side of Coventry, just off the A45 and A46. The fort is situated off the Coventry Road.   Map Ref: 12

Priory Visitor Centre
Priory Gardens, Coventry CV1 5EX   Tel: 024 7655 2242   Fax: 024 7683 2410   Email: priory.visitorscentre@coventry.gov.uk
Web: www.coventrymuseum.org.uk

Coventry City Council

On the site of Coventry's medieval Priory and Cathedral. It tells the story of the site from the time of Lady Godiva to the Dissolution by King Henry VIII using archaeological finds from recent excavations.

Opening Times: Mon to Sat 10:00-17:30, Sun 12:00-16:00. Admission: Free. Location: In city centre, near Holy Trinity Church and Coventry Cathedral.   Map Ref: 11

St Mary's Guildhall
Bayley Lane, Coventry   Tel: 024 7683 2381   Fax: 024 7683 2410
Email: artsandheritage@coventry.gov.uk
Web: www.coventrymuseum.org.uk

Coventry City Council

St Mary's Guildhall is one of the finest surviving medieval Guildhalls in England. It dates from the 1340s and includes the imposing Great Hall with its stained glass windows and a Tournai tapestry dated 1500.

Opening Times: Easter to end Sep Sun to Thu 10:00-16:00. Admission: Free. Location: City centre, near Coventry Cathedral.   Map Ref: 11

Haden Hill House
Off Barrs Road, Cradley Heath   Tel: 01384 569444   Email: oakhouse@sandwell.gov.uk
Web: www.smbc.sandwell.gov.uk

A Victorian furnished house with a collection of social history relating to the Haden Family.

Opening Times: Mon to Thu 10:00-17:00, Fri 10:00-16:30, Sat & Sun 13:00-17:00
Admission: Free Location: Off Barrs Road, Cradley Heath near the Leisure Centre
                                                          Map Ref: 13

Warwickshire & West Midlands

Black Country Living Museum

Tipton Road, Dudley DY1 4SQ   Tel: 0121 557 9643   Fax: 0121 557 4242
Email: info@bclm.co.uk   Web: www.bclm.co.uk

The Black Country Living Museum was established in 1975 to collect, preserve research and display items relating to the social and industrial history of the Black Country. There is a collection of well over 30,000 items, ranging from hand made nails to whole buildings. Together, the mine, the foundry and the many houses, shops and workshops rebuilt on its 26 acre site represent the Black Country when it was the heart of industrial Britain. Much of the collection

Policeman

consists of the fixtures and fittings that make these buildings complete

St. James's School

and accurate to the last detail, but in addition, Black Country products, both past and present, are continually being added to the collection. The most recent addition is a representative collection of cars and motorcycles made in Wolverhampton, an important centre of the automotive industry in the 1920s and 30s. The modern exhibition halls, opened in 2000, display selections of Black Country products. The centrepiece is a permanent display of items that defined the area across the world: chain and anchor made in Netherton for the great ocean liners, world class saddles made in Walsall, crystal glass made in Stourbridge and hardware made in Cradley Heath and exported throughout the British Empire.

Opening Times: Mar to Oct daily 10:00-17:00, Nov to Feb Wed to Sun 10:00-16:00.
Admission: Adult £9.60, Child £5.50, OAP £8.50, Family (2 adults and 3 children) £27.00.
(2003 prices). Location: Three miles from junction 2 of the M5, six miles from junction 10 of the M6, ten miles from Birmingham City Centre. Exhibitions & Events 2004 : For details please contact.   Map Ref: 14

Dudley Museum & Art Gallery

St James's Road, Dudley DY1 1HU   Tel: 01384 815575   Fax: 01384
815576   Web: www.dudley.gov.uk

Geological gallery with definitive collection of local Silurian and carboniferous fossils. Brooke Robinson museum of European paintings, furniture and ceramics. Temporary exhibitions throughout the year.

Opening Times: Mon to Sat 10:00-16:00. Closed BH Mon.   Admission: Free.   Location: Town centre.   Map Ref: 14

Broadfield House Glass Museum

Compton Drive, Kingswinford DY6 9NS   Tel: 01384 812745   Fax: 01384
812746   Email: glass.museum@dudley.gov.uk
Web: www.glassmuseum.org.uk

Situated in the historic glass quarter, Broadfield House celebrates the art of glassmaking. Glass artists can be watched in the studio and attractive gifts bought from the shop.

Opening Times: Tue to Sun & BH Mon 10:00-16:00.   Admission: Free.   Location: Near town centre, on main bus route.   Map Ref: 15

---

www.mghh.co.uk

For current information on the outstanding Collections in over 1600 Museums,
Galleries & Historic Houses in England, Scotland, Wales and Ireland

Warwickshire & West Midlands

Leamington Spa Art Gallery & Museum, Royal Pump Rooms

The Parade, Leamington Spa CV32 4AA   Tel: 01926 742700

Award winning art gallery and museum with services on offer including: fine art collection, exhibition on the history of Royal Leamington Spa, cabinet of curiosities, gallery of interactive exhibits, Hammam (restored Turkish bath), changing programme of visual

arts, history and local interest exhibitions and educational parties by arrangement. Fine art collection includes 16th and 17th century Dutch and Flemish, 18th and 21st century British artists, local

artists, sculpture, ceramics and glassware. Recent acquisitions include works of art by Mark Quinn, Damien Hirst and Catherine Yass. Other key artists in the collection include Stanley Spencer, L S Lowry, Gillian Wearing, Vanessa Bell, Patrick Caulfield, Sir Terry Frost, Walter Sickert and Graham Sutherland. Facilities at The Royal Pump Rooms also include a café, library, tourist information centre and assembly rooms.

Opening Times: Tue, Wed, Fri & Sat 10:30-17:00, Thu 13:30-20:00, Sun 11:00-16:00. Closed Mon. Admission: Free. Location: 500 metres from Leamington Spa Railway Station. The Royal Pump Room is situated on The Parade, two minute walk from the main shopping area. Exhibitions & Events 2004 : For Exhibitions and Events please telephone for details. Map Ref: 16

Arbury Hall

Nuneaton CV10 7PT   Tel: 024 7638 2804   Fax: 024 7664 1147
Email: brenda.newell@arburyhall.net

Arbury Hall has been the home of the Newdegate family since the 16th century. Arbury contains important collections of paintings, furniture, glass and china collected through the centuries by successive generations.

Opening Times: Easter to Sep BH week-ends Sun & Mon Hall: 14:00-17:00, Garden: 13:30-18:00. Admission: Hall & Gardens: Adult £6.50, Child £4.00, Family (2 adults and 2 children) £16.00. Garden only: Adult £4.50, Child £3.00.   Map Ref: 17

Museum & Art Gallery

Riversley Park, Nuneaton CV11 5TU   Tel: 024 7635 0720   Fax: 024 7634 3559
Email: museum@nuneaton-bedworthbc.gov.uk   Web: www.nuneatonandbedworth.gov.uk

The Museum and Art Gallery boasts a varied collection which includes George Eliot memorabilia, local history and paintings. As well as the permanent displays of its collections, there is a lively temporary exhibition programme showing regional artists, quality touring displays and subjects of local interest.

Opening Times: Tue to Sat 10:30-16:30, Sun 14:00-16:30. Closed Mon except BH. Admission: Free.
Location: Pleasant location in Riversley Park close to town centre.   Map Ref: 18

Recreation of George Eliot's Drawing Room

Rugby Art Gallery & Museum

Little Elborow Street, Rugby CV21 3BZ   Tel: 01788 533201   Fax: 01788 533204
Email: rugbyartgallery&museum@rugby.gov.uk   Web: www.rugbygalleryandmuseum.org.uk

Tripontium collection of Roman artefacts. Rugby's social history including touchscreen kiosk about Rugby's industrial heritage. Rugby Collection of 20th century and contemporary British art. Changing programme of contemporary art and craft exhibitions.

Opening Times: Tue & Thu 10:00-20:00, Wed & Fri 10:00-17:00, Sat 10:00-16:00, Sun & BH 13:00-17:00. Closed Mon. Admission: Free. Location: Town centre. Map Ref: 19

Webb Ellis Football Museum

5 St Matthews Street, Rugby CV21 3BY Tel: 01788 567777 Fax: 01788 537400
Email: pat@james-gilbert.com Web: www.gilbertrugby.com

Visit the museum and trace the history of the game and its evolution. Soak up the history of this noble game through memorabilia from its beginnings to the World Cup of 1999. Multi-screen show, The Rugby Experience.

Opening Times: Mon to Sat 09:00-17:00. Admission: Free. Location: Opposite Rugby School. Map Ref: 19

Baddesley Clinton

Rising Lane, Baddesley, Knowle, Solihull B93 0DQ Tel: 01564 783294
Fax: 01564 782706 Email: baddesleyclintion@nationaltrust.org.uk
Web: www.nationaltrust.org.uk

The Great Hall constructed in
1570s by Henry Ferrers

A romantic moated manor house, dating from the 15th century. There is simple oak furniture which has been enriched with ornamental carvings. In the Elizabethan era it was a haven for persecuted Catholics, with no fewer than three priest-holes. There are delightful gardens with stewponds and a lake walk.

Opening Times: 3 Mar to 30 Apr Wed to Sun 13:30-17:00, 1 May to 30 Sep Wed to Sun 13:30-17:30. 1 Oct to 7 Nov Wed to Sun 13:30-17:00. Open BH Mons. Admission: Adult £6.20, Child £3.10, Family £15.50. Group (15+): £5.00. NT Members Free. Location: Three quarters of a mile west of A4141 Warwick-Birmingham road, at Chadwick End. Seven and a half miles north west of Warwick, six miles south of M42 junction 5. Map Ref: 20

National Motorcycle Museum

Coventry Road, Bickenhill, Solihull B92 0EJ Tel: 01675 443311 Fax: 01675 443310
Email: sales@nationalmotorcyclemuseum.co.uk Web: nationalmotorcyclemuseum.co.uk

Wartime machines on view at the
National Motorcycle Museum

The National Motorcycle Museum houses a breathtaking collection of over 700 British motorcycles dating from 1898, each painstakingly restored to its original specification. Facilities at the Museum include a restaurant/snack bar, bookshop and souvenir shop.

Opening Times: Daily 10:00-18:00. Closed Xmas. Please note following a severe fire in Sep 2003, the Museum will be closed until Dec 2004. Admission: Adult £4.95, Child/OAP £3.75. Location: The Museum is situated on the A45 junction 6 of M42, opposite the National Exhibition Centre. Map Ref: 21

Packwood House

Lapworth, Solihull B94 6AT Tel: 01564 783294 Fax: 01564 782706
Email: packwood@nationaltrust.org.uk
Web: www.nationaltrust.org.uk

This 16th century house has a character of the 1920s. There is a fine collection of furniture, tapestries and a mixed collection of paintings. The gardens have renowned herbacious borders and a famous collection of yews.

Opening Times: 3 Mar to 7 Nov Wed to Sun 12:00-16:30. Open BH Mons. Admission: Adult £5.60, Child £2.80, Family £14.00. Group (15+) £4.50. Garden only; Adult £2.80, Child £1.40. NT Members Free. Location: Two miles east of Hockley Heath (on A3400), 11 miles south east of central Birmingham. Map Ref: 22

Warwickshire & West Midlands

STRATFORD-UPON-AVON *Warwicks*

Royal Shakespeare Company Collection

Royal Shakespeare Theatre, Waterside, Stratford-upon-Avon CV37 6BB Tel: 01789 262870/412617 Fax: 01789 262870 Email: info@rsc.org.uk Web: www.rsc.org.uk

Exhibition featuring costumes worn by famous actors in past productions. Historic paintings, drawings and prints of scenes and characters. Regularly updated to complement repertoire. Displays of memorabilia and theatre history.

Opening Times: Mon to Fri 13:30-18:30, Sat 10:30-18:30, Sun 12:00-16:00. Admission: Adult £1.50, Concession £1.00. Location: Near town centre on the banks of River Avon.

Map Ref: 23

Shakespeare Birthplace Trust

The Shakespeare Centre, Henley Street, Stratford-upon-Avon CV37 6QW
Tel: 01789 204016 Fax: 01789 263138 Email: info@shakespeare.org.uk
Web: www.shakespeare.org.uk

Elizabethan mans's signet ring which may have belonged to Shakespeare

The Trust administers the five Shakespeare properties which house the museum collections: Shakespeare's Birthplace, Anne Hathaway's Cottage, New Place/Nash's House, Mary Arden's House and the Shakespeare Countryside Museum and Halls Croft. The collections include Elizabethan and Jacobean domestic furniture, ceramic, metal ware and textiles; Shakespeare memorabilia; archaeological and social history material relating to the Stratford-upon-Avon district; local craft and agricultural tools, vehicles and machinery; coins and medals; oil and watercolours paintings, including important portraits of Shakespeare. The Trust also administers Harvard House and the Museum of British Pewter with a large collection of pewter dating from Romano-British times. The Trust also has an important Shakespeare Library and a Records Office.

Reconstruction of John Shakespeare's glove-making workshop

Opening Times: Nash's House/New Place and Hall's Croft: Nov to Mar Mon to Sat 11:00-16:00, Sun 11:00-16:00, Apr to May & Sep to Oct daily 11:00-17:00, Jun to Aug Mon to Sat 09:30-17:00, Sun 10:00-17:00. Anne Hathaway's Cottage: Nov to Mar Mon to Sat 10:00-16:00, Sun 10:30-16:00, Apr to May & Sep to Oct Mon to Sat 09:30-17:00, Sun 10:00-17:00, Jun to Aug Mon to Sat 09:00-17:00, Sun 09:30-17:00. Mary Arden's House: Nov to Mar Mon to Sat 10:00-16:00, Sun 10:30-16:00, Apr to May & Sep to Oct Mon to Sat 10:00-17:00, Sun 10:30-17:00, Jun to Aug Mon to Sat 09:30-17:00, Sun 10:00-17:00. Shakespeare's Birthplace: Nov to Mar Mon to Sat 10:00-16:00, Sun 10:30-16:00, Apr to May & Sep to Oct Mon to Sat 10:00-17:00, Sun 10:30-17:00, Jun to Aug Mon to Sat 09:00-17:00, Sun 09:30-17:00. Admission: Nash's House/New Place and Hall's Croft: Single Ticket Adult £3.50, Child £1.70, Concession £3.00, Family £9.00. Anne Hathaway's Cottage Single Ticket: Adult £5.20, Child £2.00, Concession £4.00, Family £12.00. Mary Arden's House Single Ticket: Adult £5.70, Child £2.50, Concession £5.00, Family £13.50. Shakespeare's Birthplace Single Ticket: Adult £6.70, Child £2.60, Concession £5.50, Family £15.00. Multiple House Tickets - Three In-Town Houses: Adult £10.00, Child £5.00, Concession £8.00, Family £20.00. All Five Houses: Adult £13.00, Child £6.50, Concession £12.00, Family £29.00. Group rates available telephone 01789 201806.

Map Ref: 23

Warwickshire & West Midlands

Jerome K Jerome Birthplace Museum

Belsize House, Bradford Street, Walsall WS1 1PN
Tel: 01922 653116

Jerome K Jerome is Walsall's most distinguished literary figure, born here on 2 May 1859. The Museum, located on the ground floor, includes an 1850s Victorian parlour and an exhibition charting his life and times. Items on display include his World War One ambulance driver's uniform and first editions of his work.

Opening Times: Mon to Fri 09:00-17:00, Sat 12:00-14:00. Closed BH. Admission: Free. Location: Bradford Street, two minutes walk from the Bridge. Map Ref: 24

Jerome's birthplace, Belsize House

New Art Gallery Walsall

Gallery Square, Walsall WS2 8LG Tel: 01922 654400/info 637575
Fax: 01922 654401 Email: info@artatwalsall.org.uk
Web: www.artatwalsall.org.uk

On permanent display is The Garman Ryan Collection which was donated to the people of Walsall by Lady Kathleen Garman, widow of sculptor Sir Jacob Epstein, in 1973. The gallery is also home to a Discovery Gallery, which creates an introduction to a three storey children's house, including an artist's studio and activity room. The temporary exhibition galleries are dedicated to exhibiting the best of contemporary and historic art.

Opening Times: Tue to Sat 10:00-17:00, Sun 12:00-17:00. Open BH. Admission: Free. Location: Two minutes away from the town centre and is sign posted from all major routes into Walsall Town Centre and M6 junction 7, 8 & 10. Map Ref: 24

The Garman Ryan Collection

Charlecote Park

Warwick CV35 9ER Tel: 01789 470277
Fax: 01789 470544
Email: charlecote.park@nationaltrust.org.uk
Web: www.nationaltrust.org.uk

This Tudor house was the home of the Lucy family for over 700 years. The early Victorian interior contains a good collection of family portraits, furniture, books and porcelain. The formal garden opens on to a fine deer park.

Opening Times: 6 Mar to 28 Sep Fri to Tue 12:00-17:00, 1 Oct to 2 Nov Fri to Tue 12:00-16:30. Open Weds in July & Aug and after BHs. Admission: Adult £6.40, Child £3.20, Family £16.00. Group (15+) £5.40. Grounds only: Adult £3.00, Child £ 1.50. NT Members Free. Location: One mile west of Wellesbourne, five miles east of Stratford-upon-Avon, six miles south of Warwick on north side of B4086. Map Ref: 25

Original armorial stained glass at Charlecote

Heritage Motor Centre

Banbury Road, Gaydon, Warwick CV35 0BJ Tel: 01926 641188 Fax: 01926 645103
Email: enquiries@heritage-motor-centre.co.uk Web: www.heritage-motor-centre.co.uk

Home to the world's largest collection of historic British cars. Revealing more than a century of British motor industry heritage. Extensive archive of original documents, film and photographs.

Opening Times: Daily 10:00-17:00. Closed 24-26 Dec. Admission: Adult £8.00, Child £6.00, OAP £7.00, Family (2 adults and 3 children) £25.00. Location: Two minutes from junction 12 on M40. Map Ref: 26

WARWICK *Warwicks (continued)*

The Queen's Own Hussars Museum

Lord Leycester Hospital, High Street, Warwick CV34 4BH   Tel / Fax: 01926 492035
Email: trooper@qohm.tsnet.co.uk

The Early Years display includes Sheriffmuir, the first action in which both the 3rd and 7th Hussars took part. The Wars against the French include Dettingen and the story of Thomas Brown. The Napoleonic War cases highlight Peninsular Campaign and lead up to Waterloo. 19th century and Colonial Wars are illustrated through life sized tableaux. In the Guildhall section there are numerous displays including one on the Second World War.

Opening Times: Summer Tue to Sun 10:30-17:00. Winter Tue to Sun 10:30-16:00. Closed Xmas.
Admission: Hospital: Adult £3.00, Child £2.00, OAP £2.50. No charge to enter Museum.   Location: Housed in Lord Leycester Hospital, one minute walk from Market Square.   Map Ref: 27

Royal Regiment of Fusiliers Museum (Royal Warwickshire)

St Johns House, Warwick CV34 4NF   Tel: 01926 491653   Fax: 01869 257633

Museum tells the story of the Sixth Foot (Royal Warwickshire Regiment) from its origins in 1674 to the Fusiliers of today. The displays are an exciting mix of real objects, models and activities. You can see uniforms, weapons, equipment, medals, documents, paintings and curios from all ranks of soldier - Private to Field Marshal.

Opening Times: Jan to Dec, Tue to Sat 10:00-17:00, May to Sep, Sun 14:30-17:00
Admission: Free.   Location: Five minute from Warwick Railway Station, near town centre.
                                                                                                       Map Ref: 27

St Johns House

St Johns, Warwick CV34 4NF   Tel: 01926 412021/412132   Fax: 01926 419840
Email: museum@warwickshire.gov.uk   Web: www.warwickshire.gov.uk/museum

Social history of Warwickshire, displayed in a 17th century house with gardens. Victorian schoolroom and kitchen, costume gallery, Discovery Room for the under 5s.

Opening Times: Tue to Sat & BH Mon 10:00-17:00, May to Sep also Sun 14:30-17:00.
Admission: Free.   Location: Near town centre and St Nicholas Park, two minute walk from Warwick Railway Station.   Map Ref: 27

Key to Classifications

see Classifications Index on page 423

Anthropology	Horticultural	Police, Prisons
Archaeological	Jewellery	& Dungeons
Art Galleries	Literature & Libraries	Railways
Arts, Crafts & Textiles	Maritime	Religion
China, Glass & Ceramics	Military & Defence	Roman
Communications	Multicultural	Science - Earth & Planetary
Egyptian	Music & Theatre	Sculpture
Fashion	Natural History	Sporting History
Geology	Oriental	Toy & Childhood
Health & Medicine	Palaces	Transport
Historic Houses	Photography	Victoriana

Warwickshire & West Midlands

WARWICK *Warwicks (continued)*

Warwick Doll Museum

Okens House, Castle Street, Warwick CV34 4BP   Tel: 01926 495546/412500   Fax: 01926 419840   Email: museum@warwickshire.gov.uk   Web: www.warwickshire.gov.uk/museum

Dolls, teddies, toys and games from days gone by, displayed in Okens House - a 15th century timber-framed building. Shop catering for serious doll collectors and casual visitors.

Opening Times: Apr to Oct Mon to Sat 10:00-17:00, Sun 11:30-17:00, Nov to Mar Sat only 10:00-16:00. Admission: Adult £1.00, Child/Concession 70p, Family £3.00. Location: Near town centre, on route from Warwick Castle.   Map Ref: 27

Warwickshire Museum

Market Place, Warwick CV34 4SA   Tel: 01926 412500   Fax: 01926 419840   Email: museum@warwickshire.gov.uk   Web: www.warwickshire.gov.uk/museum

Displays on the archaeology, geology and natural history of Warwickshire and a temporary exhibition gallery. Highlights include a huge brown bear, the Sheldon Tapestry Map of Warwickshire, live bees, fossils and ancient jewellery.

Opening Times: Tue to Sat & BH Mon 10:00-17:00, May to Sep also Sun 11:30-17:00. Admission: Free. Location: Town centre, in the Market Square.   Map Ref: 27

WEDNESBURY *W Midlands*

Wednesbury Museum & Art Gallery

Holyhead Road, Wednesbury WS10 7DF   Tel: 0121 556 0683   Email: oakhouse@sandwell.gov.uk   Web: www.smbc.sandwell.gov.uk

Houses a Fine art collection and the world's largest public collection of Ruskin Pottery. Also has a Family fun room, changing exhibition and workshop programme.

Opening Times: Mon, Wed & Fri 10:00-17:00, Thu & Sat 10:00-13:00, closed Sun. Admission: Free. Location: Off the old A41 in Wednesbury, three minute walk from bus station, five minute walk from Great Western Street Metro Station.   Map Ref: 28

WEST BROMWICH *W Midlands*

Bishop Asbury Cottage

Newton Road, Great Barr, West Bromwich B43 6HN   Tel: 0121 553 0759   Fax: 0121 525 5167   Email: oakhouse@sandwell.gov.uk   Web: www.smbc.sandwell.gov.uk

18th century furniture and artefacts connected with Bishop Frances Asbury, the first Methodist Bishop of America.

Opening Times: Open by appointment only, two open days a year. Admission: Groups £2.50 per person (min charge £25.00 per group). Location: On the A4041, Newton Road. Parking at Maltshovel Public House next door.   Map Ref: 29

Oak House Museum

Oak Road, West Bromwich B70 8HJ   Tel: 0121 553 0759   Email: oakhouse@sandwell.gov.uk   Web: www.smbc.sandwell.gov.uk

A Yeoman farmer's residence surrounded by pleasant grounds, housing Jacobean and Tudor furniture.

Opening Times: Apr to Sep, Mon, Tue, Wed & Fri 10:00-17:00, Sat & Sun 14:00-17:00. Oct to Mar, Mon, Tue, Wed & Fri 10:00-16:00, Sat 13:30-16:00. Closed Sun and Thu. Admission: Free Location: Near Town Centre, Ten minutes walk from Lodge Road Metro Station   Map Ref: 30

WOLVERHAMPTON *W Midlands*

Bantock House & Park

Finchfield Road, Wolverhampton WV3 9LQ   Tel: 01902 552195   Fax: 01902 552196   Web: www.wolverhamptonart.org.uk

Visitors can discover the history of Wolverhampton, from market town to metropolis, as well as finding out the history of the 19th century house and park. There are activities for all ages throughout.

Opening Times: Nov to Mar Fri to Sun 12:00-16:00, Apr to Oct Tue to Sun 10:00-17:00. Admission: Free. Location: One mile from the centre of Wolverhampton, good bus links.
                                                                       Map Ref: 31

Warwickshire & West Midlands

Wightwick Manor

Wightwick Bank, Wolverhampton WV6 8EE   Tel: 01902 761400
Fax: 01902 764663   Email: wightwickmanor@nationaltrust.org.uk
Web: www.nationaltrust.co.uk

Victorian manor house and garden owned by the Mauder family. The house is a wonderful example of the influence of William Morris and the Arts and Craft Movement. Pre-Raphaelite Art Collection, 17 acre Thomas Mawson garden with formal areas and woodland.

Opening Times: 4 Mar to 23 Dec Thu & Sat 13:30-17:00. Open BH Suns & Mons. Admission: Adult £6.00, Child £3.00, Family £14.00. Group (15+) Adult £5.00, Child £2.40.NT Members Free. Location: Off A454, three miles west of Wolverhampton.   Map Ref: 31

Queen Anne walnut marquetry cabinet

Wolverhampton Art Gallery

Lichfield Street, Wolverhampton WV1 1DU   Tel: 01902 552055   Fax: 01902 552053
Email: info@wolverhamptonart.org.uk   Web: www.wolverhamptonart.org.uk

Wolverhampton Art Gallery has become renowned for its innovative programme of temporary exhibitions, backed up by a lively programme of workshops and events. The contemporary collection is the finest in the region. The gallery also houses an outstanding collection of British and American Pop Art along with traditional 18th and 19th century paintings by artists such as Gainsborough, Turner and Landseer.

Opening Times: Mon to Sat 10:00-17:00.
Admission: Free. Location: Centre of city, two minute walk from bus and train stations.   Map Ref: 31

Blakesley Hall

Blakesley Road, Yardley B25 8RN   Tel: 0121 4642193
Web: www.bmag.org.uk

BM&AG
Birmingham Museums & Art Gallery

Built in 1590 Blakesley Hall contains period furniture and fittings including the table in the great hall that is original to the house. Recently renovated it is one of the few remaining timber framed buildings left in Birmingham.

Opening Times: Tue to Sun 11:30-16:00. Closed Mon except BH. Admission: Free.
                    Map Ref: 32

Wiltshire

Salisbury, built where the rivers Avon, Bourne and Nadder meet is arguably the most perfect cathedral city in England. Salisbury Plain contains Britain's leading concentration of major prehistoric sites, the main one being Stonehenge. Malmesbury in the north boasts some of the finest Roman architecture in the country and Avebury is one of the most important megalithic monuments in Europe.

Wiltshire's heritage is well recorded in its museums and stately homes.

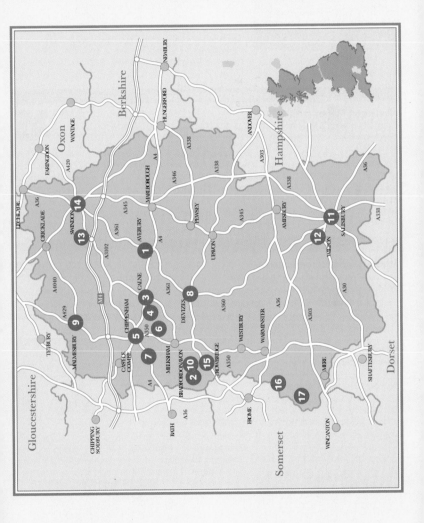

The Red Map References should be used to locate Museums etc on the pages that follow

Wiltshire

AVEBURY

Alexander Keiller Museum

High Street, Avebury SN8 1RF   Tel: 01672 539250   Fax: 01672 538038
Email: avebury@nationaltrust.org.uk   Web: www.nationaltrust.org.uk

Contains prehistoric collections from the Avebury complex of monuments, which are of similar age to Stonehenge. Admission charge also covers 'Avebury, 6000 Years of Mystery', an interactive exhibition.

Opening Times: 1 Apr to 31 Oct daily 10:00-18:00, 1 Nov to 31 Mar daily 10:00-16:00. Closed Xmas.
Admission: Adult £4.20, Child £2.10, Family £10.00 (2 adults & 3 children), Family £7.00 (1 adult & 3 children). Group (15+) Adult £3.60, Child £1.80. NT and EH Members Free. Location: Next to prehistoric stone circles. Parking five minutes walk. Reduced rate when

The Alexander Keiller Museum

arriving by public transport or cycle.   Map Ref: 1

BRADFORD-ON-AVON

Westwood Manor

Bradford-on-Avon BA15 2AF Tel: 01225 863374   Fax: 01225 867316
Web: www.nationaltrust.org.uk

A 15th century stone manor house, altered in the early 17th century. Several of the rooms have fine plasterwork and panelling. There is a collection of needlework and early keyboard instruments. The garden is laid out as a modern topiary.

Opening Times: 4 Apr to 29 Sep Tue, Wed & Sun 14:00-17:00.   Admission: Adult £4.40, Child £2.20, Family £11.20 (2 adults and 2 children). Groups at other times by written application to tenants. NT Members Free. Location: One and a half miles south west of Bradford-on-Avon, in Westwood village, beside the church.   Map Ref: 2

CALNE

Atwell-Wilson Motor Museum

Downside, Stockley Lane, Calne SN11 0NF   Tel / Fax: 01249 813119
Web: www.atwell-wilson.org

The collection began in 1962 with the Buick and Singer, Vauxhall and a Model T arrived later, and wedding work commenced in 1972. The large hall was built in 1989 when the museum opened. The contents are varied with vehicles from the 1920s to the 1980s.

Opening Times: Apr to Oct Mon to Thu & Sun 11:00-17:00. Open Good Friday. Nov to Mar Mon to Thu & Sun 11:00-16:00. Admission: Adult £3.00, Child £1.00, OAP £2.50. Location: The site is also the location of a 17th century water meadow, which is being preserved.   Map Ref: 3

Bowood House & Gardens

Estate Office, Bowood House, Calne SN11 0LZ
Tel: 01249 812102   Fax: 01249 821757
Email: houseandgardens@bowood.org   Web: www.bowood.org

Bowood House, the family home of the Marquis and Marchioness of Lansdowne, was built during the 18th century, to the designs of Henry Keene and Robert Adam. The Chapel and famous Italianate terraced gardens were added in the 19th century. The House contains important paintings & classical and 19th century sculpture. There is a fascinating collection of Indiana

Front elevation of Bowood House

(the 5th Marquis was Viceroy 1888-94). The Exhibition Rooms contain Victoriana, costume, jewellery, miniatures and fine porcelain. Among the most interesting items are the Napoleonic Collection, including Napoleon's death

The Chapel, designed by Sir Charles Cockerall, decorated for Christmas

Wiltshire

mask and Imperial porcelain, and one of the finest private collections of British watercolours, especially notable for works by Bonington, Roberts, Lear and Turner. Those who are interested in garden history will enjoy 'Capability' Brown's Park and the late 18th century 'picturesque' rockwork garden.

Opening Times: 1 Apr to 31 Oct daily 11:00-18:00. Last admission 17:00. Admission: Adult £6.40, Child 5-15yrs £4.10, 2-4yrs £3.25, OAP £5.30. Group (20+) Adult £5.45, OAP £4.65, Child 5-15yrs £3.60, 2-4yrs £3.05. Location: Off the A4 in Derry Hill village, midway between Calne and Chippenham. Exhibitions & Events 2004 : Please telephone for details. Map Ref: 4

CHIPPENHAM

Chippenham Museum & Heritage Centre
10 Market Place, Chippenham SN15 3HF Tel: 01249 705020 Fax: 01249 705025
Email: heritage@chippenham.gov.uk

Chippenham's new museum tells the story of this historic market town. Displays focus on Saxon Chippenham, Alfred the Great, Brunel's railway, and much more.

Opening Times: Mon to Sat 10:00-16:00. Closed Sun. Admission: Free. Location: Near town centre, at the historic Market Place. Map Ref: 5

Fox Talbot Museum

High Street, Lacock, Chippenham SN15 2LG Tel: 01249 730459
Fax: 01249 730501 Web: www.nationaltrust.org.uk

The Museum commemorates the achievements of a former resident of Lacock Abbey, William Henry Fox Talbot (1800-77), inventor of the negative-positive photographic process and whose decendants gave the Abbey and village to the Trust in 1944.

Opening Times: 1 Mar to 31 Oct daily 11:00-17:30 & winter weekends. Closed 25 Dec to 2 Jan. Admission: Adult £4.40, Child £2.20, Family £11.20. NT Members Free. Location: Three miles south of Chippenham off A350. Map Ref: 6

Lacock Abbey

Lacock, Chippenham SN15 2LG Tel / Fax: 01249 730227
Web: www.nationaltrust.org.uk

Founded in 1232 and converted into a country house in the mid 16th century. The monastic rooms of the Abbey have survived largely intact. There is an important Renaissance stone table, supported by 4 satyrs. Various paintings, furniture and a group of watercolours are also on display. The Victorian woodland garden has a fine display of spring flowers, magnificent trees and rose garden.

Opening Times: Abbey: 27 Mar to 31 Oct Wed to Mon 13:00-17:30. Museum: 1 Mar to 31 Oct daily 11:00-17:30. Closed Good Friday & Xmas. Admission: Adult £7.00, Child £3.50, Family £17.90 (2 adults and 2 children).

Peace and the Arts, by Cornelius Van Haarlem

Group Adult £6.30, Child £3.20. NT Members Free. Location: Three miles south of Chippenham, just east of A350. Map Ref: 6

CORSHAM

Corsham Court
Corsham SN13 0BZ Tel / Fax: 01249 701610
Email: enquiries@corsham-court.co.uk Web: corsham-court.co.uk

Notable collection of 16th & 17th Century Old Master paintings. Includes works by Lippi, Van Dyck, Anguissola, Dolci, Reynolds and Guercino: Modern British collection by appointment: Furniture by Chippendale and Adams bros.

Opening Times: 20 Mar to 30 Sep Tue, Wed, Thu, Sat & Sun 14:00-17:30. 1 Oct to 19 Mar Sat & Sun 14:00-16:30. Closed Dec. Admission: Adult £5.00, OAP £4.50, Child £2.50. Garden tickets available. Location: Six miles west of Chippenham off the A4, exit 17 from M4, nine miles east of Bath. Map Ref: 7

Wiltshire

Kennet & Avon Canal Museum

Canal Centre, The Wharf, Devizes SN10 1EB   Tel: 01380 721279/729489
Email: administrator@katrust.org

The museum has been described as 'the best little canal museum in the country'. It tells the story of the waterway from its beginnings to the present day. There is also a shop with videos, books, maps and souvenirs.

Opening Times: Feb to Xmas daily 10:00-17:00.   Admission: Adult £1.50, Child 50p, OAP £1.00.   Location: Near town centre, situated at The Wharf, beside the canal.   Map Ref: 8

Wiltshire Heritage Museum

41 Long Street, Devizes SN10 1NS   Tel: 01380 727369   Fax: 01380 722150
Email: wanhs@wiltshireheritage.org.uk   Web: www.wiltshireheritage.org.uk

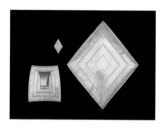

The Museum is designated for its outstanding collections, which tell the story of Wiltshire from its earliest origins at the time of the dinosaurs, up to the present day. The Museum is especially strong in prehistory, and displays some of the most important artefacts from the Bronze Age, associated with Stonehenge.

Opening Times: Mon to Sat 10:00-17:00, Sun 12:00-16:00. Closed Xmas & BH.   Admission: Free Sun & Mon. Adult £1.00, Under 16s Free.   Location: Near town centre, three minute walk from Market Place.   Map Ref: 8

Bronze age gold regalia found near Stonehenge

Athelstan Museum

Town Hall, Cross Hayes, Malmesbury SN16 9BZ   Tel / Fax: 01666 829258
Email: athelstanmuseum@northwilts.gov.uk

Collections include displays of archaeology, coins and tokens, maps, photographs. Malmesbury lace, costume, early bicycles and tricycles. Also an 18th century fire engine, Romano-British burial of a child, Malmesbury branch railway, the civil war and philosopher Thomas Hobbes.

Opening Times: Apr to Sep Tues to Sat 10:00-14:00. Oct to Mar Thu 10:00-14:00, Sat 10:00-12:00. Closed Sun and BH. Telephone for opening hours.   Admission: Free.   Location: The museum is situated within the Town Hall, Cross Hayes, one minute walk from the Abbey and centre of Malmesbury. Buses stop opposite the museum.   Map Ref: 9

Great Chalfield Manor

Melksham SN12 8NJ   Tel: 01225 782239   Fax: 01225 783379
Web: www.nationaltrust.org.uk

A 15th century manor house with a moat and gatehouse. It was restored in the early 20th century by Major R Fuller, whose family still live here. There is a collection of Flemish tapestries and oak furniture.

Opening Times: 30 Mar to 28 Oct Tue to Thu. Tours at 12:15, 14:15, 15:00, 15:45 & 16:30. Admission: Adult £4.40, child £2.20, Family £11.00 (2 adults and 2 children). Group Adult £4.00, Child £2.00. NT Members Free. Admission by guided tour only.   Location: Three miles south west of Melksham off B3107 via Broughton Gifford Common.   Map Ref: 10

John Creasey Museum/Edwin Young Gallery

Salisbury Library & Galleries, Market Place, Salisbury SP1 1BL   Tel: 01722 330606
Fax: 01722 413214   Email: peterriley@wiltshire.gov.uk

Permanent collection of contemporary art by leading artists. Temporary exhibitions on various themes from the collection plus loan exhibitions. We also hold the Edwin Young Collection of art shown twice a year, which consists of watercolour and drawings of Salisbury and environs produced primarly by Edwin Young in the 19th century.

Opening Times: Mon 10:00-19:00, Tue, Wed & Fri 09:00-19:00, Thu & Sat 09:00-17:00.
Admission: Free.   Location: Near Market Place, five minutes from bus station.   Map Ref: 11

Wiltshire

Mompesson House

The Close, Salisbury SP1 2EL   Tel: 01722 335659   Fax: 01722 321559
Email: mompessonhouse@nationaltrust.org.uk   Web: www.nationaltrust.org.uk

18th century drinking glasses

An elegant and spacious 18th century house in Cathedral Close. It has magnificent plasterwork, a fine oak staircase and good quality period furniture. The house also contains the Turnbull collection of 18th century drinking glasses. The walled garden has a pergola and herbaceous borders.

Opening Times: 9 Apr to 31 Oct Sat to Wed 11:00-17:00. Open Good Friday.   Admission: Adult £4.00, Child £2.00, Family £9.85 (2 adults and 2 children). Group £3.50. Garden only: 80p. NT Members Free.
Location: On north side of Choristers' Green in the Cathedral Close, near High Street Gate. Reduced rate when arriving by public transport.   Map Ref: 11

Royal Gloucestershire, Berkshire & Wiltshire Regiment (Salisbury) Museum

The Wardrobe, 58 The Close, Salisbury SP1 2EX   Tel: 01722 419419
Web: www.thewardrobe.org.uk

Three in one attraction of historic house, lanscaped garden to River Avon and Museum of Berkshire and Wiltshire Infantry Regiments. Museum on ground floor. Licensed tea room on site.

Opening Times: Apr to Oct 10:00-17:00, Nov Tue to Sun 10:00-17:00.   Admission: Adult £2.75, Child 75p, Concession £2.00, Family £6.00, Garden 75p.   Location: Within Salisbury's Cathedral Close and walking distance from car parks and stations.   Map Ref: 11

Salisbury & South Wiltshire Museum

The King's House, 65 The Close, Salisbury SP1 2EN   Tel: 01722 332151
Fax: 01722 325611   Email: museum@salisburymuseum.freeserve.co.uk
Web: www.salisburymuseum.org.uk

Award-winning Museum designated as having outstanding archaeology collections of national importance. Home of the re-designed Stonehenge Gallery, Warminster Jewel and Monkton Deverill gold torc. Displays of pre-history, Romans, Saxons, the medieval history of Old Sarum and Salisbury (with the renowned Giant and Hob Nob), the Pitt Rivers collection, ceramics and costume. Pictures throughout, including Turner watercolours. Temporary exhibitions all year round.

Opening Times: Mon to Sat 10:00-17:00, Sun Jul & Aug 14:00-17:00.   Admission: Adult £3.50, Child £1.00, Concession £2.30, Family £7.90.   Location: Situated in Salisbury Cathedral Close opposite the west front of the Cathedral.   Map Ref: 11

Wilton House

The Estate Office, Wilton, Salisbury SP2 0BJ   Tel: 01722 746720   Fax: 01772 744447
Email: tourism@wiltonhouse.com   Web: www.wiltonhouse.com

Inigo Jones designed house, Double Cube room arguably the finest state room in England. A very fine art collection, including many Van Dycks, important Roman, Greek and 17th century sculpture.

Opening Times: Apr to Oct 10:30-17:30.   Admission: Adult £9.75, Child £5.50, OAP £8.00.
Location: Three miles west of Salisbury.   Map Ref: 12

Lydiard House

Lydiard Park, Lydiard Tregoze, Swindon SN5 3PA   Tel: 01793 770401   Fax: 01793 877909
Web: www.swindon.gov.uk

Rescued from delapidation and now beautifully restored ancestral home of the Bolingbrokes. Fine furniture and family picture collection, painted glass window and 18th century Lady Diana Spencer Room. Audio guides and gift shop.

Opening Times: Mon to Sat 10:00-17:00, Sun 14:00-17:00. Nov to Feb closes 16:00. Closed Xmas.   Admission: Adult £1.50, Child/Concession 75p.   Location: From Swindon, follow signs to West Swindon and then pick up brown signs to Lydiard Park. From junction 16 on M4, follow brown signs.   Map Ref: 13

Wiltshire

Steam - Museum of the Great Western Railway

Kemble Drive, Swindon SN2 2TA   Tel: 01793 466646   Fax: 01793 466615
Email: steampostbox@swindon.gov.uk   Web: www.steam-museum.org.uk

King George V at the reconstructed
Station Platform

STEAM is located in a beautifully restored railway building in the heart of Swindon works where seven generations of men and women built the great locomotives and made the Great Western Railway in its heyday, the most important employer in Swindon. STEAM - Museum of the Great Western Railway, which received European Museum of the Year Special Commendation 2002, tells the story of the men and women who built, operated and travelled on 'God's Wonderful Railway'.

Hands on displays, world-famous locomotives, archive film footage and the testimonies of the ex-railway workers bring the story to life. Experience the sounds, sights and smells of the Railway Works where huge locomotives were built. Walk underneath the 'Caerphilly Castle' step up on the station platform and climb aboard the famous 'King George V'. Discover the romance and excitement of holiday travel by rail, explore hands on displays and computer interactives and discover what it was like to drive a train. Located next door the McArthurGlen Designer Outlet Great Western, STEAM offers a great day out for all. With excellent value group packages, special events and exhibitions, shop and café.

Isambard Kingdom Brunel

Opening Times: Apr to Oct Mon to Sat 10:00-17:30, Sun 11:00-17:30. Nov to Mar Mon to Sat 10:00-17:00, Sun 11:00-17:00.   Admission: Adult £5.95, Child £3.80, OAP £3.90, Family (2 Adults & 2 Children) £14.70. Group discount available.
Location: Ten minutes walk from town centre, through Railway Village.   Exhibitions & Events 2004 : Storehouse: New attraction displaying hundreds of unique railway objects from the museum stores.   Map Ref: 14

Swindon Museum & Art Gallery

Bath Road, Old Town, Swindon SN1 4BA   Tel: 01793 466556   Fax: 01793 484141
Web: www.swindon.gov.uk

Swindon
BOROUGH COUNCIL

Situated in an elegant early 19th century house, Swindon's oldest museum contains displays on the history, archaeology and geology of Swindon and surrounding area. The Art Gallery houses an outstanding collection of modern British art.

Opening Times: Mon to Sat 10:00-17:00, Sun 14:00-17:00. Closed BH.   Admission: Free.
Location: In Old Town, near town centre. Easily accessible by buses.   Map Ref: 14

TROWBRIDGE

Trowbridge Museum

The Shires, Court Street, Trowbridge BA14 8AT
Tel: 01225 751339   Fax: 01225 754608
Email: clyall@trowbridgemuseum.co.uk
Web: www.trowbridgemuseum.co.uk

Housed in a former woollen mill, museum displays tell the fascinating story of Trowbridge Town and its people. Working looms still produce cloth, which is sold within the museum. Other displays include reconstruction of Trowbridge Castle, a Victorian schoolroom, a weaver's cottage and a draper's shop. There are plenty of hands-on activities including a mouse-trail and history hunt.

Step back in time at
Trowbridge Museum

Opening Times: Tue to Fri 10:00-16:00, Sat 10:00-17:00. Closed Sun, Mon & BH.   Admission: Free.   Location: In the Shires Shopping Centre, five minutes from bus picking-up points and ten minutes from railway station.   Map Ref: 15

Wiltshire

Longleat House

Warminster BA12 7NW   Tel: 01985 844400   Fax: 01985 844885
Email: enquiries@longleat.co.uk   Web: www.longleat.co.uk

Nestling within 900 acres of 'Capability' Brown landscaped grounds, Longleat House is widely regarded as one of the best examples of high Elizabethan architecture in Britain. Priceless collections of paintings, including works by Tintoretto and Wootton, series of magnificent ceilings by John Dibblee Crace and exquisite 17th century Flemish tapestries. Also the Safari Park, 'World's Longest Hedge Maze', Safari Boats and numerous other attractions.

Opening Times: Longleat House: 1 Jan to 26 Mar weekend & school hol only, guided tours between 11:00-17:30. Oct to Dec (excluding Xmas Day) guided tours between 11:00-15:00.
Admission: Passport ticket: Adult £16.00, Child (3-14yrs) £13.00, OAP £13.00.   Location: Just off the A36 between Bath & Sailsbury (A362 Warminster to Frome).   Map Ref: 16

Stourhead House

Stourton, Warminster BA12 6QD   Tel: 01747 842030/841152   Fax: 01747 842005
Email: stourhead@nationaltrust.org.uk   Web: www.nationaltrust.org.uk

The Cabinet Room

This Palladian mansion, built in the 1720s, was home to the Hoare family, who are the owners of Britain's only surviving private bank. The interior includes an outstanding Regency library, an extensive picture collection and furniture by Chippendale the Younger. In the gardens are classical temples, including the Partheon and Temple of Apollo set around the central lake.

Opening Times: House: 19 Mar to 31 Oct Fri to Tue 11:00-17:00. Garden: Daily 09:00-19:00.
Admission: Garden & House: Adult £9.40, Child £4.50, Family £22.00. Group (15+) £8.90. NT Members Free.
Location: At Stourton, off B3092, three miles north west of Mere (A303), eight miles south of Frome (A361).   Map Ref: 17

Yorkshire

North Yorkshire is mainly rural in character, whereas South Yorkshire is industrial. West Yorkshire, on the other hand, is a mixture of both and offers magnificent Pennine and moorland scenery including the dramatic Bronte Country. Dominating the Vale of York is the historic city of York.

A fine collection of museums and galleries record the achievements of the towns and industries created by the Industrial Revolution. The artistic and cultural aspects of Yorkshire life are also well catered for.

Yorkshire

Cannon Hall Museum, Park & Gardens
Bark House Lane, Cawthorne, Barnsley S75 4AT   Tel: 01226 790270   Fax: 01226 792117
Email: cannonhall@barnsley.gov.uk   Web: www.barnsley.gov.uk

The museum has fine collections of pottery, furniture and glass. It is also home to the 13th/18th Royal Hussars Military Museum and William Harvey Collection of Dutch and Flemish paintings.

Opening Times: Apr to Oct Wed to Fri 10:30-17:00, Sat & Sun 12:00-17:00. Nov,Dec & Mar Sun only 12:00-17:00. Closed Jan & Feb.   Admission: Free.   Location: Six miles from Barnsley Town Centre, off junction 38 on M1.   Map Ref: 1

Cooper Gallery
Church Street, Barnsley S70 2AH   Tel: 01226 242905   Fax: 01226 297283
Email: coopergallery@barnsley.gov.uk   Web: www.barnsley.gov.uk

The Gallery holds a programme of contemporary art exhibitions, crafts and is home to the Trustees Collection of 17th-20th century paintings. There is also a cafe with a range of home made soups, sandwiches and delicious cakes.

Opening Times: Mon to Fri 10:30-16:00, Sat 10:00-15:00.   Admission: Free.   Map Ref: 2

Bagshaw Museum
Wilton Park, Batley WF17 0AS   Tel: 01924 326155   Fax: 01924 326164
Web: www.kirkleesmc.gov.uk

Step straight from the mystery of an Egyptian tomb into the tropical enchantment of the rainforest, taming mythical beasts on the way. With local history collections and Gothic decor.

Opening Times: Mon to Fri 11:00-17:00, Sat & Sun 12:00-17:00. Please ring for Xmas closing.
Admission: Free.   Map Ref: 3

Batley Art Gallery
Market Place, Batley WF17 5DA   Tel: 01924 326021   Web: www.kirkleesmc.gov.uk

Changing, temporary exhibitions.

Opening Times: Please ring for opening times.   Admission: Free.   Location: Town centre.
                                                                                      Map Ref: 3

Oakwell Hall & Country Park
Nutter Lane, Birstall, Batley WF17 9LG   Tel: 01924 326240   Fax: 01924 326249
Web: www.kirkleesmc.gov.uk

Built in 1583, the Hall is set out as a 1690s home, giving valuable insight into late 17th century life. One hundred acres of the original grounds are now managed as a country park.

Opening Times: Mon to Fri 11:00-17:00, Sat & Sun 12:00-17:00. Please call for Xmas closing.
Admission: There is a small admission charge from Mar to Oct.   Map Ref: 3

Beverley Art Gallery
Champney Road, Beverley HU17 8HE   Tel: 01482 392780   Fax: 01482 392778

The Gallery runs a lively temporary exhibition programme of art and craft. Selections from the permanent collection, which includes work by local Edwardian artists Fred and Mary Elwell, are displayed at times during the year.

Opening Times: Wed to Fri 10:00-17:00, Sat & Sun 10:00-12:30 & 13:30-17:00. Closed Mon & Tue.   Admission: Free.   Location: Short walk from the town centre on Champney Road, above the main Beverley Library.   Map Ref: 4

Aldborough Roman Town & Museum
Main Street, Boroughbridge YO2 3PH   Tel: 01423 322768

Aldborough was once the rich Roman city Isurium Brigantum, the principal town of the

297

Yorkshire

Brigantes - the largest tribe in Roman Britain. The museum displays a remarkable collection of finds from the town.

Opening Times: Apr to Sep daily 10:00-13:00 & 14:00-18:00, Oct daily 10:00-13:00 & 14:00-17:00. Times & prices may change. Admission: Adult £2.00, Child £1.00, Concession £1.50. EH Members Free. Location: In Aldborough, three quarters of a mile south east of Boroughbridge. Map Ref: 5

Bradford Industrial Museum & Horses At Work   ♿ 🏛 📷

Moorside Road, Eccleshill, Bradford BD2 3HP   Tel: 01274 435900

Moorside Mills, an original spinning mill, is alive with magnificent machinery which once converted raw wool into the world's worsted cloth. The mill yard rings to the sound of iron on stone as the Shire horses give rides, pull a horse tram or haul a horse-bus. In the mill, you can experience the sounds and smells of the engines which once powered the mills throughout Yorkshire.

Opening Times: Tue to Sat 10:00-17:00, Sun 12:00-17:00. Closed Mon except BH. Admission: Free. Location: Signposted from the Bradford ring road and Harrogate Road (A568). Map Ref: 6

Cartwright Hall Art Gallery   ♿ 🏛 📷

Lister Park, Bradford BD9 4NS   Tel: 01274 431212

Our collections reflect the cultural mix that makes Bradford unique, from sumptuous Indian silks and embroideries to the challenge of contemporary art and the delights of Victorian painting. The upper galleries are reserved for display of the permanent collection of Bradford Art Galleries and Museums with paintings, sculpture and decorative arts from the 19th and 20th centuries. The lower galleries are changing exhibitions.

Opening Times: Tue to Sat 10:00-17:00, Sun 13:00-17:00. Closed Mon except BH. Admission: Free. Location: In Lister Park on the A650 Keighley Road, about one mile from city centre.

Francis Derwent Wood's 'Humanity overcoming War'   Map Ref: 6

National Museum of Photography, Film & Television   ♿ 🏛 📷 🎬

Bradford BD1 1NQ   Tel: 0870 7010200   Fax: 01274 723155   Email: talk.nmpft@nmsi.ac.uk Web: www.nmpft.org.uk

Experience the past, present and future of photography, film and television with ten interactive galleries and a spectacular IMAX Cinema plus, the treasures of the Museum's Collections in Insight: Collections & Research Centre.

Opening Times: Tue to Sun 10:00-18:00. Also open BH and main school holiday Mon. Admission: Permanent Galleries Free. Charges for Imax and some exhibitions. Map Ref: 6

Sewerby Hall Museum & Art Gallery   ♿ 🏛 📷 ♿

Sewerby Hall, Church Lane, Sewerby, Bridlington YO15 1EA   Tel: 01262 677874   Fax: 01262 674265   Email: sewerbyhall@yahoo.com   Web: www.bridlington.net/sewerby

East Yorkshire history and east coast maritime art. Amy Johnson collection and temporary exhibitions of regional art and photography.

Opening Times: 18 Mar to 3 Nov daily 10:00-17:30. 4 Nov to 22 Dec Sat to Tue 11:00-16:00. Admission: Adult £3.10, Child £1.20, Over 60s £2.30, Groups half price. Location: Two miles north of Bridlington. Map Ref: 7

Smith Art Gallery   ♿ 🏛 ♿

Halifax Road, Brighouse HD6 2AF   Tel / Fax: 01484 719222 Email: Karen.Belshaw@calderdale.gov.uk   Web: www.calderdale.gov.uk

Permanent displays of 19th century art works. Also has temporary exhibition space in back gallery.

Opening Times: Mon, Tue, Thu and Fri 10:00-12:30 & 13:00-18:00, Sun 10:00-12;30 & 13:00-16:00. Admission: Free. Location: Two minutes walk from Brighouse Bus Station, ten minutes walk from Brighouse Railway Station. Map Ref: 8

Yorkshire

Red House

Oxford Road, Gomersal, Cleckheaton BD19 4JP   Tel: 01274 335100   Fax: 01274 335105
Web: www.kirkleesmc.gov.uk

Home of Charlotte Bronte's friend Mary Taylor. Charlotte featured the house as 'Briarmains' in 'Shirley'. Each room brings you closer to the 1830s and two permanent exhibitions shed light on the Brontes and life in the Spen Valley.

Opening Times: Mon to Fri 11:00-17:00, Sat & Sun 12:00-17:00. Please phone to check Xmas closing. Admission: Free.   Map Ref: 9

Dewsbury Museum

Crow Nest Park, Heckmondwike Road, Dewsbury WF13 2SG   Tel: 01924 325100
Web: www.kirkleesmc.gov.uk

Remember growing up? Dedicated to the magical theme of childhood, Dewsbury Museum will not only take you back to yours, it will give you insight into the childhood of past and future generations.

Opening Times: Mon to Fri 11:00-17:00, Sat & Sun 12:00-17:00. Please ring for Xmas closing. Admission: Free.   Map Ref: 10

Brodsworth Hall

Brodsworth, Doncaster DN5 7XJ   Tel: 01302 722598

Brodsworth Hall has survived almost completely intact since the 1860s with an extraordinary collection of 17,000 objects. These include an important group of Italian marble sculptures, an impressive collection of paintings, silver and furniture. The gardens are spectacular including a special collection of old rose varieties.

Opening Times: 1 Apr to 26 Oct Tue to Sun & BH 13:00-18:00. Pre-booked guided tours in mornings Apr to Oct. Times & prices may change.   Admission: Adult £6.00, Child £3.00, Concession £4.50. EH Members Free.   Location: In Brodsworth, five miles north west of Doncaster off A635 Barnsley Road, from junction 37 of A1(M).   Map Ref: 11

Doncaster Museum & Art Gallery

Chequer Road, Doncaster DN1 2AE   Tel: 01302 734293   Fax: 01302 735409
Email: museum@doncaster.gov.uk   Web: www.doncaster.gov.uk/museums

The Museum depicts various aspects of natural history, archaeology, local history and fine and decorative art.

Opening Times: Mon to Sat 10:00-17:00, Sun 14:00-17:00.   Admission: Free.   Location: Near town centre, ten minute walk from Rail Station.   Map Ref: 12

Kings Own Yorkshire Light Infantry Regimental Museum

Doncaster Museum and Art Gallery, Chequer Road, Doncaster DN1 2AE   Tel: 01302 734293
Fax: 01302 735409   Email: museum@doncaster.gov.uk
Web: www.doncaster.gov.uk/museums

Situated in the same building as Doncaster Museum & Art Gallery, in its own extension, the Museum reflects the history of this famous local regiment.

Opening Times: Mon to Sat 10:00-17:00, Sun 14:00-17:00.   Admission: Free.
Location: Located as part of Doncaster Museum, near town centre.   Map Ref: 12

Burton Agnes Hall

Estate Office, Burton Agnes, Driffield YO25 4NB   Tel: 01262 490324   Fax: 01262 490513   Web: www.burton-agnes.com

Elizabethan house with original carving and plasterwork. China, paintings and furniture collected over four centuries with a notable collection of modern and Impressionist paintings.

Opening Times: Apr to Oct daily 11:00-17:00.   Admission: Adult £5.20, Child £2.60, OAP £4.70.   Location: Off A166 between Driffield and Bridlington.   Map Ref: 13

Yorkshire

Sledmere House

Sledmere, Driffield YO25 3XG Tel: 01377 236637 Fax: 01377 236500

Sledmere House is a stunning 18th century Georgian Mansion set admist the Yorkshire Wolds in a Capability Brown Park. The magnificent plasterwork was designed by Joseph Rose, the most famous plasterer of the 18th century, his finest work was carried out at Sledmere. The house contains a fine collection of Chippendale and French furniture, antique statuary and paintings, the blue tiled Turkish room is unique in Britain. Sledmere is home to one of Britain's finest country house Organs, the console is housed at the base of the grand staircase, the pipes in a great glass dome which dominates the main staircase. The organ is played for visitors Wednesday to Friday and Sunday afternoons.

Opening Times: Easter weekend & May to Sep 11:30-16:30. Closed Mon & Sat.
Admission: Adult £5.00, OAP £4.50, Child £2.00.   Location: Sledmere House is situated an approximate half an hour drive form York, Beverley, Scarborough and Bridlington, off the A166 between York and Bridlington.   Map Ref: 14

Goole Museum & Art Gallery

Carlisle Street, Goole DN14 5DS Tel: 01405 768963 Fax: 01482 392782
Email: janet.tierney@eastriding.gov.uk

History of the development of the town and port of Goole, including ship models, photographs, social history and marine paintings by Goole-born artist Reuben Chappell.

Opening Times: Mon 14:00-17:00, Tue to Fri 10:00-17:00, Sat 09:00-13:00. Closed BH and Xmas & New Year. Admission: Free. Location: Town centre 12 minutes from bus station, five minutes from railway station.   Map Ref: 15

Bankfield Museum

Boothtown Road, Halifax HX3 6HG Tel: 01422 352334 Fax: 01422 349020
Email: Bankfield.Museum@calderdale.gov.uk Web: www.calderdale.gov.uk

Once the home of a mill owner, the magnificent Renaissance style Victorian mansion houses one of the finest collections of costumes and textiles in the country. There are also temporary exhibitions, workshops and activities. The museum also houses the Duke of Wellington's Regimental Collection.

Opening Times: Tue to Sat and BH Mon 10:00-17:00, Sun 14:00-17:00   Admission: Free
Location: 20 Minutes walk from Halifax Bus Station   Map Ref: 16

Piece Hall Art Gallery

Piece Hall, Halifax HX1 1RE Tel: 01422 358300 Fax: 01422 300878
Email: Karen.Belshaw@calderdale.gov.uk Web: www.calderdale.gov.uk

An exciting and diverse range of temporary exhibitions of art, crafts and local history situated in the historic Piece Hall.

Opening Times: Tue to Sun and BH 10:00-17:00. Admission: Free. Location: Two minutes walk from Halifax Bus Station and railway station.   Map Ref: 16

Yorkshire

Shibden Hall

Listers Road, Halifax HX3 6XG   Tel: 01422 321455/352246   Fax: 01422 348440
Email: shibden.hall@calderdale.gov.uk

Built in 1420, Shibden Hall with its oak panelled interiors and atmospheric room settings is Halifax's Historic Home. The Folk Museum and Barn also offer you a world without electricity, where craftsmen worked in wood and iron.

Opening Times: Mar to Nov Mon to Sat 10:00-17:00, Sun 12:00-17:00. Dec to Feb Mon to Sat 10:00-16:00, Sun 12:00-16:00.   Admission: Adult £3.50, Concession £2.50, Family £10.00.
Prices are subject to change.   Map Ref: 16

Harlow Carr Museum of Gardening

Crag Lane, Harrogate HG3 1QB   Tel: 01423 565418

The Museum, which is situated within the Plant Centre at RHS Garden Harlow Carr, houses displays of gardening equipment, tools and related items such as catalogues and seed packets. It includes a 1930s 'potting shed'.

Opening Times: Mon to Sat 09:30-17:30. Sun 11:00-16:30.   Admission: Adult £4.50, Child £1.00, Under 11s Free, OAP £4.00, RHS Members Free. NB. charge is for Gardens entrance, no charge for Museum.   Location: Off B6162, on the outskirts of Harrogate.   Map Ref: 17

Mercer Art Gallery

Swan Road, Harrogate HG1 2SA   Tel: 01423 566188   Fax: 01423 556130
Email: lg12@harrogate.gov.uk   Web: www.harrogate.gov.uk/museums

Originally built in 1806 as Harrogate's first spa building, 'The Promenade Room' has been restored to its former glory. The Gallery hosts a diverse programme of events and exhibitions, ranging from national touring shows of painting, photography, sculpture and crafts, to the display of work by Yorkshire artists. Also home to Harrogate's fine art collection.

Opening Times: Tue to Sat 10:00-17:00, Sun & BH 14:00-17:00. Closed Mon, 24-26 Dec & New Year. Admission: Free.   Location: Near town centre.   Map Ref: 17

Ripley Castle

Ripley, Harrogate HG3 3AY   Tel: 01423 770152
Fax: 01423 771745   Email: enquiries@ripleycastle.co.uk Web: www.ripleycastle.co.uk

When Sir Thomas Ingilby married Edeline Thweng in 1308/9 he received a fantastic dowry: Ripley Castle and a large chunk of the beautiful countryside around it. Seven hundred years later that legacy flourishes: the Ingilbys still live in the Castle and its walls exude the spirit of centuries of turbulent history. The colourful and occasionally eccentric behaviour of the Ingilby family proves to be a rich source of anecdotes and the guided tours, which last approx 75 minutes, are informative, entertaining and much enjoyed by adults and children. Trooper Jane Ingilby held Cromwell prisoner at pistol point in the Library. The family managed to erect an ornate ceiling in the Tower Room at just four days notice when they heard that the king was on his way to stay. A secret priest's hiding place was discovered behind the Tudor panelling in the Knight's Chamber, which also contains a collection of 17th Century Royal Greenwich Armour. An extensive walled garden features the national hyacinth collection, massive herbaceous borders, collections of tropical plants, ferns, fruit trees, rare vegetables and herbs. The deer park forms a natural ampitheatre around a large ornamental lake and contains a collection of ancient oak trees, some believed to be over a thousand years old. There is extensive free car and coach parking, and several shops, a tearoom and a pub are all within easy strolling distance.

Opening Times: Sep to Jun Tue, Thu, Sat & Sun 10:30-15:00. Jul to Aug daily.   Admission: Adult £6.00, Child £3.50, OAP £5.00.
Location: A61 north of Harrogate (three miles).   Map Ref: 17

Yorkshire

Royal Pump Room Museum   ♿ ❉

Crown Place, Harrogate HG1 2RY
Tel: 01423 556188 Fax: 01423 556130
Email: lg12@harrogate.gov.uk
Web: www.harrogate.gov.uk/museums

Housed in Harrogate's premier Spa building and site of Europe's strongest Sulphur Well, the Royal Pump Room Museum tells the story of Harrogate as a spa. You can still see the sulphur wells, and no visit to the museum is complete without a taste of the water.

Opening Times: Mon to Sat 10:00-17:00 (except Nov to Mar close 16:00), Sun 14:00-17:00 (Sun in Aug open 11:00). Closed 24-26 Dec & New Year. Admission: 2003 prices: Adult £2.50, Child £1.25, Concession £1.50, Family £6.50. Group rates, season and combined tickets available. Location: Near town centre. Map Ref: 17

Dales Countryside Museum   ♿ ❉ 🚊
Station Yard, Hawes DL8 3NT Tel: 01969 667494 Fax: 01969 667165
Email: dcm@yorkshiredales.org.uk

Fascinating museum telling the story of the people and landscape of the Yorkshire Dales, past and present. Static steam locomotive and carriages with video and displays. Hands-on exhibits, special events, demonstrations and temporary exhibitions. Tourist information and National Park Centre.

Opening Times: Daily 10:00-17:00, except Xmas. Admission: Adult £3.00, OAP £2.00, Child Free, Group rate available. Location: East end of market town centre. Map Ref: 18

Heptonstall Museum
Heptonstall, Hebden Bridge Tel: 01422 843738 Email: polly.salter@calderdale.gov.uk
Web: www.calderdale.gov.uk

17th century building with original school furniture and items of local, domestic, historic and agricultural interest including a coins exhibition.

Opening Times: Easter to Oct Sat, Sun & BH 13:00-17:00. Admission: Adult £2.00, Concession £1.00. Location: Buses from Hebden Bridge and Halifax. A646 to Hebden Bridge, then up to Heptonstall. Map Ref: 19

Rievaulx Abbey   ♿ ❉ 🚊
Rievaulx, Helmsley YO6 5LB Tel: 01439 798228

Founded in 1132, Rievaulx Abbey was the first Cistercian abbey in the north of England. The collection includes medieval floor tiles, stone sculpture, late medieval cutlery and other finds from the abbey.

Opening Times: Apr to Sep daily 10:00-18:00, Oct daily 10:00-17:00, Nov to Mar daily 10:00-16:00. Closed Xmas & New Year. Times & prices may change. Admission: Adult £3.80, Child £1.90, Concession £2.90. EH Members Free. Location: In Rievaulx, just over two miles west of Helmsley. Map Ref: 20

Hornsea Museum   ℮ ❉ 📷
11 Newbegin, Hornsea HU18 1AB Tel: 01964 533443 Web: www.hornseamuseum.com

Historic farmhouse, home of the Burns family for 200 years. Rooms, including Victorian farmhouse kitchen and parlour are displayed to show how the Burns lived worked and played 100 years ago. Also large garden, school room and Hornsea pottery collection.

Opening Times: Tue to Sat 11:00-17:00, Sun 14:00-17:00. Closed Mon except School Holidays. Admission: Adult £2.00, Concession £1.50, Family Ticket £6.00. Location: Near town centre. Map Ref: 21

Yorkshire

Colne Valley Museum

Cliffe Ash, Golcar, Huddersfield HD7 4PY   Tel: 01484 659762

Experience the atmosphere of a hand weaver's home and working life c.1840-50, with working hand looms and spinning jenny, a gas lit Cloggers Shop that's fully equipped with period tools and equipment from 1910.

Opening Times: Sat, Sun & BH 14:00-17:00. Closed Xmas & New Year.   Admission: Adult £1.40, Child/OAP 70p.   Map Ref: 22

Huddersfield Art Gallery

Princess Alexandra Walk, Huddersfield HD1 2SU   Tel: 01484 221964
Web: www.kirkleesmc.gov.uk

A lively programme, showcasing the best contemporary art from regional, national and international artists. In addition, the Kirklees Collection contains over 2000 items representing British art of the past 150 years.

Opening Times: Mon to Fri 10:00-17:00, Sat 10:00-16:00.   Admission: Free.   Location: Town centre.   Map Ref: 22

Tolson Memorial Museum

Wakefield Road, Huddersfield HD5 8DJ   Tel: 01484 223830   Fax: 01484 223843
Web: www.kirkleesmc.gov.uk

The history book of a typical Yorkshire town. Tolson Museum draws a vivid and intriguing picture of Huddersfield and its people, from the prehistoric to the present.

Opening Times: Mon to Fri 11:00-17:00, Sat & Sun 12:00-17:00.   Admission: Free.
                                                            Map Ref: 22

Victoria Tower

Castle Hill, Lumb Lane, Almondbury, Victoria Tower, Huddersfield   Tel: 01484 223830
Web: www.kirkleesmc.gov.uk

Shrouded in myth, history and legend, the story of Castle Hill goes back thousands of years. Despite its castle-like appearance, the Tower is a comparative newcomer. Breathtaking panoramic views of the Pennines and Peak District.

Opening Times: Easter & May Day weekends. Every Sat & Sun from Spring Bank until early Sep 12:00-16:00.   Admission: There is a small charge to the Tower.   Map Ref: 22

Burton Constable Hall

Burton Constable Foundation, Burton Constable, Skirlaugh, Hull
HU11 4LN   Tel: 01964 562400   Fax: 01964 563229
Email: enquiries@burtonconstable.com   Web: www.burtonconstable.com

Superb 18th and 19th century interiors, including a gallery, Great Hall, dining and drawing rooms, bedrooms, chapel, Chinese room and lamp room. Pictures and prints, architectural drawings, Chippendale furniture, scientific instruments, cabinet of curiosities and sporting guns.

Opening Times: Easter Sun to Oct. Closed Fri. Grounds: 12:30-17:00. Hall: 13:00-17:00. Admission: Adult £5.00, Child £2.00, OAP £4.50, Family £11.00. Grounds only: Adult £1.00, Child 50p.   Location: From Beverley (14 miles) follow A165 Bridlington Road. From Hull (seven miles) follow B1238 Sproatley. Follow Historic House signs.   Map Ref: 23

Ferens Art Gallery

Queen Victoria Square, Hull HU1 3RA   Tel: 01482 613902   Fax: 01482 613710
Email: museums@hullcc.gov.uk   Web: www.hullcc.gov.uk/museums

The award winning Ferens Art Gallery boasts a magnificent and diverse collection, from European Old Masters to contemporary video portraits, with important works by Fran Hals, Antonio Canaletto, Henry Moore, David Hockney and Helen Chadwick. The innovative Feren's Children's Gallery brings art to life for young enquiring minds - Ferens the Gallery Cat is your purrfect guide.

Opening Times: Mon to Sat 10:00-17:00, Sun 13:30-16:30. Closed New Years Day, Good Friday, Xmas (24th-28th inclusive).   Admission: Free.   Location: In city centre, five minutes walk from the bus and train stations.   Map Ref: 24

Yorkshire

Hands on History
South Church Side, Market Place, Hull HU1 1RR   Tel: 01482 613902   Fax: 01482 613710
Email: museums@hullcc.gov.uk   Web: www.hullcc.gov.uk/museums

Housed in Hull's Old Grammar School, Hands on History offers a fascinating glimpse into the life and times of the Victorians. Become part of the story of Hull and its people. A 2,600 year old mummy and unique replicas of King Tutenkhamun's treasures are the star attractions of the Egyptian Gallery.

Opening Times: Mon to Sat 10:00-17:00, Sun 13:30-16:30. Closed New Years Day, Good Friday & Xmas (24th-28th inclusive).   Admission: Free.   Location: In the city centre, five minutes walk from the bus and train stations.   Map Ref: 24

Hull & East Riding Museum
36 High Street, Hull HU1 1PS   Tel: 01482 613902   Fax: 01482 613710
Email: museums@hullcc.gov.uk   Web: www.hullcc.gov.uk/museums

Journey back 235 million years at the Hull & East Riding Museum and encounter sea-monsters, ritual burials and ancient tribes. Immense Hasholme Boat, Roos Carr figures and stunning Roman mosaics are just some of the highlights in this ever evolving museum.

Opening Times: Mon to Sat 10:00-17:00, Sun 13:30-16:30. Closed New Years Day, Good Friday & Xmas (24th-28th inclusive).   Admission: Free.   Location: In town centre, five minutes walk from the bus and train stations.   Map Ref: 24

Maritime Museum
Queen Victoria Square, Hull HU1 3DX   Tel: 01482 613902   Fax: 01482 613710
Email: museums@hullcc.gov.uk   Web: www.hullcc.gov.uk/museums

Set sail on the tide of Hull's rich and colourful maritime history at the Hull Maritime Museum - whaling, fishing and shipping displays are complimented by collections of scrimshaw and Maritime art.

Opening Times: Mon to Sat 10:00-17:00, Sun 13:30-16:30. Closed New Years Day, Good Friday & Xmas (24th-28th inclusive).   Admission: Free.   Location: In town centre, five minutes walk from the bus and train stations.   Map Ref: 24

Streetlife Museum
High Street, Hull HU1 1PS   Tel: 01482 613902   Fax: 01482 613710
Email: museums@hullcc.gov.uk   Web: www.hullcc.gov.uk/museums

Streetlife Museum brings 200 years of transport history alive, with all the sights, sounds and smells of the past. The stunning displays and authentic scenarios invite you to climb on, get in and explore. Don't miss the coach ride!

Opening Times: Mon to Sat 10:00-17:00, Sun 13:30-16:30. Closed New Years Day, Good Friday & Xmas (24th-28th inclusive).   Admission: Free.   Location: In the old town, 15 minutes walk from the bus and train stations.   Map Ref: 24

University of Hull Art Collection
The University of Hull, Cottingham Road, Hull HU6 7RX   Tel: 01482 465035
Fax: 01482 465192   Web: www.hull.ac.uk/artcoll/

Includes works by Beardsley, Sickert, Steer, Lucien Pissarro, John, Spencer, Wyndham Lewis and Ben Nicholson, with sculpture by Epstein, Gill, Gaudier-Brzeska and Moore. Also two important collections of Chinese ceramics covering the period c.618-1850.

Opening Times: Mon, Tue, Thu & Fri 14:00-16:00, Wed 12:30-16:00. Closed Sat, Sun & BH.
Admission: Free.   Location: 20 minute bus ride from town centre.   Map Ref: 24

Wilberforce House Museum
25 High Street, Hull HU1 1NQ   Tel: 01482 613902   Fax: 01482 613710
Email: museums@hullcc.gov.uk   Web: www.hullcc.gov.uk/museums

Birthplace of William Wilberforce; this seventeenth century merchant's house traces the rise and fall of the slave trade and Wilberforce's fight for its abolition. Realistic sets, videos and tools of the trade bring home the inhumanity of this once thriving traffic.

Opening Times: Mon to Sat 10:00-17:00, Sun 13:30-16:30. Closed New Years Day, Good Friday & Xmas (24th-28th inclusive).   Admission: Free.   Location: In the old town, 15 minutes walk from the bus and train stations.   Map Ref: 24

Yorkshire

Manor House Art Gallery & Museum

Castle Yard, Ilkley LS29 9DT   Tel: 01943 600066

A small museum specialising in local pre-history and artefacts from the area during Roman occupation. The museum is on the site of a Roman Fort. Parts of the Manor House date back to the 15th century and the building is of architectural interest.

Opening Times: Wed to Sat 11:00-17:00, Tue 13:00-17:00, Sun 13:00-16:00. Closed Mon (except BH) and Xmas. Admission: Free. Location: Five minutes from rail/bus station.
Map Ref: 25

Brontë Parsonage Museum

Church Street, Haworth, Keighley BD22 8DR   Tel: 01535 642323
Fax: 01535 647131   Email: bronte@bronte.org.uk
Web: www.bronte.info

Front entrance of the Parsonage

Charlotte, Emily and Anne Brontë were the authors of some of the greatest books in the English language. Haworth Parsonage was their much-loved home and Jane Eyre, Wuthering Heights and The Tenant of Wildfell Hall were all written here. Set between the unique village of Haworth, and the wild moorland beyond, this homely Georgian house still retains the atmosphere of the Brontë time. The rooms they once used daily are filled with the Brontës furniture, clothes and personal possessions. Here you can marvel at the handwriting in their tiny manuscript books, admire Charlotte's wedding bonnet and imagine meeting Emily's pets from her wonderful lifelike drawings. Gain an insight into the place and objects that inspired their work. The writing desks belonging to the three sisters are always on display, but their other personal possessions are changed on a yearly basis so you can always be sure of seeing something new. In addition to the main house, the Wade Wing houses a permanent exhibition about the whole of this remarkable creative family. Downstairs in our temporary exhibition gallery there is a changing display of manuscripts and art works from the Brontë Society collection.

Mr Brontë's Bedroom

Opening Times: Apr to Sep 10:00-17:30, Oct to Mar 11:00-17:00. Closed Xmas and 2-31 Jan. Last admission 30 mins before closing time. Admission: Adult £4.80, Child £1.50, Concession £3.50, Family £10.50. Location: Behind the church off Haworth Main Street. Exhibitions & Events 2004 : For Exhibitions and Events please telephone for details.
Map Ref: 26

Cliffe Castle Museum

Spring Gardens Lane, Keighley BD20 6LH   Tel: 01535 618231

Former Victorian mansion set in parkland, housing displays of rocks, crystals, fossils, local natural hsitory, bygones, Morris stained glass, original house furniture and temporary exhibitions. Aviaries, childrens play area and education room.

Opening Times: Tue to Sat 10:00-17:00, Sun 12:00-17:00. Closed Mon except BH.
Admission: Free. Location: Ten minutes walk from town centre, surrounded by park with playground.
Map Ref: 27

East Riddlesden Hall

Bradford Road, Keighley BD20 5EL   Tel: 01535 607075 Fax: 01535 691462
Email: yorker@smtp.ntrust.org.uk Web: www.visitbrontecountry.com

A characterful 17th century manor house and buildings with distinctive architectural details, set in delightful grounds. The house has a wonderful collection of oak furniture, needlework and textiles. The Great Barn with its oak frame, is one of the finest in the north of England.

Opening Times: 29 Mar to 29 Jun Tue, Wed, Sat & Sun 12:00-17:00, 1 Jul to 31 Aug Sat to Wed 12:00-17:00, 1 Sep to 2 Nov Tue, Wed, Sat & Sun 12:00-17:00. Open BH Mons & Good Friday. Admission: Adult £3.80, Child £1.90, Family £9.50. Group (15+) Adult £3.40, Child £1.70. NT Members Free. Location: One mile north east of Keighley on south side of the Bradford Road in Riddlesden, close to Leeds & Liverpool Canal.
Map Ref: 27

Yorkshire

Vintage Carriage Trust Museum of Rail Travel

Ingrow Railway Centre, Keighley BD22 8NJ Tel: 01535 680425 Fax: 01535 610796
Email: admin@vintagecarriagestrust.org Web: www.vintagecarriagestrust.org

Award-winning museum featuring restored railway carriages used in numerous cinema/television productions. Sit in the carriages, listen to sound presentations. Video presentations, numerous signs, posters and small exhibits.

Opening Times: Daily 11:00-16:30 or dusk if earlier. Closed Xmas. Admission: Adult £1.00, Child/OAP 75p, Family £3.00. Location: On A629 Keighley to Halifax road, one mile from Keighley Town Centre.
Map Ref: 27

KNARESBOROUGH *N Yorks*

Knaresborough Castle & Museum

Castle Grounds, Knaresborough HG5 8AS Tel: 01423 556188 Fax: 01423 556130
Email: lg12@harrogate.gov.uk Web: www.harrogate.gov.uk/museums

The home of Medieval kings, the imposing castle built by Edward III has many tales to tell. Join a guided tour and discover the mysterious underground Sallyport or explore on foot the keep and its dungeon. The castle museum houses a rare Tudor courtroom and galleries looking at Knaresborough's past, particularly the Civil War.

Opening Times: Good Friday to end Sep daily 10:30-17:00. Admission: Adult £2.00, Child £1.25, Concession £1.50, Family £5.50. (2002 prices) Group rates and Combined and Season tickets available. Location: Town centre.
Map Ref: 28

LEEDS *W Yorks*

Abbey House Museum

Abbey Walk, Abbey Road, Kirkstall, Leeds LS5 3EH

Tel: 0113 230 5492 Fax: 0113 230 5499
Email: abbeyhouse.museum@virgin.net Web: www.leeds.gov.uk

Reopened to public following complete refurbishment, new displays include an interactive childhood gallery, displays devoted to Kirkstall Abbey and a gallery exploring life in Victorian Leeds. Three reconstructed streets allow visitors to immerse themselves in the sights and sounds of late 19th century, from the glamorous art furnishers shop to the impoverished widow washerwoman and the sombre workshop of the undertaker.

Opening Times: Tue to Fri 10:00-17:00, Sat 12:00-17:00, Sun 10:00-17:00. Closed Mon. Admission: Adult £3.00, Child £1.00, Concession £2.00. Group rates available. Location: Three miles west of Leeds City Centre on A65.
Map Ref: 29

Armley Mills Industrial Museum

Canal Road, Armley, Leeds LS12 2QF Tel: 0113 263 7861
Email: armleymills.indmuseum@virgin.net Web: www.leeds.gov.uk

Formerly largest woollen mill in the world, Armley Mills now houses Leeds Industrial Museum. Located beside the River Aire, the museum explores the city's rich industrial past. Displays cover local textiles and clothing industries, printing, cinematography, photography and engineering. Working exhibits include a 1904 spinning mule and a 1920s style cinema.

Opening Times: Tue to Sat 10:00-17:00, Sun & BH 13:00-17:00. Admission: Adult £2.00, Child 50p, Concession £1.00, Family £5.00 Location: Two miles west of Leeds City Centre of A65.
Map Ref: 29

Guided or Private Tours	Disabled Access	Gift Shop or Sales Point	Café or Refreshments	Restaurant	Car Parking

Yorkshire

Harewood House

Harewood, Leeds LS17 9LQ   Tel: 0113 218 1010   Fax: 0113 218 1002
Email: business@harewood.org   Web: www.harewood.org

HAREWOOD

e A stunning house designed by John Carr with exquisite interiors by Robert Adam. Renowned for its stunning collections including Renaissance masterpieces, Turner watercolours and fine porcelain; furnished throughout by Thomas Chippendale including the spectacular State Bed; set in magnificent Capability Brown landscape and gardens, including a lakeside Bird Garden. One of the great Treasure Houses of England - and a Designated Museum.

Opening Times: Daily end Mar to end Oct and Sat & Sun Nov to 14 Dec. Admission: Mon to Sat: Adult £9.50, Child £5.25, OAP £7.75, Family £29.00. Sun: Adult

'The North Front' at Harewood House

£10.50, Child £5.75, OAP £8.75, Family £32.00. Location: On the A61 between Leeds and Harrogate, five mile from A1, 22 miles from York.   Map Ref: 30

Henry Moore Institute

74 The Headrow, Leeds LS1 3AH   Tel: 0113 246 7467 (Information) (0113) 234 3158
Fax: 0113 2461481   Email: info@henry-moore.ac.uk   Web: www.henry-moore-fdn.co.uk

A centre for the study of sculpture with a programme of temporary historical and contemporary exhibitions, accompanied by a series of talks, symposia and conferences. Pre-booking of guided tours necessary.

Opening Times: Daily 10:00-17:30, Wed 10:00-21:00. Closed BH. Admission: Free.
Location: In the centre of Leeds, a short walk from the city train station.   Map Ref: 29

Leeds City Art Gallery

The Headrow, Leeds LS1 3AA   Tel: 0113 247 8248   Web: www.leeds.gov.uk

One of the premier venues for visual arts in the north. Its nationally designated fine art collections range from early 19th to late 20th centuries. An outstanding collection of English watercolours; fine Victorian academic and pre-Raphaelite painting; late 19th century pictures as well as one of the most extensive collections of modern art. A changing exhibition programme represents reviews and explorations of 20th century art.

Opening Times: Mon to Sat 10:00-17:00, Wed 10:00-20:00, Sun 13:00-17:00. Closed BH. Admission: Free.
Location: City Centre Civil Quarter, next to the Town Hall,

junction 4 on City Centre Loop.   Map Ref: 29

Lotherton Hall

Lotherton Lane, Aberford, Leeds LS25 3EB   Tel: 0113 281 3259   Fax: 0113 281 2100
Web: www.leeds.gov.uk

The interiors of the former home of the colliery-owning Gascoigne family traces a world of high Edwardian living as well as providing rich locations for collections of costume, original art and ceramics. Also bird gardens and a deer park.

Opening Times: Tue to Sat 10:00-17:00, Sun 13:00-17:00. Admission: Adult £2.00, Child 50p, Concession £1.00, Family £5.00. Location: 13 Miles north east of Leeds City Centre and two and a half miles east of junction 47 on A1.   Map Ref: 31

Yorkshire

LEEDS *W Yorks (continued)*

Royal Armouries Museum
Armouries Drive, Leeds LS10 1LT
Tel: 08700 344 344   Fax: 0113 220 1955
Email: enquiries@armouries.org.uk

3000 years of history covered by over 8000 spectacular exhibits in stunning surroundings make this world famous collection of arms and armour a must see attraction. Experience an exciting combination of breathtaking displays, costumed demonstrations and dramatic interpretations, live action events, entertaining films, interactive technology and thrilling exhibitions. There really is something for everybody with five magnificent galleries themed on War, Tournament, the Orient, Self-defence and Hunting. You'll marvel at the priceless displays including Henry VIII's magnificent tournament armour and the awesome 16th century Mughal elephant armour. With authentic demonstrations of jousting, falconry and pollaxe combat, you are guaranteed an unforgettable day out from start to finish.

Opening Times: Daily 10:00-17:00. Closed 24-25 Dec.
Admission: Free museum entry.

Map Ref: 29

Temple Newsam House
Temple Newsam Road, off Selby Road, Leeds LS15 0AE   Tel: 0113 264 7321
Email: tnewsamho.leeds@virgin.net   Web: www.leeds.gov.uk

This magnificent Tudor-Jacobean house, was the birthplace of Lord Darnley, murderous husband of Mary, Queen of Scots, and for 300 years the home of the Ingram family until it was bought by Leeds from Lord Halifax in 1922. Inside thirty interiors display great paintings, renowned furniture including masterpieces by Chippendale, sumptuous textiles, silver, porcelain and Leeds pottery.

Opening Times: Tue to Sun 10:30-17:00   Admission: Adult £3.00, Adult joint ticket £5.00, Child £2.00, Child joint ticket £3.00, Family (2 adults and 3 children) £8.00.   Map Ref: 29

Thackray Museum
Beckett Street, Leeds LS9 7LN   Tel: 0113 244 4343   Fax: 0113 247 0219
Email: info@thackraymuseum.org   Web: www.thackraymuseum.org

Enjoy a great day out and discover how medicine has changed our lives. Experience life as a character in the Victorian slums of the 1840's, discover incredible lotions and potions, surgery without anesthetics and explore the interactive 'Bodyworks' gallery.

Opening Times: Daily 10:00-17:00. Closed 24-26 & 31 Dec & 1 Jan.   Admission: Adult £4.90, Child £3.50, Concession £3.90, Family (2 adults and 3 children) £16.00. Group rates available.
Location: Two miles from Leeds City Station.   Map Ref: 29

MALTON *N Yorks*

Malton Museum
Market Place, Malton YO17 7LP   Tel: 01635 695136

Renowned for its splendidly displayed Roman collection, gathered from many years of local excavations. Also objects from the Wharram Percy deserted medieval village. Also a temporary exhibition in upper gallery each year. 2004 '2000 days of digging at Heslerton'.

Opening Times: Easter Sat to 31st Oct Mon to Sat 10:00-16:00.   Admission: Adult £1.50, Child/OAP/Student £1.00, Family £4.00.   Location: In the town centre, a five minute walk from the railway and bus stations.   Map Ref: 32

Scampston Hall
Malton YO17 8NG   Tel: 01944 758224   Fax: 01944 758700
Email: info@scampston.co.uk

Owned by the same family since the 17th century, it was given the fine Regency interiors in the

Yorkshire

early 19th century. It contains important pictures by Gainsborough, Marlow, Scott and Wilson. The gardens include 10 acres of lakes and a Palladian bridge.

Opening Times: 18 Jun to 25 Jul Tue to Sun 13:30-17:00. Location: Five miles east of Malton.
Map Ref: 33

PICKERING N Yorks

Beck Isle Museum of Rural Life
Bridge Street, Pickering YO18 8DU Tel: 01751 473653 Fax: 01751 475996
Email: beckislemuseum@aol.com Web: www.beckislemuseum.co.uk

The museum is housed in a Regency mansion. 27 rooms containing Victorian collections, typical shops and workshops. A central yard contains farming equipment. An exhibition of Sydney Smith photographs on display all season.

Opening Times: 22 Mar to 3 Nov daily 10:00-17:00. Admission: Adult £3.00, Child £1.50, Concession £2.50, Family £7.50. Group prices available. Location: Opposite Memorial Hall just around the corner from the North Yorkshire Moors Railway Station. Map Ref: 34

PONTEFRACT W Yorks

Pontefract Museum
Salter Row, Pontefract WF8 1BA Tel: 01977 722740 Fax: 01977 722742
Web: www.wakefield.gov.uk

Chronological look at the history of Pontefract so far, including history of liquorice, life in the work house and living in old Pontefract. Hands-on exhibits and children's activities.

Opening Times: Mon to Fri 10:00-16:30, Sat 10:30-16:30. Closed Xmas Day. Admission: Free.
Location: Centre of town, next door to the library. Map Ref: 35

RICHMOND N Yorks

Green Howards Museum

Trinity Church Square, Richmond DL10 4QN Tel: 01748 822133
Fax: 01748 826561 Web: www.greenhowards.org.uk

One of the finest small military museums in the country with a unique collection of regimental uniforms, headdress, weapons, medals and silver. Display cabinets on four floors tell the story of the Green Howards in peace and war from 1688-2004. They are enhanced by touch-screen videos of WWI, WWII and the Regiment today.

Opening Times: Feb, Mar & Nov Mon to Fri 09:00-17:00. Apr to May Mon to Sat 09:00-17:00. May to Sep Mon to Sat 09:00-17:00 & Sun 14:00-17:00. Oct Mon to Sat 09:00-17:00. Admission: Adult £2.50, Child Free, OAP £2.00, Group £1.50 per person. Location: Situated in medieval church in centre of Richmond's cobbled market place. Map Ref: 36

Grandad explains the Crimean War (1854-56)

Richmond Castle

Richmond Tel: 01748 822493

Originally built by the Normans to control the north. The formidable 100 foot high keep has magnificent views over Richmond and is also reputed to be the place where the legendary King Arthur sleeps. Includes a collection of a vast range of medieval objects including pottery recovered from the well. Also a reconstruction of a conscientious objector's cell from World War 1.

Opening Times: 1 Apr to 30 Sep daily 10:00-18:00, 1-31 Oct daily 10:00-17:00, 1 Nov to 31 Mar daily 10:00-16:00. Closed 24-26 Dec & 1 Jan. Admission: Adult £3.00, Concession £2.30, Child £1.50. Location: In Richmond. Map Ref: 36

Richmondshire Museum
Ryders Wynd, Richmond DL10 4JA Tel: 01748 825611
Email: angus.goodfellow@tiscali.co.uk

Displays trace the history of Richmond and Richmondshire and cover leadmining, transport,

Yorkshire

domestic bygones, needlework, geology and archaeology. Features include a Dales post office, chemist shop and the vet's surgery set from television's 'All Creatures Great and Small'.

Opening Times: Apr to Oct daily 10:30-16:30. Admission: Adult £1.50, Child/OAP £1.00, Family £4.00. Location: Near Market Place. Map Ref: 36

RIPON *N Yorks*

Newby Hall
Ripon HG4 5AE Tel: 01423 322583 Fax: 01423 324452 Email: info@newbyhall.com
Web: www.newbyhall.com

A unique collection of sculptures and chamber pots can be viewed in Newby Hall. Within the 25 acres of award winning gardens is the national collection of cornus or dogwoods.

Opening Times: Hall: Apr to Sep Tue to Sun & BH Mon 12:00-17:00. Garden: Apr to Sep Tue to Sun & BH Mon 11:00-17:30. Admission: Prices on application.. Location: Between Ripon and Boroughbridge off B6265. Map Ref: 37

Norton Conyers
Wath, Ripon HG4 5EQ Tel / Fax: 01765 640333 Email: norton.conyers@ripon.org

Medieval house with later additions. Home of the Grahams since 1624. Family pictures, furniture and costumes on display. Visited by Charlotte Brontë - an original of 'Thornheld Hall in 'Jane Eyre'. Map Ref: 38

Yorkshire Law & Order Museums at Ripon
Allhallowgate, Ripon HG4 1LE Tel: 01765 690799 Email: ripon.museums@btclick.com
Web: www.riponmuseums.co.uk

Solitary confinemen

Walk the law and order trail and discover life for the law-breaker, the poor and the homeless in Victorian Ripon. The Prison & Police Museum - reopening following major refurbishment/improved access, partially funded by an HLF grant, will feature exciting new displays in this forbidding small town Gaol. In the Georgian Courthouse (recognise Ashfordly Magistrates Court from YTV's Heartbeat?) sentences ranged from a term in the debtors' gaol to transportation to Australia. The Workhouse Museum - 'bath, bed & board for vagrants; payment - breaking stones and chopping wood.'

Opening Times: 1 Apr to 31 Oct daily 13:00-16:00. School holidays, Jul & Aug 11:00-16:00. (Groups welcome at any time by arrangement). Admission: Adult £1.00 to £2.50. Combined 3 in 1 Ticket available. Map Ref: 37

ROTHERHAM *S Yorks*

Rotherham Art Gallery
Rotherham Arts Centre, Walker Place, Rotherham S65 1JH Tel: 01709 823635 Fax: 01709 823631 Email: wendy.foster@rotherham.gov.uk Web: www.rotherham.gov.uk

Whilst Clifton Park Museum is closed for a major facelift, Rotherham Art Gallery is temporarily being used as a Learning Resource Centre for The Museum Collections.

Opening Times: Mon to Sat 09:30-17:00. Closed Sun & BH. Admission: Free.
Location: Town centre, three minute walk from bus station. Map Ref: 39

York & Lancaster Regimental Museum
Rotherham Arts Centre, Walker Place, Rotherham S65 1JH Tel: 01709 323621 Fax: 01709 823653 Email: georgina.kersey@rotherham.gov.uk Web: www.rotherham.gov.uk

The York and Lancaster Regimental Museum tells the 200 year story of the men who served in the York and Lancaster Regiment.

Opening Times: Mon to Fri 09:30-17:00, Sat 09:30-16:00. Closed Sun & BH. Admission: Free.
Location: In town centre, three minute walk from central bus station. Map Ref: 39

Yorkshire

Rotunda Museum of Archaeology & Local History

Museum Terrace, Vernon Road, Scarborough YO11 2NN   Tel: 01723 232323

Finest purpose-built museum of its age in the UK, built to a design suggested by 'Father of English Geology', William Smith. The museum displays archaeological finds from the internationally important site at Star Carr and 'Gristhorpe Man' a Bronze Age tree trunk burial. Also items of Victorian Scarborough.

Opening Times: Jun to Sep Tue to Sun 10:00-17:00. Oct to May Tue, Sat & Sun 11:00-16:00. Summer opening school holidays and BH.   Admission: Museum 'S' Pass, valid 12 months all three Scarborough museum/gallery sites. Adult £2.50, Concession £1.50, Family £6.00.
Location: On Foreshore, less than 100 yards from the South Bay beach.   Map Ref: 40

Scarborough Art Gallery

The Crescent, Scarborough YO11 2PW   Tel: 01723 232323

Displays of Scarborough's fine art collection which features seascapes and views of Scarborough including works by Grimshaw, HB Carter, Frank Mason and Ernest Dade. Lively temporary exhibitions programme featuring both contemporary work from the region and works from the permanent collection.

Opening Times: Jun to Sep Tue to Sun 10:00-17:00. Oct to May Thu, Fri & Sat 11:00-16:00. Additional opening during school holidays and BH.   Admission: Museum 'S' Pass, valud 12 months all three Scarborough museum/gallery sites. Adult £2.50, Concession £1.50, Family £6.00.   Location: Near town centre.   Map Ref: 40

Wood End Museum

The Crescent, Scarborough YO11 2PW   Tel: 01723 367326

Displays featuring local wildlife, rocks and fossils and tunny fishing. Also, 'Making Sense', four large scale artworks to stimulate the senses inspired by the natural world.

Opening Times: Jun to Sep Tue to Sun 10:00-17:00. Oct to May Wed, Sat & Sun 11:00-16:00. Summer opening for school holidays & BH.   Admission: Museum 'S' Pass, valid 12 months all three Scarborough museum/gallery sites. Adult £2.50, Concession £1.50, Family £6.00.
Location: Near town centre.   Map Ref: 40

Bishops' House
Norton Lees Lane, Sheffield S8 9BE
Tel: 0114 278 2600   Fax: 0114 278 2604
Email: info@sheffieldgalleries.org.uk
Web: www.sheffieldgalleries.org.uk

Sheffield Galleries & Museums Trust

Bishops' House dates from around 1500 and is the best surviving timber-framed house in Sheffield. It retains many of its original features and gives visitors a tantalising flavour of Stuart England. The Great Parlour is restored as a typical dining room and the first floor chamber contains the original bedroom furniture and fittings listed in a 17th century inventory of contents.

Opening Times: Sat 10:00-16:30 & Sun 11:00-16:30. Mon to Fri pre-booked groups only. Admission: Free. Location: Approx two miles from Sheffield City Centre.   Map Ref: 41

Graves Art Gallery

Surrey Street, Sheffield S1 1XZ   Tel: 0114 278 2600   Fax: 0114 273 4705 Email: info@sheffieldgalleries.org.uk

Graves Art Gallery   **Sheffield Galleries & Museums Trust**

Web: www.sheffieldgalleries.org.uk

The Graves Art Gallery is home to Sheffield's outstanding collection of British and European 19th and 20th century art, including works by artists such as Stanley Spencer, Matisse, Picasso and Cezanne. The gallery also shows a superb range of touring exhibitions chosen to complement the permanent displays.

Opening Times: Mon to Sat 10:00-17:00. Admission: Free.
Location: In the town centre.   Map Ref: 41

Millennium Galleries

Arundel Gate, Sheffield S1 2PP   Tel: 0114 278 2600

Fax: 0114 278 2604
Email: info@sheffieldgalleries.org.uk
Web: www.sheffieldgalleries.org.uk

Four different galleries mean there is something to please every visitor. Enjoy blockbuster exhibitions from Britain's national galleries and museums, including the Victoria & Albert Museum and Tate. See the best craft and design, both contemporary and historical. Be dazzled by Sheffield's internationally important collection of metalwork and silverware and discover a wonderful array of treasures inside the world-renowned Ruskin Gallery.

Opening Times: Mon to Sat 10:00-17:00, Sun 11:00-17:00.
Admission: Free, apart from Special Exhibition Gallery: Adult £4.00, Child £2.00, Concession £3.00, Family £9.00.   Location: In the city centre.   Map Ref: 41

Thirsk Museum

14/16 Kirkgate, Thirsk YO7 1PQ   Tel: 01845 527707
Email: thirskmuseum@supanet.com   Web: www.thirskmuseum.org

Local history in birthplace of Thomas Lord; life and times of James Herriot's town. Bones of the Saxon giant and finds from Castle Garth. Legend of the Busby Stoop Chair.

Opening Times: Easter to end Oct Mon to Wed, Fri & Sat 10:00-16:00.   Admission: Adult £1.50, Child 75p, Family £3.50.   Location: In Kirkgate, off Market Place - free car park 100 yards.   Map Ref: 42

Clarke Hall

Aberford Road, Wakefield WF1 4AL   Tel: 01924 302700   Fax: 01924 302701
Email: info@clarke-hall.co.uk   Web: www.clarke-hall.co.uk

Clarke Hall is completely furnished as the family home of a late 17th century gentleman, Benjamin Clarke who owned it between 1677 and 1688. It includes a knot garden, maze and herb garden. New exhibition centre.

Opening Times: Please telephone.   Admission: Open days: Adult £3.50, Child Free, Concession £2.00. Group rates available.   Location: One mile from the centre of Wakefield and three miles from junction 30 of M62. Opposite Pinderfields Hospital.   Map Ref: 43

National Coal Mining Museum For England

Caphouse Colliery, New Road, Overton, Wakefield WF4 4RH   Tel: 01924 848806   Fax: 01924 840694   Email: info@ncm.org.uk   Web: www.ncm.org.uk

A unique opportunity to go 140 metres underground, where models and machinery depict methods of mining from the 1800s to the present day. Above ground, visit the pit ponies, exhibitions, steam winder and pit head baths.

Opening Times: Daily 10:00-17:00. Closed 24-26 December & New Years Day.
Admission: Free.   Location: On the main A642 Wakefield to Huddersfield road.   Map Ref: 44

Key to Classifications

see Classifications Index on page 423

Anthropology	Horticultural	Police, Prisons
Archaeological	Jewellery	& Dungeons
Art Galleries	Literature & Libraries	Railways
Arts, Crafts & Textiles	Maritime	Religion
China, Glass & Ceramics	Military & Defence	Roman
Communications	Multicultural	Science - Earth & Planetary
Egyptian	Music & Theatre	Sculpture
Fashion	Natural History	Sporting History
Geology	Oriental	Toy & Childhood
Health & Medicine	Palaces	Transport
Historic Houses	Photography	Victoriana

Yorkshire

This Dolls House dates from 1735

Nostell Priory

Doncaster Road, Wakefield WF4 1QE
Tel: 01924 863892 Fax: 01924 865282
Web: www.nationaltrust.org.uk

Built in 1733 the house is an architectural masterpiece by James Paine. The State Rooms were later completed by Robert Adam, and are magnificent examples of 18th century interior style. The Priory houses one of England's best collections of Chippendale furniture, designed specially for the house. There is an outstanding art collection, and another treasure is the John Harrison long case clock with its rare movement made of wood. The remarkable 18th century doll's house is complete with original fittings and Chippendale-style furniture. In the grounds there are delightful lakeside walks.

View of the Breakfast Room

Opening Times: 22 Mar to 2 Nov Wed to Sun 13:00-17:00, 6 Nov to 19 Dec Sat & Sun only 12:00-16:00. Open BH Mons. Admission: House: Adult £5.00, Child £2.50, Family £12.50. Group (20+) £4.50. NT Members Free.
Location: On the A638 five miles south east of Wakefield towards Doncaster.   Map Ref: 45

Wakefield Art Gallery

Wentworth Terrace, Wakefield WF1 3QW Tel: 01924 305796 Fax: 01924 305770
Web: www.wakefield.gov.uk (click on Culture)

Collection of 20th century art, fine examples of work by international sculptors Henry Moore and Barbara Hepworth - both born locally. There is also an important collection of 19th and 20th century paintings.

Opening Times: Tue to Sat 10:30-16:30, Sun 14:00-16:30. Closed Mon. Admission: Free.
Location: Approximately one mile from town centre, near to Wakefield College.   Map Ref: 43

Wakefield Museum

Wood Street, Wakefield WF1 2EW Tel: 01924 305356
Fax: 01924 305353 Web: www.wakefield.gov.uk (click on Culture)

Discover the world of Charles Waterton, conservationist and creator of the first nature reserve. Follow him on his journey through the rainforest of South America. Upstairs is the 'Story of Wakefield' - from ancient man through to the miners' strikes in the 1980s. 8000 photographs to view and print.

Opening Times: Mon to Sat 10:30-16:30, Sun 14:00-16:30.
Admission: Free. Location: Close to town centre, next to Town Hall and opposite main Police Station.   Map Ref: 43

Exploring the Touchy Feely Tree in the Waterton Gallery

Yorkshire Sculpture Park

West Bretton, Wakefield WF4 4LG Tel: 01924 830302 Fax: 01924 832600
Email: info@ysp.co.uk Web: www.ysp.co.uk

Set in the beautiful grounds of the 18th century Bretton Estate, Yorkshire Sculpture Park is one of the world's leading open-air galleries presenting a changing programme of international sculpture exhibitions. Three galleries and YSP centre with restaurant, shop and all-weather visitor facilities.

Opening Times: Daily 10:00-17:00 in winter, 10:00:18:00 in summer. Closed 22 to 26 Dec.
Admission: Free (£2.00 car parking a day). Location: One mile from junction 38 on the M1.
Map Ref: 46

Guided or Private Tours	Disabled Access	Gift Shop or Sales Point	Café or Refreshments	Restaurant	Car Parking

Yorkshire

Bramham Park

Wetherby LS23 6ND Tel: 01937 846000 Fax: 01937 846007
Email: enquiries@bramhampark.co.uk
Web: www.bramhampark.co.uk

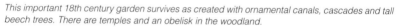
BRAMHAM

This important 18th century garden survives as created with ornamental canals, cascades and tall beech trees. There are temples and an obelisk in the woodland.

Opening Times: Apr to Sep 11:30-16:30. Closed 7-14 Jun & 16 Aug to 4 Sep (Bramham Horse Trials). House open by appointment only. Admission: Adult £4.00, Child £2.00, OAP £2.00.
Location: One mile west of A1, five miles south of Wetherby.   Map Ref: 47

Captain Cook Memorial Museum

Grape Lane, Whitby YO22 4BA Tel / Fax: 01947 601900
Email: captcookmuseumwhitby@ukgateway.net Web: www.cookmuseumwhitby.co.uk

House on the harbour where the young James Cook lodged as an apprentice and learnt his seamanship. Superb collections about his explorations. Paintings, models, special exhibition. Stunning site.

Opening Times: Mar Sat & Sun 11:00-15:00. Apr to end Oct daily 09:45-17:00.
Admission: Adult £3.00, Child £2.00, OAP £2.50, Student £2.00, Family £8.50. School rate £1.50 per pupil. Location: Town centre near swing bridge.   Map Ref: 48

Museum of Victorian Whitby

4 Sandgate, Whitby YO22 4DB Tel: 01947 601221 Fax: 01947 825805

Displays representing a stimulating re-creation of daily life in Victorian Whitby. Scenes including fisherman's cottage, barber's shop, cooper's yard and tallow chandlers, to mention but a few. The Bridge of the 19th Century Whaling Ship is also featured.

Opening Times: Daily 09:00-18:00. Admission: Adult £1.50, Child £1.00. Location: Museum is situated on first floor and basement of property.   Map Ref: 48

The RNLI Whitby Lifeboat Museum

Pier Road, Whitby YO21 3PU Tel: 01947 602 001 Web: www.lifeboats.org.uk

Last pulling and sailing lifeboat in service on display, Robert & Ellen Robson. Models, photographs, memorabilia.

Opening Times: Easter to Oct daily, Nov to March Sat & Sun only. Admission: Free.
Location: Pier Road.   Map Ref: 48

Whitby Abbey

Whitby YO22 4JT Tel: 01947 603568

Whitby Abbey was founded by St Hilda in 657. The original community was destroyed by the Danes, but was refounded as a Benedictine priory in 1078. The new museum and visitor centre contains excavated finds and replicas.

Opening Times: Apr to Sep daily 10:00-18:00, Oct daily 10:00-17:00, Nov to Mar daily 10:00-16:00. Closed Xmas & New Year. Times & prices may change. Admission: Adult £3.80, Child £1.90, Concession £2.90. EH Members Free. Location: On cliff top east of Whitby. Railway station half a mile away.   Map Ref: 48

Whitby Museum

Pannett Park, Whitby YO21 1RE Tel: 01947 602908 Fax: 01947 897638
Email: graham@durain.demon.co.uk Web: www.whitby-museum.org.uk

An Edwardian/Victorian 'museum within a museum' with a very wide set of collections, relating to Whitby and the surrounding area.

Opening Times: May to Sep Mon to Fri 09:30-17:30, Sun 14:00-17:00. Oct to Apr Tue 10:00-13:00, Wed to Sat 10:00-16:00, Sun 14:00-16:00, closed Mon. Admission: Adult £2.50, Child £1.00, Family £6.00. OAP £2.00, Group/School rates available. Location: Near town centre.
Map Ref: 48

Yorkshire

Withernsea Lighthouse Museum

Hull Road, Withernsea HU19 2DY Tel: 01964 614834 Email: lighthouse@widehorizon.net

Maritime exhibits - RNLI and HM Coastguard, photos of shipwrecks, local history, photos of Victorian and Edwardian Withernsea including pier and promenade. Also model railway. Kay Kendall Memorial including wedding dress and excerpts of films on video.

Opening Times: Mar to Oct Sat, Sun & BH 13:00-17:00. Mid Jun to mid Sep Mon to Fri 11:00-17:00. Closed Good Friday. Admission: Adult £2.00, Child £1.00, Under 5s Free, OAP £1.50, Family £5.50. Location: Centre of town.   Map Ref: 49

Beningbrough Hall & Gardens

York YO30 1DD Tel: 01904 470666 Fax: 01904 470002 Web: www.nationaltrust.org.uk

This imposing Georgian mansion was built in 1716 and contains one of the most impressive baroque interiors in England. There is an unusual central corridor running the length of the house. It is filled with 18th century treasures including over 100 pictures on loan from the National Portrait Gallery. There is also a fully equipped Victorian laundry. There is a delightful walled garden, potting shed, excellent facilities for children, shop and restaurant.

The Great Hall, an impressive English Baroque interior

Opening Times: 29 Mar to 30 Jun Sat to Wed 12:00-17:00, 1 Jul to 31 Aug Fri to Wed 12:00-17:00, 1 Sep to 31 Oct Sat To Wed 12:00-17:00. Open Good Friday.

Admission: Adult £6.00, Child £3.00, Family £14.00. Group (15+) Adult £5.50, Child £2.75. NT Members Free. Location: Eight miles north west of York, two miles west of Shipton, two miles south east of Linton-on-Ouse (A19).   Map Ref: 50

Castle Howard

York YO60 7DA Tel: 01653 648333 Fax: 01653 648501
Email: house@castlehoward.co.uk Web: www.castlehoward.co.uk

CASTLE *HOWARD*

Magnificent 18th century house with extensive collection and breathtaking grounds featuring temples, lakes and fountains. Additional attractions include historical characters, outdoor daily tours, archaeological dig and summer events programme.

Opening Times: 14 Feb to 31 Oct daily 10:00.
Admission: Adult £9.50, OAP £8.50, Child £6.50.
Location: 25 minutes north east of York, just off the A64.
                                           Map Ref: 51

Impressions Gallery of Photography

impressionsgallery

29 Castlegate, York YO1 9RN Tel: 01904 654724 Fax: 01904 651509

Email: enquiries@impressions-gallery.com
Web: www.impressions-gallery.com

Impressions Gallery opened in 1972 as one of the first specialist contemporary photography galleries in Europe. Since then we have established ourselves as a leading international exhibition space for photography and digital art. We support and promote innovative and creative work that extends the boundaries of current photographic practice. Digital imagery, film and video are essential resources for the contemporary artist, and this is reflected in our programme.

From the exhibition Gathering Light by Richard Ross

Opening Times: Tue to Sat 10:00-17:30. Admission: Free.
Location: Located in the Coppergate Centre, near Clifford's Tower and the Jorvik Centre.   Map Ref: 51

Exterior view of Impressions Gallery

Yorkshire

JORVIK

Coppergate, York YO1 9WT   Tel: 01904 543403/643211   Fax: 01904 627097
Email: jorvik@yorkarchaeology.co.uk   Web: www.vikingjorvik.com

Rare remains of timber buildings and 1,000 year old artefacts excavated by York Archaeological Trust. Representing all aspects of daily life, these objects inform JORVIK's faithful recreation of Viking-age York.

Opening Times: Apr to Oct daily 10:00-17:00, Nov to Mar daily 10:00-16:00. Closed Xmas Day. For full details please phone 01904 543402/3 Admission: Please ring for details. Location: In York City Centre, railway station and Park & Ride stops all within easy walking distance.

Map Ref: 51

Merchant Adventurers' Hall

Fossgate, York YO1 9XD Tel / Fax: 01904 654818 Email: enquiries@theyorkcompany.co.uk
Web: www.theyorkcompany.co.uk

The Hall is a scheduled monument of national importance. A truly unique and stunning Medieval Guildhall with timbered Great Hall, Undercroft and Chapel below. Displays of furniture from the 12th Century, paintings, rare silver and archaeology.

Opening Times: 5 Jan to 28 Mar & 4 Oct to 21 Dec Mon to Sat 09:00-15:30. 29 Mar to 03 Oct Mon to Thu 09:00-17:00, Fri to Sat 09:00-15:30, Sun 12:00-16:00. Closed Xmas & New Year. Admission: Adult £2.00, Child 70p, Under 7s Free, OAP/Student £1.70. Group rates by arrangement. Location: Town centre, between Piccadilly and Fossgate, opposite Marks & Spencer Home Store. Fully accessible from Fossgate.

Map Ref: 51

National Railway Museum

Leeman Road, York YO26 4XJ Tel: 01904 621261, 01904 686286 (info line)
Fax: 01904 611112 Email: nrm@nmsi.ac.uk Web: www.nrm.org.uk

Bullet Train Exhibition

The National Railway Museum mixes fascination and education with hours of fun. Our collection includes 103 locomotives and 177 other items of rolling stock and tells the story of the train from Rocket to Eurostar. Permanent displays include 'Palace on Wheels' with royal saloons dating back to pre Victorian times. We also have on display the only Bullet Train outside Japan.

Opening Times: Daily 10:00-18:00. Closed 24 to 26 Dec. Admission: Free, except during 'Day out with Thomas' events. Location: 540 metres from York Railway Station. Exhibitions & Events 2004 : 17 Jan to 4 Apr: Guild of Railway Artists Exhibition, 24 & 25 Jan: Residents First, 14-19 Feb: Day Out With Thomas, 13 & 14 Mar: Cab It.

Map Ref: 51

Nunnington Hall

A toy farmyard laid out on the flloo of the Nursery in Nunnington Hall

Nunnington, York YO62 5UY Tel: 01439 748283
Fax: 01439 748284 Web: www.nationaltrust.org.uk

A mainly 17th century property, the west wing dates from 1580 but was badly damaged during the Civil War by a Parliamentarian garrison. This was extensively remodelled in 1685 and again in the 1920s. The robust interior has stone flagged floors with a magnificent oak panelled hall. There is a mixed collection of pictures including mezzotints and watercolours. The family rooms include the nursery, the haunted room and attics, which house the Carlisle collection of miniature period rooms. The attractive walled garden was restored in the 1980s.

Opening Times: 22 Mar to 30 Apr Wed to Sun 13:30-16:30, 1-31 May Wed to Sun 13:30-17:00, 1 Jun to 31 Aug Tue to Sun 13:30-17:00, 1-30 Sep Wed to Sun, 13:30-17:00, 1-31 Oct Wed to Sun 13:30-16:30. Open BH Mons. Admission: Adult £5.00, Child £2.50, Family £12.50. Group (15+) £4.50. NT Members Free. Location: In Ryedale, four and a half miles south east of Helmsley (A170) Helmsley-Pickering road; one and a half miles north of B1257 Malton-Helmsley road. 21 Miles north of York (B1363).

Map Ref: 52

Yorkshire

The Royal Dragoon Guards

3 Tower Street, York YO1 9SB   Tel / Fax: 01904 642036   Email: rdgmuseum@onetel.net.uk
Web: www.rdg.co.uk

Artefacts, standards and medals of four famous cavalry regiments covering all their battles of the past 300 years. A new six seat cinema showing 20 minute films has recently been installed. Co-located with The Prince of Wales's Own Regiment of Yorkshire.

Opening Times: Mon to Sat 09:30-16:30. Closed 22 Dec to 2 Jan.   Admission: Adult £2.00, Child/OAP £1.00. Groups 2 for the price of 1.   Location: Centre of town, next to Cliffords Tower.

Map Ref: 51

Shandy Hall

Coxwold, York YO61 4AD   Tel / Fax: 01347 868465   Web: www.shandy-hall.org.uk

Shandy Hall houses the world's foremost collection of editions of Laurence Sterne's novels, plus an interesting background of contemporary prints and paintings illustrating his work.

Opening Times: House: May to Sep Wed 14:00-16:30, Sun 14:30-16:30. Garden: May to Sep Sun to Fri 11:00-16:30. Admission: House & Garden £4.50. Garden £2.50. Location: Above church, last house west end of village.

Map Ref: 53

Sutton Park

Sutton-on-the-Forest, York YO61 1DP   Tel: 01347 810249   Fax: 01347 811251
Email: suttonpark@fsbd.co.uk   Web: www.statelyhome.co.uk

Rich collection of 18th century furniture and paintings. Important collection of porcelain. Plaster work by Cortese, rare Chinese wallpaper.

Opening Times: Good Friday & Easter Mon then Wed, Sun & BH Mon until 29 Sep.
Admission: Adult £5.50, Child £3.00, OAP £4.50. Group rates available. Location: Eight miles north of York on B1363 York to Helmsley Road.

Map Ref: 54

Treasurer's House

Minster Yard, York YO1 7JL   Tel: 01904 624247   Fax: 01904 647372
Email: yorkth@smtp.ntrust.org.uk   Web: www.nationaltrust.org.uk

View of the Kings Room

Named after the Treasurer of York Minster and built over a Roman Road, the house is not all that it seems. Carefully restored, it has a huge hall with a half timbered gallery supported by classical columns, a fine carved and gilded 18th century chimney piece. The collection of 18th century furniture, china and glass provides an insight into the taste of Edwardian connoisseurs. The garden and terrace walls contain architectural fragments from many rebuildings of the Minster.

Opening Times: 22 Mar to 31 Oct Sat to Thu 11:00-16:30.   Admission: Adult £4.50, Child £2.20, Family £11.00. Group (15) Adult £3.50 Child £1.70. NT Members Free.   Location: In Minster Yard, on north side of Minster.

Map Ref: 51

York Archaeological Trust for Excavation & Research Ltd

Cromwell House, 13 Ogleforth, York YO1 7FG   Tel: 01904 619264   Fax: 01904 663024
Email: cmcdonnell@yorkarchaeology.co.uk   Web: www.yorkarchaeology.co.uk

Internationally important collection representing aspects of life in York from the Roman period through to late Medieval. Access for academic study and exhibition loans through the curatorial department.

Opening Times: By prior arrangement.   Location: In York City Centre. Railway station and Park & Ride stops all within easy walking distance.

Map Ref: 51

---

www.mghh.co.uk

For current information on the outstanding Collections in over 1600 Museums, Galleries & Historic Houses in England, Scotland, Wales and Ireland

York Art Gallery

Exhibition Square, York YO1 7EW   Tel: 01904 687687
Email: art.gallery@ymt.org.uk   Web: www.york.art.museum

Seven centuries of European painting from early Italian gold-ground panels to the art of the present day. Changing exhibitions of modern and contemporary art. Events for all the family.

Opening Times: Daily 10:00-17:00.   Admission: Free.
Location: Three minutes from Minster, ten minutes from railway station.   Map Ref: 51

William Marlow (1740-1813): Ouse Bridge, York

York Castle Museum

Eye of York, York YO1 9RY   Tel: 01904 687687   Fax: 01904 671078
Email: castle.museum@ymt.org.uk   Web: www.york.castle.museum

Venture into the prison cell of notorious highwayman Dick Turpin. Wander through Victorian and Edwardian streets and experience four hundred years of fascinating social history. Famous for its collections of costume, textiles, military and social history, York Castle Museum brings history back to life. With over 100,000 items on show you'll be amazed at what's here!

Opening Times: Daily 10:00-17:00. Closed 25 & 26 Dec & 1 Jan. Admission: Adult £6.00, Child/Concession £3.50, Family £16.00. Location: Centre of York, close to Clifford's Tower and the Coppergate Shopping Centre.
Map Ref: 51

'Kirkgate' York Castle Museum

York Minster Undercroft Treasury & Crypt

YORK MINSTER

York Minster, Deangate, York YO1 7JF
Tel: 01904 557216   Fax: 01904 557218
Email: visitors@yorkminster.org   Web: www.yorkminster.org

York Minster is the chief church in the Northern Province of the Church of England and is the seat of the Archbishop of York. The present building is the largest Gothic cathedral in Northern Europe, and is the setting for some of the finest 14th and 15th century stained glass windows in existence. Whether you come to York Minster as a tourist or pilgrim, we hope that as you walk round you will understand why the cathedral has inspired people of every generation since its completion. Prayer has been offered to God on this site for nearly 1,000 years. We invite you to join us in worship and experience the real purpose for which the Minster was built. Newly refurbished, the Undercroft and Crypt uncovers the remarkable history of York Minster from its early Norman foundations to the 20th century engineering that supports the central tower. The Undercroft also contains the remains of York's Roman Legionary fortress, Viking gravestones and historic artefacts from the Minster's collection.

The West End of York Minster

Opening Times: 09:30-18:00 last entry 17:00. Admission: Adult £2.50, Child £1.00, Concession £1.50. Includes free audio tour.
Location: City centre   Map Ref: 51

12th Century Stained Glass depicting Christ

Yorkshire Air Museum & Allied Air Forces Memorial

Halifax Way, Elvington, York YO41 4AU   Tel: 01904 608595   Fax: 01904 608246
Email: museum@yorkshireairmuseum.co.uk   Web: www.yorkshireairmuseum.co.uk

Experience the tremendous atmosphere of the Yorkshire Air Museum & Allied Air Forces Memorial whilst admiring fascinating displays, such as the restored Control Tower, Air Gunners Museum, Archives, Airborne Forces Display, Squadron Memorial Rooms and Gardens and much more. See the pioneering Cayley Glider and Wright Flyer, unique Halifax Bomber and modern jets such as the Harrier GR3. Our exciting 2004 Events Programme highlights the 60th Anniversaries of Allied campaigns leading to the Liberation of Europe. The excellent NAAFI Restaurant & Bar provides hot and cold meals, snacks and refreshments.

Opening Times: 10:00-17:00 Summer Time. 10:00-15.30 Winter Time. Closed Xmas & Boxing Day. Admission: Adult £5.00, OAP £4.00, Child 5-15 £3.00, Under 5's free. Reduced Rates for Groups of 8 or more on enquiry. Some events charged at different rates. Location: Five miles south east of York, good regional road access. Map Ref: 55

Yorkshire Museum

Museum Gardens, York YO1 7FR   Tel: 01904 687687
Email: yorkshire.museum@ymt.org.uk   Web: www.york.yorkshire.museum

Set in ten acres of botanical gardens, the Yorkshire Museum houses some of the richest archaeological finds in Europe and covers over 1000 years of local history. Discover Roman, Anglo-Saxon, Viking and Medieval life and meet the Jurassic sea-dragons. Exciting temporary exhibitions on display throughout the year. Call for details.

Opening Times: Daily 10:00-17:00. Admission: Adult £4.00, Child/Concession £2.50, Family £10.00. Group rates available. Location: City centre location, five minute walk from York Railway Station. Map Ref: 51

Edinburgh, Glasgow & Southern Scotland

This is the region of Sir Walter Scott and Robert Burns, writers who did much to familiarise the world with romantic Scotland. Edinburgh is a stunning city renowned for its castle and the architecture of the city displayed at its best in New Town, the most impressive area of Georgian architecture in the whole of Europe. Glasgow now rates as the second favourite city to visit in Britain, the cathedral being the central point of the oldest part of the city.

Scotland is a nation with a proud and ancient heritage, and the world-class museums and galleries of Edinburgh and Glasgow provide a wonderful source of culture but there is also a wealth of smaller museums throughout southern Scotland each with their particular story to tell.

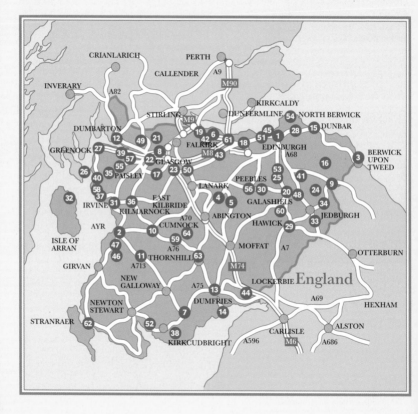

The Red Map References should be used to locate Museums etc on the pages that follow

Edinburgh, Glasgow & Southern Scotland

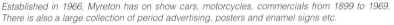
ABERLADY *E Lothian*

Myreton Motor Museum

Aberlady EH32 0PZ   Tel: 01875 870288/(07947) 066666

Established in 1966, Myreton has on show cars, motorcycles, commercials from 1899 to 1969. There is also a large collection of period advertising, posters and enamel signs etc.

Opening Times: Apr to Oct daily 11:00-16:00, Nov to March Sun 13:00-15:00. For special appointment telephone 07947 066666.   Admission: Adult £5.00, Child £2.00, OAP/Student £4.00.   Location: One mile from village of Aberlady, East Lothian.   Map Ref: 1

AYR *S Ayrshire*

Burns Cottage & Museum

Burns Cottage, Alloway, Ayr KA7 4PY   Tel: 01292 441215   Fax: 01292 441750
Email: burnscottage@netscapeonline.co.uk   Web: www.robertburns.org

Birthplace of Robert Burns (1759-96), Scotland's National Poet. Museum contains many exhibits of Burns' songs, poems, letters and personal belongings. Original manuscripts of 'Auld Lang Syne' and 'Tam O'Shanter'.

Opening Times: Apr to Sep daily 09:00-17:30. Oct to Mar 10:00-17:00.   Admission: Adult £3.00, Child/OAP £1.50, Family £9.00.   Location: Two miles south of Ayr. One mile off A77 Glasgow to Stranraer.   Map Ref: 2

Rozelle House Gallery

Rozelle Park, Monument Road, Ayr KA7 4NQ   Tel: 01292 445447   Fax: 01292 612634

The Goudie Collection, an exciting series of paintings which vividly depict Burn's haunting tale of Tam O'Shanter is the focus for Rozelle Galleries. Interspersed with this will be a programme of art, craft and museum exhibitions and there is a craft shop.

Opening Times: Mon to Sat 10:00-17:00, Apr to Oct also Sun 14:00-17:00.   Admission: Free.
Location: Approximately two miles from Ayr Town Centre in Rozelle Park, Alloway near Burns Cottage.   Map Ref: 2

BERWICK-UPON-TWEED *Scottish Borders*

Paxton House, Gallery and Country Park

Berwick-upon-Tweed TD15 1SZ   Tel: 01289 386291
Fax: 01289 386660   Email: info@paxtonhouse.com
Web: www.paxtonhouse.com

One of the finest 18th century Palladian country houses in Britain, featuring Adam Interiors and finest collection of Chippendale furniture. Largest picture gallery in a Scottish country house, now housing over 70 paintings from the National Galleries of Scotland, rehung for 2003. Twelve period rooms, 80 acres of gardens, woodland and riverside walks, gift shop, tea-room, adventure playground, picnic areas and exhibitions.

Opening Times: 1 Apr to 31 Oct daily 11:00-17:00. Grounds close at sunset.   Admission: Adult £6.00, Child £3.00, Group £5.00, Family £16.00.   Location: Signposted three miles from A1 Berwick-upon-Tweed Bypass on B6461. Berwick East Coast line ten minutes, No.32 bus from Berwick daily except Sun. Exhibitions & Events 2004 :   20 Jun: Paxton House 4th Vintage Rally, 16 to 25 Jul: Summer Music Festival of Classical Music.   Map Ref: 3

BIGGAR *S Lanarks*

Biggar Gasworks Museum

Moat Park, Biggar ML12 6DT   Tel / Fax: 01899 221050
Email: margaret@bmtrust.freeserve.co.uk   Web: www.biggar-net.co.uk

The only remaining gas works in Scotland. By 1839 Biggar had its own gasworks. A major reconstruction in 1914 brought Biggar Gasworks more or less into its present form. Closed down in 1973, but not demolished, it has been preserved for future generations.

Opening Times: May to Sep Mon to Sun 14:00-17:00.   Admission: £1.00.   Location: Near town centre.   Map Ref: 4

Edinburgh, Glasgow & Southern Scotland

Gladstone Court Museum

North Back Road, Biggar ML12 6DT   Tel / Fax: 01899 221050
Email: margaret@bmtrust.freeserve.co.uk   Web: www.biggar-net.co.uk

Gladstone Court is for all the family, its small shops and offices displaying small town life as the old remember it and the young imagine it. Here is an ironmonger's store, a bank, photographers, chemist, dressmaker, watchmaker, millner, printer and bootmaker, together with a village library and schoolroom.

Opening Times: Easter to mid Oct Mon to Sat 11.00:16:30, Sun 14:00-16:30. Admission: Adult £2.00, Child £1.00, Concessions £1.50, Family £4.00, Group discounts. Location: Near town centre.   Map Ref: 4

Greenhill Farmhouse Museum

Burn Braes, Biggar ML12 6DT   Tel / Fax: 01899 221050
Email: margaret@bmtrust.freeserve.co.uk   Web: www.biggar-net.co.uk

Rebuilt in the lovely Burn Braes, Biggar, stands Greenhill Farmhouse. The Museum Trust rescued it in a derelict condition and moved the house to Biggar as a home for its Covenanting Museum.

Opening Times: May to Sep Sat & Sun 14:00-16:30 or by appointment weekdays. Admission: Adult £1.00 Child 50p Concession 75p. Location: Near town centre, 5 mins walk.   Map Ref: 4

John Buchan Centre

Broughton, Biggar ML12 6HQ   Tel / Fax: 01899 221050
Email: margaret@bmtrust.freeserve.co.uk   Web: www.biggar-net.co.uk

In the Old Free Kirk at Broughton, John Buchan, a young supply clergyman, met his wife, Helen Masterton. The Kirk now houses a display commemorating the life and work of their eldest son, John, poet, statesman and author of many popular novels. Broughton was his childhood holiday home, held in great affection by himself and his sister Anna, who also wrote under the pen name of O Douglas.

Opening Times: May to Sep daily 14:00-17:00. Admission: Adult £1.50, Child 50p.
Location: Old Free Kirk, Broughton.   Map Ref: 5

Moat Park Heritage Centre

Moat Park, Kirkstyle, Biggar ML12 6DT   Tel / Fax: 01899 221050
Email: margaret@bmtrust.freeserve.co.uk   Web: www.biggar-net.co.uk

The Moat Park Heritage Centre was opened by HRH The Princess Royal in June 1988. One can see here how the Clyde and Tweed valleys were formed millions of years ago, rub shoulders with an Iron Age family or encounter a blood thirsty Roman soldier and other figures from our past. Splendid models display early dwellings, mottes, castles and farmhouses. There is also a magnificent Victorian patchwork.

Opening Times: Easter to mid Oct Mon to Sat 11:00-16:30, Sun 14:00-16:30. Admission: Adult £2.00, Child £1.00, Concession £1.50, Family £4.00. Location: Near town centre.   Map Ref: 4

Scottish Railway Preservation Society
Bo'ness & Kinneil Railway, Bo'ness Station, Union Street, Bo'ness EH51 9AQ
Tel: 01506 822298/825855   Fax: 01506 828766
Email: srps@srps.org.uk   Web: www.srps.org.uk

Bo'ness & Kinneil Railway is home to an exciting collection of railway buildings, locomotives, equipment, carriages and wagons. Your journey through the Forth Valley takes you to the Caverns of Birkhill Fireclay Mine. On your return you can visit the Scottish Railway Exhibition depicting the history of railways in Scotland.

Opening Times: Weekends Apr to Oct. July & Aug daily. Admission: Entry to museum is free, Rail Fares - Adult £4.50, Child £2.00, Concession £3.50, Family (2 adults and 2 children) £11.00. Scottish Railway Exhibition: Adult £1.00, Child Free. Location: In town of Bo'ness. From Edinburgh M9 leave junction 3, follow A904 to Bo'ness,

Caledonian Railway Locomotive
CR419 at Bo'ness Station

from West leave M9 at junction 5, follow signs to Bo'ness. Exhibitions & Events 2004 : Special events include Easter Egg Specials, Diesel Galas, Day out with Thomas Weekends, Caledonian Weekend, Vehicle Rallies, Santa Steam Specials and Black Bun Specials.   Map Ref: 6

Edinburgh, Glasgow & Southern Scotland

Castle Douglas Art Gallery

Market Street, Castle Douglas DG7 1BE   Tel / Fax: 01557 331643
Email: davidd@dumgal.gov.uk   Web: www.dumgal.gov.uk/museums

The Gallery plays host to an annual programme of exhibitions ranging from fine art, craft, photography. Touring exhibitions are regularly displayed at the Gallery.

Opening Times: Opening times may vary, please contact.   Admission: Free.   Location: Town centre.   Map Ref: 7

Threave

Castle Douglas DG7 1RX   Tel: 01556 502575   Fax: 01556 502683
Email: threave@nts.org.uk

The principal rooms in Threave House opened for the first time in 2002. They have been restored to their appearance in the 1930s and include interesting collections of furniture and local bygones (in the visitor centre). There are impressive views of the Galloway countryside.

Opening Times: House: 1 Mar to 31 Oct Wed to Fri & Sun 11:00-16:00. Guided tours only, maximum 10 people. Estate & garden: All year, daily 09:30 to sunset.   Admission: Adult £9.00, Concession £ 6.50, Family £23.00. NTS/NT Members Free.   Location: Off A75, one mile west of Castle Douglas.   Map Ref: 7

Summerlee Heritage Park

Heritage Way, Coatbridge ML5 1QD   Tel: 01236 431261
Fax: 01236 440429

'4 star' graded visitor attraction. 22 acre site with operational tramway, re-created addit mine and miners' row. Exhibition hall with working machinery and extensive displays of social and industrial heritage.

Opening Times: Apr to Oct daily 10:00-17:00, Nov to Mar daily 10:00-16:00.   Admission: Free.
Location: To the west of Coatbridge town centre, by the central station.   Map Ref: 8

Coldstream Museum

12 Market Square, Coldstream TD12 4BD   Tel: 01890 882630

Local history and Coldstream Guards.

Opening Times: Easter to Sep Mon to Sat 10:00-16:00, Sun 14:00-16:00. Oct Mon to Sat 13:00-16:00.   Admission: Free.   Location: Near town centre.   Map Ref: 9

Baird Institute Museum

3 Lugar Street, Cumnock KA18 1AD   Tel / Fax: 01290 421701

A local museum featuring temporary and permanent exhibitions. Displays include Cumnock Pottery, Mauchline Boxware and Ayrshire Embroidery. A room is dedicated to Keir Hardy, founder of the Labour Party. Family history information is available.

Opening Times: Mon, Tue, Thu & Fri 10:00-13:00 & 13:30-16:30.   Admission: Free.
Location: Near Cumnock Town Centre.   Map Ref: 10

Doon Valley Museum

Cathcartston, Dalmellington KA6 7QY   Tel: 01292 550633   Fax: 01292 550937
Email: stanley.sarsfield@east-ayrshire.gov.uk

A local history museum with a fine collection of photographs and maps showing the Doon Valley over the centuries. Local history displays combined with changing art exhibitions and a weaving tableau.

Opening Times: Mon to Fri 10:00-16:30.   Admission: Free.   Location: In the centre of Dalmellington, off the main square.   Map Ref: 11

Denny Ship Model Experimental Tank

Castle Street, Dumbarton G82 1QS   Tel: 01389 763444   Fax: 01389 743093

Step back into the world of the Victorian ship designer, fully restored and still used for testing ship designs.

Opening Times: Mon to Sat 10:00-16:00.   Admission: Adult £1.50, Child/OAP 75p, Family £3.00.   Location: Near town centre, two minutes walk from railway station.   Map Ref: 12

Dumfries & Galloway Aviation Museum

Former Control Tower, Heathhall Industrial Estate, Dumfries DG1 3PH   Tel: 01387 251623
Web: www.dumfriesaviationmuseum.com

Based around the original control tower of RAF Dumfries, the museum is a fascinating collection of aircraft and memorabilia from the earliest days of flight to recent times.

Opening Times: Easter to Oct Sat & Sun 10:00-17:00. Oct to Easter Sun only 11:00-15:30. Jul and Aug Wed to Fri 11:00-13:30.   Admission: Adult £2.50, Child £1.50, Family (2 Adults & 2 or more Children) £7.00   Location: Heathhall Industrial Estate, off A701.   Map Ref: 13

Dumfries Museum & Camera Obscura

The Observatory, Dumfries DG2 7SW   Tel: 01387 253374   Fax: 01387 265081
Email: dumfriesmuseum@dumgal.gov.uk   Web: www.dumgal.gov.uk/museums

A treasure house of the history of Dumfries and Galloway telling the story of the land and people of the region.

Opening Times: Apr to Sep Mon to Sat 10:00-17:00, Sun 14:00-17:00. Oct to Mar Tue to Sat 10:00-13:00 & 14:00-17:00.   Admission: Museum free. Camera Obscura Adult £1.50 Concession 75p.   Location: Five minutes walk from Whitesands.   Map Ref: 13

Gracefield Arts Centre

29 Edinburgh Road, Dumfries DG1 1JQ   Tel: 01387 262084   Fax: 01387 255173

Gracefield presents a changing display of contemporary exhibitions by local, national and international artists and craftspeople. Selected exhibitions from the permanent collection of Scottish paintings, drawings and prints dating from the 1840s are shown 3 to 4 times per year.

Opening Times: Tue to Sat 10:00-17:00.   Admission: Free.   Location: Five minute walk from train station and town centre.   Map Ref: 13

Old Bridge House
Mill Street, Dumfries DG2 7BE   Tel: 01387 256904   Fax: 01387 265081
Email: dumfriesmuseum@dumgal.gov.uk   Web: www.dumgal.gov.uk/museums

Built in 1660 into the sandstone of the 15th century Devorgilla Bridge, Dumfries' oldest house is now a museum of everyday life in the town.

Opening Times: Apr to Sep Mon to Sat 10:00-17:00. Sun 14:00-17:00.   Admission: Free.
Location: One minutes walk from Whitesands.   Map Ref: 13

Robert Burns Centre

Mill Road, Dumfries DG2 7BE   Tel / Fax: 01387 264808
Email: dumfriesmuseum@dumgal.gov.uk   Web: www.dumgal.gov.uk/museums

Situated in the town's 18th century watermill on the West Bank of the River Nith, The Robert Burns Centre tells the story of Robert Burns' last years spent in the bustling streets and lively atmosphere of Dumfries in the late 18th century.

Opening Times: Apr to Sep Mon to Sat 10:00-20:00, Sun 14:00-17:00. Oct to Mar Tue to Sat 10:00-13:00 & 14:00-17:00.   Admission: Free.   Location: West Bank of River Nith, opposite Whitesands.   Map Ref: 13

Edinburgh, Glasgow & Southern Scotland

Robert Burns House

Burns Street, Dumfries DG1 2PS   Tel: 01387 255297   Fax: 01387 265081
Email: dumfriesmuseum@dumgal.gov.uk   Web: www.dumgal.gov.uk/museums

Simple sandstone house in a quiet Dumfries street where Robert Burns, Scotland's National Poet, spent the last years of his brilliant life.

Opening Times: Apr to Sep Mon to Sat 10:00-17:00, Sun 14:00-17:00. Oct to Mar Tue to Sat 10:00-13:00 & 14:00-17:00.   Admission: Free.   Location: One minute walk from Broons Road car park.   Map Ref: 13

Shambellie House Museum of Costume

New Abbey, Dumfries DG2 8HQ   Tel: 01387 850375   Fax: 01387 850461

Email: info@nms.ac.uk
Web: www.nms.ac.uk/costume

Step back in time and experience Victorian and Edwardian grace and refinement. Set in attractive wooded grounds, Shambellie is a beautiful Victorian country house which offers visitors the chance to see period clothes, from the 1850s to the 1950s, in appropriate room settings, with accessories, furniture and decorative art. Part of the National Museums of Scotland.

Opening Times: Apr to Oct 11:00-17:00.   Admission: Adult £2.50, Child Free, Concession £1.50.   Location: Seven miles south of Dumfries, on the A710.   Map Ref: 14

Shambellie House display

Dunbar Town House Museum

Dunbar Town House, High Street, Dunbar EH42 1ER   Tel: 01368 863734   Fax: 01620 828201
Email: elms@eastlothian.gov.uk   Web: www.dunbarmuseum.org

Dunbar Town House Museum is based in a 16th century building. There is an archaeology display, a local history room and a different local history exhibition each year.

Opening Times: Apr to Oct 12:30-16:30.   Admission: Free.   Location: High Street.
Map Ref: 15

John Muir's Birthplace

126 High Street, Dunbar EH42 1ER   Tel: 01368 865899   Fax: 01620 828201
Email: info@jmbt.org.uk   Web: www.jmbt.org.uk

The birthplace of the environmentalist John Muir, includes displays about Muir's life and ideas, and the conservation movement.

Opening Times: Apr to Oct Mon to Sat 10:00-17:00, Sun 13:00-17:00. Nov to Mar closed Mon & Tue.   Admission: Free.   Location: High Street.   Map Ref: 15

Jim Clark Room

44 Newton Street, Duns TD11 3AU   Tel: 01361 883960

Museum dedicated to local driver Jim Clark.

Opening Times: Easter to Sep daily 10:30-13:00 & 14:00-16:30, Sun 14:00-16:00. Oct Mon to Sat 13:00-16:00.   Admission: Adult £1.30, SBC Residents Free.   Location: In main town centre.   Map Ref: 16

Manderston

Duns TD11 3PP   Tel: 01361 883450   Fax: 01361 882010
Email: palmer@manderston.co.uk   Web: www.manderston.co.uk

Biscuit Tin Museum contains a rare collection of commemorative and decorative tins from Huntley & Palmer. Based in a period Edwardian mansion.

Opening Times: Mid May to End Sep Thu & Sun 14:00-17:00.   Admission: £6.50 (includes tour of house & gardens).   Location: On A6105 two miles east of Duns, 12 miles west of Berwick-upon-Tweed.   Map Ref: 16

Edinburgh, Glasgow & Southern Scotland

Museum of Scottish Country Life

Wester Kittochside, East Kilbride G76 9HR Tel: 01355 224181 Fax: 01355 571290 Email: info@nms.ac.uk Web: www.nms.ac.uk/countrylife

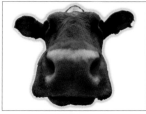

Go wild in the country!

Go wild in the country at Scotland's fantastic working farm and museum! This award-winning Museum shows how country people lived and worked in Scotland in the past and how this has shaped the countryside of today. The site includes an exhibition building housing the National Country Life Collections, the original Georgian farmhouse, historical working farm and events area. Part of the National Museums of Scotland.

Opening Times: Daily 10:00-17:00. Admission: Adult £3.00, Child Free, Concessions £1.50.
Location: Situated between East Kilbride and Glasgow.
Map Ref: 17

EDINBURGH

Brass Rubbing Centre

Trinity Apse, Chalmers Close, Royal Mile, Edinburgh EH1 1SS
Tel: 0131 556 4364 Web: www.cac.org.uk

·EDINBVRGH·
THE CITY OF EDINBURGH COUNCIL
CULTURE AND LEISURE

BRASS RUBBING CENTRE

Edinburgh Brass Rubbing Centre

The Brass Rubbing Centre occupies Trinity Apse, the sole surviving fragment of the Gothic Trinity College Church founded about 1460. It contains a fascinating collection of replicas moulded from ancient Pictish stones, and medieval church brasses. No experience is required to make a rubbing, and staff are on hand to assist. The Centre also stocks high-quality, ready-made rubbings and brass rubbing kits.

Opening Times: Apr to Sep Mon to Sat 10:00-17:00, Sun during Aug 12:00-17:00. Last rubbings begins one hour prior to closing. Closed Oct to Mar. Admission: Free.
Cost to make rubbing.
Map Ref: 18

City Art Centre

2 Market Street, Edinburgh EH1 1DE

·EDINBVRGH·
THE CITY OF EDINBURGH COUNCIL
CULTURE AND LEISURE

The City Art Centre

Tel: 0131 529 3993
Fax: 0131 529 3986
Email: cac.admin@edinburgh.gov.uk
Web: www.cac.org.uk

The City Art Centre is both home to Edinburgh's outstanding collection of Scottish art and one of the United Kingdom's premier temporary exhibition spaces. Since it opened in 1980, the City Art Centre has mounted a huge range of exhibitions, from rare Egyptian antiquities to the most innovative contemporary art, from Michelangelo drawings to Star Wars. The scale and range of the exhibition programme has made the gallery one of Britain's most visited exhibition centres. The city's fine art collection consists of almost 4,000 works of Scottish art: paintings, watercolours, drawings, prints, photographs, sculpture and tapestries, including work by McTaggart, Fergusson, Peploe and Eardley. The collection reflects all of the significant influences and movements in Scottish art, ranging from early portraiture, through the Glasgow Boys, the Edinburgh School and the Colourists.

Opening Times: Mon to Sat 10:00-17:00, Sun during Aug 12:00-17:00. Admission: Free. Charging for occasional   Map Ref: 18

The Blue Hat

Edinburgh, Glasgow & Southern Scotland

Dean Gallery

73 Belford Road, Edinburgh EH4 3DS   Tel: 0131 624 6200   Fax: 0131 623 7126
Email: deaninfo@nationalgalleries.org   Web: www.nationalgalleries.org

The Dean Gallery just opposite the Gallery of Modern Art, holds an extensive collection of Dada and Surrealist art including works by Dali, Ernst, Magritte, Man Ray and Miro. It is also home to an impressive collection of works by Sir Eduardo Paolozzi including a substantial number of plaster sculptures, prints and drawings. Spectacular city views and beautiful sculpture park.

Opening Times: Daily 10:00-17:00, late night Thu until 19:00. Admission: Free to permanent collection, admission charges for special exhibitions. Location: Ten minutes walk from West End Princes Street, or catch free

Joan Miró 1893-1983 Maternity (Maternité) 1924

bus from Scottish National Portrait Gallery.   Exhibitions & Events 2004 : Until 29 Feb: Artists Design Textiles (Free), 29 May to 31 Oct: Jeff Koons (tbc), 4 Dec to 13 Mar 05: Paolozzi at 80 (tbc).   Map Ref: 18

Edinburgh University - Historical Musical Instruments

Reid Concert Hall, Bistro Square, Edinburgh EH8 9AG   Tel: 0131 650 4367   Fax: 0131 650 2425   Email: euchmi@ed.ac.uk   Web: www.music.ed.ac.uk/euchmi

Outstanding display of over 1000 musical instruments showing 400 years of history of folk and domestic music, bands and orchestras, plus interactive devices.

Opening Times: Mon to Fri 14:00-17:00, Wed 15:00-17:00, Sat 10:00-13:00. Closed Xmas & New Year. Admission: Free. Location: Bristo Square, next to McEwan Hall   Map Ref: 18

The Fruitmarket Gallery

THE FRUITMARKET GALLERY

45 Market Street, Edinburgh EH1 1DF   Tel: 0131 225 2383   Fax: 0131 220 3130
Email: info@fruitmarket.co.uk   Web: www.fruitmarket.co.uk

Situated in one of the world's most beautiful cities, Edinburgh's Fruitmarket Gallery is an acclaimed international art space which has operated as a contemporary gallery since 1974. The gallery shows a programme of exciting, thought-provoking exhibitions of Scottish, British and international contemporary art. The Fruitmarket Gallery exhibition programme is complemented by an ambient, street-level glass fronted café and innovative bookshop.

Upper Gallery, Inka Essenhigh exhibition 2003.
Photo Alan Dimmick

Opening Times: Mon to Sat 11:00-18:00, Sun 12:00-17:00. Admission: All exhibitions free. Location: Very central location, next to Waverley Station. Exhibitions &

Events 2004 : May to Jul: Nathan Coley British artist, Aug to Sep: Fred Tomaselli American painter/collagist.   Map Ref: 18

The Georgian House

7 Charlotte Square, Edinburgh EH2 4DR   Tel / Fax: 0131 226 3318

The Georgian House is part of Robert Adam's masterpiece of urban design, Charlotte Square. It dates from 1776, when those who could afford it began to escape the cramped, squalid conditions of Edinburgh's Old Town to settle in the fashionable New Town. The house's beautiful china, shining silver, exquisite paintings and furniture all reflect the domestic surroundings and social conditions of the times.

Opening Times: 1-31 Mar & 1 Nov to 24 Dec daily 11:00-15:00, 1 Apr to 31 Oct daily 10:00-17:00.

Entrance to the Georgian House
7 Charlotte Square

Admission: Adult £5.00, Concession £3.75, Family £13.50. NTS/NT Members Free. Location: Two minutes from west end of Princes Street, ten minutes from Tourist Information Centre.   Map Ref: 18

The Grand Lodge of Scotland Museum

Freemasons Hall, 96 George Street, Edinburgh EH2 3DH   Tel: 0131 225 5304   Fax: 0131 225 3953   Email: grandsecretary@sol.co.uk   Web: www.grandlodgescotland.com

All objects relating to Scottish Freemasonry, including glassware, ceramics, coins, photographs and books.

Opening Times: Mon to Fri 09:30-16:30. Closed Sat, Sun & BH.   Admission: Free.
Location: Town centre.   Map Ref: 18

Lauriston Castle

Cramond Road South, Davidson's Mains, Edinburgh EH4 5QD   Tel: 0131 336 2060   Web: www.cac.org.uk

A 16th century tower house with later additions, Lauriston Castle stands in tranquil grounds overlooking the Forth at Cramond. The preserved Edwardian interior is an ideal backdrop to the rich collection of fine and decorative art assembled by the last private owners. The Castle and its grounds are host to a year round programme of art and craft based workshops, study days and family events.

Opening Times: By guided tour only Apr to Oct 11:20, 12:20, 14:20, 15:20 & 16:20. Closed Fri. Nov to Mar Sat & Sun 14:20 & 15:20. Admission: Adult £4.50, Concession £3.00.   Map Ref: 18

Lothian & Borders Fire Brigade, Museum of Fire

Brigade Headquarters, Lauriston Place, Edinburgh EH3 9DE   Tel: 0131 228 2401
Fax: 0131 229 8359   Email: neil.dinwoodie@lbfire.org.uk   Web: www.lbfire.org.uk

The Museum tells the history of the oldest fire brigade in the UK (formed 1824), showing the development of fire fighting, displaying a range of engines along with many other fire related items.

Opening Times: Mon to Fri 09:00-16:30. Closed Xmas & New Year also first two weeks Aug. Viewing is normally by appointment. Admission: Free. Location: City Centre, next to Art College.   Map Ref: 18

Museum of Childhood

42 High Street, Royal Mile, Edinburgh EH1 1TG

Tel: 0131 529 4142
Fax: 0131 558 3103
Email: admin@museumofchildhood.fsnet.co.uk
Web: www.cac.org.uk

It is a treasure house crammed full of memories of childhood past and present. There are toys and games galore from all around the world, ranging from dolls and teddy bears to train sets and tricycles. Listen to children chanting multiplication tables in the 1930s schoolroom. Watch the street games played by Edinburgh children filmed in 1951. Find out how children were brought up, dressed and educated in decades gone by.

Opening Times: Mon to Sat 10:00-17:00, Sun during Jul & Aug 12:00-17:00. Admission: Free.   Map Ref: 18

Museum of Edinburgh

Huntly House, 142 Canongate, Royal Mile, Edinburgh EH8 8DD
Tel: 0131 529 4143 Fax: 0131 557 3346 Web: www.cac.org.uk

Housing collections relating to the story of Edinburgh from pre-historic times to the present day, the museum's treasures include the National Covenant, the great charter demanding religious freedoms, signed in 1638. The museum also includes the feeding bowl and collar presented to 'Greyfriars Bobby', the little Skye Terrier dog that maintained a vigil by the grave of his master and won the hearts of the people of Edinburgh.

Opening Times: Mon to Sat 10:00-17:00. Sun during Aug 12:00-17:00. Admission: Free. Map Ref: 18

National Gallery of Scotland

The Mound, Edinburgh EH2 2EL Tel: 0131 624 6200 Fax: 0131 623 7126
Email: nginfo@nationalgalleries.org Web: www.nationalgalleries.org

Scotland's greatest collection of European paintings, drawings and prints dating from the early Renaissance to the late 19th century. The collection includes works by Raphael, Titian, Velazquez, Poussin, Rembrandt, Vermeer, Rubens, Turner and the Impressionists. Also houses the national collection of Scottish art with works by Ramsay, Raeburn, Wilkie and McTaggart.

Opening Times: Daily 10:00-17:00, late night Thu until 19:00.
Admission: Free to permanent collection, charges for special exhibitions. Location: Right in the centre of Edinburgh, just off Princes Street. Exhibitions & Events 2004 : 1-31 Jan: The Vaughan Bequest of Turner Watercolours (Free), 9 Jan to 21 Mar: Travels with Edward Lear (Free). Map Ref: 18

National War Museum of Scotland

Edinburgh Castle, Castlehill, Edinburgh EH1 2NG Tel: 0131 225 7534
Fax: 0131 225 3848 Email: info@nms.ac.uk
Web: www.nms.ac.uk/war

Explore the Scottish experience of war and military service over the last 400 years. The lives of many thousands of Scots have been dominated by this experience - the objects in the Museum and the individuals and events to which they relate make this clear. The Museum also reveals the extent to which war and military service have influenced Scotland's history, identity and reputation abroad. Part of the National Museums of Scotland.

Opening Times: Apr to Oct 09:45-17:45, Nov to Mar 09:45-16:45.
Admission: Included in admission to Edinburgh Castle.
Location: In city centre, five minutes walk from Princes Street.
Map Ref: 18

Guided or Private Tours	Disabled Access	Gift Shop or Sales Point	Café or Refreshments	Restaurant	Car Parking

Nelson Monument

Calton Hill, Edinburgh EH7 5AA
Tel: 0131 556 2716   Web: www.cac.org.uk

High on Calton Hill, this monument to Admiral Lord Nelson and Trafalgar was built between 1807 and 1815. In 1853 a large time ball was introduced. It is lowered each day as the one o'clock gun is fired from Edinburgh Castle. The panoramic view from the monument is framed by Fife to the north, the Forth estuary to the east, the Moorfoot Hills to the south and the Forth Rail and Road Bridges to the west.

Opening Times: Apr to Sep Mon 13:00-18:00, Tue to Sat 10:00-18:00. Oct to Mar Mon to Sat 10:00-15:00.   Admission: Adult £2.00.
Map Ref: 18

Newhaven Heritage Museum

24 Pier Place, Newhaven Harbour, Edinburgh EH6 4LP
Tel: 0131 551 4165   Web: www.cac.org.uk

What was it like to live in the tightly-knit fishing community of Newhaven, earning a living as a fishwife or fisherman braving the sea to bring home the catch? Discover the answer in the historic fishmarket, overlooking picturesque Newhaven Harbour.

Opening Times: Mon to Sun 12:00-16:45.
Admission: Free.
Map Ref: 18
The lively and informative Newhaven Heritage Museum

No 28 Charlotte Square

28 Charlotte Square, Edinburgh EH2 4ET
Tel: 0131 243 9300   Fax: 0131 243 9301

Situated in Edinburgh's renowned New Town, it is considered by many as the finest Georgian square in Britain. It was the last commission of Robert Adam, one of the world's most influential architects. On display is a collection of 20th century Scottish paintings, Regency furniture and objets d'art.

Opening Times: Gallery: Mon to Fri 11:00-15:00.   Admission: Free
Location: In Edinburgh city centre, two minutes from west end of Princes Street.
Map Ref: 18
'Still Life of Roses and Mirror' by S J Peploe © The Hutchison Collection

---

The People's Story

Canongate Tolbooth, Royal Mile, Edinburgh EH8 8BN
Tel: 0131 529 4057   Fax: 0131 556 3439
Web: www.cac.org.uk

Situated in the Canongate Tolbooth, opposite the Museum of Edinburgh in the Royal Mile, The People's Story Museum uses oral history, reminiscence, written sources and reconstructed set to tell the story of the lives, work and leisure of the ordinary people of Edinburgh from the late 18th century to the present day.

Opening Times: Mon to Sat 10:00-17:00. Sun during Aug 12:00-17:00.   Admission: Free.
Map Ref: 18
The People's Story Museum

Edinburgh, Glasgow & Southern Scotland

The Queen's Gallery

Palace of Holyroodhouse, Edinburgh EH8 8DX   Tel: 0131 556 5100   Email: information@royalcollection.org.uk
Web: www.royal.gov.uk

The new Queen's Gallery will host a programme of changing exhibitions from the Royal Collection. Exhibitions include King of the World: The Padshahnama, An Imperial Mughal Manuscript. 24 Oct 2003 - 3 May 2004. These exquisite 17th century paintings record life at the court of Shah-Jahan, builder of the Taj Mahal. Enchanting the Eye: Dutch Paintings of the Golden Age, 14 May 2004, brings together 50 outstanding examples of Dutch 17th century paintings from the Royal Collection.

The Queens Gallery, Palace of Holyroodhouse - interior. Photo by EZM. The Royal Collection © 2003

Opening Times: Daily Apr to Oct 09:30-18:00 (last admission 17:15). Nov to Mar 09:30-16:30 (last admission 15:45). Entry by timed ticket.   Admission: Adult £4.50, Child £2.50, Under 5s Free, OAP/Student £3.50, Family (2 adults and 3 children) £11.50.   Map Ref: 18

Royal Museum & Museum of Scotland

Chambers Street, Edinburgh EH1 1JF   Tel: 0131 227 4422
Fax: 0131 220 4819   Email: info@nms.ac.uk   Web: www.nms.ac.uk

These two 'must-see' Museums stand side-by-side in the centre of the city, minutes from the historic Royal Mile and Edinburgh Castle. The striking Museum of Scotland which celebrates it's 5th birthday this year, presents the history of Scotland - it's land, it's people and their achievements - through the rich national collections. The stunning series of galleries take you on a journey from the country's

Double Coffin, Ancient Egypt Gallery, Royal Museum

geological beginnings through time to the twentieth century. Incorporated in the galleries are striking figures sculpted by Sir Eduardo Paolozzi, installations by Andy Goldsworthy and a new artwork by Ian Hamilton Findlay. Next door is the Royal Museum. In this elegant Victorian building, distinguished by it's soaring glass-topped roof and stunning Main Hall, you will discover outstanding

Lewis Chessman, Museum of Scotland

international collections which reflect the diversity of life on Earth and ingenuity of humankind. Don't miss the new Communicate! Gallery, part of the BT Connected Earth network, which combines stunning displays with interactive exhibits to bring you the past, present and future of telecommunications. There are exciting temporary exhibitions and special events, for all the family, throughout the year as well as fascinating free daily guided tours of the collections.

Opening Times: Mon to Fri 10:00-17:00, Tue 10:00-20:00, Sun 12:00-17:00.   Admission: Free.
Location: Near city centre, five minute walk from Princes Street and Royal Mile.   Map Ref: 18

Royal Scots Regimental Museum

The Castle, Edinburgh EH1 2YT   Tel: 0131 310 5016/5017   Fax: 0131 310 5019

The Royal Scots is the oldest Regiment in the British Army and as such is the Senior Infantry Regiment of the Line. It was raised in 1633 and through paintings, artefacts, silver and medals their fascinating story is told from formation to the present day.

Opening Times: Apr to Sep daily 09:30-17:30. Oct to Mar Mon to Fri 09:30-16:00.
Admission: Free.   Location: Edinburgh Castle.   Map Ref: 18

Royal Scottish Academy Building

&

The Mound, Edinburgh EH2 2EL   Tel: 0131 624 6200   Fax: 0131 623 7126

Email: enquiries@nationalgalleries.org
Web: www.nationalgalleries.org

This recently refurbished art gallery will display major international exhibitions.

Opening Times: Daily 10:00-17:00, late night Thu until 19:00. Admission: Varied charges for exhibitions. Location: The Mound, Edinburgh. Exhibitions & Events 2004 : Until 29 Feb: Degas and the Italians in Paris (£6.50/£4.50), 4 Aug to 5 Dec: The Age of Titian (£6.50/£4.50).

Map Ref: 18

Scott Monument

·ЄDINBVRGH·
THE CITY OF EDINBURGH COUNCIL
CULTURE AND LEISURE

East Princes Street Gardens, Edinburgh EH2 2EJ
Tel: 0131 529 4068
Web: www.cac.org.uk

Designed by George Meikle Kemp, this monument to the great Scottish writer opened in August 1846. In the years since then millions of people have climbed the 200 foot structure to admire its commanding views of the city, the exhibition on the life of Sir Walter Scott and the statuettes of characters from his works which adorn the monument.

Opening Times: Apr to Sep Mon to Sat 09:00-18:00, Sun 10:00-18:00. Oct to Mar Mon to Sat 09:00-15:00, Sun 10:00-15:00. Admission: £2.50.

Map Ref: 18

The Scott Monument, Edinburgh

Scottish National Gallery of Modern Art

& 🕮 ▢ ◑ ♿

75 Belford Road, Edinburgh EH4 3DR

Tel: 0131 624 6200   Fax: 0131 623 7126
Email: gmainfo@nationalgalleries.org
Web: www.nationalgalleries.org

Scotland's finest collection of 20th and 21st century paintings, sculpture and graphic art including works by Picasso, Matisse, Giacometti, Sickert and Hockney. Significant holdings of Surrealism and German Expressionism along with an unrivalled collection of 20th and 21st century Scottish art, from the Colourists right up to the present day.

Sculptures by Moore, Hepworth and Paolozzi in surrounding grounds.

Opening Times: Daily 10:00-17:00, late night Thu until 19:00. Admission: Free to permanent collection, admission charges for special exhibitions. Location: Ten minutes walk from West End Princes Street, or catch the free bus. Exhibitions & Events 2004 : Until 7 Mar: Cindy Sherman (£4/£3), Until 7 Mar: Bill Viola (Free), 3 Apr to 13 Jun: Ben Nicholson & The St Ives School (Free), 3 Apr to 13 Jun: Lucian Freud: Prints (Free), 10 Jul to 19 Sep: Jasper Johns since 1983 (tbc).

Lichtenstein 'In the Car'

Map Ref: 18

Scottish National Portrait Gallery

1 Queen Street, Edinburgh EH2 1JD   Tel: 0131 624 6200
Fax: 0131 623 7126   Email: pginfo@nationalgalleries.org
Web: www.nationalgalleries.org

A visual history of Scotland from the 16th century to the present day, told through portraits of the people who shaped it: royals and rebels, poets and philosophers, heroes and villains. Among the most famous are Mary, Queen of Scots and Robert Burns. Also houses the National Photography Collection, including vast holdings of work by Hill and Adamson, the Scottish pioneers of photography.

Opening Times: Daily 10:00-17:00, late night Thu until 19:00.
Admission: Free to permanent collection, admission charges for special exhibitions.   Location: Just a two minute walk from Princes Street (Eastend) and one minute walk from central bus station in St Andrew Square.   Exhibitions & Events 2004 :   17 Jan to 18 Apr: Patrick Geddes and France (Free), 12 Feb to 31 May: Below Stairs (£4/£3), 13 May to 5 Sep: Portrait Miniatures: Albion Collection (Free).   Map Ref: 18

Henry Raeburn - Walter Scott

Surgeons' Hall Museum

Royal College of Surgeons, 18 Nicolson Street, Edinburgh EH8 9DW   Tel: 0131 527 1649
Fax: 0131 557 6406   Email: museum@rcsed.ac.uk   Web: www.rcsed.ac.uk

History of Surgery Exhibition - The Royal College of Surgeons of Edinburgh, founded in 1505, has the largest medical/anatomical/surgical collection in Scotland. Follow the story of surgery in Scotland from its earliest days, through the Burke and Hare murders to modern keyhole surgery. William Playfair's 1832 Pathology Museum - Includes the Charles Bell collections of anatomical preparations and original oil paintings from the Napoleonic Wars. Items belonging to Robert Knox, Robert Liston, James Syme, Joseph Lister, James Young Simpson and Joseph Bell are among surgical ephemera dating from Roman times.

Sir Jules Thorn Hall

Opening Times: Mon to Fri 12:00-16:00. Closed Sat, Sun, BH & diploma days.
Admission: Free. Guided group tours of Pathology Museum for groups (min 12 max 24 people) can be arranged through the Museum office - price on application.   Location: Opposite Festival Theatre and University Old College (3/4 mile from Princes Street).   Exhibitions & Events 2004 :   Apr/May: The Syringe, Aug: Sport & Surgery.   Map Ref: 18

Talbot Rice Gallery

University of Edinburgh, Old College, South Bridge, Edinburgh EH8 9YL
Tel: 0131 650 2210   Fax: 0131 650 2213

The Talbot Rice Gallery at the University of Edinburgh is a public gallery comprising of two exhibition spaces. The Georgian Gallery houses the permanent display of the University's Old Master paintings and bronzes. The White Gallery shows around seven contemporary art exhibitions every year and is accompanied by the round room programme of experimental projects and small exhibitions. The Gallery has an active public events programme accompanying all exhibitions; admission to all of the exhibitions spaces and public events is free.

The Torrie Collection

Opening Times: Tue to Sat 10:00-17:00, please phone for further details.   Admission: Free.   Location: Five minutes walk from Royal Mile, next to Royal Museum of Scotland.   Map Ref: 18

EDINBURGH (continued)

The Writers' Museum

Lady Stair's House, Lady Stair's Close, Lawnmarket, Royal
Mile, Edinburgh EH1 2PA   Tel: 0131 529 4901

THE WRITERS' MUSEUM

·ЄDINBVRGH·
THE CITY OF EDINBURGH COUNCIL
CULTURE AND LEISURE

Fax: 0131 220 5057
Email: enquiries@writersmusuem.demon.co.uk
Web: www.cac.org.uk

The Museum is dedicated to Scotland's great literary figures: Robert Burns (1759-1796), Sir Walter Scott (1771-1832) and Robert Louis Stevenson (1850-1895). Other prominent Scottish writers are featured in the museum's temporary exhibition programme. In the adjacent Makars' Court, which takes its name from the Scots word for a writer or poet, commemorative flagstones celebrate the work of Scottish writers from the 14th century to the present day.

Opening Times: Mon to Sat 10:00-17:00. Sun during Aug 12:00-17:00.   Admission: Free.   Map Ref: 18

The Writers' Museum, Edinburgh

FALKIRK

Callendar House

Callendar Estate, Falkirk FK1 1YR   Tel: 01324 503770   Fax: 01324 503771

CALLENDAR
HOUSE

600 years of Scottish history; costumed interpreters, working Georgian kitchen, exhibitions, Georgian gardens, gift shop, conference facilities, tea shop at the stables, the Park Gallery and maginificent grounds. Open all year.

Opening Times: Mon to Sat all year 10:00-16:00, Apr to Sep Sun 14:00-17:00.   Admission: Adults £3.00, Child £1.00, OAP £1.50   Map Ref: 19

GALASHIELS *Scottish Borders*

Old Gala House

Scott Crescent, Galashiels TD1 3JS   Tel / Fax: 01896 752611

Museum and art gallery, former home of Laird of Gala.

Opening Times: Easter to Sep Tue to Sat 10:00-16:00. Jul to Aug Mon to Sat 10:00-16:00, Sun 14:00-16:00. Oct Tue to Sat 13:00-16:00.   Admission: Free.   Location: Five minute walk from town centre.   Map Ref: 20

GLASGOW

Auld Kirk Museum

The Auld Kirk Museum,The Cross, Kirkintilloch, Glasgow G66 1AB   Tel: 0141 578 0144
Fax: 0141 578 0140

Find out about Romans, the Forth & Clyde Canal and iron founding at this award winning museum.

Opening Times: Tue to Sat 10:00-13:00, 2:00-17:00.   Location: Kirkintilloch   Map Ref: 21

Key to Classifications

see Classifications Index on page 423

Anthropology	Horticultural	Police, Prisons
Archaeological	Jewellery	& Dungeons
Art Galleries	Literature & Libraries	Railways
Arts, Crafts & Textiles	Maritime	Religion
China, Glass & Ceramics	Military & Defence	Roman
Communications	Multicultural	Science - Earth & Planetary
Egyptian	Music & Theatre	Sculpture
Fashion	Natural History	Sporting History
Geology	Oriental	Toy & Childhood
Health & Medicine	Palaces	Transport
Historic Houses	Photography	Victoriana

Edinburgh, Glasgow & Southern Scotland

The Burrell Collection

2060 Pollokshaws Road, Glasgow G43 1AT
Tel: 0141 287 2550   Fax: 0141 287 2597
Web: www.glasgowmuseums.com

The Burrell Collection consists of some 9000 items of European, Near Eastern and Oriental fine and decorative art. Highlights of the collection include the spectacular medieval European stained glass, tapestries and furniture; Egyptian, Greek and Roman antiquities; 19th century French art including works by Degas and Cezanne; Islamic art and Chinese art. The collections are housed in a award winning building in the woodland surroundings of Pollok Country Park. They were a gift to the city from the great shipping magnate and collector Sir William Burrell.

The Warrick Vase from the Emperor Hadrian's villa of Tivoli

Rodin, The Thinker

Opening Times: Mon to Thu & Sat 10:00-17:00, Fri & Sun 11:00-17:00.   Admission: Free.   Location: Pollok Country Park.
Map Ref: 22

Clydebuilt - Scottish Maritime Museum

Kings Inch Road, Braehead, Glasgow G51 4BN   Tel: 0141 886 1013   Fax: 0141 886 1015
Email: clydebuilt@tinyworld.co.uk

The story of Glasgow, its river and people over 300 years from tobacco to shipbuilding with floating exhibits.

Opening Times: Mon to Thu & Sat 10:00-18:00 Sun 11:00-17:00. Closed Fri.   Admission: Adult £3.50, Child/OAP £1.75, Family £8.00.   Location: Next to Braehead Shopping Centre.
Map Ref: 22

Collins Gallery

University of Strathclyde, 22 Richmond Street, Glasgow G1 1XQ   Tel: 0141 548 2558
Fax: 0141 552 4053   Email: collinsgallery@strath.ac.uk
Web: www.collinsgallery.strath.ac.uk/collections

Lively, annual programme of temporary exhibitions covering contemporary Fine and Applied Art from British and International artists, both new and established. Artwork is usually for sale.

Opening Times: Mon to Fri 10:00-17:00, Sat 12:00-16:00. Closed Sun, public holidays and exhibition installations.   Admission: Free.   Location: City centre, five minute walk from railway stations and underground.
Map Ref: 22

David Livingstone Centre

165 Station Road, Blantyre, Glasgow G72 9BT   Tel: 01698 823140

Scotland's most famous explorer and missionary was born here in Shuttlerow in 1813. Today the 18th century tenement commemorates David Livingstone's life and work.

Opening Times: 1 Apr to 24 Dec Mon to Sat 10:00-17:00, Sun 12:30-17:00.   Admission: Adult £3.50, Concession £2.60, Family £9.50. NTS/NT Members Free.   Location: Just off junction 5 of M74 via A725 and A724, in Blantyre.
Map Ref: 23

Fossil Grove

Victoria Park, Glasgow G14 1BN
Tel: 0141 287 2000
Web: www.glasgowmuseums.com

330 million year old fossilised tree stumps. The fossils represented the giant clubmoss, which grew in swampy tropical forests during the carboniferous or coal age. Designated a Site of Special Scientific Interest by Scottish National Heritage.

Opening Times: Apr to Sep. Daily 12:00-17:00.
Admission: Free.   Location: Victoria Park.
Map Ref: 22

Gallery of Modern Art

Royal Exchange Square, Glasgow G1 3AH
Tel: 0141 229 1996 Fax: 0141 204 5316
Web: www.glasgowmuseums.com

Opened in 1996, the gallery is housed in the elegant, neo-classical Royal Exchange Building, in the heart of Glasgow city centre. The displays are constantly changing as a result of an active programme of temporary exhibitions and new acquisitions. The Gallery of Modern Art aims to widen public access to contemporary art; in particular targeting young adults aged 16-25 years. A thought-provoking programme of temporary exhibitions and workshops focuses upon contemporary social issues, often featuring groups marginalized in today's society.

'Patriots' by Peter Howson

Opening Times: Mon to Wed & Sat 10:00-17:00, Thu 10:00-20:00, Fri & Sun 11:00-17:00. Admission: Free.
Location: In city centre. Map Ref: 22

Glasgow Museums Resource Centre

200 Woodhead Road, South Nitshill Industrial Estate, Glasgow G53 7NN

The new Glasgow Museums Resource Centre

Tel: 0141 276 9300 Fax: 0141 276 9305
Web: www.glasgowmuseums.com

Glasgow Museums Resource Centre is a new purpose-built resource centre. It will house the collections from Kelvingrove Art Gallery and Museum during the refurbishment of the building. The Resource Centre will be open for visits, tours and research.

Opening Times: To be confirmed, please telephone for details or visit our website. Admission: Free.
Map Ref: 22

The Glasgow School of Art

167 Renfrew Street, Glasgow G3 6RQ Tel: 0141 353 4526 Fax: 0141 353 4746
Email: shop@gsa.ac.uk Web: www.gsa.ac.uk

Charles Rennie Mackintosh's architectural masterpiece. Still a working art school, the regular guided tours let visitors see inside this fascinating building that includes the breathtaking Mackintosh Library.

Opening Times: Tour times: Mon to Fri 11:00 & 14:00, Sat 10:30 & 11:30. Additional times in Jul & Aug Sat 13:00, Sun 10:30, 11:30 & 13:00. Admission: Adult £5.00, Concession £4.00.
Location: City centre, 15 minute walk from Queen Street Station. Map Ref: 22

Hunterian Art Gallery

University of Glasgow, Hillhead Street, Glasgow G12 8QQ
Tel: 0141 330 5431 Fax: 0141 330 3618
Email: hunter@museum.gla.ac.uk Web: www.hunterian.gla.ac.uk

The Hunterian Art Gallery holds a remarkable collection of European art. The founding collection of Dr William Hunter includes outstanding paintings by Rembrandt, Koninck, Chardin and Stubbs. Unrivalled holdings of work by James McNeil Whistler including paintings, pastels and prints. A popular feature of the Charles Rennie Mackintosh collection is the reconstruction of the interiors of The Mackintosh House. There are major displays of paintings by the Scottish Colourists, Fergusson, Peploe, Cadell and Hunter. The graphics collection, one of the most important in Scotland,

The Mackintosh House © Hunterian Art Gallery

holds some 30,000 prints. These may be seen in the Print Room by prior appointment or in the Gallery's exhibition programme. Selections from the collection can be seen in regular exhibitions drawn from the Print Room.

Opening Times: Mon to Sat 09:30-17:00. Closed Sun. Mackintosh House closes daily 12:30-13:30. Admission: Free. Location: In Westend of Glasgow, 15 minutes from city centre. Exhibitions & Events 2004 : 24 Oct to 17 Jan: A Hundred Objects for 100 Years - A National Art Collections Fund Centenary Exhibition, Spring to Autumn: 20th Century Painting from the Permanent Collection, Spring to Autumn: Scottish Art 1800-1900, 12 Jun to 2 Oct: Stubbs and the Hunters. Map Ref: 22

Red & Black: The Fan, J M Whistler © Hunterian Art Gallery

Hunterian Museum

The University of Glasgow, University Avenue, Glasgow G12 8QQ   Tel: 0141 330 4221
Fax: 0141 330 3617   Email: hunter@museum.gla.ac.uk   Web: www.hunterian.gla.ac.uk

Scotland's first public museum was established in 1807 based on the vast collections of Dr William Hunter (1718-83). A student at Glasgow University in the 1730s, Dr Hunter later acquired fame and fortune as a physician and medical teacher in London. Many items from his valuable collections are on display. Since Dr Hunter's time, the collections have grown into one of the largest collections in the United Kingdom with new and exciting additions every year. The Hunterian Museum is located within the Gothic splendour of the University of Glasgow. It has unique

The Bearsden Shark © Hunterian Museum

exhibits of Romans in Scotland, Scottish fossils including the 325 million year old Bearsden shark, dinosaurs from Scotland, Scottish minerals and scientific instruments. The Coin Centre houses one of the world's finest collections of coins and medals.

Opening Times: Mon to Sat 09:30-17:00. Closed Sun & BH. Admission: Free. Location: In West End of Glasgow, part of University of Glasgow campus.

Greek Coin Catana © Hunterian Museum

Exhibitions & Events 2004 : 31 Jan to 17 Apr:
Rosengarten, 2 Apr to 30 Sep: 2004 A Space Oddity - The Bicentenary of Glasgow's Meteorite, 8 May to 28 Aug: The World of Chaucer - Medieval Books and Manuscripts, 8 May to 1 Aug: Wildlife Photographer of the Year. Map Ref: 22

Kelvingrove Art Gallery & Museum

Kelvingrove, Glasgow G3 8AG   Tel: 0141 287 2699

Kelvingrove Art Gallery & Museum is closed until 2006 for extensive refurbishment. Highlights of the Collection are on show at the McLellan Galleries and stored at the new Glasgow Museums Resource Centre. Map Ref: 22

McLellan Galleries

270 Sauchiehall Street, Glasgow G2 3EH
Tel: 0141 565 4137   Fax: 0141 565 4111
Web: www.glasgowmuseums.com

Built in 1856, the Galleries are named after their builder, Archibald McLellan. Situated in the centre of Glasgow, the Galleries are home to the exhibition 'Art Treasures of Kelvingrove', highlights from Kelvingrove's fine and decorative art collections, until Nov 2005.

Opening Times: Mon to Thu & Sat 10:00-17:00, Fri & Sun 11:00-17:00. Admission: Free. Map Ref: 22

Museum of Transport
1 Bunhouse Road, Glasgow G3 8DP   Tel: 0141 287 2720   Fax: 0141 287 2692
Web: www.glasgowmuseums.com

The history of transport and technology with a Glasgow focus. Horse-drawn vehicles, the world's oldest bicycle, cars, fire engines, trains, locomotives and ship models illustrating the history of Clyde shipbuilding. Kelvin Way recreates an old Glasgow street with a cinema showing films about Glasgow transport.

Opening Times: Mon to Thu & Sat 10:00-17:00, Fri & Sun 11:00-17:00. Admission: Free.   Map Ref: 22

The Clyde Room: models from the great days of Glasgow shipyards

---

People's Palace Museum and Winter Gardens
Glasgow Green, Glasgow G40 1AT

Tel: 0141 554 0223
Fax: 0141 550 0892
Web: www.glasgowmuseums.com

The historical, social and cultural history of Glasgow, especially the East End, presented through a range of displays including audio-visual shows and reconstructions including a flat, a shop and an air-raid shelter. Objects range from suffragette banners to Billy Connolly's banana boots. Winter Gardens is an elegant Victorian glasshouse featuring tropical plants and café area.

Opening Times: Mon to Thu & Sat 10:00-17:00, Fri & Sun 11:00-17:00. Admission: Free.   Map Ref: 22

The Big Yin: Billy Connolly's stage costume

Pollok House
2060 Pollokshaws Road, Glasgow G43 1AT Tel: 0141 616 6410 Fax: 0141 616 6521

The Maxwell family is known to have been established at Pollok by 1269. The present house (c.1750) replaced three earlier structures and was extended in 1890. It is set within Pollok Country Park, also the home of the Burrell Collection. The house contains an internationally important collection of paintings, silver and ceramics, displayed as they were around 1931.

Opening Times: Daily 10:00-17:00. Closed Xmas & New Year. Admission: Adult £5.00, Concession £3.75, Family £13.50. NTS/NT Members Free. Location: Off junctions 1 or 2 of M77, follow signs for Burrell Collection, three miles south of Glasgow's city centre.   Map Ref: 22

Provand's Lordship
3 Castle Street, Glasgow G4 0RB Tel: 0141 553 8819 Fax: 0141 552 4744
Web: www.glasgowmuseums.com

The oldest house in Glasgow, built in 1471 as a manse for the St Nicholas Hospital, just opposite Glasgow Cathedral. Period display and furniture. Tranquil recreated medieval herb garden.

Opening Times: Mon to Thu & Sat 10:00-17:00, Fri & Sun 11:00-17:00. Admission: Free.   Map Ref: 22

Historic domestic interior

Royal Highland Fusiliers Regimental Museum

518 Sauchiehall Street, Glasgow G2 3LW   Tel: 0141 332 0961   Fax: 0141 353 1493
Email: assregsec@rhf.org.uk   Web: www.rhf.org.uk

The museum tells the story of three hundred and thirty years continuous service with the use of silver, weapons, artwork, medals, uniforms etc.

Opening Times: Mon to Fri 08:30-16:00.   Admission: Free.   Location: Charring Cross, three minutes from underground station.
Map Ref: 22

St Mungo Museum of Religious Life & Art

2 Castle Street, Glasgow G4 0RH
Tel: 0141 553 2557   Fax: 0141 552 4744
Web: www.glasgowmuseums.com

The museum explores the importance of religion in people's lives across the world and through time. There are galleries of religious art, including Dali's Christ of St John of the Cross, religious life (and death) and Britain's first permanent Zen garden, symbolising the harmony between people and nature. Aims to promote understanding and respect between people of different faiths and none.

Opening Times: Mon to Thu & Sat 10:00-17:00, Fri & Sun 11:00-17:00.   Admission: Free.
Map Ref: 22

Salvador Dali, Christ of St John of the Cross

Scotland Street School, Museum of Education

225 Scotland Street, Glasgow G5 8QB   Tel: 0141 287 0500   Fax: 0141 287 0515
Web: www.glasgowmuseums.com

The building is a Glasgow Board School designed by Charles Rennie Mackintosh. The collection relates to education in the region from c.1830 to the present day, including furniture, books, photographs, documents, toys and costumes. Reconstructed period classroom and craft room.

Opening Times: Mon to Thu & Sat 10:00-17:00, Fri & Sun 11:00-17:00.   Admission: Free.   Location: On south side of city.
Map Ref: 22

World War II Classroom

The Tenement House

145 Buccleuch Street, Glasgow G3 6QN   Tel: 0141 333 0183
Email: tenementhouse@nts.org.uk

Glasgow is associated with tenements. This first-floor flat is a typical late Victorian example, consisting of four rooms and retaining most of its original features such as its bed recesses, kitchen range, coal bunker and bathroom. The furniture, furnishings and personal possessions present a fascinating picture of domestic life in the early 20th century.

Opening Times: 1 Mar to 31 Oct daily 13:00-17:00.   Admission: Adult £3.50, Concession £2.60, Family £9.50.   NTS/NT Members Free.   Location: Third left off Rose Street or Cambridge Street. North west of Sauchiehall

The Tenement House Kitchen

Street pedestrian shopping area.
Map Ref: 22

Guided or Private Tours	Disabled Access	Gift Shop or Sales Point	Café or Refreshments	Restaurant	Car Parking

Edinburgh, Glasgow & Southern Scotland

GORDON *Scottish Borders*

Mellerstain House

Gordon TD3 6LG   Tel: 01573 410225   Fax: 01573 410636
Email: mellerstain.house@virgin.net   Web: www.muses.calligrafix.co.uk/mellerstain

The Music Room at Mellerstain House

Home of the Earl and Countess of Haddington. Superb Adam (William and Robert) mansion, with very fine interiors decorations and plasterwork. Original period furniture. Art collection with portraits by Van Dyke, Ramsey, Gainsborough, Maes and Van Der Heist. Set in beautiful award-winning gardens with magnificent views to the Cheviot Hills. Riverside walk, thatched Tea Cottage, tea room and small shop.

Opening Times: Easter (4 days) 1 May to 30 Sep 12:30-17:00. Closed Sat & Tue. Open at other times for booked parties. Admission: Adult £5.50, Child Free. Gardens £3.00. Location: Six miles north of Kelso on A6089, 40 miles south of Edinburgh via A68. Map Ref: 24

GOREBRIDGE *Mid-Lothian*

Arniston House

Gorebridge EH23 4RY Tel / Fax: 01875 830515
Email: henrietta.d.bekker2@btinternet.com Web: www.arniston-house.co.uk

The Dundas family home, a William Adam mansion house. Fine stucco work, Scottish portraiture and period furniture.

Opening Times: Apr, May & Jun Tue & Wed tours at 14:00 & 15:30. Jul to Mid Sep Sun to Fri tours at 14:00 & 15:30. Grounds open at 12:00. Admission: Adult £5.00, Child £2.00, Concession £4.00. Location: Turn off A7 onto B6372 towards Temple. Arniston is one mile on the right. Map Ref: 25

GREAT CUMBRAE ISLAND *N Ayrshire*

Museum of the Cumbraes

Garrison Stables, Garrison Grounds, Millport, Great Cumbrae Island KA28 0DG Tel: 01475 531191 Web: www.northayrshiremuseums.org.uk

The Museum of the Cumbraes was originally housed in Millport's Garrison House. The collection focuses on social and local history of the area. The village and the Garrison House are excellent examples of Victorian architecture.

Opening Times: Apr to Sep, please telephone for times. Admission: Free. Map Ref: 26

GREENOCK *Inverclyde*

McLean Museum & Art Gallery

15 Kelly Street, Greenock PA16 8JX Tel: 01475 715624 Fax: 01475 715626
Email: val.boa@inverclyde.gov.uk Web: www.inverclyde.gov.uk/museum/index.htm

Permanent displays on local history, James Watt, ship and engine models, big game mounts and items from foreign lands. Temporary exhibition programme and fine art collection.

Opening Times: Mon to Sat 10:00-17:00. Closed Sun & BH. Admission: Free.
Location: West end of Greenock, close to bus station and Greenock West Railway Station. Map Ref: 27

HADDINGTON *E Lothian*

Lennoxlove

Haddington EH41 4NZ Tel: 01620 823720 Email: info@lennoxlove.org
Web: www.lennoxlove.org

A strong and well preserved keep or Pele tower is at the heart of this delightful castle. It now contains the Dukes of Hamilton collection of pictures, furniture and porcelain. The Death mask and other mementoes of Mary Queen of Scots.

Opening Times: Easter to Oct, Wed, Thu & Sun. Guided tours only Location: 20 miles south east of Edinburgh, near Haddington. Map Ref: 28

Edinburgh, Glasgow & Southern Scotland

Drumlanrigs Tower

High Street, Hawick   Tel: 01450 377615   Fax: 01450 378506

Hawick's oldest building is a fortified tower enveloped inside an 18th century town house. The Tower displays the history of Hawick during medieval times, to the industrial revolution to the present day.

Opening Times: Easter to Oct Mon to Sat 10:00-17:00, Sun 12:00-16:00. Jun & Sep closed 17:30. Jul & Aug closed 18:00.   Admission: Adult £2.50, SBC Residents Free.   Map Ref: 29

Hawick Museum & the Scott Gallery

Wilton Lodge Park, Hawick TD9 7JL   Tel: 01450 373457   Fax: 01450 378506
Email: fionacolton@hotmail.com

The museum and custom-built art gallery house the Jimmie Guthrie Motorcycle exhibition and the Scott Art Gallery. The Museum and Scott Gallery reflect the town's history and provide a venue for visiting exhibitions.

Opening Times: Apr to Sep Mon to Fri 10:00-12:00 & 13:00-17:00, Sat & Sun 14:00-17:00. Oct to Mar Mon to Fri 13:00-16:00, Sun 14:00-16:00.   Admission: Free.   Location: In local park, ten minute walk from town centre.   Map Ref: 29

Traquair House

Innerleithen EH44 6PW   Tel: 01896 830323   Fax: 01896 830639
Email: enquiries@traquair.co.uk   Web: www.traquair.co.uk

Where Alexander I signed a charter over 800 years ago and where the 'modern wings' were completed in 1680. Once a pleasure ground for Scottish kings in times of peace, then a refuge for Catholic priests in times of terror.

Opening Times: Jun to Aug 10:30-17:30, Oct 12:30-16:30.   Admission: Adult £5.50, Child £3.00, OAP £5.20, Family £16.00.   Location: Innerleithen, one and a half miles from Traquair.
        Map Ref: 30

Scottish Maritime Museum

Laird Forge Buildings, Gottries Road, Irvine KA12 8QE   Tel: 01294 278283   Fax: 01294 313211   Email: smm@tildesley.fsbusiness.co.uk   Web: www.scottishmaritimemuseum.org

The museum holds Scotland's best collection of smaller ships and boats. Also displayed in former Alexander Stephens of Linthouse shipbuilding engine shop, shipyard machinery and tools.

Opening Times: Apr to Oct 10:00-17:00, Nov to Mar 10:00-16:00.   Admission: Adult £2.50, Child/OAP £1.75, Family £5.00.   Location: Near town centre, two minute walk from Irvine Railway Station.   Map Ref: 31

Vennel Gallery

10 Glasgow Vennel, Irvine KA12 0BD   Tel / Fax: 01294 275059   Email: vennel@north-ayrshire.gov.uk   Web: www.northayrshiremuseums.org.uk

The Gallery has a programme of changing exhibitions of contemporary art and crafts. The gallery includes the Heckling Shop and the Lodging House where Robert Burns worked and lived in 1781.

Opening Times: Fri to Sun 10:00-13:00 & 14:00-17:00. Closed Wed.   Admission: Free.
Location: Just down the lane from The Porthead Tavern.   Map Ref: 31

Arran Heritage Museum

Rosaburn, Brodick, Isle of Arran KA27 8DP   Tel: 01770 302636
Email: arranmuseum@biinternet.com

The museum reflects the social history, archaeology and geology of the island.

Opening Times: Apr to Oct daily 10:30-16:30.   Admission: Adult £2.25, Child £1.00, OAP £1.50, Family £6.00.   Location: One mile from ferry terminal on main road north.   Map Ref: 32

Edinburgh, Glasgow & Southern Scotland

Brodick Castle Gardens & Country Park

Brodick, Isle of Arran KA27 8HY   Tel: 01770 302202   Fax: 01770 302312

The site of this ancient seat of the Dukes of Hamilton was a fortress even in Viking times. The 13th century fortified tower was developed in the 16th century and extended by Cromwell in the 17th century. Some furniture dates from the 17th century, with superb paintings, porcelain and silver collected by the Hamiltons and William Beckford, whose daughter was married to the 10th Duke of Hamilton.

Opening Times: 1 Apr to 31 Oct daily 11:00-16:30 (closes 15:30 in Oct). Reception centre, shop & restaurant - also open 1 Nov to 21 Dec Fri to Sun 10:00-

Brodick Castle - Entrance Hall

15:30.   Admission: Adult £7.00, Concession £5.25, Family £19.00. NTS/NT Members Free.
Location: Ferry from Ardrossan to Brodick and connecting bus to Reception Centre. Map Ref: 32

Jedburgh Castle Jail & Museum

Castlegate, Jedburgh TD8 6QD   Tel: 01835 863254   Fax: 01835 864750

Comprehensive guide to Jedburgh's history. Also jail cells in two two-storey blocks. Garden and grounds for picnics and functions. Audio tours - touch screen and video.

Opening Times: Apr to Oct Mon to Sat 10:00-16:30, Sun 13:00-16:00.   Admission: Adult £2.00, Child Free, Concession £1.50.   Location: Within walking distance of the town.   Map Ref: 33

Mary Queen of Scots House

Queen Street, Jedburgh TD8 6EN   Tel / Fax: 01835 863331

Museum dedicated to Mary Queen of Scots.

Opening Times: Mar to Nov Mon to Sat 10:00-16:30, Sun 11:00-16:30.   Admission: Adult £2.50, SBC Residents Free.   Location: Five minute walk from town centre.   Map Ref: 33

Floors Castle

Roxburghe Estates Office, Kelso TD5 7SF   Tel: 01573 223333   Fax: 01573 226056
Email: marketing@floorscastle.com   Web: www.floorscastle.com

The largest inhabited castle in Scotland is home to the Duke of Roxburghe. The interiors are filled with outstanding collection of French 17th and 18th century furniture, magnificent tapestries, Chinese and European porcelain and many other fine works of art. Enhanced with family photographs and beautiful plants grown on the estate.

Opening Times: Apr to Oct 10:00-16:30. Last admission 16:00.   Admission: Adult £5.75, Child £3.25, OAP/Student £4.75, Under 5s Free. Group rates available.   Location: Roxburghe Estate Office.   Map Ref: 34

Weaver's Cottage

The Cross, Kilbarchan PA10 2JG   Tel: 01505 705588

This typical handloom weaver's cottage, built in 1723, houses the last of the 800 looms working in this village in the 1930s. It is now in use again weaving traditional fabrics. Locally woven shawls cover the box beds, and 19th century domestic items present an appealing display. Plants and herbs used to make natural dyes are a feature of the cottage garden.

Opening Times: 1 Apr to 30 Sep   Admission: Adult £3.50, Concession £2.60, Family £9.50. NTS/NT Members Free.   Location: M8 junction 28A, A737, follow signs for Kilbarchan. 12 miles south west of Glasgow.   Map Ref: 35

Dean Castle

Dean Road, Kilmarnock KA3 1XB   Tel: 01563 574916   Fax: 01563 554720
Email: bruce.morgan@east-ayrshire.gov.uk

Dean Castle is a magnificent collection of restored buildings dating from the 1350s. Important

Edinburgh, Glasgow & Southern Scotland

collections of arms and armour, musical instruments and manuscripts by Robert Burns are on display in public rooms.

Opening Times: Apr to Oct 12:00-17:00. Oct to Apr Sat & Sun only 12:00-16:00.
Admission: Free. Location: 15 minutes walk from Kilmarnock Railway Station, set in grounds off the main road into Kilmarnock. Map Ref: 36

Dick Institute
Elmbank Avenue, Kilmarnock KA1 3BU Tel: 01563 554343 Fax: 01563 554344
Email: jason.sutcliffe@east-ayrshire.gov.uk

Temporary and permanent exhibitions over two floors of this grand Victorian building. Fine art, social and natural history collections are upstairs, whilst downstairs galleries house temporary exhibitions.

Opening Times: Mon & Tue, Thu & Fri 09:00-20:00, Wed & Sat 09:00-17:00. Admission: Free.
Location: Near Kilmarnock town centre, ten minutes from railway station. Map Ref: 36

Dalgarven Mill Museum of Ayrshire Country Life & Costume

Dalgarven Mill Trust, Dalgarven, Kilwinning KA13 6PL Tel / Fax: 01294 552448
Email: admin@dalgarvenmill.org.uk Web: www.dalgarvenmill.org.uk

Collection of machinery, memorabilia, furnishings and archives illustrating life in pre-industrial rural Ayrshire. Superb collection of costume spanning two centuries from 1775, beautifully displayed with changing exhibitions.

Opening Times: Easter to end Oct Tue to Sun 10:00-17:00. Oct to Easter Tue to Fri 10:00-16:00,
Sat & Sun 10:00-17:00. Admission: Admission charged. Location: Rural situation, two miles from Kilwinning, two miles from Dalry on A737. Map Ref: 37

Broughton House & Garden
12 High Street, Kirkcudbright DG6 4JX Tel: 01557 330437/(01721) 726003
Fax: 01557 330437

18th century town house of the Murrays of Broughton and Cally. Bought by E A Hornel, renowned artist, in 1901, the House still contains many of Hornel's works, paintings by other artists, an extensive collection of Scottish books and local history material.

Opening Times: 25 Mar to 28 Jun Mon to Sat 12:00-17:00, Sun 13:00-17:00, 29 Jun to 1 Sep Mon to Sat 10:00-18:00, Sun 13:00-17:00, 2 Sep to 27 Oct Mon to Sat 12:00-17:00, Sun 13:00-17:00. Admission: Adult £3.50, Concession £2.60, Family £9.50. NTS/NT Members Free. Location: Off A711/A755. Map Ref: 38

Broughton House Gallery

Stewartry Museum
St Mary Street, Kirkcudbright DG6 4AQ Tel / Fax: 01557 331643
Email: DavidD@dumgal.gov.uk Web: www.dumgal.gov.uk/museums

The Stewartry Museum was founded in 1879. As the collections grew, the present purpose-built museum was opened in 1893 and it still retains its charm as a traditional late Victorian museum. Its collections chiefly relate to the human and natural history of the Stewartry. The permanent collection includes the 'Siller Gun' - Britain's earliest surviving sporting trophy, and works by Kirkcudbrightshire artists including Jessie M King. Temporary exhibitions highlight different aspects of the collection and Museums Service activities.

Opening Times: Mon to Sat 11:00-16:00. Longer hours Jun to Sep including Sun 14:00-17:00.
Location: Town Centre. Map Ref: 38

Tolbooth Art Centre
High Street, Kirkcudbright DG6 4JL Tel: 01557 331556 Fax: 01557 331643
Email: DavidD@dumgal.gov.uk Web: www.dumgal.gov.uk/museums

The Tolbooth Art Centre is based in Kirkcudbright's 17th century Tolbooth. Find out about Kirkcudbright's famous artists, such as E A Hornel, Jessie M King, E A Taylor and Charles

Oppenheimer in the audio-visual shows and see their works on permanent display. The top floor of the Tolbooth, formerly the debtor's prison, is now used as a gallery for ever changing contemporary art and craft exhibitions.

Opening Times: Mon to Sat 11:00-16:00. Longer hours Jun to Sep including Sun 14:00-17:00.
Admission: Adult £1.50, Child Free, Concession 75p. Location: Town centre. Map Ref: 38

LANGBANK *Renfrews*

The Dolly Mixture
Finlaystone Country Estate, Langbank PA14 6TJ Tel / Fax: 01475 540505
Email: info@finlaystone.co.uk Web: www.finlaystone.co.uk

All sorts of dolls from around the world, collected since 1903 by mother and daughter Clare Spurgin and Jane MacMillan. Set within a country estate with extensive gardens and woodland play areas.

Opening Times: Apr to Sep 12:00-17:00. Oct to Mar Sat & Sun 12:00-17:00.
Admission: Estate: Adult £3.00, Child/OAP £2.00. Location: Ten minutes west Glasgow Airport on A8. Map Ref: 39

LARGS *N Ayrshire*

Kelburn Castle
Fairlie, Largs KA29 0BE Tel: 01475 568685 Fax: 01475 568121
Email: admin@kelburncountrycentre.com Web: www.kelburncountrycentre.com

The home of the Earls of Glasgow, probably the oldest castle in Scotland to have been continuously inhabited by the same family, incorporating a Norman Keep (1200), a Z-plan castle (1580), a 1700 mansion house and a Victorian wing (1882). Famous glen, unique trees and historic gardens. Also exhibitions, riding school, falconry centre, children's play areas and the 'Secret Forest'.

The 1700 facade of Kelburn Castle

Opening Times: Easter to Oct daily 10:00-18:00 (Castle open Jul & Aug or for guided tours available all year round for booked groups). Admission: Adult £5.00, Child/OAP £3.50 (£1.50 extra for castle). Location: On the A78 between Largs and Fairlie. Map Ref: 40

LAUDER *Scottish Borders*

Thirlestane Castle
Lauder TD2 6RU Tel: 01578 722430 Fax: 01578 722761
Email: admin@thirlestancastle.co.uk Web: www.thirlestanecastle.co.uk

Nestling in the gentle Border Hills, with its rose pink sandstone and fairytale turrets, Thirlestane Castle holds a uniquely important place in Scottish history. It is one of the oldest and finest castles in the land, and home to one of the country's most distinguished families.

Opening Times: Good Friday, Easter Monday, 1 May to end of second week in Oct Mon to Sun 10:30-16:50 (last admissions 15:30) Admission: Castle & Grounds: Adult £5.50, Child £3.00, OAP £5.00, Family (2 adults and 3 children) £15.00. Grounds only: Adult £2.00, Child £1.00.

The Chinese Room

Location: 28 miles south of Edinburgh, off A68 at Lauder. Map Ref: 41

LINLITHGOW *W Lothian*

Canal Museum
Linlithgow Canal Centre, Canal Basin, Manse Road, Linlithgow EH49 6AJ Tel: 01506 671215
Email: info@lucs.org.uk Web: www.lucs.org.uk

Display of photographs, documents, tools and other objects illustrating the history of the Union Canal, its construction, and its working life. Video.

Opening Times: Easter to mid Oct Sat & Sun 14:00-17:00. Jul & Aug daily 14:00-17:00.
Admission: Free. Location: Five minute walk from Linlithgow Station. Map Ref: 42

Edinburgh, Glasgow & Southern Scotland

LINLITHGOW *W Lothian (continued)*

House of the Binns

Linlithgow EH49 7NA   Tel: 0150683 4255   Email: houseofthebinns@nts.org.uk

The House of the Binns is the historic home of the Dalyells family, among them General Tam Dalyell who raised the Royal Scots Greys here in 1681. There are important moulded ceilings in four of the main rooms. The collection of furniture mostly dates from the 18th and 19th century. There is an excellent run of family portraits and an interesting collection of china.

Opening Times: House: 1 Jun to 30 Sep daily expect Fri 14:00-17:00. Parkland: 1 Apr to 31 Oct daily 10:00-17:00, 1 Nov to 31 Mar daily 10:00-16:00. Admission: Adult £5.00, Concession £3.75, Family £13.50, NTS/NT

The High Hall

Members Free. Location: On top of a hill, three quarters of a mile from main road, four miles east of Linlithgow and railway station.   Map Ref: 42

LIVINGSTON *W Lothian*

Almond Valley Heritage Trust

Livingston Mill, Millfield, Livingston EH54 7AR

Tel: 01506 414957
Fax: 01506 497771
Email: rac@almondvalley.co.uk
Web: www.almondvalley.co.uk

An innovative museum exploring the history and environment of West Lothian. Includes displays of Scotland's Shale Oil industry and other local manufacturing. Health, food, sanitation and hands-on environment science. Working watermill, farm, narrow-gauge railway, nature trail and play areas.

Opening Times: Daily 10:00-17:00. Admission: Adult £3.00, Child £2.00, Family (2 adult and 4 children) £10.00. Location: Two miles from junction 3 on the M8.   Map Ref: 43

LOCKERBIE *Dumfries & Galloway*

Thomas Carlyle's Birthplace

The Arched House, Ecclefechan, Lockerbie DG11 3DG   Tel: 01576 300666

The Arched House, in which Thomas Carlyle was born on 4 December 1795, was built by his father and uncle in 1791. He was a great writer and historian and one of the most powerful influences on 19th century British thought. The interior of the house is furnished to reflect domestic life at the time. Also on show is a collection of portraits and his belongings.

Opening Times: 1 May to 30 Sep Thu to Mon 13:00-17:00. Admission: Adult £2.50, Concession £1.90, Family £7.00. NTS/NT Members Free. Location: Off M74, on A74 in Ecclefechan. Five and a half miles south east of Lockerbie, six miles north west of Gretna Green.
                                                                    Map Ref: 44

LONGNIDDRY *E Lothian*

Gosford House

Longniddry   Tel: 01875 870201

The mansion set in a striking maritime situation was designed by Robert Adamin Roman thermae style. There is an outstanding art collection and famous Marble Hall of Staffordshire alabaster.

Opening Times: June to Aug   Location: Two miles north east of Longniddry.   Map Ref: 45

MAUCHLINE *E Ayrshire*

Burns House Museum

Castle Street, Mauchline   Tel: 01290 550045   Email: stanley.sarsfield@east-ayrshire.gov.uk
Web: www.east-ayrshire.gov.uk

MAUCHLINE *E Ayrshire (continued)*

Redesigned museum focuses on Burns during the period he wrote Kilmarnock Edition and lived in the house. The museum brings the words and songs of Burns to life through interactives.

Opening Times: Tue to Sat 10:00-17:00 Tournament Year.   Admission: Free.   Map Ref: 36

MAYBOLE *E Ayrshire*

Blairquhan Castle
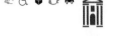
Maybole KA19 7LZ Tel: 01655 770239 Fax: 01655 770278
Email: enquiries@blairquhan.co.uk Web: www.blairquhan,co.uk

Blairquhan was built for Sir David Hunter Blair 3rd Bart in 1821-1824 by William Burn. It has all its original furniture, a picture gallery and fine gardens. It is approached by a three mile private drive.

Opening Times: 24 Jul to 22 Aug except Mon 13:30-16:15 (last admission to house). Grounds open till 18:00. Open by appointment all year.   Admission: Adult £5.00, Child £3.00, Concession £4.00.   Location: Seven miles SE of Maybole.   Map Ref: 46

Culzean Castle & Country Park

Maybole KA19 8LE Tel: 01655 884455 Fax: 01655 884503
Email: culzean@nts.org.uk Web: www.culzeancastle.net

Robert Adam converted the fortified tower house into an elegant residence for David Kennedy, 10th Earl of Cassillis, between 1777 and 1792. The Castle contains a fine collection of paintings and furniture, and a display of weapons in the Armoury. The Country Park contains a wealth of natural and historical interest with garden areas including a Walled Garden and terraced Fountain Court.

Opening Times: Castle: 1 Apr to 31 Oct daily 10:30-17:00. Visitor Centre: 1 Apr to 31 Oct daily 09:00-17:30, 1 Nov to 31 Mar, Sat & Sun 11:00-16:00. Country Park: Daily 09:30 to sunset. Admission: Combined ticket: Adult £9.00, Concession £6.50, Family £23.00. Country Park only: Adult £5.00, Concession £3.75, Family £13.50. NTS/NT Members Free.   Location: 12 miles south of Ayr on A719, four miles west of Maybole, off A77.   Map Ref: 47

MELROSE *Scottish Borders*

Abbotsford

Melrose TD6 9BQ Tel: 01896 752043 Fax: 01896 752916
Email: abbotsford@melrose.bordernet.co.uk
Web: www.melrose.bordernet.co.uk/abbbotsford

Home of the 19th Century poet and novelist Sir Walter Scott, author of Waverley, Ivanhoe, Lady of the Lake, etc. With a vast collection of memorabilia and a special ambience.

Opening Times: 15 Mar to 31 Oct Mon to Sat 09:30-17:00. Mar, Apr, May & Oct Sun 14:00-17:00. Jun, Jul, Aug & Sep Sun 09:30-17:00.   Admission: Adult £4.20, Child £2.10 (2003 prices). Group rates available.   Map Ref: 48

MILNGAVIE

Lillie Art Gallery
East Dunbartonshire Museums, Station Road, Milngavie G62 8BZ Tel: 0141 578 8847

Collection of 20th century Scottish painting. Temporary exhibition programme of fine and applied art, and also from the permanent collection.

Opening Times: Tue to Sat 10:00-13:00 & 14:00-17:00.   Admission: Free.   Location: Opposite Milngavie Railway Station. A short drive from Glasgow City Centre, off the A81.   Map Ref: 49

MOTHERWELL *N Lanarks*

Motherwell Heritage Centre

1 High Road, Motherwell ML1 3HU Tel: 01698 251000 Fax: 01698 268867
Email: devaneyr@northlan.gov.uk Web: motherwellheritage.freeserve.com

The gallery features a year round programme of both in-house and touring exhibitions. Don't miss the permanent 'Technopolis' display on the area's heritage. Also local history research library.

MOTHERWELL *N Lanarks (continued)*

Opening Times: Wed to Sat 10:00-17:00, Thu 10:00-19:00. Sun 12:00-17:00. Closed Mon and Tue. Admission: Free. Location: Top of Hamilton Road, by Bentley Hotel, three minutes from Motherwell Station. Map Ref: 50

MUSSELBURGH *E Lothian*

The Library

Newhailes

Newhailes Road, Musselburgh EH21 6RY
Tel: 0131 653 5599

A fine late 17th century house with impressive 18th century additions. The house was built in 1686 and bought by Sir David Dalrymple, of the legal and political dynasty. He was responsible for the addition of one of the most important rococo interiors in Scotland. The house contains a fine collection of paintings, portraits and a library described as 'the most learned room in Europe'.

Opening Times: House: 1 Apr to 30 Sep Thu to Mon 12:00-17:00, 1-31 Oct Sat & Sun 12:00-17:00. By guided tour only.
Admission: Adult £7.00, Concession £5.25, Family £7.00. NTS/NT Members Free. Location: Off A6095 Newhailes Road.
Map Ref: 51

NEWTON STEWART *Dumfries & Galloway*

Creetown Gem Rock Museum

Chain Road, Creetown, Newton Stewart DG8 7HJ Tel: 01671 820357 Fax: 01671 820554
Email: gem.rock@btinternet.com Web: www.gemrock.net

Famous collection of gems, crystals, rocks and fossils from around the world. New prospectors pantry, internet cafe, A J professors study, crystal cave and workshop. A new outside activity area.

Opening Times: Good Friday to Sep daily 09:30-17:30, Oct to Nov & Mar to Good Friday daily 10:00-16:00, Dec to Feb Sat & Sun 10:00-16:00. Closed Xmas & New Year. Admission: Adult £3.50, Concession £3.00, Child 5-15 years £2.00, Family £9.00 (2 Adults and up to 3 Children). Under 5's Free. Location: In the village of Creetown, follow signposts from village square.
Map Ref: 52

NEWTONGRANGE *Mid-Lothian*

Scottish Mining Museum

Lady Victoria Colliery, Newtongrange EH22 4QN Tel: 0131 663 7519 Fax: 0131 654 1618
Email: enquiries@scottishminingmuseum.com Web: www.scottishminingmuseum.com

Scotland's National Coal Mining Museum, historic buildings and extensive collections and archives. Retail, catering, events and hospitality venue. Engineering brilliance and the highs and lows of mining life.

Opening Times: Feb to Oct daily 10:00-17:00, Nov to Feb 10:00-16:00. Admission: Adult £4.00, Child/OAP £2.20, Family £10.00. Group: Adult £3.50, Concession £2.00.
Location: Newtongrange, eight miles from Edinburgh on A7. Map Ref: 53

NORTH BERWICK *E Lothian*

Museum of Flight

East Fortune Airfield, East Fortune EH39 5LF Tel: 01620 880308
Fax: 01620 880355 Email: info@nms.ac.uk Web: www.nms.ac.uk/flight

Scotland's national aviation collection. Discover some of the most extraordinary machines in the world that map the development of human flight. See the oldest aircraft in Britain, an original Wright Brothers' engine, Europe's biggest rocket and some of the fastest machines ever built. Based at historic East Fortune Airfield - launch site of the R34 Airship, the first aircraft to cross the Atlantic, east to west. Part of the National Museums of Scotland.

Opening Times: Daily Apr to Oct 10:00-17:00, Nov to Mar 11:00 to 16:00 Weekends only. Closed 25, 26 Dec and 1 Jan. Admission: Adult £3.00, Child Free, Concessions £1.50. Location: 20 miles east of Edinburgh. Map Ref: 54

PAISLEY *Renfrews*

Coats Observatory
49 Oakshaw Street West, Paisley PA1 2DR   Tel: 0141 889 2013   Fax: 0141 889 9240
Email: museum-els@renfrewshire.gov.uk   Web: www.renfrewshire.gov.uk

Architecturally stunning, the Observatory was built by the Coats family in 1883 and is a working Victorian Observatory. Displays on astronomy, astronautics, seismology and meteorology. Meteorological and astronomical information has been recorded here since 1882. Public telescopic viewing, weather permitting, on Thursday evenings in winter. Very active Renfrewshire Astronomical Society.

Opening Times: Tue to Sat 10:00-17:00, Sun 14:00-17:00. Oct to Mar Thu 19:00-21:30.
Admission: Free. Location: Access via Oakshaw Street or through Paisley Museum. Less than
ten minutes from railway station.   Map Ref: 55

Paisley Museum & Art Galleries
High Street, Paisley PA1 2BA   Tel: 0141 889 3151   Fax: 0141 889 9240
Email: museum.els@renfrewshire.gov.uk   Web: www.renfrewshire.gov.uk

Home to the world's largest collection of Paisley Shawls, a selection of which are always on display. Art Galleries show 19th century Scottish paintings and studio ceramics. Also displays on local and natural history. Museum shop has wide range of Paisley pattern products and exclusive gifts. A-listed historic 1871 building.

Opening Times: Tue to Sat 10:00-17:00, Sun 14:00-17:00, BH 10:00-17:00. Admission: Free. Location: Less than ten minute walk from Paisley Gilmour Street Railway Station.   Map Ref: 55

PEEBLES *Scottish Borders*

Tweeddale Museum
Chambers Institute, High Street, Peebles EH45 8AJ   Tel: 01721 724820   Fax: 01721 724424
Email: rhannay@scotborders.gov.uk

Local history museum.

Opening Times: Mon to Fri 10:00-12:00 & 14:00-17:00, Apr to Oct also Sat 10:00-13:00 & 14:00-16:00. Closed Sun. Admission: Free. Location: In town centre.   Map Ref: 56

PRESTONPANS *E Lothian*

Prestongrange Museum
Morison's Haven, Prestongrange, Prestonpans EH32 9RX   Tel: 0131 653 2904   Fax: 01620
828201 Email: elms@eastlothian.gov.uk   Web: www.prestongrangemuseum.org

Prestongrange Museum is based in the Old Prestongrange Colliery at Morison's Haven, Prestonpans. There is a Cornish bean engine on site, unique to Scotland. We also feature an annual educational exhibition.

Opening Times: Apr to Oct 11:00-16:00. Admission: Free. Location: Between Musselburgh
and Prestonpans, easily accessible from the A1 and on public transport.   Map Ref: 51

RENFREW *Renfrews*

Renfrew Community Museum
The Brown Institute, 41 Canal Street, Renfrew PA4 8QA   Tel: 0141 886 3149   Fax: 0141 886
2300 Email: museums.els@renfrewshire.gov.uk   Web: www.renfrewshire.gov.uk

This museum was opened for the Renfrew 600 Celebrations in 1997 in the former Brown Institute Building, when Renfrew celebrated 600 years of Royal Burgh status. Displays of local history.

Opening Times: Tue to Sat 10:00-13:00 & 14:00-17:00. Admission: Free. Location: Few
minutes walk from centre of Renfrew.   Map Ref: 57

SALTCOATS *N Ayrshire*

North Ayrshire Museum
Manse Street, Kirkgate, Saltcoats KA21 5AA   Tel / Fax: 01294 464174
Email: namuseum@north-ayrshire.gov.uk   Web: www.northayrshiremuseums.org.uk

Edinburgh, Glasgow & Southern Scotland

The Museum shows the history of North Ayrshire with displays on archaeology, costume, transport and popular culture. There is a maritime history section and a reconstruction of an Ayrshire cottage interior.

Opening Times: Mon to Sat 10:00-13:00 & 14:00-17:00, closed Wed & Sun. Admission: Free.
Location: In church grounds between Safeways and the Post Office.   Map Ref: 58

SANQUHAR Dumfries & Galloway

Sanquhar Tolbooth Museum

High Street, Sanquhar DG4 6BN Tel: 01659 50186 Fax: 01387 265081
Email: dumfriesmuseum@dumgal.gov.uk Web: www.dumgal.gov.uk/museums

Discover Sanquhar's world famous knitting tradition and the story of the mines and miners of Sanquhar and Kirkconnel. How did the ordinary people of Upper Nithsdale live and work? All this and more can be found in the town's fine 18th century Tolbooth.

Opening Times: Apr to Sep Tue to Sat 10:00-13:00 & 14:00-17:00, Sun 14:00-17:00.
Admission: Free. Location: On High Street.   Map Ref: 59

SELKIRK Scottish Borders

Bowhill House & Country Park

Bowhill, Selkirk TD7 5ET Tel / Fax: 01750 22204 Email: bht@buccleuch.com

Scottish Borders home of the Duke and Duchess of Buccleuch set in magnificent scenery. Outstanding collection of art, silverware, porcelain and French furniture. Historic relics include Monmouth's saddle and execution shirt, Sir Walter Scott's plaid and some proof editions. Queen Victoria's letters and gifts to successive Duchess of Buccleuch, her Mistress of the Robes. James Hogg Exhibition.

Opening Times: House: June Thu & Sun 13:00-16:00. Jul Daily 13:00-17:00. Aug please telephone for details.

Bowhill set amid magnificent scenery

Country Park: Easter to end of Aug. Times vary. Please telephone for details. Admission: House & Park: Adult £6.00, OAP £4.50, Child £2.00. Park only: £2.00, Under 5s and wheelchair users free. Family tickets and group tickets available.
Location: Three miles west of Selkirk on A708.   Map Ref: 60

Sir Walter Scotts Courtroom (Selkirk Town Hall)

Market Place, Selkirk TD7 4BT Tel: 01750 20096 Fax: 01750 23282
Email: dmabon@scotborders.gov.uk

Museum dedicated to local Sheriff of Selkirk - Sir Walter Scott.

Opening Times: Easter to Sep Mon to Sat 10:00-16:00, Jun to Sep also Sun 14:00-16:00, Oct Mon to Sat 13:00-16:00. Admission: Free. Location: In town centre.   Map Ref: 60

SOUTH QUEENSFERRY W Lothian

Dalmeny House

South Queensferry EH30 9TQ Tel: 0131 331 1888 Fax: 0131 331 1788
Email: linda.edgar@dalmeny.co.uk Web: www.dalmeny.co.uk

Rothschild 18th century French furniture, tapestries and porcelain. One of the world's most important Napoleonic collections, assembled by the fifth Earl, Prime Minister, historian and owner of three Derby winners.

Opening Times: Jul & Aug Sun, Mon & Tues 14:00-17:30. Last admission 16:30.
Admission: Adult £4.00. Location: Seven miles from centre of Edinburgh.   Map Ref: 61

Hopetoun House

South Queensferry EH30 9SL Tel: 0131 331 2451 Fax: 0131 319 1885
Web: www.hopetounhouse.com

A magnificient palace on the shores of the Firth of Forth designed by William Adam and his sons. It is the largest country house in Scotland. The gilded state apartments have much of the original furniture from the 1760s. There is a good art collection, Meissen porcelain and 17th century tapestries. The 100 acres of parkland include fine walks and a red deer park.

Opening Times: 9 Apr to 26 Sep daily 10:00-17:30. Admission: Adult £6.50, Child 5+ £3.50,
Family £18.00. Location: Two and a half miles west of Forth Road Bridge.   Map Ref: 61

Queensferry Museum

53 High Street, South Queensferry EH30 9HP
Tel: 0131 331 5545 Web: www.cac.org.uk

Situated in the historic former Royal Burgh of Queensferry, the museum commands magnificent views of the great bridges spanning the Forth. The museum traces the history of the people of Queensferry and Dalmeny, the historic ferry passage to Fife, the construction of the rail and road bridges and takes a look at the wildlife of the Forth estuary.

Opening Times: Mon, Thu, Fri & Sat 10:00-13:00 & 14:15-17:00, Sun 12:00-17:00. Last admission 30 minutes before closing. Closed Tue & Wed. Admission: Free.

Queensferry Museum, South Queensferry   Map Ref: 61

STRANRAER *Dumfries & Galloway*

Castle of St John

Castle Street, Stranraer DG9 7RT Tel: 01776 705088 Fax: 01776 705544
Email: JohnPic@dumgal.gov.uk Web: www.dumgal.gov.uk/museums

The Castle of St John is a medieval tower house. Over the centuries the Castle has been used as a home, a local court, a military garrison and a prison. Videos and reconstructions are used to tell the story of the Castle. There is an activity room for families and children.

Opening Times: Easter to mid Sep Mon to Sat 10:00-13:00 & 14:00-17:00. Location: Town centre, within walking distance of ferry terminal.   Map Ref: 62

Stranraer Museum

The Old Town Hall, George Street, Stranraer DG9 7JP Tel: 01776 705088 Fax: 01776 705835
Email: JohnPic@dumgal.gov.uk Web: www.dumgal.gov.uk/museums

Displays on archaeology, local history, farming and dairying. Temporary exhibitions held throughout the year and activities for all the family.

Opening Times: Mon to Fri 10:00-17:00, Sat 10:00-13:00 & 14:00-17:00. Closed Xmas & New Year, Easter & May BH. Admission: Free. Location: Near town centre.   Map Ref: 62

THORNHILL *Dumfries & Galloway*

Drumlanrig Castle, Gardens & Country Park

Thornhill DG3 4AQ Tel: 01848 330248 Fax: 01848 331682
Email: bre@drumlanrigcastle.org.uk Web: www.buccleuch.com

Dumfriesshire home of the Duke of ·Buccleuch and Queensberry KT, built between 1679 and 1691 by William Douglas, 1st Duke of Queensberry. Magnificent art collection, including works by Rembrandt and Holbein. Associations with Bonnie Prince Charlie and Mary Queen of Scots. French furniture, 300 year old silver chandelier as well as cabinets made for Louis XIV's Versailles.

Opening Times: Castle: 9 Apr to Mon 12 Apr, Sat 1 May to·Sun 22 Aug inclusive. Weekdays 11.00-16:00, Sun 12:00-16:00. Gardens & Country Park: 9 Apr to Tue 30 Sep daily 11:00-17:00. Admission: Castle & Country Park: Adult £6.00, Child £2.00, OAP/Student £4.00, Family (2 adults and 4 children) £14.00. Country Park Only: Adult £3.00, Child £2.00, Family (2 adults and 4 children) £8.00. Location: 18 miles north of Dumfries on A76. 16 miles from M74 at Elvanfoot.   Map Ref: 63

WANLOCKHEAD *Dumfries & Galloway*

Museum of Lead Mining

Wanlockhead ML12 6UT Tel: 01659 74387 Fax: 01659 74481
Email: brianwmont@goldpan.co.uk Web: www.leadminingmuseum.co.uk

Scotland's only visitor lead mine. Fabulous mineral collection. Visit 18th and 19th century miners' cottages. Scotland's second oldest miners' library.

Opening Times: Apr to end Oct daily 10:00-17:00. Admission: Adult £3.95, Child £2.50, Concession £2.75, Family £9.80. Group Adult £3.00, Group Child £2.00.   Map Ref: 64

There are few aspects of Scottish history, folklore and legend that cannot be examined within the great variety of museums in this central eastern region of Scotland. St Andrews, Aberdeen, Dundee, Perth and Stirling all have a variety of interesting museums, there are ancient Scottish castles with fine collections, and many smaller towns whose museums display the life, work and aspirations of their locality.

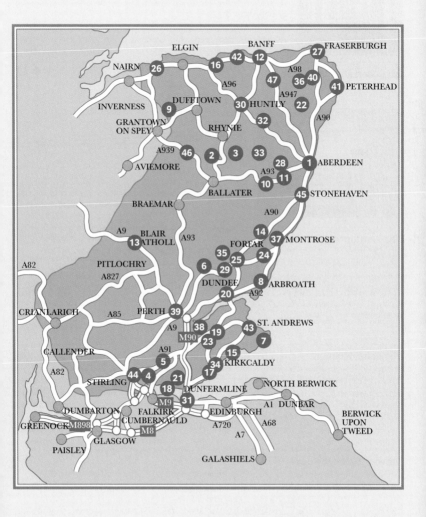

The Red Map References should be used to locate Museums etc on the pages that follow

Central, East & Notheast Scotland

Aberdeen Art Gallery
Schoolhill, Aberdeen AB10 1FQ
Tel: 01224 523700 Fax: 01224 632133
Email: info@aagm.co.uk Web: www.aberdeencity.gov.uk

One of the city's most popular tourist attractions, Aberdeen's splendid art gallery houses an important fine art collection with particularly good examples of 19th and 20th century works, a rich and diverse applied art collection and an exciting programme of special exhibitions.

Opening Times: Mon to Sat 10:00-17:00, Sun 14:00-17:00.
Admission: Free. Location: Centrally located via Belmont Street, from Union Street. Map Ref: 1

Aberdeen Maritime Museum
Shiprow, Aberdeen AB11 5BY Tel: 01224 337700 Fax: 01224 213066
Email: info@aagm.co.uk Web: www.aberdeencity.gov.uk

The city's award-winning maritime museum brings the history of the North Sea to life. View multi-media displays and exciting exhibitions on the offshore oil industry, shipbuilding, fishing and clipper ships, then visit the museum shop and licensed café.

Opening Times: Mon to Sat 10:00-17:00, Sun 12:00-15:00. Admission: Free. Location: Situated facing the harbour, accessible from Union Street via Adelphi. Map Ref: 1

The Gordon Highlanders Museum
St Lukes, Viewfield Road, Aberdeen AB15 7XH Tel: 01224 311200 Fax: 01224 319323
Email: museum@gordonhighlanders.com Web: www.gordonhighlanders.com

Regimental collection of The Gordon Highlanders, including 12 Victoria Crosses. History of the Regiment told through audio-visual and traditional displays. Tea room, gardens and gift shop.

Opening Times: Apr to Oct Tue to Sat 10:30-16:30, Sun 13:30-16:30. Open by appointment only at all other times. Admission: Adult £2.50, Child £1.00, OAP/Student £1.50. By appointment visits £3.50. Location: West end of Aberdeen, just off Queens Road by Anderson Drive Roundabout. Map Ref: 1

Marischal Museum
Marischal College, Aberdeen AB10 1YS Tel: 01224 274301 Fax: 01224 274302
Email: museum@abdn.ac.uk Web: www.abdn.ac.uk/marischal_museum

Major display of North-East identity from the first settlers to the present day; other gallery displays material from the rest of the world through the collections of donors - ancient Egypt, gold buddhas, African masks and Greek vases, etc.

Opening Times: Mon to Fri 10:00-17:00, Sun 14:00-17:00. Admission: Free. Location: In city centre. Map Ref: 1

Provost Skene's House
Guestrow, Aberdeen AB10 1AS Tel: 01224 641086 Fax: 01224 632133
Email: info@aagm.co.uk Web: www.aberdeencity.gov.uk

Dating from 1545, Provost Skene's House now houses an attractive series of period room settings recalling the elegant furnishings of earlier times. Visitors can see an intriguing series of religious paintings in the Painted Gallery, changing fashions in the Costume Gallery and enjoy displays of local interest, coins and archaeology on the top floor.

Opening Times: Mon to Sat 10:00-17:00, Sun 13:00-16:00. Admission: Free. Location: Guestrow is off Broad Street, opposite Marischal College. Map Ref: 1

Central, East & Notheast Scotland

Craigievar Castle

Alford AB33 8JF   Tel: 013398 83635
Fax: 013398 83280

This fairytale-like castle is an example of the best of Scottish Baronial architecture. The Great Tower stands just as it was when it was completed in 1626.The interior houses a collection of family portraits and 17th and 18th century furniture.

Opening Times: 1 Apr to 30 Sep Fri to Tue 12:00-17:30. Guided tours only. Grounds open all year.   Admission: Adult £9.00, Concession £6.50, Family £23.00. NTS/NT Members Free.
Location: On A980, six miles south of Alford and 26 miles west of Aberdeen.   Map Ref: 2

The Hall

Grampian Transport Museum Trust

Alford AB33 8AE   Tel: 019755 62292   Fax: 019755 62180   Email: info@gtm.org.uk
Web: www.gtm.org.uk

The land travel and transport history of Aberdeenshire housed in a large road gallery and restored railway station. Road vehicles include the famous Craigievar Express, a 19th century steam tricycle and the world's oldest Sentinel Steam Waggon.

Opening Times: Daily Apr to Sep 10:00-17:00, Oct 10:00-16:00.   Admission: 2003 Prices: Adult £4.80, Child £2.30, OAP £4.20, Family (2 adults & up to 3 children) £12.00.   Location: 25 miles west of Aberdeen, on the A944. Town centre, off free public car park.   Map Ref: 3

Alloa Tower

Alloa Park, Alloa FK10 1PP   Tel: 01259 211701   Fax: 01259 218744

The largest surviving keep in Scotland, dates from the 14th century. It was home to successive generations of the Earls of Mar, who played host to many Scots monarchs. The original medieval features such as the dungeon, first floor well and magnificient oak roof timbers have been retained. There is a unique collection of family portraits and silver.

Opening Times: 1 Apr to 31 Oct daily 13:00-17:00.   Admission: Adult £3.50, Concession £2.60, Family £9.50. NTS/NT Members Free.   Location: Off A907, in Alloa, close to town centre.
Map Ref: 4

Clackmannanshire Council Museum & Heritage Service

Speirs Centre, 29 Primrose Street, Alloa FK10 1JJ   Tel: 01259 216913   Fax: 01259 721313
Email: smills@clacks.gov.uk   Web: www.clacksweb.org.uk

Growing collections of archaeology, social and industrial history, including large assemblage of W & J A Bailey's Alloa Pottery and artefacts from Patons & Baldwins, Alloa wool-spinning mill, memorabilia from breweries in Alloa. Expanding art collection. Small exhibition gallery.

Opening Times: Tue to Fri 13:30-17:00. Closed Sat, Sun & BH. Also open by arrangement or appointment.   Admission: Free.   Location: Near town centre, two minutes walk main car park & bus station.   Map Ref: 5

Alyth Museum

Commercial Street, Alyth PH11 8AF   Tel: 01738 632488   Fax: 01738 443505
Email: museum@pkc.gov.uk   Web: www.pkc.gov.uk/ah

This small and welcoming local museum provides a fascinating insight into Alyth and the surrounding area through displays of domestic and agricultural items and local photographs.

Opening Times: May to Sep Wed to Sun 13:00-17:00.   Admission: Free.   Location: In town centre.   Map Ref: 6

Kellie Castle

Pittenweem, Anstruther KY10 2RF   Tel: 01333 720271   Fax: 01333 720326
Kellie Castle is a very fine example of the domestic architecture of Lowland Scotland

Central, East & Notheast Scotland

(dating from 1360). Sympathetically restored around 1878, it contains magnificent plaster ceilings, painted panelling and furniture designed by Sir Robert Lorimer.

Opening Times: Good Friday to Easter Monday & 1 Jun to 30 Sep daily 13:00-17:00.
Admission: Adult £5.00, Concession £3.75, Family £13.50. NTS/NT Members Free.
Location: On B9171, three miles north west of Pittenweem. Map Ref: 7

The Scottish Fisheries Museum Trust Ltd
St Ayles, Harbourhead, Anstruther KY10 3AB   Tel / Fax: 01333 310628   Email: tom@scottish-fisheries-museum.org   Web: www.scottish-fisheries-museum.org

This award-winning National Museum tells the story of the Scottish fishing industry and its people from the earliest times to the present day.

Opening Times: Apr to Sep Mon to Sat 10:00-17:30, Sun 11:00-17:00. Oct to Mar Mon to Sat 10:00-16:30, Sun 12:00-16:30.   Admission: Adult £4.50, Accompanied Child Free, Concession £3.50. Group rates available.   Location: By Anstruther Harbour. Map Ref: 7

Arbroath Art Gallery
Hill Terrace, Arbroath DD11 1AH   Tel: 01241 875598   Fax: 01241 439263
Email: signal.tower@angus.gov.uk   Web: www.angus.gov.uk/history.htm

Two galleries show temporary exhibitions of artists in the local area and from our Angus Council Collections which includes two works by 'Breughel the Younger' and works by James Watterston Herald.

Opening Times: Mon & Wed 09:30-20:00, Tues 10:00-18:00, Thu 09:30-18:00, Fri & Sat 09:30-17:00.   Admission: Free.   Location: Ten minute walk from bus and railway stations. Town centre location above Public Library. Map Ref: 8

Arbroath Museum
Signal Tower, Ladyloan, Arbroath DD11 1PU   Tel: 01241 875598   Fax: 01241 439263
Email: signal.tower@angus.gov.uk   Web: www.angus.gov.uk/history.htm

Arbroath's fishing, flax, engineering and social history and the Bell Rock Lighthouse, the 1813 Shore Station of which is the museum building.

Opening Times: Mon to Sat 10:00-17:00 all year, Jul to Aug Sun 14:00-17:00.
Admission: Free.   Location: On A92 on seafront beside harbour. Seven minutes walk from bus/railway station. Map Ref: 8

Ballindalloch Castle
Ballindalloch AB37 9AX   Tel: 01807 500206   Fax: 01807 500210
Email: enquiries@ballindallochcastle.co.uk   Web: www.ballindallochcastle.co.uk

Ballindalloch Castle is the family home of the Macpherson-Grants, Lairds of Ballindalloch since 1546. This beautiful castle houses the most important private collection of 17th century Spanish paintings in Scotland.

Opening Times: Easter to Sep 10:30-17:00.   Admission: Charges on application.
Location: On A95 seven miles southwest of Aberlour. Map Ref: 9

Banchory Museum
Bridge Street, Banchory AB31 5SX   Tel: 01771 622906

Exhibition on Banchory-born Scott Skinner - the 'Strathspey King'. Displays of Royal commemorative china, nineteenth century tartans and Deeside natural history.

Opening Times: May, Jun & Sep Mon to Sat 11:00-13:00 & 14:00-16:30. Jul to Aug Mon to Sat 11:00-13:00 & 14:00-16:30. Sun 14:00-16:30. For Apr & Oct - times 01771 622906.
Admission: Free.   Location: In Bridge Street, one minute walk from main car park in Dee Street. Map Ref: 10

| Guided or Private Tours | Disabled Access | Gift Shop or Sales Point | Café or Refreshments | Restaurant | Car Parking |

Central, East & Notheast Scotland

Crathes Castle

Banchory AB31 5QJ   Tel: 01330 844525
Fax: 01330 844797

King Robert the Bruce granted the lands of Leys to the Burnett family in 1323. The ancient Horn of Leys was presented by Bruce to the family as a symbol of his gift. The castle, built in the 16th century, is an excellent example of a tower house of the period. Some rooms retain original painted ceilings and collections of family portraits and furniture.

Opening Times: 1 Apr to 30 Sep daily 10:00-17:30, 1 to 31 Oct daily 10:00-16:30. Admission: Adult £9.00, Concession £6.50, Family £23.00. NTS/NT Members Free. Location: Three miles east of Banchory.   Map Ref: 10

Crathes Castle - Muses Ceiling

Drum Castle

Drumoak, Banchory AB31 5EY   Tel: 01330 811204   Fax: 01330 811962

The keep is one of the three oldest tower houses surviving in Scotland. The original house was enlarged with the creation of a very fine Jacobean mansion in 1619 and a later addition during the reign of Queen Victoria. Inside the house there is an excellent collection of portraits and good Georgian furniture.

Opening Times: 1 Apr to 31 May daily 12:30-17:30, 1 Jun to 31 Aug daily 10:00-17:30. Admission: Adult £7.00, Concession £5.25, Family £19.00. NTS/NT Members Free. Location: Off A93, three miles west of Peterculter.

The Library
                                                                       Map Ref: 11

Banff Museum

High Street, Banff AB45 1AE   Tel: 01771 622906

One of Scotland's oldest museums, founded in 1828. Award-winning natural history display and the life of Thomas Edward, the 'Banff Naturalist'. Nationally important collection of Banff silver.

Opening Times: Jun to Sep Mon to Sat 14:00-16:30. Admission: Free. Location: In High Street, one minute walk from St Mary's car park.   Map Ref: 12

Blair Castle

Blair Atholl PH18 5TL
Tel: 01796 481207   Fax: 01796 481487
Email: office@blair-castle.co.uk   Web: www.blair-castle.co.uk

Five star attraction set in stunning Highland Perthshire, Blair Castle has been the ancient home and fortress of the Earls and Dukes of Atholl for over 725 years. Some 30 rooms of infinite variety display beautiful furniture, fine collections of paintings, arms and armour, china, costume, lace and embroidery, Jacobite relics and other unique treasures. Function & Event venue, civil wedding licence held.

Opening Times: 1 Apr to 29 Oct Daily 09:30-17:00 (Last entry 16:30). Admission: Adult £6.70, Child £4.20, OAP £5.70, Student £5.40, Family £17.00. Exhibitions & Events 2004 : 26 Mar: Perthshire Tourism Fair, 23 to 25 Apr: Tartan Exhibition, 21 to 23 May: Galloway Antiques Fair, 29 May: Atholl Highlanders Parade, 30 May: Atholl Gathering and Highland Games, 21 Jul: Blair Castle Highland Night, 26 to 29 Aug: Bowmore International Horse Trials and Country Fair, 10 to 12 Sep: Galloway Antiques Fair, 30 Oct: Glenfiddich Piping Championships, 31 Oct: Glenfiddich Fiddling Championships.   Map Ref: 13

Central, East & Notheast Scotland

BRECHIN *Angus*

Brechin Town House Museum

28 High Street, Brechin DD9 6EU   Tel: 01356 625536   Email: brechin.musuem@angus.gov.uk
Web: www.angus.gov.uk/history.htm

Social history of this tiny Cathedral City includes local ecclesiastical, industrial history and works of art by David Waterson.

Opening Times: Mon, Tue, Thu, Fri & Sat 10:00-17:00, Wed 10:00-13:00.   Admission: Free.
Location: In town centre.   Map Ref: 14

BUCKHAVEN *Fife*

Buckhaven Museum

College Street, Buckhaven   Tel: 01592 412860   Fax: 01592 412870

The display features the town's history with a focus on the fishing industry. See the stained glass windows made by local people with the help of the community artist and a replica of a kitchen from the 1920s.

Opening Times: Open library hours.   Admission: Free.   Location: Above Buckhaven Library.
Map Ref: 15

BUCKIE *Moray*

The Buckie Drifter Maritime Heritage Centre

Freuchny Road, Buckie AB56 1TT   Tel: 01542 834646   Fax: 01542 835995
Email: buckie.drifter@moray.gov.uk   Web: www.moray.org/bdrifter

Enter the Buckie Drifter for a journey back in time to when the herring was king, glimpse the lives of the fishing communities, recreated fishing boat and quayside display. RNLI lifeboat on display.

Opening Times: Apr to Oct Mon to Sat 10:00-17:00, Sun 12:00-17:00.   Admission: Adult £2.75, Child/OAP £1.75. Group rates available.   Location: Situated at the harbour across the road from the lifeboat station.   Map Ref: 16

Peter Anson Gallery

Town House West, Cluny Place, Buckie AB56 1HB   Tel: 01309 673701   Fax: 01309 675863
Email: museums@moray.gov.uk   Web: www.moray.org/museums

Examples of drawings/paintings by maritime artist Peter Anson.

Opening Times: Mon to Fri 10:00-20:00, Sat 10:00-12:00. Closed Sun.   Admission: Free.
Location: Shared building with Buckie Library near town centre.   Map Ref: 16

BURNTISLAND *Fife*

Burntisland Museum

102 High Street, Burntisland   Tel: 01592 412860   Fax: 01592 412870

Visit the exciting reproduction Edwardian fairground display and find out more about Burntisland's history.

Opening Times: Open library hours.   Admission: Free.   Map Ref: 17

CULROSS *Fife*

Culross Palace

Culross KY12 8JH   Tel: 01383 880359   Fax: 01383 882675

Culross Palace was built between 1597 and 1611 and features original interiors with painted woodwork. There is 17th and 18th century furniture, decorative items and a fine collection of Staffordshire and Scottish pottery. A model 17th century garden has been built to the rear of the Palace which contains a variety of unusual vegetables and herbs that were all available in 1600.

Opening Times: Good Friday to 30 Sep, daily, 12:00-17:00.   Admission: Adult £5.00, Concession £3.75, Family £13.50. NTS/NT Members Free.   Location: Off A985, 12 miles west of Forth Road Bridge, four miles east of Kincardine Bridge, six miles west of Dumfermline, 15 miles west of Edinburgh city centre.   Map Ref: 18

Central, East & Notheast Scotland

Hill of Tarvit Mansion House

Cupar KY15 5PB   Tel / Fax: 01334 653127   Email: hilloftarvit@nts.org.uk

Home to a notable collection including French, Chippendale-style and vernacular furniture, Dutch paintings and pictures by Raeburn and Ramsay, Flemish tapestries and Chinese porcelain and bronzes. The interior is very much in the Edwardian fashion.

Opening Times: 1 Apr to 30 Sep daily 13:00-17:00, 1 to 31 Oct Sat & Sun 13:00-17:00.
Admission: Adult £5.00, Concession £3.75, Family £13.50. NTS/NT Members Free.
Location: Off A916, two miles south of Cupar.   Map Ref: 19

Broughty Castle Museum

Castle Approach, Broughty Ferry, Dundee DD5 2TF   Tel: 01382 436916   Fax: 01382 436951
Email: broughty@dundeecity.gov.uk   Web: www.dundeecity.gov.uk/broughtycastle

15th century fort at the mouth of the Tay Estuary, housing fascinating displays on the history and natural history of the local area. Enjoy magnificent views over the river from our Observation Gallery.

Opening Times: Apr to Sep Mon to Sat 10:00-16:00, Sun 12:30-16:00. Oct to Mar Tue to Sat 10:00-16:00, Sun 12:30-16:00. Admission: Free. Location: Situated on the seafront beside Broughty Ferry harbour. Three miles from Dundee City Centre off the A930.   Map Ref: 20

Discovery Point & RRS Discovery

Discovery Quay, Dundee DD1 4XA   Tel: 01382 201245   Fax: 01382 225891
Email: info@dundeeheritage.co.uk   Web: www.rrsdiscovery.com

Come face to face with The Heroes of the Ice and experience life with Scott and his crew on their epic adventure to Antarctica where they survived for 2 winters on board RRS Discovery locked in the Antarctic ice.

Opening Times: Apr to Oct 10:00-18:00, Sun 11:00-18:00. Nov to Mar 10:00-17:00, Sun 11:00-17:00. Closed 25 & 26 Dec and 1 & 2 Jan. Admission: Adult £6.25, Child £3.85, Concession £4.70. Group rates available. Location: Near town centre, one minute walk from central railway station.   Map Ref: 20

McManus Galleries

Albert Square, Dundee DD1 1DA   Tel: 01382 432350   Fax: 01382 432369
Email: leisure.arts@dundeecity.gov.uk   Web: www.dundeecity.gov.uk/mcmanus

A remarkable Gothic building housing one of Scotland's most impressive collections of fine and decorative art and award-winning displays of local history, archaeology, wildlife and the environment. There's always something new to see and do with a changing programme of exhibitions, activities, events and displays. Café serving refreshments and a gallery shop selling a variety of prints, cards, books and gifts.

Gallery 4 - 'Europe and Beyond'

Opening Times: Mon to Sat 10:30-17:00, Thu 10:30-19:00, Sun 12:30-16:00. Admission: Free.
Location: Situated in Dundee City Centre, ten minutes walk from bus and rail stations.   Map Ref: 20

Mills Observatory

Glamis Road, Balgay Park, Dundee DD2 2UB   Tel: 01382 435967   Fax: 01382 435962
Email: mills.observatory@dundeecity.gov.uk   Web: www.dundeecity.gov.uk/mills

Mills Observatory is the UK's only full-time public observatory. See the stars and planets through an impressive Victorian telescope. Fascinating displays on astronomy and space exploration. Public planetarium shows take place monthly during the winter.

Opening Times: Apr to Sep Tue to Fri 11:00-17:00, Sat & Sun 12:30-16:00. Oct to Mar Mon to Fri 16:00-22:00, Sat & Sun 12:30-16:00. Admission: Free. Location: Balgay Park, one mile west of Dundee City Centre.   Map Ref: 20

Central, East & Notheast Scotland

Verdant Works

West Hendersons Wynd, Dundee DD1 5BT   Tel: 01382 225282
Fax: 01382 221612   Email: admin@dundeeheritage.co.uk
Web: www.verdantworks.com

Step back into a 'Time Capsule' of yester-year and experience the history of the great Jute textile days of Dundee. With original working machinery and multi media film shows, this award winning museum brings the past to life.

Opening Times: Apr to Oct 10:00-18:00, Sun 11:00-17:00. Nov to Mar 10:30-16:30, Sunday 11:00-16:30. Closed Mon & Tue throughout Nov to Mar.   Admission: Adult £5.95, Child £3.85, Concession £4.45. Rates valid until 31/03/04. Group rates available for groups of 15 or more.

Map Ref: 20

Andrew Carnegie Birthplace Museum

Moodie Street, Dunfermline KY12 7PL   Tel: 01383 724302   Fax: 01383 721862
Email: carnegiebirthplace@hotmail.com   Web: www.carnegiebirthplace.com

Andrew Carnegie's birthplace, cottage and memorial hall house the many treasures which he acquired during his eventful life. They include freedom caskets, keys and items from his study in Skibo Castle.

Opening Times: Apr to Oct Mon to Sat 11:00-17:00, Sun 14:00-17:00.   Admission: Adult £2.00, Child (accompanied) Free, Concession £1.00.   Location: Near town centre, 400 yards downhill from Dunfermline Abbey.

Map Ref: 21

Dunfermline Museum

Viewfield Terrace, Dunfermline KY12 7HY   Tel: 01383 313838   Fax: 01383 313837
Email: lesley.botten@fife.gov.uk

Linen history and Dunfermline's civic and local history. Dunfermline Museum is the headquarters for West Fife Museums Service which also includes Pittencrieff House Museum, Inverkeithing Museum and St Margaret's Cave.

Opening Times: By appointment only.   Admission: Free.   Location: Five minutes walk from bus station.

Map Ref: 21

Pittencrieff House Museum

Pittencrieff Park, Dunfermline KY12 8QH   Tel: 01383 722935/313838

Temporary exhibition gallery, displays about local history and the Dunfermline Giant.

Opening Times: 1 Apr to 30 Sep 11:00-17:00. 1 Oct to 31 Mar 11:00-16:00.   Admission: Free.
Location: In Pittencrieff Park, western edge of Dunfermline.

Map Ref: 21

Haddo House

Methlick, Ellon AB41 7EQ   Tel: 01651 851440   Fax: 01651 851888
Email: haddo@nts.org.uk

Designed by William Adam for the 2nd Earl of Aberdeen in 1732, but refurbished in the 1880s. The House elegantly blends crisp Georgian architecture with sumptuous late Victorian interiors by Wright and Mansfield. Haddo is noted for its fine furniture, paintings and objets d'art. It also boasts a delightful terrace garden with geometric rosebeds and a fountain.

Opening Times: 1 to 30 June Fri to Mon 11:00-16:30, 1 Jul to 31 Aug daily 11:00-16:30. Guided tours only.

Admission: Adult £7.00, Concession £5.25, Family £19.00. NTS/NT Members Free.   Location: Off B999, four miles north of Pitmedden.

The Drawing Room

Map Ref: 22

Central, East & Notheast Scotland

Falkland Palace

Cupar, Falkland KY15 7BU   Tel: 01337 857397   Fax: 01337 857980

The Royal Palace of Falkland was the country residence of Stuart kings and queens. The palace contains fine portraits of the Stuart monarchs and two sets of 17th century tapestry hangings. The garden was designed and built by Percy Cane, and contains three herbaceous borders with many varieties of shrubs and trees.

Opening Times: 1 Mar to 31 Oct Mon to Sat 10:00-18:00, Sun 13:00-17:00.   Admission: Adult £7.00, Concession £5.25, Family £19.00. NTS/NT Members Free.
Location: A912, ten miles from junction 8 of M90, 11 miles north of Kirkcaldy.   Map Ref: 23

Falkland Palace - Chapel Royal

House of Pitmuies

Guthrie, Forfar DD8 2SN   Tel: 01241 828245

Two semi-formal walled gardens shelter long herbaccous borders, old-fashioned roses and superb delphiniums. River and lockside walks have fine trees, a wide variety of shrubs and massed spring bulbs.

Opening Times: Apr to Oct daily 10:00-17:00.   Admission: Adult £2.50.   Map Ref: 24

The Meffan, Forfar Museum & Gallery

Meffan Institute, 20 West High Street, Forfar DD8 1BB   Tel: 01307 464123/467017   Fax: 01307 468451   Email: the.meffan@angus.gov.uk   Web: www@angus.gov.uk/history.htm

Stunning Pictish Stones and archaeology. A street of quaint old shops including weaver, shoemaker, sweet shop, clock maker and baker. Art galleries with frequently changing exhibitions. A witch's trial prior to her execution all in realistic life size displays.

Opening Times: Mon to Sat 10:00-17:00.   Admission: Free.   Location: In town centre.
Map Ref: 25

Brodie Castle

Brodie Castle, Brodie, Forres IV36 2TE
Tel: 01309 641371   Fax: 01309 641600
Email: brodiecastle@nts.org.uk

The castle is a fine 16th century Z-plan tower house set in peaceful parkland. It contains fine French furniture, English, Continental and Chinese porcelain and a major collection of paintings, including 17th century Dutch art, 19th century English watercolours, Scottish Colourists and early 20th century works.The magnificent library contains 6000 volumes.

Opening Times: 1 to 30 Apr & 1 Jul to 31 Aug daily 12:00-16:00, 1 May to 30 Jun & 1 to 30 Sep Sun to Thu 12:00-16:00.
Admission: Adult £5.00, Concession £3.75, Family £13.50. NTS/NT Members Free.   Location: Off A96, four and a half miles west of Forres.   Map Ref: 26

'Jane, Duchess of Gordon and her son', from the Studio of George Romney

Falconer Museum

Tolbooth Street, Forres IV36 1PH   Tel: 01309 673701   Fax: 01309 675863
Email: museums@moray.gov.uk   Web: www.moray.org/museums

Information about the Royal Burgh of Forres, its people and history. Collection about the popular folk singing duo 'The Corries'.

Opening Times: Apr to Oct Mon to Sat 10:00-17:00. Closed Sun. Nov to Mar Mon to Thu 11:00-12:30 & 13:00-15:30. Closed Fri, Sat, Sun.   Admission: Free.   Location: Just off the High Street on Tolbooth Street, opposite The Tolbooth.   Map Ref: 26

Central, East & Notheast Scotland

Nelson Tower

c/o Falconer Museum, Tolbooth Street, Forres IV36 1PH   Tel: 01309 673701   Fax: 01309 675863   Email: museums@moray.gov.uk   Web: www.moray.org/museums

Memorabilia associated with Lord Nelson and his various battles. Pictures of Forres and surrounding area in bygone days. Spectacular views of Forres and Findhorn Bay.

Opening Times: May to Sep Tue to Sun 14:00-16.00. Admission: Free. Location: Around a mile from town centre.   Map Ref: 26

Museum of Scottish Lighthouses

Kinnaird Head, Fraserburgh AB43 9DU   Tel: 01346 511022   Fax: 01346 511033
Web: www.lighthousemuseum.co.uk

The new Museum of Scottish Lighthouses boasts the largest and best collection of lighthouse lenses and equipment in the UK. Discover the unique story of the Stevenson family, lighthouse engineers to the world.

Opening Times: Apr to Oct Mon to Sat 11:00-17:00, Sun 12:00-17:00. July to Aug Mon to Sat 10:00-18:00, Sun 11:00-18:00. Nov to Mar Mon to Sat 11:00-16:00, Sun 12:00-16:00. Admission: Adult £5.00, Child £2.00, Concession £4.00, Family £12.00/£14.20/£16.00. Group rates available. Location: Fraserburgh, 15 minute walk from bus station.   Map Ref: 27

Sandhaven Meal Mill

Sandhaven, Fraserburgh AB43 4EP   Tel: 01771 622906

Restored typical 19th century Scottish meal mill. Guided tours and working demonstration model.

Opening Times: May to Sep Sat & Sun 14:00-16:30. Admission: Free. Location: On B9031 at eastern end of Sandhaven village.   Map Ref: 27

Garlogie Mill Power House Museum

Garlogie AB32 6RX   Tel: 01771 622906

Unique beam engine - only one of its type still in situ - which powered this 19th century woollen spinning mill. Award-winning AV presentation and displays on the history of textiles in the area.

Opening Times: May to Sep Sat & Sun 14:00-16:30. Admission: Free. Location: At west end of Garlogie village, behind Village Hall.   Map Ref: 28

Angus Folk Museum

Kirkwynd Cottage, Glamis DD8 1RT   Tel: 01307 840288   Fax: 01307 840233

Housing one of Scotland's finest folk collection, this museum presents a vivid insight into how the rural workforce used to live.

Opening Times: 1 Apr to 30 Jun & 1 to 30 Sep Fri to Tue 12:00-17:00, 1 Jul to 31 Aug daily 12:00-17:00. Admission: Adult £5.00, Concession £3.75, Family £13.50. NTS/NT Members Free. Location: Off A94 in Glamis, five miles south west of Forfar.   Map Ref: 29

Glamis Castle

Glamis DD8 1RJ   Tel: 01307 840393   Fax: 01307 840733
Email: admin@glamis-castle.co.uk   Web: www.glamis-castle.co.uk

Family home of the Earls of Strathmore and Kinghorne since 1372. Childhood home of Her Majesty Queen Elizabeth the Queen Mother and setting for Shakespeare's famous play 'Macbeth'.

Opening Times: 29 Mar to 31 Oct 10:30-17:30. Jul & Aug from 10:00. Admission: Adult £6.80, Child £3.70, OAP/Student £5.50. Group rates available.   Map Ref: 29

Brander Museum

The Square, Huntly AB54 8AE   Tel: 01771 622906

Display on Huntly-born author George Macdonald. Extensive collection of communion tokens.

Central, East & Notheast Scotland

19th century arms and armour from Sudan. Archaeological finds from Huntly Castle and other aspects of local history.

Opening Times: Tue to Sat 14:00-16:30. Closed BH. Admission: Free. Location: In The Square, town centre.

Map Ref: 30

Leith Hall

Huntly AB54 4NQ Tel: 01464 831216 Fax: 01464 831594
Email: leithhall@nts.org.uk

Leith Hall is a charming and intimate Scottish family home. The house offers a unique insight into the lives, loves and tragedies of the Leith-Hay family over the last four centuries. There is an interesting variety of family furniture, artwork, tapestries and military memorabilia. The garden features a fine collection of alpines and primulas in the rock garden.

'The Storming of San Sebastian' by Denis Dighton

Opening Times: Good Friday to Easter Monday daily 12;00-17:00, 1 May to 30 Sep Fri to Tue 12:00-17:00. Admission: Adult £7.00, Concession £5.25, Family £19.00. NTS/NT Members Free. Location: On B9002, one mile west of Kennethmont.

Map Ref: 30

Inverkeithing Museum

The Friary, Queen Street, Inverkeithing KY11 1LS Tel: 01383 313838/313594

Local history displays and local collections, featuring Admiral Samuel Greig, 'Father of the Russian Navy'.

Opening Times: Thu to Sun 11:00-12:30 & 13:00-16:00. Admission: Free. Location: Upstairs in The Friary, just off the High Street.

Map Ref: 31

Carnegie Museum

The Square, Inverurie AB51 3SN Tel: 01771 622906

Extensive archaeological displays, showing finds from New Stone Age to Bronze Age, as well as Early Christian carved stones. Displays on Inverurie's canal and railway history and the 19th century Volunteer Movement.

Opening Times: Mon & Wed to Fri 14:00-16:30, Sat 10:00-13:00 & 14:00-16:00. Closed BH. Admission: Free. Location: In The Square, above Inverurie Library, in town centre.

Map Ref: 32

Castle Fraser

Sauchen, Inverurie AB51 7LD Tel: 01330 833463 Fax: 01330 833819
Email: castlefraser@nts.org.uk

The most elaborate Z-plan castle in Scotland was built between 1575 and 1636 by the sixth laird, Michael Fraser. The castle contains many Fraser family portraits, including one by Raeburn, and fine 18th and 19th century carpets, curtains and bed hangings. One of its most evocative rooms is the strikingly simple Great Hall.

The Dining Room

Opening Times: 1 Apr to 30 Jun & 1 to 30 Sep Fri to Tue 12:00-17:30, 1 Jul to 31 Aug daily 11:00-17:30. Admission: Adult £7.00, Concession £5.25, Family £19.00. NTS/NT Members Free. Location: Off A944, four miles north of Dunecht and 16 miles west of Aberdeen.

Map Ref: 33

John McDouall Stuart Museum

Rectory Lane, Dysart, Kirkaldy Tel: 01592 412860 Fax: 01592 412870

This house is the birthplace of John McDouall Stuart, the first European explorer to make a return journey across Australia in 1861-1862. Displays describe his harrowing journeys, the Australian wilderness and the Aborigines who made a life there.

Opening Times: 1 Jun to 31 Aug 14:00-17:00. Admission: Free. Location: In town centre.
Map Ref: 34

Kirkaldy Museum & Art Gallery

War Memorial Gardens, Kirkaldy KY1 1YG Tel: 01592 412860 Fax: 01592 412870

Set in lovely grounds, Kirkaldy Museum & Art Gallery, features superb collection of 19th and 20th century Scottish paintings, an award-winning permanent local history gallery and a lively changing exhibition programme. Gallery shop for cards, crafts and local publications. Café incorporating Wemyss Ware Pottery displays. Enquiry and outreach service.

Opening Times: Mon to Sat 10:30-17:00, Sun 14:00-17:00. Closed Xmas & New Year. Admission: Free. Location: Five minute walk from town centre, adjacent to railway station.
Map Ref: 34

Blue and White Teapot by S J Peploe

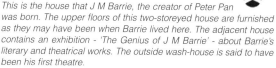

J M Barrie's Birthplace

9 Brechin Road, Kirriemuir DD8 4BX Tel: 01575 572646

This is the house that J M Barrie, the creator of Peter Pan was born. The upper floors of this two-storeyed house are furnished as they may have been when Barrie lived here. The adjacent house contains an exhibition - 'The Genius of J M Barrie' - about Barrie's literary and theatrical works. The outside wash-house is said to have been his first theatre.

Opening Times: 1 Apr to 30 Jun & 1 to 30 Sep Fri to Tue 12:00-17:00, 1 Jul to 31 Aug daily 12:00-17:00. Admission: Adult £5.00, Concession 3.75, Family £13.50. NTS/NT Members Free. Location: A90/A926, in Kirriemuir, six miles north west of Forfar.
Kitchen/Box Bed
Map Ref: 35

Kirriemuir Gateway to the Glens Museum

The Town House, 32 High Street, Kirriemuir DD8 4BB Tel: 01575 575479
Email: kirriegateway@angus.gov.uk Web: www.angus.gov.uk/history.htm

Social history of Kirriemuir and the Western Angus Glens including wildlife and archaeology. Museum of the Year in 2001.

Opening Times: Mon to Wed, Fri & Sat 10:00-17:00, Thu 13:00-17:00. Admission: Free.
Location: In town centre.
Map Ref: 35

Maud Railway Museum

Maud Station, Maud AB42 5LY Tel: 01771 622906

Housed in the former Maud Railway Station buildings, this museum illustrates the history of north east railways from the GNSR period, through LNER days into the era of British Rail.

Opening Times: Easter to Sep Sat, Sun & BH 14:00-16:30. Admission: Free. Location: In centre of Maud Village, at old railway station site.
Map Ref: 36

Methil Heritage Centre

The Old Post Office Building, 272 High Street, Lower Methil, Methil KY8 3EQ Tel: 01333 422100 Fax: 01333 422101 Web: www.methilheritage.co.uk

A lively local history museum and gallery located in the town of Methil. The museum features an exciting new permanent display 'Levenmouth Lives' as well as a temporary exhibition programme and associated events.

Opening Times: Tue to Thu 11:00-16:30, Sat 13:00-16:30. Admission: Free. Map Ref: 15

Central, East & Notheast Scotland

House of Dun

Montrose DD10 9LQ   Tel: 01674 810264   Fax: 01674 810722
Email: houseofdun@nts.org.uk

The Red Bedroom

A Georgian house designed and built by William Adam in 1730 for David Erskine, Lord Dun. There is a family collection of portraits, furniture and porcelain. The small walled garden has been largely restored to a late Victorian period and includes a range of plants typical of the 1880s.

Opening Times: 1 Apr to 30 Jun & 1-30 Sep Fri to Tue 12:00-17:00. 1 Jul to 31 Aug daily 12:00-17:00. Guided tours only. Admission: Adult £7.00, Concession £5.25, Family £19.00. NTS/NT Members Free. Location: On A935, three miles west of Montrose.   Map Ref: 37

Montrose Museum & Art Gallery

Panmure Place, Montrose DD10 8HE   Tel: 01674 673232
Email: montrose.museum@angus.gov.uk   Web: www.angus.gov.uk/history.htm

Montrose's maritime and social history. The wildlife of Angus Gallery covering from sea to mountain top. Art Gallery with constantly changing exhibitions.

Opening Times: Mon to Sat 10:00-17:00. Admission: Free. Location: Two minutes walk from town centre, ten minutes walk from railway station.   Map Ref: 37

William Lamb Sculpture Studio

Market Street, Montrose DD10 8NB   Tel: 01674 673232
Email: montrose.museum@angus.gov.uk   Web: www.angus.gov.uk/history.htm

Bronze, plaster and stone sculpture, wood carvings, watercolours and etchings by William Lamb (1893-1951) who was commissioned by the Royal Family. The studio collection includes heads of the Queen Mother, and our present Queen and Princess Margaret as children.

Opening Times: Jul to early Sep Mon to Sun 14:00-17:00. Admission: Free. Location: In secluded close between High Street and Market Street, in town centre.   Map Ref: 37

Laing Museum

High Street, Newburgh KY14 6DX   Tel: 01337 883017   Fax: 01334 413214
Email: museums.east@fife.gov.uk

First opened in 1896 to house Alexander Laing's Museum Collection and Reference Library, now a fascinating local history museum. It still displays Laing's material alongside the history of Newburgh.

Opening Times: Apr to Sep 12:00-17:00. Oct to Mar open by appointment. Admission: Free. Location: Town centre, High Street.   Map Ref: 38

Black Watch Museum

Balhousie Castle, Perth PH1 5HR   Tel: 0131 310 8530   Fax: 0131 310 8525
Email: museum@theblackwatch.co.uk   Web: www.theblackwatch

Over 260 years of history of Scotland's oldest Highland Regiment: on display are paintings, uniforms, silver medals, weapons and memorabilia which brings the past alive, also displays from today. Well stocked gift shop with souvenirs, replica badges etc, on sale.

Opening Times: Oct to Apr Mon to Fri 10:00-15:30. Closed last Sat in Jun. May to Sep Mon to Sat 10:00-16:30. Admission: Free. Donations welcome. Location: Hay Street next to Bells Sports Centre.   Map Ref: 39

Central, East & Notheast Scotland

The Fergusson Gallery

Marshall Place, Perth PH2 8NU Tel: 01738 441944 Fax: 01738 443505
Email: museum@pkc.gov.uk Web: www.pkc.gov.uk/ah

Houses the most extensive collection of the work of J D Fergusson, one of the leading figures in 20th century Scottish art.

Opening Times: Temporarily closed for renovation. Collection rehoused in Perth Museum & Art Gallery where it will be on show in a series of exhibitions. Reopening in spring 2005.
Admission: Free. Location: On southern edge of town centre, five minute walk from railway and bus stations.
Map Ref: 39

Perth Museum & Art Gallery

George Street, Perth PH1 5LB Tel: 01738 632488 Fax: 01738 443505
Email: museum@pkc.gov.uk Web: www.pkc.gov.uk/ah

One of the oldest museums in Britain, found in the centre of the fair city of Perth. Exhibitions are drawn from our fantastic collections of fine and Applied Art, Archaeology, Photography and Human and Natural History. Changing exhibitions throughout the year. Until spring 2005, works by the Scottish colourist J.D. Fergusson will be on show, while the Ferguson Gallery is renovated.

Opening Times: Mon to Sat 10:00-17:00. Closed Sun, Xmas to New Year. Admission: Free. Location: In city centre. Exhibitions & Events 2004 : See our website for details of our events and exhibitions.
Map Ref: 39

Perth Museum and Art Gallery

Scone Palace

Perth PH2 6BD Tel: 01738 552300 Fax: 01738 552588
Email: visits@scone-palace.co.uk Web: www.scone-palace.co.uk

Family home of the Earls of Mansfield. Housing a magnificent and varied collection of works of art. Set in mature and historic grounds. Once the crowning place of the Kings of Scotland, Scone Palace offers a fascinating day out for all the family.

Opening Times: 09:30-17:30. Last entry 17:00.
Admission: Adult £6.75, Child £3.80, OAP/Concession £5.70. Exhibitions & Events 2004 : 3 & 4 Jul: Game Fair.
The State Drawing Room
Map Ref: 39

Aberdeenshire Farming Museum

Aden Country Park, Mintlaw, Peterhead AB42 5FQ Tel: 01771 622906

The main museum exhibitions cover the story of farming in north east Scotland and the life of an estate before the First World War. The working farm illustrates life in the 1950s.

Opening Times: Apr & Oct Sat, Sun & school holidays 12:00-16:30. May to Sep daily 11:00-16:30. Admission: Free. Location: In Aden Country Park, one mile west of A952/A950 crossroads at Mintlaw.
Map Ref: 40

Arbuthnot Museum

St Peter Street, Peterhead AB42 1QD Tel: 01779 477778

Fishing, shipping and whaling displays. Local history, coins and Inuit art. Temporary exhibitions gallery.

Opening Times: Mon to Tue, Thu to Sat 11:00-13:00 & 14:00-16:30, Wed 11:00-13:00. Closed BH. Admission: Free. Location: In town centre, at St Peter Street/Queen Street crossroads, above Peterhead Library.
Map Ref: 41

Peterhead Maritime Heritage Visitor Centre

South Road, Lido, Peterhead AB42 0YP Tel: 01779 477778

Award-winning building presenting aspects of Peterhead's maritime heritage. Interactive displays on fishing, whaling, navigation and the oil industry. AV presentation on maritime life.

Opening Times: Jun to Aug Mon to Sat 10:30-17:00, Sun 11:30-17:00.   Admission: Phone for details.   Location: One mile south of Peterhead Town Centre on South Road (A952).
Map Ref: 41

Fordyce Joiners Workshop & Visitor Centre

Fordyce, Portsoy AB45 2SL Tel: 01224 664228

Late 19th/early 20th century rural joiner's workshop. Displays of hand tools and workshop machinery and AV presentation. See a craftsman at work and relax in a Victorian-style garden.

Opening Times: Summertime: Thu to Mon 10:00-20:00, Wintertime: Fri to Mon 12:00-18:00.
Admission: Free. Location: In Church Street, one minute from car park beside Fordyce Parish Church.
Map Ref: 42

British Golf Museum

Bruce Embankment, St Andrews KY16 9AB Tel: 01334 460046 Fax: 01334 460064 Email: hilarywebster@randagc.org Web: www.britishgolfmuseum.co.uk

A visit to the British Golf Museum will transport you down a pathway of surprising facts and striking feats from 500 years of golf history. Using diverse displays and exciting exhibits, the Museum traces the history of the game, both in Britain and abroad, from the middle ages to the present day. A must for golfers and non-golfers alike.

Opening Times: Apr to Oct 9:30-17:30. For winter opening times call the museum. Admission: Adult £4.00, Child £2.00, OAP £3.00, Student £3.00, Group (10+) 50p off all charges.(2002 charges). Location: Ten minute walk from town centre, five minute walk from bus station. R/A Clubhouse, beside beach.

Fun in the 18th Hole Gallery

Map Ref: 43

St Andrews Museum

Kinburn Park, Doubledykes Road, St Andrews KY16 9DP Tel: 01334 412690 Fax: 01334 413214 Email: museums.east@fife.gov.uk

Telling the history of this ancient town and showing changing exhibitions about the local environment and Fife as a whole. This museum always has something new to see and do.

Opening Times: Apr to Sep 10:00-17:00. Oct to Mar 10:30-16:00. Admission: Free.
Location: On western edge of town centre, near bus station.
Map Ref: 43

St Andrews Preservation Trust Museum

12 North Street, St Andrews KY16 9PW Tel: 01334 477629
Web: www.standrewspreservationtrust.co.uk

This charming 16th century house contains a wealth of fascinating material on the history of St Andrews and its people. There are displays depicting a variety of old shops and businesses - a grocers, chemists, dentists workroom and much more.

Opening Times: May to Sep, Easter week, last week Nov daily 14:00-17:00. Admission: Free.
Location: Near the Cathedral.
Map Ref: 43

Central, East & Notheast Scotland

Scotland's Secret Bunker

Crown Buildings, Troywood, St Andrews KY16 8QH   Tel: 01333 310301   Fax: 01333 312040
Email: mod@secretbunker.co.uk   Web: www.secretbunker.co.uk

Hidden beneath a Scottish Farmhouse, a tunnel leads to Scotland's Secret Bunker. 24,000 square feet of secret accommodation on two levels, 100 feet underground. Discover the twilight world of the Government Cold War, and take the opportunity to discover how they would have survived and you wouldn't!!! One of Scotland's DEEPEST and best kept secrets.

Opening Times: Apr to Oct daily 10:00-17:00. Map Ref: 43
Operations Room

STIRLING

Argyll & Sutherland Highlanders Regimental Museum

Stirling Castle, Stirling FK8 1EH   Tel: 01786 475165   Fax: 01786 446038
Email: museum@argylls.co.uk   Web: www.argylls.co.uk

The Museum, containing displays of silver, paintings and medals, provides visitors with tales of those who have served Britain in the ranks of the Regiment.

Opening Times: Easter to Sep daily 09:30-17:00. Oct to Easter daily 10:00-16:15.
Admission: Free, although there is a Castle entry fee.   Location: Within Stirling Castle.

Map Ref: 44

Stirling Smith Art Gallery & Museum

Dumbarton Road, Stirling FK8 2RQ   Tel: 01786 471917   Fax: 01786 449523
Email: elspeth.king@smithartgallery.demon.co.uk
Web: www.smithartgallery.demon.co.uk

Founded in 1874, the Smith has a collection of Scottish and European paintings and a collection of artefacts illustrating the story of Stirling. These include the world's oldest football (c.1540) and curling stone (1511), the Stirling Jug of 1457, and artefacts relating to the story of Wallace and Bruce. The Smith is an ideal place from which to explore the rest of Stirling.

Opening Times: Tue to Sat 10:30-17:00, Sun 14:00-17:00. Closed Mon.   Admission: Free.   Location: Dumbarton Road, 200 metres from Albert Hall and Tourist Information Centre.

Smith Art Gallery & Museum

Map Ref: 44

University of Stirling Art Collection

University of Stirling, Stirling FK9 4LA   Tel: 01786 466050

The Collection comprises over 300 works including paintings, prints, sketches, tapestries, sculpture and silver. There is a sculpture trail through the beautiful university grounds.

Opening Times: Daily 09:00-22:00. Closed Xmas & New Year.   Admission: Free.
Location: Ten minutes from bus/railway stations.

Map Ref: 44

Central, East & Notheast Scotland

STONEHAVEN *Aberdeens*

Tolbooth Museum

The Harbour, Stonehaven AB39 2JU   Tel: 01224 664228

Stonehaven's oldest building - the Earl Marischal's 16th century storehouse which served as the County Tolbooth of Kincardineshire 1600-1767. Displays of local bygones and the building's links with the Scottish Episcopal Church.

Opening Times: May to Oct Wed to Mon 13:30-16:30.   Admission: Free.   Location: On Stonehaven Harbourfront.

Map Ref: 45

TOMINTOUL *Moray*

Tomintoul Museum & Visitor Centre

The Square, Tomintoul AB37 9ET   Tel: 01309 673701   Fax: 01309 675863
Email: museum@moray.gov.uk   Web: www.moray.org/museums

Displays on local history and wildlife.

Opening Times: Mar to May & Oct Mon to Fri 09:30-16:00, Jun to Aug Mon to Sat 09:30-16:30, Sep Mon to Sat 09:30-16:00.   Admission: Free.

Map Ref: 46

TURRIFF *Aberdeens*

Fyvie Castle

Fyvie, Turriff AB53 8JS
Tel: 01651 891266
Fax: 01651 891107

Fyvie was once a royal stronghold, one of a chain of fortresses throughout medieval Scotland. The oldest part dates from the 13th century, and an air of mystery is created by the ghosts and legends associated with it. A rich portrait collection includes works by Batoni, Raeburn, Romney, Gainsborough, Opie and Hoppner. Also a fine collection of arms and armour, and 17th century tapestries.

Opening Times: 1 Apr to 30 Jun & 1 to 30 Sep Fri to Tue 12:00-17:00, 1 Jul to 31 Aug daily 11:00-17:00.   Admission: Adult £7.00, Concession £5.25, Family £19.00. NTS/NT Members Free.
Location: Off A947, eight miles south east of Turriff.   Map Ref: 47

The Entrance Hall

Highlands & Islands

The Highlands and Islands present a back cloth of awesome mountains and majestic coastal scenery. The Western Isles are a 130 mile long chain of islands rich in culture. The Orkney Islands have the remains of a Stone Age fishing village preserved from 3000 BC.

There are fascinating museums scattered throughout the region capturing the Highland heritage illustrating the local archaeology, geology, and natural, social and local history

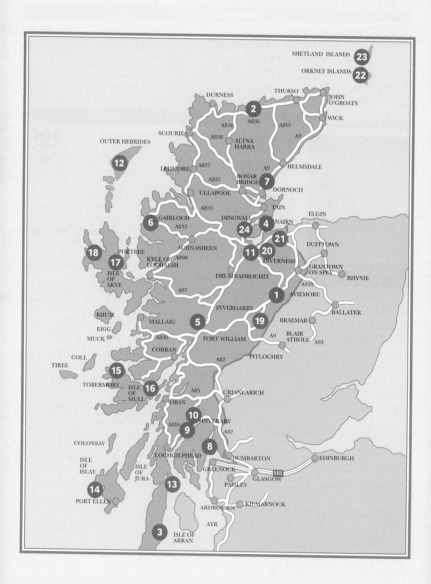

The Red Map References should be used to locate Museums etc on the pages that follow

Highlands & Islands

Strathspey Railway

Aviemore Station, Dalfaber Road, Aviemore PH22 1PY   Tel: 01479 810725
Email: information@strathspeyrailway.co.uk   Web: www.strathspeyrailway.co.uk

*Scotland's 'Steam Railway in The Highlands',
operating from Aviemore to Boat of Garten and Broomhill
(Nethy Bridge and Dulnain Bridge close by. Broomhill is
Glenbogle station in the BBC Series Monarch of the Glen).
Splendid views of the Cairngorm Mountain range and the
River Spey can be had from the carriage windows. While
on board the train you can enjoy tea, coffee, or something
stronger, along with light snacks.*

Opening Times: 7 to 14 Apr & Jun to Sep 09:30-17:30,
Apr Sun & Wed 09:30-17:30, May & Oct Sat, Sun, Wed &
Thu 09:30-17:30.   Admission: Adult £9.00, Child £4.50, OAP £6.30, Family £22.50.
Location: In centre of Aviemore and Boat of Garten. Bromhill Station is off A95 approx three and
a half miles south of Grantown-on-Spey.   Exhibitions & Events 2004 : 29-31 May: , 14-22 Aug:
Day out with Thomas the Tank Engine.   Map Ref: 1

Strathnaver Museum

Bettyhill by Thurso KW14 7ST   Tel: 01641 521418   Email: strathnavermus@ukonline.co.uk

*Strathnaver Museum is a locally run museum which first opened in 1976. It is housed in what was
St Columba's Parish Church at the eastern end of Bettyhill. The Strath area abounds with
archaeological sites; finds may be seen in the museum.*

Opening Times: Apr to Oct Mon to Sat 10:00-13:00 & 14:00-17:00.   Admission: Adult £1.90,
Child 50p, OAP £1.20, Student £1.00, Group £1.00 per person.   Location: Half a mile from
village.   Map Ref: 2

Campbeltown Museum

Hall Street, Campbeltown PA28 6BS   Tel: 01586 552366   Fax: 01369 705797
Email: mary.vanhelmond@angyll-bute.gov.uk

*Good display of local archaeology, geology and natural history. Programme of small temporary
exhibitions in foyer of the Public Library.*

Opening Times: Tue to Sat 10:00-13:00 & 14:00-17:00, Tue & Thu 17:30-19:30.
Admission: Free.   Location: Near town centre, five minute walk from Tourist Information Centre,
in the building of the Public Library.   Map Ref: 3

Hugh Millers Cottage

Church Street, Cromarty IV11 8XA   Tel: 01381 600245

Complete set of Hugh Miller's works

*Home of eminent geologist, stonemason, editor
and writer Hugh Miller. The furnished thatched cottage,
built c1698 by his great-grandfather, contains an exhibition
and captioned video programme on his life and work. A
reading room has been opened offering the chance to
browse among Miller's works. New artworks on display
include a tapestry, sculpture and silver medallion.*

Opening Times: Good Friday to 30 Sep daily 12:00-
17:00, 1 to 31 Oct Sun to Wed 12:00-17:00.
Admission: Adult £2.50, Concession £1.90, Family £7.00.
NTS/NT Members Free.   Location: Via Kessock Bridge
and A832 in Cromarty.   Map Ref: 4

Highlands & Islands

Treasures of the Earth

Road of the Isles A830, Corpach, Fort William PH33 7JL
Tel: 01397 772283 Fax: 01397 772133

A stunning collection of gemstones and crystals, displayed in fascinating simulation of cave, cavern and mining scenes. Priceless gemstones, beautiful crystals and exotic minerals light your path as they glisten and sparkle in cavities set against the scene back drop of ancient forest and tumbling waterfalls. Nuggets of gold, silver, aqua-marines, rubies and opals.

Opening Times: 1 Feb to 2 Jan 10:00-17:00 (Jul, Aug & Sep 09:30-19:00). Admission: Adult £3.50, Child £2.00, OAP £3.00. Location: At Corpach four miles from Fort William on the A830. Map Ref: 5

The West Highland Museum

Cameron Square, Fort William PH33 6AJ Tel: 01397 702169 Fax: 01397 701927

Old fashioned, traditional museum, world famous for its Jacobite collections. Excellent social and local history collections including the Alexander Carmichael collection and exhibitions on charms, costume, etc. Usually there is a temporary exhibition.

Opening Times: Oct to May Mon to Sat 10:00-16:00. Jun to Sep 10:00-17:00. Sun Jul & Aug 14:00-17:00. Admission: Adult £3.00, Child up to 16 free, Concession £2.00.
Location: Central Square in town, next door to Tourist Office. Map Ref: 5

Gairloch Heritage Museum

Achtercairn, Gairloch IV21 2BP Tel: 01445 712287
Email: info@gairlochheritagemuseum.org.uk Web: www.gairlochheritagemuseum.org.uk

Reflects the history of the parish of Gairloch: its people, their life and work, customs, the landscape, local skills such as spinning, fishing etc. Also to be seen is the light from the Rubha Reidh Light House. Children welcome.

Opening Times: Apr to Sep Mon to Sat 10:00-17:00, Oct Mon to Fri 10:00-13:30. Closed Nov to Mar. Open during winter by appointment only. Admission: Adult £3.00, Child 50p, Under 5s Free, OAP £2.00. Location: Situated five minutes walk from the shores of the loch, within easy reach of shops and hotels. Map Ref: 6

Dunrobin Castle Museum

Dunrobin Castle, Golspie KW10 6SF Tel: 01408 633177 Fax: 01408 634081
Email: info@dunrobincastle.net Web: www.highlandescape.com

Pictish stones. Collection of natural history. Sutherland family artefacts. Falconry.

Opening Times: Apr to 15 Oct Mon to Sat 10:30-16:30, Sun 12:00-16:30. Admission: Adult £6.60, Child £4.50, OAP £5.70, Family £18.00. Group rates available. Location: One and a half miles from Golspie. Map Ref: 7

The Hill House

Upper Colquhoun Street, Helensburgh G84 9AJ
Tel: 01436 673900 Fax: 01436 674685

The finest of Charles Rennie Mackintosh's domestic creations, The Hill House sits high above the Clyde commanding fine views of the river estuary. Walter Blackie commissioned not only the house and garden but much of the furniture and all the interior fittings and decorative schemes. Displays include work of new designers, demonstration of the effects of the wonderful stained glass, and a selection of original fabrics.

The Drawing Room

Opening Times: 1 Apr to 31 Oct daily 13:30-17:30.

Highlands & Islands

Admission: Adult £7.00, Concession £5.25, Family £19.00. Groups must book. NTS/NT Members Free. Location: Eastern side of Helensburgh. Map Ref: 8

INVERARAY *Argyllshire*

Auchindrain Township: Open Air Museum

By Inveraray PA32 8XN Tel: 01499 500235

A restored original farming village, furnished and equipped to provide a fascinating glimpse of Highland life in bygone days.

Opening Times: Apr to Sep daily 10:00-17:00. Admission: Adult £3.80, Child £1.80, OAP £3.00. Map Ref: 9

Inveraray Castle

Argyll Estates Office, Cherry Park, Inveraray PA32 8XE Tel: 01499 302203
Fax: 01499 302421 Email: enquiries@inveraray-castle.com
Web: www.inveraray-castle.com

The Castle was erected between 1745 and 1785 to replace an earlier traditional fortified keep. It was designed by Roger Morris and Robert Mylne. On display one can see the famous Armoury Collection, French Tapestries, fine examples of Scottish and European Furniture and a wealth of other works of art together with a genealogical display in the clan room.

Opening Times: Apr, May, Oct Mon to Sat 10:00-13:00 & 14:00-17:45 Sun 13:00-17:45. Jun to Sep Mon to Sat 10:00-17:45 Sun 13:00-17:45. Admission: Adult £5.90, Student/OAP £4.90, Child £3.90, Family £16.00.

Reduction for groups of 20 or more. Location: Off the A83 Trunk Road from Glasgow to Campbeltown. Map Ref: 10

Inveraray Maritime Museum

The Pier, Inveraray PA32 8UY Tel: 01499 302213

Displays, artefacts and archive film of Clyde and West Scotland maritime history. Hands-on activities and special displays of Highland Clearances and author Neil Munro of Para Handy fame.

Opening Times: Apr to Sep 10:00-18:00, Oct to Mar 10:00-17:00. Admission: Adult £3.80, Child £2.20, OAP £2.80, Family £11.00. Location: Near town centre at Pier. Map Ref: 10

INVERNESS *Highland*

Inverness Museum & Art Gallery

Castle Wynd, Inverness IV2 3EB Tel: 01463 237114 Fax: 01463 225293
Email: inverness.museum@highland.gov.uk Web: www.highland.gov.uk

Discovery Centre

Enjoy real Highland heritage in displays, exhibitions and events - an extravaganza of archaeology, art, natural and local history. Discover silver and taxidermy from Inverness, weapons and bagpipes from the Highlands and Scottish contemporary art. The ever-changing temporary exhibitions gallery presents a range of events and displays which reflect the cultural activity of the city. Progamme of talks, events and recitals. Activities for children and adults. Public enquiry service, identifying objects and providing information. Roll up your sleeves and discover the Highlands in the brand new interactive discovery centre, with hundreds of interesting artefacts to see and handle. Video macroscope to project objects onto a large screen, computer controlled roof top camera and satellite weather reports from around the world. Museum shop with a range of gifts, books and Highland souvenirs.

Opening Times: Mon to Sat 09:00-17:00. Closed Sun. Admission: Free. Location: In city centre, five minutes walk from car parks, railway station and bus station. Exhibitions & Events 2004 : For Exhibitions and Events please telephone for details. Map Ref: 10

Highlands & Islands

Regimental Museum,
The Queen's Own Highlanders Collection
Fort George, Ardersier, Inverness IV2 7TD   Tel: 01463 224380

Unique collection of uniform, medals, paintings, prints, weapons of Queen's Own Highlanders, Seaforth Highlanders, The Queen's Own Cameron Highlanders, Lovat Scouts, includes regular militia, territorial battalions. Comprehensive library and archive collection, available by appointment.

Opening Times: Apr to Sep daily 10:00-18:00. Oct to Mar Mon to Fri 10:00-16:00.
Admission: Free. (Visitors to Fort George must pay entrance fee to Historic Scotland)
Location: Within Fort George, 12 miles east of Inverness.   Map Ref: 11

ISLAND OF BENBECULA

Museum Nan Eilean
Sgoil Lionacleit, Lionacleit, Island of Benbecula HS7 5PJ   Tel: 01870 602864   Fax: 01870 602817   Email: dmacphee1a@eileanansiar.biblio.net   Web: www.cne-siar.gov.uk

Artefacts, photographs illustrating archaeology, local history and way of life in the Uists. Programme of temporary exhibitions.

Opening Times: Mon, Wed & Thu 09:00-16:00. Tue, Fri & Sat 11:00-13:00 & 14:00-16:00.
Admission: Free. Location: Centrally situated on Island of Benbecula.   Map Ref: 12

ISLE OF BUTE *Argyllshire*

Bute Museum
Stuart Street, Rothesay, Isle of Bute PA20 0EP   Tel: 01700 505067

Illustrative of the natural history, archaeology and social history of the Islands of Bute and Inchmarnock.

Opening Times: Apr to Sep Mon to Sat 10:30-16:30, Sun 14:30-16:30. Oct to Mar Tue to Sat 14:30-16:30.   Admission: Adult £1.50, Child 50p, OAP £1.00.   Location: In town centre behind castle.   Map Ref: 13

ISLE OF ISLAY *Argyllshire*

Museum of Islay Life
Daal Terrace, Port Charlotte, Isle of Islay PA48 7UA   Tel / Fax: 01496 850358
Email: imt@islaymuseum.freeserve.co.uk   Web: www.islaymuseum.freeserve.co.uk

The collection covers Islay life from earliest times, including archaeological artefacts. Domestic items are displayed in room settings. Traditional industries - whisky, joinery, crafting and fishing are well represented.

Opening Times: Apr to Oct Mon to Sat 10:00-17:00, Sun 14:00-17:00. Nov to Mar opening times advertised locally/by appointment for Groups.   Admission: Adult £2.50, Child £1.50, Concession £1.50, Family £7.00. Coach reduction - 20%.   Location: At edge of small village - good parking, one minute from bus stop.   Map Ref: 14

ISLE OF LEWIS

Museum Nan Eilean
Francis Street, Stornoway, Isle of Lewis HS1 2NF   Tel: 01851 709266   Fax: 01851 706318
Email: rlanghorne@cne-slar.gov.uk   Web: www.cne-siar.gov.uk

The collections feature local archaeology, objects and photographs relating to local history, domestic life, crofting, agrriculture, crafts and fishing.

Opening Times: Apr to Sep Mon to Sat 10:00-17:30. Oct to Mar Tue to Fri 10:00-17:00, Sat 10:00-13:00.   Admission: Free.   Location: Short walk from town centre.   Map Ref: 12

Highlands & Islands

Isle of Mull Museum

Main Street, Tobermory, Isle of Mull PA75 6NY

Historical artefacts and informative displays about the Isle of Mull from its geological beginnings to the present day.

Opening Times: Mon to Fri 10:00-16:00. Admission: Adult £1.00, Child 20p. Location: On Tobermory Main Street next to Clydesdale Bank. Map Ref: 15

Torosay Castle

Craignure, Isle of Mull PA65 6AY   Tel: 01680 812421   Fax: 01680 812470
Email: torosay@aol.com   Web: www.torosay.com

Relax in a beautiful David Bryce designed Victorian home, explore the spectacular gardens containing a large collection of chilean plants and a set of 19 Italian statues by Antonnio Bonazza.

Opening Times: 1 Apr to 31 Oct House: 10:30-17:00. Gardens: All year 09:00-19:00.
Admission: Adult £5.00, Concession £4.00, Child £1.75, Family £12.00. Location: Inner Hebrides. Map Ref: 16

Dualchas-Skye & Lochalsh Area Museums & Heritage Service

The Highland Council, Park Lane, Portree, Isle of Skye IV51 9GP   Tel: 01478 613857/613856
Web: www.highland.gov.uk/cl/default.htm

The Heritage Service provides detailed information on the history and culture of the area through its varied and extensive collections including the Dualchas Collection, The Archives and the Dualchas Library.

Opening Times: Mon to Fri 10:00-17:00. Closed Sat, Sun & BH. Please phone for an appointment. Admission: Free. Location: Portree, Isle of Skye. Map Ref: 17

Dunvegan Castle

Dunvegan, Isle of Skye IV55 8WF   Tel: 01470 521206
Fax: 01470 521205   Email: info@dunvegancastle.com
Web: www.dunvegancastle.com

The stronghold of the Chiefs of MacLeod for nearly 800 years and it remains their home. Built on a rock once surrounded entirely by salt water, it is unique in Scotland as the only house of such antiquity to have retained its family and its roof throughout the centuries, surviving the extremes of feast, famine and the intermittent periods of warring with neighbouring clans.

Opening Times: Daily mid Mar to Oct 10:00-17:30 (last entry 17:00), Nov to mid Mar 11:00-16:00 (last entry 15:30). Admission: Adult £6.50, Child £3.50, OAP/ Student/Group £5.50. Location: One and a half miles from village of Dunvegan, follow signposts. Map Ref: 18

Romantic & Historic Dunvegan Castle

Highland Folk Museum

Duke Street, Kingussie PH21 1JG   Tel: 01540 661307   Fax: 01540 661631
Email: highland.folk@highland.gov.uk   Web: www.highlandfolk.com

Award winning museum on two sites recreating the social history of the Scottish Highlands with a reconstructed 18th century farming township, Victorian water-powered sawmill, pre-war school and Isle of Lewis Blackhouse. Art Gallery features local artists.

Opening Times: Easter to Oct, please phone to confirm times. Admission: Adult £5.00, Child/OAP £3.00. Location: Kingussie Museum is five minutes from bus stop and railway station. Newtonmore Museum is 15 minutes from railway station. Map Ref: 19

Guided or Private Tours	Disabled Access	Gift Shop or Sales Point	Café or Refreshments	Restaurant	Car Parking

Cawdor Castle from
the flower garden

Cawdor Castle

Cawdor Castle, Nairn IV12 5RD
Tel: 01667 404401   Fax: 01667 404674
Email: info@cawdorcastle.com   Web: www.cawdorcastle.com

Cawdor Castle, the most romantic Castle in the Highlands, has a magical name linked with Macbeth by Shakespeare. The medieval tower and drawbridge are intact and generations of art lovers are responsible for the eclectic collections of paintings, tapestries, furniture and books in the castle. Beautiful gardens, nature trails, 9-hole golf course and putting green.

Opening Times: May to mid Oct daily 10:00-17:00.
Admission: Adult £6.50, Child £3.70, OAP £5.50, Family £19.20.
Groups of 20+ £5.70.   Location: Situated between Inverness and Nairn on the B9090 off the A96.   Map Ref: 20

Nairn Museum

Viewfield House, Viewfield Drive, Nairn IV12 4EE   Tel: 01667 456791   Fax: 01667 455399
Email: manager@nairnmuseum.freeserve.co.uk   Web: www.nairnmuseum.co.uk

The two Nairn museums amalgamated in 2000. Our permanent displays cover fishermen and farmers, adventures and Nairnshire notables. Changing monthly exhibitions. Children's area. Family and local history research facilities.

Opening Times: End Mar to end Oct Mon to Sat 10:00-16:30.   Admission: Adult £2.00, Child 50p, Family £4.00. Groups discount available.   Location: Near town centre, three minute walk from bus station.   Map Ref: 21

ORKNEY

Corrigall Farm Museum

Harray, Orkney   Tel / Fax: 01856 771411   Email: museum@orkney.gov.uk
Web: www.orkneyheritage.com

Interprets 19th/early 20th Century Orkney farming; peat fire; livestock; warm welcome; hands-on activities.

Opening Times: Mar to Sep Mon to Sat 09:00-17:00, Sun 14:00-17:00.   Admission: Free.
Location: Midhouse.   Map Ref: 22

Kirbuster Museum

Birsay, Orkney   Tel / Fax: 01856 771268   Email: museum@orkney.gov.uk
Web: www.orkneyheritage.com

Unique authentic survival in northern Europe of central hearth homestead. Site dates from 16th century. Peat fires; livestock; putting green.

Opening Times: Mar to Sep Mon to Sat 09:00-17:00, Sun 14:00-17:00.   Admission: Free.
Map Ref: 22

Orkney Museum, Tankerness House

Broad Street, Kirkwall, Orkney KW15 1DH   Tel: 01856 873191   Fax: 01856 875160
Email: museum@orkney.gov.uk   Web: www.orkneyheritage.com

The story of Orkney, from the Stone Age to modern times. Vivid displays, including the Picts and Vikings. Internationally important artefacts housed in a historic 16th century laird's town house.

Opening Times: Oct to Apr Mon to Sat 10:30-12:30 & 13:30-17:00. May to Sep Mon to Sat 10:30-17:00, Sun 14:00-17:00.   Admission: Free.   Location: Opposite St Magnus Cathedral.
Map Ref: 22

Orkney Wireless Museum

Kiln Corner, Junction Road, Kirkwall, Orkney KW15 1ES   Tel: 01856 871400
Web: www.owm.org.uk

Wartime communications equipment from Scapa Flow, history of domestic radio, working crystal set and valve set, Gimmick transistor radios, Orkney Wartime Photographic Archive.

Opening Times: Apr to Sep Mon to Sat 10:00-16:30, Sun 14:30-16:30.   Admission: Adult £2.00, Child £1.00.   Location: Next to harbour.   Map Ref: 22

Highlands & Islands

The Pier Arts Centre

Stromness, Orkney KW16 3AA   Tel: 01856 850 209   Fax: 01856 851 462

A permanent collection of 20th century British art including work by Ben Nicholson, Barbara Hepworth, Terry Frost, Roger Hilton, Alfred Wallis and Peter Lanyon and temporary exhibition programme of contemporary art by international and local artists.

Opening Times: Tue to Sat 10:30-12:30 & 13:30-17:00. Admission: Free. Location: One minute walk from bus station.   Map Ref: 22

Scapa Flow Visitor Centre & Museum
Lyness, Hoy, Orkney KW16 3NT   Tel: 01856 791300   Fax: 01856 875160
Email: museum@orkney.gov.uk   Web: www.orkneyheritage.com

The history of Scapa Flow, Britain's main naval base in both World Wars and the grave of the German High Seas Fleet. Historic buildings, photographs and artefacts.

Opening Times: Oct to May Mon to Fri 09:00-16:30. Jun to Oct daily 09:00-16:30.
Admission: Free.   Location: Lyness, Hoy.   Map Ref: 22

Stromness Museum
52 Alfred Street, Stromness, Orkney KW16 3DF   Tel: 01856 850025

Orkney maritime and natural history, including ships and fishing, Hudsons Bay log, Arctic whaling, German fleet in Scapa Flow, birds, seashells, moths and butterflies, fossils and ethnology.

Opening Times: Apr to Sep Sun to Sat 10:00-17:00. Oct to Mar Mon to Sat 11:00-15:30 .
Admission: Adult £2.50, Child 50p, OAP £2.00. Schools Free.   Location: 15 minute walk from town centre.   Map Ref: 22

Böd of Gremista
Gremista, Lerwick, Shetland   Tel: 01595 695057   Web: www.shetland-museum.org.uk

Renovated late 18th century house and fishing booth. Three-storey, stone-roofed bulding. Restored rooms with period furniture. Displays on line fishing and merchant marine trade. Biography of A Anderson, co-founder of P & O.

Opening Times: Jun to mid Sep Tue to Sun 10:00-13:00 & 14:00-17:00. Admission: Free - donations welcome   Location: Outskirts of town, one mile from ferry terminal.   Map Ref: 23

Shetland Croft House Museum
Voe, Dunrossness, Shetland Tel: 01595 695057 Fax: 01595 696729
Web: www.shetland-museum.org.uk

Restored mid-19th century steading, comprising house, byre, barn and mill. Stone walls and straw thatched traditional building with authentic contents. Locally-made furniture and agricultural implements.

Opening Times: May to Sep 10:00-13:00 & 14:00-17:00. Admission: Free - donations welcome.   Location: Near Boddam, five miles from airport.   Map Ref: 23

Shetland Museum
Lower Hillhead, Lerwick, Shetland ZE1 0EL   Tel: 01595 695057   Fax: 01595 696729
Email: tommy.watt@sic.shetland.gos.uk   Web: www.shetland-museum.org.uk

Comprehensive history of Shetland, geology, archaeology from Stone Age to medieval, including Iron Age farm finds and Early Christian treasure. Agriculture and fisheries 18th to 20th century. Social history, textiles.

Opening Times: Mon Wed & Fri 10:00-19:00, Tue, Thu & Sat 10:00-17:00. Admission: Free.
Location: Town centre, one minutes walk from Town Hall.   Map Ref: 23

Highland Museum of Childhood
The Old Station, Strathpeffer IV14 9DH   Tel / Fax: 01997 421031
Email: info@hmoc.freeserve.co.uk   Web: www.hmoc.freeserve.co.uk

Discover the customs and traditions of Highland childhood through audio-visual displays, childhood treasures and a fascinating doll and toy collection. Hands-on activities for children.

Opening Times: 1 Apr to 31 Oct Mon to Sat 10:00-17:00, Sun 14:00-17:00. Admission: Adult £2.00, Concession £1.50, Family £5.00. Location: Strathpeffer, Ross & Cromarty, Highlands.
Map Ref: 24

South & Southwest Wales

Wales has a strong tradition of music, literature and art, and this tradition is well represented in the museums and galleries of South Wales. Cardiff and Swansea have exceptional museums and galleries - Welsh heritage, the social history of coal mining, steam railways and maritime history are the focus of museums throughout this region.

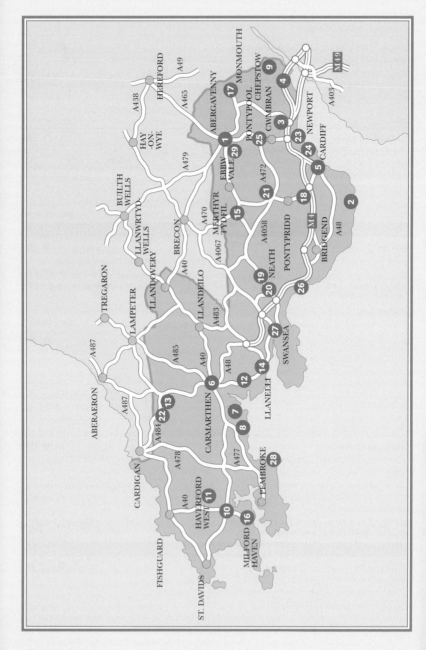

The Red Map References should be used to locate Museums etc on the pages that follow

South & Southwest Wales

ABERGAVENNY *Monmouthshire*

Abergavenny Museum & Castle

Castle Street, Abergavenny NP7 5EE   Tel: 01873 854282   Fax: 01873 736004
Email: abergavennymuseum@monmouthshire.gov.uk

The history of Abergavenny from prehistoric to present, housed in a Regency hunting lodge amid the ruins of the Norman Castle. Displays include 1950s shop interior, farm kitchen, saddlers shop. Regular exhibitions and events.

Opening Times: Open all year. Admission: Free. Location: Near town centre, parking nearby.   Map Ref: 1

BARRY

Fonmon Castle

Barry CF62 3ZN   Tel: 01446 710206

This medieval castle has been occupied as a home since the 13th century. It has exceptional Georgian interiors and is surrounded by extensive gardens.

Opening Times: Apr to Sep   Location: 15 miles west of Cardiff, one mile west of Cardiff airport.
                                                                                    Map Ref: 2

BARRY ISLAND *Vale of Glamorgan*

Vale of Glamorgan Railway Co

Barry Island Station, Barry Island CF62 5TH   Tel: 01446 748816   Fax: 01446 749018
Email: valeofglamrail@hotmail.com   Web: www.valeglamrail.co.uk

Operating steam railway between Barry Island and Barry Waterfront, with new extension to Woodham Halt due to open in Spring 2004. Museum of South Wales Railways, rolling stock viewing at Plymouth Road Depot. Please contact the Station for information on special events.

Opening Times: Easter to mid Sep Sat, Sun & BH 11:00-16:00   Admission: Adult £3.00, Child £2.00, Family £8.00. Special fares for special events.   Location: Barry Island Railway Station (connects with Valleys Lines) one minute walk from beach.   Map Ref: 2

CAERLEON *Newport*

Roman Legionary Museum

High Street, Caerleon NP18 1AE   Tel: 01633 423134   Fax: 01633 422869
Web: www.nmgw.ac.uk

Discover what made the Romans such a formidable force. See how they lived, slept and ate, how they marched and prepared for battle and which gods they worshipped.

Opening Times: Mon to Sat 10:00-17:00, Sun 14:00-17:00.   Admission: Free.   Location: On Caerleon High Street, in town centre.   Map Ref: 3

CALDICOT *Monmouthshire*

Caldicot Castle

Caldicot Castle, Church Road, Caldicot NP26 4HU   Tel: 01291 420241   Fax: 01291 435094
Email: caldicotcastle@monmouthshire.gov.uk   Web: www.caldicotcastle.co.uk

Founded by the Normans, developed in Royal hands as a medieval stronghold and restored as a Victorian family home, the castle has a colourful and romantic history.

Opening Times: Mar to Oct daily 11:00-17:00.   Admission: Adult £3.00, Concessions and Family rates available.   Location: Five minutes from Caldicot Centre, between Chepstow and Newport.   Map Ref: 4

CARDIFF

Cardiff Castle

Cardiff Street, Cardiff CF10 3RB   Tel: 029 2087 8100
Fax: 029 2023 1417   Email: cardiffcastle@cardiff.gov.uk
Web: www.cardiff.gov.uk/castle

Discover 2000 years of history in the heart of the city from the arrival of the Romans, through the Norman Conquest to lavish Victorian design - all have left their mark on the castle for you to explore. The Castle collections include original furnishings by the architect William Burges (1827-81). A collection of his architectural drawings and textiles

South & Southwest Wales

by Burges may be seen by appointment. Plus traditional Welsh banquets for a great night out (booking essential).

Opening Times: Mar to Oct daily 09:30-18:00 (last entry 17:00), Nov to Feb daily 09:30-17:00 (last entry 16:00). Admission: Adult £5.80, Child/Concession £3.50, Student £4.60, Family £16.60. Location: Cardiff City Centre. Quarter mile from central bus and train station.
Map Ref: 5

Museum of Welsh Life

St Fagans, Cardiff CF5 6XB   Tel: 029 2057 3500   Fax: 029 2057 3490
Web: www.nmgw.ac.uk

One of Europe's most outstanding open air museums. See how we have lived, worked, played and worshipped in over 40 buildings that have been moved from all over Wales.

Opening Times: Daily 10:00-17:00. Admission: Free. Location: In the village of St Fagans, approx six miles from Cardiff City Centre.
Map Ref: 5

National Museum & Gallery Cardiff

Cathays Park, Cardiff CF10 3NP   Tel: 029 2039 7951   Fax: 029 2037 3219
Web: www.nmgw.ac.uk

The National Museum & Gallery Cardiff is unique amongst British museums and galleries in its range of arts and science displays. The elegant Art Galleries house dazzling works of art by French Impressionists while the Evolution of Wales takes you on an amazing journey through 4600 million years of history. Don't miss the interactive Glanely Gallery where you can enjoy a changing programme of hands-on activities.

Opening Times: Tue to Sun 10:00-17:00, open BH Mon. Admission: Free. Location: In Cardiff's Civic Centre, approx five minutes walk from Cardiff City Centre.
Map Ref: 5

Techniquest
Stuart Street, Cardiff Bay, Cardiff CF10 5BW   Tel: 029 2047 5475   Fax: 029 2048 2517
Email: info@techniquest.org   Web: www.techniquest.org

Techniquest - the UK's most family friendly science centre with more than 150 hands-on exhibits and puzzles, Science Theatre, Planetarium, Discovery Room, Laboratory and The Hub.

Opening Times: Mon to Fri 09:30-16:30, Sat, Sun, BH 10:30-17:00. School holidays 09:30-17:00. Admission: Adult £6.75, Child £4.65, Concession £4.65, Family £18.50. Group rates available. Location: Cardiff Bay, waterfront location - five minutes from Cardiff Bay Station.
Map Ref: 5

Welch Regiment Museum (41st/69th Foot) of the Royal Regiment of Wales

The Black and Barbican Towers, Cardiff Castle, Cardiff CF10 2RB   Tel: 029 2022 9367
Email: welch@rrw.org.uk   Web: www.rrw.org.uk

The museum commemorates the service of the Infantry of South Wales namely the Welch Regiment (41st/69th Foot), also associated militia, volunteer and territorial forces, 1719-1969. Also the Royal Regiment of Wales 24th/41st Foot 1969 to date.

Opening Times: Mar to Oct daily 10:00-17:30, closed Tue. Nov to Feb daily 10:00-16:30, closed Tue. Closed Xmas & New Year. Admission: Museum: Free. Castle: Adult £2.90, Child/OAP £1.80, Student £2.30, Family £8.40. Subject to change. Location: The Museum is situated within Cardiff Castle and is within ten minutes walking time of the main train and bus station, also city centre multi-storey car parks.
Map Ref: 5

Carmarthenshire County Museum

Abergwili, Carmarthen SA31 2JG   Tel: 01267 231691   Fax: 01267 223830
Email: cdelaney@carmarthenshire.gov.uk   Web: www.carmarthenshire.gov.uk

One of Wales' finest regional museums housed in the one-time Palace of the Bishop of St Davids. On show are paintings, furniture, Roman archaeology and much more. Set in own parkland with walks and picnic sites.

Opening Times: Mon to Sat 10:00-16:30. Closed Xmas & New Year. Admission: Free. Location: At Abergwili - one and a half miles from Carmarthen on the A40. Public transport - buses for Llandeilo.
Map Ref: 6

South & Southwest Wales

Dylan Thomas Boathouse

Dylans Walk, Laugharne, Carmarthen SA3 4SD   Tel: 01994 427420
Web: www.dylanthomasboathouse.com

The Boathouse, where Dylan and Caitlin lived with their children from 1949-1953 is now a heritage centre. The house now contains audio visual presentations, original furnishings and memorabilia, a themed bookshop, tea room, viewing platform and terrace.

Opening Times: May to Oct and Easter weekend daily 10:00-17:30, Nov to Apr daily 10:30-15:30.   Admission: Adult £2.75, Under 7s Free.   Map Ref: 7

Museum of Speed

Pendine, Carmarthen SA33 4NY   Tel: 01994 453488   Fax: 01267 223830
Email: cdelaney@carmarthenshire.gov.uk   Web: www.carmarthenshire.gov.uk

Explores the history of Pendine's role in racing. The main exhibition, July and August is the car 'Babs', record breaking and fast vehicles and bikes at other times.

Opening Times: Easter to Sep daily 10:00-13:00 & 13:30-17:00. Oct Fri to Mon 10:00-13:00 & 13:30-17:00. Closed Nov to Easter.   Admission: Free.   Location: On the seafront at Pendine A4066 from the A40.   Map Ref: 8

Chepstow Museum

Bridge Street, Chepstow NP16 5EZ   Tel: 01291 625981

Museum reveals the rich and varied past of this ancient Wye Valley port and market centre. Wine trade, ship building and salmon fishing feature in displays which also recall Wye tourism and local social history.

Opening Times: Mon to Sat, Sun afternoon.   Admission: Free.   Location: In lower town, opposite Chepstow Castle.   Map Ref: 9

Haverfordwest Town Museum

Castle House, The Castle, Haverfordwest SA61 2EF   Tel: 01437 763087
Web: www.haverfordwest-town-museum.org.uk

The Haverfordwest Town Museum is situated in the Old Prison Governor's House in the grounds of Haverfordwest Castle. It reflects on the history of Haverfordwest from Norman times to the present day. The museum contains a wide variety of artefacts, photographs, paintings and uses multi-media computer facilities with touch screen. The oldest letter box in Wales, fully restored, is in the museum. Each room in the museum reflects on a distinct theme. The castle and reception room informs visitors about the history of the castle and its use as a prison.

The exterior of Haverfordwest Town Museum

Opening Times: Easter to Oct Mon to Sat 10:00-16:00.
Admission: Adults £1.00, Child/OAP/Student £0.50, Family £3.00   Location: In the grounds of Haverfordwest Castle, in the Old Governor's House. Signposted from town centre.   Map Ref: 10

Picton Castle

Haverfordwest SA62 4AS   Tel / Fax: 01437 751326
Email: pct@pictoncastle.freeserve.co.uk   Web: www.pictoncastle.co.uk

Picton, built in the 13th century by Sir John Wogan, is still the family home of his direct descendants the Philippses. The medieval castle was remodelled above the undercroft in the 1750s providing fine Georgian interiors. Around 1790 a new wing was added which included a dining room and drawing room. The 40 acres of gardens are part of The Royal Horticultural Society access scheme for beautiful gardens. The woodland gardens have a unique collection of rhododendrons, azaleas, mature trees, unusual shrubs, wild flowers, a new fern walk, and a recently restored dewpond. The walled garden has a fishpond with a

South & Southwest Wales

fountain, fernery, herbaceous borders and a large collection of herbs labelled with their herbal remedies. Children can enjoy the maze and the nature trail.

Opening Times: 1 Apr to 30 Sep Tue to Sun (open BH Mon) 10:30-17:00. Castle: by guided tour only between 12:00-16:00. Gardens only: daily 10:30 to dusk. Admission: Castle, Garden & Gallery: Adult £4.95, OAP £4.75, Child £1.95. Garden & Gallery: Adult £3.95, OAP £3.75, Child £1.95. Group reductions available please phone for details. Location: Four miles east of Haverfordwest, just off the A40. Exhibitions & Events 2004 : The Gallery has regular art exhibitions. Events including garden lectures and plant sales are held throughout the season. Please telephone for details. Map Ref: 10

Scolton Manor Museum

Spittal, Haverfordwest SA62 5QL Tel: 01437 731328 Fax: 01437 779500

Manor house built 1842 furnished to around 1900, also with costume and art galleries. Stable block also featuring blacksmith and carpenter's workshops. Railway area with signal box and 'Margaret' locomotive. Exhibition Hall displaying agricultural machinery and other local industries, World War II and railway galleries.

Opening Times: Apr to Oct Tue to Sun & BH 10:30-17:30. Admission: Adult £2.00, Child £1.00, Concession £1.50. Location: Five miles outside Haverfordwest on the B4329 (Cardigan Road). Map Ref: 11

Kidwelly Industrial Museum

Broadford, Kidwelly SA17 4LW Tel: 01554 891078 Fax: 01267 223830
Email: cdelaney@carmarthenshire.gov.uk Web: www.carmarthenshire.gov.uk

A unique opportunity to see how tinplate was made. The museum has buildings and machinery of the tinplate industry, coal mining and much more, in a delightful rural setting.

Opening Times: Easter BH, Spring BH to 31 Aug Mon to Fri 10:00-17:00, Sat & Sun 12:00-17:00. Admission: Free. Location: Signposted from the A484 on the outskirts of Kidwelly. Map Ref: 12

Museum of the Welsh Woollen Industry

Dre-fach Felindre, Llandysul SA44 5UP Tel: 01559 370929 Fax: 01559 371592
Web: www.nmgw.ac.uk

The Museum of the Welsh Woollen Industry tells the fascinating story of the most traditional of rural industries and still houses a thriving, working woollen mill, producing for the modern market.

Opening Times: Please phone for details, re-opening in mid-spring following re-developments. Admission: Free. Location: Four miles east of Newcastle Emlyn, 16 miles north west of Carmarthen, four miles off A484, in village of Dre-Fach Felindre. Map Ref: 13

Parc Howard Museum & Art Gallery

Felinfoel Road, Llanelli SA15 3LJ Tel: 01554 772029 Fax: 01267 223830
Email: cdelaney@carmarthenshire.gov.uk Web: www.carmarthenshire.gov.uk

Situated in a fine public park, Parc Howard has the largest collection of Llanelly Pottery, paintings and other items from Llanelli's past.

Opening Times: Apr to Sep Mon to Fri 11:00-13:00 & 14:00-18:00, Sat & Sun 14:00-18:00. Oct to Mar Mon to Fri 11:00-13:00 & 14:00-16:00, Sat & Sun 14:00-16:00. Admission: Free. Location: Half a mile north of Llanelli town on the A476. Map Ref: 14

Cyfarthfa Castle Museum & Art Gallery

Brecon Road, Merthyr Tydfil CF47 8RE Tel / Fax: 01685 723112
Email: cyfarthfacastle@fsmail.net

Georgian castellated mansion, originally Crawshay family home, set in 160 acre park. Collection includes: local history, fine art, porcelain, costume collection, brass instruments, Egypt collection, several temporary exhibitions.

South & Southwest Wales

Opening Times: Apr to Sep daily 10:00-17:30. Oct to Mar Tue to Fri 10:00-16:00, Sat & Sun 12:00-16:00. Closed Mon. Admission: Free. Location: Cyfarthfa Park on Brecon Road, one mile north of Merthyr Town Centre. Map Ref: 15

Joseph Parrys Ironworkers Cottage

4 Chapel Row, Georgetown, Merthyr Tydfil CF48 1BN Tel / Fax: 01685 723112
Email: museum@cyfarthfapark.freeserve.co.uk

1840s ironworkers cottage, direct contrast to Cyfarthfa Castle. Home to Parry family and birthplace of Joseph Parry, musician and composer of Myfanwy. Ground floor recreates 1841; upper floor, exhibition of Parry's life and local industry.

Opening Times: Apr to Sep Thu to Sun 14:00-17:00. Other times by appointment.
Admission: Free. Location: Town centre, five minutes from bus station. Map Ref: 15

Milford Haven Maritime & Heritage Museum

The Old Custom House, Sybil Way, The Docks, Milford Haven SA73 3AF Tel: 01646 694496
Fax: 01646 699454

Building of Milford from early whaling to fishing, oil refining to marina. Television shows on history of town and docks. Brass rubbing, hands-on and off exhibits.

Opening Times: Mon to Sat 11:00-17:00, Sun, BH & school holidays 11:00-17:00. Also group booking in advance outside these times. Admission: Adult £1.20, Child/OAP 60p, Under 5s Free. Location: Near town centre, on Milford Haven Marina. Map Ref: 16

Castle & Regimental Museum

The Castle, Monmouth NP25 3BS Tel: 01600 772175
Email: curator@monmouthcastlemuseum.org.uk Web: www.monmouthcastlemuseum.org.uk

The regimental museum of the Royal Monmouthshire Royal Engineers, and of the preceding Monmouthshire Militia. With some history of Monmouth Castle and Henry V. Also a small medieval-style herb garden.

Opening Times: Apr to Oct daily 14:00-17:00, Nov to Easter Sat & Sun 14:00-16:00. Admission: Free - donations welcome. Location: At the highest point of the town centre. Map Ref: 17

Nelson Museum & Local History Centre

Priory Street, Monmouth NP25 3XA Tel: 01600 710630
Email: nelsonmuseum@monmouthshire.gov.uk

The life, loves, death and commemoration of the famous admiral in one of Britain's major Nelson collections. In the same building Monmouth's history is displayed, including a section on Charles Rolls, co-founder of Rolls Royce.

Opening Times: Mon to Sat 10:00-13:00, 14:00-17:00. Sun 14:00-17:00. Admission: Free.
Location: Town centre, parking nearby. Map Ref: 17

Nantgarw China Works Museum

Tyla Gwyn, Nantgarw CF15 7TB Tel: 01443 841703 Fax: 01443 841826
Email: cvm@rhondda-cynon-taff.gov.uk Web: www.friendsofncwm.org

Dedicated to William Billingsley, the 19th century porcelain manufacturer and decorator, and the Pardoe family, domestic earthen utilityware manufacturers. Grounds contain remains of factory buildings and bottle kilns. Please ring or email for details.

Opening Times: Please ring or email for details. Admission: Please ring or email for details.
Location: Ten miles north of Cardiff, five miles south of Pontypridd. Map Ref: 18

Cefn Coed Colliery Museum

Neath Road, Crynant, Neath SA10 Tel: 01639 750556 Fax: 01639 645726

The museum is located on the site of the former Cefn Coed Colliery. It tells the story of life and work in what was once the deepest anthracite mine in the world.

Opening Times: Apr to Oct daily 10:30-17:00. Admission: Free. Location: Four miles north of Neath, south of Crynant on A4109. Map Ref: 19

South & Southwest Wales

NEATH (continued)

Neath Museum

Gwyn Hall, Orchard Street, Neath SA11 1DT   Tel: 01639 645726

It is a small but lively museum of local history, displaying Neath's rich history from prehistoric times through Roman, medieval, Victorian and on. It also houses an art gallery for temporary art and photographic exhibitions.

Opening Times: Tue to Sat 10:00-16:00. Closed for lunch, Sun & BH & Xmas week.
Admission: Free   Location: Centre of town, one minute walk from the Bus Station, five minutes walk from Train Station.   Map Ref: 20

NELSON *Caerphilly*

Llancaiach Fawr Manor

Nelson CF46 6ER   Tel: 01443 412248   Fax: 01443 412688   Email: allens@caerphilly.gov.uk
Web: www.caerphilly.gov.uk/visiting

Costumed interpreters guide visitors around the Manor which is set in the year 1645.

Opening Times: Mon to Fri 10:00-17:00. Sat & Sun 10:00-18:00. Closed Mon in Nov to Feb. Last admission one and a half hours before closing.   Admission: Adult £4.50, Child/Concession £3.00. Group rates available for over 20 persons.   Location: 20 miles north of Cardiff. 11 miles south of Merthyr Tydfil.   Map Ref: 21

NEWCASTLE EMLYN *Carmarthenshire*

The National Coracle Centre

Cenarth, Newcastle Emlyn SA38 9JL   Tel: 01239 710980   Email: martin.cenarthmill@virgin.net
Web: www.coraclecentre.co.uk

A unique collection of coracles from Wales and around the world, set in the grounds of a 17th century flour mill, overlooking the salmon leap.

Opening Times: Easter to Oct Sun to Fri 10:30-17:30 and by appointment.   Admission: Adult £3.00, Child £1.00, OAP £2.50.   Location: Centre of Cenarth village, beside the river and falls.
                                                                                     Map Ref: 22

NEWPORT

Newport Museum

John Frost Square, Newport NP20 1PA   Tel: 01633 840064

Houses fascinating displays of the natural and human history of Newport. Archaeology displays including important material from this Roman town of Caerwent; social history displays including the chartists; natural history displays including local geology; art exhibitions of watercolours, oils and prints, John Wait teapot display and Fox collection of contemporary art. There is a temporary exhibition programme.

Opening Times: Mon to Thu 09:30-17:00, Fri 09:30-16:30, Sat 09:30-16:00. Admission: Free.
Location: Town centre, near car parks and bus station.   Map Ref: 23

Tredegar House
Coedkernew, Newport NP1 8YW   Tel: 01633 815880   Fax: 01633 815895
Email: tredegar.house@newport.gov.uk

Enjoy a lively informative tour of this magnificent country house and discover what life was like for the Lords of Tredegar and their servants. Craft workshops and formal gardens.

Opening Times: 11 Apr to 29 Sep Wed to Sun, Sat & Sun in Oct. Special Halloween & Christmas opening.   Admission: Please ring for prices.   Map Ref: 24

---

www.mghh.co.uk

For current information on the outstanding Collections in over 1600 Museums, Galleries & Historic Houses in England, Scotland, Wales and Ireland

South & Southwest Wales

Amgueddfa Pontypool Museum

Park Buildings, Pontypool NP4 6JH   Tel: 01495 752036   Fax: 01495 752043
Email: pontypoolmuseum@hotmail.com   Web: www.pontypoolmuseum.org.uk

The museum has a collection of different displays including art and craft, a new art gallery and a Japanware display. Telling the history of the Torfaen area - industrial and social, and is set in a Georgian stable block.

Opening Times: Mon to Fri 10:00-17:00, Sat & Sun 14:00-17:00. Closed Xmas & New Year.
Admission: Adult £1.20, Concession 60p, Family £2.40. Group bookings 10% discount.
Location: Close to town centre and Pontypool Park.   Map Ref: 25

South Wales Miners Museum

Afan Argoed Countryside Centre, Cynonville, Port Talbot SA13 3HG
Tel: 01639 850564   Fax: 01639 850446

Set in the beautiful Afan Valley, The South Wales Miners Museum, gives information on the social history of coal mining. It tells us of the communities, family life and leisure activities.

Opening Times: Summer Mon to Fri 10:30-17:00, Sat & Sun 10:30-18:00. Winter Mon to Fri 10:30-16:00, Sat & Sun 10:30-17:00. Closed Xmas.   Admission: Adult £1.20, Child/OAP 60p.
Location: Approx six miles from nearest town. The South Wales Miners Museum is in Afan Argoed in Afan Forest Park.   Map Ref: 26

Egypt Centre

University of Swansea, Singleton Park, Swansea SA2 8PP   Tel: 01792 295960

The largest collection of Egyptian antiquities in Wales. Includes coffins, jewellery, tools and weapons etc.

Opening Times: Tue to Sat 10:00-16:00. Closed Sun, Mon & BH.   Admission: Free.
Location: On University Campus, ten minutes by car from Swansea.   Map Ref: 27

Glynn Vivian Art Gallery

Alexandra Road, Swansea SA1 5DZ   Tel: 01792 516900
Fax: 01792 651713   Email: glynn.vivian.gallery@swansea.gov.uk
Web: www.swansea.gov.uk

A changing exhibition programme of contemporary visual arts. Plus a broad spectrum of visual arts form the original bequest of Richard Glynn Vivian (1835-1910) which includes work by Old Masters as well as an international collection of porcelain and Swansea china. The 20th century is also well represented with modern painting and sculpture by Hepworth, Nicholson, Nash alongside Welsh artists such as Ceri Richards, Gwen John and Augustus John.

Opening Times: Tue to Sun 10:00-17:00. Closed Mon except BH.
Admission: Free.   Location: One minute walk from railway station.
Sculpture Court with David Nash Sculpture   Map Ref: 27

Swansea Museum

Victoria Road, Maritime Quarter, Swansea SA1 1SN   Tel: 01792 653763   Fax: 01792 652585
Email: swansea.museum@swansea.gov.uk   Web: www.swansea.gov.uk

Diverse range of collection reflecting the passions of the Victorian founders. The museum displays an exceptional collection of Swansea China. A quirky collection of artefacts provides infinite variety in the 'Cabinet of Curiosities'.

Opening Times: Tue to Sun & BH 10:00-17:00. Closed Xmas & New Year. Admission: Free. Location: Central location, five minutes from city centre.   Map Ref: 27

South & Southwest Wales

TENBY *Pembrokeshire*

Tenby Museum & Art Gallery

Castle Hill, Tenby SA70 7BP   Tel / Fax: 01834 842809   Email: tenbymuseum@hotmail.com
Web: www.tenbymuseum.free.online.co.uk

Two art galleries with regularly changing exhibitions, works by Gwen John and Augustus John.
Local history, maritime, archaeology, geology and natural history. Activities for children.

Opening Times: Daily Easter to end Oct 10:00-17:00, Nov to Easter Mon to Fri 10:00-17:00.
Admission: Adult £2.00, Child £1.00, Concession £1.50, Family £4.50.   Location: Centre of
town, above the harbour.   Map Ref: 28

Tudor Merchants House

Quay Hill, Tenby SA70 7BX   Tel / Fax: 01834 842279
Web: www.nationaltrust.org.uk

This late 15th century town house is characteristic of the area and of the time when Tenby was a
thriving port. The ground floor chimney is a fine vernacular example, and the original roof-trusses
survive. The remains of early frescos can be seen on interior walls and the house is furnished from
the Tudor period onwards. There is access to a small herb garden.

Opening Times: 1 Apr to 30 Sep daily 10:00-17:00, 1 Oct to 31 Oct daily 10:00-15:00.
Admission: Adult £2.00, Child £1.00, Family £5.00. Group: Adult £1.60, Child 80p. NT Members
Free.   Location: Centre of Tenby off Tudor Square.   Map Ref: 28

TORFAEN

Big Pit National Mining Museum

Big Pit, Blaenafon, Torfaen NP4 9XP   Tel: 01495 790311
Fax: 01495 792618   Web: www.nmgw.ac.uk

In the heart of the recently declared World Heritage Site at Blaenafon, Big Pit offers an experience
unparalleled in Britain and unique to Wales. Guided by an ex-miner, you will descend 300 feet to
the very depths of the mine and experience the inky blackness that the miners worked in day after
day. Complete your visit on the surface and explore the colliery buildings, pit head baths and
winding engine house.

Opening Times: Mid Feb to 30 Nov daily 09:30-17:00   Admission: Free.   Location: In the
town of Blaenafon, approx 16 miles north of Newport. Signposted from junction 25A of M4.

Map Ref: 29

Glorious unspoilt border country with little traffic and described as 'one of the lost wildernesses of Britain'. The Brecon Beacons National Park offers a wide variety of majestic sights including the Black Mountains.

Museums and galleries are not exactly prolific and generally focus on local history, and the arts and crafts of the region.

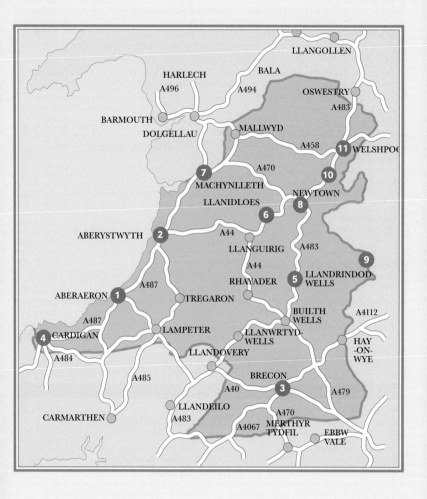

The Red Map References should be used to locate Museums etc on the pages that follow

Mid-Wales

Llanerchaeron

Ciliau Aeron, Aberaeron, SA48 8DG   Tel: 01545 570200
Fax: 01545 571759   Web: www.nationaltrust.org.uk

This is a small 18th century estate built and designed by John Nash. It was a self sufficient estate and today is a working organic farm. There are extensive walks around the estate and parkland.

Opening Times: 31 Mar to 31 Oct Wed to Sun 11:30-16:30. Open BH Mons.   Admission: Adult £5.00, Child £2.50, Family £12.00. Group (15+) Adult £4.00, Child £2.00. NT Members Free.
Location: Two and a half miles east of Aberaeron off A482.   Map Ref: 1

Ceredigion Museum & Gallery

Coliseum, Terrace Road, Aberystwyth SY23 2AQ   Tel: 01970 633088   Fax: 01970 633084
Email: museum@ceredigion.gov.uk   Web: www.ceredigion.gov.uk/coliseum

Local history museum in a restored Edwardian Theatre with exhibitions on archaeology, seafaring, agriculture, furniture etc. Changing temporary exhibition. Art Gallery.

Opening Times: Mon to Sat 10:00-17:00.   Admission: Free.   Location: Town centre, next to Tourist Information Centre.   Map Ref: 2

School of Art Gallery & Museum : Ceramics Collection

Arts Centre, Penglais, Aberystwyth SY23 3DE   Tel: 01970 622460   Fax: 01970 622461
Email: mov@aber.ac.uk   Web: www.aber.ac.uk/ceramics

Contemporary British, European, American and Japanese studio pottery; 18th and 19th century Welsh and English slip ware; Swansea and Nantgarw porcelain; Art Pottery and Oriental ceramics; and an outstanding collection of early 20th century British pioneer studio pottery. Changing displays.

Opening Times: Mon to Sat 09:30-17:00, also most evenings. Closed Sun, Easter & Xmas.
Admission: Free.   Location: On University Campus, one mile from town centre and railway station.   Map Ref: 2

School of Art Gallery & Museum

University of Wales, Buarth Mawr, Aberystwyth SY23 1NG   Tel: 01970 622460   Fax: 01970 622461   Email: neh@aber.ac.uk   Web: www.aber.ac.uk/art/ or /museum

University's collection of fine and decorative art: watercolours, drawings, and European prints from 15th century to present; art in Wales since 1945; contemporary Welsh and post-war Italian photography. Changing exhibitions from the collection, touring shows and exhibitions by invited artists. Study collection by appointment. Housed in magnificent Edwardian building overlooking Cardigan Bay.

Opening Times: Mon to Fri 10:00-17:30. Closed Sat, Sun Easter & Xmas.   Admission: Free.
Location: Near town centre, four minute walk from railway station and town centre.   Map Ref: 2

Brecknock Museum & Art Gallery

Captains Walk, Brecon LD3 7DW   Tel: 01874 624121   Fax: 01874 611281
Email: brecknock.museum@powys.gov.uk

Located in the centre of Brecon Beacons National Park it explores the past, natural environment and art of Brecknockshire. A Victorian Assize Court is interpreted with figures, sound and light. A lively exhibition programme features contemporary art and crafts from Wales.

Opening Times: Mon to Fri 10:00-17:00. Apr to Sep Sun 12:00-17:00, 4 Nov to Feb Sat 10:00-13:00 & 14:00-17:00.   Admission: Adult £1.00, Child Free, Concession 50p, Residents of Powys Free.   Location: Near town centre.   Map Ref: 3

South Wales Borderers & Monmouthshire Regimental Museum

The Barracks, Brecon LD3 7EB   Tel: 01874 613310   Fax: 01874 613275
Email: swb@rrw.org.uk   Web: www.rrw.org.uk

The Royal Regiment of Wales Museum with artefacts from the 1879 Anglo-Zulu War and equipment and war mementoes spanning 300 years.

Opening Times: Apr to Sep daily 09:00-17:00, Oct to Mar Mon to Fri 09:00-17:00.
Admission: Adult £3.00, Child Free. Group rates available.   Location: The Museum is adjacent to the Barracks in Brecon in The Walton (B4601)   Map Ref: 3

Mid-Wales

Cardigan Heritage Centre

Teifi Wharf, Castle Street, Cardigan SA43 3AA   Tel: 01239 614404

A Heritage Centre situated on the ground floor of an 18th Century warehouse on the Teifi river. There are collections on the history of Cardigan from Norman times to the present day. Also a Café, Craft/Book Shop and riverside terrace.

Opening Times: Easter to Oct 10:00-17:00 daily.   Admission: Adults £2.00, Child £1.00, Family £5.00 plus concessions.   Location: On the Riverside by Cardigan Bridge.   Map Ref: 4

Radnorshire Museum

Temple Street, Llandrindod Wells LD1 5DL   Tel: 01597 824513   Fax: 01597 825781

An unrivalled collection of photographs of Llandrindod from Victorian times to the present day. Archaeological collections from Castal Collen (site of main defence of Roman times), Capel Maelog and a unique Sheela-na-Gig.

Opening Times: Tue to Thu 10:00-17:00, Fri 10:00-16:30, closed between 13:00-14:00. Weekends - winter Sat 10:00-13:00, summer Sat 10:00-17:00, Sun 13:00-17:00. Closed Mon. Admission: Adult £1.00, Child Free, OAP 50p, Powys Residents Free.   Location: Next to Tourist Information, two minute walk from train station.   Map Ref: 5

Llanidloes Museum

The Town Hall, Great Oak Street, Llanidloes   Tel: 01686 413777

Three display areas reflecting the nature and type of the collections including local history, Victorian life and a Natural History Gallery.

Opening Times: Mon & Tue, Thu & Fri 11:00-13:00 & 14:00-17:00. May to Sep Sat & Sun 11:00-13:00 & 14:00-17:00. Oct to Apr Sat 10:00-13:00.   Admission: Adult £1.00, Child/Residents of Powys Free, Concession 50p.   Location: In the Town Hall.   Map Ref: 6

MOMA WALES

Heol Penrallt, Machynlleth SY20 8AJ   Tel: 01654 703355   Fax: 01654 702160   Email: info@momawales.org.uk   Web: www.momawales.org.uk

Y TABERNACL

Museum Of Modern Art, Wales

The Museum Of Modern Art, Wales has grown up alongside The Tabernacle, a former Wesleyan chapel which in 1986 reopened as a centre for the performing arts. MOMA WALES has six beautiful exhibition spaces which house, throughout the year, Modern Welsh Art and The Tabernacle Collection. Individual artists are spotlighted in a series of temporary exhibitions which are often accompanied by Workshops. In August expert judges and then the public choose the winners of the Tabernacle Art Competition. Many works of art in MOMA WALES are for sale. The adjacent auditorium has perfect acoustics and pitch-pine pews to seat 350 people. It is ideal for chamber and choral music, drama, lectures and conferences. Translation booths, recording facilities and a cinema screen have been installed; the oak-beamed Foyer has a bar; and extensive access for disabled people is made possible by a lift and a ramped approach.

Skinwalker 1, by Kathryn Dodd

Opening Times: Mon to Sat 10:00-16:00. Closed Xmas & New Year.   Admission: Free. Location: In town centre, five minutes walk from railway station.   Exhibitions & Events 2004 : Modern Welsh Art and Exhibitions throughout the year.   Map Ref: 7

Mid-Wales

Newtown Textile Museum
5/7 Commercial Street, Newtown   Tel: 01686 622024

The museum is housed in a typical early 19th century weaving shop, it focuses on the history of the woollen industry in Newtown from 1790 to the beginning of the 20th century.

Opening Times: May to Sep Mon, Tue, Thu, Fri, Sat & BH 10:00-17:00.   Admission: Adult £1.00, Child 50p. Free to local residents.   Location: Near town centre, five minutes walk from central bus station.   Map Ref: 8

The Judge's Lodging
Broad Street, Presteigne LD8 2AD   Tel: 01544 260650   Fax: 01544 260652
Email: info@judgeslodging.org.uk   Web: www.judgeslodging.org.uk

Stunningly restored 1860s judge's apartments, servants' quarters, courtroom and cells with displays on the Radnor borders region, local history and the Radnorshire Constabulary. A totally hands-on, national award-winning historic house.

Opening Times: 1 Mar to 22 Dec daily from 10:00. Closed Mon & Tue in Nov & Dec. Admission: Adult £4.50, Concession £3.95, Child £3.50, Family £13.50, Group rates available.   Map Ref: 9

Andrew Logan Museum of Sculpture
Berriew, Welshpool SY21 8PJ   Tel: 01686 640689   Fax: 01686 640764
Email: info@andrewlogan.com   Web: www.andrewlogan.com

Enter the glittering, fantasy wonderland where horses fly, butterflies are larger than birds and a throne is a velvet lily. 17th in The Independent's Guide to Top 50 Small Museums.

Opening Times: Easter to Oct Wed to Sun 12:00-18:00. Nov & Dec Sat & Sun 12:00-16:00. Admission: Adult £2.00, Concession £1.00.   Map Ref: 10

Powis Castle & Garden
Welshpool SY21 8RF   Tel: 01938 551929   Fax: 01938 554336
Email: powiscastle@nationaltrust.org.uk   Web: www.nationaltrust.org.uk

Bust of Lord Herbert of Chirbury,
by Hubert Le Sueur dated 1631

This medieval castle contains one of the finest collections in Wales. It is furnished with a wealth of fine paintings and furniture. There is pottery, marbles and busts including antique Roman pieces. A beautiful collection of treasures from India is displayed in the Clive Museum. Laid out under the influence of Italian and French styles, the garden retains its original lead statues, an orangery and an aviary on the terraces. In the 18th century an informal woodland wilderness was created on the opposing ridge with fine views over the Severn Valley.

Opening Times: Castle & Museum: 21 Mar to 29 Mar Thu to Mon 13:00-16:00, 1 Apr to 30 Sep Thu to Mon 13:00-17:00, 1 Oct to 31 Oct Thu to Mon 13:00-16:00. Admission: Adult £8.40, Child £4.20, Family £21.00. Group (15+) £7.40. Garden only; Adult £5.80, Child £2.90, Family £14.40. Group (15+) £4.80. NT Members Free. Location: One mile south of Welshpool, signposted from main road to Newtown (A483).   Map Ref: 11

A sword, shield and helmet in the Clive Museum

Powysland Museum & Montgomery Canal Centre
The Canal Wharf, Welshpool SY21 7AQ   Tel: 01938 554656

The museum is housed in a restored 19th century warehouse by the Montgomery Canal. It illustrates the history of the county from pre-historic settlers to the 21st century population.

Opening Times: Mon & Tue Thu & Fri 11:00-13:00 & 14:00-17:00. May to Sep Sat & Sun 10:00-13:00 & 14:00-17:00. Oct to Apr Sat 14:00-17:00.   Admission: Adult £1.00, Child/Resident of Powys Free, Concession 50p.   Location: Near town centre, five minutes walk from railway station.   Map Ref: 11

North Wales

North Wales contains Snowdonia National Park including the highest mountains in England and Wales. The north coast boasts the queen of the Welsh resorts, Llandudno, the town retaining much of its Victorian charm. The Isle of Anglesey is a delight with fine beaches and a remarkable number of Neolithic ruins.

There is a fine selection of museums and galleries throughout the region which cover both social history and local history as well as subjects as diverse as tramways, steam railways, Roman remains, the style and times of David Lloyd George and Maritime history.

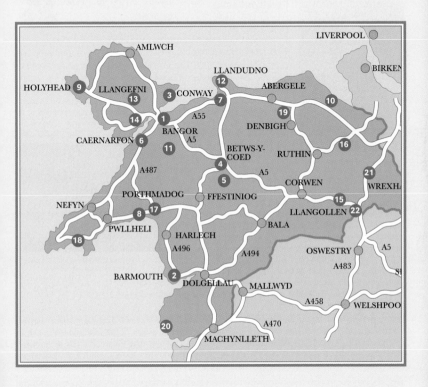

The Red Map References should be used to locate Museums etc on the pages that follow

North Wales

Gwynedd Museum & Art Gallery

Ffordd Gwynedd, Bangor LL57 1DT   Tel: 01248 353368
Email: gwyneddmuseum@gwynedd.gov.uk   Web: www.gwynedd.gov.uk/museums

Gwynedd's only general museum where you can learn about the ways of life led by previous generations which helps us to place our own experiences in the context of an unfolding story.

Opening Times: Tue to Fri 12:30-16:30, Sat 10:30-16:30.   Admission: Free.   Location: By the main bus stop near the town centre.   Map Ref: 1

Industrial Railway Museum

Penrhyn Castle

Bangor LL57 4HN   Tel: 01248 353084
Fax: 01248 371281
Email: penrhyncastle@nationaltrust.org.uk
Web: www.nationaltrust.org.uk

Built on the profits of Jamaican sugar and Welsh slate, Penrhyn is a massive 19th century neo-Norman castle crammed with fascinating things including a one-ton slate bed made for Queen Victoria and a spectacular grand staircase that took ten years to build. It houses one of the best art collections in Wales, including paintings by Rembrandt, Gainsborough and Canaletto. The castle's interiors are decorated with elaborate carvings, hand-made wallpapers and stained glass, and its furniture collection includes many original pieces made of

The Dining Room view
towards the vast family portrait

Penrhyn oak and designed by the architect Thomas Hopper. Penrhyn is surrounded by 45 acres of grounds, including parkland, wooded walks and semi-tropical areas. Its Victorian walled garden contains exotic plants and shrubs from all over the world. Taking full advantage of its location, the castle offers stunning views of the mountains of Snowdonia and the Menai Strait. The stable block houses an Industrial Railway Museum with full-sized locomotives, rolling stock and track, and the Railway Model Museum. Displayed in the Doll Museum are over 500 dolls from around the world. The stable block's two exhibition galleries hold high quality temporary art exhibitions by local and internationally renowned artists.

Opening Times: 27 Mar to 30 Jun Wed to Mon 12:00-17:00, 1 Jul to 30 Aug Wed to Mon 11:00-17:00 1 Sep to 31 Oct Wed to Mon 12:00-17:00.   Admission: Adult £7.00, Child £3.50, Family £17.50. Group: (15+) £5.50. NT Members Free.   Location: One mile east of Bangor, at Llandygai on A5122. Signposted from junction 11 of A55 and A5.   Exhibitions & Events 2004: There is a wide programme of exhibitions and events. Please telephone for details.   Map Ref: 1

Barmouth Sailors Institute & Ty Gwyn & Ty Crwn

The Quay, Barmouth LL42 1ET   Tel: 01341 241333

The presentations of photographs and pictures in all buildings portray Barmouth's maritime heritage since the Tudor period. The reading room in the Sailors' Institute dates from 1890 and is the last example of its kind in Wales.

Opening Times: Ty Gwyn & Ty Crwn: Apr to Sep daily 09:00-19:00. Barmouth Sailors' Institute: Mon to Sat 09:00-18:00 all year round.   Admission: Free.   Location: On the Quay, five minutes walk from town centre.   Map Ref: 2

---

www.mghh.co.uk

For current information on the outstanding Collections in over 1600 Museums, Galleries & Historic Houses in England, Scotland, Wales and Ireland

North Wales

Beaumaris Gaol & Courthouse

Beaumaris LL58 8ED   Tel: 01248 810921

Crime and punishment related collections including prison and court furniture, legal robes, chains, police equipment.

Opening Times: Easter to end Sep daily 10:30-17:00.   Admission: Adult £3.50, Child/OAP £2.50.   Location: Court House, opposite Castle in Main Street, gaol two minute walk from Main Street.   Map Ref: 3

Museum of Childhood Memories

1 Castle Street, Beaumaris LL58 8AP   Tel: 01248 712498
Web: www.aboutbritain.com/museumofchildhoodmemories.htm

A independent museum located in a Georgian house. The nine rooms each display a different theme showing the happier side of family life over the past 150 years.

Opening Times: Mar to Oct 10:30-17:00. Closed Nov to Feb.   Admission: Adult £3.50, Child £2.00, OAP/Student £3.00.   Location: Opposite Beaumaris Castle, Anglesey.   Map Ref: 3

Conwy Valley Railway Museum

The Old Goods Yard, Betws-y-Coed LL24 0AL   Tel: 01690 760568   Fax: 01690 710132

Dioramas featuring LNW Railway by the late Jack Nelson quarter full size working model 15' gauge steam locomotive 'Britannia'. Exhibits and working layouts London and North Western Railway.

Opening Times: Apr to Oct daily 10:15-17:30, Nov to Mar daily 10:00-16:00.   Admission: Adult £1.00, Child/OAP 50p, Family £2.50.   Location: Adjacent to railway station, four minute walk from town centre.   Map Ref: 4

Ty Mawr Wybrnant

Penmachno, Betws-y-Coed LL25 0HJ   Tel: 01690 760213
Web: www.nationaltrust.org.uk

Ty Mawr was the birthplace of Bishop William Morgan, first translator of the entire Bible into Welsh. The house has been restored to its probable 16th-17th century appearance and houses a display of Welsh Bibles.

Opening Times: 1 Apr to 30 Sep Thu to Sun 12:00-17:00, 1 Oct to 31 Oct Thu to Sun 12:00-16:00.Open BH Mons.   Admission: Adult £2.40, Child £1.20, Family £6.00. Group (15+): Adult £2.00, Child £1.00. NT Members Free.   Location: From A5 three miles south of Betws-y-Coed,take B4406 to Penmachno. House is two and a half miles north west of Penmachno by forest road.   Map Ref: 5

Ty'n-y-Coed Uchaf

Penmachno, Betws-y-Coed LL24 0PS   Tel: 01690 760229
Web: www.nationaltrust.org.uk

A traditional smallholding with 19th century farmhouse and outbuildings, providing a record of an almost vanished way of life.

Opening Times: 1 Apr to 30 Sep Thu, Fri & Sun 12:00-17:00, 1 Oct to 31 Oct Thu, Fri & Sun 12:00-16:00.   Admission: Adult £2.40, Child £1.20, Family £6.00. Group (15+): Adult £2.00, Child £1.00. NT Members Free.   Location: One and a half miles south of Betws-y-Coed on the A5. Turn right at the sign for TyMawr, then follow B4404 for half a mile.   Map Ref: 5

Caernarfon Maritime Museum

Victoria Dock, Caernarfon   Tel: 01248 752083

The museum illustrates the rich maritime and industrial history of the port and town of Caernarfon, including its seafarers. A display illustrates the operation of the dredger Seiont II through a recreation of parts of the bridge and engine room, and another the training ship HMS Conway (including an anchor outside the museum).

Opening Times: Sun to Fri 11:00-16:00. Closed Sat.   Admission: Adult £1.00, Child Free.
Location: Near town centre, just outside town walls on Victoria Dock.   Map Ref: 6

North Wales

Royal Welch Fusiliers Regimental Museum

Queen's Tower, Caernarfon Castle, Caernarfon LL55 2AY Tel: 01286 673362
Email: rwfusiliers@callnetuk.com Web: www.rwfmuseum.org.uk

Extensive collection of uniforms, paintings, weapons and memorabilia displayed in five refurbished galleries. Outstanding collection of medals and works relating to Great War poets and authors, Siegfried Sassoon, Robert Graves, David Jones, Dr J C Dunn and Frank Richards.

Opening Times: 09:30-18:00 daily in summer. Please phone for details of winter opening. Admission: Free, within entry to Caernarfon Castle. Location: Town centre, five minute walk from central bus station.

Mounting the Queen's Guard in London, September, 1975   Map Ref: 6

CONWY

Aberconwy House

2 Castle Street, Conwy LL32 8AY   Tel: 01492 592246
Web: www.nationaltrust.org.uk

This 14th century house is the last remaining medieval merchant's house in Conwy to have survived the turbulent history of this walled town. Furnished rooms show daily life from different periods in history.

Opening Times: 27 Mar to 31 Oct Wed to Mon 11:00-17:00. Closed Tue. Admission: Adult £2.40, Child £1.20, Family £6.00. Group: Adult £2.00, Child £1.00. NT Members Free.
Location: At junction of Castle Street and High Street.   Map Ref: 7

Royal Cambrian Academy

Crown Lane, Conwy LL32 8AN   Tel / Fax: 01492 593413   Email: rca@rcaconwy.org
Web: www.rcaconwy.org

Nine temporary art exhibitions per year. A variety of contemporary and historical work from the best Welsh artists.

Opening Times: Tue to Sat 11:00-17:00, Sun 13:00-16:30. Closed Mon. Admission: Free except special exhibitions. Location: One minute walk from railway station and bus stop, just off Conwy High Street, behind 'Plas Mawr'.   Map Ref: 7

CRICCIETH *Gwynedd*

Lloyd George Museum & Highgate Cottage

Llanystumdwy, Criccieth LL52 0SH   Tel / Fax: 01766 522071   Email: amgueddfeydd-museum@gwynedd.gov.uk Web: www.gwynedd.gov.uk/museums

The Museum traces the life and times of David Lloyd George featuring freedom caskets and scrolls, medals, paintings, photographs and documents such as the Treaty of Versailles. A visit to Highgate, the Victorian cottage where he lived as a child is included, which also features a Victorian garden and shoemaker's workshop.

Opening Times: Easter, May Mon to Fri 10:30-17:00. Jun Mon to Sat 10:30-17:00. Jul to Sep daily 10:30-17:00. Oct Mon to Fri 11:00-16:00. Admission: Adult £3.00, Child/Over 60's/Concession £2.00, Family £7.00. Location: Centre of the village, opposite Moriah Chapel.
    Map Ref: 8

North Wales

HOLYHEAD *Anglesey*

Holyhead Maritime Museum

8 Llainfain Estate, Llaingoch, Holyhead LL65 1NF   Tel / Fax: 01407 769745
Email: johncave4@AOL   Web: geocities.com/dickburnel

The Museum, located at the old Lifeboat House (c.1858) facing the famous breakwater, displays models, photographs and artefacts relating to the maritime history of Holyhead and district from Roman times until the present.

Opening Times: Spring to autumn daily 13:00-17:00. Closed Mon except BH.
Admission: Adult £2.00, Child 50p, OAP £1.50, Family £5.00.   Location: Newry Beach,
Holyhead.   Map Ref: 9

HOLYWELL *Flintshire*

Greenfield Valley Museum

Basingwerk House, Greenfield Valley Heritage Park, Holywell CH8 7GH   Tel: 01352 714172
Fax: 01352 714791   Email: info@greenfieldvalley.com   Web: www.greenfieldvalley.com

Museum and farm complex within a 70 acre heritage park. Period buildings including Victorian cottage, 17th century cottage, Victorian schoolroom as well as farming exhibitions, adventure playgound, small animals and weekend events.

Opening Times: Apr to Oct daily 10:00-16:30. Nov to Mar by arrangement only for Groups.
Admission: Adult £2.65, Child £1.60, Under 5s Free, Concession £2.20, Saver Ticket (2 adults and 2 children) £7.00. Group rates available.   Location: Close to Basingwerk Abbey and St Winefride's Holy Well. Follow brown signs from A55 through Holywell or A548 coast road.
                                                                                               Map Ref: 10

LLANBERIS *Gwynedd*

Welsh Slate Museum

Welsh Slate Museum, Gilfach Ddu, Llanberis LL55 4TY   Tel: 01286 870630
Fax: 01286 871906   Web: www.nmgw.ac.uk

A living, working piece of history, the museum tells the story of the slate industry in Wales, from nurturing traditional crafts and skills to the harsh realities of quarrying life for over 15,000 men (and boys) of Gwynedd.

Opening Times: 1 Nov to Easter Sun to Fri 10:00-16:00, Easter to End Oct daily 10:00-17:00.
Admission: Free.   Location: In the middle of Padarn Country Park, Llanberis, on the A4086.
                                                                                               Map Ref: 11

LLANDUDNO

Great Orme Tramway

Victoria Station, Church Walks, Llandudno   Tel: 01492 575275   Fax: 01492 879346
Email: enq@greatormetramway.com   Web: www.greatormetramway.com

The Great Orme Tramway is over 100 years old and remains the only cable hauled tramway in Britain, an amazing way to reach the top of Llandudno's famous mountain. The tramway journey takes in the wonderful panorama of the resort, the Great Orme Country Park and a 4000 year old copper mine. From the summit, views of the Lake District mountains and the Isle of Man can be seen on a clear day.

Opening Times: Late Mar to late Oct daily 10:00-18:00.
Admission: Adult Return £3.95, Child Return £2.80,
Family Tickets and Group discounts available.
Location: Five minutes walk from town centre, two minute walk from Pier entrance.   Map Ref: 12

Llandudno Museum

17/19 Gloddaeth Street, Llandudno LL30 2DD   Tel / Fax: 01492 876517
Email: llandudno.museum@lineone.net

Painting and sculptures, objets d'art, local history from archaeology, Roman objects, town resort, war memorabilia and Welsh kitchen, etc. Temporary exhibitions from art to local history.

Opening Times: Easter to Oct Tue to Sat 10:30-13:00 & 14:00-17:00, Sun 14:15-17:00. Nov to Easter Tue to Sat 13:30-16:30. Open BH. Closed Xmas. Admission: Adult £1.50, Child 75p, Concession £1.20, Family £2.25/£3.50.   Location: Near town centre, three minute walk from pier/promenade.   Map Ref: 12

North Wales

Anglesey Heritage Gallery/Oriel Ynys Mon

Rhosmeirch, Llangefni LL77 7TQ   Tel: 01248 724444   Fax: 01248 750282

Oriel Ynys Mon comprises a museum depicting the culture and history of Anglesey, encompassing archaeology, art, history, industry and agriculture. A separate art gallery presents a changing programme of arts exhibitions by local, regional and nationally acclaimed artists. The museum's core collection includes art works by such artists as Charles Tunnicliffe and Kyffin Williams, social history and archaeology collection.

Opening Times: Tue to Sun 10:30-17:00. Closed Mon except BH.   Admission: Art Gallery: Free. Museum: Adult £2.25, Child/OAP £1.25.   Location: Close to town centre, on main bus route.

Map Ref: 13

Plas Newydd

Plas Newydd, Llanfairpwll, Llangefni LL61 6DQ   Tel: 01248 714795   Fax: 01248 713673   Email: plasnewydd@nationaltrust.org.uk   Web: www.nationaltrust.org.uk

An impressive 18th century house by James Wyatt housing Rex Whistler's largest painting and an exhibition about his work. Also a military museum containing campaign relics of the 1st Marquess of Anglesey. There is a fine spring garden and Australasian arboretum.

Opening Times: House; 27 Mar to 3 Nov Sat to Wed 12:00-17:00. Garden: 27 Mar to 3 Nov Sat to Wed 11:00-17:30. Open Good Friday.   Admission: Adult £5.00, Child £2.50, Family £12.00. Group (15+) £4.50. Garden only; Adult £3.00, Child £1.50. NT Members Free. Location: Two miles south west of Llanfairpwll and A5 on A4080 to Brynsiecyn; turn off A5 at west end of Britannia Bridge.

Map Ref: 14

The east front, viewed across the Menai Strait from the Faenol Estate

Llangollen Motor Museum

Pentrefelin, Llangollen LL20 8EE   Tel: 01978 860324
Web: www.llangollenmotormuseum.co.uk

Sixty plus vehicles from 1910 to 1970, a 50s garage village scene complete with owner's quarters, toys, tools, motor reference library and a small exhibition showing the history and development of our canal network.

Opening Times: Mar to Oct Tue to Sun 10:00-17:00.   Admission: Adult £2.50, OAP £2.00, Family £6.00.   Location: One mile outside Llangollen.

Map Ref: 15

Plas Newydd

Hill Street, Llangollen LL20 8AW   Tel: 01978 861314   Fax: 01824 708258
Email: rose.mcmahon@denbighshire.gov.uk   Web: www.denbighshire.gov.uk

The romantic home of the famous Ladies of Llangollen between 1780 and 1829. They eloped to live in the rural retreat, their gothicisation of a once humble cottage and grounds still fascinates.

Opening Times: Apr to Oct daily 10:00-17:00. Last recommended admission 4:15.
Admission: Adult £3.00, Child £2.00, OAP £2.00, Family (2 adults and 2 children) £8.00. Group rates of 30+ 10% off usual tickets.   Location: Ten minute walk from the centre of Llangollen.

Map Ref: 15

Daniel Owen Museum & Heritage Centre

Mold Library,Museum and Gallery, Earl Road, Mold CH7 1AP   Tel: 01352 754791

Displays reflect the development of the market town, the industrial heritage, the social and cultural life including the work of local poets and composers, Richard Wilson, the painter, and Daniel Owen, father of the Welsh of Novel.

Opening Times: Mon, Tue, Thu & Fri 09:30-19:00, Wed 09:30-17:30, Sat 09:30-12:30. Closed BH.   Admission: Free.   Location: Town centre.

Map Ref: 16

North Wales

Porthmadog Maritime Museum

Oakley Wharf No 1, The Harbour, Porthmadog LL49 9LU   Tel: 01766 513736

Models, paintings, drawings, charts, navigation instruments, shipbuilding tools and personal property - all relating to shipbuilding industry and the export of slates quarried at Blaenan Ffestiniog.

Opening Times: Easter week and from May BH to end Sep daily 11:00-17:00.
Admission: Adult £1.00, Child/OAP 50p, Family £2.50. Groups by arrangement.   Location: On wharf near bridge, opposite Harbour Station, behind Tourist Centre.   Map Ref: 17

Plas yn Rhiw

Rhiw, Pwllheli LL53 8AB   Tel: 01758 780219   Web: www.nationaltrust.org.uk

This small manor house was rescued from neglect and restored by the three Keating sisters in 1938. The original house was 16th century and contains watercolours of local views and a mixture of oak furniture. The ornamental gardens contain many flowering trees and shrubs.

Opening Times: 27 Mar to 31 May Thu to Mon 12:00-17:00, 2 Jun to 1 Oct Wed to Mon 12:00-17:00, 2 Oct to 24 Oct Sat & Sun 12:00-17:00, 25 Oct to 31 Oct Daily 12:00-17:00.
Admission: Adult £3.40, Child £1.70, Family £8.00. Group: Adult £2.70, Child £1.30. Garden only; Adult £2.00, Child £1.00, Family £5.00. Group: £1.60. NT Members Free.
Location: Follow A499 and B4413 from Pwlheli. 16 Miles from Pwlheli.   Map Ref: 18

Bodelwyddan Castle

Bodelwyddan, St Asaph LL18 5YA   Tel: 01745 584060   Fax: 01745 584563
Email: enquiries@bodelwyddan-castle.co.uk   Web: www.bodelwyddan-castle.co.uk

The Welsh home of the National Portrait Gallery. New galleries with interactive displays of Victorian portraiture. Sculpture from the Royal Academy of Arts. Victorian games gallery. Free audio tour.

Opening Times: Open daily 10:30-17:00. Closed Mon & Fri Nov to Mar.   Admission: Adult £4.50, Child £2.00, OAP £4.00, Family £12.00.   Location: Junction 25 of A55 expressway.   Map Ref: 19

Narrow Gauge Railway Museum

Talyllyn Railway, Wharf Station, Tywyn LL36 9EY   Tel: 01654 710472   Fax: 01654 711755
Email: enquiries@ngrm.net   Web: www.talyllyn.co.uk

A representative selection of predominately Welsh narrow gauge exhibits ranging from photographs to locomotives, adjacent to the Talyllyn Railway.

Opening Times: All year 09:30-17:00, longer between 23 Mar and 2 Oct when trains run daily.
Admission: Train tickets, Day Rover: Adult £9.50, Child £2.00, Concession £8.50. Intermediate fares available.   Location: Five minutes from Tywyn station (Wales and Borders), five minutes from town centre.   Map Ref: 20

Bersham Ironworks & Heritage Centre

Bersham, Wrexham LL14 4HT   Tel: 01978 261529   Fax: 01978 361703
Email: bershamheritage@wrexham.gov.uk   Web: www.wrexham.gov.uk

Exhibitions and collections largely based on the iron, steel and coal industries, particularly John Wilkinson and nearby Bersham Ironworks. Also temporary exhibition programme.

Opening Times: Heritage Centre: Easter to Oct Mon to Fri 10:00-16:30, Sat & Sun 12:00-16:30 (Oct to Mar closing 15:30). Ironworks: Easter & summer school holidays Thu to Mon 12:00-16:30.   Admission: Free.   Location: Two miles from town centre.   Map Ref: 21

North Wales

Chirk Castle

Chirk, Wrexham LL14 5AF   Tel: 01691 777701   Fax: 01691 774706
Email: chirkcastle@nationaltrust.org.uk   Web: www.nationaltrust.org.uk

This is the only Edwardian fortress in North Wales to have been continuously occupied since it was built in the 14th century. The elegant state rooms inside house elaborate plasterwork, Adam-style furniture, tapestries and portraits. There is a collection of arms and armour. The formal garden has clipped yews and rose garden, while there is also a rock garden and shrubbery.

The Saloon showing the harpsichord, chimneypiece and settees

Opening Times: 20 Mar to 30 Sep Wed to Sun 12:00-17:00, 1 Oct to 31 Oct Wed to Sun 12:00-16:00. Open BH Mons.   Admission: Adult £6.00, Child £3.00, Family £15.00. Group (15+) Adult £4.80, Child £2.40. NT Members Free.   Location: Entrance one mile off A5, two miles west of Chirk village; seven miles south of Wrexham, signposted off A483.   Map Ref: 22

Erddig

Wrexham LL13 0YT   Tel: 01978 355314   Fax: 01978 313333
Email: erddig@nationaltrust.org.uk   Web: www.nationaltrust.org.uk

Erddig is one of the most fascinating houses in Britain. The state rooms display most of their original 18th and 19th century furniture and furnishings, including some exquisite Chinese wallpaper. The garden has been restored to its 18th century formal design and has a Victorian Parterre, and yew walk.

The Entrance Hall (Music Room)

Opening Times: 20 Mar to 29 Sep Sat to Wed 12:00-17:00, 2 Oct to 31 Oct Sat to Wed 12:00-16:00. Open Good Friday.   Admission: Adult £7.00, Child £3.50, Family £17.50. Group: (15+) Adult £5.50, Child £2.80. NT Members Free.   Location: Two miles south of Wrexham.   Map Ref: 21

Minera Lead Mines

Wern Road, Minera, Wrexham LL11 3DU   Tel: 01978 261529
Email: mineraleadmines@wrexham.gov.uk   Web: www.wrexham.gov.uk

Displays relating to lead mining including a small museum, reconstructed pumping engine, ore processing etc.

Opening Times: Easter & summer school holidays, Thu to Sun 12:00-16:30. Closed Tue and Wed.   Admission: Free.   Location: Five miles from town centre.   Map Ref: 22

Wrexham County Borough Museum

County Buildings, Regent Street, Wrexham LL11 1RB   Tel: 01978 317970   Fax: 01978 317982
Email: museum@wrexham.gov.uk   Web: www.wrexham.gov.uk

Mainly social history collections, exhibitions include 'Brymbo Man - A Bronze Age Burial', The Welsh National Football Collection and exhibitions about the town and surrounding area. Also two temporary exhibition galleries and A N Palmer Centre for archives local studies.

Opening Times: Mon to Fri 10:00-16:30, Sat 10:30-15:00.   Admission: Free.   Location: In town centre.   Map Ref: 21

Northern Ireland

A country steeped in history with its capital city of Belfast and its beautiful sandstone castle. To the west is Londonderry encircled by a 17th century stone wall considered to be the best preserved fortification in Europe. Omagh in the 'wild' county of Tyrone has an outstanding variety of landscapes - mountains, rivers and moorlands. County Fermanagh is the 'Lakeland County' including Devenish Island with its sixth century monastery. To the east in County Armagh the 'Garden of Ulster', and finally County Down with the Mourne Mountains cannot be rivalled for its history and wildlife.

There are 35 interesting Museums and heritage sites depicting Northern Ireland's history, culture, folklife, emigration, archaeology, geology, and natural environment.

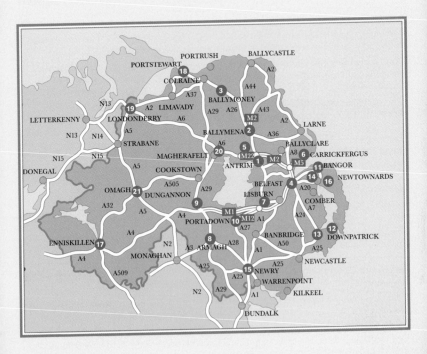

The Red Map References should be used to locate Museums etc on the pages that follow

Northern Ireland

Clotworthy Arts Centre

Antrim Castle Gardens, Randalstown Road, Antrim BT41 4LH   Tel: 028 9442 8000
Email: clotworthyarts@antrim.gov.uk

Arts Centre with three galleries and a small theatre. Housed in former coach yard of Antrim Castle and set within 17th century Antrim Castle Gardens.

Opening Times: Mon to Fri 09:30-21:30, Sat 10:00-17:00, Sun Jul & Aug 14:00-17:00.
Admission: Free. Guided Tours £2.00 per person - must be pre-booked.   Location: Five minute walk from town centre via Market Square. By road off A6 to Randalstown, 150 metres from junction with A26 to Ballymena.

Map Ref: 1

Ballymena Museum

3 Wellington Court, Ballymena, Co Antrim BT43 6EG   Tel: 028 25 642166   Fax: 028 25 638582
Email: ballymena.museum@ballymena.gov.uk   Web: www.ballymena.gov.uk

Mixed social history/local collection providing an insight into the rich local cultural heritage of Mid-Antrim. Temporary exhibitions and events, permanent displays, community outreach and historical enquiry service.

Opening Times: Mon to Fri 10:00-13:00 & 14:00-17:00, Sat 10:00-13:00. Closed Sun & BH.
Admission: Free.   Location: Town centre, between Wellington Street and Church Street.

Map Ref: 2

Royal Irish Regiment Museum

HQ The Royal Irish Regiment, St Patrick's Barracks, Ballymena, Co Antrim BT43 7NX   Tel: 028 2566 1383   Fax: 028 2566 1378   Email: hqrirish@royalirishregiment.co.uk
Web: www.royalirishregiment.co.uk

Collection takes the visitor on a journey from the formation of the regiment in 1689 to the present day.

Opening Times: Wed & Sat 14:00-17:00. Also by prior arrangement.   Admission: Adult £2.00, Child/OAP £1.00.   Location: In St Patrick's Barracks.

Map Ref: 2

Leslie Hill Open Farm

Ballymoney, Co Antrim BT53 6QL   Tel: 028 2766 3109/2766 6803

Comprehensive collection of horse-drawn farm implements, carts, mobile threshers, barn threshres and hand tools, governess cart, jaunting car and travelling coach. Household items of the past.

Opening Times: Open all Easter week 11:00-18.00. Apr & May Sun & BH 14:00-18:00. Jun Sat & Sun 14:00-18:00, Jul & Aug Mon to Sat 11:00-18:00, Sun 14:00-18:00.   Admission: Adult £3.00, Child £2.00. Group rates available.   Location: One mile north west of Ballymoney.

Map Ref: 3

Fernhill House 'The Peoples Museum'

Fernhill House, Glencairn Park, Belfast BT13   Tel: 028 9071 5599   Fax: 028 9071 3810

Fernhill House is a community museum which explores the history of the Geater Shankill and tells the story of the people from the early 19th century until the present day.

Opening Times: Mon to Sat 10:00-16:00, Sun 13:00-16:00.   Admission: Adult £2.00, Child £1.00, OAP 50p, Student £1.50, Family £4.00.   Location: 15 minute drive from Belfast City Centre.

Map Ref: 4

Ormeau Baths Gallery

18A Ormeau Avenue, Belfast BT2 8HQ   Tel: 028 9032 1402   Fax: 028 9031 2232   Email: admin@obgonline.net   Web: www.obgonline.net

The Gallery is dedicated to the presentation of innovative exhibitions of contemporary visual art across a wide range of disciplines, by leading Irish and international artists.

Opening Times: Tue to Sat 10:00-18:00.   Admission: Free.   Location: Five minutes from Belfast City Hall via Bedford or Linenhall Street.

Map Ref: 4

Northern Ireland

Royal Ulster Rifles Regimental Museum

5 Waring Street, Belfast BT1 2EW   Tel / Fax: 028 9023 2086   Email: rurmuseum@yahoo.co.uk
Web: www.rurmuseum.tripod.com/

Over 4000 artefacts on show in the museum, including uniforms, trophies, badges, medals and other interesting items for the military historian, such as photograph albums, war diaries, pictures and muniments.

Opening Times: Mon to Thu 10:00-12:30 & 14:00-16:00, Fri 10:00-12:30. Admission: Adult £1.00, Child/OAP Free. Free to former Members of the Regiment. Location: City centre location, five minute walk from Laganside Bus Station. Convenient parking nearby.   Map Ref: 4

Ulster Museum

Botanic Gardens, Belfast BT9 5AB   Tel: 028 9038 3000

The museum holds collections of art, history, botany and zoology, geology, antiquities and ethnography. The fine art collection of the Ulster Museum embraces a wide range of periods and schools; British painting from the 17th century to the present day, including works by Gainsborough, Reynolds and Turner; a small but significant collection of Dutch, Flemish and Italian Old Masters; an extensive holding of Irish art from the 17th century to the present; and 20th century British, European and American art.

Opening Times: Mon to Fri 10:00-17:00, Sat 13:00-17:00, Sun 14:00-17:00. Closed 12 Jul and Xmas. Admission: Free. Location: One mile from city centre, beside Queen's University.
Map Ref: 4

Bellaghy Bawn

Castle Street, Bellaghy, Co Antrim BT45 8LA   Tel: 028 7938 6812   Fax: 028 9054 3111

Library of living poets of Northern Ireland including films, audio and art prints of Seamus Heaney. History displays from 17th to 19th century.

Opening Times: Daily 10:00-17:00. Admission: Adult £1.50. Location: At top of Castle Street.
Map Ref: 5

Flame: The Gasworks Museum of Ireland

44 Irish Quarter West, Carrickfergus, Co Antrim BT38 8AT   Tel: 028 9336 9575
Web: www.gasworksflame.com

The site contains one only surviving coal-gas manufacturing plant in Ireland and the largest set of horizontal retorts in western Europe. Collection of gas-related appliances and extensive research library.

Opening Times: Available on application. Admission: Adult £2.50, Child/OAP £1.50, Under 5s Free. Groups £2.00 per person. School groups £1.00 per person. Family group £7.00.
Location: Near town centre, four minute walk from Tourist Office and Castle. (signposted)
Map Ref: 6

Ballance House

118A Lisburn Road, Glenavy, Co Antrim BT29 4NY   Tel: 02892 648492   Fax: 02892 648098
Email: ballancen3@aol.com   Web: www.ballance.utvinternet.com

Artefacts relating to the life of New Zealand Prime Minister, John Ballance (1839-93) Liberal politician and welfare state reformer. Also illustrating the history of emigration from Ireland to New Zealand.

Opening Times: Apr to Sep Wed, Sun & BH 14:00-17:00, Other times by appointment. Closed 12 Jul. Admission: Adult £3.00, Child 50p. Group rates available. Location: On the A30, seven miles from Lisburn, two miles from Glenavy.
Map Ref: 7

Northern Ireland

Armagh County Museum

The Mall East, Armagh BT61 9BE
Tel: 028 3752 3070   Web: www.magni.org.uk

The collections of the museum reflect the lives of the people who live, work and are associated with County Armagh. The museum has an extensive reference library. A range of special exhibitions are held throughout the year. Armagh County Museum is part of the Museums & Galleries of Northern Ireland (MAGNI).

Opening Times: Mon to Fri 10:00-17:00, Sat 10:00-13:00 & 14:00-17:00. Closed Sun. Admission: Free. Location: On the Mall, an area of urban parkland a few minutes walk from the centre of the city.
Map Ref: 8

Royal Irish Fusiliers Museum

Sovereigns House, The Mall, Armagh BT61 9DL   Tel / Fax: 028 3752 2911
Email: rylirfusiliermus@cs.com   Web: www.rirfus-museum.freeserve.co.uk

Housed in a Georgian listed building, the collection is dedicated to the history of the regiment from 1793 to 1968. An extensive medal display includes two Victoria Crosses from the Great War.

Opening Times: Mon to Fri & BH 10:00-12:30 & 13:30-16:00. Closed Xmas & New Year.
Admission: Free. Location: Beside The Mall, near town centre and two minute walk from bus station.
Map Ref: 8

The Argory

Moy, Dungannon, Co Armagh BT71 6NA   Tel: 028 8778 4753
Fax: 028 8778 9598   Email: uagest@smtp.ntrust.org.uk   Web: www.ntni.org.uk

The Argory is a treasure trove, where the clock ticks but time stands still, and where nothing has been thrown away for 100 years. A guided tour will take you deep into this handsome Aladdin's Cave of Victorian and Edwardian taste and interests. Watch out for the musical tours when the Bishop's cabinet barrel organ is played.

Opening Times: House: 13 Mar to end May Sat, Sun & BH/PH (inc 9-18 Apr) 13:00-18:00, Jun to Aug daily 13:00-18:00, Sep Sat & Sun 13:00-18:00. Oct 2-10 Sat & Sun 13:00-17:00. Grounds: May to Sep 10:00-20:00 daily, Oct to Apr 10:00-16:00 daily. Admission: House Tour -
Adult £4.30, Child £2.30, Family £10.80. Group £3.90. Grounds: Car £2.30. NT Members Free.
Location: Four miles from Moy, three miles from M1, exit 13 or 14 (signposted).
Map Ref: 9

Ardress House

64 Ardress Road, Portadown, Co Armagh BT62 1SQ   Tel: 028 3885 1236
Email: ardress@nationaltrust.org.uk   Web: www.ntni.org.uk

Built before 1705 for Thomas Clarke. A beautiful Adamesque drawing room wasa later addition. There is fine plasterwork depicting scenes from classical mythology and good early Irish furniture.

Opening Times: 13 Mar to end Sep Sat, Sun & BH/PH 14:00-18:00. Admission: Adult £3.00, Child £1.50, Family £7.50. Group £2.50. NT Members Free. Location: 64 Ardress Road, Portadown, Co. Armagh.
Map Ref: 10

North Down Heritage Centre

Town Hall, Bangor, Co Down BT20 4BT   Tel: 028 9127 1200   Fax: 028 9127 1370
Email: bangor_heritage_centre@yahoo.com   Web: www.northdown.gov.uk/heritage

Concentrates on the glorious Early Christian monastery, the heyday of seaside holidays and local archaeology. Unique collection relating to Irish entertainer Percy French.

Opening Times: Tue to Sat 10:30-16:30, Sun 14:00-16:30, Jul & Aug closed 17:30.
Admission: Free. Location: Rear of Town Hall, Castle Park.
Map Ref: 11

Castle Ward

Strangford, Downpatrick, Co Down BT30 7LS
Tel: 028 4488 1204 Fax: 028 4488 1729
Email: castleward@ntrust.org.uk Web: www.ntni.org.uk

Castle Ward is full of personality. Situated in a stunning location overlooking Strangford Lough, the lawns roll up to one of the curios of the 18th century. Discover the full story on a house tour, which unravels the mystery to why the intriguing mansion was built, inside and out, in two distinct architectural styles, Classical and Strawberry Hill Gothik.

Opening Times: House: 13 Mar to end Apr Sat, Sun & BH/PH (inc 9-18 Apr) 13:00-18:00. May Wed to Mon 13:00-18:00. Jun to Aug daily 13:00-18:00. Grounds: Oct-Apr daily 10:00-16:00, May to Sep daily 10:00-20:00. Sep to Oct Sat & Sun 13:00-18-00.

Castle Ward, Gothik Boudoir

Admission: House & Grounds: Adult £5.00, Child £2.30, Family £10.80, Group £4.00. Grounds only: Adult £3.50, Child £1.50, Family £8.00, Group £2.50. NT Members Free. Location: Seven miles north east of Downpatrick, one and a half miles west of Strangford village on A25, on south shore of Strangford Lough. Map Ref: 12

Down County Museum

The Mall, Downpatrick, Co Down BT30 6AH Tel: 028 44 615218 Fax: 028 44 615590
Email: lmckenna@downclc.gov.uk Web: www.downcountymuseum.com

Collections relating to the history of County Down from early times to today. Museum is located in restored 18th century gaol of Down.

Opening Times: Mon to Fri 10:00-17:00, Sat & Sun 13:00-17:00. Admission: Free.
Location: Located between Downpatrick Courthouse and Down Cathedral. Follow brown signs.
Map Ref: 13

Downpatrick Railway Museum

The Railway Station, Downpatrick, Co Down BT30 6LZ Tel: 028 4461 5779
Email: walter.burke@tesco.net Web: www.downpatricksteamrailway.co.uk

Through the rolling drumlins of County Down, the Downpatrick Railway Museum houses and operates a unique collection of artefacts from the bygone railway golden age, the only such operating collection in Ulster and indeed Ireland. Now operating between Downpatrick & Inch Abbey - 2 miles.

Opening Times: Jul to Sep Sat & Sun 14:00-17:00, also 17 Mar, Easter Sun & Mon, Halloween weekend & 2nd and 3rd weekend Dec 14:00-17:00. Admission: Tours: Adult £1.50, Child 50p. Train: Adult £4.50, Child/OAP £2.50. Location: In Downpatrick Town Centre, adjacent to Ulsterbus Station. Map Ref: 13

Ulster Folk & Transport Museum

 ULSTER FOLK AND TRANSPORT MUSEUM

Cultra, Holywood, Co Down BT18 0EU Tel: 028 9042 8428
Web: www.magni.org.uk

Take time to explore one of Ireland's foremost visitor attractions, recapturing a disappearing way of life, preserving traditional skills and celebrating transport history. Just minutes from Belfast the Ulster Folk & Transport Museum is situated in over 177 acres of park and grassland. At the Open Air Folk Museum 60 acres are devoted to illustrating the way of life of people in Northern Ireland in the early 1900s. Visitors can stroll through yesteryear's countryside with its farms, cottages, crops and livestock and visit a typical 1900s Ulster town with its shops, churches, and terraced housing. Indoors the Folk Gallery features a number of exhibitions. The indoor

The Corner Shop, 1900s Ballycultra Town

Transport Museum boasts the most comprehensive transport collection in Ireland. The Irish Railway Collection is displayed in an award-winning gallery, explaining the history and impact of both standard and narrow gauge railways in Ireland. The Road Transport Galleries boast a fine collection of vehicles ranging from cycles, motorcycles, trams, buses, fire engines and cars. The Museum also has a varied programme of major events and activities from Vehicle Days to the Rare

CO DOWN (continued)

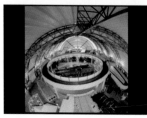

The award winning Irish Railway Collection

Breeds Show and sale. Skills once commonly practised such as lace sampler making, spinning, weaving, woodturning and forge work, and basket making are among many demonstrated and taught at the Museum.

Opening Times: Mar to Jun Mon to Fri 10:00-17:00, Sat 10:00-18:00, Sun 11:00-18:00. Jul to Sep Mon to Sat 10:00-18:00, Sun 11:00-18:00. Oct to Feb Mon to Fri 10:00-16:00, Sat 10:00-18:00, Sun 11:00-17:00. Admission: Adult £6.00, Child £3.00, Under 5s Free, Concession £3.00, Family £16.00. Group Rates available. Location: On the main Belfast to Bangor Road, just ten minutes outside Belfast with excellent access by road, rail and bus. Exhibitions & Events 2004 : For Exhibitions and Events please telephone for details. Map Ref: 14

Newry Museum

1A Bank Parade, Newry, Co Down BT35 6HP   Tel: 028 3026 6232   Fax: 028 3026 6839

The museum incorporates architectural features from a now demolished Georgian house including a fully furnished panelled room. Highlights of the collection include a table reputed to have been on HMS Victory, an Order of St Patricks Robe and a Gelston Clock dating from 1770.

Opening Times: Mon to Fri 10:30-13:00 & 14:00-16:30. Closed BH.   Admission: Free. Location: Located in Newry Arts Centre. Two minute walk from bus station on the Mall. In town centre. Map Ref: 15

Mount Stewart House, Garden & Temple of the Winds

Newtownards, Co Down BT22 2AS   Tel: 028 4278 8387/8487   Fax: 028 4278 8569 Email: mountstewart@ntrust.org.uk   Web: www.ntni.org.uk

Mount Stewart south front Spanish Garden

Situated on the tranquil shores of Strangford Lough, the impressive house and gardens of Mount Stewart have a unique story to tell. This year you will enjoy seeing and hearing many new stories about the Londonderry family, their home, their prominent guests and the people who have worked there over the centuries.

Opening Times: House: 13 Mar to end Apr Sat, Sun & BH/PH (inc 9-18 Apr) 12:00-18:00. May to Jun Wed to Mon 13:00-18:00, 12:00-18:00 Sat & Sun. Jul to Aug daily 12:00-18:00. Sep 12:00-18:00 Wed to Mon. Oct Sat & Sun 12:00-18:00. Admission: House & Gardens: Adult £5.20, Child £2.50, Family £10.80, Group £4.50. Gardens only: Adult £4.20, Child £2.20, Family £9.30, Group £3.90. NT Members Free. Location: 15 Miles south east of Belfast on Newtownards-Portaferry road, A20, five miles south east of Newtownards. Map Ref: 16

The Somme Heritage Centre

233 Bangor Road, Newtownards, Co Down BT23 7PH   Tel: 028 9182 3202 Fax: 028 9182 3214   Email: sommeassociation@dnet.co.uk   Web: irishsoldier.org

The centre has a collection of around 5000 pieces related to Irish participation in the First World War. The centre is also starting to collect World War Two material.

Opening Times: Apr to Jun & Sep Mon to Thu 10:00-16:00, Sat 12:00-16:00. Jul to Aug Mon to Fri 10:00-17:00, Sat & Sun 12:00-17:00. Oct to Mar Mon to Thu 10:00-16:00.   Admission: Adult £3.75, Child/Concession £2.75, Family £10.00. Map Ref: 16

Guided or Private Tours	Disabled Access	Gift Shop or Sales Point	Café or Refreshments	Restaurant	Car Parking

Northern Ireland

Castle Coole

Enniskillen, Co Fermanagh BT74 6JY

Tel: 028 6632 2690   Fax: 028 6632 5665
Email: castlecoole@ntrust.org.uk
Web: www.ntni.org.uk

If you are looking for stately grandeur then Castle Coole is a rare treat. Situated in a stunning landscaped parkland on the edge of Enniskillen this majestic 18th century house built by James Wyatt was built to impress. Soak up the opulent Regency interior with rich decoration and furnishings, including the ornate state bedroom prepared for George IV in 1821.

Opening Times: House: 13 Mar to end May Sat, Sun & BH/PH (inc 9-18 Apr) 12:00-18:00. Jun Wed to Mon 12:00-18:00. Jul to Aug daily 12:00-18:00. Sep Sat & Sun 12:00-18:00. Oct 2-10 Sat & Sun 13:00-17:00. Grounds: Apr to Sep 10:00-20:00 daily, Oct to Mar 10:00-16:00 daily.   Admission: House & Grounds: Adult £4.00, Child £2.00, Family £10.00, Group £3.00. NT Members Free.   Location: One and a half miles south east of Enniskillen on main Belfast-Enniskillen road (A4).

Castle Coole lobby with gallery

Map Ref: 17

Fermanagh County Museum

Enniskillen Castle, Castle Barracks, Enniskillen, Co Fermanagh BT74 7HL
Tel: 028 6632 5000   Fax: 028 6632 7342   Email: castle@fermanagh.gov.uk
Web: www.enniskillencastle.co.uk

Fermanagh County Museum collections represent Fermanagh's history, folklife, archaeology and environment. There are a variety of permanent displays relating to these topics as well as a rich and varied programme of events, education programmes and temporary exhibitions on subjects such as art, literature, music and history.

Opening Times: All year Mon 14:00-17:00, Tue to Fri 10:00-17:00. May to Sep Sat 14:00-17:00, Jul & Aug Sun 14:00-17:00.   Admission: Adult £2.25, Child £1.25, OAP/Student £1.75, Under 5s Free, Family (2 adults and 2 children) £5.50.   Location: Near town centre, two minute walk from Ulster Bus Station and Tourist Information Centre.

Enniskillen Castle

Map Ref: 17

Florence Court

Demesne Road, Enniskillen, Co Fermanagh BT92 1DB   Tel: 028 6634 8249
Fax: 028 6634 8873   Email: florencecourt@ntrust.org.uk   Web: www.ntni.org.uk

Florence Court is a truly welcoming home. Since the recent return of much of the Enniskillen family belongings to this fine mid 18th century house and estate, it has recaptured its warm and gentle atmosphere. House tours take you inside the heart of the house, and as each new door opens you discover more about family and the staff.

Opening Times: House: 13 Mar to end May Sat, Sun & BH/PH (inc 9-18 Apr) 12:00-18:00. June Mon to Fri 13:00-18:00, Sat & Sun 12:00-18:00. Jul & Aug daily 12:00-18:00. Sep Sat & Sun 12:00-18:00. Oct 2-10 Sat & Sun 13:00-17:00. Grounds: Apr to Sep daily 10:00-20:00, Oct to Mar daily 10:00-16:00.   Admission: House Tour: Adult £4.00, Child £2.00, Family £10.00. Group £3.00. Grounds: Car £2.50. NT Members Free.   Location: eight miles south west of Enniskillen via A4 Sligo road and A32 Swanlinbar road, four miles from Marble Arch Caves.

Florence Court East Front

Map Ref: 17

Royal Inniskilling Fusiliers Regimental Museum

Enniskillen Castle, Castle Barracks, Enniskillen, Co Fermanagh BT74 7HL   Tel: 02866 323142
Fax: 02866 320359   Email: museum@inniskilling.com   Web: www.inniskilling.com

Housed in Enniskillen Castle, the museum traces the history of the Regiment from its formation on this site in 1689 to its amalgamation in 1968. It features a wide range of uniforms, weapons, regimental memorabilia and medals including eight Victoria crosses.

Opening Times: All year Mon 14:00-17:00 Tue to Fri 10:00-17:00. May to Sep Sat 14:00-17:00. Jul Aug Sun 14:00-17:00.   Admission: Adult £2.25, Child £1.25 (In conjunction with Fermanagh County Museum).   Location: Two minute walk from Ulster bus station and tourist information centre.   Map Ref: 17

CO LONDONDERRY

Hezlett House

107 Sea Road, Castlerock, Coleraine, Co Londonderry BT51 4TW
Tel: 028 7084 8728   Email: hezletthouse@nationaltrust.org.uk
Web: www.ntni.org.uk

This 17th century thatched cottage was built for the rector of Dunboe. It was taken over by Isaac Hezlett in 1761 and his family continued to live there until 1976. There is a display of furnishings and parts of the interior have been left bare to expose the structural details.

Opening Times: 13 Mar to end May Sat, Sun & BH/PH (inc 9-18 Apr) 13:00-18:00, Jun to Aug Wed to Mon 13:00-18:00. Sep Sat & Sun 13:00-18:00. Oct 2-10 Sat & Sun 13:00-17:00. Admission: Adult £3.60, Child £2.10, Family £ 8.30. Group £3.10. NT Members Free. Location: Five miles west of Coleraine on Coleraine-Downhill coast road, A2.   Map Ref: 18

Harbour Museum

Harbour Square, Derry, Co Londonderry BT48 6AF   Tel: 028 7137 7331   Fax: 028 7137 7633
Email: museums@derrycity.gov.uk

A traditional museum, with emphasis on the city's maritime connections - temporary exhibitions are regularly displayed.

Opening Times: Mon to Fri 10:00-13:00, 14:00-16:30.   Admission: Free.   Location: City centre location - one minute from central bus station.   Map Ref: 19

Tower Museum

Union Hall Place, Derry, Co Londonderry BT48 6LU   Tel: 028 7137 2411
Email: museums@derrycity.gov.uk

The Tower Museum looks at the history of Derry from its geological formation through to the present day. There are special features on the Plantation of Ulster, the Siege of Derry and the 'Troubles'.

Opening Times: Sep to Jun Tue to Sat & BH 10:00-17:00, Jul to Aug Mon to Sat 10:00-17:00, Sun 14:00-17:00.   Admission: Admission charged.   Location: City centre location - just inside the City Walls.   Map Ref: 19

Workhouse Museum

Glendermott Road, Waterside, Derry, Co Londonderry BT47 6BG   Tel: 028 7131 8328
Email: museums@derrycity.gov.uk

First Floor - World War II display on Derry's part in protecting Atlantic convoys. Video presentations plus two rooms for temporary exhibitions. Second Floor - display on Irish and African famines. Also dormitory display.

Opening Times: Mon to Thu & Sat 10:00-16:30. Closed Fri & Sun. Jul to Aug Fri 10:00-16:00, Sun 14:00-16:30.   Admission: Free.   Location: One mile from city centre, on main bus route.
                                                                                              Map Ref: 19

Northern Ireland

Springhill

20 Springhill Road, Magherafelt, Co Londonderry BT45 7NQ   Tel / Fax: 028 8674 8210 Email: springhill@ntrust.org.uk Web: www.ntni.org.uk

Springhill has a beguiling spirit that captures the heart of every visitor. Its welcoming charm has much to do with the lovely gardens, its very pretty 'Plantation' house and 300 years of intriguing history. The stunning collection of colourful haute couture and day-to-day clothing and accessories is a mirror of history, with some pieces dating back to the 17th century.

Opening Times: 13 Mar to end Jun Sat, Sun & BH/PH (inc 09:00-18 Apr) 12:00-18:00. 1 Jul to 31 Aug daily 12:00-18:00. Sep Sat & Sun 12:00-18:00. Oct 2-10 Sat & Sun 12:00-17:00. Admission: House & Costume Collection Tour: Adult £3.90, Child £2.10, Family £8.50. Group £3.50. NT Members Free. Location: One mile from Moneymore on Moneymore-Coagh road, B18.   Map Ref: 20

CO TYRONE

Ulster American Folk Park

Mellon Road, Castletown, Omagh, Co Tyrone BT78 5QY   Tel: 028 8224 3292

A museum of Emigration and Folk Life telling the story of the floods of Emigrants who left these shores in the 18th and 19th centuries. Visit the Old and New Worlds joined by a full-sized Emigrant Sailing Ship. Explore 28, mainly original exhibit buildings from both sides of the Atlantic. Costumed interpreters tell the emigrant's story and demonstrate a wide range of traditional crafts daily. Emigrants exhibition explores related themes and the Centre for Migration Studies allows for further research. Facilities include Residential Centre, Educational programmes, shop and restaurant. Voted Visitor Attraction of The Year.

Opening Times: Apr to Sep Mon to Sat 10:30-18:00, Sun & BH 11:00-18:00. Oct to Apr Mon to Fri 10:30-17:00. Admission: Adult £4.00, Child £2.50, OAP £3.50. Location: A5 - three miles from Omagh on Strabane Road. Exhibitions & Events 2004 : For Exhibitions and Events please telephone for details.   Map Ref: 21

Ireland

Ireland is a country with a unique history and is renowned for its music and literature, particularly Dublin with its narrow cobbled streets and the superb collections in its museums and art galleries. Wherever one travels in Ireland there are castles, heritage centres and sites, abbeys and in many towns museums that together provide a fascinating record of the local history and crafts, maritime history and military history and indeed the Irish way of living and their culture.

The Red Map References should be used to locate Museums etc on the pages that follow

Ireland - Dublin & The East

CO DUBLIN

Chester Beatty Library

✏ ♿ 🌐 ⓞ

Dublin Castle, Dublin 2 Tel: +353 (0)1 407 0750   Fax: +353 (0)1 407 0760
Email: info@cbl.ie   Web: www.cbl.ie

The exhibition galleries open a window on the artistic treasures of the great cultures and religions of the world. The Library's rich collection of manuscripts, prints, icons, miniature paintings, early printed books and objets d'art represent numerous cultures and countries. European Museum of the Year 2002.

Opening Times: May to Sep Mon to Fri 10:00-17:00, Oct to Apr Tue to Fri 10:00-17:00, every Sat 11:00-17:00, every Sun 13:00-17:00. Closed BH Mon, 24-26 Dec, 1 Jan & Good Friday.
Admission: Free.   Location: Ten minutes walk from Trinity College/Grafton Street.   Map Ref: 1

The Douglas Hyde Gallery

✏ ♿ 🌐

Trinity College, Nassau Street, Dublin 2   Tel: +353 (0)1 608 1116
Fax: +353 (0)1 670 8330   Email: dhgallery@tcd.ie   Web: www.douglashydegallery.com

The Gallery has a diverse programme of exhibitions, embracing both Irish and international contemporary art. A wide range of gallery activities - tours, lectures, discussion groups - encourages audience participation and evaluation of the work on exhibition. An information leaflet accompanies every show. The Gallery has a small bookshop which stocks a wide range of art magazines, including Artforum, Frieze and Circa.

Opening Times: Mon to Fri 11:00-18:00, Thu 11:00-19:00, Sat 11:00-16:45. Closed Xmas, Easter and BH.   Admission: Free.   Location: Trinity College, Nassau Street, Dublin 2.   Map Ref: 1

Dublin City Gallery, the Hugh Lane

✏ ♿ 🌐 💬

Charlemont House, Parnell Square North, Dublin 1
Tel: +353 (0)1 874 1903   Fax: +353 (0)1 872 2182
Email: info@hughlane.ie   Web: www.hughlane.ie

The collection includes Impressionist masterpieces by Renoir, Monet, Degas and Morisot. A fine collection of 20th century Irish art and works by contemporary Irish and international artists. The Gallery also houses Francis Bacon's reconstructed studio accompanied by an audio visual room, a micro gallery with touch screen terminals and an exhibition gallery with works by Francis Bacon.

Opening Times: Tue to Thu 9:30-18:00, Fri & Sat 9:30-17:00, Sun 11:00-17:00. Closed Mon and Xmas.   Admission: Free to permanent collection. Admission to Francis Bacon Studio - Adult €7.00, Concession €3.50.   Location: City centre, at the end of O'Connell Street, on the north side of Parnell Square. A ten minute walk Tara Street or Connolly Street Railway Station.

Interior Francis Bacon Studio. Photo Perry Ogden   Map Ref: 1

Dublin Civic Museum

City Assembly House, 58 South William Street, Dublin 2   Tel: +353 (0)1 679 4260

Experience aspects of life in Dublin through the ages. Collections include: streets and buildings of Dublin, traders, industry, transport, political history, maps and views.

Opening Times: Tue to Sat 10:00-18:00, Sun 11:0-14:00. Closed Mon.   Admission: Free.
Map Ref: 1

Dublin Writers Museum

✏ 🌐 💬 ⓞ 🚌

18 Parnell Square, Dublin 1   Tel: +353 (0)1 872 2077   Fax: +353 (0)1 872 2231
Email: writers@dublintourism.ie   Web: www.visitdublin.com

The collection features the lives and works of Dublin's literary celebrities over the past 200 years. Swift, Sheridan, Shaw, Wilde, Yeats, Joyce and Beckett are among those presented through their books, letters, portraits and personal items.

Opening Times: Jan to Dec Mon to Sat 10:00-17:00, Sun & BH 11:00-17:00. Late opening Jun, Jul & Aug Mon to Fri 10:00-18:00.   Admission: Adult €6.25, Child €3.75, Concession €5.25, Family €17.50.   Location: In Dublin City Centre, five minute walk from O'Connell Street.
Map Ref: 1

Dublin's City Hall - The Story of the Capital

City Hall, Dame Street, Dublin 2

Dublin City
Baile Átha Cliath

Tel: +353 (0)1 672 2204   Fax: +353 (0)1 672 2620
Email: cityhall@dublincity.ie   Web: www.dublincity.ie/cityhall

This multi-media exhibition traces the evolution of the city from 1170 to the present day with particular emphasis on the development of civic governance. The Civic Regalia, including the Great City Sword and Great Mace are on display along with computer interactives, archive films, models and costumes. Located in City Hall, one of Dublin's finest neo-classical buildings, which dates from 1779, this exhibition brings to life the changes in the city over the centuries.

Opening Times: Mon to Fri 10:00-17:15, Sun & BH 14:00-17:00.
Admission: Adult €4.00, Child €1.50, Students/OAPs €2.00,
Family €10.00.   Map Ref: 1

James Joyce Museum

Joyce Tower, Sandycove   Tel / Fax: +353 (0)1 280 9265   Email: joycetower@dublintourism.ie
Web: www.visitdublin.com

The collection includes letters, photographs, portraits and personal possessions of Joyce. There are first editions of his work including his early broadsides and the celebrated edition of 'Ulysses' illustrated by Henri Matisse.

Opening Times: Feb to Oct Mon to Sat 10:00-17:00, Sun & BH 14:00-18:00. Closed 13:00-14:00.   Admission: Adult €6.25, Child €3.75, Concession €5.25, Family €17.50.
Location: Eight miles south of Dublin City.   Map Ref: 1

Kilmainham Gaol

Inchicore Road, Dublin 8   Tel: +353 (0)1 453 5984

Access to the Gaol is by guided tour only. The tour lasts approx one hour and 15 minutes and includes the social and political history of the Gaol. In addition to the tour the public have an opportunity to visit the museum at their own convenience. The museum is on three levels it is the only museum that deals with modern Irish and political history spanning from 1796-1924. Among the highlights of the collection there are artefacts from the 1798 Rebellion, the last letters of the leaders of the 1916 Rebellion, along with documents and artefacts from the Irish War of Independence and Civil War. The Gaol also plays host to a wide range of temporary exhibitions, including art and historical exhibitions etc.

Opening Times: Oct to Mar Mon to Sat 09:30-17:30, Sun 10:00-18:00, Apr to Sep Mon to Sun 09:30-18:00. Closed Xmas.   Admission: Adult €4.40, Child/Student €1.90, OAP/Group €3.10, Family €10.10.   Location: Three miles from city centre. Bus 79, 51B, 78A from Aston Quay.
Exhibitions & Events 2004 : Please phone for details.   Map Ref: 1

National Gallery of Ireland

Merrion Square West, Dublin 2   Tel: +353 (0)1 661 5133   Fax: +353 (0)1 661 5372
Email: artgall@eircom.net   Web: www.nationalgallery.ie

The National Gallery of Ireland has a superb collection of western European art, from the Middle Ages to the 20th century. It also holds the most important collection of Irish art in the world including the National Portrait Gallery and the Yeates Museum. Artists on display include Caravaggio, Canova, Vermeer, Rembrant, Poussin, Monet, Velazquez, Picasso, Goya, Turner, Gainsborough and all the major painters of Irish school, including the Yeates family.

Architects Model of the New Millennium Wing
opened in January 2002

Opening Times: Mon to Sat 09:30-17:30, Thur 09:30-20:30, Sun 12:00-17:30. Closed Good Friday and Xmas.
Admission: Free.   Location: City centre, five minutes from DART. Meter parking available.   Map Ref: 1

National Museum of Archaeology & History

museum

National Museum of Ireland
Árd-Mhúsaem na hÉireann

Kildare Street, Dublin 2   Tel: +353 (0)1 677 7444
Email: marketing@museum.ie
Web: www.museum.ie

This branch of the National Museum of Ireland houses the most wonderful collection of artefacts dating from 7000BC to the 20th Century, including the Ardagh Chalice, the Tara Brooch and the Derrynaflan Hoard. Special exhibitions include 'Ór - Ireland's Gold', a stunning collection of prehistoric gold ornaments, as well as 'Prehistoric Ireland' and 'Viking Age Ireland'. The 'Road to Independance' tells the story of Ireland's history during War of Independance (1919-1921). In the recently opened, 'Medieval Ireland 1150-1550' life in later medieval Ireland is explored through surviving artefacts divided into three galleries, titled 'Power', 'Work' and 'Prayer'.

Archaeology & History Museum

Opening Times: Tue to Sat 10:00-17:00, Sun 14:00-17:00. Closed Mon (incl. BH). Admission: Free. Location: Nearest DART Station, Pearse Street.

Map Ref: 1

National Museum of Decorative Arts & History

museum

National Museum of Ireland
Árd-Mhúsaem na hÉireann

Collins Barracks, Dublin 7   Tel: +353 (0)1 677 7444
Email: marketing@museum.ie   Web: www.museum.ie

Collins Barracks could be said to be the National Museum of Ireland's largest Irish artefact, having had a unique history all its own in another life. It now completes the picture for the National Museum in Dublin and joins the two already famous buildings in the possession of the Museum. On display, you'll find silver, ceramics, glassware, weaponry, furniture, folklife, clothing, jewellery, coins and medals. All of these displayed with imagination in innovative and contemporary galleries, which entice you to go further, look harder and examine more closely. New approaches to exhibiting major collections in individual galleries include Irish Period Furniture, Irish Country Furniture, 'The Way We Wore' and the recently opened exhibition of 'Airgead - A Thousand Years of Irish Coins & Currency'. While you're with us in Collins Barracks, come and see the work of one of the most influential designers and architects of the 20th century, Irish-born Eileen Gray.

Decorative Arts & History Museum

Opening Times: Tue to Sat 10:00-17:00, Sun 14:00-17:00. Closed Mon (incl. BH).
Admission: Free. Location: Opposite Heuston Station on Wolfe Tone Quay.

Map Ref: 1

National Museum of Natural History

museum

National Museum of Ireland
Árd-Mhúsaem na hÉireann

Merrion Street, Dublin 2
Tel: +353 (0)1 677 7444
Email: marketing@museum.ie   Web: www.museum.ie

Opened in 1857 as the museum of the Royal Dublin Society the 'Natural History Museum' has developed as a cabinet style zoological museum with animals from all over the world. The history of collecting extends over two centuries and has resulted in a rich variety of animals, many of which are now endangered or extinct. Exhibitions in this museum have changed little in style for over a century, adding to the charm and rarity of this national treasure. The tradition of collecting and research continues and only a fraction of the two million specimens is on display.

Natural History Museum

Opening Times: Tue to Sat 10:00-17:00, Sun 14:00-17:00. Closed Mon (incl. BH). Admission: Free. Location: Nearest DART Station, Pearse Street.

Map Ref: 1

Ireland - Dublin & The East

Royal Hibernian Academy

Gallagher Gallery, 15 Ely Place, Dublin 2   Tel: +353 (0)1 661 2558   Fax: +353 (0)1 661 0762
Email: rhaagallery@eircom.net   Web: www.royalhibernianacademy.com

Established in 1823, the Royal Hibernian Academy is an artist led organisation run by artists for artists. It presents an innovative exhibition programme of leading Irish and international artists. Commercial shows are in the Ashford Gallery which represents emerging artists and Academicians.

Opening Times: Tue to Sat 11:00-17:00, Thu 11:00-20:00, Sun 14:00-17:00. Closed Mon.
Admission: Free.   Location: City Centre, one minute from St Stephen's Green.   Map Ref: 1

Shaw Birthplace

33 Synge Street, Dublin 8   Tel: +353 (0)1 475 0854   Fax: +353 (0)1 872 2231
Email: shawhouse@dublintourism.ie   Web: www.visitdublin.com

The first home of the Shaw family and the renowned playwright, restored to its Victorian elegance and charm. The house contains photographs, original documents and letters that throw light on G B Shaw's long and impressive career.

Opening Times: May to Sep Mon to Sat 10:00-13:00 & 14:00-17:00, Sun & BH 11:00-17:00.
Closed 13:00-14:00.   Admission: Adult €6.25, Child €3.75, Concession €5.25, Family €17.50.
Location: Ten minute walk from St Stephen's Green.   Map Ref: 1

Trinity College Library Dublin

Trinity College Library

Trinity College Library, College Street, Dublin 2
Tel: +353 (0)1 677 2941   Fax: +353 (0)1 671 9003

The Old Library is home to the famous 19th gospel manuscript the Book of Kells. Also on view is The Book of Kells 'Turning Darkness into Light' Exhibition which explains the background of the Book of Kells and other related manuscripts, the Book of Armagh, the Book of Durrow, the Book of Mulling and the Book of Dimma.

Opening Times: Mon to Sat 09:30-17:00, Sun (Oct to May) 12:00-16:30, Sun (Jun to Sep) 09:30-16:30. BH Oct to May 12:00-16:30.
Closed Xmas & New Year.   Admission: Adult €7.50, Child Free, Student/OAP €6.50, Family (2 adults and 4 children) €15.00.
Location: City centre.   Map Ref: 1

Fry Model Railway

Malahide Castle Demesne, Malahide, Co Dublin   Tel: +353 (0)1 846 3779   Fax: +353 (0)1 846 3723   Email: fryrailway@dublintourism.ie   Web: www.visitdublin.com

This is a unique collection of hand-made models of Irish trains, from the beginning of rail travel to modern times. One of the world's largest miniature railways. The exhibition is unique in that it is a working railway covering an area of 2500 sq ft.

Opening Times: Apr to Sep Mon to Sat 10:00-13:00 & 14:00-17:00 Sun & BH 14:00-18:00.
Admission: Adult €6.25, Child €3.75, Concession €5.25, Family €17.50.   Location: Eight miles north of Dublin City Centre, four miles from Dublin Airport.   Map Ref: 2

Malahide Castle

Malahide, Co Dublin   Tel: +353 (0)1 846 2184   Fax: +353 (0)1 846 2537
Email: malahidecastle@dublintourism.ie   Web: www.visitdublin.com

The Talbot family lived here for nearly 800 years. The Castle is furnished with beautiful Irish period furniture together with an extensive collection of Irish portrait paintings, mainly from the National Gallery of Ireland.

Opening Times: Jan to Dec Mon to Sat 10:00-17:00. Apr to Oct Sun & BH 11:00-18:00, Nov to Mar Sun & BH 11:00-17:00. Closed 13:00-14:00.   Admission: Adult €6.25, Child €3.75, Concession €5.25, Family €17.50.   Location: Eight miles north of Dublin City, four miles from Dublin Airport.   Map Ref: 2

Ireland - Dublin & The East

Athy Museum

Town Hall, Athy, Co Kildare   Tel: +353 (0)507 33075   Fax: +353 (0)507 33076
Email: oriordanmargaret@eircom.net   Web: www.kildare.ie/athyonline

Athy Heritage Centre holds Ireland's only permanent exhibition on polar explorer, Sir Ernest Shackleton who was born locally. It includes a faithful 5th scale replica model of his ship Endurance and various artefacts from his expeditions including a sledge and harness. The centre also relates the history of the town with an exhibition on the 1903 Gordon Bennett Race, the precursor to todays Grand Prix racing.

Opening Times: Jan to Dec Mon to Sat 10:00-18:00, Sun & BH 14:00-18:00. Nov to Feb closed Sun. Admission: Adult €2.00, Child €1.00, OAP/Student €1.50, Family (2 adults and 2 children) €5.00.   Map Ref: 3

Athy Heritage Town

The Steam Museum

Straffan, Co Kildare   Tel: +353 (0)1 627 3155   Fax: +353 (0)1 627 3477
Email: info@steam-museum.ie   Web: www.steam-museum.ie

The Steam Museum houses two complementary collections. The Richard Guinness Hall contains contemporary, inventors and prototype models. The Power Hall has seven full sized stationary steam engines in steam at weekends. Both housed in the rebuilt Gothic church from Inchicore. Lodge Park Walled Garden (also open) is beside the Museum, also the Steaming Kettle Tearoom and the gift and garden shop.

Opening Times: Jun, Jul & Aug Wed to Sun 14:00-18:00, May & Sep by appointment in advance. Admission: Adult €7.50, Child/OAP/Student €5.00, Family €20.00, Groups of 20 €5.00.   Map Ref: 4

Millmount Museum & Tower

Millmount, Drogheda, Co Louth   Tel: +353 (0)41 983 3097   Fax: +353 (0)41 984 1599
Email: info@millmount.net   Web: www.millmount.net

The museum is housed in the former officers' mess of a military complex built in 1808 and contains a wide variety of local and national artefacts. Perhaps its most prized possessions are the three large banners of the 18th century broguemakers, carpenters and weavers guilds. These are the only surviving Guilds' banners in the country. The beautifully woven drapes are wonderfully rich in detail and have been recognised by the National Museum as being of special significance. One of the most popular exhibits is the authentic Folk Kitchen which accurately recreates a 19th century Irish kitchen with items that include vintage utensils, a traditional dresser, a settle bed, examples of the earliest washing machines, fire utensils and a range of butter churns and all the equipment needed for butter making. Many visitors are intrigued by the Curiosities Section which contains unique early cinema

posters, vintage typewriters and many other weird and wonderful objects. The Industrial Room of the museum explores Drogheda's industrial heritage, highlighting industries that flourished here during the 19th and 20th centuries - spinning, weaving, brewing, pipe and shoemaking, iron works and shipbuilding. St Oliver Plunkett spent much of his time as Primate of Armagh living in Drogheda and his story is detailed in the Religious Exhibition along with local penal crosses and other religious artefacts. The museum is especially proud of its

Geological Collection which contains more than 300 examples of granites and marbles from around the world. Local rock types and an exotic exhibit of an iron meteorite from Australia are displayed alongside naturally occurring diamonds, amethyst and gold rocks.

Opening Times: Mon to Sat 10:00-18:00, Sun & BH 14:30-17:30. Admission: Please phone for details. Location: Five minute walk from town centre.   Map Ref: 5

CO KILKENNY

Butler Gallery

The Castle, Kilkenny   Tel: +353 (0)56 61106

Public funded gallery. Exhibitions include Tony Cragg, Bill Woodrow, Sol le Wit, James Turrell, Petah Coyne, Jean Scully and Roman Signer. Collection contains contemporary sculpture, paintings and photography.

Opening Times: Oct to Mar daily 10:30-17:00, Apr to Sep daily 10:00-19:00.   Admission: Free.

Map Ref: 6

Rothe House Museum

Parliament Street, Kilkenny   Tel: +353 (0)56 22893   Email: rothehouse@eircom.net

Rothe House was built by prosperous merchant John Rothe in 1594. The Kilkenny Archaeological Society bought and restored the house. Within the house are various exhibitions from folk to costume and accessories.

Opening Times: Mon to Sat 10:30-17:00, Sun 15:00-17:00. Opening hours may vary off-season.
Location: City centre - five minutes from rail/bus station.

Map Ref: 6

CO TIPPERARY

Bolton Library

GPA Building, John Street, Cashel, Co Tipperary   Tel / Fax: +353 (0)62 61944
Email: boltonlibrary@oceanfree.net   Web: www.heritagetowns.com/cashel

A unique collection of two Archbishops over 12,000 volumes. Manuscript collections, early printing from 12th century. 20 titles prior to 1500, spectacular copy of Nuremburg Chronicle (1493) and many more. Visit the Georgian Cathedral in grounds and Cashel City walls 14th century.

Opening Times: Mar to Oct Tue to Sat 09:30-17:30, Oct to Feb Mon to Fri 09:30-17:30.   Admission: Adult €1.50, Child €0.50, OAP/Student €1.00.

Map Ref: 7

CO WEXFORD

Wexford County Museum

The Castle, Enniscorthy, Co Wexford
Tel / Fax: +353 (0)54 35926   Email: wexmus@iol.ie

The County Museum is in four main sections which illustrate in a dramatic way the stories and history of County Wexford through the centuries - military, agriculture, writing, crafts, industrial and ecclesiastical. The museum is a veritable treasure house of information for anyone interested in Irish ways of living, culture and heritage.

Opening Times: Mar to Sep 10:00-17:30, Sun 14:00-17:30.
Admission: Adult €4.50, Student/Senior €3.00, Child €1.00, Family €11.00.   Location: Town centre.

Map Ref: 8

Irish Agricultural Museum

Johnstown Castle Old Farmyard, Wexford   Tel: +353 (0)53 42888   Fax: +353 (0)53 42213

Extensive displays on rural transport, farming and the activities of the farmyard and the farmhouse. Nationally important collection of Irish country furniture - over 100 pieces. Also Famine Exhibition, Ferguson System and gardening displays

Opening Times: Mon to Fri 09:00-17:00, Apr to Nov also Sat & Sun 14:00-17:00.
Admission: Adult €5.00, Child €3.00, Family €15.00. Group rates available.   Location: Four miles south west of Wexford Town.

Map Ref: 9

Ireland - The South & Southwest

Bantry House

Bantry, Co Cork   Tel: +353 (0)27 50047   Fax: +353 (0)27 50795   Email: info@bantryhouse.ie
Web: www.bantryhouse.ie

Bantry House and Gardens has been home to the White family since 1739, and is one of the finest stately homes in Ireland. The house contains a unique collection of tapestries, furniture, carpets and art treasures, collected mainly by the second Earl in the 19th century. These include Russian icons, 18th century French, Flemish and Irish furniture, Gobelin tapestries and Aubusson carpets.

Opening Times: Mid Mar to end Oct daily 09:00-17:00.
Location: Near town centre on N71, ten minute walk.
Exhibitions & Events 2004 : 26/06/ to 04/07: WCM.

Map Ref: 10

Cobh Museum

Scots Church, High Road, Cobh, Co Cork   Tel: +353 (0)21 481 4240   Fax: +353 (0)21 481 1018   Email: cobhmuseum@eircom.net

The museum is housed in the former Scots Presbyterian Church. Exhibitions reflect the social and cultural history of the town of Cobh (Queenstown), the Great Island and the harbour.

Opening Times: Easter to Oct Mon to Sat 11:00-13:00 & 14:00-18:00, Sun 15:00-18:00.
Admission: Adult €1.50, Child/OAP €0.75, Family €3.75.   Location: Five minutes walk from town centre, near Tourist Office and station.

Map Ref: 11

Cork Public Museum

Fitzgerald Park, Mardyke, Cork   Tel: +353 (0)21 427 0679   Fax: +353 (0)21 427 0931
Email: museum@corkcity.ie

General collection outlining the history of Cork from earliest times to present day, includes archaeology, geology, history - social and political. Cork silver and glass.

Opening Times: Mon to Fri 11:00-13:00 & 14:15-17:00 (Jun & Aug to 18:00), Sun 15:00-17:00. Closed Sat and BH weekends.   Admission: Free Mon to Fri. Sun - Adult €1.50, Family/Group €3.00.   Location: Ten minute walk from town centre, two minute walk from number 8 bus stop on Western Road.

Map Ref: 12

Crawford Municipal Art Gallery

Emmet Place, Cork   Tel: +353 (0)21 427 3377   Fax: +353 (0)21 480 5043
Email: crawfordgallery@eircom.net   Web: www.crawfordartgallery.com

In a collection of (mostly) Irish art from the last three centuries, highlights include works by James Barry, Daniel Maclise, Walter Osborne, Sean Keating, Jack B Yeats, Louis le Brocquy, Paul Seawright and Kathy Prendergast.

Opening Times: Mon to Sat 10:00-17:00. Closed Sun & BH.   Admission: Free.   Location: City centre.

Map Ref: 12

Kerry County Museum

Ashe Memorial Hall, Denny Street, Tralee, Co Kerry   Tel: +353 (0)66 712 7475/712 7777

Kerry County Museum, Tralee is Ireland's most visited regional museum. Located in the splendidly restored Ashe Memorial Hall in Tralee Town Centre it traces the history and archaeology of Kerry from earliest times. The Museum comprises four elements: Kerry in Colour - a widescreen audio-visual presentation on Kerry's spectacular scenery, its heritage sites and traditions. Permanent Museum Galleries - with the Treasures of Kerry divided into ten sections chronologically from the Stone Age to the Present Day. Geraldine Tralee Medieval Experience - a reconstruction of Tralee in 1451 when it was headquarters of the Munster Geraldines. Temporary Exhibition Area - that houses major international temporary exhibitions in conjunction with overseas institutions.

Ireland - The South & Southwest

Opening Times: Jan to Mar Tue to Fri 10:00-16:30, Apr to May Tue to Sat 09:30-17:30, June to Aug Daily 09:30-17:30, Sept to Dec Tue to Sat 09:30-17:00.   Admission: Adult €8.00, Child €5.00, OAP/Student €6.00, Family €22.00.   Location: In town centre.   Exhibitions & Events 2004 : Please telephone for details.   Map Ref: 13

CO LIMERICK

The Hunt Museum

The Custom House, Rutland Street, Limerick   Tel: +353 (0)61 312833   Fax: +353 (0)61 312834   Email: info@huntmuseum.com   Web: www.huntmuseum.com

A magnificent collection of art and antiquity - donated to the 'people of Ireland' by John and Gertrude Hunt. Exhibited in an 18th century Custom House, with gift shop and a riverside restaurant.

Opening Times: All year Mon to Sat 10:00-17:00, Sun 14:00-17:00.   Admission: Adult €6.50, Child €3.50, Family €15.00.   Location: Two minute walk from Limerick Tourist Information Office.   Map Ref: 14

Limerick City Gallery of Art

Carnegie Building, Pery Square, Limerick   Tel: +353 (0)61 310633

The permanent collection consists of some 600 works in a wide variety of media and styles dating from the 18th century to contemporary practice, it is mostly Irish or Irish related in origin with exceptional examples of work by leading Irish artists of all periods. The permanent collection also houses the National Collection of Contemporary Drawing with a published catalogue and the Michael O'Connor Poster Collection, which consists of 3,800 works of international design.

Opening Times: Mon to Wed & Fri 10:00-18:00, Thu 10:00-19:00, Sat 10:00-17:00, Sun 14:00-17:00.   Admission: Free.   Location: One minute walk from train and bus station.   Map Ref: 14

Limerick Museum

Castle Lane, Nicholas Street, Limerick   Tel: +353 (0)61 417826   Fax: +353 (0)61 415266 Email: lwalsh@limerickcity.ie   Web: www.limerickcity.ie

Regional museum covering all aspects of the past of Limerick City and the region. Principal themes include archaeology, Limerick silver, Limerick lace, numismatics, printing, labour history, manufacturers, national independence movements, topographical paintings, prints, old photographs, postcards, etc.

Opening Times: Tue to Sat 10:00-13:00 & 14:15-17:00. Closed Sun, Mon and BH. Admission: Free. Location: Limerick City, beside King John's Castle.

A Section of the Display Galleries   Map Ref: 14

414

Ireland - The West & Northwest

Clare Museum

Arthur's Row, Ennis, Co Clare   Tel: +353 (0)65 682 3382   Fax: +353 (0)65 684 2119
Email: claremuseum@eircom.net   Web: www.clarelibrary.ie

The Riches of Clare Exhibition tells 6000 years of Clare's history, using the authentic artifacts, computer inter-actives, and audio-visual presentations. Includes artifacts from the National Museum of Ireland.

Opening Times: Jan to Apr Tue to Sat 09:30-17:30, May to Sep Mon to Sat 09:30-17:30, Sun 14:00-17:30, Oct to Dec Tue to Sat 09:30-17:30.   Admission: Adult €3.50, Student €2.50, Family €10.00.   Location: Centre of Ennis, off O'Connell Square.   Map Ref: 15

Donegal County Museum

High Road, Letterkenny, Co Donegal   Tel: +353 (0)74 9124613   Fax: +353 (0)74 9126522
Email: jmccarthy@donegalcoco.ie

The museum is housed in a stone building which was once part of Letterkenny Workhouse built in 1846. The museum houses and displays a fascinating range of artefacts covering all aspects of the history of County Donegal.

Opening Times: Mon to Fri 10:00-12:30 & 13:00-16:30, Sat 13:00-16:30.   Admission: Free.
Location: Signposted in Letterkenny, five minute walk from town centre.   Map Ref: 16

Glebe House & Gallery

Churchill, Letterkenny, Co Donegal   Tel: +353 (0)74 37071

Regency house, 1828, set in woodland gardens, decorated with William Morris textiles, Islamic and Japanese art. Collection includes works by leading 20th century artists - Picasso, Kokoshka as well as Irish and Italian artists.

Opening Times: Mid May to end Sep Sat to Thu 11:00-18:30.   Admission: Adult €2.50, Child €1.20, OAP/Group €1.90, Family €6.30.   Map Ref: 17

National Museum of Country Life

Turlough Park, Castlebar, Co Mayo   Tel: +353 (0)94 90 31773
Fax: +353 (0)94 90 31628   Email: tpark@museum.ie   Web: www.museum.ie

The National Museum of Ireland - Country Life is located in Turlough village, four miles east of Castlebar, Co. Mayo (off the N5). Visitors to the Museum's Exhibition Galleries are invited to experience the story of Irish country life between 1850 and 1950 through the innovative combination of artefacts and displays, archival video footage and interactive screens. Visitors can enjoy a range of public programmes including weekly craft demonstrations, and workshops. Admission to these events is free but booking is necessary. (Bookings +353 (0)94 31751/31498, e-mail educationtph@museum.ie).

Opening Times: Tue to Sat 10:00-17:00, Sun 14:00-17:00. Closed Mon. Admission: Free.
Map Ref: 18

Sligo County Museum

Stephen Street, Sligo   Tel: +353 (0)71 47190   Fax: +353 (0)71 46798
Email: sligolib@sligococo.ie   Web: www.sligococo.ie

There is a Yeats Collection and an accumulation of local artefacts. Yeats Collection comprises photographs, prints, letters, drawings and medals awarded to W B Yeats as Nobel Prize for Literature 1923.

Opening Times: Oct to May Tue to Sat 14:00-17:00. Jun to Sep Tue to Sat 10:00-12:00 & 14:00-17:00.   Admission: Free.   Location: Near town centre.   Map Ref: 19

Ireland - The Midlands

Cavan County Museum

Virginia Road, Ballyjamesduff, Co Cavan   Tel: +353 (0)49 854 4070   Fax: +353 (0)49 854 4332   Email: ccmuseum@eircom.net   Web: www.cavanmuseum.ie

Cavan County Museum, a magnificent 19th century building, which is beautifully situated amid extensive grounds, houses the material culture of County Cavan and is an ideal starting point for a relaxing family day out.

Opening Times: Tue to Sat 10:00-17:00, also May to Oct Sun & BH 14:00-18:00.
Location: Five minute walk from town centre.   Map Ref: 20

Cavan Crystal

Dublin Road, Cavan   Tel: +353 (0)49 433 1800   Fax: +353 (0)49 433 1198
Email: sales@cavancrystaldesign.com   Web: www.cavancrystandesign.com

Cavan Crystal, established since 1969, maintains its tradition for making top quality, hand made crystal glassware and giftware. Perfect gifts for every occasion in both traditional and contemporary designs.

Opening Times: Mon to Fri 09:30-18:00, Sat 10:00-17:00, Sun 12:00-18:00.   Map Ref: 21

Monaghan County Museum

1/2 Hill Street, Monaghan   Tel: +353 (0)47 82928   Fax: +353 (0)47 71189
Email: comuseum@monaghancoco.ie

The extensive and rapidly growing collections at Monaghan County Museum range from ancient Stone Age right up to modern times. A purpose built gallery houses temporary/travelling exhibitions.

Opening Times: Tue to Fri 10:00-13:00 & 14:00-17:00, Sat 11:00-13:00 & 14:00-17:00. Closed Sun & Mon. Guided tours on request. Admission: Free. Location: Town centre. Map Ref: 22

National Irish Famine Museum

Strokestown, Co Roscommon   Tel: +353 (0)78 33013   Fax: +353 (0)78 33712
Email: info@strokestownpark.ie   Web: www.strokestownpark.ie

Famine museum uses original documents from the house estate. The history of the Irish famine is explained and draws parallels to the occurrance of famine today in the developing world.

Opening Times: Apr to Oct daily 11:00-17:30.
Admission: Adult House/Museum/Gardens €9.00, House only/Museum only €3.50, Gardens only €4.50.
OAP/Student/Group discounts available. Location: In town on N5 main Dublin/Ballina road.

Map Ref: 23

Belvedere House, Gardens and Park

Mullingar, Co Westmeath   Tel: +353 (0)44 49060   Fax: +353 (0)44 49002
Email: info@belvedere-house.ie   Web: www.belvedere-house.ie

One of the finest Irish historic houses, and together with walled garden and landscaped park has been exquisitely restored. Explore 6 kilometres of woodland trails and discover intriguing follies throughout. Remarkable Visitor Centre with multimedia displays and excellent facilities. The gem of the Irish Midlands - where history lives on.

Opening Times: May to Aug Mon to Fri 09:30-18:00, Sat & Sun 10:30-19:00. Sep to Oct 10:30-18:00. Nov to Apr 10:30-16:30. Admission: Adult €6.00, Child €4.00, OAP/Student €5.00, Family €17.00, Group rates available. Location: 50 miles from Dublin and five miles from Mullingar on the N52.   Map Ref: 24

Isle of Man

The National Museum Service operates 11 National Heritage Museum sites with visitor facilities and interpretive services. These sites are located in towns and villages throughout the Island.

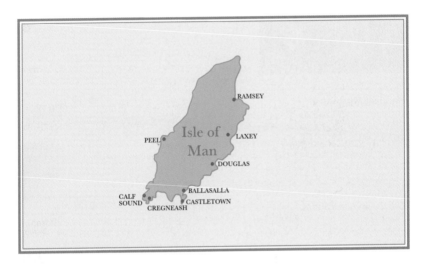

Manx National Heritage

Manx Museum, Kingswood Grove, Douglas IM1 3LY   Tel: 01624 648000
Fax: 01624 648001   Email: enquiries@mnh.gov.im   Web: www.gov.im/mnh

Manx National Heritage is a major award winning and unique organisation in Europe. The portfolio of Heritage responsibilities include:- The National Museum Service, The National Monuments Service, The National Trust Service, The National Archives and The National Art Gallery.

Rushen Abbey

Ballasalla   Tel: 01624 648000   Fax: 01624 648001
Email: enquiries@mnh.gov.im   Web: www.gov.im/mnh

Rushen Abbey is the most substantial and important medieval religious site in the Isle of Man. Discover what life was like for the Cistercian community, walk through the remains of substantial medieval buildings and see where archaeology research has revealed traces of buildings below ground. This is a highlight of a 'Christian Heritage' route around the Island.

Opening Times: 1 Apr to Oct (date tbc) daily 10:00-17:00.

Calf Sound

Calf Sound   Tel: 01624 648000   Fax: 01624 648001
Email: enquiries@mnh.gov.im   Web: www.gov.im/mnh

Visitor centre sited and styled to address this unique setting of beautiful landscape, sea and the Calf. Information and audio visual presentations about history and wildlife in this area.

Opening Times: Daily 10:00-17:00. Closed Xmas & New Year.   Admission: Free.
Location: One and a half miles from Cregneash.

Isle of Man

Castle Rushen

Castletown   Tel: 01624 648000   Fax: 01624 648001
Email: enquiries@mnh.gov.im   Web: www.gov.im/mnh

One of Britains best preserved 12th century medieval castles, Castle Rushen is a limestone fortress rising out of the heart of the old capital of the Island, Castletown. Once the fortress of the Kings and Lords of Mann, Rushen is brought alive with rich decorations, sounds and smells of a bygone era.

Opening Times: 1 Apr to Oct (date tbc) daily 10:00-17:00.   Location: In the town centre.

Castle Rushen, Castletown

Nautical Museum

Manx National Heritage

10 Bridge Street, Castletown   Tel: 01624 648000   Fax: 01624 648001
Email: enquiries@mnh.gov.im   Web: www.gov.im/mnh

Set at the mouth of Castletown harbour, this museum is home to an 18th century armed yacht. A replica sailmaker's loft, ship model and photographs bring alive Manx maritime life and trade in the days of sail.

Opening Times: 1 Apr to Oct (date tbc) daily 10:00-17:00.

Old Grammar School

Manx National Heritage

Castletown   Tel: 01624 648000   Fax: 01624 648001
Email: enquiries@mnh.gov.im   Web: www.gov.im/mnh

The former capital's first church was built around 1200AD and was a school from 1570 to 1930. The main wing is the oldest roofed structure in the Island.

Opening Times: 1 Apr to Oct (tbc) daily 10:00-17:00.   Admission: Free.

Old House of Keys

Manx National Heritage

Parliament Square, Castletown   Tel: 01624 648000   Fax: 01624 648001
Email: enquiries@mnh.gov.im   Web: www.gov.im/mnh

The history of the Old House of Keys building is one chapter in the long, and often turbulent, history of Manx politics which stretches back to the ninth and tenth centuries when the Viking Kings ruled the Isle of Man. It has been restored to its appearance in 1866 and provides an insight into the political life and times of the Island through interactive audio presentations.

Opening Times: 1 Apr to Oct (date tbc) daily 10:00-17:00.   Location: Opposite Castle Rushen in the town centre.

Manx Museum

Kingswood Grove, Douglas IM1 3LY   Tel: 01624 648000   Fax: 01624 648001
Email: enquiries@mnh.gov.im   Web: www.gov.im/mnh

The natural point to begin your exploration of the Island and the fascinating 10,000 year old 'Story of Mann'. Displays of Manx archaeology, history, folk life and natural science. Also houses the National Art Gallery and the Island's national archive and reference library. In a matter of hours you'll discover all kinds of facts and intriguing features that bring the past to life.

Opening Times: Mon-Sat 10:00-17:00. Closed Xmas & New Year.   Admission: Free.

Manx Museum, Douglas

Isle of Man

The Great Laxey Wheel & Mines Trail

Manx National Heritage

Laxey   Tel: 01624 648000   Fax: 01624 648001
Email: enquiries@mnh.gov.im   Web: www.gov.im/mnh

Built in 1854 and 22 metres in diameter, the Great Laxey Wheel - christened 'Lady Isabella' after the wife of the then Lieutenant Governor of the Isle of Man, is the largest working water wheel in Europe, and has remained one of the Island's most dramatic tourist attractions. It was designed to pump water from the lead and zinc mines and is an acknowledged masterpiece of Victorian engineering.

Opening Times: 1 Apr to Oct (date tbc) daily 10:00-17:00.
The Great Laxey Wheel, Laxey

House of Manannan

Manx National Heritage

East Quay, Peel   Tel: 01624 648000   Fax: 01624 648001
Email: enquiries@mnh.gov.im   Web: www.gov.im/mnh

Using reconstructions, interactive displays, audio visual presentations and original material, the House of Manannan explores the Celtic, Viking and Maritime traditions of the Isle of Man. It brings to life themes which are both ancient and modern. Experience two hours of drama, colour and excitement by the harbour in the City of Peel.

Opening Times: Daily 10:00-17:00. Closed Xmas & New Year. Location: By Peel Harbour.
House of Manannan, Peel

Peel Castle

Manx National Heritage

Peel   Tel: 01624 648000   Fax: 01624 648001
Email: enquiries@mnh.gov.im   Web: www.gov.im/mnh

In the 11th century the Castle was the ruling seat of the Norse Kingdom of Mann. Stroll through the remains of the Round Tower, 13th century Cathedral and site of the 90ft long giant's grave.

Opening Times: 1 Apr to Oct (date tbc) daily 10:00-17:00.

Cregneash Village Folk Museum

Manx National Heritage

Cregneash, Port St Mary   Tel: 01624 648000   Fax: 01624 648001
Email: enquiries@mnh.gov.im   Web: www.gov.im/mnh

Experience what life was really like in a Manx crofting village during the early 19th century. Stroll around this attractive village set in beautiful countryside, call into Harry Kelly's Cottage, The Turner's Shed, a Weaver's House and the Blacksmith's Smithy. Grazing nearby will be the Manx four horned Loghtan sheep along with other animals from the village farm. Home baked refreshments in the village café will complete your visit.

Opening Times: 1 Apr to Oct (date tbc) daily 10:00-17:00.
Cregneash Village Folk Museum, Cregneash

The Grove Rural Life Museum

Manx National Heritage

Andreas Road, Ramsey   Tel: 01624 648000   Fax: 01624 648001
Email: enquiries@mnh.gov.im   Web: www.gov.im/mnh

Victorian time capsule, a country house built as a summer retreat for a Liverpool shipping merchant. Rooms are filled with period and often original furnishings and outbuildings house 19th century vehicles and farming tools.

Opening Times: 1 Apr to Oct (date tbc) daily 10:00-17:00.

Channel Islands

Alderney Society Museum

The Old School, Alderney GY9 3TG   Tel: 01481 823222   Fax: 01481 824979
Email: alderneymuseum@alderney.net   Web: www.alderneymuseum.org

A museum of local interest. Special features - Iron Age pottery, Elizabethan shipwreck, German occupation and fortifications, 19th century harbour and fortifications.

Opening Times: Easter to end Oct Mon to Fri 10:00-12:00 & 14:00-16:00, Sat & Sun 10:00-12:00.   Admission: Adult £2.00, Child Free.   Location: High Street.

Castle Cornet

St Peter Port   Tel: 01481 721657   Fax: 01481 740719
Email: administration@museums.gov.gg   Web: www.museum.guernsey.net

Maritime Museum, Royal Guernsey Militia Museum, 'The Story of Castle Cornet', 201 Squadron RAF Museum, four period gardens and a season of storytelling and outdoor theatre.

Opening Times: Apr to Sep daily 10:00-17:00.   Admission: Adult £6.00, Child Free, OAP £4.00.   Location: St Peter Port, ten minute walk from bus station.

Fort Grey Shipwreck Museum

Rocquaine, St Peters GY7 9BY   Tel: 01481 265036   Fax: 01481 236279
Email: administration@museums.gov.gg   Web: www.museum.guernsey.net

Martello Tower housing objects recovered from the many wrecks off Guernsey's west coast, dating from 1777 to 1973.

Opening Times: Apr to Sep daily 10:00-17:00.   Admission: Adult £2.50, Child Free, OAP £1.25.   Location: South west coast of Guernsey - Rocquaine Bay.

German Occupation Museum

Forest GY8 0BG   Tel: 01481 238205

Unique collection of German occupation items recreated street scene, restored fortifications audio-visual experience. Tearoom and garden.

Opening Times: Apr to Oct daily 10:00-16:30. Nov to Mar daily 10:00-13:00.   Admission: Adult £3.00, Child £2.00, Groups £2.50.   Location: 15 minutes from town centre.

Guernsey Folk Museum

Saumarez Park, Castel GY5 7UJ   Tel / Fax: 01481 255384   Web: www.nationaltrust-gsy.org.gg

Social/agricultural history of Guernsey from Victorian period. Recreated rooms and displays set in old farm complex around central farm courtyard. Original and reproduction period costumes on display.

Opening Times: 25 Mar to 31 Oct daily 10:00-17:00.   Admission: Adult £3.00, Child/Concession £1.00. Group rates available.   Location: Set in Saumarez Park, public park. On regular bus route.

Guernsey Museum & Art Gallery

Candie, St Peter Port GY1 1UG   Tel: 01481 726518   Fax: 01481 715177
Email: administration@museums.gov.gg   Web: www.museum.guernsey.net

Museum - 'The Story of Guernsey'. Art Gallery - exhibitions Feb to Dec.

Opening Times: Feb to Dec daily 10:00-17:00. Winter closing 16:00.   Admission: Adult £3.50, Child Free, OAP £2.50.   Location: Candie Gardens, four minute walk from centre of St Peter Port.

Hauteville House - Victor Hugo's House of Exile

38 Hauteville, St Peter Port GY1 1DG   Tel: 01481 721911   Fax: 01481 715913

The house was bought in 1856 by the famous French writer Victor Hugo and decorated with china, pieces of furniture, tapestries and Delft tiles in a unique and original way. Visit the garden also.

Opening Times: Apr to Sep Mon to Sat 10:00-12:00 & 14:00-17:00. Jul & Aug 10:00-17:00. Closed Sun & BH.   Admission: Adult £5.00.   Location: Near town centre, five minutes walk from central bus station.

Channel Islands

Sausmarez Manor

St Martins GY4 6SG Tel: 01481 235571   Fax: 01481 235572
Email: peter@desausmarezmanor.co.uk Web: www.artparks.co.uk

Historic house lived in by descendents of Seigneurs going back to c1220. With subtropical garden, sculpture park, dolls house collection, pitch & putt, adventure play area and ride on train.

Opening Times: Apr to Oct daily 10:00-17:00. Admission: Overall admission & carpark free, attractions individually priced.

JERSEY

Channel Islands Military Museum

The Five Mile Road, St Ouen Tel: 01534 723136

The island's finest collection of original military and civilian occupation items to be seen on the island, housed in a restored bunker which formed part of Hitler's Atlantic wall defence.

Opening Times: 25 Mar to 31 Oct daily 10:00-17:00. Admission: Adult £3.00, Child £1.00.
Location: At the rear of Jersey Woollen Mills and across from Jersey Pearl.

Elizabeth Castle

St Helier Tel: 01534 723971 Fax: 01534 610338 Email: marketing@jerseyheritagetrust.org
Web: www.jerseyheritagetrust.org

A magnificent fortress that hosts a number of fine exhibitions detailing its past and those who have been stationed there. Noon-day gun fired daily.

Opening Times: Apr to Nov daily 10:00-18:00. Closed winter. Admission: Adult £5.10, Concession £4.30, Under 5s Free, 15% Group Discount available. Location: Located in the Bay of St Aubin.

Hamptonne Country Life Museum

Rue de la Patente, St Lawrence Tel: 01534 863955 Fax: 01534 863935
Email: marketing@jerseyheritagetrust.org Web: www.jerseyheritagetrust.org

A unique collection of restored farm houses and buildings tracing 600 years of Jersey's rural past.

Opening Times: Apr to Nov daily 10:00-17:00. Closed winter. Admission: Adult £4.95, Concession £4.20, Under 5s Free, 15% Group Discount available. Location: Centre of Jersey.

Jersey Battle of the Flowers Museum

La Robeline, Mont des Corvees, St Ouen JE3 2ES Tel: 01534 482408

The Battle of Flowers Museum presents the show of the year, so why not come on safari and see a wonderland of animals, meet the zebras, lions, and the 101 dalmations and lots of other interesting animals.

Opening Times: Daily 10:00-17:00. Admission: Adult £3.50, Child £1.50, OAP £3.25.
Location: West of island, seven miles from town.

Jersey Museum

The Weighbridge, St Helier JE2 3NF Tel: 01534 633300 Fax: 01534 633301
Email: marketing@jerseyheritagetrust.org Web: www.jerseyheritagetrust.org

The start point to any visit to Jersey. This award winning museum traces Jersey's past from the Ice Age to the present day. Also includes a fine art gallery and three floors of restored Victorian merchant's house.

Opening Times: Apr to Nov daily 10:00-17:00, winter 10:00-16:00. Admission: Adult £5.10, Concession £4.30, Under 5s Free, 15% Group Discount available. Location: Located next to bus office.

La Hougue Bie Museum

Grouville Tel: 01534 353823 Fax: 01534 866472 Email: marketing@jerseyheritagetrust.org
Web: www.jerseyheritagetrust.org

A loft neolithic mound dominates this site that also includes an extensive geology and archaeology museum, neolithic encampment and memorial bunker to the slave workers of the occupation years.

Opening Times: Apr to Nov daily 10:00-17:00. Closed winter. Admission: Adult £5.10, Concession £4.30, Under 5s Free, 15% Group Discount available. Location: On major bus route from St Helier.

Isle of Man

Maritime Museum & Occupation Tapestry Gallery

New North Quay, St Helier   Tel: 01534 811043   Fax: 01534 874099
Email: marketing@jerseyheritagetrust.org   Web: www.jerseyheritagetrust.org

Interactive fun, discovery and art commissions this museum is ideal for the maritime enthusiast and family alike. The 12 panels of the tapestry movingly record the privation and suffering of occupied people.

Opening Times: Apr to Nov daily 10:00-17:00, Winter 10:00-16:00. Admission: Adult £5.80, Concession £4.95, Under 5s Free, 15% Group Discount available. Location: One minute walk from Jersey Tourism Visitor Centre.

Mont Orgueil Castle

Gorey, St Martin   Tel: 01534 853292   Fax: 01534 854303
Email: marketing@jerseyheritagetrust.org   Web: www.jerseyheritagetrust.org

A mediaeval castle built in the 13th century, Mont Orgueil dominates the Royal Bay of Granville. It remains one of the most complete castles of its type and commands some of Jersey's finest views.

Opening Times: Apr to Nov daily 10:00-18:00, winter times available on request.
Admission: Adult £4.95, Concession £4.20, Under 5s Free, 15% Group Discount available.
Location: South east coast of Jersey.

Noirmont Command Bunker

Noirmont Point, St Brelade   Tel: 01534 746795   Email: m.costard@spoor.co.uk

Built by the German occupying forces during WWII, this impressive artillery command bunker has been restored to a high standard. The adjacent battery and observation tower may also be visited.

Opening Times: Please contact for details.   Admission: Adults £1.50, Accompanied Child Free.

Sir Francis Cook Gallery

Augres, Trinity   Tel: 01534 863333   Fax: 01534 633301
Email: marketing@jerseyheritagetrust.org   Web: www.jerseyheritagetrust.org

Hosting Jersey artists, this venue holds regular exhibitions of their work.

Opening Times: Dependent on exhibitions, please phone for details. Location: Main bus route to north of Jersey.

Classification Index

see Classifications List on page 9

Anthropology

Archaeological

Classification Index

Art Galleries

Classification Index

Classification Index

Art, Crafts & Textiles

Classification Index

China, Porcelain, Glass & Ceramics

Classification Index

Communications

Egyptian

Fashion

Classification Index

Geology

Health & Medicine

Historic Houses

Classification Index

Classification Index

Classification Index

Classification Index

Maritime

Military & Defence

Classification Index

Oriental

Palaces

Photography

Police, Prisons & Dungeons

Railways

Classification Index

Classification Index

Sporting History

Toys & Childhood

Transport

Classification Index

Victoriana

Town Index

Town Index

Town Index

Town Index

Town Index

Town Index

Index to Entries

Index to Entries

Index to Entries

Index to Entries

Index to Entries

Index to Entries

Index to Entries

Index to Entries

Index to Entries

Index to Entries

Index to Entries

Index to Entries

Index to Entries

Notes

Notes